EQUITY INVESTMENTS

CFA® Program Curriculum
2025 • LEVEL I • VOLUME 5

WILEY

©2024 by CFA Institute. All rights reserved. This copyright covers material written expressly for this volume by the editor/s as well as the compilation itself. It does not cover the individual selections herein that first appeared elsewhere. Permission to reprint these has been obtained by CFA Institute for this edition only. Further reproductions by any means, electronic or mechanical, including photocopying and recording, or by any information storage or retrieval systems, must be arranged with the individual copyright holders noted.

CFA®, Chartered Financial Analyst®, AIMR-PPS®, and GIPS® are just a few of the trademarks owned by CFA Institute. To view a list of CFA Institute trademarks and the Guide for Use of CFA Institute Marks, please visit our website at www.cfainstitute.org.

This publication is designed to provide accurate and authoritative information in regard to the subject matter covered. It is sold with the understanding that the publisher is not engaged in rendering legal, accounting, or other professional service. If legal advice or other expert assistance is required, the services of a competent professional should be sought.

All trademarks, service marks, registered trademarks, and registered service marks are the property of their respective owners and are used herein for identification purposes only.

ISBN 9781961409026 (paper)
ISBN 9781961409149 (ebook)
May 2024

SKYBE73E575-1953-49D5-84C8-3FFCCB850F2A_032624

Please visit our website at
www.WileyGlobalFinance.com.

CONTENTS

How to Use the CFA Program Curriculum ... ix
    CFA Institute Learning Ecosystem (LES) ... ix
    Designing Your Personal Study Program ... ix
    Errata ... x
    Other Feedback ... x

Equity Investments

Learning Module 1   **Market Organization and Structure** ... 3
    Introduction ... 4
    The Functions of the Financial System ... 4
        Helping People Achieve Their Purposes in Using the Financial System ... 5
        Determining Rates of Return ... 10
        Capital Allocation Efficiency ... 11
    Assets and Contracts ... 12
        Classifications of Assets and Markets ... 13
    Securities ... 15
        Fixed Income ... 15
        Equities ... 16
        Pooled Investments ... 17
    Currencies, Commodities, and Real Assets ... 18
        Commodities ... 19
        Real Assets ... 19
    Contracts ... 22
        Forward Contracts ... 23
        Futures Contracts ... 24
        Swap Contracts ... 25
        Option Contracts ... 26
        Other Contracts ... 27
    Financial Intermediaries ... 27
        Brokers, Exchanges, and Alternative Trading Systems ... 28
        Dealers ... 29
        Arbitrageurs ... 30
    Securitizers, Depository Institutions and Insurance Companies ... 32
        Depository Institutions and Other Financial Corporations ... 34
        Insurance Companies ... 35
    Settlement and Custodial Services and Summary ... 36
        Summary ... 38
    Positions and Short Positions ... 39
        Short Positions ... 40
    Leveraged Positions ... 41
    Orders and Execution Instructions ... 44
        Execution Instructions ... 45
    Validity Instructions and Clearing Instructions ... 49

	Stop Orders	49
	Clearing Instructions	51
Primary Security Markets		51
	Public Offerings	51
	Private Placements and Other Primary Market Transactions	53
	Importance of Secondary Markets to Primary Markets	55
Secondary Security Market and Contract Market Structures		55
	Trading Sessions	55
	Execution Mechanisms	56
	Market Information Systems	59
Well-functioning Financial Systems		60
Market Regulation		62
Summary		*65*
Practice Problems		*68*
Solutions		*76*

Learning Module 2

Security Market Indexes — 81

Introduction		81
Index Definition and Calculations of Value and Returns		82
	Calculation of Single-Period Returns	83
	Calculation of Index Values over Multiple Time Periods	85
Index Construction		86
	Target Market and Security Selection	87
	Index Weighting	87
Index Management: Rebalancing and Reconstitution		95
	Rebalancing	96
	Reconstitution	96
Uses of Market Indexes		97
	Gauges of Market Sentiment	98
	Proxies for Measuring and Modeling Returns, Systematic Risk, and Risk-Adjusted Performance	98
	Proxies for Asset Classes in Asset Allocation Models	98
	Benchmarks for Actively Managed Portfolios	98
	Model Portfolios for Investment Products	99
Equity indexes		99
	Broad Market Indexes	99
	Multi-Market Indexes	100
	Sector Indexes	101
	Style Indexes	101
Fixed-income indexes		102
	Construction	102
	Types of Fixed-Income Indexes	103
Indexes for Alternative Investments		105
	Commodity Indexes	105
	Real Estate Investment Trust Indexes	106
	Hedge Fund Indexes	107
Summary		*109*
Practice Problems		*111*

Contents

	Solutions	*118*
Learning Module 3	**Market Efficiency**	**123**
	Introduction	123
	The Concept of Market Efficiency	125
	The Description of Efficient Markets	125
	Market Value versus Intrinsic Value	127
	Factors Affecting Market Efficiency Including Trading Costs	128
	Market Participants	129
	Information Availability and Financial Disclosure	130
	Limits to Trading	131
	Transaction Costs and Information-Acquisition Costs	131
	Forms of Market Efficiency	132
	Weak Form	133
	Semi-Strong Form	134
	Strong Form	137
	Implications of the Efficient Market Hypothesis	137
	Fundamental Analysis	138
	Technical Analysis	138
	Portfolio Management	138
	Market Pricing Anomalies - Time Series and Cross-Sectional	139
	Time-Series Anomalies	140
	Cross-Sectional Anomalies	142
	Other Anomalies, Implications of Market Pricing Anomalies	142
	Closed-End Investment Fund Discounts	143
	Earnings Surprise	143
	Initial Public Offerings (IPOs)	144
	Predictability of Returns Based on Prior Information	145
	Implications for Investment Strategies	145
	Behavioral Finance	146
	Loss Aversion	146
	Herding	146
	Overconfidence	147
	Information Cascades	147
	Other Behavioral Biases	148
	Behavioral Finance and Investors	148
	Behavioral Finance and Efficient Markets	148
	Summary	*149*
	References	*150*
	Practice Problems	*152*
	Solutions	*156*
Learning Module 4	**Overview of Equity Securities**	**159**
	Importance of Equity Securities	159
	Equity Securities in Global Financial Markets	160
	Characteristics of Equity Securities	165
	Common Shares	166
	Preference Shares	168

	Private Versus Public Equity Securities	170
	Non-Domestic Equity Securities	173
	Direct Investing	174
	Depository Receipts	175
	Risk and Return Characteristics	178
	Return Characteristics of Equity Securities	178
	Risk of Equity Securities	179
	Equity and Company Value	180
	Accounting Return on Equity	181
	The Cost of Equity and Investors' Required Rates of Return	185
	Summary	*186*
	References	*189*
	Practice Problems	*190*
	Solutions	*194*
Learning Module 5	**Company Analysis: Past and Present**	**197**
	Introduction	197
	Company Research Reports	201
	Determining the Business Model	205
	Revenue Analysis	217
	Revenue Drivers	217
	Pricing Power	219
	Top-Down Revenue Analysis	221
	Operating Profitability and Working Capital Analysis	224
	Operating Costs and Their Classification	224
	Behavior with Output: Fixed and Variable Costs	225
	Natural and Functional Operating Cost Classifications and Measures of Operating Profitability	229
	Working Capital	232
	Capital Investments and Capital Structure	236
	Sources and Uses of Capital	236
	Evaluating Capital Investments and Capital Structure	237
	Practice Problems	*242*
	Solutions	*244*
Learning Module 6	**Industry and Competitive Analysis**	**245**
	Introduction	245
	Uses of Industry Analysis	248
	Why Analyze an Industry?	249
	Improve Forecasts	249
	Identify Investment Opportunities	250
	Industry and Competitive Analysis Steps	250
	Industry Classification	251
	Third-Party Industry Classification Schemes	252
	Limitations of Third-Party Industry Classification Schemes	254
	Alternative Methods of Grouping Companies	256
	Industry Survey	258
	Industry Size and Historical Growth Rate	258

	Characterizing Industry Growth	259
	Industry Profitability Measures	260
	Market Share Trends and Major Players	260
	Industry Structure and External Influences	265
	Assessing the Five Forces: A Checklist Approach	266
	External Influences on Industry Growth	271
	Competitive Positioning	276
	References	*280*
	Practice Problems	*281*
	Solutions	*283*
Learning Module 7	**Company Analysis: Forecasting**	**285**
	Introduction	285
	Forecast Objects, Principles, and Approaches	288
	What to Forecast?	289
	Focus on Objects That Are Regularly Disclosed	290
	Forecast Approaches	290
	Selecting a Forecast Horizon	294
	Forecasting Revenues	295
	Forecast Objects for Revenues	296
	Forecast Approaches for Revenues	297
	Forecasting Operating Expenses and Working Capital	301
	Cost of Sales and Gross Margins	301
	SG&A Expenses	303
	Working Capital Forecasts	306
	Forecasting Capital Investments and Capital Structure	311
	Scenario Analysis	318
	References	*331*
	Practice Problems	*332*
	Solutions	*334*
Learning Module 8	**Equity Valuation: Concepts and Basic Tools**	**335**
	Introduction	336
	Estimated Value and Market Price	336
	Categories of Equity Valuation Models	338
	Background for the Dividend Discount Model	340
	Dividends: Background for the Dividend Discount Model	340
	Dividend Discount Model (DDM) and Free-Cash-Flow-to-Equity Model (FCFE)	343
	Preferred Stock Valuation	346
	The Gordon Growth Model	349
	Multistage Dividend Discount Models	354
	Multipler Models and Relationship Among Price Multiples, Present Value Models, and Fundamentals	358
	Relationships among Price Multiples, Present Value Models, and Fundamentals	359
	Method of Comparables and Valuation Based on Price Multiples	362
	Illustration of a Valuation Based on Price Multiples	365

Enterprise Value	367
Asset-Based Valuation	370
Summary	*374*
References	*376*
Practice Problems	*377*
Solutions	*384*

Glossary — **G-1**

How to Use the CFA Program Curriculum

The CFA® Program exams measure your mastery of the core knowledge, skills, and abilities required to succeed as an investment professional. These core competencies are the basis for the Candidate Body of Knowledge (CBOK™). The CBOK consists of four components:

- A broad outline that lists the major CFA Program topic areas (www.cfainstitute.org/programs/cfa/curriculum/cbok/cbok)
- Topic area weights that indicate the relative exam weightings of the top-level topic areas (www.cfainstitute.org/en/programs/cfa/curriculum)
- Learning outcome statements (LOS) that advise candidates about the specific knowledge, skills, and abilities they should acquire from curriculum content covering a topic area: LOS are provided at the beginning of each block of related content and the specific lesson that covers them. We encourage you to review the information about the LOS on our website (www.cfainstitute.org/programs/cfa/curriculum/study-sessions), including the descriptions of LOS "command words" on the candidate resources page at www.cfainstitute.org/-/media/documents/support/programs/cfa-and-cipm-los-command-words.ashx.
- The CFA Program curriculum that candidates receive access to upon exam registration

Therefore, the key to your success on the CFA exams is studying and understanding the CBOK. You can learn more about the CBOK on our website: www.cfainstitute.org/programs/cfa/curriculum/cbok.

The curriculum, including the practice questions, is the basis for all exam questions. The curriculum is selected or developed specifically to provide candidates with the knowledge, skills, and abilities reflected in the CBOK.

CFA INSTITUTE LEARNING ECOSYSTEM (LES)

Your exam registration fee includes access to the CFA Institute Learning Ecosystem (LES). This digital learning platform provides access, even offline, to all the curriculum content and practice questions. The LES is organized as a series of learning modules consisting of short online lessons and associated practice questions. This tool is your source for all study materials, including practice questions and mock exams. The LES is the primary method by which CFA Institute delivers your curriculum experience. Here, candidates will find additional practice questions to test their knowledge. Some questions in the LES provide a unique interactive experience.

DESIGNING YOUR PERSONAL STUDY PROGRAM

An orderly, systematic approach to exam preparation is critical. You should dedicate a consistent block of time every week to reading and studying. Review the LOS both before and after you study curriculum content to ensure you can demonstrate the knowledge, skills, and abilities described by the LOS and the assigned reading. Use the LOS as a self-check to track your progress and highlight areas of weakness for later review.

Successful candidates report an average of more than 300 hours preparing for each exam. Your preparation time will vary based on your prior education and experience, and you will likely spend more time on some topics than on others.

ERRATA

The curriculum development process is rigorous and involves multiple rounds of reviews by content experts. Despite our efforts to produce a curriculum that is free of errors, in some instances, we must make corrections. Curriculum errata are periodically updated and posted by exam level and test date on the Curriculum Errata webpage (www.cfainstitute.org/en/programs/submit-errata). If you believe you have found an error in the curriculum, you can submit your concerns through our curriculum errata reporting process found at the bottom of the Curriculum Errata webpage.

OTHER FEEDBACK

Please send any comments or suggestions to info@cfainstitute.org, and we will review your feedback thoughtfully.

Equity Investments

LEARNING MODULE

1

Market Organization and Structure

by Larry Harris, PhD, CFA.

Larry Harris, PhD, CFA, is at the USC Marshall School of Business (USA).

LEARNING OUTCOMES	
Mastery	The candidate should be able to:
☐	explain the main functions of the financial system
☐	describe classifications of assets and markets
☐	describe the major types of securities, currencies, contracts, commodities, and real assets that trade in organized markets, including their distinguishing characteristics and major subtypes
☐	describe types of financial intermediaries and services that they provide
☐	compare positions an investor can take in an asset
☐	calculate and interpret the leverage ratio, the rate of return on a margin transaction, and the security price at which the investor would receive a margin call
☐	compare execution, validity, and clearing instructions
☐	compare market orders with limit orders
☐	define primary and secondary markets and explain how secondary markets support primary markets
☐	describe how securities, contracts, and currencies are traded in quote-driven, order-driven, and brokered markets
☐	describe characteristics of a well-functioning financial system
☐	describe objectives of market regulation

1. INTRODUCTION

Financial analysts gather and process information to make investment decisions, including those related to buying and selling assets. Generally, the decisions involve trading securities, currencies, contracts, commodities, and real assets such as real estate. Consider several examples:

- Fixed income analysts evaluate issuer credit-worthiness and macroeconomic prospects to determine which bonds and notes to buy or sell to preserve capital while obtaining a fair rate of return.
- Stock analysts study corporate values to determine which stocks to buy or sell to maximize the value of their stock portfolios.
- Corporate treasurers analyze exchange rates, interest rates, and credit conditions to determine which currencies to trade and which notes to buy or sell to have funds available in a needed currency.
- Risk managers work for producers or users of commodities to calculate how many commodity futures contracts to buy or sell to manage inventory risks.

Financial analysts must understand the characteristics of the markets in which their decisions will be executed. This reading, by examining those markets from the analyst's perspective, provides that understanding.

This reading is organized as follows. Section 2 examines the functions of the financial system. Section 3 introduces assets that investors, information-motivated traders, and risk managers use to advance their financial objectives and presents ways practitioners classify these assets into markets. These assets include such financial instruments as securities, currencies, and some contracts; certain commodities; and real assets. Financial analysts must know the distinctive characteristics of these trading assets.

Section 4 is an overview of financial intermediaries (entities that facilitate the functioning of the financial system). Section 5 discusses the positions that can be obtained while trading assets. You will learn about the benefits and risks of long and short positions, how these positions can be financed, and how the financing affects their risks. Section 6 discusses how market participants order trades and how markets process those orders. These processes must be understood to achieve trading objectives while controlling transaction costs.

Section 7 focuses on describing primary markets. Section 8 describes the structures of secondary markets in securities. Sections 9 and 10 close the reading with discussions of the characteristics of a well-functioning financial system and of how regulation helps make financial markets function better. A summary reviews the reading's major ideas and points, and practice problems conclude.

2. THE FUNCTIONS OF THE FINANCIAL SYSTEM

☐ explain the main functions of the financial system

The financial system includes markets and various financial intermediaries that help transfer financial assets, real assets, and financial risks in various forms from one entity to another, from one place to another, and from one point in time to another. These transfers take place whenever someone exchanges one asset or financial contract for another. The assets and contracts that people (people act on behalf of themselves, companies, charities, governments, etc., so the term "people" has a broad definition in this reading) trade include notes, bonds, stocks, exchange-traded funds, currencies, forward contracts, futures contracts, option contracts, swap contracts, and certain commodities. When the buyer and seller voluntarily arrange their trades, as is usually the case, the buyer and the seller both expect to be better off.

People use the financial system for six main purposes:

1. to save money for the future;
2. to borrow money for current use;
3. to raise equity capital;
4. to manage risks;
5. to exchange assets for immediate and future deliveries; and
6. to trade on information.

The main functions of the financial system are to facilitate:

1. the achievement of the purposes for which people use the financial system;
2. the discovery of the rates of return that equate aggregate savings with aggregate borrowings; and
3. the allocation of capital to the best uses.

These functions are extremely important to economic welfare. In a well-functioning financial system, transaction costs are low, analysts can value savings and investments, and scarce capital resources are used well.

Sections 2.1 through 2.3 expand on these three functions. The six subsections of Section 2.1 cover the six main purposes for which people use the financial system and how the financial system facilitates the achievement of those purposes. Sections 2.2 and 2.3 discuss determining rates of return and capital allocation efficiency, respectively.

Helping People Achieve Their Purposes in Using the Financial System

People often arrange transactions to achieve more than one purpose when using the financial system. For example, an investor who buys the stock of an oil producer may do so to move her wealth from the present to the future, to hedge the risk that she will have to pay more for energy in the future, and to exploit insightful research that she conducted that suggests the company's stock is undervalued in the marketplace. If the investment proves to be successful, she will have saved money for the future, managed her energy risk exposure, and obtained a return on her research.

The separate discussions of each of the six main uses of the financial system by people will help you better identify the reasons why people trade. Your ability to identify the various uses of the financial system will help you avoid confusion that often leads to poor financial decisions. The financial intermediaries that are mentioned in these discussions are explained further in Section 4.

Saving

People often have money that they choose not to spend now and that they want available in the future. For example, workers who save for their retirements need to move some of their current earnings into the future. When they retire, they will use their savings to replace the wages that they will no longer be earning. Similarly, companies save money from their sales revenue so that they can pay vendors when their bills come due, repay debt, or acquire assets (for example, other companies or machinery) in the future.

To move money from the present to the future, savers buy notes, certificates of deposit, bonds, stocks, mutual funds, or real assets such as real estate. These alternatives generally provide a better expected rate of return than simply storing money. Savers then sell these assets in the future to fund their future expenditures. When savers commit money to earn a financial return, they commonly are called investors. They invest when they purchase assets, and they divest when they sell them.

Investors require a fair rate of return while their money is invested. The required fair rate of return compensates them for the use of their money and for the risk that they may lose money if the investment fails or if inflation reduces the real value of their investments.

The financial system facilitates savings when institutions create investment vehicles, such as bank deposits, notes, stocks, and mutual funds, that investors can acquire and sell without paying substantial transaction costs. When these instruments are fairly priced and easy to trade, investors will use them to save more.

Borrowing

People, companies, and governments often want to spend money now that they do not have. They can obtain money to fund projects that they wish to undertake now by borrowing it. Companies can also obtain funds by selling ownership or equity interests (covered in Section 2.1.3). Banks and other investors provide those requiring funds with money because they expect to be repaid with interest or because they expect to be compensated with future disbursements, such as dividends and capital gains, as the ownership interest appreciates in value.

People may borrow to pay for such items as vacations, homes, cars, or education. They generally borrow through mortgages and personal loans, or by using credit cards. People typically repay these loans with money they earn later.

Companies often require money to fund current operations or to engage in new capital projects. They may borrow the needed funds in a variety of ways, such as arranging a loan or a line of credit with a bank, or selling fixed income securities to investors. Companies typically repay their borrowing with income generated in the future. In addition to borrowing, companies may raise funds by selling ownership interests.

Governments may borrow money to pay salaries and other expenses, to fund projects, to provide welfare benefits to their citizens and residents, and to subsidize various activities. Governments borrow by selling bills, notes, or bonds. Governments repay their debt using future revenues from taxes and in some instances from the projects funded by these debts.

Borrowers can borrow from lenders only if the lenders believe that they will be repaid. If the lenders believe, however, that repayment in full with interest may not occur, they will demand higher rates of interest to cover their expected losses and to compensate them for the discomfit they experience wondering whether they will lose their money. To lower the costs of borrowing, borrowers often pledge assets as collateral for their loans. The assets pledged as collateral often include those that will be purchased by the proceeds of the loan. If the borrowers do not repay their loans, the lenders can sell the collateral and use the proceeds to settle the loans.

Lenders often will not loan to borrowers who intend to invest in risky projects, especially if the borrowers cannot pledge other collateral. Investors may still be willing to supply capital for these risky projects if they believe that the projects will likely produce valuable future cash flows. Rather than lending money, however, they will contribute capital in exchange for equity in the projects.

The financial system facilitates borrowing. Lenders aggregate from savers the funds that borrowers require. Borrowers must convince lenders that they can repay their loans, and that, in the event they cannot, lenders can recover most of the funds lent. Credit bureaus, credit rating agencies, and governments promote borrowing; credit bureaus and credit rating agencies do so by collecting and disseminating information that lenders need to analyze credit prospects and governments do so by establishing bankruptcy codes and courts that define and enforce the rights of borrowers and lenders. When the transaction costs of loans (i.e., the costs of arranging, monitoring, and collecting them) are low, borrowers can borrow more to fund current expenditures with credible promises to return the money in the future.

Raising Equity Capital

Companies often raise money for projects by selling (issuing) ownership interests (e.g., corporate common stock or partnership interests). Although these equity instruments legally represent ownership in companies rather than loans to the companies, selling equity to raise capital is simply another mechanism for moving money from the future to the present. When shareholders or partners contribute capital to a company, the company obtains money in the present in exchange for equity instruments that will be entitled to distributions in the future. Although the repayment of the money is not scheduled as it would be for loans, equity instruments also represent potential claims on money in the future.

The financial system facilitates raising equity capital. Investment banks help companies issue equities, analysts value the securities that companies sell, and regulatory reporting requirements and accounting standards attempt to ensure the production of meaningful financial disclosures. The financial system helps promote capital formation by producing the financial information needed to determine fair prices for equity. Liquid markets help companies raise capital. In these markets, shareholders can easily divest their equities as desired. When investors can easily value and trade equities, they are more willing to fund reasonable projects that companies wish to undertake.

EXAMPLE 1

Financing Capital Projects

1. As a chief financial officer (CFO) of a large industrial firm, you need to raise cash within a few months to pay for a project to expand existing and acquire new manufacturing facilities. What are the primary options available to you?

Solution:

Your primary options are to borrow the funds or to raise the funds by selling ownership interests. If the company borrows the funds, you may have the company pledge some or all of the project as collateral to reduce the cost of borrowing.

Managing Risks

Many people, companies, and governments face financial risks that concern them. These risks include default risk and the risk of changes in interest rates, exchange rates, raw material prices, and sale prices, among many other risks. These risks are often managed by trading contracts that serve as hedges for the risks.

For example, a farmer and a food processor both face risks related to the price of grain. The farmer fears that prices will be lower than expected when his grain is ready for sale whereas the food processor fears that prices will be higher than expected when she has to buy grain in the future. They both can eliminate their exposures to these risks if they enter into a binding forward contract for the farmer to sell a specified quantity of grain to the food processor at a future date at a mutually agreed upon price. By entering into a forward contract that sets the future trade price, they both eliminate their exposure to changing grain prices.

In general, hedgers trade to offset or insure against risks that concern them. In addition to forward contracts, they may use futures contracts, option contracts, or insurance contracts to transfer risk to other entities more willing to bear the risks (these contracts will be covered in Section 3.4). Often the hedger and the other entity face exactly the opposite risks, so the transfer makes both more secure, as in the grain example.

The financial system facilitates risk management when liquid markets exist in which risk managers can trade instruments that are correlated (or inversely correlated) with the risks that concern them without incurring substantial transaction costs. Investment banks, exchanges, and insurance companies devote substantial resources to designing such contracts and to ensuring that they will trade in liquid markets. When such markets exist, people are better able to manage the risks that they face and often are more willing to undertake risky activities that they expect will be profitable.

Exchanging Assets for Immediate Delivery (Spot Market Trading)

People and companies often trade one asset for another that they rate more highly or, equivalently, that is more useful to them. They may trade one currency for another currency, or money for a needed commodity or right. Following are some examples that illustrate these trades:

- Volkswagen pays its German workers in euros, but the company receives dollars when it sells cars in the United States. To convert money from dollars to euros, Volkswagen trades in the foreign exchange markets.
- A Mexican investor who is worried about the prospects for peso inflation or a potential devaluation of the peso may buy gold in the spot gold market. (This transaction may hedge against the risk of devaluation of the peso because the value of gold may increase with inflation.)
- A plastic producer must buy carbon credits to emit carbon dioxide when burning fuel to comply with environmental regulations. The carbon credit is a legal right that the producer must have to engage in activities that emit carbon dioxide.

In each of these cases, the trades are considered spot market trades because the instruments trade for immediate delivery. The financial system facilitates these exchanges when liquid spot markets exist in which people can arrange and settle trades without substantial transaction costs.

Information-Motivated Trading

Information-motivated traders trade to profit from information that they believe allows them to predict future prices. Like all other traders, they hope to buy at low prices and sell at higher prices. Unlike pure investors, however, they expect to earn a return on their information in addition to the normal return expected for bearing risk through time.

Active investment managers are information-motivated traders who collect and analyze information to identify securities, contracts, and other assets that their analyses indicate are under- or overvalued. They then buy those that they consider undervalued and sell those that they consider overvalued. If successful, they obtain a greater return than the unconditional return that would be expected for bearing the risk in their positions. The return that they expect to obtain is a conditional return earned on the basis of the information in their analyses. Practitioners often call this process active portfolio management.

The Functions of the Financial System

Note that the distinction between pure investors and information-motivated traders depends on their motives for trading and not on the risks that they take or their expected holding periods. Investors trade to move wealth from the present to the future whereas information-motivated traders trade to profit from superior information about future values. When trading to move wealth forward, the time period may be short or long. For example, a bank treasurer may only need to move money overnight and might use money market instruments trading in an interbank funds market to accomplish that. A pension fund, however, may need to move money 30 years forward and might do that by using shares trading in a stock market. Both are investors although their expected holding periods and the risks in the instruments that they trade are vastly different.

In contrast, information-motivated traders trade because their information-based analyses suggest to them that prices of various instruments will increase or decrease in the future at a rate faster than others without their information or analytical models would expect. After establishing their positions, they hope that prices will change quickly in their favor so that they can close their positions, realize their profits, and redeploy their capital. These price changes may occur almost instantaneously, or they may take years to occur if information about the mispricing is difficult to obtain or understand.

The two categories of traders are not mutually exclusive. Investors also are often information-motivated traders. Many investors who want to move wealth forward through time collect and analyze information to select securities that will allow them to obtain conditional returns that are greater than the unconditional returns expected for securities in their asset classes. If they have rational reasons to expect that their efforts will indeed produce superior returns, they are information-motivated traders. If they consistently fail to produce such returns, their efforts will be futile, and they would have been better off simply buying and holding well-diversified portfolios.

EXAMPLE 2

Investing versus Information-Motivated Trading

1. The head of a large labor union with a pension fund asks you, a pension consultant, to distinguish between investing and information-motivated trading. You are expected to provide an explanation that addresses the financial problems that she faces. How would you respond?

Solution:

The object of investing for the pension fund is to move the union's pension assets from the present to the future when they will be needed to pay the union's retired pensioners. The pension fund managers will typically do this by buying stocks, bonds, and perhaps other assets. The pension fund managers expect to receive a fair rate of return on the pension fund's assets without paying excessive transaction costs and management fees. The return should compensate the fund for the risks that it bears and for the time that other people are using the fund's money.

The object of information-motivated trading is to earn a return in excess of the fair rate of return. Information-motivated traders analyze information that they collect with the hope that their analyses will allow them to predict better than others where prices will be in the future. They then buy assets that they think will produce excess returns and sell those that they think will underperform. Active investment managers are information-motivated traders.

> The characteristic that most distinguishes investors from information-motivated traders is the return that they expect. Although both types of traders hope to obtain extraordinary returns, investors rationally expect to receive only fair returns during the periods of their investments. In contrast, information-motivated traders expect to make returns in excess of required fair rates of return. Of course, not all investing or information-motivated trading is successful (in other words, the actual returns may not equal or exceed the expected returns).

The financial system facilitates information-motivated trading when liquid markets allow active managers to trade without significant transaction costs. Accounting standards and reporting requirements that produce meaningful financial disclosures reduce the costs of being well informed, but do not necessarily help informed traders profit because they often compete with each other. The most profitable well-informed traders are often those that have the most unique insights into future values.

Summary

People use the financial system for many purposes, the most important of which are saving, borrowing, raising equity capital, managing risk, exchanging assets in spot markets, and information-motivated trading. The financial system best facilitates these uses when people can trade instruments that interest them in liquid markets, when institutions provide financial services at low cost, when information about assets and about credit risks is readily available, and when regulation helps ensure that everyone faithfully honors their contracts.

Determining Rates of Return

Saving, borrowing, and selling equity are all means of moving money through time. Savers move money from the present to the future whereas borrowers and equity issuers move money from the future to the present.

Because time machines do not exist, money can travel forward in time only if an equal amount of money is travelling in the other direction. This equality always occurs because borrowers and equity sellers create the securities in which savers invest. For example, the bond sold by a company that needs to move money from the future to the present is the same bond bought by a saver who needs to move money from the present to the future.

The aggregate amount of money that savers will move from the present to the future is related to the expected rate of return on their investments. If the expected return is high, they will forgo current consumption and move more money to the future. Similarly, the aggregate amount of money that borrowers and equity sellers will move from the future to the present depends on the costs of borrowing funds or of giving up ownership. These costs can be expressed as the rate of return that borrowers and equity sellers are expected to deliver in exchange for obtaining current funds. It is the same rate that savers expect to receive when delivering current funds. If this rate is low, borrowers and equity sellers will want to move more money to the present from the future. In other words, they will want to raise more funds.

Because the total money saved must equal the total money borrowed and received in exchange for equity, the expected rate of return depends on the aggregate supply of funds through savings and the aggregate demand for funds. If the rate is too high, savers will want to move more money to the future than borrowers and equity issuers will want to move to the present. The expected rate will have to be lower to discourage the savers and to encourage the borrowers and equity issuers. Conversely, if the rate is too low, savers will want to move less money forward than borrowers and equity issuers will want to move to the present. The expected rate will have to be higher to

The Functions of the Financial System

encourage the savers and to discourage the borrowers and equity issuers. Between rates too high and too low, an expected rate of return exists, in theory, in which the aggregate supply of funds for investing (supply of funds saved) and the aggregate demand for funds through borrowing and equity issuing are equal.

Economists call this rate the equilibrium interest rate. It is the price for moving money through time. Determining this rate is one of the most important functions of the financial system. The equilibrium interest rate is the only interest rate that would exist if all securities were equally risky, had equal terms, and were equally liquid. In fact, the required rates of return for securities vary by their risk characteristics, terms, and liquidity. For a given issuer, investors generally require higher rates of return for equity than for debt, for long-term securities than for short-term securities, and for illiquid securities than for liquid ones. Financial analysts recognize that all required rates of return depend on a common equilibrium interest rate plus adjustments for risk.

EXAMPLE 3

Interest Rates

1. For a presentation to private wealth clients by your firm's chief economist, you are asked to prepare the audience by explaining the most fundamental facts concerning the role of interest rates in the economy. You agree. What main points should you try to convey?

Solution:

Savers have money now that they will want to use in the future. Borrowers want to use money now that they do not have, but they expect that they will have money in the future. Borrowers are loaned money by savers and promise to repay it in the future.

The interest rate is the return that lenders, the savers, expect to receive from borrowers for allowing borrowers to use the savers' money. The interest rate is the price of using money.

Interest rates depend on the total amount of money that people want to borrow and the total amount of money that people are willing to lend. Interest rates are high when, in aggregate, people value having money now substantially more than they value having money in the future. In contrast, if many people with money want to use it in the future and few people presently need more money than they have, interest rates will be low.

Capital Allocation Efficiency

Primary capital markets (primary markets) are the markets in which companies and governments raise capital (funds). Companies may raise funds by borrowing money or by issuing equity. Governments may raise funds by borrowing money.

Economies are said to be **allocationally efficient** when their financial systems allocate capital (funds) to those uses that are most productive. Although companies may be interested in getting funding for many potential projects, not all projects are worth funding. One of the most important functions of the financial system is to ensure that only the best projects obtain scarce capital funds; the funds available from savers should be allocated to the most productive uses.

In market-based economies, savers determine, directly or indirectly, which projects obtain capital. Savers determine capital allocations directly by choosing which securities they will invest in. Savers determine capital allocations indirectly by giving funds to financial intermediaries that then invest the funds. Because investors fear the loss of their money, they will lend at lower interest rates to borrowers with the best credit prospects or the best collateral, and they will lend at higher rates to other borrowers with less secure prospects. Similarly, they will buy only those equities that they believe have the best prospects relative to their prices and risks.

To avoid losses, investors carefully study the prospects of the various investment opportunities available to them. The decisions that they make tend to be well informed, which helps ensure that capital is allocated efficiently. The fear of losses by investors and by those raising funds to invest in projects ensures that only the best projects tend to be funded. The process works best when investors are well informed about the prospects of the various projects.

In general, investors will fund an equity project if they expect that the value of the project is greater than its cost, and they will not fund projects otherwise. If the investor expectations are accurate, only projects that should be undertaken will be funded and all such projects will be funded. Accurate market information thus leads to efficient capital allocation.

> **EXAMPLE 4**
>
> ### Primary Market Capital Allocation
>
> 1. How can poor information about the value of a project result in poor capital allocation decisions?
>
> ### Solution:
>
> Projects should be undertaken only if their value is greater than their cost. If investors have poor information and overestimate the value of a project in which its true value is less than its cost, a wealth-diminishing project may be undertaken. Alternatively, if investors have poor information and underestimate the value of a project in which its true value is greater than its cost, a wealth-enhancing project may not be undertaken.

3 ASSETS AND CONTRACTS

☐ describe classifications of assets and markets

People, companies, and governments use many different assets and contracts to further their financial goals and to manage their risks. The most common assets include financial assets (such as bank deposits, certificates of deposit, loans, mortgages, corporate and government bonds and notes, common and preferred stocks, real estate investment trusts, master limited partnership interests, pooled investment products, and exchange-traded funds), currencies, certain commodities (such as gold and oil), and real assets (such as real estate). The most common contracts are option, futures, forward, swap, and insurance contracts. People, companies, and governments use these assets and contracts to raise funds, to invest, to profit from information-motivated trading, to hedge risks, and/or to transfer money from one form to another.

Classifications of Assets and Markets

Practitioners often classify assets and the markets in which they trade by various common characteristics to facilitate communications with their clients, with each other, and with regulators.

The most actively traded assets are securities, currencies, contracts, and commodities. In addition, real assets are traded. Securities generally include debt instruments, equities, and shares in pooled investment vehicles. **Currencies** are monies issued by national monetary authorities. Contracts are agreements to exchange securities, currencies, commodities or other contracts in the future. Commodities include precious metals, energy products, industrial metals, and agricultural products. Real assets are tangible properties such as real estate, airplanes, or machinery. Securities, currencies, and contracts are classified as financial assets whereas commodities and real assets are classified as physical assets.

Securities are further classified as debt or equity. Debt instruments (also called fixed-income instruments) are promises to repay borrowed money. Equities represent ownership in companies. Pooled investment vehicle shares represent ownership of an undivided interest in an investment portfolio. The portfolio may include securities, currencies, contracts, commodities, or real assets. Pooled investment vehicles, such as exchange-traded funds, which exclusively own shares in other companies, generally are also considered equities.

Securities are also classified by whether they are public or private securities. Public securities are those registered to trade in public markets, such as on exchanges or through dealers. In most jurisdictions, issuers must meet stringent minimum regulatory standards, including reporting and corporate governance standards, to issue publicly traded securities.

Private securities are all other securities. Often, only specially qualified investors can purchase private equities and private debt instruments. Investors may purchase them directly from the issuer or indirectly through an investment vehicle specifically formed to hold such securities. Issuers often issue private securities when they find public reporting standards too burdensome or when they do not want to conform to the regulatory standards associated with public equity. Venture capital is private equity that investors supply to companies when or shortly after they are founded. Private securities generally are illiquid. In contrast, many public securities trade in liquid markets in which sellers can easily find buyers for their securities.

Contracts are derivative contracts if their values depend on the prices of other underlying assets. Derivative contracts may be classified as physical or financial depending on whether the underlying instruments are physical products or financial securities. Equity derivatives are contracts whose values depend on equities or indexes of equities. Fixed-income derivatives are contracts whose values depend on debt securities or indexes of debt securities.

Practitioners classify markets by whether the markets trade instruments for immediate delivery or for future delivery. Markets that trade contracts that call for delivery in the future are forward or futures markets. Those that trade for immediate delivery are called **spot markets** to distinguish them from forward markets that trade contracts on the same underlying instruments. Options markets trade contracts that deliver in the future, but delivery takes place only if the holders of the options choose to exercise them.

When issuers sell securities to investors, practitioners say that they trade in the **primary market**. When investors sell those securities to others, they trade in the **secondary market**. In the primary market, funds flow to the issuer of the security from the purchaser. In the secondary market, funds flow between traders.

Practitioners classify financial markets as money markets or capital markets. **Money markets** trade debt instruments maturing in one year or less. The most common such instruments are repurchase agreements (defined in Section 3.2.1), negotiable certificates of deposit, government bills, and commercial paper. In contrast, **capital markets** trade instruments of longer duration, such as bonds and equities, whose values depend on the credit-worthiness of the issuers and on payments of interest or dividends that will be made in the future and may be uncertain. Corporations generally finance their operations in the capital markets, but some also finance a portion of their operations by issuing short-term securities, such as commercial paper.

Finally, practitioners distinguish between **traditional investment markets** and **alternative investment markets**. Traditional investments include all publicly traded debts and equities and shares in pooled investment vehicles that hold publicly traded debts and/or equities. Alternative investments include **hedge funds**, private equities (including venture capital), commodities, real estate securities and real estate properties, securitized debts, operating leases, machinery, collectibles, and precious gems. Because these investments are often hard to trade and hard to value, they may sometimes trade at substantial deviations from their intrinsic values. The discounts compensate investors for the research that they must do to value these assets and for their inability to easily sell the assets if they need to liquidate a portion of their portfolios.

The remainder of this section describes the most common assets and contracts that people, companies, and governments trade.

EXAMPLE 5

Asset and Market Classification

The investment policy of a mutual fund only permits the fund to invest in public equities traded in secondary markets. Would the fund be able to purchase:

1. Common stock of a company that trades on a large stock exchange?

Solution to 1:

Yes. Common stock is equity. Those common stocks that trade on large exchanges invariably are public equities that trade in secondary markets.

2. Common stock of a public company that trades only through dealers?

Solution to 2:

Yes. Dealer markets are secondary markets and the security is a public equity.

3. A government bond?

Solution to 3:

No. Although government bonds are public securities, they are not equities. They are debt securities.

4. A single stock futures contract?

Solution to 4:

No. Although the underlying instruments for single stock futures are invariably public equities, single stock futures are derivative contracts, not equities.

5. Common stock sold for the first time by a properly registered public company?

Solution to 5:

No. The fund would not be able to buy these shares because a purchase from the issuer would be in the primary market. The fund would have to wait until it could buy the shares from someone other than the issuer.

6. Shares in a privately held bank with €10 billion of capital?

Solution to 6:

No. These shares are private equities, not public equities. The public prominence of the company does not make its securities public securities unless they have been properly registered as public securities.

SECURITIES

☐ describe the major types of securities, currencies, contracts, commodities, and real assets that trade in organized markets, including their distinguishing characteristics and major subtypes

People, companies, and governments sell securities to raise money. Securities include bonds, notes, commercial paper, mortgages, common stocks, preferred stocks, warrants, mutual fund shares, unit trusts, and depository receipts. These can be classified broadly as fixed-income instruments, equities, and shares in pooled investment vehicles. Note that the legal definition of a security varies by country and may or may not coincide with the usage here. Securities that are sold to the public or that can be resold to the public are called issues. Companies and governments are the most common issuers.

Fixed Income

Fixed-income instruments contractually include predetermined payment schedules that usually include interest and principal payments. Fixed-income instruments generally are promises to repay borrowed money but may include other instruments with payment schedules, such as settlements of legal cases or prizes from lotteries. The payment amounts may be pre-specified or they may vary according to a fixed formula that depends on the future values of an interest rate or a commodity price. Bonds, notes, bills, certificates of deposit, commercial paper, repurchase agreements, loan agreements, and mortgages are examples of promises to repay money in the future. People, companies, and governments create fixed-income instruments when they borrow money.

Corporations and governments issue bonds and notes. Fixed-income securities with shorter maturities are called "notes," those with longer maturities are called "bonds." The cutoff is usually at 10 years. In practice, however, the terms are generally used interchangeably. Both become short-term instruments when the remaining time until maturity is short, usually taken to be one year or less.

Some corporations issue convertible bonds, which are typically convertible into stock, usually at the option of the holder after some period. If stock prices are high so that conversion is likely, convertibles are valued like stock. Conversely, if stock prices are low so that conversion is unlikely, convertibles are valued like bonds.

Bills, certificates of deposit, and commercial paper are respectively issued by governments, banks, and corporations. They usually mature within a year of being issued; certificates of deposit sometimes have longer initial maturities.

Repurchase agreements (repos) are short-term lending instruments. The term can be as short as overnight. A borrower seeking funds will sell an instrument—typically a high-quality bond—to a lender with an agreement to repurchase it later at a slightly higher price based on an agreed upon interest rate.

Practitioners distinguish between short-term, intermediate-term, and long-term fixed-income securities. No general consensus exists about the definition of short-term, intermediate-term, and long-term. Instruments that mature in less than one to two years are considered short-term instruments whereas those that mature in more than five to ten years are considered long-term instruments. In the middle are intermediate-term instruments.

Instruments trading in money markets are called money market instruments. Such instruments are traded debt instruments maturing in one year or less. Money market funds and corporations seeking a return on their short-term cash balances typically hold money market instruments.

Equities

Equities represent ownership rights in companies. These include common and preferred shares. Common shareholders own residual rights to the assets of the company. They have the right to receive any dividends declared by the boards of directors, and in the event of liquidation, any assets remaining after all other claims are paid. Acting through the boards of directors that they elect, common shareholders usually can select the managers who run the corporations.

Preferred shares are equities that have preferred rights (relative to common shares) to the cash flows and assets of the company. Preferred shareholders generally have the right to receive a specific dividend on a regular basis. If the preferred share is a cumulative preferred equity, the company must pay the preferred shareholders any previously omitted dividends before it can pay dividends to the common shareholders. Preferred shareholders also have higher claims to assets relative to common shareholders in the event of corporate liquidation. For valuation purposes, financial analysts generally treat preferred stocks as fixed-income securities when the issuers will clearly be able to pay their promised dividends in the foreseeable future.

Warrants are securities issued by a corporation that allow the warrant holders to buy a security issued by that corporation, if they so desire, usually at any time before the warrants expire or, if not, upon expiration. The security that warrant holders can buy usually is the issuer's common stock, in which case the warrants are considered equities because the warrant holders can obtain equity in the company by exercising their warrants. The warrant **exercise price** is the price that the warrant holder must pay to buy the security.

> **EXAMPLE 6**
>
> **Securities**
>
> 1. What factors distinguish fixed-income securities from equities?
>
> **Solution:**
>
> Fixed-income securities generate income on a regular schedule. They derive their value from the promise to pay a scheduled cash flow. The most common fixed-income securities are promises made by people, companies, and governments to repay loans.
>
> Equities represent residual ownership in companies after all other claims—including any fixed-income liabilities of the company—have been satisfied. For corporations, the claims of preferred equities typically have priority over the claims of common equities. Common equities have the residual ownership in corporations.

Pooled Investments

Pooled investment vehicles are mutual funds, trusts, depositories, and hedge funds, that issue securities that represent shared ownership in the assets that these entities hold. The securities created by mutual funds, trusts, depositories, and hedge fund are respectively called *shares*, *units*, *depository receipts*, and *limited partnership interests* but practitioners often use these terms interchangeably. People invest in pooled investment vehicles to benefit from the investment management services of their managers and from diversification opportunities that are not readily available to them on an individual basis.

Mutual funds are investment vehicles that pool money from many investors for investment in a portfolio of securities. They are often legally organized as investment trusts or as corporate investment companies. Pooled investment vehicles may be open-ended or closed-ended. Open-ended funds issue new shares and redeem existing shares on demand, usually on a daily basis. The price at which a fund redeems and sells the fund's shares is based on the net asset value of the fund's portfolio, which is the difference between the fund's assets and liabilities, expressed on a per share basis. Investors generally buy and sell open-ended mutual funds by trading with the mutual fund.

In contrast, closed-end funds issue shares in primary market offerings that the fund or its investment bankers arrange. Once issued, investors cannot sell their shares of the fund back to the fund by demanding redemption. Instead, investors in closed-end funds must sell their shares to other investors in the secondary market. The secondary market prices of closed-end funds may differ—sometimes quite significantly—from their net asset values. Closed-end funds generally trade at a discount to their net asset values. The discount reflects the expenses of running the fund and sometimes investor concerns about the quality of the management. Closed-end funds may also trade at a discount or a premium to net asset value when investors believe that the portfolio securities are overvalued or undervalued. Many financial analysts thus believe that discounts and premiums on closed-end funds measure market sentiment.

Exchange-traded funds (ETFs) and exchange-traded notes (ETNs) are open-ended funds that investors can trade among themselves in secondary markets. The prices at which ETFs trade rarely differ much from net asset values because a class of investors, known as authorized participants (APs), has the option of trading directly with the ETF. If the market price of an equity ETF is sufficiently below its net asset value, APs will buy shares in the secondary market at market price and redeem shares at net asset value with the fund. Conversely, if the price of an ETF is sufficiently above its net asset value, APs will buy shares from the fund at net asset value and sell shares in the secondary market at market price. As a result, the market price and net asset values of ETFs tend to converge.

Many ETFs permit only in-kind deposits and redemptions. Buyers who buy directly from such a fund pay for their shares with a portfolio of securities rather than with cash. Similarly, sellers receive a portfolio of securities. The transaction portfolio generally is very similar—often essentially identical—to the portfolio held by the fund. Practitioners sometimes call such funds "depositories" because they issue depository receipts for the portfolios that traders deposit with them. The traders then trade the receipts in the secondary market. Some warehouses holding industrial materials and precious metals also issue tradable warehouse receipts.

Asset-backed securities are securities whose values and income payments are derived from a pool of assets, such as mortgage bonds, credit card debt, or car loans. These securities typically pass interest and principal payments received from the pool of assets through to their holders on a monthly basis. These payments may depend on formulas that give some classes of securities—called tranches—backed by the pool more value than other classes.

Hedge funds are investment funds that generally organize as limited partnerships. The hedge fund managers are the general partners. The limited partners are qualified investors who are wealthy enough and well informed enough to tolerate and accept substantial losses, should they occur. The regulatory requirements to participate in a hedge fund and the regulatory restrictions on hedge funds vary by jurisdiction. Most hedge funds follow only one investment strategy, but no single investment strategy characterizes hedge funds as a group. Hedge funds exist that follow almost every imaginable strategy ranging from long–short arbitrage in the stock markets to direct investments in exotic alternative assets.

The primary distinguishing characteristic of hedge funds is their management compensation scheme. Almost all funds pay their managers with an annual fee that is proportional to their assets and with an additional performance fee that depends on the wealth that the funds generate for their shareholders. A secondary distinguishing characteristic of many hedge funds is the use of leverage to increase risk exposure and to hopefully increase returns.

5. CURRENCIES, COMMODITIES, AND REAL ASSETS

☐ describe the major types of securities, currencies, contracts, commodities, and real assets that trade in organized markets, including their distinguishing characteristics and major subtypes

Currencies are monies issued by national monetary authorities. Approximately 180 currencies are currently in use throughout the world. Some of these currencies are regarded as reserve currencies. Reserve currencies are currencies that national central banks and other monetary authorities hold in significant quantities. The primary reserve currencies are the US dollar and the euro. Secondary reserve currencies include the British pound, the Japanese yen, and the Swiss franc.

Currencies, Commodities, and Real Assets

Currencies trade in foreign exchange markets. In spot currency transactions, one currency is immediately or almost immediately exchanged for another. The rate of exchange is called the spot exchange rate. Traders typically negotiate institutional trades in multiples of large quantities, such as US$1 million or ¥100 million. Institutional trades generally settle in two business days.

Retail currency trades most commonly take place through commercial banks when their customers exchange currencies at a location of the bank, use ATM machines when travelling to withdraw a different currency than the currency in which their bank accounts are denominated, or use credit cards to buy items priced in different currencies. Retail currency trades also take place at airport kiosks, at store front currency exchanges, or on the street.

Commodities

Commodities include precious metals, energy products, industrial metals, agricultural products, and carbon credits. Spot commodity markets trade commodities for immediate delivery whereas the forward and futures markets trade commodities for future delivery. Managers seeking positions in commodities can acquire them directly by trading in the spot markets or indirectly by trading forward and futures contracts.

The producers and processors of industrial metals and agricultural products are the primary users of the spot commodity markets because they generally are best able to take and make delivery and to store physical products. They undertake these activities in the normal course of operating their businesses. Their ability to handle physical products and the information that they gather operating businesses also gives them substantial advantages as information-motivated traders in these markets. Many producers employ financial analysts to help them analyze commodity market conditions so that they can best manage their inventories to hedge their operational risks and to speculate on future price changes.

Commodities also interest information-motivated traders and investment managers because they can use them as hedges against risks that they hold in their portfolios or as vehicles to speculate on future price changes. Most such traders take positions in the futures markets because they usually do not have facilities to handle most physical products nor can they easily obtain them. They also cannot easily cope with the normal variation in qualities that characterizes many commodities. Information-motivated traders and investment managers also prefer to trade in futures markets because most futures markets are more liquid than their associated spot markets and forward markets. The liquidity allows them to easily close their positions before delivery so that they can avoid handling physical products.

Some information-motivated traders and investment managers, however, trade in the spot commodity markets, especially when they can easily contract for low-cost storage. Commodities for which delivery and storage costs are lowest are nonperishable products for which the ratio of value to weight is high and variation in quality is low. These generally include precious metals, industrial diamonds, such high-value industrial metals as copper, aluminum, and mercury, and carbon credits.

Real Assets

Real assets include such tangible properties as real estate, airplanes, machinery, or lumber stands. These assets normally are held by operating companies, such as real estate developers, airplane leasing companies, manufacturers, or loggers. Many institutional investment managers, however, have been adding real assets to their portfolios as direct investments (involving direct ownership of the real assets) and indirect investments (involving indirect ownership, for example, purchase of securities of companies that invest in real assets or real estate investment trusts). Investments in real assets are attractive to them because of the income and tax benefits that they often generate, and because changes in their values may have a low correlation with other investments that the managers hold.

Direct investments in real assets generally require substantial management to ensure that the assets are maintained and used efficiently. Investment managers investing in such assets must either hire personnel to manage them or hire outside management companies. Either way, management of real assets is quite costly.

Real assets are unique properties in the sense that no two assets are alike. An example of a unique property is a real estate parcel. No two parcels are the same because, if nothing else, they are located in different places. Real assets generally differ in their conditions, remaining useful lives, locations, and suitability for various purposes. These differences are very important to the people who use them, so the market for a given real asset may be very limited. Thus, real assets tend to trade in very illiquid markets.

The heterogeneity of real assets, their illiquidity, and the substantial costs of managing them are all factors that complicate the valuation of real assets and generally make them unsuitable for most investment portfolios. These same problems, however, often cause real assets to be misvalued in the market, so astute information-motivated traders may occasionally identify significantly undervalued assets. The benefits from purchasing such assets, however, are often offset by the substantial costs of searching for them and by the substantial costs of managing them.

Many financial intermediaries create entities, such as real estate investment trusts (REITs) and master limited partnerships (MLPs), to securitize real assets and to facilitate indirect investment in real assets. The financial intermediaries manage the assets and pass through the net benefits after management costs to the investors who hold these securities. Because these securities are much more homogenous and divisible than the real assets that they represent, they tend to trade in much more liquid markets. Thus, they are much more suitable as investments than the real assets themselves.

Of course, investors seeking exposure to real assets can also buy shares in corporations that hold and operate real assets. Although almost all corporations hold and operate real assets, many specialize in assets that particularly interest investors seeking exposure to specific real asset classes. For example, investors interested in owning aircraft can buy an aircraft leasing company such as Waha Capital (Abu Dhabi Securities Exchange) and Aircastle Limited (NYSE).

EXAMPLE 7

Assets and Contracts

Consider the following assets and contracts:

Bank deposits	Hedge funds
Certificates of deposit	Master limited partnership interests
Common stocks	Mortgages
Corporate bonds	Mutual funds
Currencies	Stock option contracts
Exchange-traded funds	Preferred stocks
Lumber forward contracts	Real estate parcels
Crude oil futures contracts	Interest rate swaps
Gold	Treasury notes

Currencies, Commodities, and Real Assets

1. Which of these represent ownership in corporations?

Solution to 1:

Common and preferred stocks represent ownership in corporations.

2. Which of these are debt instruments?

Solution to 2:

Bank deposits, certificates of deposit, corporate bonds, mortgages, and Treasury notes are all debt instruments. They respectively represent loans made to banks, corporations, mortgagees (typically real estate owners), and the Treasury.

3. Which of these are created by traders rather than by issuers?

Solution to 3:

Lumber forward contracts, crude oil futures contracts, stock option contracts, and interest rate swaps are created when the seller sells them to a buyer.

4. Which of these are pooled investment vehicles?

Solution to 4:

Exchange-traded funds, hedge funds, and mutual funds are pooled investment vehicles. They represent shared ownership in a portfolio of other assets.

5. Which of these are real assets?

Solution to 5:

Real estate parcels are real assets.

6. Which of these would a home builder most likely use to hedge construction costs?

Solution to 6:

A builder would buy lumber forward contracts to lock in the price of lumber needed to build homes.

7. Which of these would a corporation trade when moving cash balances among various countries?

Solution to 7:

Corporations often trade currencies when moving cash from one country to another.

6. CONTRACTS

> describe the major types of securities, currencies, contracts, commodities, and real assets that trade in organized markets, including their distinguishing characteristics and major subtypes

A contract is an agreement among traders to do something in the future. Contracts include forward, futures, swap, option, and insurance contracts. The values of most contracts depend on the value of an **underlying** asset. The underlying asset may be a commodity, a security, an index representing the values of other instruments, a currency pair or basket, or other contracts.

Contracts provide for some physical or cash settlement in the future. In a physically settled contract, settlement occurs when the parties to the contract physically exchange some item, such as avocados, pork bellies, or gold bars. Physical settlement also includes the delivery of such financial instruments as bonds, equities, or futures contracts even though the delivery is electronic. In contrast, cash settled contracts settle through cash payments. The amount of the payment depends on formulas specified in the contracts.

Financial analysts classify contracts by whether they are physical or financial based on the nature of the underlying asset. If the underlying asset is a physical product, the contract is a physical; otherwise, the contract is a financial. Examples of assets classified as physical include contracts for the delivery of petroleum, lumber, and gold. Examples of assets classified as financial include option contracts, and contracts on interest rates, stock indexes, currencies, and credit default swaps.

Contracts that call for immediate delivery are called spot contracts, and they trade in spot markets. Immediate delivery generally is three days or less, but depends on each market. All other contracts involve what practitioners call futurity. They derive their values from events that will take place in the future.

EXAMPLE 8

Contracts for Difference

Contracts for difference (CFD) allow people to speculate on price changes for an underlying asset, such as a common stock or an index. Dealers generally sell CFDs to their clients. When the clients sell the CFDs back to their dealer, they receive any appreciation in the underlying asset's price between the time of purchase and sale (open and close) of the contract. If the underlying asset's price drops over this interval, the client pays the dealer the difference.

1. Are contracts for difference derivative contracts?

Solution to 1:

Contracts for difference are derivative contracts because their values are derived from changes in the prices of the underlying asset on which they are based.

2. Are contracts for difference based on copper prices cash settled or physically settled?

Solution to 2:

All contracts for difference are cash settled contracts regardless of the underlying asset on which they are based because they settle in cash and not in the underlying asset.

Forward Contracts

A **forward contract** is an agreement to trade the underlying asset in the future at a price agreed upon today. For example, a contract for the sale of wheat after the harvest is a forward contract. People often use forward contracts to reduce risk. Before planting wheat, farmers like to know the price at which they will sell their crop. Similarly, before committing to sell flour to bakers in the future, millers like to know the prices that they will pay for wheat. The farmer and the miller both reduce their operating risks by agreeing to trade wheat forward.

Practitioners call such traders hedgers because they use their contractual commitments to hedge their risks. If the price of wheat falls, the wheat farmer's crop will drop in value on the spot market but he has a contract to sell wheat in the future at a higher fixed price. The forward contract has become more valuable to the farmer. Conversely, if the price of wheat rises, the miller's future obligation to sell flour will become more burdensome because of the high price he would have to pay for wheat on the spot market, but the miller has a contract to buy wheat at a lower fixed price. The forward contract has become more valuable to the miller. In both cases, fluctuations in the spot price are hedged by the forward contract. The forward contract offsets the operating risks that the hedgers face.

Consider a simple example of hedging. An avocado farmer in Mexico expects to harvest 15,000 kilograms of avocados and that the price at harvest will be 60 pesos per kilogram. That price, however, could fluctuate significantly before the harvest. If the price of avocados drops to 50 pesos, the farmer would lose 10 pesos per kilogram (60 pesos − 50 pesos) relative to his expectations, or a total of 150,000 pesos. Now, suppose that the farmer can sell avocados forward to Del Rey Avocado at 58 pesos for delivery at the harvest. If the farmer sells 15,000 kilograms forward, and the price of avocados drops to 50 pesos, the farmer would still be able to sell his avocados for 58 pesos, and thus would not suffer from the drop in the price of avocados below this level.

EXAMPLE 9

Hedging Gold Production

A Zimbabwean gold producer invests in a mine expansion project on the expectation that gold prices will remain at or above $1,200 USD per ounce when the new project starts producing ore.

1. What risks does the gold producer face with respect to the price of gold?

Solution to 1:

The gold producer faces the risk that the price of gold could fall below $1,200 USD before it can sell its new production. If so, the investment in the expansion project will be less profitable than expected, and may even generate losses for the mine.

> 2. How might the gold producer hedge its gold price risk?
>
> **Solution to 2:**
>
> > The gold producer could hedge the gold price risk by selling gold forward, hopefully at a price near $1,200 USD. Even if the price of gold falls, the gold producer would get paid the contract price.

Forward contracts are very common, but two problems limit their usefulness for many market participants. The first problem is counterparty risk. **Counterparty risk** is the risk that the other party to a contract will fail to honor the terms of the contract. Concerns about counterparty risk ensure that generally only parties who have long-standing relationships with each other execute forward contracts. Trustworthiness is critical when prices are volatile because, after a large price change, one side or the other may prefer not to settle the contract.

The second problem is liquidity. Trading out of a forward contract is very difficult because it can only be done with the consent of the other party. The liquidity problem ensures that forward contracts tend to be executed only among participants for whom delivery is economically efficient and quite certain at the time of contracting so that both parties will want to arrange for delivery.

The counterparty risk problem and the liquidity problem often make it difficult for market participants to obtain the hedging benefits associated with forward contracting. Fortunately, futures contracts have been developed to mitigate these problems.

Futures Contracts

A **futures contract** is a standardized forward contract for which a clearinghouse guarantees the performance of all traders. The buyer of a futures contract is the side that will take physical delivery or its cash equivalent. The seller of a futures contract is the side that is liable for the delivery or its cash equivalent. A **clearinghouse** is an organization that ensures that no trader is harmed if another trader fails to honor the contract. In effect, the clearinghouse acts as the buyer for every seller and as the seller for every buyer. Buyers and sellers, therefore, can trade futures without worrying whether their counterparties are creditworthy. Because futures contracts are standardized, a buyer can eliminate his obligation to buy by selling his contract to anyone. A seller similarly can eliminate her obligation to deliver by buying a contract from anyone. In either case, the clearinghouse will release the trader from all future obligations if his or her long and short positions exactly offset each other.

To protect against defaults, futures clearinghouses require that all participants post with the clearinghouse an amount of money known as **initial margin** when they enter a contract. The clearinghouse then settles the margin accounts on a daily basis. All participants who have lost on their contracts that day will have the amount of their losses deducted from their margin by the clearinghouse. The clearinghouse similarly increases margins for all participants who gained on that day. Participants whose margins drop below the required **maintenance margin** must replenish their accounts. If a participant does not provide sufficient additional margin when required, the participant's broker will immediately trade to offset the participant's position. These **variation margin** payments ensure that the liabilities associated with futures contracts do not grow large.

Contracts

> ### EXAMPLE 10
>
> ### Futures Margin
>
> 1. NYMEX's Light Sweet Crude Oil futures contract specifies the delivery of 1,000 barrels of West Texas Intermediate Crude Oil when the contract finally settles. A broker requires that its clients post an initial overnight margin of $7,763 per contract and an overnight maintenance margin of $5,750 per contract. A client buys ten contracts at $75 per barrel through this broker. On the next day, the contract settles for $72 per barrel. How much additional margin will the client have to provide to his broker?
>
> ### Solution:
>
> The client lost three dollars per barrel (he is the side committed to take delivery or its cash equivalent at $75 per barrel). This results in a $3,000 loss on each of his 10 contracts, and a total loss of $30,000. His initial margin of $77,630 is reduced by $30,000 leaving $47,630 in his margin account. Because his account has dropped below the maintenance margin requirement of $57,500, the client will get a margin call. The client must provide an additional $30,000 = $77,630 − $47,630 to replenish his margin account; the account is replenished to the amount of the initial margin. The client will only receive another margin call if his account drops to below $57,500 again.

Futures contracts have vastly improved the efficiency of forward contracting markets. Traders can trade standardized futures contracts with anyone without worrying about counterparty risk, and they can close their positions by arranging offsetting trades. Hedgers for whom the terms of the standard contract are not ideal generally still use the futures markets because the contracts embody most of the price risk that concerns them. They simply offset (close out) their futures positions, at the same time they enter spot contracts on which they make or take ultimate delivery.

> ### EXAMPLE 11
>
> ### Forward and Futures Contracts
>
> 1. What feature most distinguishes futures contracts from forward contracts?
>
> ### Solution:
>
> A futures contract is a standardized forward contract for which a clearinghouse guarantees the performance of all buyers and sellers. The clearinghouse reduces the counterparty risk problem. The clearinghouse allows a buyer who has bought a contract from one person and sold the same contract to another person to net out the two obligations so that she is no longer liable for either side of the contract; the positions are closed. The ability to trade futures contracts provides liquidity in futures contracts compared with forward contracts.

Swap Contracts

A **swap contract** is an agreement to exchange payments of periodic cash flows that depend on future asset prices or interest rates. For example, in a typical **interest rate swap**, at periodic intervals, one party makes fixed cash payments to the counterparty in exchange for variable cash payments from the counterparty. The variable payments are based on a pre-specified variable interest rate such as the London Interbank Offered Rate (Libor). This swap effectively exchanges fixed interest payments for variable interest payments. Because the variable rate is set in the future, the cash flows for this contract are uncertain when the parties enter the contract.

Investment managers often enter interest rate swaps when they own a fixed long-term income stream that they want to convert to a cash flow that varies with current short-term interest rates, or vice versa. The conversion may allow them to substantially reduce the total interest rate risk to which they are exposed. Hedgers often use swap contracts to manage risks.

In a **commodity swap**, one party typically makes fixed payments in exchange for payments that depend on future prices of a commodity such as oil. In a **currency swap**, the parties exchange payments denominated in different currencies. The payments may be fixed, or they may vary depending on future interest rates in the two countries. In an **equity swap**, the parties exchange fixed cash payments for payments that depend on the returns to a stock or a stock index.

EXAMPLE 12

Swap and Forward Contracts

1. What feature most distinguishes a swap contract from a cash-settled forward contract?

Solution:

Both contracts provide for the exchange of cash payments in the future. A forward contract only has a single cash payment at the end that depends on an underlying price or index at the end. In contrast, a swap contract has several scheduled periodic payments, each of which depends on an underlying price or index at the time of the payment.

Option Contracts

An **option contract** allows the holder (the purchaser) of the **option** to buy or sell, depending on the type of option, an underlying instrument at a specified price at or before a specified date in the future. Those that do buy or sell are said to **exercise** their contracts. An option to buy is a **call option**, and an option to sell is a **put** option. The specified price is called the strike price (exercise price). If the holders can exercise their contracts only when they mature, they are **European-style** contracts. If they can exercise the contracts earlier, they are **American-style** contracts. Many exchanges list standardized option contracts on individual stocks, stock indexes, futures contracts, currencies, swaps, and precious metals. Institutions also trade many customized option contracts with dealers in the over-the-counter derivative market.

Option holders generally will exercise call options if the strike price is below the market price of the underlying instrument, in which case, they will be able to buy at a lower price than the market price. Similarly, they will exercise put options if the strike price is above the underlying instrument price so that they sell at a higher price than the market price. Otherwise, option holders allow their options to expire as worthless.

The price that traders pay for an option is the option premium. Options can be quite expensive because, unlike forward and futures contracts, they do not impose any liability on the holder. The premium compensates the sellers of options—called option writers—for giving the call option holders the right to potentially buy below market prices and put option holders the right to potentially sell above market prices. Because the writers must trade if the holders exercise their options, option contracts may impose substantial liabilities on the writers.

> **EXAMPLE 13**
>
> ### Option and Forward Contracts
>
> 1. What feature most distinguishes option contracts from forward contracts?
>
> **Solution:**
>
> The holder of an option contract has the right, but not the obligation, to buy (for a call option) or sell (for a put option) the underlying instrument at some time in the future. The writer of an option contract must trade the underlying instrument if the holder exercises the option.
>
> In contrast, the two parties to a forward contract must trade the underlying instrument (or its equivalent value for a cash-settled contract) at some time in the future if either party wants to settle the contract.

Other Contracts

Insurance contracts pay their beneficiaries a cash benefit if some event occurs. Life, liability, and automobile insurance are examples of insurance contracts sold to retail clients. People generally use insurance contracts to compensate for losses that they will experience if bad things happen unexpectedly. Insurance contracts allow them to hedge risks that they face.

Credit default swaps (CDS) are insurance contracts that promise payment of principal in the event that a company defaults on its bonds. Bondholders use credit default swaps to convert risky bonds into more secure investments. Other creditors of the company may also buy them to hedge against the risk they will not be paid if the company goes bankrupt.

Well-informed traders who believe that a corporation will default on its bonds may buy credit default swaps written on the corporation's bonds if the swap prices are sufficiently low. If they are correct, the traders will profit if the payoff to the swap is more than the cost of buying and maintaining the swap position.

People sometimes also buy insurance contracts as investments, especially in jurisdictions where payouts from insurance contracts are not subject to as much taxation as are payouts to other investment vehicles. They may buy these contracts directly from insurance companies, or they may buy already issued contracts from their owners. For example, the life settlements market trades life insurance contracts that people sell to investors when they need cash.

FINANCIAL INTERMEDIARIES

7

- [ ] describe types of financial intermediaries and services that they provide

Financial intermediaries help entities achieve their financial goals. These intermediaries include commercial, mortgage, and investment banks; credit unions, credit card companies, and various other finance corporations; brokers and exchanges; dealers and arbitrageurs; clearinghouses and depositories; mutual funds and hedge funds; and insurance companies. The services and products that financial intermediaries provide allow their clients to solve the financial problems that they face more efficiently than they could do so by themselves. Financial intermediaries are essential to well-functioning financial systems.

Financial intermediaries are called intermediaries because the services and products that they provide help connect buyers to sellers in various ways. Whether the connections are easy to identify or involve complex financial structures, financial intermediaries stand between one or more buyers and one or more sellers and help them transfer capital and risk between them. Financial intermediaries' activities allow buyers and sellers to benefit from trading, often without any knowledge of the other.

This section introduces the main financial intermediaries that provide services and products in well-developed financial markets. The discussion starts with those intermediaries whose services most obviously connect buyers to sellers and then proceeds to those intermediaries whose services create more subtle connections. Because many financial intermediaries provide many different types of services, some are mentioned more than once. The section concludes with a general characterization of the various ways in which financial intermediaries add value to the financial system.

Brokers, Exchanges, and Alternative Trading Systems

Brokers are agents who fill orders for their clients. They do not trade with their clients. Instead, they search for traders who are willing to take the other side of their clients' orders. Individual brokers may work for large brokerage firms, the brokerage arm of banks, or at exchanges. Some brokers match clients to clients personally. Others use specialized computer systems to identify potential trades and help their clients fill their orders. Brokers help their clients trade by reducing the costs of finding counterparties for their trades.

Block brokers provide brokerage service to large traders. Large orders are hard to fill because finding a counterparty willing to do a large trade is often quite difficult. A large buy order generally will trade at a premium to the current market price, and a large sell order generally will trade at a discount to the current market price. These price concessions encourage other traders to trade with the large traders. They also make large traders reluctant, however, to expose their orders to the public before their trades are arranged because they do not want to move the market. Block brokers, therefore, carefully manage the exposure of the orders entrusted to them, which makes filling them difficult.

Investment banks provide advice to their mostly corporate clients and help them arrange transactions such as initial and seasoned securities offerings. Their corporate finance divisions help corporations finance their business by issuing securities, such as common and preferred shares, notes, and bonds. Another function of corporate finance divisions is to help companies identify and acquire other companies (i.e., in mergers and acquisitions).

Exchanges provide places where traders can meet to arrange their trades. Historically, brokers and dealers met on an exchange floor to negotiate trades. Increasingly, exchanges arrange trades for traders based on orders that brokers and dealers submit to them. Such exchanges essentially act as brokers. The distinction between exchanges and brokers has become quite blurred. Exchanges and brokers that use electronic order matching systems to arrange trades among their clients are functionally indistinguishable in this respect. Examples of exchanges include the NYSE, Eurex, Frankfurt Stock Exchange, the Chicago Mercantile Exchange, the Tokyo Stock Exchange, and the Singapore Exchange.

Exchanges are easily distinguished from brokers by their regulatory operations. Most exchanges regulate their members' behavior when trading on the exchange, and sometimes away from the exchange.

Many securities exchanges regulate the issuers that list their securities on the exchange. These regulations generally require timely financial disclosure. Financial analysts use this information to value the securities traded at the exchange. Without such disclosure, valuing securities could be very difficult and market prices might not reflect the fundamental values of the securities. In such situations, well-informed participants may profit from less-informed participants. To avoid such losses, the less-informed participants may withdraw from the market, which can greatly increase corporate costs of capital.

Some exchanges also prohibit issuers from creating capital structures that would concentrate voting rights in the hands of a few owners who do not own a commensurate share of the equity. These regulations attempt to ensure that corporations are run for the benefit of all shareholders and not to promote the interests of controlling shareholders who do not have significant economic stakes in the company.

Exchanges derive their regulatory authority from their national or regional governments, or through the voluntary agreements of their members and issuers to subject themselves to the exchange regulations. In most countries, government regulators oversee the exchange rules and the regulatory operations. Most countries also impose financial disclosure standards on public issuers. Examples of government regulatory bodies include the Japanese Financial Services Agency, the British Financial Conduct Authority, the German Federal Financial Supervisory Authority (BaFin), the US Securities and Exchange Commission, the Ontario Securities Commission, and the Argentine National Securities Commission (CNV).

Alternative trading systems (ATSs), also known as **electronic communications networks** (ECNs) or **multilateral trading facilities** (MTFs) are trading venues that function like exchanges but that do not exercise regulatory authority over their subscribers except with respect to the conduct of their trading in their trading systems. Some ATSs operate electronic trading systems that are otherwise indistinguishable from the trading systems operated by exchanges. Others operate innovative trading systems that suggest trades to their customers based on information that their customers share with them or that they obtain through research into their customers' preferences. Many ATSs are known as **dark pools** because they do not display the orders that their clients send to them. Large investment managers especially like these systems because market prices often move to their disadvantage when other traders know about their large orders. ATSs may be owned and operated by broker–dealers, exchanges, banks, or by companies organized solely for this purpose, many of which may be owned by a consortia of brokers–dealers and banks. Examples of ATSs include MATCHNow (Canada), BATS (United States), POSIT (United States), Liquidnet (United States), Baxter-FX (Ireland), and Turquoise (Europe). Many of these ATSs provide services in many markets besides the ones in which they are domiciled.

Dealers

Dealers fill their clients' orders by trading with them. When their clients want to sell securities or contracts, dealers buy the instruments for their own accounts. If their clients want to buy securities, dealers sell securities that they own or have borrowed. After completing a transaction, dealers hope to reverse the transaction by trading with another client on the other side of the market. When they are successful, they effectively connect a buyer who arrived at one point in time with a seller who arrived at another point in time.

The service that dealers provide is liquidity. **Liquidity** is the ability to buy or sell with low transactions costs when you want to trade. By allowing their clients to trade when they want to trade, dealers provide liquidity to them. In over-the-counter markets, dealers offer liquidity when their clients ask them to trade with them. In exchange markets, dealers offer liquidity to anyone who is willing to trade at the prices that the dealers offer at the exchange. Dealers profit when they can buy at prices that on average are lower than the prices at which they sell.

Dealers may organize their operations within proprietary trading houses, investment banks, and hedge funds, or as sole proprietorships. Some dealers are traditional dealers in the sense that individuals make trading decisions. Others use computerized trading to make all trading decisions. Examples of companies with large dealing operations include Deutsche Bank (Germany), RBC Capital Markets (Canada), Nomura Securities (Japan), Timber Hill (United States), Goldman Sachs (United States), and IG Group (United Kingdom). Almost all investment banks have large dealing operations.

Most dealers also broker orders, and many brokers deal to their customers. Accordingly, practitioners often use the term **broker–dealer** to refer to dealers and brokers. Broker–dealers have a conflict of interest with respect to how they fill their customers' orders. When acting as a broker, they must seek the best price for their customers' orders. When acting as dealers, however, they profit most when they sell to their customers at high prices or buy from their customers at low prices. The problem is most serious when the customer allows the broker–dealer to decide whether to trade the order with another trader or to fill it as a dealer. Consequently, when trading with a broker–dealer, some customers specify how they want their orders filled. They may also trade only with pure agency brokers who do not also deal.

Primary dealers are dealers with whom central banks trade when conducting monetary policy. They buy bills, notes, and bonds when the central banks sell them to decrease the money supply. The dealers then sell these instruments to their clients. Similarly, when the central banks want to increase the money supply, the primary dealers buy these instruments from their clients and sell them to the central banks.

EXAMPLE 14

Brokers and Dealers

1. What characteristic *most likely* distinguishes brokers from dealers?

Solution:

Brokers are agents that arrange trades on behalf of their clients. They do not trade with their clients. In contrast, dealers are proprietary traders who trade with their clients.

Arbitrageurs

Arbitrageurs trade when they can identify opportunities to buy and sell identical or essentially similar instruments at different prices in different markets. They profit when they can buy in one market for less than they sell in another market. Arbitrageurs are financial intermediaries because they connect buyers in one market to sellers in another market.

The purest form of arbitrage involves buying and selling the same instrument in two different markets. Arbitrageurs who do such trades sell to buyers in one market and buy from sellers in the other market. They provide liquidity to the markets because they make it easier for buyers and sellers to trade when and where they want to trade.

Because dealers and arbitrageurs both provide liquidity to other traders, they compete with each other. The dealers connect buyers and sellers who arrive in the same market at different times whereas the arbitrageurs connect buyers and sellers who arrive at the same time in different markets. In practice, traders who profit from offering liquidity rarely are purely dealers or purely arbitrageurs. Instead, most traders attempt to identify and exploit every opportunity they can to manage their inventories profitably.

If information about prices is readily available to market participants, pure arbitrages involving the same instrument will be quite rare. Traders who are well informed about market conditions usually route their orders to the market offering the best price so that arbitrageurs will have few opportunities to match traders across markets when they want to trade the exact same instrument.

Arbitrageurs often trade securities or contracts whose values depend on the same underlying factors. For example, dealers in equity option contracts often sell call options in the contract market and buy the underlying shares in the stock market. Because the values of the call options and of the underlying shares are closely correlated (the value of the call increases with the value of the shares), the long stock position hedges the risk in the short call position so that the dealer's net position is not too risky.

Similar to the pure arbitrage that involves the same instrument in different markets, these arbitrage trades connect buyers in one market to sellers in another market. In this case, however, the buyers and sellers are interested in different instruments whose values are closely related. In the example, the buyer is interested in buying a call options contract, the value of which is a nonlinear function of the value of the underlying stock; the seller is interested in selling the underlying stock.

Options dealers buy stock and sell calls when calls are overpriced relative to the underlying stocks. They use complicated financial models to value options in relation to underlying stock values, and they use financial engineering techniques to control the risk of their portfolios. Successful arbitrageurs must know valuation relations well and they must manage the risk in their portfolios well to trade profitably. They profit by buying the relatively undervalued instrument and selling the relatively overvalued instrument.

Buying a risk in one form and selling it another form involves a process called replication. Arbitrageurs use various trading strategies to replicate the returns to securities and contracts. If they can substantially replicate those returns, they can use the replication trading strategy to offset the risk of buying or selling the actual securities and contracts. The combined effect of their trading is to transform risk from one form to another. This process allows them to create or eliminate contracts in response to the excess demand for, and supply of, contracts.

For example, when traders want to buy more call contracts than are presently available, they push the call contract prices up so that calls become overvalued relative to the underlying stock. The arbitrageurs replicate calls by using a particular financial engineering strategy to buy the underlying stock, and then create the desired call option contracts by selling them short. In contrast, if more calls have been created than traders want to hold, call prices will fall so that calls become undervalued relative to the underlying stock. The arbitrageurs will trade stocks and contracts to absorb the excess contracts. Arbitrageurs who use these strategies are financial intermediaries because they connect buyers and sellers who want to trade the same underlying risks but in different forms.

> **EXAMPLE 15**
>
> ### Dealers and Arbitrageurs
>
> 1. With respect to providing liquidity to market participants, what characteristics most clearly distinguish dealers from arbitrageurs?
>
> **Solution:**
>
> Dealers provide liquidity to buyers and sellers who arrive at the same market at different times. They move liquidity through time. Arbitrageurs provide liquidity to buyers and sellers who arrive at different markets at the same time. They move liquidity across markets.

8. SECURITIZERS, DEPOSITORY INSTITUTIONS AND INSURANCE COMPANIES

☐ describe types of financial intermediaries and services that they provide

Banks and investment companies create new financial products when they buy and repackage securities or other assets. For example, mortgage banks commonly originate hundreds or thousands of residential mortgages by lending money to homeowners. They then place the mortgages in a pool and sell shares of the pool to investors as mortgage pass-through securities, which are also known as mortgage-backed securities. All payments of principal and interest are passed through to the investors each month, after deducting the costs of servicing the mortgages. Investors who purchase these pass-through securities obtain securities that in aggregate have the same net cash flows and associated risks as the pool of mortgages.

The process of buying assets, placing them in a pool, and then selling securities that represent ownership of the pool is called securitization.

Mortgage-backed securities have the advantage that default losses and early repayments are much more predictable for a diversified portfolio of mortgages than they are for individual mortgages. They are also attractive to investors who cannot efficiently service mortgages but wish to invest in mortgages. By securitizing mortgage pools, the mortgage banks allow investors who are not large enough to buy hundreds of mortgages to obtain the benefits of diversification and economies of scale in loan servicing.

Securitization greatly improves liquidity in the mortgage markets because it allows investors in the pass-through securities to buy mortgages indirectly that they otherwise would not buy. Because the financial risks associated with mortgage-backed securities (debt securities with specified claims on the cash flows of a portfolio of mortgages) are much more predictable than those of individual mortgages, mortgage-backed securities are easier to price and thus easier to sell when investors need to raise cash. These characteristics make the market for mortgage-backed securities much more liquid than the market for individual mortgages. Because investors value liquidity—the ability to sell when they want to—they will pay more for securitized mortgages than for individual mortgages. The homeowners benefit because higher mortgage prices imply lower interest rates.

The mortgage bank is a financial intermediary because it connects investors who want to buy mortgages to homeowners who want to borrow money. The homeowners sell mortgages to the bank when the bank lends them money.

Some mortgage banks form mortgage pools from mortgages that they buy from other banks that originate the loans. These mortgage banks are also financial intermediaries because they connect sellers of mortgages to buyers of mortgage-backed securities. Although the sellers of the mortgages are the originating lenders and not the borrowers, the benefits of creating liquid mortgage-backed securities ultimately flow back to the borrowers.

The creation of the pass-through securities generally takes place on the accounts of the mortgage bank. The bank buys mortgages and sells pass-through securities whose values depend on the mortgage pool. The mortgages appear on the bank's accounts as assets and the mortgage-backed securities appear as liabilities.

In many securitizations, the financial intermediary avoids placing the assets and liabilities on its balance sheet by setting up a special corporation or trust that buys the assets and issues the securities. That corporation or trust is called a **special purpose vehicle** (SPV) or alternatively a **special purpose entity** (SPE). Conducting a securitization through a special purpose vehicle is advantageous to investors because their interests in the asset pool are better protected in an SPV than they would be on the balance sheet of the financial intermediary if the financial intermediary were to go bankrupt.

Financial intermediaries securitize many assets. Besides mortgages, banks securitize car loans, credit card receivables, bank loans, and airplane leases, to name just a few assets. As a class, these securities are called asset-backed securities.

When financial intermediaries securitize assets, they often create several classes of securities, called tranches, that have different rights to the cash flows from the asset pool. The tranches are structured so that some produce more predictable cash flows than do others. The senior tranches have first rights to the cash flow from the asset pool. Because the overall risk of a given asset pool cannot be changed, the more junior tranches bear a disproportionate share of the risk of the pool. Practitioners often call the most junior tranche toxic waste because it is so risky. The complexity associated with slicing asset pools into tranches can make the resulting securities difficult to value. Mistakes in valuing these securities contributed to the financial crisis that started in 2007.

Investment companies also create pass-through securities based on investment pools. For example, an exchange-traded fund is an asset-backed security that represents ownership in the securities and contracts held by the fund. The shareholders benefit from the securitization because they can buy or sell an entire portfolio in a single transaction. Because the transaction cost savings are quite substantial, exchange-traded funds often trade in very liquid markets. The investment companies (and sometimes the arbitrageurs) that create exchange-traded funds are financial intermediaries because they connect the buyers of the funds to the sellers of the assets that make up the fund portfolios.

More generally, the creators of all pooled investment vehicles are financial intermediaries that transform portfolios of securities and contracts into securities that represent undivided ownership of the portfolios. The investors in these funds thus indirectly invest in the securities held by the fund. They benefit from the expertise of the investment manager and from obtaining a portfolio that may be more diversified than one they might otherwise be able to hold.

Depository Institutions and Other Financial Corporations

Depository institutions include commercial banks, savings and loan banks, credit unions, and similar institutions that raise funds from depositors and other investors and lend it to borrowers. The banks give their depositors interest and transaction services, such as check writing and check cashing, in exchange for using their money. They may also raise funds by selling bonds or equity in the bank.

These banks are financial intermediaries because they transfer funds from their depositors and investors to their borrowers. The depositors and investors benefit because they obtain a return (in interest, transaction services, dividends, or capital appreciation) on their funds without having to contract with the borrowers and manage their loans. The borrowers benefit because they obtain the funds that they need without having to search for investors who will trust them to repay their loans.

Many other financial corporations provide credit services. For example, acceptance corporations, discount corporations, payday advance corporations, and factors provide credit to borrowers by lending them money secured by such assets as consumer loans, machinery, future paychecks, or accounts receivables. They finance these loans by selling commercial paper, bonds, and shares to investors. These corporations are intermediaries because they connect investors to borrowers. The investors obtain investments secured by a diversified portfolio of loans while the borrowers obtain funds without having to search for investors.

Brokers also act as financial intermediaries when they lend funds to clients who want to buy securities on margin. They generally obtain the funds from other clients who deposit them in their accounts. Brokers who provide these services to hedge funds and other similar institutions are called prime brokers.

Banks, financial corporations, and brokers can only raise money from depositors and other lenders because their equity owners retain residual interests in the performance of the loans that they make. If the borrowers default, the depositors and other lenders have priority claims over the equity owners. If insufficient money is collected from the borrowers, shareholders' equity is used to pay their depositors and other lenders. The risk of losing capital focuses the equity owners' and management's attention so that credit is not offered foolishly.

Because the ability of these companies to cover their credit losses is limited by the capital that their owners invest in them, the depositors and other investors who lend them money pay close attention to how much money the owners have at risk. For example, if a finance corporation is poorly capitalized, its shareholders will lose little if its clients default on the loans that the finance corporation makes to them. In that case, the finance corporation will have little incentive to lend only to creditworthy borrowers and to effectively manage collection on those loans once they have been made. Worse, it may even choose to lend to borrowers with poor credit because the interest rates that they can charge such borrowers are higher. Until those loans default, the higher income will make the corporation appear to be more profitable than it actually is. Depositors and other investors are aware of these problems and generally pay close attention to them. Accordingly, poorly capitalized financial institutions cannot easily borrow money to finance their operations at favorable rates.

Depository banks and financial corporations are similar to securitized asset pools that issue pass-through securities. Their depositors and investors own securities that ultimately are backed by an asset pool consisting of their loan portfolios. The depositors generally hold the most senior tranche, followed by the other creditors. The shareholders hold the most junior tranche. In the event of bankruptcy, they are paid only if everyone else is paid.

EXAMPLE 16

Commercial Banks

1. What services do commercial banks provide that make them financial intermediaries?

Solution:

Commercial banks collect deposits from investors and lend them to borrowers. They are intermediaries because they connect lenders to borrowers. Commercial banks also provide transaction services that make it easier for the banks' depository customers to pay bills and collect funds from their own customers.

Insurance Companies

Insurance companies help people and companies offset risks that concern them. They do this by creating insurance contracts (policies) that provide a payment in the event that some loss occurs. The insured buy these contracts to hedge against potential losses. Common examples of insurance contracts include auto, fire, life, liability, medical, theft, and disaster insurance contracts.

Credit default swaps are also insurance contracts, but historically they have not been subject to the same reserve requirements that most governments apply to more traditional insurance contracts. They may be sold by insurance companies or by other financial entities, such as investment banks or hedge funds.

Insurance contracts transfer risk from those who buy the contracts to those who sell them. Although insurance companies occasionally broker trades between the insured and the insurer, they more commonly provide the insurance themselves. In that case, the insurance company's owners and creditors become the indirect insurers of the risks that the insurance company assumes. Insurance companies also often transfer risks that they do not wish to bear by buying reinsurance policies from reinsurers.

Insurers are financial intermediaries because they connect the buyers of their insurance contracts with investors, creditors, and reinsurers who are willing to bear the insured risks. The buyers benefit because they can easily obtain the risk transfers that they seek without searching for entities that would be willing to assume those risks.

The owners, creditors, and reinsurers of the insurance company benefit because the company allows them to sell their tolerance for risk easily without having to manage the insurance contracts. Instead, the company manages the relationships with the insured—primarily collections and claims—and hopefully controls the various problems—fraud, moral hazard, and adverse selection—that often plague insurance markets. Fraud occurs when people deliberately cause or falsely report losses to collect on insurance. Moral hazard occurs when people are less careful about avoiding insured losses than they would be if they were not insured so that losses occur more often than they would otherwise. Adverse selection occurs when only those who are most at risk buy insurance so that insured losses tend to be greater than average.

Everyone benefits because insurance companies hold large diversified portfolios of policies. Loss rates for well-diversified portfolios of insurance contracts are much more predictable than for single contracts. For such contracts as auto insurance in which losses are almost uncorrelated across policies, diversification ensures that the financial performance of a large portfolio of contracts will be quite predictable and so holding the portfolio will not be very risky. The insured benefit because they do not have to pay the insurers much to compensate them for bearing risk (the expected loss is quite predictable so the risk is relatively low). Instead, their insurance premiums primarily reflect the expected loss rate in the portfolio plus the costs of running and financing the company.

9. SETTLEMENT AND CUSTODIAL SERVICES AND SUMMARY

☐ describe types of financial intermediaries and services that they provide

In addition to connecting buyers to sellers through a variety of direct and indirect means, financial intermediaries also help their customers settle their trades and ensure that the resulting positions are not stolen or pledged more than once as collateral.

Clearinghouses arrange for final settlement of trades. In futures markets, they guarantee contract performance. In other markets, they may act only as escrow agents, transferring money from the buyer to the seller while transferring securities from the seller to the buyer.

The members of a clearinghouse are the only traders for whom the clearinghouse will settle trades. To ensure that their members settle the trades that they present to the clearinghouse, clearinghouses require that their members have adequate capital and post-performance bonds (margins). Clearinghouses also limit the aggregate net (buy minus sell) quantities that their members can settle.

Brokers and dealers who are not members of the clearinghouse must arrange to have a clearinghouse member settle their trades. To ensure that the non-member brokers and dealers can settle their trades, clearinghouse members require that their customers (the non-member brokers and dealers) have adequate capital and post-margins. They also limit the aggregate net quantities that their customers can settle and they monitor their customers' trading to ensure that they do not arrange trades that they cannot settle.

Brokers and dealers similarly monitor the trades made by their retail and institutional customers, and regulate their customers to ensure that they do not arrange trades that they cannot settle.

This hierarchical system of responsibility generally ensures that traders settle their trades. The brokers and dealers guarantee settlement of the trades they arrange for their retail and institutional customers. The clearinghouse members guarantee settlement of the trades that their customers present to them, and clearinghouses guarantee settlement of all trades presented to them by their members. If a clearinghouse member fails to settle a trade, the clearinghouse settles the trade using its own capital or capital drafted from the other members.

Reliable settlement of all trades is extremely important to a well-functioning financial system because it allows strangers to confidently contract with each other without worrying too much about **counterparty risk**, the risk that their counterparties will not settle their trades. A secure clearinghouse system thus greatly increases liquidity because it greatly increases the number of counterparties with whom a trader can safely arrange a trade.

In many national markets, clearinghouses clear all securities trades so that traders can trade securities through any exchange, broker, alternative trading system, or dealer. These clearinghouse systems promote competition among these exchange service providers.

Settlement and Custodial Services and Summary

In contrast, most futures exchanges have their own clearinghouses. These clearinghouses usually will not accept trades arranged away from their exchanges so that a competing exchange cannot trade another exchange's contracts. Competing exchanges may create similar contracts, but moving traders from one established market to a new market is extraordinarily difficult because traders prefer to trade where other traders trade.

Depositories or custodians hold securities on behalf of their clients. These services, which are often offered by banks, help prevent the loss of securities through fraud, oversight, or natural disaster. Broker–dealers also often hold securities on behalf of their customers so that the customers do not have to hold the securities in certificate form. To avoid problems with lost certificates, securities increasingly are issued only in electronic form.

EXAMPLE 17

Financial Intermediaries

1. As a relatively new member of the business community, you decide it would be advantageous to join the local lunch club to network with businessmen. Upon learning that you are a financial analyst, club members soon enlist you to give a lunch speech. During the question and answer session afterwards, a member of the audience asks, "I keep reading in the newspaper about the need to regulate 'financial intermediaries', but really don't understand exactly what they are. Can you tell me?" How do you answer?

Solution:

Financial intermediaries are companies that help their clients achieve their financial goals. They are called intermediaries because, in some way or another, they stand between two or more people who would like to trade with each other, but for various reasons find it difficult to do so directly. The intermediary arranges the trade for them, or more often, trades with both sides.

For example, a commercial bank is an intermediary that connects investors with money to borrowers who need money. The investors buy certificates of deposit from the bank, buy bonds or stock issued by the bank, or simply are depositors in the bank. The borrowers borrow this money from the bank when they arrange loans. Without the bank's intermediation, the investors would have to find trustworthy borrowers themselves, which would be difficult, and the borrowers would have to find trusting lenders, which would also be difficult.

Similarly, an insurance company is an intermediary because it connects customers who want to insure risks with investors who are willing to bear those risks. The investors own shares or bonds issued by the insurance company, or they have sold reinsurance contracts to the insurance company. The insured benefit because they can more easily buy a policy from an insurance company than they can find counterparties who would be willing to bear their risks. The investors benefit because the insurance company creates a diversified portfolio of risks by selling insurance to thousands or millions of customers. Diversification ensures that the net risk borne by the insurance company and its investors will be predictable and thus financially manageable.

In both cases, the financial intermediary also manages the relationships with its customers and investors so that neither side has to worry about the

> credit-worthiness or trust-worthiness of its counterparties. For example, the bank manages credit quality and collections on its loans and the insurance company manages risk exposure and collections on its policies. These services benefit both sides by reducing the costs of connecting investors to borrowers or of insured to insurers.
>
> These are only two examples of financial intermediation. Many others involve firms engaged in brokerage, dealing, arbitrage, securitization, investment management, and the clearing and settlement of trades. In all cases, the financial intermediary stands between a buyer and a seller, offering them services that allow them to better achieve their financial goals in a cost effective and efficient manner.

Summary

By facilitating transactions among buyers and sellers, financial intermediaries provide services essential to a well-functioning financial system. They facilitate transactions the following ways:

1. Brokers, exchanges, and various alternative trading systems match buyers and sellers interested in trading the same instrument at the same place and time. These financial intermediaries specialize in discovering and organizing information about who wants to trade.

2. Dealers and arbitrageurs connect buyers to sellers interested in trading the same instrument but who are not present at the same place and time. Dealers connect buyers to sellers who are present at the same place but at different times whereas arbitrageurs connect buyers to sellers who are present at the same time but in different places. These financial intermediaries trade for their own accounts when providing these services. Dealers buy or sell with one client and hope to do the offsetting transaction later with another client. Arbitrageurs buy from a seller in one market while simultaneously selling to a buyer in another market.

3. Many financial intermediaries create new instruments that depend on the cash flows and associated financial risks of other instruments. The intermediaries provide these services when they securitize assets, manage investment funds, operate banks and other finance corporations that offer investments to investors and loans to borrowers, and operate insurance companies that pool risks. The instruments that they create generally are more attractive to their clients than the instruments on which they are based. The new instruments also may be differentiated to appeal to diverse clienteles. Their efforts connect buyers of one or more instruments to sellers of other instruments, all of which in aggregate provide the same cash flows and risk exposures. Financial intermediaries thus effectively arrange trades among traders who otherwise would not trade with each other.

4. Arbitrageurs who conduct arbitrage among securities and contracts whose values depend on common factors convert risk from one form to another. Their trading connects buyers and sellers who want to trade similar risks expressed in different forms.

5. Banks, clearinghouses, and depositories provide services that ensure traders settle their trades and that the resulting positions are not stolen or pledged more than once as collateral.

POSITIONS AND SHORT POSITIONS

☐ compare positions an investor can take in an asset

People generally solve their financial and risk management problems by taking positions in various assets or contracts. A **position** in an asset is the quantity of the instrument that an entity owns or owes. A portfolio consists of a set of positions.

People have **long positions** when they own assets or contracts. Examples of long positions include ownership of stocks, bonds, currencies, contracts, commodities, or real assets. Long positions benefit from an appreciation in the prices of the assets or contracts owned.

People have **short positions** when they have sold assets that they do not own, or when they write and sell contracts. Short positions benefit from a decrease in the prices of the assets or contracts sold. Short sellers profit by selling at high prices and repurchasing at lower prices. Information-motivated traders sell assets and contracts short positions when they believe that prices will fall.

Hedgers also often sell instruments short. They short securities and contracts when the financial risks inherent in the instruments are positively correlated with the risks to which they are exposed. For example, to hedge the risk associated with holding copper inventories, a wire manufacturer would sell short copper futures. If the price of copper falls, the manufacturer will lose on his copper inventories but gain on his short futures position. (If the risk in an instrument is inversely correlated with a risk to which hedgers are exposed, the hedgers will hedge with long positions.)

Contracts have long sides and short sides. The long side of a forward or futures contract is the side that will take physical delivery or its cash equivalent. The short side of such contracts is the side that is liable for the delivery. The long side of a futures contract increases in value when the value of the underlying asset increases in value.

The identification of the two sides can be confusing for option contracts. The long side of an option contract is the side that holds the right to exercise the option. The short side is the side that must satisfy the obligation. Practitioners say that that the long side *holds* the option and the short side *writes* the option, so the long side is the holder and the short side is the writer. The put contracts are the source of the potential confusion. The put contract holder has the right to sell the underlying to the writer. The holder will benefit if the price of the underlying falls, in which case the price of the put contract will rise. The holder is long the put contract and has an indirect short position in the underlying instrument. Analysts call the indirect short position short exposure to the underlying. The put contract holders have long exposure to their option contract and short exposure to the underlying instrument.

Exhibit 1: Option Positions and Their Associated Underlying Risk Exposures

Type of Option	Option Position	Exposure to Underlying Risk
Call	Long	Long
Call	Short	Short
Put	Long	Short
Put	Short	Long

The identification of the long side in a swap contract is often arbitrary because swap contracts call for the exchange of contractually determined cash flows rather than for the purchase (or the cash equivalent) of some underlying instrument. In general, the side that benefits from an increase in the quoted price is the long side.

The identification of the long side in currency contracts also may be confusing. In this case, the confusion stems from symmetry in the contracts. The buyer of one currency is the seller of the other currency, and vice versa for the seller. Thus, a long forward position in one currency is a short forward position in the other currency. When practitioners describe a position, they generally will say, "I'm long the dollar against the yen," which means they have bought dollars and sold yen.

Short Positions

Short sellers create short positions in contracts by selling contracts that they do not own. In a sense, they become the issuers of the contract when they create the liabilities associated with their contracts. This analogy will also help you better understand risk when you study corporate finance: Corporations create short positions in their bonds when they issue bonds in exchange for cash. Although bonds are generally considered to be securities, they are also contracts between the issuer and the bondholder.

Short sellers create short positions in securities by borrowing securities from security lenders who are long holders. The short sellers then sell the borrowed securities to other traders. Short sellers close their positions by repurchasing the securities and returning them to the security lenders. If the securities drop in value, the short sellers profit because they repurchase the securities at lower prices than the prices at which they sold the securities. If the securities rise in value, they will lose. Short sellers who buy to close their positions are said to cover their positions.

The potential gains in a long position generally are unbounded. For example, the stock prices of such highly successful companies as Yahoo! have increased more than 50-fold since they were first publicly traded. The potential losses on long positions, however, are limited to no more than 100 percent—a complete loss—for long positions without any associated liabilities.

In contrast, the potential gains on a short position are limited to no more than 100 percent whereas the potential losses are unbounded. The unbounded potential losses on short positions make short positions very risky in volatile instruments. As an extreme example of this, if you had shorted 100 shares of Yahoo! in July 1996 at $20 and kept the position open for four years, you would have lost $148,000 on your $2,000 initial short position. During this period, Yahoo! rose 75-fold to $1,500 on a split-adjusted equivalent basis.

Although security lenders generally believe that they are long the securities that they lend, in fact, they do not actually own the securities during the periods of their loans. Instead, they own promises made by the short sellers to return the securities. These promises are memorialized in security lending agreements. These agreements specify that the short sellers will pay the long sellers all dividends or interest that they otherwise would have received had they not lent their securities. These payments are called payments-in-lieu of dividends (or of interest), and they may have different tax treatments than actual dividends and interest. The security lending agreements also protect the lenders in the event of a stock split.

To secure the security loans, lenders require that the short seller leave the proceeds of the short sale on deposit with them as collateral for the stock loan. They invest the collateral in short-term securities, and they rebate the interest to the short sellers at rates called short rebate rates. The short rebate rates are determined in the market and generally are available only to institutional short-sellers and some large retail traders. If a security is hard to borrow, the rebate rate may be very small or even negative.

Such securities are said to be "on special". Most security lending agreements require various margin payments to keep the credit risk among the parties from growing when prices change.

Securities lenders lend their securities because the short rebate rates they pay on the collateral are lower than the interest rates they receive from investing the collateral. The difference is because of the implicit loan fees that they receive from the borrowers for borrowing the stock. The difference also compensates lenders for risks that the lenders take when investing the collateral and for the risk that the borrowers will default if prices rise significantly.

> **EXAMPLE 18**
>
> ### Short Positions in Securities and Contracts
>
> 1. How is the process of short selling shares of Siemens different from that of short selling a Siemens equity call option contract?
>
> ### Solution:
>
> To short sell shares of Siemens, the seller (or his broker) must borrow the shares from a long holder so that he can deliver them to the buyer. To short sell a Siemens equity call option contract, the seller simply creates the contract when he sells it to the buyer.

LEVERAGED POSITIONS

11

☐ calculate and interpret the leverage ratio, the rate of return on a margin transaction, and the security price at which the investor would receive a margin call

In many markets, traders can buy securities by borrowing some of the purchase price. They usually borrow the money from their brokers. The borrowed money is called the **margin loan**, and they are said to buy on margin. The interest rate that the buyers pay for their margin loan is called the **call money rate**. The call money rate is above the government bill rate and is negotiable. Large buyers generally obtain more favorable rates than do retail buyers. For institutional-size buyers, the call money rate is quite low because the loans are generally well secured by securities held as collateral by the lender.

Trader's equity is that portion of the security price that the buyer must supply. Traders who buy securities on margin are subject to minimum margin requirements. The **initial margin requirement** is the minimum fraction of the purchase price that must be trader's equity. This requirement may be set by the government, the exchange, or the exchange clearinghouse. For example, in the United States, the Federal Reserve Board sets the initial margin requirement through Regulation T. In Hong Kong SAR, the Securities and Futures Commission sets the margin requirements. In all markets, brokers often require more equity than the government-required minimum from their clients when lending to them.

Many markets allow brokers to lend their clients more money if the brokers use risk models to measure and control the overall risk of their clients' portfolios. This system is called portfolio margining.

Buying securities on margin can greatly increase the potential gains or losses for a given amount of equity in a position because the trader can buy more securities on margin than he could otherwise. The buyer thus earns greater profits when prices rise and suffers greater losses when prices fall. The relation between risk and borrowing is called **financial leverage** (often simply called leverage). Traders leverage their positions when they borrow to buy more securities. A highly leveraged position is large relative to the equity that supports it.

The leverage ratio is the ratio of the value of the position to the value of the equity investment in it. The leverage ratio indicates how many times larger a position is than the equity that supports it. The maximum leverage ratio associated with a position financed by the minimum margin requirement is one divided by the minimum margin requirement. If the requirement is 40 percent, then the maximum leverage ratio is 2.5 = 100% position ÷ 40% equity.

The leverage ratio indicates how much more risky a leveraged position is relative to an unleveraged position. For example, if a stock bought on 40 percent margin rises 10 percent, the buyer will experience a 25 percent (2.5 × 10%) return on the equity investment in her leveraged position. But if the stock falls by 10 percent, the return on the equity investment will be –25 percent (before the interest on the margin loan and before payment of commissions).

Financial analysts must be able to compute the total return to the equity investment in a leveraged position. The total return depends on the price change of the purchased security, the dividends or interest paid by the security, the interest paid on the margin loan, and the commissions paid to buy and sell the security. The following example illustrates the computation of the total return to a leveraged purchase of stock that pays a dividend.

EXAMPLE 19

Computing Total Return to a Leveraged Stock Purchase

A buyer buys stock on margin and holds the position for exactly one year, during which time the stock pays a dividend. For simplicity, assume that the interest on the loan and the dividend are both paid at the end of the year.

Purchase price	$20/share
Sale price	$15/share
Shares purchased	1,000
Leverage ratio	2.5
Call money rate	5%
Dividend	$0.10/share
Commission	$0.01/share

1. What is the total return on this investment?

Solution to 1:

To find the return on this investment, first determine the initial equity and then determine the equity remaining after the sale. The total purchase price is $20,000. The leverage ratio of 2.5 indicates that the buyer's equity financed 40 percent = (1 ÷ 2.5) of the purchase price. Thus, the equity investment is $8,000 = 40% of $20,000. The $12,000 remainder is borrowed. The actual investment is slightly higher because the buyer must pay a commission of $10

Leveraged Positions

= $0.01/share × 1,000 shares to buy the stock. The total initial investment is $8,010.

At the end of the year, the stock price has declined by $5/share. The buyer lost $5,000 = $5/share × 1,000 shares as a result of the price change. In addition, the buyer has to pay interest at 5 percent on the $12,000 loan, or $600. The buyer also receives a dividend of $0.10/share, or $100. The trader's equity remaining after the sale is computed from the initial equity investment as follows:

Initial investment	$8,010
Purchase commission	−10
Trading gains/losses	−5,000
Margin interest paid	−600
Dividends received	100
Sales commission paid	−10
Remaining equity	$2,490

or

Proceeds on sale	$15,000
Payoff loan	−12,000
Margin interest paid	−600
Dividends received	100
Sales commission paid	−10
Remaining equity	$2,490

so that the return on the initial investment of $8,010 is (2,490 − 8,010)/8,010 = −68.9%.

2. Why is the loss greater than the 25 percent decrease in the market price?

Solution to 2:

The realized loss is substantially greater than the stock price return of ($15 − $20)/$20 = −25%. Most of the difference is because of the leverage with the remainder primarily the result of the interest paid on the loan. Based on the leverage alone and ignoring the other cash flows, we would expect that the return on the equity would be −62.5% = 2.5 leverage times the −25% stock price return.

In the above example, if the stock dropped more than the buyer's original 40 percent margin (ignoring commissions, interest, and dividends), the trader's equity would have become negative. In that case, the investor would owe his broker more than the stock is worth. Brokers often lose money in such situations if the buyer does not repay the loan out of other funds.

To prevent such losses, brokers require that margin buyers always have a minimum amount of equity in their positions. This minimum is called the **maintenance margin requirement**. It is usually 25 percent of the current value of the position, but it may be higher or lower depending on the volatility of the instrument and the policies of the broker.

If the value of the equity falls below the maintenance margin requirement, the buyer will receive a **margin call**, or request for additional equity. If the buyer does not deposit additional equity with the broker in a timely manner, the broker will close the position to prevent further losses and thereby secure repayment of the margin loan.

When you buy securities on margin, you must know the price at which you will receive a margin call if prices drop. The answer to this question depends on your initial equity and on the maintenance margin requirement.

EXAMPLE 20

Margin Call Price

1. A trader buys stock on margin posting 40 percent of the initial stock price of $20 as equity. The maintenance margin requirement for the position is 25 percent. Below what price will a margin call occur?

Solution:

The trader's initial equity is 40 percent of the initial stock price of $20, or $8 per share. Subsequent changes in equity per share are equal to the share price change so that equity per share is equal to $8 + (P − 20) where P is the current share price. The margin call takes place when equity drops below the 25 percent maintenance margin requirement. The price below which a margin call will take place is the solution to the following equation:

$$\frac{\text{Equity/share}}{\text{Price/share}} = \frac{\$8 + P - 20}{P} = 25\%$$

which occurs at P = 16. When the price drops below $16, the equity will be under $4/share, which is less than 25 percent of the price.

Traders who sell securities short are also subject to margin requirements because they have borrowed securities. Initially, the trader's equity supporting the short position must be at least equal to the margin requirement times the initial value of the short position. If prices rise, equity will be lost. At some point, the short seller will have to contribute additional equity to meet the maintenance margin requirement. Otherwise, the broker will buy the security back to cover the short position to prevent further losses and thereby secure repayment of the stock loan.

12 ORDERS AND EXECUTION INSTRUCTIONS

- [ ] compare execution, validity, and clearing instructions
- [ ] compare market orders with limit orders

Buyers and sellers communicate with the brokers, exchanges, and dealers that arrange their trades by issuing **orders**. All orders specify what instrument to trade, how much to trade, and whether to buy or sell. Most orders also have other instructions attached to them. These additional instructions may include execution instructions, validity instructions, and clearing instructions. **Execution instructions** indicate how to fill the order, **validity instructions** indicate when the order may be filled, and **clearing instructions** indicate how to arrange the final settlement of the trade.

Orders and Execution Instructions

In this section, we introduce various order instructions and explain how traders use them to achieve their objectives. We discuss execution mechanisms—how exchanges, brokers and dealers fill orders—in the next section. To understand the concepts in this section, however, you need to know a little about order execution mechanisms.

In most markets, dealers and various other proprietary traders often are willing to buy from, or sell to, other traders seeking to sell or buy. The prices at which they are willing to buy are called **bid** prices and those at which they are willing to sell are called **ask** prices, or sometimes **offer** prices. The ask prices are invariably higher than the bid prices.

The traders who are willing to trade at various prices may also indicate the quantities that they will trade at those prices. These quantities are called **bid sizes** and **ask sizes** depending on whether they are attached to bids or offers.

Practitioners say that the traders who offer to trade make a market. Those who trade with them take the market.

The highest bid in the market is the **best bid**, and the lowest ask in the market is the **best offer**. The difference between the best bid and the best offer is the **market bid–ask spread**. When traders ask, "What's the market?" they want to know the best bid and ask prices and their associated sizes. Bid–ask spreads are an implicit cost of trading. Markets with small bid–ask spreads are markets in which the costs of trading are small, at least for the sizes quoted. Dealers often quote both bid and ask prices, and in that case, practitioners say that they quote a two-sided market. The market spread is never more than any dealer spread.

Execution Instructions

Market and limit orders convey the most common execution instructions. A **market order** instructs the broker or exchange to obtain the best price immediately available when filling the order. A **limit order** conveys almost the same instruction: Obtain the best price immediately available, but in no event accept a price higher than a specified limit price when buying or accept a price lower than a specified limit price when selling.

Many people mistakenly believe that limit orders specify the prices at which the orders will trade. Although limit orders do often trade at their limit prices, remember that the first instruction is to obtain the best price available. If better prices are available than the limit price, brokers and exchanges should obtain those prices for their clients.

Market orders generally execute immediately if other traders are willing to take the other side of the trade. The main drawback with market orders is that they can be expensive to execute, especially when the order is placed in a market for a thinly traded security, or more generally, when the order is large relative to the normal trading activity in the market. In that case, a market buy order may fill at a high price, or a market sell order may fill at a low price if no traders are willing to trade at better prices. High purchase prices and low sale prices represent price concessions given to other traders to encourage them to take the other side of the trade. Because the sizes of price concessions can be difficult to predict, and because prices often change between when a trader submits an order and when the order finally fills, the execution prices for market orders are often uncertain.

Buyers and sellers who are concerned about the possibility of trading at unacceptable prices add limit price instructions to their orders. The main problem with limit orders is that they may not execute. Limit orders do not execute if the limit price on a buy order is too low, or if the limit price on a sell order is too high. For example, if an investment manager submits a limit order to buy at the limit price of 20 (buy limit 20) and nobody is willing to sell at or below 20, the order will not trade. If prices never drop to 20, the manager will never buy. If the price subsequently rises, the manager will have lost the opportunity to profit from the price rise.

Whether traders use market orders or limit orders when trying to arrange trades depends on their concerns about price, trading quickly, and failing to trade. On average, limit orders trade at better prices than do market orders, but they often do not trade. Traders generally regret when their limit orders fail to trade because they usually would have profited if they had traded. Limit buy orders do not fill when prices are rising, and limit sell orders do not fill when prices are falling. In both cases, traders would be better off if their orders had filled.

The probability that a limit order will execute depends on where the order is placed relative to market prices. An aggressively priced order is more likely to trade than is a less aggressively priced order. A limit buy order is aggressively priced when the limit price is high relative to the market bid and ask prices. If the limit price is placed above the best offer, the buy order generally will partially or completely fill at the best offer price, depending on the size available at the best offer. Such limit orders are called **marketable limit orders** because at least part of the order can trade immediately. A limit buy order with a very high price relative to the market is essentially a market order.

If the buy order is placed above the best bid but below the best offer, traders say the order makes a new market because it becomes the new best bid. Such orders generally will not immediately trade, but they may attract sellers who are interested in trading. A buy order placed at the best bid is said to make market. It may have to wait until all other buy orders at that price trade first. Finally, a buy order placed below the best bid is **behind the market**. It will not execute unless market prices drop. Traders call limit orders that are waiting to trade **standing limit orders**.

Sell limit orders are aggressively priced if the limit price is low relative to market prices. The limit price of a marketable sell limit order is below the best bid. A limit sell order placed between the best bid and the best offer makes a new market on the sell side, one placed at the best offer makes market, and one placed above the best offer is behind the market.

Exhibit 2 presents a simplified **limit order book** in which orders are presented ranked by their limit prices for a hypothetical market. The market is "26 bid, offered at 28" because the best bid is 26 and the best offer (ask) is 28.

Exhibit 2: Terms Traders Use to Describe Standing Limit Orders

	Order Prices	
Bids	Offers (Asks)	
	33	The least aggressively priced sell orders are far from the market.
	32	
	31	These sell orders are *behind the market*. We also say that they are *away from the market*.
	30	
	29	
	28	← The *best offer* is *at the market*.
		The space between the current best bid and offer is *inside the market*. If a new limit order arrives here, it *makes a new market*.
The best bid and best offer *make the market*.		
26		← The *best bid* is *at the market*.
25		
24		These buy orders *are behind the market*. We also say that they are *away from the market*.
23		
22		
21		The least aggressively priced buy orders are *far from the market*.

Source: *Trading and Exchanges*.[1]

EXAMPLE 21

Making and Taking

1. What is the difference between making a market and taking a market?

Solution to 1:

A trader makes a market when the trader offers to trade. A trader takes a market when the trader accepts an offer to trade.

2. What order types are most likely associated with making a market and taking a market?

Solution to 2:

Traders place standing limit orders to give other traders opportunities to trade. Standing limit orders thus make markets. In contrast, traders use market orders or marketable limit orders to take offers to trade. These marketable orders take the market.

---

[1] Harris, Larry. 2003. *Trading and Exchanges: Market Microstructure for Practitioners*. New York: Oxford University Press.

A trade-off exists between how aggressively priced an order is and the ultimate trade price. Although aggressively priced orders fill faster and with more certainty then do less aggressively priced limit orders, the prices at which they execute are inferior. Buyers seeking to trade quickly must pay higher prices to increase the probability of trading quickly. Similarly, sellers seeking to trade quickly must accept lower prices to increase the probability of trading quickly.

Some order execution instructions specify conditions on size. For example, **all-or-nothing (AON) orders** can only trade if their entire sizes can be traded. Traders can similarly specify minimum fill sizes. This specification is common when settlement costs depend on the number of trades made to fill an order and not on the aggregate size of the order.

Exposure instructions indicate whether, how, and perhaps to whom orders should be exposed. **Hidden orders** are exposed only to the brokers or exchanges that receive them. These agencies cannot disclose hidden orders to other traders until they can fill them. Traders use hidden orders when they are afraid that other traders might behave strategically if they knew that a large order was in the market. Traders can discover hidden size only by submitting orders that will trade with that size. Thus, traders can only learn about hidden size after they have committed to trading with it.

Traders also often indicate a specific **display size** for their orders. Brokers and exchanges then expose only the display size for these orders. Any additional size is hidden from the public but can be filled if a suitably large order arrives. Traders sometimes call such orders **iceberg orders** because most of the order is hidden. Traders specify display sizes when they do not want to display their full sizes, but still want other traders to know that someone is willing to trade at the displayed price. Traders on the opposite side who wish to trade additional size at that price can discover the hidden size only if they trade the displayed size, at which point the broker or exchange will display any remaining size up to the display size. They also can discover the hidden size by submitting large orders that will trade with that size.

EXAMPLE 22

Market versus Limit and Hidden versus Displayed Orders

You are the buy-side trader for a very clever investment manager. The manager has hired a commercial satellite firm to take regular pictures of the parking lots in which new car dealers store their inventories. It has also hired some part-time workers to count the cars on the lots. With this information and some econometric analyses, the manager can predict weekly new car sale announcements more accurately than can most analysts. The manager typically makes a quarter percent each week on this strategy. Once a week, a day before the announcements are made, the manager gives you large orders to buy or sell car manufacturers based on his insights into their dealers' sales. What primary issues should you consider when deciding whether to:

1. use market or limit orders to fill his orders?

Solution to 1:

The manager's information is quite perishable. If his orders are not filled before the weekly sales are reported to the public, the manager will lose the opportunity to profit from the information as prices immediately adjust to the news. The manager, therefore, needs to get the orders filled quickly. This consideration suggests that the orders should be submitted as market orders. If submitted as limit orders, the orders might not execute and the firm would lose the opportunity to profit.

Large market orders, however, can be very expensive to execute, especially if few people are willing to trade significant size on the other side of the market. Because transaction costs can easily exceed the expected quarter percent return, you should submit limit orders to limit the execution prices that you are willing to accept. It is better to fail to trade than to trade at losing prices.

2. display the orders or hide them?

Solution to 2:

Your large orders could easily move the market if many people were aware of them, and even more so if others were aware that you are trading on behalf of a successful information-motivated trader. You thus should consider submitting hidden orders. The disadvantage of hidden orders is that they do not let people know that they can trade the other side if they want to.

VALIDITY INSTRUCTIONS AND CLEARING INSTRUCTIONS   13

☐ compare execution, validity, and clearing instructions

Validity instructions indicate when an order may be filled. The most common validity instruction is the **day order**. A day order is good for the day on which it is submitted. If it has not been filled by the close of business, the order expires unfilled.

Good-till-cancelled orders (GTC) are just that. In practice, most brokers limit how long they will manage an order to ensure that they do not fill orders that their clients have forgotten. Such brokers may limit their GTC orders to a few months.

Immediate or cancel orders (IOC) are good only upon receipt by the broker or exchange. If they cannot be filled in part or in whole, they cancel immediately. In some markets these orders are also known as **fill or kill** orders. When searching for hidden liquidity, electronic algorithmic trading systems often submit thousands of these IOC orders for every order that they fill.

Good-on-close orders can only be filled at the close of trading. These orders often are market orders, so traders call them **market-on-close** orders. Traders often use on-close orders when they want to trade at the same prices that will be published as the closing prices of the day. Mutual funds often like to trade at such prices because they value their portfolios at closing prices. Many traders also use **good-on-open** orders.

Stop Orders

A **stop order** is an order in which a trader has specified a stop price condition. The stop order may not be filled until the stop price condition has been satisfied. For a sell order, the stop price condition suspends execution of the order until a trade occurs at or below the stop price. After that trade, the stop condition is satisfied and the order becomes valid for execution, subject to all other execution instructions attached to it. If the market price subsequently rises above the sell order's stop price before the order trades, the order remains valid. Similarly, a buy order with a stop condition becomes valid only after a price rises above the specified stop price.

Traders often call stop orders **stop-loss orders** because many traders use them with the hope of stopping losses on positions that they have established. For example, a trader who has bought stock at 40 may want to sell the stock if the price falls below 30. In that case, the trader might submit a "GTC, stop 30, market sell" order. If the price falls to or below 30, the market order becomes valid and it should immediately execute at the best price then available in the market. That price may be substantially lower than 30 if the market is falling quickly. The stop-loss order thus does not guarantee a stop to losses at the stop price. If potential sellers are worried about trading at too low of a price, they can attach stop instructions to limit orders instead of market orders. In this example, if the trader is unwilling to sell below 25, the trader would submit a "GTC, stop 30, limit 25 sell" order.

If a trader wants to guarantee that he can sell at 30, the trader would buy a put option contract struck at 30. The purchase price of the option would include a premium for the insurance that the trader is buying. Option contracts can be viewed as limit orders for which execution is guaranteed at the strike price. A trader similarly might use a stop-buy order or a call option to limit losses on a short position.

A portfolio manager might use a stop-buy order when the manager believes that a security is undervalued but is unwilling to trade without market confirmation. For example, suppose that a stock currently trades for 50 RMB and a manager believes that it should be worth 100 RMB. Further, the manager believes that the stock will much more likely be worth 100 RMB if other traders are willing to buy it above 65 RMB. To best take advantage of this information, the manager would consider issuing a "GTC, stop 65 RMB, limit 100 RMB buy" order. Note that if the manager relies too much on the market when making this trading decision, however, he may violate CFA Standard of Professional Conduct V.A.2, which requires that all investment actions have a reasonable and adequate basis supported by appropriate research and investigation.

Because stop-sell orders become valid when prices are falling and stop-buy orders become valid when prices are rising, traders using stop orders contribute to market momentum as their sell orders push prices down further and their buy orders push prices up. Execution prices for stop orders thus are often quite poor.

EXAMPLE 23

Limit and Stop Instructions

1. In what ways do limit and stop instructions differ?

Solution:

Although both limit and stop instructions specify prices, the role that these prices play in the arrangement of a trade are completely different. A limit price places a limit on what trade prices will be acceptable to the trader. A buyer will accept prices only at or lower than the limit price whereas a seller will accept prices only at or above the limit price.

In contrast, a stop price indicates when an order can be filled. A buy order can only be filled once the market has traded at a price at or above the stop price. A sell order can only be filled once the market has traded at a price at or below the stop price.

Both order instructions may delay or prevent the execution of an order. A buy limit order will not execute until someone is willing to sell at or below the limit price. Similarly, a sell limit order will not execute until someone is

> willing to buy at or above the limit sell price. In contrast, a stop-buy order will not execute if the market price never rises to the stop price. Similarly, a stop-sell order will not execute if the market price never falls to the stop price.

Clearing Instructions

Clearing instructions tell brokers and exchanges how to arrange final settlement of trades. Traders generally do not attach these instructions to each order—instead they provide them as standing instructions. These instructions indicate what entity is responsible for clearing and settling the trade. For retail trades, that entity is the customer's broker. For institutional trades, that entity may be a custodian or another broker. When a client uses one broker to arrange trades and another broker to settle trades, traders say that the first broker gives up the trade to the other broker, who is often known as the prime broker. Institutional traders provide these instructions so they can obtain specialized execution services from different brokers while maintaining a single account for custodial services and other prime brokerage services, such as margin loans.

An important clearing instruction that must appear on security sale orders is an indication of whether the sale is a long sale or a short sale. In either case, the broker representing the sell order must ensure that the trader can deliver securities for settlement. For a long sale, the broker must confirm that the securities held are available for delivery. For a short sale, the broker must either borrow the security on behalf of the client or confirm that the client can borrow the security.

PRIMARY SECURITY MARKETS 14

☐ define primary and secondary markets and explain how secondary markets support primary markets

When issuers first sell their securities to investors, practitioners say that the trades take place in the **primary markets**. An issuer makes an **initial public offering** (IPO)—sometimes called a placing—of a security issue when it sells the security to the public for the first time. A seasoned security is a security that an issuer has already issued. If the issuer wants to sell additional units of a previously issued security, it makes a **seasoned offering** (sometimes called a secondary offering). Both types of offerings occur in the **primary market** where issuers sell their securities to investors. Later, if investors trade these securities among themselves, they trade in **secondary markets**. This section discusses primary markets and the procedures that issuers use to offer their securities to the public.

Public Offerings

Corporations generally contract with an investment bank to help them sell their securities to the public. The investment bank then lines up subscribers who will buy the security. Investment bankers call this process **book building**. In London, the book builder is called the book runner. The bank tries to build a book of orders to which they can sell the offering. Investment banks often support their book building by providing investment information and opinion about the issuer to their clients and to the public. Before the offering, the issuer generally makes a very detailed disclosure of its business, of the risks inherent in it, and of the uses to which the new funds will be placed.

When time is of the essence, issuers in Europe may issue securities through an **accelerated book build**, in which the investment bank arranges the offering in only one or two days. Such sales often occur at discounted prices.

The first public offering of common stock in a company consists of newly issued shares to be sold by the company. It may also include shares that the founders and other early investors in the company seek to sell. The initial public offering provides these investors with a means of liquidating their investments.

In an **underwritten offering**—the most common type of offering—the investment bank guarantees the sale of the issue at an offering price that it negotiates with the issuer. If the issue is undersubscribed, the bank will buy whatever securities it cannot sell at the offering price. In the case of an IPO, the underwriter usually also promises to make a market in the security for about a month to ensure that the secondary market will be liquid and to provide price support, if necessary. For large issues, a syndicate of investment banks and broker–dealers helps the **lead underwriter** build the book. The issuer usually pays an underwriting fee of about 7 percent for these various services. The underwriting fee is a placement cost of the offering.

In a **best effort offering**, the investment bank acts only as broker. If the offering is undersubscribed, the issuer will not sell as much as it hoped to sell.

For both types of offerings, the issuer and the bank usually jointly set the offering price following a negotiation. If they set a price that buyers consider too high, the offering will be undersubscribed, and they will fail to sell the entire issue. If they set the price too low, the offering will be oversubscribed, in which case the securities are often allocated to preferred clients or on a pro-rata basis.

(Note that CFA Standard of Professional Conduct III.B—fair dealing—requires that the allocation be based on a written policy disclosed to clients and suggests that the securities be offered on a pro-rata basis among all clients who have comparable relationships with their broker–dealers.)

Investment banks have a conflict of interest with respect to the offering price in underwritten offerings. As agents for the issuers, they generally are supposed to select the offering price that will raise the most money. But as underwriters, they have strong incentives to choose a low price. If the price is low, the banks can allocate valuable shares to benefit their clients and thereby indirectly benefit the banks. If the price is too high, the underwriters will have to buy overvalued shares in the offering and perhaps also during the following month if they must support the price in the secondary market, which directly costs the banks. These considerations tend to lower initial offering prices so that prices in the secondary market often rise immediately following an IPO. They are less important in a seasoned offering because trading in the secondary market helps identify the proper price for the offering.

First time issuers generally accept lower offering prices because they and many others believe that an undersubscribed IPO conveys very unfavorable information to the market about the company's prospects at a time when it is most vulnerable to public opinion about its prospects. They fear that an undersubscribed initial public offering will make it substantially harder to raise additional capital in subsequent seasoned offerings.

Primary Security Markets

EXAMPLE 24

The Healthybots Initial Public Offering

Healthybots is a health care company that treats diseases using artificial intelligence–based solutions. Healthybots raised approximately £265 million gross through an initial public offering of 103,142,466 ordinary shares at £2.57 per ordinary share. After the initial public offering, Healthybots had 213,333,333 ordinary shares issued and outstanding.

Healthybots received gross proceeds of approximately £34.3 million and net proceeds of £31.8 million. The ordinary shares that were sold to the public represented approximately 48 percent of Healthybots' total issued ordinary shares.

The shares commenced trading at 8:00 a.m. on the AIM market of the London Stock Exchange, where Healthybots opened at £2.74, traded 37 million shares between £2.68 and £2.74, and closed at £2.73.

1. Approximately how many new shares were issued by the company and how many shares were sold by the company's founders? What fraction of their holdings in the company did the founders sell?

Solution to 1:

Healthybots received gross proceeds of £34.3 million at £2.57 per share, so the company issued and sold 13,346,304 shares (= £34.3 million/£2.57 per share). The total placement was for 103,142,466 shares, so the founders sold 89,796,162 shares (= 103,142,466 shares − 13,346,304 shares). Because approximately 200 million shares (= 213.3 million shares − 13.3 million shares) were outstanding before the placement, the founders sold approximately 45 percent (= 90 million shares/200 million shares) of the company.

2. Approximately what return did the subscribers who participated in the IPO make on the first day it traded?

Solution to 2:

The subscribers bought the stock for £2.57 per share, and it closed at £2.73. The first day return thus was 6.2% $= \frac{2.73 - 2.57}{2.57} \times 100$.

3. Approximately how much did Healthybots pay in placement costs as a percentage of the new funds raised?

Solution to 3:

Healthybots obtained gross proceeds of £34.3 million but only raised net proceeds of £31.8 million. The £2.5 million difference was the total cost of the placement to the firm, which is 7.9 percent of net proceeds, or new funds raised (£2.5 million/£31.8 million).

Private Placements and Other Primary Market Transactions

Corporations sometimes issue their securities in private placements. In a **private placement**, corporations sell securities directly to a small group of qualified investors, usually with the assistance of an investment bank. Qualified investors have sufficient knowledge and experience to recognize the risks that they assume, and sufficient wealth to assume those risks responsibly. Most countries allow corporations to do private placements without nearly as much public disclosure as is required for public offerings. Private placements, therefore, may be cheaper than public offerings, but the buyers generally require higher returns (lower purchase prices) because they cannot subsequently trade the securities in an organized secondary market.

Corporations sometimes sell new issues of seasoned securities directly to the public on a piecemeal basis via a shelf registration. In a **shelf registration**, the corporation makes all public disclosures that it would for a regular offering, but it does not sell the shares in a single transaction. Instead, it sells the shares directly into the secondary market over time, generally when it needs additional capital. Shelf registrations provide corporations with flexibility in the timing of their capital transactions, and they can alleviate the downward price pressures often associated with large secondary offerings.

Many corporations may also issue shares via dividend reinvestment plans (DRPs or DRIPs, for short) that allow their shareholders to reinvest their dividends in newly issued shares of the corporation (in particular, DRPs specify that the corporation issue new shares for the plan rather than purchase them on the open market). These plans sometimes also allow existing shareholders and other investors to buy additional stock at a slight discount to current prices.

Finally, corporations can issue new stock via a rights offering. In a rights offering, the corporation distributes rights to buy stock at a fixed price to existing shareholders in proportion to their holdings. Because the rights need not be exercised, they are options. The exercise price, however, is set below the current market price of the stock so that buying stock with the rights is immediately profitable. Consequently, shareholders will experience dilution in the value of their existing shares. They can offset the dilution loss by exercising their rights or by selling the rights to others who will exercise them. Shareholders generally do not like rights offerings because they must provide additional capital (or sell their rights) to avoid losses through dilution. Financial analysts recognize that these securities, although called rights, are actually short-term stock warrants and value them accordingly.

The national governments of financially strong countries generally issue their bonds, notes, and bills in public auctions organized by a government agency (usually associated with the finance ministry). They may also sell them directly to dealers.

Smaller and less financially secure national governments and most regional governments often contract with investment banks to help them sell and distribute their securities. The laws of many governments, however, require that they auction their securities.

EXAMPLE 25

Private and Public Placements

1. In what ways do private placements differ from public placements?

Solution:

Issuers make private placements to a limited number of investors that generally are financially sophisticated and well informed about risk. The investors generally have some relationship to the issuer. Issuers make public placements when they sell securities to the general public. Public placements generally require substantially more financial disclosure than do private placements.

Importance of Secondary Markets to Primary Markets

Corporations and governments can raise money in the primary markets at lower cost when their securities will trade in liquid secondary markets. In a **liquid market**, traders can buy or sell with low transaction costs and small price concessions when they want to trade. Buyers value liquidity because they may need to sell their securities to meet liquidity needs. Investors thus will pay more for securities that they can easily sell than for those that they cannot easily sell. Higher prices translate into lower costs of capital for the issuers.

SECONDARY SECURITY MARKET AND CONTRACT MARKET STRUCTURES

15

- ☐ define primary and secondary markets and explain how secondary markets support primary markets
- ☐ describe how securities, contracts, and currencies are traded in quote-driven, order-driven, and brokered markets

Trading is the successful outcome to a bilateral search in which buyers look for sellers and sellers look for buyers. Many market structures have developed to reduce the costs of this search. Markets are liquid when the costs of finding a suitable counterparty to a trade are low.

Trading in securities and contracts takes place in a variety of market structures. The structures differ by when trades can be arranged, who arranges the trades, how they do so, and how traders learn about possible trading opportunities and executed trades. This section introduces the various market structures used to trade securities and contracts. We first consider trading sessions, then execution mechanisms, and finally market information systems.

Trading Sessions

Markets are organized as call markets or as continuous trading markets. In a **call market**, trades can be arranged only when the market is called at a particular time and place. In contrast in a **continuous trading market**, trades can be arranged and executed anytime the market is open.

Buyers can easily find sellers and vice versa in call markets because all traders interested in trading (or orders representing their interests) are present at the same time and place. Call markets thus have the potential to be very liquid when they are called. But they are completely illiquid between trading sessions. In contrast, traders can arrange and execute their trades at any time in continuous trading markets, but doing so can be difficult if the buyers and sellers (or their orders) are not both present at the same time.

Most call markets use single price auctions to match buyers to sellers. In these auctions, the market constructs order books representing all buy orders and all seller orders. The market then chooses a single trade price that will maximize the total volume of trade. The order books are supply and demand schedules, and the point at which they cross determines the trade price.

Call markets usually are organized just once a day, but some markets organize calls at more frequent intervals.

Many continuous trading markets start their trading with a call market auction. During a pre-opening period, traders submit their orders for the market call. At the opening, any possible trades are arranged and then trading continues in the continuous trading session. Some continuous trading markets also close their trading with a call. In these markets, traders who are only interested in trading in the closing call submit market- or limit-on-close orders.

EXAMPLE 26

Call Markets and Continuous Trading Markets

1. What is the main advantage of a call market compared with a continuous trading market?

Solution to 1:

By gathering all traders to the same place at the same time, a call market makes it easier for buyers to find sellers and vice versa. In contrast, if buyers and sellers (or their orders) are not present at the same time in a continuous market, they cannot trade.

2. What is the main advantage of a continuous trading market compared with a call market?

Solution to 2:

In a continuous trading market, a willing buyer and seller can trade at any time the market is open. In contrast, in a call market trading can take place only when the market is called.

Execution Mechanisms

The three main types of market structures are quote-driven markets (sometimes called price-driven or dealer markets), order-driven markets, and brokered markets. In **quote-driven markets**, customers trade with dealers. In **order-driven markets**, an order matching system run by an exchange, a broker, or an alternative trading system uses rules to arrange trades based on the orders that traders submit. Most exchanges and ECNs organize order-driven markets. In **brokered markets**, brokers arrange trades between their customers. Brokered markets are common for transactions of unique instruments, such as real estate properties, intellectual properties, or large blocks of securities. Many trading systems use more than one type of market structure.

Quote-Driven Markets

Worldwide, most trading, other than in stocks, takes place in quote-driven markets. Almost all bonds and currencies and most spot commodities trade in quote-driven markets. Traders call them quote-driven (or price-driven or dealer) because customers trade at the prices quoted by dealers. Depending on the instrument traded, the dealers work for commercial banks, for investment banks, for broker–dealers, or for proprietary trading houses.

Quote-driven markets also often are called over-the-counter (OTC) markets because securities used to be literally traded over the dealer's counter in the dealer's office. Now, most trades in OTC markets are conducted over proprietary computer communications networks, by telephone, or sometimes over instant messaging systems.

Order-Driven Markets

Order-driven markets arrange trades using rules to match buy orders to sell orders. The orders may be submitted by customers or by dealers. Almost all exchanges use order-driven trading systems, and every automated trading system is an order-driven system.

Because rules match buyers to sellers, traders often trade with complete strangers. Order-driven markets thus must have procedures to ensure that buyers and sellers perform on their trade contracts. Otherwise, dishonest traders would enter contracts that they would not settle if a change in market conditions made settlement unprofitable.

Two sets of rules characterize order-driven market mechanisms: Order matching rules and trade pricing rules. The order matching rules match buy orders to sell orders. The trade pricing rules determine the prices at which the matched trades take place.

Order Matching Rules

Order-driven trading systems match buyers to sellers using rules that rank the buy orders and the sell orders based on price, and often along with other secondary criteria. The systems then match the highest-ranking buy order with the highest-ranking sell order. If the buyer is willing to pay at least as much as the seller is willing to receive, the system will arrange a trade for the minimum of the buy and sell quantities. The remaining size, if any, is then matched with the next order on the other side and the process continues until no further trades can be arranged.

The **order precedence hierarchy** determines which orders go first. The first rule is **price priority**: The highest priced buy orders and the lowest priced sell orders go first. They are the most aggressively priced orders. **Secondary precedence rules** determine how to rank orders at the same price. Most trading systems use time precedence to rank orders at the same price. The first order to arrive has precedence over other orders. In trading systems that permit hidden and partially hidden orders, displayed quantities at a given price generally have precedence over the undisplayed quantities. So the complete precedence hierarchy is given by price priority, display precedence at a given price, and finally time precedence among all orders with the same display status at a given price. These rules give traders incentives to improve price, display their orders, and arrive early if they want to trade quickly. These incentives increase market liquidity.

Trade Pricing Rules

After the orders are matched, the trading system then uses its trade pricing rule to determine the trade price. The three rules that various order-driven markets use to price their trades are the uniform pricing rule, the discriminatory pricing rule, and the derivative pricing rule.

Call markets commonly use the uniform pricing rule. Under this rule, all trades execute at the same price. The market chooses the price that maximizes the total quantity traded.

Continuous trading markets use the **discriminatory pricing rule**. Under this rule, the limit price of the order or quote that first arrived—the standing order—determines the trade price. This rule allows a large arriving trader to discriminate among standing limit orders by filling the most aggressively priced orders first at their limit prices and then filling less aggressively priced orders at their less favorable (from the point of view of the arriving trader) limit prices. If trading systems did not use this pricing rule, large traders would break their orders into pieces to price discriminate on their own.

EXAMPLE 27

Filling a Large Order in a Continuous Trading Market

1. Before the arrival of a large order, the Tokyo Stock Exchange has the following limit orders standing on its book:

Buyer	Bid Size	Limit Price(¥)	Offer Size	Seller
Takumi	15	100.1		
Hiroto	8	100.2		
Shou	10	100.3		
		100.4	4	Hina
		100.5	6	Sakura
		100.6	12	Miku

Tsubasa submits a day order to buy 15 contracts, limit ¥100.5. With whom does he trade, what is his average trade price, and what does the limit order book look like afterward?

Solution:

Tsubasa's buy order first fills with the most aggressively priced sell order, which is Hina's order for four contracts. A trade takes place at ¥100.4 for four contracts, Hina's order fills completely, and Tsubasa still has 11 more contracts remaining.

The next most aggressively priced sell order is Sakura's order for six contracts. A second trade takes place at ¥100.5 for six contracts, Sakura's order fills completely, and Tsubasa still has five more contracts remaining.

The next most aggressively priced sell order is Miku's order at ¥100.6. No further trade is possible, however, because her limit sell price is above Tsubasa's limit buy price. Tsubasa's average trade price is $¥100.46 = \frac{4 \times ¥100.4 + 6 \times ¥100.5}{4 + 6}$.

Because Tsubasa issued a day order, the remainder of his order is placed on the book on the buy side at ¥100.5. The following orders are then on the book:

Buyer	Bid Size	Limit Price (¥)	Offer Size	Seller
Takumi	15	100.1		
Hiroto	8	100.2		
Shou	10	100.3		
		100.4		
Tsubasa	5	100.5		
		100.6	12	Miku

If Tsubasa had issued an immediate-or-cancel order, the remaining five contracts would have been cancelled.

Crossing networks use the derivative pricing rule. **Crossing networks** are trading systems that match buyers and sellers who are willing to trade at prices obtained from other markets. Most systems cross their trades at the midpoint of the best bid and ask quotes published by the exchange at which the security primarily trades.

This pricing rule is called a **derivative pricing rule** because the price is derived from another market. In particular, the price does not depend on the orders submitted to the crossing network. Some crossing networks are organized as call markets and others as continuously trading markets. The most important crossing market is the equity trading system POSIT.

Brokered Markets

The third execution mechanism is the **brokered market**, in which brokers arrange trades among their clients. Brokers organize markets for instruments for which finding a buyer or a seller willing to trade is difficult because the instruments are unique and thus of interest only to a limited number of people or institutions. These instruments generally are also infrequently traded and expensive to carry in inventory. Examples of such instruments include very large blocks of stock, real estate properties, fine art masterpieces, intellectual properties, operating companies, liquor licenses, and taxi medallions. Because dealers generally are unable or unwilling to hold these assets in their inventories, they will not make markets in them. Organizing order-driven markets for these instruments is not sensible because too few traders would submit orders to them.

Successful brokers in these markets try to know everyone who might now or in the future be willing to trade. They spend most of their time on the telephone and in meetings building their networks.

EXAMPLE 28

Quote-Driven, Order-Driven, and Brokered Markets

1. What are the primary advantages of quote-driven, order-driven, and brokered markets?

Solution:

In a quote-driven market, dealers generally are available to supply liquidity. In an order-driven market, traders can supply liquidity to each other. In a brokered market, brokers help find traders who are willing to trade when dealers would not be willing to make markets and when traders would not be willing to post orders.

Market Information Systems

Markets vary in the type and quantity of data that they disseminate to the public. Traders say that a market is pre-trade transparent if the market publishes real-time data about quotes and orders. Markets are post-trade transparent if the market publishes trade prices and sizes soon after trades occur.

Buy-side traders value transparency because it allows them to better manage their trading, understand market values, and estimate their prospective and actual transaction costs. In contrast, dealers prefer to trade in opaque markets because, as frequent traders, they have an information advantage over those who know less than they do. Bid–ask spreads tend to be wider and transaction costs tend to be higher in opaque markets because finding the best available price is harder for traders in such markets.

16. WELL-FUNCTIONING FINANCIAL SYSTEMS

☐ describe characteristics of a well-functioning financial system

The financial system allows traders to solve financing and risk management problems. In a well-functioning financial system:

- investors can easily move money from the present to the future while obtaining a fair rate of return for the risks that they bear;
- borrowers can easily obtain funds that they need to undertake current projects if they can credibly promise to repay the funds in the future;
- hedgers can easily trade away or offset the risks that concern them; and
- traders can easily trade currencies for other currencies or commodities that they need.

If the assets or contracts needed to solve these problems are available to trade, the financial system has **complete markets**. If the costs of arranging these trades are low, the financial system is **operationally efficient**. If the prices of the assets and contracts reflect all available information related to fundamental values, the financial system is informationally efficient.

Well-functioning financial systems are characterized by:

- the existence of well-developed markets that trade instruments that help people solve their financial problems (complete markets);
- liquid markets in which the costs of trading—commissions, bid–ask spreads, and order price impacts—are low (operationally efficient markets);
- timely financial disclosures by corporations and governments that allow market participants to estimate the fundamental values of securities (support **informationally efficient markets**); and
- prices that reflect fundamental values so that prices vary primarily in response to changes in fundamental values and not to demands for liquidity made by uninformed traders (informationally efficient markets).

Such complete and operationally efficient markets are produced by financial intermediaries who:

- organize exchanges, brokerages, and alternative trading systems that match buyers to sellers;
- provide liquidity on demand to traders;
- securitize assets to produce investment instruments that are attractive to investors and thereby lower the costs of funds for borrowers;
- run banks that match investors to borrowers by taking deposits and making loans;
- run insurance companies that pool uncorrelated risks;
- provide investment advisory services that help investors manage and grow their assets at low cost;
- organize clearinghouses that ensure everyone settles their trades and contracts; and
- organize depositories that ensure nobody loses their assets.

The benefits of a well-functioning financial system are huge. In such systems, investors who need to move money to the future can easily connect with entrepreneurs who need money now to develop new products and services. Similarly, producers who would otherwise avoid valuable projects because they are too risky can easily transfer those risks to others who can better bear them. Most importantly, these transactions generally can take place among strangers so that the benefits from trading can be derived from an enormous number of potential matches.

In contrast, economies that have poorly functioning financial systems have great difficulties allocating capital among the many companies who could use it. Financial transactions tend to be limited to arrangements within families when people cannot easily find trustworthy counterparties who will honor their contracts. In such economies, capital is allocated inefficiently, risks are not easily shared, and production is inefficient.

An extraordinarily important byproduct of an operationally efficient financial system is the production of informationally efficient prices. Prices are informationally efficient when they reflect all available information about fundamental values. Informative prices are crucially important to the welfare of an economy because they help ensure that resources go where they are most valuable. Economies that use resources where they are most valuable are allocationally efficient. Economies that do not use resources where they are most valuable waste their resources and consequently often are quite poor.

Well-informed traders make prices informationally efficient. When they buy assets and contracts that they think are undervalued, they tend to push the assets' prices up. Similarly, when they sell assets and contracts that they think are overvalued, they tend to push the assets' prices down. The effect of their trading thus causes prices to reflect their information about values.

How accurately prices reflect fundamental information depends on the costs of obtaining fundamental information and on the liquidity available to well-informed traders. Accounting standards and reporting requirements that produce meaningful and timely financial disclosures reduce the costs of obtaining fundamental information and thereby allow analysts to form more accurate estimates of fundamental values. Liquid markets allow well-informed traders to fill their orders at low cost. If filling orders is very costly, informed trading may not be profitable. In that case, information-motivated traders will not commit resources to collect and analyze data and they will not trade. Without their research and their associated trading, prices would be less informative.

EXAMPLE 29

Well-Functioning Financial Systems

1. As a financial analyst specializing in emerging market equities, you understand that a well-functioning financial system contributes to the economic prosperity of a country. You are asked to start covering a new small market country. What factors will you consider when characterizing the quality of its financial markets?

Solution:

In general, you will consider whether:

- the country has markets that allow its companies and residents to finance projects, save for the future, and exchange risk;
- the costs of trading in those markets is low; and

- prices reflect fundamental values.

You may specifically check to see whether:

- fixed income and stock markets allow borrowers to easily obtain capital from investors;
- corporations disclose financial and operating data on a timely basis in conformity to widely respected reporting standards, such as IFRS;
- forward, futures, and options markets trade instruments that companies need to hedge their risks;
- dealers and arbitrageurs allow traders to trade when they want to;
- bid–ask spreads are small;
- trades and contracts invariably settle as expected;
- investment managers provide high-quality management services for reasonable fees;
- banks and other financing companies are well capitalized and thus able to help investors provide capital to borrowers;
- securitized assets are available and represent reasonable credit risks;
- insurance companies are well capitalized and thus able to help those exposed to risks insure against them; and
- price volatility appears consistent with changes in fundamental values.

17. MARKET REGULATION

☐ describe objectives of market regulation

Government agencies and practitioner organizations regulate many markets and the financial intermediaries that participate in them. The regulators generally seek to promote fair and orderly markets in which traders can trade at prices that accurately reflect fundamental values without incurring excessive transaction costs. This section identifies the problems that financial regulators hope to solve and the objectives of their regulations.

Regrettably, some people will steal from each other if given a chance, especially if the probability of detection is low or if the penalty for being caught is low. The number of ways that people can steal or misappropriate wealth generally increases with the complexity of their relationships and with asymmetries in their knowledge. Because financial markets tend to be complex, and because customers are often much less sophisticated than the professionals that serve them, the potential for losses through various frauds can be unacceptably high in unregulated markets.

Regulators thus ensure that systems are in place to protect customers from fraud. In principle, the customers themselves would demand such systems as a condition of doing business. When customers are unsophisticated or poorly informed, however, they may not know how to protect themselves. When the costs of learning are large—as they often are in complex financial markets—having regulators look out for the public interest can be economically efficient.

More customer money is probably lost in financial markets through negligence than through outright fraud. Most customers in financial markets use various agents to help them solve problems that they do not understand well. These agents include securities brokers, financial advisers, investment managers, and insurance agents. Because customers generally do not have much information about market conditions, they find it extremely difficult to measure the added value they obtain from their agents. This problem is especially challenging when performance has a strong random component. In that case, determining whether agents are skilled or lucky is very difficult. Moreover, if the agent is a good salesman, the customer may not critically evaluate their agent's performance. These conditions, which characterize most financial markets, ensure that customers cannot easily determine whether their agents are working faithfully for them. They tend to lose if their agents are unqualified or lazy, or if they unconsciously favor themselves and their friends over their clients, as is natural for even the most honest people.

Regulators help solve these agency problems by setting minimum standards of competence for agents and by defining and enforcing minimum standards of practice. CFA Institute provides significant standard setting leadership in the areas of investment management and investment performance reporting through its Chartered Financial Analyst Program, in which you are studying, and its Global Investment Performance Standards. In principle, regulation would not be necessary if customers could identify competent agents and effectively measure their performance. In the financial markets, doing so is very difficult.

Regulators often act to level the playing field for market participants. For example, in many jurisdictions, insider trading in securities is illegal. The rule prevents corporate insiders and others with access to corporate information from trading on material information that has not been released to the public. The purpose of the rule is to reduce the profits that insiders could extract from the markets. These profits would come from other traders who would lose when they trade with well-informed insiders. Because traders tend to withdraw from markets when they lose, rules against insider trading help keep markets liquid. They also keep corporate insiders from hoarding information.

Many situations arise in financial markets in which common standards benefit everyone involved. For example, having all companies report financial results on a common basis allows financial analysts to easily compare companies. Accordingly, the International Accounting Standards Board (IASB) and the US-based Financial Accounting Standards Board (FASB), among many others, promulgate common financial standards to which all companies must report. The benefits of having common reporting standards has led to a very successful and continuing effort to converge all accounting standards to a single worldwide standard. Without such regulations, investors might eventually refuse to invest in companies that do not report to a common standard, but such market-based discipline is a very slow regulator of behavior, and it would have little effect on companies that do not need to raise new capital.

Regulators generally require that financial firms maintain minimum levels of capital. These capital requirements serve two purposes. First, they ensure that the companies will be able to honor their contractual commitments when unexpected market movements or poor decisions cause them to lose money. Second, they ensure that the owners of financial firms have substantial interest in the decisions that they make. Without a substantial financial interest in the decisions that they make, companies often take too many risks and exercise poor judgment about extending credit to others. When such companies fail, they impose significant costs on others. Minimum capital requirements reduce the probability that financial firms will fail and they reduce the disruptions associated with those failures that do occur. In principle, a firm's customers and counterparties could require minimum capital levels as a condition of doing business with the firm, but they have more difficulty enforcing their contracts than do governments who can imprison people.

Regulators similarly regulate insurance companies and pension funds that make long-term promises to their clients. Such entities need to maintain adequate reserves to ensure that they can fund their liabilities. Unfortunately, their managers have a tendency to underestimate these reserves if they will not be around when the liabilities come due. Again, in principle, policyholders and employees could regulate the behavior of their insurance funds and their employers by refusing to contract with them if they do not promise to adequately fund their liabilities. In practice, however, the sophistication, information, and time necessary to write and enforce contracts that control these problems are beyond the reach of most people. The government thus is a sensible regulator of such problems.

Many regulators are self-regulating organizations (SROs) that regulate their members. Exchanges, clearinghouses, and dealer trade organizations are examples of self-regulating organizations. In some cases, the members of these organizations voluntarily subject themselves to the SRO's regulations to promote the common good. In other cases, governments delegate regulatory and enforcement authorities to SROs, usually subject to the supervision of a government agency, such as a national securities and exchange authority. Exchanges, dealer associations, and clearing agencies often regulate their members with these delegated powers.

By setting high standards of behavior, SROs help their members obtain the confidence of their customers. They also reduce the chance that members of the SRO will incur losses when dealing with other members of the SRO.

When regulators fail to solve the problems discussed here, the financial system does not function well. People who lose money stop saving and borrowers with good ideas cannot fund their projects. Similarly, hedgers withdraw from markets when the costs of hedging are high. Without the ability to hedge, producers become reluctant to specialize because specialization generally increases risk. Because specialization also decreases costs, however, production becomes less efficient as producers chose safer technologies. Economies that cannot solve the regulatory problems described in this section tend to operate less efficiently than do better regulated economies, and they tend to be less wealthy.

To summarize, the objectives of market regulation are to:

1. control fraud;
2. control agency problems;
3. promote fairness;
4. set mutually beneficial standards;
5. prevent undercapitalized financial firms from exploiting their investors by making excessively risky investments; and
6. ensure that long-term liabilities are funded.

Regulation is necessary because regulating certain behaviors through market-based mechanisms is too costly for people who are unsophisticated and uninformed. Effectively regulated markets allow people to better achieve their financial goals.

EXAMPLE 30

Bankrupt Traders

You are the chief executive officer of a brokerage that is a member of a clearinghouse. A trader who clears through your firm is bankrupt at midday, but you do not yet know it even though your clearing agreement with him explicitly requires that he immediately report significant losses. The trader knows that if he takes a large position, prices might move in his favor so that he will no longer be bankrupt. The trader attempts to do so and succeeds. You find out about this later in the evening.

1. Why does the clearinghouse regulate its members?

Solution to 1:

The clearinghouse regulates its members to ensure that no member imposes costs on another member by failing to settle a trade.

2. What should you do about the trader?

Solution to 2:

You should immediately end your clearing relationship with the trader and confiscate his trading profits. The trader was trading with your firm's capital after he became bankrupt. Had he lost, your firm would have borne the loss.

3. Why would the clearinghouse allow you to keep his trading profits?

Solution to 3:

If the clearinghouse did not permit you to keep his trading profits, other traders similarly situated might attempt the same strategy.

SUMMARY

This reading introduces how the financial system operates and explains how well-functioning financial systems lead to wealthy economies. Financial analysts need to understand how the financial system works because their analyses often lead to trading decisions.

The financial system consists of markets and the financial intermediaries that operate in them. These institutions allow buyers to connect with sellers. They may trade directly with each other when they trade the same instrument or they only may trade indirectly when a financial intermediary connects the buyer to the seller through transactions with each that appear on the intermediary's balance sheet. The buyer and seller may exchange instruments, cash flows, or risks.

The following points, among others, were made in this reading:

- The financial system consists of mechanisms that allow strangers to contract with each other to move money through time, to hedge risks, and to exchange assets that they value less for those that they value more.
- Investors move money from the present to the future when they save. They expect a normal rate of return for bearing risk through time. Borrowers move money from the future to the present to fund current projects and expenditures. Hedgers trade to reduce their exposure to risks they prefer not to take. Information-motivated traders are active investment managers who try to identify under- and overvalued instruments.
- Securities are first sold in primary markets by their issuers. They then trade in secondary markets.

- People invest in pooled investment vehicles to benefit from the investment management services of their managers.
- Forward contracts allow buyers and sellers to arrange for future sales at predetermined prices. Futures contracts are forward contracts guaranteed by clearinghouses. The guarantee ensures that strangers are willing to trade with each other and that traders can offset their positions by trading with anybody. These features of futures contract markets make them highly attractive to hedgers and information-motivated traders.
- Many financial intermediaries connect buyers to sellers in a given instrument, acting directly as brokers and exchanges or indirectly as dealers and arbitrageurs.
- Financial intermediaries create instruments when they conduct arbitrage, securitize assets, borrow to lend, manage investment funds, or pool insurance contracts. These activities all transform cash flows and risks from one form to another. Their services allow buyers and sellers to connect with each other through instruments that meet their specific needs.
- Financial markets work best when strangers can contract with each other without worrying about whether their counterparts are able and willing to honor their contract. Clearinghouses, variation margins, maintenance margins, and settlement guarantees made by creditworthy brokers on behalf of their clients help manage credit risk and ultimately allow strangers to contract with each other.
- Information-motivated traders short sell when they expect that prices will fall. Hedgers short sell to reduce the risks of a long position in a related contract or commodity.
- Margin loans allow people to buy more securities than their equity would otherwise permit them to buy. The larger positions expose them to more risk so that gains and losses for a given amount of equity will be larger. The leverage ratio is the value of a position divided by the value of the equity supporting it. The returns to the equity in a position are equal to the leverage ratio times the returns to the unleveraged position.
- To protect against credit losses, brokers demand maintenance margin payments from their customers who have borrowed cash or securities when adverse price changes cause their customer's equity to drop below the maintenance margin ratio. Brokers close positions for customers who do not satisfy these margin calls.
- Orders are instructions to trade. They always specify instrument, side (buy or sell), and quantity. They usually also provide several other instructions.
- Market orders tend to fill quickly but often at inferior prices. Limit orders generally fill at better prices if they fill, but they may not fill. Traders choose order submission strategies on the basis of how quickly they want to trade, the prices they are willing to accept, and the consequences of failing to trade.
- Stop instructions are attached to other orders to delay efforts to fill them until the stop condition is satisfied. Although stop orders are often used to stop losses, they are not always effective.
- Issuers sell their securities using underwritten public offerings, best efforts public offerings, private placements, shelf registrations, dividend reinvestment programs, and rights offerings. Investment banks have a conflict of interests when setting the initial offering price in an IPO.

- Well-functioning secondary markets are essential to raising capital in the primary markets because investors value the ability to sell their securities if they no longer want to hold them or if they need to disinvest to raise cash. If they cannot trade their securities in a liquid market, they will not pay as much for them.
- Matching buyers and sellers in call markets is easy because the traders (or their orders) come together at the same time and place.
- Dealers provide liquidity in quote-driven markets. Public traders as well as dealers provide liquidity in order-driven markets.
- Order-driven markets arrange trades by ranking orders using precedence rules. The rules generally ensure that traders who provide the best prices, display the most size, and arrive early trade first. Continuous order-driven markets price orders using the discriminatory pricing rule. Under this rule, standing limit orders determine trade prices.
- Brokers help people trade unique instruments or positions for which finding a buyer or a seller is difficult.
- Transaction costs are lower in transparent markets than in opaque markets because traders can more easily determine market value and more easily manage their trading in transparent markets.
- A well-functioning financial system allows people to trade instruments that best solve their wealth and risk management problems with low transaction costs. Complete and liquid markets characterize a well-functioning financial system. Complete markets are markets in which the instruments needed to solve investment and risk management problems are available to trade. Liquid markets are markets in which traders can trade when they want to trade at low cost.
- The financial system is operationally efficient when its markets are liquid. Liquid markets lower the costs of raising capital.
- A well-functioning financial system promotes wealth by ensuring that capital allocation decisions are well made. A well-functioning financial system also promotes wealth by allowing people to share the risks associated with valuable products that would otherwise not be undertaken.
- Prices are informationally efficient when they reflect all available information about fundamental values. Information-motivated traders make prices informationally efficient. Prices will be most informative in liquid markets because information-motivated traders will not invest in information and research if establishing positions based on their analyses is too costly.
- Regulators generally seek to promote fair and orderly markets in which traders can trade at prices that accurately reflect fundamental values without incurring excessive transaction costs. Governmental agencies and self-regulating organizations of practitioners provide regulatory services that attempt to make markets safer and more efficient.
- Mandated financial disclosure programs for the issuers of publicly traded securities ensure that information necessary to estimate security values is available to financial analysts on a consistent basis.

PRACTICE PROBLEMS

1. Akihiko Takabe has designed a sophisticated forecasting model, which predicts the movements in the overall stock market, in the hope of earning a return in excess of a fair return for the risk involved. He uses the predictions of the model to decide whether to buy, hold, or sell the shares of an index fund that aims to replicate the movements of the stock market. Takabe would *best* be characterized as a(n):

    A. hedger.

    B. investor.

    C. information-motivated trader.

2. James Beach is young and has substantial wealth. A significant proportion of his stock portfolio consists of emerging market stocks that offer relatively high expected returns at the cost of relatively high risk. Beach believes that investment in emerging market stocks is appropriate for him given his ability and willingness to take risk. Which of the following labels *most appropriately* describes Beach?

    A. Hedger.

    B. Investor.

    C. Information-motivated trader.

3. Lisa Smith owns a manufacturing company in the United States. Her company has sold goods to a customer in Brazil and will be paid in Brazilian real (BRL) in three months. Smith is concerned about the possibility of the BRL depreciating more than expected against the US dollar (USD). Therefore, she is planning to sell three-month futures contracts on the BRL. The seller of such contracts generally gains when the BRL depreciates against the USD. If Smith were to sell these future contracts, she would *most appropriately* be described as a(n):

    A. hedger.

    B. investor.

    C. information-motivated trader.

4. Which of the following is *not* a function of the financial system?

    A. To regulate arbitrageurs' profits (excess returns).

    B. To help the economy achieve allocational efficiency.

    C. To facilitate borrowing by businesses to fund current operations.

5. An investor primarily invests in stocks of publicly traded companies. The investor wants to increase the diversification of his portfolio. A friend has recommended investing in real estate properties. The purchase of real estate would *best* be characterized as a transaction in the:

    A. derivative investment market.

    B. traditional investment market.

Practice Problems

    C. alternative investment market.

6. A hedge fund holds its excess cash in 90-day commercial paper and negotiable certificates of deposit. The cash management policy of the hedge fund is *best* described as using:

    A. capital market instruments.

    B. money market instruments.

    C. intermediate-term debt instruments.

7. An oil and gas exploration and production company announces that it is offering 30 million shares to the public at $45.50 each. This transaction is *most likely* a sale in the:

    A. futures market.

    B. primary market.

    C. secondary market.

8. Consider a mutual fund that invests primarily in fixed-income securities that have been determined to be appropriate given the fund's investment goal. Which of the following is *least likely* to be a part of this fund?

    A. Warrants.

    B. Commercial paper.

    C. Repurchase agreements.

9. A friend has asked you to explain the differences between open-end and closed-end funds. Which of the following will you *most likely* include in your explanation?

    A. Closed-end funds are unavailable to new investors.

    B. When investors sell the shares of an open-end fund, they can receive a discount or a premium to the fund's net asset value.

    C. When selling shares, investors in an open-end fund sell the shares back to the fund whereas investors in a closed-end fund sell the shares to others in the secondary market.

10. The Standard & Poor's Depositary Receipts (SPDRs) is an investment that tracks the S&P 500 stock market index. Purchases and sales of SPDRs during an average trading day are *best* described as:

    A. primary market transactions in a pooled investment.

    B. secondary market transactions in a pooled investment.

    C. secondary market transactions in an actively managed investment.

11. Which of the following statements about exchange-traded funds is *most correct*?

    A. Exchange-traded funds are not backed by any assets.

B. The investment companies that create exchange-traded funds are financial intermediaries.

C. The transaction costs of trading shares of exchange-traded funds are substantially greater than the combined costs of trading the underlying assets of the fund.

12. The usefulness of a forward contract is limited by some problems. Which of the following is *most likely* one of those problems?

    A. Once you have entered into a forward contract, it is difficult to exit from the contract.

    B. Entering into a forward contract requires the long party to deposit an initial amount with the short party.

    C. If the price of the underlying asset moves adversely from the perspective of the long party, periodic payments must be made to the short party.

13. Tony Harris is planning to start trading in commodities. He has heard about the use of futures contracts on commodities and is learning more about them. Which of the following is Harris *least likely* to find associated with a futures contract?

    A. Existence of counterparty risk.

    B. Standardized contractual terms.

    C. Payment of an initial margin to enter into a contract.

14. A German company that exports machinery is expecting to receive $10 million in three months. The firm converts all its foreign currency receipts into euros. The chief financial officer of the company wishes to lock in a minimum fixed rate for converting the $10 million to euro but also wants to keep the flexibility to use the future spot rate if it is favorable. What hedging transaction is *most likely* to achieve this objective?

    A. Selling dollars forward.

    B. Buying put options on the dollar.

    C. Selling futures contracts on dollars.

15. A book publisher requires substantial quantities of paper. The publisher and a paper producer have entered into an agreement for the publisher to buy and the producer to supply a given quantity of paper four months later at a price agreed upon today. This agreement is a:

    A. futures contract.

    B. forward contract.

    C. commodity swap.

16. The Standard & Poor's Depositary Receipts (SPDRs) is an exchange-traded fund in the United States that is designed to track the S&P 500 stock market index. The latest price of a share of SPDRs is $290. A trader has just bought call options on shares of SPDRs for a premium of $3 per share. The call options expire in six months and have an exercise price of $305 per share. On the expiration date, the trader will exercise the call options (ignore any transaction costs) if and only if

the shares of SPDRs are trading:

A. below $305 per share.

B. above $305 per share.

C. above $308 per share.

17. Jason Schmidt works for a hedge fund and he specializes in finding profit opportunities that are the result of inefficiencies in the market for convertible bonds—bonds that can be converted into a predetermined amount of a company's common stock. Schmidt tries to find convertibles that are priced inefficiently relative to the underlying stock. The trading strategy involves the simultaneous purchase of the convertible bond and the short sale of the underlying common stock. The above process could best be described as:

A. hedging.

B. arbitrage.

C. securitization.

18. Pierre-Louis Robert just purchased a call option on shares of the Michelin Group. A few days ago he wrote a put option on Michelin shares. The call and put options have the same exercise price, expiration date, and number of shares underlying. Considering both positions, Robert's exposure to the risk of the stock of the Michelin Group is:

A. long.

B. short.

C. neutral.

19. An online brokerage firm has set the minimum margin requirement at 55 percent. What is the maximum leverage ratio associated with a position financed by this minimum margin requirement?

A. 1.55.

B. 1.82.

C. 2.22.

20. A trader has purchased 200 shares of a non-dividend-paying firm on margin at a price of $50 per share. The leverage ratio is 2.5. Six months later, the trader sells these shares at $60 per share. Ignoring the interest paid on the borrowed amount and the transaction costs, what was the return to the trader during the six-month period?

A. 20 percent.

B. 33.33 percent.

C. 50 percent.

21. Jason Williams purchased 500 shares of a company at $32 per share. The stock was bought on 75 percent margin. One month later, Williams had to pay interest on the amount borrowed at a rate of 2 percent per month. At that time, Williams received a dividend of $0.50 per share. Immediately after that he sold the shares

at $28 per share. He paid commissions of $10 on the purchase and $10 on the sale of the stock. What was the rate of return on this investment for the one-month period?

A. −12.5 percent.

B. −15.4 percent.

C. −50.1 percent.

22. Caroline Rogers believes the price of Gamma Corp. stock will go down in the near future. She has decided to sell short 200 shares of Gamma Corp. at the current market price of €47. The initial margin requirement is 40 percent. Which of the following is an appropriate statement regarding the margin requirement that Rogers is subject to on this short sale?

A. She will need to contribute €3,760 as margin.

B. She will need to contribute €5,640 as margin.

C. She will only need to leave the proceeds from the short sale as deposit and does not need to contribute any additional funds.

23. The current price of a stock is $25 per share. You have $10,000 to invest. You borrow an additional $10,000 from your broker and invest $20,000 in the stock. If the maintenance margin is 30 percent, at what price will a margin call first occur?

A. $9.62.

B. $17.86.

C. $19.71.

24. A market has the following limit orders standing on its book for a particular stock. The bid and ask sizes are number of shares in hundreds.

Bid Size	Limit Price (€)	Offer Size
5	9.73	
12	9.81	
4	9.84	
6	9.95	
	10.02	5
	10.10	12
	10.14	8

What is the market?

A. 9.73 bid, offered at 10.14.

B. 9.81 bid, offered at 10.10.

C. 9.95 bid, offered at 10.02.

25. Consider the following limit order book for a stock. The bid and ask sizes are

Practice Problems

number of shares in hundreds.

Bid Size	Limit Price (¥)	Offer Size
3	122.80	
8	123.00	
4	123.35	
	123.80	7
	124.10	6
	124.50	7

A new buy limit order is placed for 300 shares at ¥123.40. This limit order is said to:

A. take the market.

B. make the market.

C. make a new market.

26. Currently, the market in a stock is "$54.62 bid, offered at $54.71." A new sell limit order is placed at $54.62. This limit order is said to:

    A. take the market.

    B. make the market.

    C. make a new market.

27. You have placed a sell market-on-open order—a market order that would automatically be submitted at the market's open tomorrow and would fill at the market price. Your instruction, to sell the shares at the market open, is a(n):

    A. execution instruction.

    B. validity instruction.

    C. clearing instruction.

28. Jim White has sold short 100 shares of Super Stores at a price of $42 per share. He has also simultaneously placed a "good-till-cancelled, stop 50, limit 55 buy" order. Assume that if the stop condition specified by White is satisfied and the order becomes valid, it will get executed. Excluding transaction costs, what is the maximum possible loss that White can have?

    A. $800.

    B. $1,300.

    C. Unlimited.

29. You own shares of a company that are currently trading at $30 a share. Your technical analysis of the shares indicates a support level of $27.50. That is, if the price of the shares is going down, it is more likely to stay above this level rather than fall below it. If the price does fall below this level, however, you believe that the price may continue to decline. You have no immediate intent to sell the shares but are concerned about the possibility of a huge loss if the share price declines below the support level. Which of the following types of orders could you place

to most appropriately address your concern?

A. Short sell order.

B. Good-till-cancelled stop sell order.

C. Good-till-cancelled stop buy order.

30. In an underwritten offering, the risk that the entire issue may not be sold to the public at the stipulated offering price is borne by the:

A. issuer.

B. investment bank.

C. buyers of the part of the issue that is sold.

31. A British company listed on AIM (formerly the Alternative Investment Market) of the London Stock Exchange announced the sale of 6,686,665 shares to a small group of qualified investors at £0.025 per share. Which of the following *best* describes this sale?

A. Shelf registration.

B. Private placement.

C. Initial public offering.

32. A German publicly traded company, to raise new capital, gave its existing shareholders the opportunity to subscribe for new shares. The existing shareholders could purchase two new shares at a subscription price of €4.58 per share for every 15 shares held. This is an example of a(n):

A. rights offering.

B. private placement.

C. initial public offering.

33. Consider an order-driven system that allows hidden orders. The following four sell orders on a particular stock are currently in the system's limit order book. Based on the commonly used order precedence hierarchy, which of these orders will have precedence over others?

Order	Time of Arrival (HH:MM:SS)	Limit Price (€)	Special Instruction (If any)
I	9:52:01	20.33	
II	9:52:08	20.29	Hidden order
III	9:53:04	20.29	
IV	9:53:49	20.29	

A. Order I (time of arrival of 9:52:01).

B. Order II (time of arrival of 9:52:08).

C. Order III (time of arrival of 9:53:04).

34. Zhenhu Li has submitted an immediate-or-cancel buy order for 500 shares of a

Practice Problems

company at a limit price of CNY 74.25. There are two sell limit orders standing in that stock's order book at that time. One is for 300 shares at a limit price of CNY 74.30 and the other is for 400 shares at a limit price of CNY 74.35. How many shares in Li's order would get cancelled?

A. None (the order would remain open but unfilled).

B. 200 (300 shares would get filled).

C. 500 (there would be no fill).

35. A market has the following limit orders standing on its book for a particular stock:

Buyer	Bid Size (Number of Shares)	Limit Price (£)	Offer Size (Number of Shares)	Seller
Keith	1,000	19.70		
Paul	200	19.84		
Ann	400	19.89		
Mary	300	20.02		
		20.03	800	Jack
		20.11	1,100	Margaret
		20.16	400	Jeff

Ian submits a day order to sell 1,000 shares, limit £19.83. Assuming that no more buy orders are submitted on that day after Ian submits his order, what would be Ian's average trade price?

A. £19.70.

B. £19.92.

C. £20.05.

36. A financial analyst is examining whether a country's financial market is well functioning. She finds that the transaction costs in this market are low and trading volumes are high. She concludes that the market is quite liquid. In such a market:

A. traders will find it hard to make use of their information.

B. traders will find it easy to trade and their trading will make the market less informationally efficient.

C. traders will find it easy to trade and their trading will make the market more informationally efficient.

37. The government of a country whose financial markets are in an early stage of development has hired you as a consultant on financial market regulation. Your first task is to prepare a list of the objectives of market regulation. Which of the following is *least likely* to be included in this list of objectives?

A. Minimize agency problems in the financial markets.

B. Ensure that financial markets are fair and orderly.

C. Ensure that investors in the stock market achieve a rate of return that is at least equal to the risk-free rate of return.

SOLUTIONS

1. C is correct. Takabe is best characterized as an information-motivated trader. Takabe believes that his model provides him superior information about the movements in the stock market and his motive for trading is to profit from this information.

2. B is correct. Beach is an investor. He is simply investing in risky assets consistent with his level of risk aversion. Beach is not hedging any existing risk or using information to identify and trade mispriced securities. Therefore, he is not a hedger or an information-motivated trader.

3. A is correct. Smith is a hedger. The short position on the BRL futures contract offsets the BRL long position in three months. She is hedging the risk of the BRL depreciating against the USD. If the BRL depreciates, the value of the cash inflow goes down in USD terms but there is a gain on the futures contracts.

4. A is correct. Regulation of arbitrageurs' profits is not a function of the financial system. The financial system facilitates the allocation of capital to the best uses and the purposes for which people use the financial system, including borrowing money.

5. C is correct. The purchase of real estate properties is a transaction in the alternative investment market.

6. B is correct. The 90-day commercial paper and negotiable certificates of deposit are money market instruments.

7. B is correct. This transaction is a sale in the primary market. It is a sale of shares from the issuer to the investor and funds flow to the issuer of the security from the purchaser.

8. A is correct. Warrants are least likely to be part of the fund. Warrant holders have the right to buy the issuer's common stock. Thus, warrants are typically classified as equity and are least likely to be a part of a fixed-income mutual fund. Commercial paper and repurchase agreements are short-term fixed-income securities.

9. C is correct. When investors want to sell their shares, investors of an open-end fund sell the shares back to the fund whereas investors of a closed-end fund sell the shares to others in the secondary market. Closed-end funds are available to new investors but they must purchase shares in the fund in the secondary market. The shares of a closed-end fund trade at a premium or discount to net asset value.

10. B is correct. SPDRs trade in the secondary market and are a pooled investment vehicle.

11. B is correct. The investment companies that create exchange-traded funds (ETFs) are financial intermediaries. ETFs are securities that represent ownership in the assets held by the fund. The transaction costs of trading shares of ETFs are substantially lower than the combined costs of trading the underlying assets of the ETF.

12. A is correct. Once you have entered into a forward contract, it is difficult to exit from the contract. As opposed to a futures contract, trading out of a forward contract is quite difficult. There is no exchange of cash at the origination of a

Solutions

forward contract. There is no exchange on a forward contract until the maturity of the contract.

13. A is correct. Harris is least likely to find counterparty risk associated with a futures contract. There is limited counterparty risk in a futures contract because the clearinghouse is on the other side of every contract.

14. B is correct. Buying a put option on the dollar will ensure a minimum exchange rate but does not have to be exercised if the exchange rate moves in a favorable direction. Forward and futures contracts would lock in a fixed rate but would not allow for the possibility to profit in case the value of the dollar three months later in the spot market turns out to be greater than the value in the forward or futures contract.

15. B is correct. The agreement between the publisher and the paper supplier to respectively buy and supply paper in the future at a price agreed upon today is a forward contract.

16. B is correct. The holder of the call option will exercise the call options if the price is above the exercise price of $305 per share. Note that if the stock price is above $305 but less than $308, the option would be exercised even though the net result for the option buyer after considering the premium is a loss. For example, if the stock price is $307, the option buyer would exercise the option to make $2 = $307 − $305 per share, resulting in a loss of $1 = $3 − $2 after considering the premium. It is better to exercise and have a loss of only $1, however, rather than not exercise and lose the entire $3 premium.

17. B is correct. The process can best be described as arbitrage because it involves buying and selling instruments, whose values are closely related, at different prices in different markets.

18. A is correct. Robert's exposure to the risk of the stock of the Michelin Group is long. The exposure as a result of the long call position is long. The exposure as a result of the short put position is also long. Therefore, the combined exposure is long.

19. B is correct. The maximum leverage ratio is 1.82 = 100% position ÷ 55% equity. The maximum leverage ratio associated with a position financed by the minimum margin requirement is one divided by the minimum margin requirement.

20. C is correct. The return is 50 percent. If the position had been unleveraged, the return would be 20% = (60 − 50)/50. Because of leverage, the return is 50% = 2.5 × 20%.

    Another way to look at this problem is that the equity contributed by the trader (the minimum margin requirement) is 40% = 100% ÷ 2.5. The trader contributed $20 = 40% of $50 per share. The gain is $10 per share, resulting in a return of 50% = 10/20.

21. B is correct. The return is −15.4 percent.

    Total cost of the purchase = $16,000 = 500 × $32
    Equity invested = $12,000 = 0.75 × $16,000
    Amount borrowed = $4,000 = 16,000 − 12,000
    Interest paid at month end = $80 = 0.02 × $4,000
    Dividend received at month end = $250 = 500 × $0.50
    Proceeds on stock sale = $14,000 = 500 × $28

Total commissions paid = $20 = $10 + $10

Net gain/loss = −$1,850 = −16,000 − 80 + 250 + 14,000 − 20

Initial investment including commission on purchase = $12,010

Return = −15.4% = −$1,850/$12,010

22. A is correct. She will need to contribute €3,760 as margin. In view of the possibility of a loss, if the stock price goes up, she will need to contribute €3,760 = 40% of €9,400 as the initial margin. Rogers will need to leave the proceeds from the short sale (€9,400 = 200 × €47) on deposit.

23. B is correct. A margin call will first occur at a price of $17.86. Because you have contributed half and borrowed the remaining half, your initial equity is 50 percent of the initial stock price, or $12.50 = 0.50 × $25. If P is the subsequent price, your equity would change by an amount equal to the change in price. So, your equity at price P would be 12.50 + (P − 25). A margin call will occur when the percentage margin drops to 30 percent. So, the price at which a margin call will occur is the solution to the following equation.

$$\frac{\text{Equity/Share}}{\text{Price/Share}} = \frac{12.50 + P - 25}{P} = 30\%$$

The solution is P = $17.86.

24. C is correct. The market is 9.95 bid, offered at 10.02. The best bid is at €9.95 and the best offer is €10.02.

25. C is correct. This order is said to make a new market. The new buy order is at ¥123.40, which is better than the current best bid of ¥123.35. Therefore, the buy order is making a new market. Had the new order been at ¥123.35, it would be said to make the market. Because the new buy limit order is at a price less than the best offer of ¥123.80, it will not immediately execute and is not taking the market.

26. A is correct. This order is said to take the market. The new sell order is at $54.62, which is at the current best bid. Therefore, the new sell order will immediately trade with the current best bid and is taking the market.

27. B is correct. An instruction regarding when to fill an order is considered a validity instruction.

28. B is correct. The maximum possible loss is $1,300. If the stock price crosses $50, the stop buy order will become valid and will get executed at a maximum limit price of $55. The maximum loss per share is $13 = $55 − $42, or $1,300 for 100 shares.

29. B is correct. The most appropriate order is a good-till-cancelled stop sell order. This order will be acted on if the stock price declines below a specified price (in this case, $27.50). This order is sometimes referred to as a good-till-cancelled stop loss sell order. You are generally bullish about the stock, as indicated by no immediate intent to sell, and would expect a loss on short selling the stock. A stop buy order is placed to buy a stock when the stock is going up.

30. B is correct. The investment bank bears the risk that the issue may be undersubscribed at the offering price. If the entire issue is not sold, the investment bank underwriting the issue will buy the unsold securities at the offering price.

31. B is correct. This sale is a private placement. As the company is already publicly traded, the share sale is clearly not an initial public offering. The sale also does

Solutions

not involve a shelf registration because the company is not selling shares to the public on a piecemeal basis.

32. A is correct. This offering is a rights offering. The company is distributing rights to buy stock at a fixed price to existing shareholders in proportion to their holdings.

33. C is correct. Order III (time of arrival of 9:53:04) has precedence. In the order precedence hierarchy, the first rule is price priority. Based on this rule, sell orders II, III, and IV get precedence over order I. The next rule is display precedence at a given price. Because order II is a hidden order, orders III and IV get precedence. Finally, order III gets precedence over order IV based on time priority at same price and same display status.

34. C is correct. The order for 500 shares would get cancelled; there would be no fill. Li is willing to buy at CNY 74.25 or less but the minimum offer price in the book is CNY 74.30; therefore, no part of the order would be filled. Because Li's order is immediate-or-cancel, it would be cancelled.

35. B is correct. Ian's average trade price is:

$$£19.92 = \frac{300 \times £20.02 + 400 \times £19.89 + 200 \times £19.84}{300 + 400 + 200}$$

Ian's sell order first fills with the most aggressively priced buy order, which is Mary's order for 300 shares at £20.02. Ian still has 700 shares for sale. The next most aggressively priced buy order is Ann's order for 400 shares at £19.89. This order is filled. Ian still has 300 shares for sale. The next most aggressively priced buy order is Paul's order for 200 shares at £19.84. A third trade takes place. Ian still has 100 shares for sale.

The next buy order is Keith's order for 1,000 shares at £19.70. However, this price is below Ian's limit price of £19.83. Therefore, no more trade is possible.

36. C is correct. In such a market, well-informed traders will find it easy to trade and their trading will make the market more informationally efficient. In a liquid market, it is easier for informed traders to fill their orders. Their trading will cause prices to incorporate their information and the prices will be more in line with the fundamental values.

37. C is correct. Ensure that investors in the stock market achieve a rate of return that is at least equal to the risk-free rate of return is least likely to be included as an objective of market regulation. Stocks are risky investments and there would be occasions when a stock market investment would not only have a return less than the risk-free rate but also a negative return. Minimizing agency costs and ensuring that financial markets are fair and orderly are objectives of market regulation.

LEARNING MODULE 2

Security Market Indexes

by Paul D. Kaplan, PhD, CFA, and Dorothy C. Kelly, CFA.

Paul D. Kaplan, PhD, CFA, is at Morningstar (Canada). Dorothy C. Kelly, CFA, is at McIntire School of Commerce, University of Virginia (USA).

LEARNING OUTCOMES	
Mastery	The candidate should be able to:
☐	describe a security market index
☐	calculate and interpret the value, price return, and total return of an index
☐	describe the choices and issues in index construction and management
☐	compare the different weighting methods used in index construction
☐	calculate and analyze the value and return of an index given its weighting method
☐	describe rebalancing and reconstitution of an index
☐	describe uses of security market indexes
☐	describe types of equity indexes
☐	compare types of security market indexes
☐	describe types of fixed-income indexes
☐	describe indexes representing alternative investments

1. INTRODUCTION

Investors gather and analyze vast amounts of information about security markets on a continual basis. Because this work can be both time consuming and data intensive, investors often use a single measure that consolidates this information and reflects the performance of an entire security market.

Security market indexes were first introduced as a simple measure to reflect the performance of the US stock market. Since then, security market indexes have evolved into important multi-purpose tools that help investors track the performance of various security markets, estimate risk, and evaluate the performance of investment managers. They also form the basis for new investment products.

> **in·dex**, *noun* (*pl.***in·dex·es** *or* **in·di·ces**) Latin *indic-*, *index*, from *indicare* to indicate: an indicator, sign, or measure of something.

ORIGIN OF MARKET INDEXES

Investors had access to regularly published data on individual security prices in London as early as 1698, but nearly 200 years passed before they had access to a simple indicator to reflect security market information. To give readers a sense of how the US stock market in general performed on a given day, publishers Charles H. Dow and Edward D. Jones introduced the Dow Jones Average, the world's first security market index, in 1884. The index, which appeared in *The Customers' Afternoon Letter*, consisted of the stocks of nine railroads and two industrial companies. It eventually became the Dow Jones Transportation Average. Convinced that industrial companies, rather than railroads, would be "the great speculative market" of the future, Dow and Jones introduced a second index in May 1896—the Dow Jones Industrial Average (DJIA). It had an initial value of 40.94 and consisted of 12 stocks from major US industries. Today, investors can choose from among thousands of indexes to measure and monitor different security markets and asset classes.

This reading is organized as follows. Section 2 defines a security market index and explains how to calculate the price return and total return of an index for a single period and over multiple periods. Section 3 describes how indexes are constructed and managed. Section 4 discusses the use of market indexes. Sections 5, 6, and 7 discuss various types of indexes, and the final section summarizes the reading. Practice problems follow the conclusions and summary.

2. INDEX DEFINITION AND CALCULATIONS OF VALUE AND RETURNS

- [ ] describe a security market index
- [ ] calculate and interpret the value, price return, and total return of an index

A **security market index** represents a given security market, market segment, or asset class. Most indexes are constructed as portfolios of marketable securities.

The value of an index is calculated on a regular basis using either the actual or estimated market prices of the individual securities, known as **constituent securities**, within the index. For each security market index, investors may encounter two versions of the same index (i.e., an index with identical constituent securities and weights): one version based on price return and one version based on total return. As the name suggests, a **price return index**, also known as a **price index**, reflects *only* the prices of the constituent securities within the index. A **total return index**, in contrast, reflects not only the prices of the constituent securities but also the reinvestment of all income received since inception.

Index Definition and Calculations of Value and Returns

At inception, the values of the price and total return versions of an index are equal. As time passes, however, the value of the total return index, which includes the reinvestment of all dividends and/or interest received, will exceed the value of the price return index by an increasing amount. A look at how the values of each version are calculated over multiple periods illustrates why.

The value of a price return index is calculated as:

$$V_{PRI} = \frac{\sum_{i=1}^{N} n_i P_i}{D} \qquad (1)$$

where

V_{PRI} = the value of the price return index

n_i = the number of units of constituent security i held in the index portfolio

N = the number of constituent securities in the index

P_i = the unit price of constituent security i

D = the value of the divisor

The **divisor** is a number initially chosen at inception. It is frequently chosen so that the price index has a convenient initial value, such as 1,000. The index provider then adjusts the value of the divisor as necessary to avoid changes in the index value that are unrelated to changes in the prices of its constituent securities. For example, when changing index constituents, the index provider may adjust the divisor so that the value of the index with the new constituents equals the value of the index prior to the changes.

Index return calculations, like calculations of investment portfolio returns, may measure price return or total return. **Price return** measures only price appreciation or percentage change in price. **Total return** measures price appreciation plus interest, dividends, and other distributions.

Calculation of Single-Period Returns

For a security market index, price return can be calculated in two ways: either the percentage change in value of the price return index, or the weighted average of price returns of the constituent securities. The price return of an index can be expressed as:

$$PR_I = \frac{V_{PRI1} - V_{PRI0}}{V_{PRI0}} \qquad (2)$$

where

PR_I = the price return of the index portfolio (as a decimal number, i.e., 12 percent is 0.12)

V_{PRI1} = the value of the price return index at the end of the period

V_{PRI0} = the value of the price return index at the beginning of the period

Similarly, the price return of each constituent security can be expressed as:

$$PR_i = \frac{P_{i1} - P_{i0}}{P_{i0}} \qquad (3)$$

where

PR_i = the price return of constituent security i (as a decimal number)

P_{i1} = the price of constituent security i at the end of the period

P_{i0} = the price of constituent security i at the beginning of the period

Because the price return of the index equals the weighted average of price returns of the individual securities, we can write:

$$PR_I = \sum_{i=1}^{N} w_i PR_i = \sum_{i=1}^{N} w_i \left(\frac{P_{i1} - P_{i0}}{P_{i0}} \right) \quad (4)$$

where:

PR_I = the price return of index portfolio (as a decimal number)

PR_i = the price return of constituent security i (as a decimal number)

N = the number of individual securities in the index

w_i = the weight of security i (the fraction of the index portfolio allocated to security i)

P_{i1} = the price of constituent security i at the end of the period

P_{i0} = the price of constituent security i at the beginning of the period

Equation 4 can be rewritten simply as:

$$PR_I = w_1 PR_1 + w_2 PR_2 + \ldots + w_N PR_N \quad (5)$$

where

PR_I = the price return of index portfolio (as a decimal number)

PR_i = the price return of constituent security i (as a decimal number)

w_i = the weight of security i (the fraction of the index portfolio allocated to security i)

N = the number of securities in the index

Total return measures price appreciation plus interest, dividends, and other distributions. Thus, the **total return** of an index is the price appreciation, or change in the value of the price return index, plus income (dividends and/or interest) over the period, expressed as a percentage of the beginning value of the price return index. The total return of an index can be expressed as:

$$TR_I = \frac{V_{PRI1} - V_{PRI0} + Inc_I}{V_{PRI0}} \quad (6)$$

where

TR_I = the total return of the index portfolio (as a decimal number)

V_{PRI1} = the value of the price return index at the end of the period

V_{PRI0} = the value of the price return index at the beginning of the period

Inc_I = the total income (dividends and/or interest) from all securities in the index held over the period

Index Definition and Calculations of Value and Returns

The total return of an index can also be calculated as the weighted average of total returns of the constituent securities. The total return of each constituent security in the index is calculated as:

$$TR_i = \frac{P_{1i} - P_{0i} + Inc_i}{P_{0i}} \qquad (7)$$

where

TR_i = the total return of constituent security i (as a decimal number)

P_{1i} = the price of constituent security i at the end of the period

P_{0i} = the price of constituent security i at the beginning of the period

Inc_i = the total income (dividends and/or interest) from security i over the period

Because the total return of an index can be calculated as the weighted average of total returns of the constituent securities, we can express total return as:

$$TR_I = \sum_{i=1}^{N} w_i TR_i = \sum_{i=1}^{N} w_i \left(\frac{P_{1i} - P_{0i} + Inc_i}{P_{0i}} \right) \qquad (8)$$

Equation 8 can be rewritten simply as

$$TR_I = w_1 TR_1 + w_2 TR_2 + \ldots + w_N TR_N \qquad (9)$$

where

TR_I = the total return of the index portfolio (as a decimal number)

TR_i = the total return of constituent security i (as a decimal number)

w_i = the weight of security i (the fraction of the index portfolio allocated to security i)

N = the number of securities in the index

Calculation of Index Values over Multiple Time Periods

The calculation of index values over multiple time periods requires geometrically linking the series of index returns. With a series of price returns for an index, we can calculate the value of the price return index with the following equation:

$$V_{PRIT} = V_{PRI0}(1 + PR_{I1})(1 + PR_{I2})\ldots(1 + PR_{IT}) \qquad (10)$$

where

V_{PRI0} = the value of the price return index at inception

V_{PRIT} = the value of the price return index at time t

PR_{IT} = the price return (as a decimal number) on the index over period t, $t = 1, 2, \ldots, T$

For an index with an inception value set to 1,000 and price returns of 5 percent and 3 percent for Periods 1 and 2 respectively, the values of the price return index would be calculated as follows:

Period	Return (%)	Calculation	Ending Value
0		1,000(1.00)	1,000.00
1	5.00	1,000(1.05)	1,050.00
2	3.00	1,000(1.05)(1.03)	1,081.50

Similarly, the series of total returns for an index is used to calculate the value of the total return index with the following equation:

$$V_{TRIT} = V_{TRI0}(1 + TR_{I1})(1 + TR_{I2})...(1 + TR_{IT}) \qquad (11)$$

where

V_{TRI0} = the value of the index at inception

V_{TRIT} = the value of the total return index at time t

TR_{It} = the total return (as a decimal number) on the index over period t, $t = 1, 2, ..., T$

Suppose that the same index yields an additional 1.5 percent return from income in Period 1 and an additional 2.0 percent return from income in Period 2, bringing the total returns for Periods 1 and 2, respectively, to 6.5 percent and 5 percent. The values of the total return index would be calculated as follows:

Period	Return (%)	Calculation	Ending Value
0		1,000(1.00)	1,000.00
1	6.50	1,000(1.065)	1,065.00
2	5.00	1,000(1.065)(1.05)	1,118.25

As illustrated above, as time passes, the value of the total return index, which includes the reinvestment of all dividends and/or interest received, exceeds the value of the price return index by an increasing amount.

3. INDEX CONSTRUCTION

- [ ] describe the choices and issues in index construction and management
- [ ] compare the different weighting methods used in index construction
- [ ] calculate and analyze the value and return of an index given its weighting method

Constructing and managing a security market index is similar to constructing and managing a portfolio of securities. Index providers must decide the following:

1. Which target market should the index represent?
2. Which securities should be selected from that target market?
3. How much weight should be allocated to each security in the index?
4. When should the index be rebalanced?
5. When should the security selection and weighting decision be re-examined?

Target Market and Security Selection

The first decision in index construction is identifying the target market, market segment, or asset class that the index is intended to represent. The target market may be defined very broadly or narrowly. It may be based on asset class (e.g., equities, fixed income, real estate, commodities, hedge funds); geographic region (e.g., Japan, South Africa, Latin America, Europe); the exchange on which the securities are traded (e.g., Shanghai, Toronto, Tokyo), and/or other characteristics (e.g., economic sector, company size, investment style, duration, or credit quality).

The target market determines the investment universe and the securities available for inclusion in the index. Once the investment universe is identified, the number of securities and the specific securities to include in the index must be determined. The constituent securities could be nearly all those in the target market or a representative sample of the target market. Some equity indexes, such as the S&P 500 Index and the FTSE 100, fix the number of securities included in the index and indicate this number in the name of the index. Other indexes allow the number of securities to vary to reflect changes in the target market or to maintain a certain percentage of the target market. For example, the Tokyo Stock Price Index (TOPIX) represents and includes all of the largest stocks, known as the First Section, listed on the Tokyo Stock Exchange. To be included in the First Section—and thus the TOPIX—stocks must meet certain criteria, such as the number of shares outstanding, the number of shareholders, and market capitalization. Stocks that no longer meet the criteria are removed from the First Section and also the TOPIX. Objective or mechanical rules determine the constituent securities of most, but not all, indexes. The S&P Bombay Stock Exchange Sensitive Index, also called the S&P BSE SENSEX and the S&P 500, for example, use a selection committee and more subjective decision-making rules to determine constituent securities.

Index Weighting

The weighting decision determines how much of each security to include in the index and has a substantial impact on an index's value. Index providers use a number of methods to weight the constituent securities in an index. Indexes can be price weighted, equal weighted, market-capitalization weighted, or fundamentally weighted. Each weighting method has its advantages and disadvantages.

Price Weighting

The simplest method to weight an index and the one used by Charles Dow to construct the Dow Jones Industrial Average is **price weighting**. In price weighting, the weight on each constituent security is determined by dividing its price by the sum of all the prices of the constituent securities. The weight is calculated using the following formula:

$$w_i^P = \frac{P_i}{\sum_{i=1}^{N} P_i} \quad (12)$$

Exhibit 1 illustrates the values, weights, and single-period returns following inception of a price-weighted equity index with five constituent securities. The value of the price-weighted index is determined by dividing the sum of the security values (101.50) by the divisor, which is typically set at inception to equal the initial number of securities in the index. Thus, in our example, the divisor is 5 and the initial value of the index is calculated as 101.50 ÷ 5 = 20.30.

Exhibit 1: Example of a Price-Weighted Equity Index

Security	Shares in Index	BOP Price	Value (Shares × BOP Price)	BOP Weight (%)	EOP Price	Dividends Per Share	Value (Shares × EOP Price)	Total Dividends	Price Return (%)	Total Return (%)	BOP Weight × Price Return (%)	BOP Weight × Total Return (%)	EOP Weight (%)
A	1	50.00	50.00	49.26	55.00	0.75	55.00	0.75	10.00	11.50	4.93	5.66	52.38
B	1	25.00	25.00	24.63	22.00	0.10	22.00	0.10	-12.00	-11.60	-2.96	-2.86	20.95
C	1	12.50	12.50	12.32	8.00	0.00	8.00	0.00	-36.00	-36.00	-4.43	-4.43	7.62
D	1	10.00	10.00	9.85	14.00	0.05	14.00	0.05	40.00	40.50	3.94	3.99	13.33
E	1	4.00	4.00	3.94	6.00	0.00	6.00	0.00	50.00	50.00	1.97	1.97	5.72
Total			101.50	100.00			105.00	0.90			3.45	4.33	100.00
Index Value			20.30				21.00	0.18	3.45	4.33			

Divisor = 5
BOP = Beginning of period
EOP = End of period

Type of Index	BOP Value	Return (%)	EOP Value
Price Return	20.30	3.45	21.00
Total Return	20.30	4.33	21.18

Index Construction

As illustrated in this exhibit, Security A, which has the highest price, also has the highest weighting and thus will have the greatest impact on the return of the index. Note how both the price return and the total return of the index are calculated on the basis of the corresponding returns on the constituent securities.

A property unique to price-weighted indexes is that a stock split on one constituent security changes the weights on all the securities in the index.[1] To prevent the stock split and the resulting new weights from changing the value of the index, the index provider must adjust the value of the divisor as illustrated in Exhibit 2. Given a 2-for-1 split in Security A, the divisor is adjusted by dividing the sum of the constituent prices *after* the split (77.50) by the value of the index *before* the split (21.00). This adjustment results in changing the divisor from 5 to 3.69 so that the index value is maintained at 21.00.

The primary advantage of price weighting is its simplicity. The main disadvantage of price weighting is that it results in arbitrary weights for each security. In particular, a stock split in any one security causes arbitrary changes in the weights of all the constituents' securities.

Exhibit 2: Impact of 2-for-1 Split in Security A

Security	Price before Split	Weight before Split (%)	Price after Split	Weight after Split (%)
A	55.00	52.38	27.50	35.48
B	22.00	20.95	22.00	28.39
C	8.00	7.62	8.00	10.32
D	14.00	13.33	14.00	18.07
E	6.00	5.72	6.00	7.74
Total	105.00	100.00	77.50	100.00
Divisor	5.00		3.69	
Index Value	21.00		21.00	

Equal Weighting

Another simple index weighting method is **equal weighting**. This method assigns an equal weight to each constituent security at inception. The weights are calculated as:

$$w_i^E = \frac{1}{N} \qquad (13)$$

where

w_i = fraction of the portfolio that is allocated to security *i* or weight of security *i*

N = number of securities in the index

To construct an equal-weighted index from the five securities in Exhibit 1, the index provider allocates one-fifth (20 percent) of the value of the index (at the beginning of the period) to each security. Dividing the value allocated to each security by each security's individual share price determines the number of shares of each security to include in the index. Unlike a price-weighted index, where the weights are arbitrarily determined by the market prices, the weights in an equal-weighted index are arbitrarily assigned by the index provider.

---

1 A stock split is an increase in the number of shares outstanding and a proportionate decrease in the price per share such that the total market value of equity, as well as investors' proportionate ownership in the company, does not change.

Exhibit 3 illustrates the values, weights, and single-period returns following inception of an equal-weighted index with the same constituent securities as those in Exhibit 1. This example assumes a beginning index portfolio value of 10,000 (i.e., an investment of 2,000 in each security). To set the initial value of the index to 1,000, the divisor is set to 10 (10,000 ÷ 10 = 1,000).

Exhibit 1 and Exhibit 3 demonstrate how different weighting methods result in different returns. The 10.4 percent price return of the equal-weighted index shown in Exhibit 3 differs significantly from the 3.45 percent price return of the price-weighted index in Exhibit 1.

Like price weighting, the primary advantage of equal weighting is its simplicity. Equal weighting, however, has a number of disadvantages. First, securities that constitute the largest fraction of the target market value are underrepresented, and securities that constitute a small fraction of the target market value are overrepresented. Second, after the index is constructed and the prices of constituent securities change, the index is no longer equally weighted. Therefore, maintaining equal weights requires frequent adjustments (rebalancing) to the index.

Market-Capitalization Weighting

In **market-capitalization weighting**, or value weighting, the weight on each constituent security is determined by dividing its market capitalization by the total market capitalization (the sum of the market capitalization) of all the securities in the index. Market capitalization or value is calculated by multiplying the number of shares outstanding by the market price per share.

The market-capitalization weight of security i is:

$$w_i^M = \frac{Q_i P_i}{\sum_{j=1}^{N} Q_j P_j} \qquad (14)$$

where

w_i = fraction of the portfolio that is allocated to security i or weight of security i

Q_i = number of shares outstanding of security i

P_i = share price of security i

N = number of securities in the index

Exhibit 4 illustrates the values, weights, and single-period returns following inception of a market-capitalization-weighted index for the same five-security market. Security A, with 3,000 shares outstanding and a price of 50 per share, has a market capitalization of 150,000 or 26.29 percent (150,000/570,500) of the entire index portfolio. The resulting index weights in the exhibit reflect the relative value of each security as measured by its market capitalization.

As shown in Exhibit 1, Exhibit 3, and Exhibit 4, the weighting method affects the index's returns. The price and total returns of the market-capitalization index in Exhibit 4 (1.49 percent and 2.13 percent, respectively) differ significantly from those of the price-weighted (3.45 percent and 4.33 percent, respectively) and equal-weighted (10.40 percent and 10.88 percent respectively) indexes. To understand the source and magnitude of the difference, compare the weights and returns of each security under each of the weighting methods. The weight of Security A, for example, ranges from 49.26 percent in the price-weighted index to 20 percent in the equal-weighted index. With a price return of 10 percent, Security A contributes 4.93 percent to the price return of the price-weighted index, 2.00 percent to the price return of the equal-weighted index, and 2.63 percent to the price return of the market-capitalization-weighted index. With

Index Construction

Exhibit 3: Example of an Equal-Weighted Equity Index

Security	Shares in Index	BOP Price	Value (Shares × BOP Price)	Weight (%)	EOP Price	Dividends Per Share	Value (Shares × EOP Price)	Total Dividends	Price Return (%)	Total Return (%)	Weight × Price Return (%)	Weight × Total Return (%)	EOP Weight (%)
A	40	50.00	2,000	20.00	55.00	0.75	2,200	30	10.00	11.50	2.00	2.30	19.93
B	80	25.00	2,000	20.00	22.00	0.10	1,760	8	−12.00	−11.60	−2.40	−2.32	15.94
C	160	12.50	2,000	20.00	8.00	0.00	1,280	0	−36.00	−36.00	−7.20	−7.20	11.60
D	200	10.00	2,000	20.00	14.00	0.05	2,800	10	40.00	40.50	8.00	8.10	25.36
E	500	4.00	2,000	20.00	6.00	0.00	3,000	0	50.00	50.00	10.00	10.00	27.17
Total			10,000	100.00			11,040	48			10.40	10.88	100.00
Index Value			1,000				1,104	4.80	10.40	10.88			

Divisor = 10
BOP = Beginning of period
EOP = End of period

Type of Index	BOP Value	Return (%)	EOP Value
Price Return	1,000.00	10.40	1,104.00
Total Return	1,000.00	10.88	1,108.80

Exhibit 4: Example of a Market-Capitalization-Weighted Equity Index

Stock	Shares Out-standing	BOP Price	BOP Market Cap	BOP Weight (%)	EOP Price	Dividends Per Share	EOP Market Cap	Total Dividends	Price Return (%)	Total Return (%)	BOP Weight × Price Return (%)	BOP Weight × Total Return (%)	EOP Weight (%)
A	3,000	50.00	150,000	26.29	55.00	0.75	165,000	2,250	10.00	11.50	2.63	3.02	28.50
B	10,000	25.00	250,000	43.82	22.00	0.10	220,000	1,000	−12.00	−11.60	−5.26	−5.08	38.00
C	5,000	12.50	62,500	10.96	8.00	0.00	40,000	0	−36.00	−36.00	−3.95	−3.95	6.91
D	8,000	10.00	80,000	14.02	14.00	0.05	112,000	400	40.00	40.50	5.61	5.68	19.34
E	7,000	4.00	28,000	4.91	6.00	0.00	42,000	0	50.00	50.00	2.46	2.46	7.25
Total			570,500	100.00			579,000	3,650			1.49	2.13	100.00
Index Value			1,000				1,014.90	6.40	1.49	2.13			

Divisor = 570.50

BOP = Beginning of period
EOP = End of period

Type of Index	BOP Value	Return (%)	EOP Value
Price Return	1,000.00	1.49	1,014.90
Total Return	1,000.00	2.13	1,021.30

Index Construction

a total return of 11.50 percent, Security A contributes 5.66 percent to the total return of the price-weighted index, 2.30 percent to the total return of the equal-weighted index, and 3.02 percent to the total return of the market-capitalization-weighted index.

Float-Adjusted Market-Capitalization Weighting

In **float-adjusted market-capitalization weighting**, the weight on each constituent security is determined by adjusting its market capitalization for its **market float**. Typically, market float is the number of shares of the constituent security that are available to the investing public. For companies that are closely held, only a portion of the shares outstanding are available to the investing public (the rest are held by a small group of controlling investors). In addition to excluding shares held by controlling shareholders, most float-adjusted market-capitalization-weighted indexes also exclude shares held by other corporations and governments. Some providers of indexes that are designed to represent the investment opportunities of global investors further reduce the number of shares included in the index by excluding shares that are not available to foreigner investors. The index providers may refer to these indexes as "free-float-adjusted market-capitalization-weighted indexes."

Float-adjusted market-capitalization-weighted indexes reflect the shares available for public trading by multiplying the market price per share by the number of shares available to the investing public (i.e., the float-adjusted market capitalization) rather than the total number of shares outstanding (total market capitalization). Currently, most market-capitalization-weighted indexes are float adjusted. Therefore, unless otherwise indicated, for the remainder of this reading, "market-capitalization" weighting refers to float-adjusted market-capitalization weighting.

The float-adjusted market-capitalization weight of security i is calculated as:

$$w_i^M = \frac{f_i Q_i P_i}{\sum_{j=1}^{N} f_j Q_j P_j} \qquad (15)$$

where

f_i = fraction of shares outstanding in the market float

w_i = fraction of the portfolio that is allocated to security i or weight of security i

Q_i = number of shares outstanding of security i

P_i = share price of security i

N = number of securities in the index

Exhibit 5 illustrates the values, weights, and single-period returns following inception of a float-adjusted market-capitalization-weighted equity index using the same five securities as before. The low percentage of shares of Security D in the market float compared with the number of shares outstanding indicates that the security is closely held.

The primary advantage of market-capitalization weighting (including float adjusted) is that constituent securities are held in proportion to their value in the target market. The primary disadvantage is that constituent securities whose prices have risen the most (or fallen the most) have a greater (or lower) weight in the index (i.e., as a security's price rises relative to other securities in the index, its weight increases; and as its price decreases in value relative to other securities in the index, its weight decreases). This weighting method leads to overweighting stocks that have risen in price (and may be overvalued) and underweighting stocks that have declined in price (and may be undervalued). The effect of this weighting method is similar to a momentum investment strategy in that over time, the securities that have risen in price the most will have the largest weights in the index.

Exhibit 5: Example of Float-Adjusted Market-Capitalization-Weighted Equity Index

Stock	Shares Out-standing	% Shares in Market Float	Shares in Index	BOP Price	BOP Float-Adjusted Market Cap	BOP Weight (%)	EOP Price	EOP Dividends Per Share	Ending Float-Adjusted Market Cap	Total Dividends	Price Return (%)	Total Return (%)	BOP Weight × Price Return (%)	BOP Weight × Total Return (%)	EOP Weight (%)
A	3,000	100	3,000	50.00	150,000	35.40	55.00	0.75	165,000	2,250	10.00	11.50	3.54	4.07	39.61
B	10,000	70	7,000	25.00	175,000	41.31	22.00	0.10	154,000	700	−12.00	−11.60	−4.96	−4.79	36.97
C	5,000	90	4,500	12.50	56,250	13.28	8.00	0.00	36,000	0	−36.00	−36.00	−4.78	−4.78	8.64
D	8,000	25	2,000	10.00	20,000	4.72	14.00	0.05	28,000	100	40.00	40.50	1.89	1.91	6.72
E	7,000	80	5,600	4.00	22,400	5.29	6.00	0.00	33,600	0	50.00	50.00	2.65	2.65	8.06
Total					423,650	100.00			416,600	3,050			−1.66	−0.94	100.00
Index Value					1,000				983.36	7.20	−1.66	−0.94			

Divisor = 423.65

BOP = Beginning of period
EOP = End of period

Type of Index	Initial Value	Return (%)	Ending Value
Price Return	1,000.00	−1.66	983.36
Total Return	1,000.00	−0.94	990.56

Fundamental Weighting

Fundamental weighting attempts to address the disadvantages of market-capitalization weighting by using measures of a company's size that are independent of its security price to determine the weight on each constituent security. These measures include book value, cash flow, revenues, earnings, dividends, and number of employees.

Some fundamental indexes use a single measure, such as total dividends, to weight the constituent securities, whereas others combine the weights from several measures to form a composite value that is used for weighting.

Letting F_i denote a given fundamental size measure of company i, the fundamental weight on security i is:

$$w_i^F = \frac{F_i}{\sum_{j=1}^{N} F_j} \qquad (16)$$

Relative to a market-capitalization-weighted index, a fundamental index with weights based on such an item as earnings will result in greater weights on constituent securities with earnings yields (earnings divided by price) that are higher than the earnings yield of the overall market-weighted portfolio. Similarly, stocks with earnings yields less than the yield on the overall market-weighted portfolio will have lower weights. For example, suppose there are two stocks in an index. Stock A has a market capitalization of €200 million, Stock B has a market capitalization of €800 million, and their aggregate market capitalization is €1 billion (€1,000 million). Both companies have earnings of €20 million and aggregate earnings of €40 million. Thus, Stock A has an earnings yield of 10 percent (20/200) and Stock B has an earnings yield of 2.5 percent (20/800). The earnings weight of Stock A is 50 percent (20/40), which is higher than its market-capitalization weight of 20 percent (200/1,000). The earnings weight of Stock B is 50 percent (20/40), which is less than its market-capitalization weight of 80 percent (800/1,000). Relative to the market-cap-weighted index, the earnings-weighted index over-weights the high-yield Stock A and under-weights the low-yield Stock B.

The most important property of fundamental weighting is that it leads to indexes that have a "value" tilt. That is, a fundamentally weighted index has ratios of book value, earnings, dividends, etc. to market value that are higher than its market-capitalization-weighted counterpart. Also, in contrast to the momentum "effect" of market-capitalization-weighted indexes, fundamentally weighted indexes generally will have a contrarian "effect" in that the portfolio weights will shift away from securities that have increased in relative value and toward securities that have fallen in relative value whenever the portfolio is rebalanced.

INDEX MANAGEMENT: REBALANCING AND RECONSTITUTION

4

describe rebalancing and reconstitution of an index

So far, we have discussed index construction. Index management entails the two remaining questions:

- When should the index be rebalanced?
- When should the security selection and weighting decisions be re-examined?

Rebalancing

Rebalancing refers to adjusting the weights of the constituent securities in the index. To maintain the weight of each security consistent with the index's weighting method, the index provider rebalances the index by adjusting the weights of the constituent securities on a regularly scheduled basis (rebalancing dates)—usually quarterly. Rebalancing is necessary because the weights of the constituent securities change as their market prices change. Note, for example, that the weights of the securities in the equal-weighted index (Exhibit 3) at the end of the period are no longer equal (i.e., 20 percent):

Security A	19.93%
Security B	15.94
Security C	11.60
Security D	25.36
Security E	27.17

In rebalancing the index, the weights of Securities D and E (which had the highest returns) would be decreased and the weights of Securities A, B, and C (which had the lowest returns) would be increased. Thus, rebalancing creates turnover within an index.

Price-weighted indexes are not rebalanced because the weight of each constituent security is determined by its price. For market-capitalization-weighted indexes, rebalancing is less of a concern because the indexes largely rebalance themselves. In our market-capitalization index, for example, the weight of Security C automatically declined from 10.96 percent to 6.91 percent, reflecting the 36 percent decline in its market price. Market-capitalization weights are only adjusted to reflect mergers, acquisitions, liquidations, and other corporate actions between rebalancing dates.

Reconstitution

Reconstitution is the process of changing the constituent securities in an index. It is similar to a portfolio manager deciding to change the securities in his or her portfolio. Reconstitution is part of the rebalancing cycle. The reconstitution date is the date on which index providers review the constituent securities, re-apply the initial criteria for inclusion in the index, and select which securities to retain, remove, or add. Constituent securities that no longer meet the criteria are replaced with securities that do meet the criteria. Once the revised list of constituent securities is determined, the weighting method is re-applied. Indexes are reconstituted to reflect changes in the target market (bankruptcies, de-listings, mergers, acquisitions, etc.) and/or to reflect the judgment of the selection committee.

Reconstitution creates turnover in a number of different ways, particularly for market-capitalization-weighted indexes. When one security is removed and another is added, the index provider has to change the weights of the other securities in order to maintain the market-capitalization weighting of the index.

The frequency of reconstitution is a major issue for widely used indexes and their constituent securities. The Russell 2000 Index, for example, reconstitutes annually. It is used as a benchmark by numerous investment funds, and each year, prior to the index's reconstitution, the managers of these funds buy stocks they think will be added to the index—driving those stocks' prices up—and sell stocks they think will be deleted from the index—driving those stocks' prices down. Exhibit 6 illustrates a historical example of the potential impact of these decisions. Beginning in late April 2009, some managers began acquiring and bidding up the price of Uranium Energy Corporation (UEC) because they believed that it would be included in the reconstituted Russell 2000 Index. On 12 June, Russell listed UEC as a preliminary addition to the Russell 2000 Index and the Russell 3000 Index.[2] By that time, the stock value had increased by more than 300 percent. Investors continued to bid up the stock price in the weeks following the announcement, and the stock closed on the reconstitution date of 30 June at USD2.90, up nearly 400 percent for the quarter.

Exhibit 6: Three-Month Performance of Uranium Energy Corporation and NASDAQ April through June 2009

Source: Yahoo! Finance and Capital IQ.

USES OF MARKET INDEXES

☐ describe uses of security market indexes

Indexes were initially created to give a sense of how a particular security market performed on a given day. With the development of modern financial theory, their uses in investment management have expanded significantly. Some of the major uses of indexes include:

- gauges of market sentiment;
- proxies for measuring and modeling returns, systematic risk, and risk-adjusted performance;
- proxies for asset classes in asset allocation models;
- benchmarks for actively managed portfolios; and
- model portfolios for such investment products as index funds and exchange-traded funds (ETFs).

---

2 According to the press release, final membership in the index would be published after market close on Friday, 26 June.

Investors using security market indexes must be familiar with how various indexes are constructed in order to select the index or indexes most appropriate for their needs.

Gauges of Market Sentiment

The original purpose of stock market indexes was to provide a gauge of investor confidence or market sentiment. As indicators of the collective opinion of market participants, indexes reflect investor attitudes and behavior. The Dow Jones Industrial Average has a long history, is frequently quoted in the media, and remains a popular gauge of market sentiment. It may not accurately reflect the overall attitude of investors or the "market," however, because the index consists of only 30 of the thousands of US stocks traded each day.

Proxies for Measuring and Modeling Returns, Systematic Risk, and Risk-Adjusted Performance

The capital asset pricing model (CAPM) defines beta as the systematic risk of a security with respect to the entire market. The market portfolio in the CAPM consists of all risky securities. To represent the performance of the market portfolio, investors use a broad index. For example, the Tokyo Price Index (TOPIX) and the S&P 500 often serve as proxies for the market portfolio in Japan and the United States, respectively, and are used for measuring and modeling systematic risk and market returns.

Security market indexes also serve as market proxies when measuring risk-adjusted performance. The beta of an actively managed portfolio allows investors to form a passive alternative with the same level of systematic risk. For example, if the beta of an actively managed portfolio of global stocks is 0.95 with respect to the MSCI World Index, investors can create a passive portfolio with the same systematic risk by investing 95 percent of their portfolio in a MSCI World Index fund and holding the remaining 5 percent in cash. Alpha, the difference between the return of the actively managed portfolio and the return of the passive portfolio, is a measure of risk-adjusted return or investment performance. Alpha can be the result of manager skill (or lack thereof), transaction costs, and fees.

Proxies for Asset Classes in Asset Allocation Models

Because indexes exhibit the risk and return profiles of select groups of securities, they play a critical role as proxies for asset classes in asset allocation models. They provide the historical data used to model the risks and returns of different asset classes.

Benchmarks for Actively Managed Portfolios

Investors often use indexes as benchmarks to evaluate the performance of active portfolio managers. The index selected as the benchmark should reflect the investment strategy used by the manager. For example, an active manager investing in global small-capitalization stocks should be evaluated using a benchmark index, such as the FTSE Global Small Cap Index, which includes approximately 4,400 liquid small-capitalization stocks across 47 countries as of August 2018.

The choice of an index to use as a benchmark is important because an inappropriate index could lead to incorrect conclusions regarding an active manager's investment performance. Suppose that the small-cap manager underperformed the small-cap index but outperformed a broad equity market index. If investors use the broad market index as a benchmark, they might conclude that the small-cap manager is earning his or her fees and should be retained or given additional assets to invest. Using the small-cap index as a benchmark might lead to a very different conclusion.

Model Portfolios for Investment Products

Indexes also serve as the basis for the development of new investment products. Using indexes as benchmarks for actively managed portfolios has led some investors to conclude that they should invest in the benchmarks instead. Based on the CAPM's conclusion that investors should hold the market portfolio, broad market index funds have been developed to function as proxies for the market portfolio.

Investment management firms initially developed and managed index portfolios for institutional investors. Eventually, mutual fund companies introduced index funds for individual investors. Subsequently, investment management firms introduced exchange-traded funds, which are managed the same way as index mutual funds but trade like stocks.

The first ETFs were based on existing indexes. As the popularity of ETFs increased, index providers created new indexes for the specific purpose of forming ETFs, leading to the creation of numerous narrowly defined indexes with corresponding ETFs. The VanEck Vectors Vietnam ETF, for example, allows investors to invest in the equity market of Vietnam.

The choice of indexes to meet the needs of investors is extensive. Index providers are constantly looking for opportunities to develop indexes to meet the needs of investors.

EQUITY INDEXES

☐ describe types of equity indexes
☐ compare types of security market indexes

A wide variety of equity indexes exist, including broad market, multi-market, sector, and style indexes.

Broad Market Indexes

A broad equity market index, as its name suggests, represents an entire given equity market and typically includes securities representing more than 90 percent of the selected market. For example, the Shanghai Stock Exchange Composite Index (SSE) is a market-capitalization-weighted index of all shares that trade on the Shanghai Stock Exchange. In the United States, the Wilshire 5000 Total Market Index is a market-capitalization-weighted index that includes all US equities with readily available prices and is designed to represent the entire US equity market.[3] The Russell 3000, consisting of the largest 3,000 stocks by market capitalization, represents approximately 98 percent of the US equity market.

---

3 Despite its name, the Wilshire 5000 has no constraint on the number of securities that can be included. It included approximately 5,000 securities at inception.

Multi-Market Indexes

Multi-market indexes usually comprise indexes from different countries and regions and are designed to represent multiple security markets. Multi-market indexes may represent multiple national markets, geographic regions, economic development groups, and, in some cases, the entire world. World indexes are of importance to investors who take a global approach to equity investing without any particular bias toward a particular country or region. A number of index providers publish families of multi-market equity indexes.

MSCI offers a number of multi-market indexes. As shown in Exhibit 7, MSCI classifies countries and regions along two dimensions: level of economic development and geographic region. Developmental groups, which MSCI refers to as market classifications, include developed markets, emerging markets, and frontier markets. The geographic regions are largely divided by longitudinal lines of the globe: the Americas, Europe with Africa, and Asia with the Pacific. MSCI provides country- and region-specific indexes for each of the developed and emerging markets within its multi-market indexes. MSCI periodically reviews the classifications of markets in its indexes for movement from frontier markets to emerging markets and from emerging markets to developed markets and reconstitutes the indexes accordingly.

Exhibit 7: MSCI Global Investable Market Indexes (as of October 2018)

Developed Markets

Americas	Europe and Middle East	Pacific
Canada, United States	Austria, Belgium, Denmark, Finland, France, Germany, Ireland, Israel, Italy, Netherlands, Norway, Portugal, Spain, Sweden, Switzerland, United Kingdom	Australia, Hong Kong SAR, Japan, New Zealand, Singapore

Emerging Markets

Americas	Europe, Middle East, Africa	Asia
Brazil, Chile, Colombia, Mexico, Peru	Czech Republic, Egypt, Greece, Hungary, Poland, Qatar, Russia, South Africa, Turkey, United Arab Emirates	Chinese mainland, India, Indonesia, South Korea, Malaysia, Pakistan, Philippines, Taiwan region, Thailand

Frontier Markets

Americas	Europe & CIS	Africa	Middle East	Asia
Argentina	Croatia, Estonia, Lithuania, Kazakhstan, Romania, Serbia, Slovenia	Kenya, Mauritius, Morocco, Nigeria, Tunisia, WAEMU[1]	Bahrain, Jordan, Kuwait, Lebanon, Oman	Bangladesh, Sri Lanka, Vietnam

MSCI Standalone Market Indexes[2]

Europe, Middle East, and Africa	Americas	Europe and CIS	Africa	Middle East
Saudi Arabia	Jamaica, Panama,[3] Trinidad & Tobago	Bosnia Herzegovina, Bulgaria, Ukraine	Botswana, Ghana, Zimbabwe	Palestine

[1] *The West African Economic and Monetary Union (WAEMU) consists of the following countries:* Benin, Burkina Faso, Ivory Coast, Guinea-Bissau, Mali, Niger, Senegal, and Togo. Currently the MSCI WAEMU Indexes include securities classified in Senegal, Ivory Coast, and Burkina Faso.
[2] *The MSCI Standalone Market Indexes are not included in the MSCI Emerging Markets Index or MSCI*

Frontier Markets Index. However, these indexes use either the Emerging Markets or the Frontier Markets methodological criteria concerning size and liquidity.
[3] *MSCI Panama Index has been launched as a Standalone Market Index.*
Source: adapted from MSCI (https://www.msci.com/en/market-cap-weighted-indexes), October 2018.

Fundamental Weighting in Multi-Market Indexes

Some index providers weight the securities within each country/region by market capitalization and then weight each country/region in the overall index in proportion to its relative GDP, effectively creating fundamental weighting in multi-market indexes. GDP-weighted indexes were some of the first fundamentally weighted indexes created. Introduced in 1987 by MSCI to address the 60 percent weight of Japanese equities in the market-capitalization-weighted MSCI EAFE Index at the time, GDP-weighted indexes reduced the allocation to Japanese equities by half.[4]

Sector Indexes

Sector indexes represent and track different economic sectors—such as consumer goods, energy, finance, health care, and technology—on either a national, regional, or global basis. Because different sectors of the economy behave differently over the course of the business cycle, some investors may seek to overweight or underweight their exposure to particular sectors.

Sector indexes are organized as families; each index within the family represents an economic sector. Typically, the aggregation of a sector index family is equivalent to a broad market index. Economic sector classification can be applied on a global, regional, or country-specific basis, but no universally agreed upon sector classification method exists.

Sector indexes play an important role in performance analysis because they provide a means to determine whether a portfolio manager is more successful at stock selection or sector allocation. Sector indexes also serve as model portfolios for sector-specific ETFs and other investment products.

Style Indexes

Style indexes represent groups of securities classified according to market capitalization, value, growth, or a combination of these characteristics. They are intended to reflect the investing styles of certain investors, such as the growth investor, value investor, and small-cap investor.

Market Capitalization

Market-capitalization indexes represent securities categorized according to the major capitalization categories: large cap, midcap, and small cap. With no universal definition of these categories, the indexes differ on the distinctions between large cap and midcap and between midcap and small cap, as well as the minimum market-capitalization size required to be included in a small-cap index. Classification into categories can be based on absolute market capitalization (e.g., below €100 million) or relative market capitalization (e.g., the smallest 2,500 stocks).

---

[4] Steven A. Schoenfeld, *Active Index Investing* (Hoboken, NJ: John Wiley & Sons, 2004):220.

Value/Growth Classification

Some indexes represent categories of stocks based on their classifications as either value or growth stocks. Different index providers use different factors and valuation ratios (low price-to-book ratios, low price-to-earnings ratios, high dividend yields, etc.) to distinguish between value and growth equities.

Market Capitalization and Value/Growth Classification

Combining the three market-capitalization groups with value and growth classifications results in six basic style index categories:

- Large-Cap Value
- Mid-Cap Value
- Small-Cap Value
- Large-Cap Growth
- Mid-Cap Growth
- Small-Cap Growth

Because indexes use different size and valuation classifications, the constituents of indexes designed to represent a given style, such as small-cap value, may differ—sometimes substantially.

Because valuation ratios and market capitalizations change over time, stocks frequently migrate from one style index category to another on reconstitution dates. As a result, style indexes generally have much higher turnover than do broad market indexes.

7 FIXED-INCOME INDEXES

☐ describe types of fixed-income indexes
☐ compare types of security market indexes

A wide variety of fixed-income indexes exists, but the nature of the fixed-income markets and fixed-income securities leads to some very important challenges to fixed-income index construction and replication. These challenges are the number of securities in the fixed-income universe, the availability of pricing data, and the liquidity of the securities.

Construction

The fixed-income universe includes securities issued by governments, government agencies, and corporations. Each of these entities may issue a variety of fixed-income securities with different characteristics. As a result, the number of fixed-income securities is many times larger than the number of equity securities. To represent a specific fixed-income market or segment, indexes may include thousands of different securities. Over time, these fixed-income securities mature, and issuers offer new securities to meet their financing needs, leading to turnover in fixed-income indexes.

Another challenge in index construction is that fixed-income markets are predominantly dealer markets. This means that firms (dealers) are assigned to specific securities and are responsible for creating liquid markets for those securities by purchasing and selling them from their inventory. In addition, many securities do not trade frequently and, as a result, are relatively illiquid. As a result, index providers must contact dealers to obtain current prices on constituent securities to update the index or they must estimate the prices of constituent securities using the prices of traded fixed-income securities with similar characteristics.

These challenges can result in indexes with dissimilar numbers of bonds representing the same markets. The large number of fixed-income securities—combined with the lack of liquidity of some securities—has made it more costly and difficult, compared with equity indexes, for investors to replicate fixed-income indexes and duplicate their performance.

Types of Fixed-Income Indexes

The wide variety of fixed-income securities, ranging from zero-coupon bonds to bonds with embedded options (i.e., callable or putable bonds), results in a number of different types of fixed-income indexes. Similar to equities, fixed-income securities can be categorized according to the issuer's economic sector, the issuer's geographic region, or the economic development of the issuer's geographic region. Fixed-income securities can also be classified along the following dimensions:

- type of issuer (government, government agency, corporation);
- type of financing (general obligation, collateralized);
- currency of payments;
- maturity;
- credit quality (investment grade, high yield, credit agency ratings); and
- absence or presence of inflation protection.

Fixed-income indexes are based on these various dimensions and can be categorized as follows:

- aggregate or broad market indexes;
- market sector indexes;
- style indexes;
- economic sector indexes; and
- specialized indexes such as high-yield, inflation-linked, and emerging market indexes.

The first fixed-income index created, the Bloomberg Barclays US Aggregate Bond Index (formerly the Barclays Capital Aggregate Bond Index), is an example of a single-country aggregate index. Designed to represent the broad market of US fixed-income securities, it comprises approximately 8,000 securities, including US Treasury, government-related, corporate, mortgage-backed, asset-backed, and commercial mortgage-backed securities.

Aggregate indexes can be subdivided by market sector (government, government agency, collateralized, corporate); style (maturity, credit quality); economic sector, or some other characteristic to create more narrowly defined indexes. A common distinction reflected in indexes is between investment grade (e.g., those with a Standard & Poor's credit rating of BBB– or better) and high-yield securities. Investment-grade indexes are typically further subdivided by maturity (i.e., short, intermediate, or long) and by credit rating (e.g., AAA, BBB, etc.).[5] The wide variety of fixed-income indexes reflects the partitioning of fixed-income securities on the basis of a variety of dimensions.

Exhibit 8 illustrates how the major types of fixed-income indexes can be organized on the basis of various dimensions.

---

5 Credit ratings are discussed in depth in the Level I CFA Program reading "Fundamentals of Credit Analysis."

Exhibit 8: Dimensions of Fixed-Income Indexes

Market	Global			
	Regional			
	Country or currency zone			
Type	Corporate	Collateralized *Securitized* Mortgage-backed	Government agency	Government
Maturity	For example, 1–3, 3–5, 5–7, 7–10, 10+ years; short-term, medium-term, or long-term			
Credit quality	For example, AAA, AA, A, BBB, etc.; Aaa, Aa, A, Baa, etc.; investment grade, high yield			

All aggregate indexes include a variety of market sectors and credit ratings. The breakdown of the Bloomberg Barclays Global Aggregate Bond Index by market sectors and by credit rating is shown in Exhibit 9 and Exhibit 10, respectively.

Exhibit 9: Market Sector Breakdown of the Bloomberg Barclays Global Aggregate Bond Index

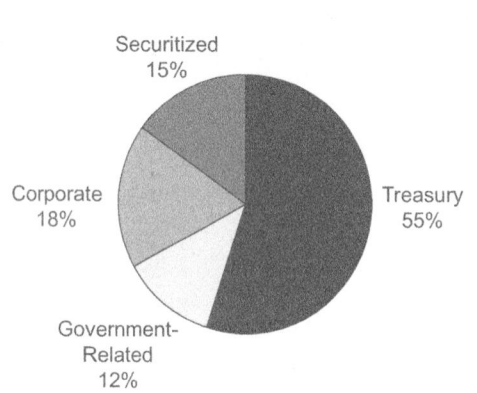

Sector Breakdown as of June 30, 2016

- Securitized 15%
- Corporate 18%
- Government-Related 12%
- Treasury 55%

Source: Bloomberg Barclays Indices, Global Aggregate Index Factsheet, August 24, 2016. https://data.bloomberglp.com/indices/sites/2/2016/08/Factsheet-Global-Aggregate.pdf.

Exhibit 10: Credit Breakdown of the Bloomberg Barclays Global Aggregate Bond Index

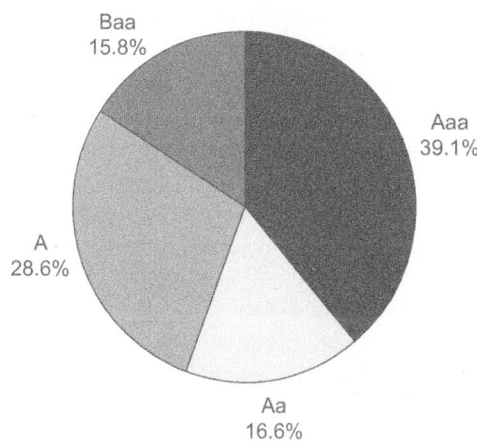

Source: Bloomberg Barclays Indices, Global Aggregate Index Factsheet, August 24, 2016. https://data.bloomberglp.com/indices/sites/2/2016/08/Factsheet-Global-Aggregate.pdf.

INDEXES FOR ALTERNATIVE INVESTMENTS

8

- ☐ describe indexes representing alternative investments
- ☐ compare types of security market indexes

Many investors seek to lower the risk or enhance the performance of their portfolios by investing in assets classes other than equities and fixed income. Interest in alternative assets and investment strategies has led to the creation of indexes designed to represent broad classes of alternative investments. Three of the most widely followed alternative investment classes are commodities, real estate, and hedge funds.

Commodity Indexes

Commodity indexes consist of futures contracts on one or more commodities, such as agricultural products (rice, wheat, sugar), livestock (cattle, hogs), precious and common metals (gold, silver, copper), and energy commodities (crude oil, natural gas).

Although some commodity indexes may include the same commodities, the returns of these indexes may differ because each index may use a different weighting method. Because commodity indexes do not have an obvious weighting mechanism, such as market capitalization, commodity index providers create their own weighting methods. Some indexes, such as the Thomson Reuters/Core Commodity CRB Index (TR/CC CRB Index), formerly known as the Commodity Research Bureau (CRB) Index, contain a fixed number of commodities that are weighted equally. The S&P

GSCI uses a combination of liquidity measures and world production values in its weighting scheme and allocates more weight to commodities that have risen in price. Other indexes have fixed weights that are determined by a committee.

The different weighting methods can also lead to large differences in exposure to specific commodities. The S&P GSCI in 2018, for example, weights the energy-sector approximately 50% higher and the agriculture sector 40% lower than the CRB Index. These differences result in indexes with very different risk and return profiles. Unlike commodity indexes, broad equity and fixed-income indexes that target the same markets share similar risk and return profiles.

The performance of commodity indexes can also be quite different from their underlying commodities because the indexes consist of futures contracts on the commodities rather than the actual commodities. Index returns are affected by factors other than changes in the prices of the underlying commodities because futures contracts must be continually "rolled over" (i.e., replacing a contract nearing expiration with a new contract). Commodity index returns reflect the risk-free interest rate, the changes in future prices, and the roll yield. Therefore, a commodity index return can be quite different from the return based on changes in the prices of the underlying commodities.

Real Estate Investment Trust Indexes

Real estate indexes represent not only the market for real estate securities but also the market for real estate—a highly illiquid market and asset class with infrequent transactions and pricing information. Real estate indexes can be categorized as appraisal indexes, repeat sales indexes, and real estate investment trust (REIT) indexes.

REIT indexes consist of shares of publicly traded REITs. REITS are public or private corporations organized specifically to invest in real estate, either through ownership of properties or investment in mortgages. Shares of public REITs are traded on the world's various stock exchanges and are a popular choice for investing in commercial real estate properties. Because REIT indexes are based on publicly traded REITs with continuous market pricing, the value of REIT indexes is calculated continuously.

The FTSE EPRA/NAREIT global family of REIT indexes shown in Exhibit 11 seeks to represent trends in real estate stocks worldwide and includes representation from the European Public Real Estate Association (EPRA) and the National Association of Real Estate Investment Trusts (NAREIT).

Exhibit 11: The FTSE EPRA/NAREIT Global REIT Index Family

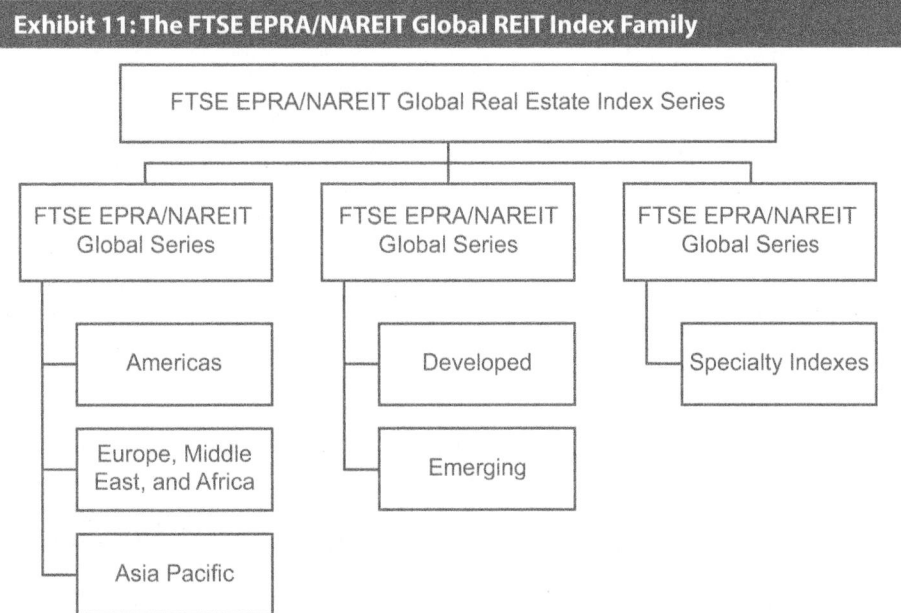

Source: FTSE International, "FTSE EPRA/NAREIT Global & Global Ex US Indices" Factsheet 2009). "FTSE®" is a trade mark of the London Stock Exchange Plc, "NAREIT®" is a trade mark of the National Association of Real Estate Investment Trusts ("NAREIT") and "EPRA®" is a trade mark of the European Public Real Estate Association ("EPRA") and all are used by FTSE International Limited ("FTSE") under license.

Hedge Fund Indexes

Hedge fund indexes reflect the returns on hedge funds. **Hedge funds** are private investment vehicles that typically use leverage and long and short investment strategies.

A number of research organizations maintain databases of hedge fund returns and summarize these returns into indexes. These database indexes are designed to represent the performance of the hedge funds on a very broad global level (hedge funds in general) or the strategy level. Most of these indexes are equal weighted and represent the performance of the hedge funds within a particular database.

Most research organizations rely on the voluntary cooperation of hedge funds to compile performance data. As unregulated entities, however, hedge funds are not required to report their performance to any party other than their investors. Therefore, each hedge fund decides to which database(s) it will report its performance. As a result, rather than index providers determining the constituents, the constituents determine the index.

Frequently, a hedge fund reports its performance to only one database. The result is little overlap of funds covered by the different indexes. With little overlap between their constituents, different global hedge fund indexes may reflect very different performance for the hedge fund industry over the same period of time.

Another consequence of the voluntary performance reporting is the potential for survivorship bias and, therefore, inaccurate performance representation. This means that hedge funds with poor performance may be less likely to report their performance to the database or may stop reporting to the database, so their returns may be excluded when measuring the return of the index. As a result, the index may not accurately reflect actual hedge fund performance so much as the performance of hedge funds that are performing well.

REPRESENTATIVE INDEXES WORLDWIDE

As indicated in this reading, the choice of indexes to meet the needs of investors is extensive. Investors using security market indexes must be careful in their selection of the index or indexes most appropriate for their needs. The following table illustrates the variety of indexes reflecting different asset classes, markets, and weighting methods.

Index	Representing	Number of Securities	Weighting Method	Comments
Dow Jones Industrial Average	US blue chip companies	30	Price	The oldest and most widely known US equity index. *Wall Street Journal* editors choose 30 stocks from among large, mature blue-chip companies.
Nikkei Stock Average	Japanese blue chip companies	225	Modified price	Known as the Nikkei 225 and originally formulated by Dow Jones & Company. Because of extreme variation in price levels of component securities, some high-priced shares are weighted as a fraction of share price.
TOPIX	All companies listed on the Tokyo Stock Exchange First Section	Varies	Float-adjusted market cap	Represents about 93 percent of the market value of all Japanese equities. Contains a large number of very small, illiquid stocks, making exact replication difficult.
MSCI All Country World Index	Stocks of 23 developed and 24 emerging markets	Varies	Free-float-adjusted market cap	Composed of companies representative of the market structure of developed and emerging market countries in the Americas, Europe/Middle East, and Asia/Pacific regions. Price return and total return versions available in both USD and local currencies.
S&P Developed Ex-US BMI Energy Sector Index	Energy sector of developed global markets outside the United States	Varies	Float-adjusted market cap	Serves as a model portfolio for the SPDR® S&P Energy Sector Exchange-Traded Fund (ETF).
Bloomberg Barclays Global Aggregate Bond Index	Investment-grade bonds in the North American, European, and Asian markets	Varies	Market cap	Formerly known as Lehman Brothers Global Aggregate Bond Index.
Markit iBoxx Euro High-Yield Bond Indexes	Sub-investment-grade euro-denominated corporate bonds	Varies	Market cap and variations	Rebalanced monthly. Represents tradable part of market. Price and total return versions available with such analytical values as yield, duration, modified duration, and convexity. Provides platform for research and structured products.
FTSE EPRA/NAREIT Global Real Estate Index	Real estate securities in the North American, European, and Asian markets	Varies	Float-adjusted market cap	The stocks of REITs that constitute the index trade on public stock exchanges and may be constituents of equity market indexes.

Indexes for Alternative Investments

Index	Representing	Number of Securities	Weighting Method	Comments
HFRX Global Hedge Fund Index	Overall composition of the HFR database	Varies	Asset weighted	Comprises all eligible hedge fund strategies. Examples include convertible arbitrage, distressed securities, market neutral, event driven, macro, and relative value arbitrage. Constituent strategies are asset weighted on the basis of asset distribution within the hedge fund industry.
HFRX Equal Weighted Strategies EUR Index	Overall composition of the HFR database	Varies	Equal weighted	Denominated in euros and is constructed from the same strategies as the HFRX Global Hedge Fund Index.
Morningstar Style Indexes	US stocks classified by market cap and value/growth orientation	Varies	Float-adjusted market cap	The nine indexes defined by combinations of market cap (large, mid, and small) and value/growth orientation (value, core, growth) have mutually exclusive constituents and are exhaustive with respect to the Morningstar US Market Index. Each is a model portfolio for one of the iShares Morningstar ETFs.

SUMMARY

This reading explains and illustrates the construction, management, and uses of security market indexes. It also discusses various types of indexes. Security market indexes are invaluable tools for investors, who can select from among thousands of indexes representing a variety of security markets, market segments, and asset classes. These indexes range from those representing the global market for major asset classes to those representing alternative investments in specific geographic markets. To benefit from the use of security market indexes, investors must understand their construction and determine whether the selected index is appropriate for their purposes. Frequently, an index that is well suited for one purpose may not be well suited for other purposes. Users of indexes must be familiar with how various indexes are constructed in order to select the index or indexes most appropriate for their needs.

Among the key points made in this reading are the following:

- Security market indexes are intended to measure the values of different target markets (security markets, market segments, or asset classes).
- The constituent securities selected for inclusion in the security market index are intended to represent the target market.
- A price return index reflects only the prices of the constituent securities.
- A total return index reflects not only the prices of the constituent securities but also the reinvestment of all income received since the inception of the index.

- Methods used to weight the constituents of an index range from the very simple, such as price and equal weightings, to the more complex, such as market-capitalization and fundamental weightings.
- Choices in index construction—in particular, the choice of weighting method—affect index valuation and returns.
- Index management includes 1) periodic rebalancing to ensure that the index maintains appropriate weightings and 2) reconstitution to ensure the index represents the desired target market.
- Rebalancing and reconstitution create turnover in an index. Reconstitution can dramatically affect prices of current and prospective constituents.
- Indexes serve a variety of purposes. They gauge market sentiment and serve as benchmarks for actively managed portfolios. They act as proxies for measuring systematic risk and risk-adjusted performance. They also serve as proxies for asset classes in asset allocation models and as model portfolios for investment products.
- Investors can choose from security market indexes representing various asset classes, including equity, fixed-income, commodity, real estate, and hedge fund indexes.
- Within most asset classes, index providers offer a wide variety of indexes, ranging from broad market indexes to highly specialized indexes based on the issuer's geographic region, economic development group, or economic sector or other factors.
- Proper use of security market indexes depends on understanding their construction and management.

PRACTICE PROBLEMS

1. A security market index represents the:
   A. risk of a security market.
   B. security market as a whole.
   C. security market, market segment, or asset class.

2. One month after inception, the price return version and total return version of a single index (consisting of identical securities and weights) will be equal if:
   A. market prices have not changed.
   B. capital gains are offset by capital losses.
   C. the securities do not pay dividends or interest.

3. The values of a price return index and a total return index consisting of identical equal-weighted dividend-paying equities will be equal:
   A. only at inception.
   B. at inception and on rebalancing dates.
   C. at inception and on reconstitution dates.

4. Security market indexes are:
   A. constructed and managed like a portfolio of securities.
   B. simple interchangeable tools for measuring the returns of different asset classes.
   C. valued on a regular basis using the actual market prices of the constituent securities.

5. When creating a security market index, an index provider must first determine the:
   A. target market.
   B. appropriate weighting method.
   C. number of constituent securities.

6. An analyst gathers the following information for an equal-weighted index comprised of assets Able, Baker, and Charlie:

Security	Beginning of Period Price (€)	End of Period Price (€)	Total Dividends (€)
Able	10.00	12.00	0.75
Baker	20.00	19.00	1.00
Charlie	30.00	30.00	2.00

   The price return of the index is:

A. 1.7%.

B. 5.0%.

C. 11.4%.

7. An analyst gathers the following information for an equal-weighted index comprised of assets Able, Baker, and Charlie:

Security	Beginning of Period Price (€)	End of Period Price (€)	Total Dividends (€)
Able	10.00	12.00	0.75
Baker	20.00	19.00	1.00
Charlie	30.00	30.00	2.00

The total return of the index is:

A. 5.0%.

B. 7.9%.

C. 11.4%.

8. An analyst gathers the following information for a price-weighted index comprised of securities ABC, DEF, and GHI:

Security	Beginning of Period Price (£)	End of Period Price (£)	Total Dividends (£)
ABC	25.00	27.00	1.00
DEF	35.00	25.00	1.50
GHI	15.00	16.00	1.00

The price return of the index is:

A. −4.6%.

B. −9.3%.

C. −13.9%.

9. An analyst gathers the following information for a market-capitalization-weighted index comprised of securities MNO, QRS, and XYZ:

Security	Beginning of Period Price (¥)	End of Period Price (¥)	Dividends per Share (¥)	Shares Outstanding
MNO	2,500	2,700	100	5,000
QRS	3,500	2,500	150	7,500
XYZ	1,500	1,600	100	10,000

The price return of the index is:

A. −9.33%.

B. −10.23%.

Practice Problems

C. −13.90%.

10. An analyst gathers the following information for a market-capitalization-weighted index comprised of securities MNO, QRS, and XYZ:

Security	Beginning of Period Price (¥)	End of Period Price (¥)	Dividends Per Share (¥)	Shares Outstanding
MNO	2,500	2,700	100	5,000
QRS	3,500	2,500	150	7,500
XYZ	1,500	1,600	100	10,000

The total return of the index is:

A. 1.04%.

B. −5.35%.

C. −10.23%.

11. When creating a security market index, the target market:

A. determines the investment universe.

B. is usually a broadly defined asset class.

C. determines the number of securities to be included in the index.

12. An analyst gathers the following data for a price-weighted index:

	Beginning of Period		End of Period	
Security	Price (€)	Shares Outstanding	Price (€)	Shares Outstanding
A	20.00	300	22.00	300
B	50.00	300	48.00	300
C	26.00	2,000	30.00	2,000

The price return of the index over the period is:

A. 4.2%.

B. 7.1%.

C. 21.4%.

13. An analyst gathers the following data for a value-weighted index:

Security	Beginning of Period		End of Period	
	Price (£)	Shares Outstanding	Price (£)	Shares Outstanding
A	20.00	300	22.00	300
B	50.00	300	48.00	300
C	26.00	2,000	30.00	2,000

The return on the value-weighted index over the period is:

A. 7.1%.

B. 11.0%.

C. 21.4%.

14. An analyst gathers the following data for an equally-weighted index:

Security	Beginning of Period		End of Period	
	Price (¥)	Shares Outstanding	Price (¥)	Shares Outstanding
A	20.00	300	22.00	300
B	50.00	300	48.00	300
C	26.00	2,000	30.00	2,000

The return on the index over the period is:

A. 4.2%.

B. 6.8%.

C. 7.1%.

15. Which of the following index weighting methods requires an adjustment to the divisor after a stock split?

A. Price weighting.

B. Fundamental weighting.

C. Market-capitalization weighting.

16. If the price return of an equal-weighted index exceeds that of a market-capitalization-weighted index comprised of the same securities, the *most likely* explanation is:

A. stock splits.

B. dividend distributions.

C. outperformance of small-market-capitalization stocks.

17. A float-adjusted market-capitalization-weighted index weights each of its constit-

uent securities by its price and:

   A. its trading volume.

   B. the number of its shares outstanding.

   C. the number of its shares available to the investing public.

18. Which of the following index weighting methods is most likely subject to a value tilt?

   A. Equal weighting.

   B. Fundamental weighting.

   C. Market-capitalization weighting.

19. Rebalancing an index is the process of periodically adjusting the constituent:

   A. securities' weights to optimize investment performance.

   B. securities to maintain consistency with the target market.

   C. securities' weights to maintain consistency with the index's weighting method.

20. Which of the following index weighting methods requires the most frequent rebalancing?

   A. Price weighting.

   B. Equal weighting.

   C. Market-capitalization weighting.

21. Reconstitution of a security market index reduces:

   A. portfolio turnover.

   B. the need for rebalancing.

   C. the likelihood that the index includes securities that are not representative of the target market.

22. Security market indexes are used as:

   A. measures of investment returns.

   B. proxies to measure unsystematic risk.

   C. proxies for specific asset classes in asset allocation models.

23. Uses of market indexes do not include serving as a:

   A. measure of systemic risk.

   B. basis for new investment products.

   C. benchmark for evaluating portfolio performance.

24. Which of the following statements regarding sector indexes is *most* accurate?

Sector indexes:

- **A.** track different economic sectors and cannot be aggregated to represent the equivalent of a broad market index.
- **B.** provide a means to determine whether an active investment manager is more successful at stock selection or sector allocation.
- **C.** apply a universally agreed upon sector classification system to identify the constituent securities of specific economic sectors, such as consumer goods, energy, finance, health care.

25. Which of the following is an example of a style index? An index based on:
    - **A.** geography.
    - **B.** economic sector.
    - **C.** market capitalization.

26. Which of the following statements regarding fixed-income indexes is *most* accurate?
    - **A.** Liquidity issues make it difficult for investors to easily replicate fixed-income indexes.
    - **B.** Rebalancing and reconstitution are the only sources of turnover in fixed-income indexes.
    - **C.** Fixed-income indexes representing the same target market hold similar numbers of bonds.

27. An aggregate fixed-income index:
    - **A.** comprises corporate and asset-backed securities.
    - **B.** represents the market of government-issued securities.
    - **C.** can be subdivided by market or economic sector to create more narrowly defined indexes.

28. Fixed-income indexes are *least likely* constructed on the basis of:
    - **A.** maturity.
    - **B.** type of issuer.
    - **C.** coupon frequency.

29. In comparison to equity indexes, the constituent securities of fixed-income indexes are:
    - **A.** more liquid.
    - **B.** easier to price.
    - **C.** drawn from a larger investment universe.

30. Commodity index values are based on:
    - **A.** futures contract prices.

Practice Problems

   B. the market price of the specific commodity.

   C. the average market price of a basket of similar commodities.

31. Which of the following statements is *most* accurate?

   A. Commodity indexes all share similar weighting methods.

   B. Commodity indexes containing the same underlying commodities offer similar returns.

   C. The performance of commodity indexes can be quite different from that of the underlying commodities.

32. Which of the following is *not* a real estate index category?

   A. Appraisal index.

   B. Initial sales index.

   C. Repeat sales index.

33. A unique feature of hedge fund indexes is that they:

   A. are frequently equal weighted.

   B. are determined by the constituents of the index.

   C. reflect the value of private rather than public investments.

34. The returns of hedge fund indexes are *most likely*:

   A. biased upward.

   B. biased downward.

   C. similar across different index providers.

SOLUTIONS

1. C is correct. A security market index represents the value of a given security market, market segment, or asset class.

2. C is correct. The difference between a price return index and a total return index consisting of identical securities and weights is the income generated over time by the underlying securities. If the securities in the index do not generate income, both indexes will be identical in value.

3. A is correct. At inception, the values of the price return and total return versions of an index are equal.

4. A is correct. Security market indexes are constructed and managed like a portfolio of securities.

5. A is correct. The first decision is identifying the target market that the index is intended to represent because the target market determines the investment universe and the securities available for inclusion in the index.

6. B is correct. The price return is the sum of the weighted returns of each security. The return of Able is 20 percent [(12 − 10)/10]; of Baker is −5 percent [(19 − 20)/20]; and of Charlie is 0 percent [(30 − 30)/30]. The price return index assigns a weight of 1/3 to each asset; therefore, the price return is 1/3 × [20% + (−5%) + 0%] = 5%.

7. C is correct. The total return of an index is calculated on the basis of the change in price of the underlying securities plus the sum of income received or the sum of the weighted total returns of each security. The total return of Able is 27.5 percent; of Baker is 0 percent; and of Charlie is 6.7 percent:

    Able: (12 − 10 + 0.75)/10 = 27.5%

    Baker: (19 − 20 + 1)/20 = 0%

    Charlie: (30 − 30 + 2)/30 = 6.7%

    An equal-weighted index applies the same weight (1/3) to each security's return; therefore, the total return = 1/3 × (27.5% + 0% + 6.7%) = 11.4%.

8. B is correct. The price return of the price-weighted index is the percentage change in price of the index: (68 − 75)/75 = −9.33%.

Security	Beginning of Period Price (£)	End of Period Price (£)
ABC	25.00	27.00
DEF	35.00	25.00
GHI	15.00	16.00
TOTAL	75.00	68.00

9. B is correct. The price return of the index is (48,250,000 − 53,750,000)/53,750,000 = −10.23%.

Solutions

Security	Beginning of Period Price (¥)	Shares Outstanding	Beginning of Period Value (¥)	End of Period Price (¥)	End of Period Value (¥)
MNO	2,500	5,000	12,500,000	2,700	13,500,000
QRS	3,500	7,500	26,250,000	2,500	18,750,000
XYZ	1,500	10,000	15,000,000	1,600	16,000,000
Total			53,750,000		48,250,000

10. B is correct. The total return of the market-capitalization-weighted index is calculated below:

Security	Beginning of Period Value (¥)	End of Period Value (¥)	Total Dividends (¥)	Total Return (%)
MNO	12,500,000	13,500,000	500,000	12.00
QRS	26,250,000	18,750,000	1,125,000	−24.29
XYZ	15,000,000	16,000,000	1,000,000	13.33
Total	53,750,000	48,250,000	2,625,000	−5.35

11. A is correct. The target market determines the investment universe and the securities available for inclusion in the index.

12. A is correct. The sum of prices at the beginning of the period is 96; the sum at the end of the period is 100. Regardless of the divisor, the price return is $100/96 - 1 = 0.042$ or 4.2 percent.

13. B is correct. It is the percentage change in the market value over the period:

    Market value at beginning of period: $(20 \times 300) + (50 \times 300) + (26 \times 2,000) = 73,000$

    Market value at end of period: $(22 \times 300) + (48 \times 300) + (30 \times 2,000) = 81,000$

    Percentage change is $81,000/73,000 - 1 = 0.1096$ or 11.0 percent with rounding.

14. C is correct. With an equal-weighted index, the same amount is invested in each security. Assuming $1,000 is invested in each of the three stocks, the index value is $3,000 at the beginning of the period and the following number of shares is purchased for each stock:

    Security A: 50 shares
    Security B: 20 shares
    Security C: 38.46 shares.

    Using the prices at the beginning of the period for each security, the index value at the end of the period is $3,213.8: ($22 × 50) + ($48 × 20) + ($30 × 38.46). The price return is $3,213.8/$3,000 − 1 = 7.1%.

15. A is correct. In the price weighting method, the divisor must be adjusted so the index value immediately after the split is the same as the index value immediately prior to the split.

16. C is correct. The main source of return differences arises from outperformance

of small-cap securities or underperformance of large-cap securities. In an equal-weighted index, securities that constitute the largest fraction of the market are underrepresented and securities that constitute only a small fraction of the market are overrepresented. Thus, higher equal-weighted index returns will occur if the smaller-cap equities outperform the larger-cap equities.

17. C is correct. "Float" is the number of shares available for public trading.

18. B is correct. Fundamental weighting leads to indexes that have a value tilt.

19. C is correct. Rebalancing refers to adjusting the weights of constituent securities in an index to maintain consistency with the index's weighting method.

20. B is correct. Changing market prices will cause weights that were initially equal to become unequal, thus requiring rebalancing.

21. C is correct. Reconstitution is the process by which index providers review the constituent securities, re-apply the initial criteria for inclusion in the index, and select which securities to retain, remove, or add. Constituent securities that no longer meet the criteria are replaced with securities that do. Thus, reconstitution reduces the likelihood that the index includes securities that are not representative of the target market.

22. C is correct. Security market indexes play a critical role as proxies for asset classes in asset allocation models.

23. A is correct. Security market indexes are used as proxies for measuring market or systematic risk, not as measures of systemic risk.

24. B is correct. Sector indexes provide a means to determine whether a portfolio manager is more successful at stock selection or sector allocation.

25. C is correct. Style indexes represent groups of securities classified according to market capitalization, value, growth, or a combination of these characteristics.

26. A is correct. The large number of fixed-income securities—combined with the lack of liquidity of some securities—makes it costly and difficult for investors to replicate fixed-income indexes.

27. C is correct. An aggregate fixed-income index can be subdivided by market sector (government, government agency, collateralized, corporate), style (maturity, credit quality), economic sector, or some other characteristic to create more narrowly defined indexes.

28. C is correct. Coupon frequency is not a dimension on which fixed-income indexes are based.

29. C is correct. The fixed-income market has more issuers and securities than the equity market.

30. A is correct. Commodity indexes consist of futures contracts on one or more commodities.

31. C is correct. The performance of commodity indexes can be quite different from that of the underlying commodities because the indexes consist of futures contracts on the commodities rather than the actual commodities.

32. B is correct. It is not a real estate index category.

Solutions

33. B is correct. Hedge funds are not required to report their performance to any party other than their investors. Therefore, each hedge fund decides to which database(s) it will report its performance. Thus, for a hedge fund index, constituents determine the index rather than index providers determining the constituents.

34. A is correct. Voluntary performance reporting may lead to survivorship bias, and poorer performing hedge funds will be less likely to report their performance.

LEARNING MODULE 3

Market Efficiency

by Sean Cleary, PhD, CFA, Howard J. Atkinson, CIMA, ICD.D, CFA, and Pamela Peterson Drake, PhD, CFA.

Sean Cleary, PhD, CFA, is at Queen's University (Canada). Howard J. Atkinson, CIMA, ICD.D, CFA, is at Horizons ETF Management (Canada) Inc. (Canada). Pamela Peterson Drake, PhD, CFA, is at James Madison University (USA).

LEARNING OUTCOMES	
Mastery	The candidate should be able to:
☐	describe market efficiency and related concepts, including their importance to investment practitioners
☐	contrast market value and intrinsic value
☐	explain factors that affect a market's efficiency
☐	contrast weak-form, semi-strong-form, and strong-form market efficiency
☐	explain the implications of each form of market efficiency for fundamental analysis, technical analysis, and the choice between active and passive portfolio management
☐	describe market anomalies
☐	describe behavioral finance and its potential relevance to understanding market anomalies

1. INTRODUCTION

Market efficiency concerns the extent to which market prices incorporate available information. If market prices do not fully incorporate information, then opportunities may exist to make a profit from the gathering and processing of information. The subject of market efficiency is, therefore, of great interest to investment managers, as illustrated in Example 1.

> **EXAMPLE 1**
>
> **Market Efficiency and Active Manager Selection**
>
> 1. The chief investment officer (CIO) of a major university endowment fund has listed eight steps in the active manager selection process that can be applied both to traditional investments (e.g., common equity and fixed-income securities) and to alternative investments (e.g., private equity, hedge funds, and real assets). The first step specified is the evaluation of market opportunity:
>
>   > What is the opportunity and why is it there? To answer this question, we start by studying capital markets and the types of managers operating within those markets. We identify market inefficiencies and try to understand their causes, such as regulatory structures or behavioral biases. We can rule out many broad groups of managers and strategies by simply determining that the degree of market inefficiency necessary to support a strategy is implausible. Importantly, we consider the past history of active returns meaningless unless we understand why markets will allow those active returns to continue into the future.[1]
>
>   The CIO's description underscores the importance of not assuming that past active returns that might be found in a historical dataset will repeat themselves in the future. **Active returns** refer to returns earned by strategies that do *not* assume that all information is fully reflected in market prices.

Governments and market regulators also care about the extent to which market prices incorporate information. Efficient markets imply informative prices—prices that accurately reflect available information about fundamental values. In market-based economies, market prices help determine which companies (and which projects) obtain capital. If these prices do not efficiently incorporate information about a company's prospects, then it is possible that funds will be misdirected. By contrast, prices that are informative help direct scarce resources and funds available for investment to their highest-valued uses.[2] Informative prices thus promote economic growth. The efficiency of a country's capital markets (in which businesses raise financing) is an important characteristic of a well-functioning financial system.

The remainder of this reading is organized as follows. Section 2 provides specifics on how the efficiency of an asset market is described and discusses the factors affecting (i.e., contributing to and impeding) market efficiency. Section 3 presents an influential three-way classification of the efficiency of security markets and discusses its implications for fundamental analysis, technical analysis, and portfolio management. Section 4 presents several market anomalies (apparent market inefficiencies that have received enough attention to be individually identified and named) and describes how these anomalies relate to investment strategies. Section 5 introduces behavioral finance and how that field of study relates to market efficiency. A summary concludes the reading.

---

1 The CIO is Christopher J. Brightman, CFA, of the University of Virginia Investment Management Company, as reported in Yau, Schneeweis, Robinson, and Weiss (2007, pp. 481–482).
2 This concept is known as allocative efficiency.

THE CONCEPT OF MARKET EFFICIENCY

☐ describe market efficiency and related concepts, including their importance to investment practitioners

☐ contrast market value and intrinsic value

The Description of Efficient Markets

An **informationally efficient market** (an **efficient market**) is a market in which asset prices reflect new information quickly and rationally. An efficient market is thus a market in which asset prices reflect all past and present information.[3]

In this section we expand on this definition by clarifying the time frame required for an asset's price to incorporate information as well as describing the elements of information releases assumed under market efficiency. We discuss the difference between market value and intrinsic value and illustrate how inefficiencies or discrepancies between these values can provide profitable opportunities for active investment. As financial markets are generally not considered being either completely efficient or inefficient, but rather falling within a range between the two extremes, we describe a number of factors that contribute to and impede the degree of efficiency of a financial market. Finally, we conclude our overview of market efficiency by illustrating how the costs incurred by traders in identifying and exploiting possible market inefficiencies affect how we interpret market efficiency.

Investment managers and analysts, as noted, are interested in market efficiency because the extent to which a market is efficient affects how many profitable trading opportunities (market inefficiencies) exist. Consistent, superior, risk-adjusted returns (net of all expenses) are not achievable in an efficient market.[4] In an efficient market, a **passive investment** strategy (i.e., buying and holding a broad market portfolio) that does not seek superior risk-adjusted returns can be preferred to an **active investment** strategy because of lower costs (for example, transaction and information-seeking costs). By contrast, in a very inefficient market, opportunities may exist for an active investment strategy to achieve superior risk-adjusted returns (net of all expenses in executing the strategy) as compared with a passive investment strategy. In inefficient markets, an active investment strategy may outperform a passive investment strategy on a risk-adjusted basis. Understanding the characteristics of an efficient market and being able to evaluate the efficiency of a particular market are important topics for investment analysts and portfolio managers.

An efficient market is a market in which asset prices reflect information quickly. But what is the time frame of "quickly"? Trades are the mechanism by which information can be incorporated into asset transaction prices. The time needed to execute trades to exploit an inefficiency may provide a baseline for judging speed of adjustment.[5]

---

[3] This definition is convenient for making several instructional points. The definition that most simply explains the sense of the word *efficient* in this context can be found in Fama (1976): "An efficient capital market is a market that is efficient in processing information" (p. 134).

[4] The technical term for *superior* in this context is *positive abnormal* in the sense of higher than expected given the asset's risk (as measured, according to capital market theory, by the asset's contribution to the risk of a well-diversified portfolio).

[5] Although the original theory of market efficiency does not quantify this speed, the basic idea is that it is sufficiently swift to make it impossible to consistently earn abnormal profits. Chordia, Roll, and Subrahmanyam (2005) suggest that the adjustment to information on the New York Stock Exchange (NYSE) is between 5 and 60 minutes.

The time frame for an asset's price to incorporate information must be at least as long as the shortest time a trader needs to execute a transaction in the asset. In certain markets, such as foreign exchange and developed equity markets, market efficiency relative to certain types of information has been studied using time frames as short as one minute or less. If the time frame of price adjustment allows many traders to earn profits with little risk, then the market is relatively inefficient. These considerations lead to the observation that market efficiency can be viewed as falling on a continuum.

Finally, an important point is that in an efficient market, prices should be expected to react only to the elements of information releases that are not anticipated fully by investors—that is, to the "unexpected" or "surprise" element of such releases. Investors process the unexpected information and revise expectations (for example, about an asset's future cash flows, risk, or required rate of return) accordingly. The revised expectations enter or get incorporated in the asset price through trades in the asset. Market participants who process the news and believe that at the current market price an asset does not offer sufficient compensation for its perceived risk will tend to sell it or even sell it short. Market participants with opposite views should be buyers. In this way the market establishes the price that balances the various opinions after expectations are revised.

EXAMPLE 2

Price Reaction to the Default on a Bond Issue

Suppose that a speculative-grade bond issuer announces, just before bond markets open, that it will default on an upcoming interest payment. In the announcement, the issuer confirms various reports made in the financial media in the period leading up to the announcement. Prior to the issuer's announcement, the financial news media reported the following: 1) suppliers of the company were making deliveries only for cash payment, reducing the company's liquidity; 2) the issuer's financial condition had probably deteriorated to the point that it lacked the cash to meet an upcoming interest payment; and 3) although public capital markets were closed to the company, it was negotiating with a bank for a private loan that would permit it to meet its interest payment and continue operations for at least nine months. If the issuer defaults on the bond, the consensus opinion of analysts is that bondholders will recover approximately $0.36 to $0.38 per dollar face value.

1. If the market for the bond is efficient, the bond's market price is *most likely* to fully reflect the bond's value after default:

    A. in the period leading up to the announcement.

    B. in the first trade prices after the market opens on the announcement day.

    C. when the issuer actually misses the payment on the interest payment date.

Solution to 1:

B is correct. The announcement removed any uncertainty about default. In the period leading up to the announcement, the bond's market price incorporated a probability of default, but the price would not have fully reflected the bond's value after default. The possibility that a bank loan might permit the company to avoid default was not eliminated until the announcement.

2. If the market for the bond is efficient, the piece of information that bond investors *most likely* focus on in the issuer's announcement is that the issuer had:

   A. failed in its negotiations for a bank loan.
   B. lacked the cash to meet the upcoming interest payment.
   C. been required to make cash payments for supplier deliveries.

Solution to 2:

A is correct. The failure of the loan negotiations first becomes known in this announcement. The failure implies default.

Market Value versus Intrinsic Value

Market value is the price at which an asset can currently be bought or sold. **Intrinsic value** (sometimes called **fundamental value**) is, broadly speaking, the value that would be placed on it by investors if they had a complete understanding of the asset's investment characteristics.[6] For a bond, for example, such information would include its interest (coupon) rate, principal value, the timing of its interest and principal payments, the other terms of the bond contract (indenture), a precise understanding of its default risk, the liquidity of its market, and other issue-specific items. In addition, market variables such as the term structure of interest rates and the size of various market premiums applying to the issue (for default risk, etc.) would enter into a discounted cash flow estimate of the bond's intrinsic value (discounted cash flow models are often used for such estimates). The word *estimate* is used because in practice, intrinsic value can be estimated but is not known for certain.

If investors believe a market is highly *efficient*, they will usually accept market prices as accurately reflecting intrinsic values. Discrepancies between market price and intrinsic value are the basis for profitable active investment. Active investors seek to own assets selling below perceived intrinsic value in the marketplace and to sell or sell short assets selling above perceived intrinsic value.

If investors believe an asset market is relatively *inefficient*, they may try to develop an independent estimate of intrinsic value. The challenge for investors and analysts is estimating an asset's intrinsic value. Numerous theories and models, including the dividend discount model, can be used to estimate an asset's intrinsic value, but they all require some form of judgment regarding the size, timing, and riskiness of the future cash flows associated with the asset. The more complex an asset's future cash flows, the more difficult it is to estimate its intrinsic value. These complexities and the estimates of an asset's market value are reflected in the market through the buying and selling of assets. The market value of an asset represents the intersection of supply and demand—the point that is low enough to induce at least one investor to buy while being high enough to induce at least one investor to sell. Because information relevant to valuation flows continually to investors, estimates of intrinsic value change, and hence, market values change.

---

6 Intrinsic value is often defined as the present value of all expected future cash flows of the asset.

> **EXAMPLE 3**
>
> ### Intrinsic Value
>
> 1. An analyst estimates that a security's intrinsic value is lower than its market value. The security appears to be:
>   - **A.** undervalued.
>   - **B.** fairly valued.
>   - **C.** overvalued.
>
> **Solution to 1:**
>
> C is correct. The market is valuing the asset at more than its true worth.
>
> 2. A market in which assets' market values are, on average, equal to or nearly equal to intrinsic values is *best described* as a market that is attractive for:
>   - **A.** active investment.
>   - **B.** passive investment.
>   - **C.** both active and passive investment.
>
> **Solution to 2:**
>
> B is correct because an active investment is not expected to earn superior risk-adjusted returns if the market is efficient. The additional costs of active investment are not justified in such a market.
>
> 3. Suppose that the future cash flows of an asset are accurately estimated. The asset trades in a market that you believe is efficient based on most evidence, but your estimate of the asset's intrinsic value exceeds the asset's market value by a moderate amount. The *most likely* conclusion is that you have:
>   - **A.** overestimated the asset's risk.
>   - **B.** underestimated the asset's risk.
>   - **C.** identified a market inefficiency.
>
> **Solution to 3:**
>
> B is correct. If risk is underestimated, the discount rate being applied to find the present value of the expected cash flows (estimated intrinsic value) will be too low and the intrinsic value estimate will be too high.

3. FACTORS AFFECTING MARKET EFFICIENCY INCLUDING TRADING COSTS

- [ ] describe market efficiency and related concepts, including their importance to investment practitioners
- [ ] explain factors that affect a market's efficiency

For markets to be efficient, prices should adjust quickly and rationally to the release of new information. In other words, prices of assets in an efficient market should "fully reflect" all information. Financial markets, however, are generally not classified at the two extremes as either completely inefficient or completely efficient but, rather, as exhibiting various degrees of efficiency. In other words, market efficiency should be viewed as falling on a continuum between extremes of completely efficient, at one end, and completely inefficient, at the other. Asset prices in a highly efficient market, by definition, reflect information more quickly and more accurately than in a less-efficient market. These degrees of efficiency also vary through time, across geographical markets, and by type of market. A number of factors contribute to and impede the degree of efficiency in a financial market.

Market Participants

One of the most critical factors contributing to the degree of efficiency in a market is the number of market participants. Consider the following example that illustrates the relationship between the number of market participants and market efficiency.

EXAMPLE 4

Illustration of Market Efficiency

Assume that the shares of a small market capitalization (cap) company trade on a public stock exchange. Because of its size, it is not considered "blue-chip" and not many professional investors follow the activities of the company.[7] A small-cap fund analyst reports that the most recent annual operating performance of the company has been surprisingly good, considering the recent slump in its industry. The company's share price, however, has been slow to react to the positive financial results because the company is not being recommended by the majority of research analysts. This mispricing implies that the market for this company's shares is less than fully efficient. The small-cap fund analyst recognizes the opportunity and immediately recommends the purchase of the company's shares. The share price gradually increases as more investors purchase the shares once the news of the mispricing spreads through the market. As a result, it takes a few days for the share price to fully reflect the information.

Six months later, the company reports another solid set of interim financial results. But because the previous mispricing and subsequent profit opportunities have become known in the market, the number of analysts following the company's shares has increased substantially. As a result, as soon as unexpected information about the positive interim results are released to the public, a large number of buy orders quickly drive up the stock price, thereby making the market for these shares more efficient than before.

A large number of investors (individual and institutional) follow the major financial markets closely on a daily basis, and if mispricings exist in these markets, as illustrated by the example, investors will act so that these mispricings disappear quickly. Besides the number of investors, the number of financial analysts who follow or analyze a security or asset should be positively related to market efficiency. The number of market participants and resulting trading activity can vary significantly through time. A lack of trading activity can cause or accentuate other market imperfections that impede market efficiency. In fact, in many of these markets, trading in many of

---

[7] A "blue-chip" share is one from a well-recognized company that is considered to be high quality but low risk. This term generally refers to a company that has a long history of earnings and paying dividends.

the listed stocks is restricted for foreigners. By nature, this limitation reduces the number of market participants, restricts the potential for trading activity, and hence reduces market efficiency.

> **EXAMPLE 5**
>
> ### Factors Affecting Market Efficiency
>
> 1. The expected effect on market efficiency of opening a securities market to trading by foreigners would *most likely* be to:
>   - **A.** decrease market efficiency.
>   - **B.** leave market efficiency unchanged.
>   - **C.** increase market efficiency.
>
> **Solution:**
>
> C is correct. The opening of markets as described should increase market efficiency by increasing the number of market participants.

Information Availability and Financial Disclosure

Information availability (e.g., an active financial news media) and financial disclosure should promote market efficiency. Information regarding trading activity and traded companies in such markets as the New York Stock Exchange, the London Stock Exchange, and the Tokyo Stock Exchange is readily available. Many investors and analysts participate in these markets, and analyst coverage of listed companies is typically substantial. As a result, these markets are quite efficient. In contrast, trading activity and material information availability may be lacking in smaller securities markets, such as those operating in some emerging markets.

Similarly, significant differences may exist in the efficiency of different types of markets. For example, many securities trade primarily or exclusively in dealer or over-the-counter (OTC) markets, including bonds, money market instruments, currencies, mortgage-backed securities, swaps, and forward contracts. The information provided by the dealers that serve as market makers for these markets can vary significantly in quality and quantity, both through time and across different product markets.

Treating all market participants fairly is critical for the integrity of the market and explains why regulators place such an emphasis on "fair, orderly, and efficient markets."[8] A key element of this fairness is that all investors have access to the information necessary to value securities that trade in the market. Rules and regulations that promote fairness and efficiency in a market include those pertaining to the disclosure of information and illegal insider trading.

For example, US Securities and Exchange Commission's (SEC's) Regulation FD (Fair Disclosure) requires that if security issuers provide nonpublic information to some market professionals or investors, they must also disclose this information to the public.[9] This requirement helps provide equal and fair opportunities, which is important in encouraging participation in the market. A related issue deals with illegal insider trading. The SEC's rules, along with court cases, define illegal insider trading as trading in securities by market participants who are considered insiders "while in

---

8 "The Investor's Advocate: How the SEC Protects Investors, Maintains Market Integrity, and Facilitates Capital Formation," US Securities and Exchange Commission (www.sec.gov/about/whatwedo.shtml).
9 Regulation FD, "Selective Disclosure and Insider Trading," 17 CFR Parts 240, 243, and 249, effective 23 October 2000.

possession of material, nonpublic information about the security."[10] Although these rules cannot guarantee that some participants will not have an advantage over others and that insiders will not trade on the basis of inside information, the civil and criminal penalties associated with breaking these rules are intended to discourage illegal insider trading and promote fairness. In the European Union, insider trading laws are generally enshrined in legislation and enforced by regulatory and judicial authorities.[11]

Limits to Trading

Arbitrage is a set of transactions that produces riskless profits. Arbitrageurs are traders who engage in such trades to benefit from pricing discrepancies (inefficiencies) in markets. Such trading activity contributes to market efficiency. For example, if an asset is traded in two markets but at different prices, the actions of buying the asset in the market in which it is underpriced and selling the asset in the market in which it is overpriced will eventually bring these two prices together. The presence of these arbitrageurs helps pricing discrepancies disappear quickly. Obviously, market efficiency is impeded by any limitation on arbitrage resulting from operating inefficiencies, such as difficulties in executing trades in a timely manner, prohibitively high trading costs, and a lack of transparency in market prices.

Some market experts argue that restrictions on short selling limit arbitrage trading, which impedes market efficiency. **Short selling** is the transaction whereby an investor sells shares that he or she does not own by borrowing them from a broker and agreeing to replace them at a future date. Short selling allows investors to sell securities they believe to be overvalued, much in the same way they can buy those they believe to be undervalued. In theory, such activities promote more efficient pricing. Regulators and others, however, have argued that short selling may exaggerate downward market movements, leading to crashes in affected securities. In contrast, some researchers report evidence indicating that when investors are unable to borrow securities, that is to short the security, or when costs to borrow shares are high, market prices may deviate from intrinsic values.[12] Furthermore, research suggests that short selling is helpful in price discovery (that is, it facilitates supply and demand in determining prices).[13]

Transaction Costs and Information-Acquisition Costs

The costs incurred by traders in identifying and exploiting possible market inefficiencies affect the interpretation of market efficiency. The two types of costs to consider are transaction costs and information-acquisition costs.

- *Transaction costs*: Practically, transaction costs are incurred in trading to exploit any perceived market inefficiency. Thus, "efficient" should be viewed as efficient within the bounds of transaction costs. For example, consider a violation of the principle that two identical assets should sell for the same price in different markets. Such a violation can be considered to be a rather simple possible exception to market efficiency because prices appear to

---

10 Although not the focus of this particular reading, it is important to note that a party is considered an insider not only when the individual is a corporate insider, such as an officer or director, but also when the individual is aware that the information is nonpublic information [Securities and Exchange Commission, Rules 10b5-1 ("Trading on the Basis of Material Nonpublic Information in Insider Trading Cases") and Rule 10b5-2 "Duties of Trust or Confidence in Misappropriation Insider Trading Cases")].

11 See the European Union's Market Abuse Regulation (Regulation (EU) no. 596/2014 of the European Parliament and of the Council of 16 April 2014 on market abuse) and Directive for Criminal Sanctions for Market Abuse (Directive 2014/57/EU of the European Parliament and of the Council of 16 April 2014 on criminal sanctions for market abuse).

12 See Deng, Mortal, and Gupta (2017) and references therein."

13 See Bris, Goetzmann, and Zhu (2009).

be inconsistently processing information. To exploit the violation, a trader could arbitrage by simultaneously shorting the asset in the higher-price market and buying the asset in the lower-price market. If the price discrepancy between the two markets is smaller than the transaction costs involved in the arbitrage for the lowest cost traders, the arbitrage will not occur, and both prices are in effect efficient within the bounds of arbitrage. These bounds of arbitrage are relatively narrow in highly liquid markets, such as the market for US Treasury bills, but could be wide in illiquid markets.

- *Information-acquisition costs:* Practically, expenses are always associated with gathering and analyzing information. New information is incorporated in transaction prices by traders placing trades based on their analysis of information. Active investors who place trades based on information they have gathered and analyzed play a key role in market prices adjusting to reflect new information. The classic view of market efficiency is that active investors incur information acquisition costs but that money is wasted because prices already reflect all relevant information. This view of efficiency is very strict in the sense of viewing a market as inefficient if active investing can recapture any part of the costs, such as research costs and active asset selection. Grossman and Stiglitz (1980) argue that prices must offer a return to information acquisition; in equilibrium, if markets are efficient, returns net of such expenses are just fair returns for the risk incurred. The modern perspective views a market as inefficient if, after deducting such costs, active investing can earn superior returns. Gross of expenses, a return should accrue to information acquisition in an efficient market.

In summary, a modern perspective calls for the investor to consider transaction costs and information-acquisition costs when evaluating the efficiency of a market. A price discrepancy must be sufficiently large to leave the investor with a profit (adjusted for risk) after taking account of the transaction costs and information-acquisition costs to reach the conclusion that the discrepancy may represent a market inefficiency. Prices may somewhat less than fully reflect available information without there being a true market opportunity for active investors.

4. FORMS OF MARKET EFFICIENCY

☐ contrast weak-form, semi-strong-form, and strong-form market efficiency

Eugene Fama developed a framework for describing the degree to which markets are efficient.[14] In his efficient market hypothesis, markets are efficient when prices reflect *all* relevant information at any point in time. This means that the market prices observed for securities, for example, reflect the information available at the time.

In his framework, Fama defines three forms of efficiency: weak, semi-strong, and strong. Each form is defined with respect to the available information that is reflected in prices.

---

14 Fama (1970).

Forms of Market Efficiency

Forms of Market Efficiency	Market Prices Reflect:		
	Past Market Data	Public Information	Private Information
Weak form of market efficiency	✓		
Semi-strong form of market efficiency	✓	✓	
Strong form of market efficiency	✓	✓	✓

A finding that investors can consistently earn **abnormal returns** by trading on the basis of information is evidence contrary to market efficiency. In general, abnormal returns are returns in excess of those expected given a security's risk and the market's return. In other words, abnormal return equals actual return less expected return.

Weak Form

In the **weak-form efficient market hypothesis**, security prices fully reflect *all past market data*, which refers to all historical price and trading volume information. If markets are weak-form efficient, past trading data are already reflected in current prices and investors cannot predict future price changes by extrapolating prices or patterns of prices from the past.[15]

Tests of whether securities markets are weak-form efficient require looking at patterns of prices. One approach is to see whether there is any serial correlation in security returns, which would imply a predictable pattern.[16] Although there is some weak correlation in daily security returns, there is not enough correlation to make this a profitable trading rule after considering transaction costs.

An alternative approach to test weak-form efficiency is to examine specific trading rules that attempt to exploit historical trading data. If any such trading rule consistently generates abnormal risk-adjusted returns after trading costs, this evidence will contradict weak-form efficiency. This approach is commonly associated with **technical analysis**, which involves the analysis of historical trading information (primarily pricing and volume data) in an attempt to identify recurring patterns in the trading data that can be used to guide investment decisions. Many technical analysts, also referred to as "technicians," argue that many movements in stock prices are based, in large part, on psychology. Many technicians attempt to predict how market participants will behave, based on analyses of past behavior, and then trade on those predictions. Technicians often argue that simple statistical tests of trading rules are not conclusive because they are not applied to the more sophisticated trading strategies that can be used and that the research excludes the technician's subjective judgment. Thus, it is difficult to definitively refute this assertion because there are an unlimited number of possible technical trading rules.

Can technical analysts profit from trading on past trends? Overall, the evidence indicates that investors cannot consistently earn abnormal profits using past prices or other technical analysis strategies in developed markets.[17] Some evidence suggests, however, that there are opportunities to profit on technical analysis in countries with developing markets, including Hungary, Bangladesh, and Turkey, among others.[18]

---

15 Market efficiency should not be confused with the random walk hypothesis, in which price changes over time are independent of one another. A random walk model is one of many alternative expected return generating models. Market efficiency does not require that returns follow a random walk.
16 Serial correlation is a statistical measure of the degree to which the returns in one period are related to the returns in another period.
17 Bessembinder and Chan (1998) and Fifield, Power, and Sinclair (2005).
18 Fifield, Power, and Sinclair (2005), Chen and Li (2006), and Mobarek, Mollah, and Bhuyan (2008).

Semi-Strong Form

In a **semi-strong-form efficient market**, prices reflect all publicly known and available information. Publicly available information includes financial statement data (such as earnings, dividends, corporate investments, changes in management, etc.) and financial market data (such as closing prices, shares traded, etc.). Therefore, the semi-strong form of market efficiency encompasses the weak form. In other words, if a market is semi-strong efficient, then it must also be weak-form efficient. A market that quickly incorporates all publicly available information into its prices is semi-strong efficient.

In a semi-strong market, efforts to analyze publicly available information are futile. That is, analyzing earnings announcements of companies to identify underpriced or overpriced securities is pointless because the prices of these securities already reflect all publicly available information. If markets are semi-strong efficient, no single investor has access to information that is not already available to other market participants, and as a consequence, no single investor can gain an advantage in predicting future security prices. In a semi-strong efficient market, prices adjust quickly and accurately to new information. Suppose a company announces earnings that are higher than expected. In a semi-strong efficient market, investors would not be able to act on this announcement and earn abnormal returns.

A common empirical test of investors' reaction to information releases is the event study. Suppose a researcher wants to test whether investors react to the announcement that the company is paying a special dividend. The researcher identifies a sample period and then those companies that paid a special dividend in the period and the date of the announcement. Then, for each company's stock, the researcher calculates the expected return on the share for the event date. This expected return may be based on many different models, including the capital asset pricing model, a simple market model, or a market index return. The researcher calculates the excess return as the difference between the actual return and the expected return. Once the researcher has calculated the event's excess return for each share, statistical tests are conducted to see whether the abnormal returns are statistically different from zero. The process of an event study is outlined in Exhibit 1.

Forms of Market Efficiency

Exhibit 1: The Event Study Process

```
Identify the period of study
            ↓
Identify the stocks associated with the event within the study period
            ↓
Estimate the expected return for each company for the announcement
            ↓
Calculate the excess return for each company in the sample as the actual
return on the announcement date, less the expected return
            ↓
Perform statistical analyses on the excess returns in the sample to see
whether these returns are different from zero
```

How do event studies relate to efficient markets? In a semi-strong efficient market, share prices react quickly and accurately to public information. Therefore, if the information is good news, such as better-than-expected earnings, one would expect the company's shares to increase immediately at the time of the announcement; if it is bad news, one would expect a swift, negative reaction. If actual returns exceed what is expected in absence of the announcement and these returns are confined to the announcement period, then they are consistent with the idea that market prices react quickly to new information. In other words, the finding of excess returns at the time of the announcement does not necessarily indicate market inefficiency. In contrast, the finding of consistent excess returns following the announcement would suggest a trading opportunity. Trading on the basis of the announcement—that is, once the announcement is made—would not, on average, yield abnormal returns.

EXAMPLE 6

Information Arrival and Market Reaction

Consider an example of a news item and its effect on a share's price. The following events related to Tesla, Inc. in August of 2018:

1 August 2018	After the market closes, Tesla, Inc., publicly reports that there was a smaller-than expected cash burn for the most recent quarter.
2 August 2018	Elon Musk, Chairman and CEO of Tesla, Inc., notifies Tesla's board of directors that he wants to take the company private. This is not public information at this point.
7 August 2018	Before the market opens, the *Financial Times* reports that a Saudi fund has a $2 billion investment in Tesla.

	During market trading, Musk announces on Twitter "Am considering taking Tesla private at $420. Funding secured." [Twitter, Elon Musk @elonmusk, 9:48 a.m., 7 August 2018]
24 August 2018	After the market closed, Musk announces that he no longer intends on taking Tesla private.

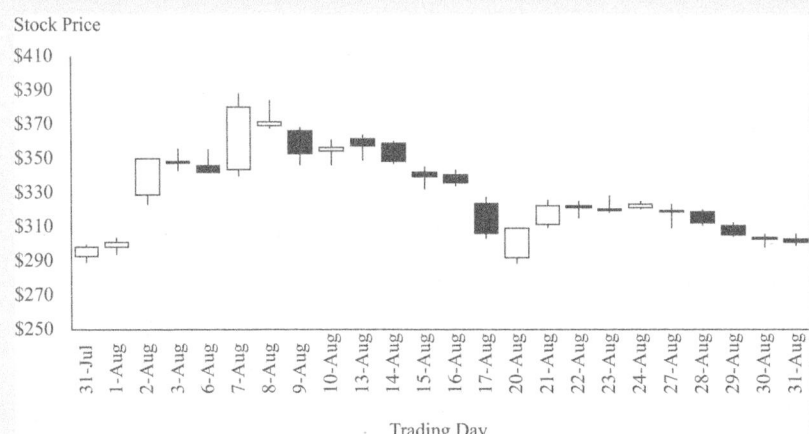

Exhibit 2: Price of Tesla, Inc. Stock: 31 July 2018–31 August 2018

Note: Open-High-Low-Close graph of Tesla's stock price, with white rectangles indicating upward movement in the day and black rectangles indicating downward movement during the day.

Source of data: Yahoo! Finance.

1. Is the fact that the price of Tesla moves up immediately on the day after the Q2 earnings (the first day of trading with this information) indicative of efficiency regarding information?

   Most likely.

2. Does the fact that the price of Tesla moves up but does not reach $420 on the day the going-private Twitter announcement is made mean that investors underreacted?

   Not necessarily. There was confusion and uncertainty about the going-private transaction at the time, so the price did not close in on the proposed $420 per share for going private.

3. Does the fact that the market price of the stock declined well before the issue of going-private was laid to rest by Musk mean that the market is inefficient?

   Not necessarily. There were numerous analyses, discussions, and other news regarding the likelihood of the transaction, all of which was incorporated in the price of the stock before the going-private transaction was dismissed by Musk.

Researchers have examined many different company-specific information events, including stock splits, dividend changes, and merger announcements, as well as economy-wide events, such as regulation changes and tax rate changes. The results of most research are consistent with the view that developed securities markets might be semi-strong efficient. But some evidence suggests that the markets in developing countries may not be semi-strong efficient.[19]

Strong Form

In a **strong-form efficient market**, security prices fully reflect both public and private information. A market that is strong-form efficient is, by definition, also semi-strong- and weak-form efficient. In the case of a strong-form efficient market, insiders would not be able to earn abnormal returns from trading on the basis of private information. A strong-form efficient market also means that prices reflect all private information, which means that prices reflect everything that the management of a company knows about the financial condition of the company that has not been publicly released. However, this is not likely because of the strong prohibitions against insider trading that are found in most countries. If a market is strong-form efficient, those with insider information cannot earn abnormal returns.

Researchers test whether a market is strong-form efficient by testing whether investors can earn abnormal profits by trading on nonpublic information. The results of these tests are consistent with the view that securities markets are not strong-form efficient; many studies have found that abnormal profits can be earned when nonpublic information is used.[20]

IMPLICATIONS OF THE EFFICIENT MARKET HYPOTHESIS

5

☐ explain the implications of each form of market efficiency for fundamental analysis, technical analysis, and the choice between active and passive portfolio management

The implications of efficient markets to investment managers and analysts are important because they affect the value of securities and how these securities are managed. Several implications can be drawn from the evidence on efficient markets for developed markets:

- Securities markets are weak-form efficient, and therefore, investors cannot earn abnormal returns by trading on the basis of past trends in price.
- Securities markets are semi-strong efficient, and therefore, analysts who collect and analyze information must consider whether that information is already reflected in security prices and how any new information affects a security's value.
- Securities markets are not strong-form efficient because securities laws are intended to prevent exploitation of private information.

---

19 See Gan, Lee, Hwa, and Zhang (2005) hnd Raja, Sudhahar, and Selvam (2009).
20 Evidence that finds that markets are not strong-form efficient include Jaffe (1974) and Rozeff and Zaman (1988).

Fundamental Analysis

Fundamental analysis is the examination of publicly available information and the formulation of forecasts to estimate the intrinsic value of assets. Fundamental analysis involves the estimation of an asset's value using company data, such as earnings and sales forecasts, and risk estimates as well as industry and economic data, such as economic growth, inflation, and interest rates. Buy and sell decisions depend on whether the current market price is less than or greater than the estimated intrinsic value.

The semi-strong form of market efficiency says that all available public information is reflected in current prices. So, what good is fundamental analysis? Fundamental analysis is necessary in a well-functioning market because this analysis helps the market participants understand the value implications of information. In other words, fundamental analysis facilitates a semi-strong efficient market by disseminating value-relevant information. And, although fundamental analysis requires costly information, this analysis can be profitable in terms of generating abnormal returns if the analyst creates a comparative advantage with respect to this information.[21]

Technical Analysis

Investors using **technical analysis** attempt to profit by looking at patterns of prices and trading volume. Although some price patterns persist, exploiting these patterns may be too costly and, hence, would not produce abnormal returns.

Consider a situation in which a pattern of prices exists. With so many investors examining prices, this pattern will be detected. If profitable, exploiting this pattern will eventually affect prices such that this pattern will no longer exist; it will be arbitraged away. In other words, by detecting and exploiting patterns in prices, technical analysts assist markets in maintaining weak-form efficiency. Does this mean that technical analysts cannot earn abnormal profits? Not necessarily, because there may be a possibility of earning abnormal profits from a pricing inefficiency. But would it be possible to earn abnormal returns on a consistent basis from exploiting such a pattern? No, because the actions of market participants will arbitrage this opportunity quickly, and the inefficiency will no longer exist.

Portfolio Management

If securities markets are weak-form and semi-strong-form efficient, the implication is that active trading, whether attempting to exploit price patterns or public information, is not likely to generate abnormal returns. In other words, portfolio managers cannot beat the market on a consistent basis, so therefore, passive portfolio management should outperform active portfolio management. Researchers have observed that mutual funds do not, on average, outperform the market on a risk-adjusted basis.[22] Mutual funds perform, on average, similar to the market before considering fees and expenses and perform worse than the market, on average, once fees and expenses are considered. Even if a mutual fund is not actively managed, there are costs to managing these funds, which reduces net returns.

So, what good are portfolio managers? The role of a portfolio manager is not necessarily to beat the market but, rather, to establish and manage a portfolio consistent with the portfolio's objectives, with appropriate diversification and asset allocation, while taking into consideration the risk preferences and tax situation of the investor.

---

21 Brealey (1983).
22 See Malkiel (1995). One of the challenges to evaluating mutual fund performance is that the researcher must control for survivorship bias.

MARKET PRICING ANOMALIES - TIME SERIES AND CROSS-SECTIONAL

☐ describe market anomalies

Although considerable evidence shows that markets are efficient, researchers have identified a number of apparent market inefficiencies or anomalies. These market anomalies, if persistent, are exceptions to the notion of market efficiency. Researchers conclude that a **market anomaly** may be present if a change in the price of an asset or security cannot directly be linked to current relevant information known in the market or to the release of new information into the market.

The validity of any evidence supporting the potential existence of a market inefficiency or anomaly must be *consistent* over reasonably long periods. Otherwise, a detected market anomaly may largely be an artifact of the sample period chosen. In the widespread search for discovering profitable anomalies, many findings could simply be the product of a process called **data mining**, also known as **data snooping**. In generally accepted research practice, an initial hypothesis is developed which is based on economic rationale. Tests are then conducted on objectively selected data to either confirm or reject the original hypothesis. However, with data mining the process is typically reversed: data are examined with the intent to develop a hypothesis, instead of developing a hypothesis first. This is done by analyzing data in various manners, and even utilizing different empirical approaches until you find support for a desired result, in this case a profitable anomaly.

Can researchers look back on data and find a trading strategy that would have yielded abnormal returns? Absolutely. Enough data snooping often can detect a trading strategy that would have worked in the past by chance alone. But in an efficient market, such a strategy is unlikely to generate abnormal returns on a consistent basis in the future. Also, although identified anomalies may appear to produce excess returns, it is generally difficult to profitably exploit the anomalies after accounting for risk, trading costs, and so on.

Several well-known anomalies are listed in Exhibit 3. This list is by no means exhaustive, but it provides information on the breadth of the anomalies. A few of these anomalies are discussed in more detail in the following sections. The anomalies are placed into categories based on the research method that identified the anomaly. Time-series anomalies were identified using time series of data. Cross-sectional anomalies were identified based on analyzing a cross section of companies that differ on some key characteristics. Other anomalies were identified by a variety of means, including event studies.

Exhibit 3: Sampling of Observed Pricing Anomalies

Time Series	Cross-Sectional	Other
January effect	Size effect	Closed-end fund discount
Day-of-the-week effect	Value effect	Earnings surprise
Weekend effect	Book-to-market ratios	Initial public offerings
Turn-of-the-month effect	P/E ratio effect	Distressed securities effect
Holiday effect	Value Line enigma	Stock splits
Time-of-day effect		Super Bowl

Time Series	Cross-Sectional	Other
Momentum		
Overreaction		

Time-Series Anomalies

Two of the major categories of time-series anomalies that have been documented are 1) calendar anomalies and 2) momentum and overreaction anomalies.

Calendar Anomalies

In the 1980s, a number of researchers reported that stock market returns in January were significantly higher compared to the rest of the months of the year, with most of the abnormal returns reported during the first five trading days in January. Since its first documentation in the 1980s, this pattern, known as the **January effect**, has been observed in most equity markets around the world. This anomaly is also known as the **turn-of-the-year effect**, or even often referred to as the "small firm in January effect" because it is most frequently observed for the returns of small market capitalization stocks.[23]

The January effect contradicts the efficient market hypothesis because excess returns in January are not attributed to any new and relevant information or news. A number of reasons have been suggested for this anomaly, including tax-loss selling. Researchers have speculated that, in order to reduce their tax liabilities, investors sell their "loser" securities in December for the purpose of creating capital losses, which can then be used to offset any capital gains. A related explanation is that these losers tend to be small-cap stocks with high volatility.[24] This increased supply of equities in December depresses their prices, and then these shares are bought in early January at relatively attractive prices. This demand then drives their prices up again. Overall, the evidence indicates that tax-loss selling may account for a portion of January abnormal returns, but it does not explain all of it.

Another possible explanation for the anomaly is so-called "window dressing", a practice in which portfolio managers sell their riskier securities prior to 31 December. The explanation is as follows: many portfolio managers prepare the annual reports of their portfolio holdings as of 31 December. Selling riskier securities is an attempt to make their portfolios appear less risky. After 31 December, a portfolio manager would then simply purchase riskier securities in an attempt to earn higher returns. However, similar to the tax-loss selling hypothesis, the research evidence in support of the window dressing hypothesis explains some, but not all, of the anomaly.

Recent evidence for both stock and bond returns suggests that the January effect is not persistent and, therefore, is not a pricing anomaly. Once an appropriate adjustment for risk is made, the January "effect" does not produce abnormal returns.[25]

Several other calendar effects, including the day-of-the-week and the weekend effects,[26] have been found. These anomalies are summarized in Exhibit 4.[27] But like the size effect, which will be described later, most of these anomalies have been eliminated

---

23 There is also evidence of a January effect in bond returns that is more prevalent in high-yield corporate bonds, similar to the small-company effect for stocks.
24 See Roll (1983).
25 See, for example, Kim (2006).
26 For a discussion of several of these anomalous patterns, see Jacobs and Levy (1988).
27 The weekend effect consists of a pattern of returns around the weekend: abnormal positive returns on Fridays followed by abnormally negative returns on Mondays. This is a day-of-the-week effect that specifically links Friday and Monday returns. It is interesting to note that in 2009, the weekend effect in the United States was inverted, with 80 percent of the gains from March 2009 onward coming from the

over time. One view is that the anomalies have been exploited such that the effect has been arbitraged away. Another view, however, is that increasingly sophisticated statistical methodologies fail to detect pricing inefficiencies.

Exhibit 4: Calendar-Based Anomalies

Anomaly	Observation
Turn-of-the-month effect	Returns tend to be higher on the last trading day of the month and the first three trading days of the next month.
Day-of-the-week effect	The average Monday return is negative and lower than the average returns for the other four days, which are all positive.
Weekend effect	Returns on weekends tend to be lower than returns on weekdays.
Holiday effect	Returns on stocks in the day prior to market holidays tend to be higher than other days.

Momentum and Overreaction Anomalies

Momentum anomalies relate to short-term share price patterns. One of the earliest studies to identify this type of anomaly was conducted by Werner DeBondt and Richard Thaler, who argued that investors overreact to the release of unexpected public information.[28] Therefore, stock prices will be inflated (depressed) for those companies releasing good (bad) information. This anomaly has become known as the overreaction effect. Using the overreaction effect, they proposed a strategy that involved buying "loser" portfolios and selling "winner" portfolios. They defined stocks as winners or losers based on their total returns over the previous three- to five-year period. They found that in a subsequent period, the loser portfolios outperformed the market, while the winner portfolios underperformed the market. Similar patterns have been documented in many, but not all, global stock markets as well as in bond markets. One criticism is that the observed anomaly may be the result of statistical problems in the analysis.

A contradiction to weak-form efficiency occurs when securities that have experienced high returns in the short term tend to continue to generate higher returns in subsequent periods.[29] Empirical support for the existence of momentum in stock returns in most stock markets around the world is well documented. If investors can trade on the basis of momentum and earn abnormal profits, then this anomaly contradicts the weak form of the efficient market hypothesis because it represents a pattern in prices that can be exploited by simply using historical price information.[30]

Researchers have argued that the existence of momentum is rational and not contrary to market efficiency because it is plausible that there are shocks to the expected growth rates of cash flows to shareholders and that these shocks induce a

---

first trading day of the week.
28 DeBondt and Thaler (1985).
29 Notice that this pattern lies in sharp contrast to DeBondt and Thaler's reversal pattern that is displayed over longer periods of time. In theory, the two patterns could be related. In other words, it is feasible that prices are bid up extremely high, perhaps too high, in the short term for companies that are doing well. In the longer term (three-to-five years), the prices of these short-term winners correct themselves and they do poorly.
30 Jegadeesh and Titman (2001).

serial correlation that is rational and short lived.[31] In other words, having stocks with some degree of momentum in their security returns may not imply irrationality but, rather, may reflect prices adjusting to a shock in growth rates.

Cross-Sectional Anomalies

Two of the most researched cross-sectional anomalies in financial markets are the size effect and the value effect.

Size Effect

The size effect results from the observation that equities of small-cap companies tend to outperform equities of large-cap companies on a risk-adjusted basis. Many researchers documented a small-company effect soon after the initial research was published in 1981. This effect, however, was not apparent in subsequent studies.[32] Part of the reason that the size effect was not confirmed by subsequent studies may be because of the fact that if it were truly an anomaly, investors acting on this effect would reduce any potential returns. But some of the explanation may simply be that the effect as originally observed was a chance outcome and, therefore, not actually an inefficiency.

Value Effect

A number of global empirical studies have shown that value stocks, which are generally referred to as stocks that have below-average price-to-earnings (P/E) and market-to-book (M/B) ratios, and above-average dividend yields, have consistently outperformed growth stocks over long periods of time.[33] If the effect persists, the value stock anomaly contradicts semi-strong market efficiency because all the information used to categorize stocks in this manner is publicly available.

Fama and French developed a three-factor model to predict stock returns.[34] In addition to the use of market returns as specified by the capital asset pricing model (CAPM), the Fama and French model also includes the size of the company as measured by the market value of its equity and the company's book value of equity divided by its market value of equity, which is a value measure. The Fama and French model captures risk dimensions related to stock returns that the CAPM model does not consider. Fama and French find that when they apply the three-factor model instead of the CAPM, the value stock anomaly disappears.

7. OTHER ANOMALIES, IMPLICATIONS OF MARKET PRICING ANOMALIES

☐ describe market anomalies

---

31 Johnson (2002).
32 Although a large number of studies documents a small-company effect, these studies are concentrated in a period similar to that of the original research and, therefore, use a similar data set. The key to whether something is a true anomaly is persistence in out-of-sample tests. Fama and French (2008) document that the size effect is apparent only in microcap stocks but not in small- and large-cap stocks and these microcap stocks may have a significant influence in studies that document a size effect.
33 For example, see Capaul, Rowley, and Sharpe (1993) and Fama and French (1998).
34 Fama and French (1995).

A number of additional anomalies has been documented in the financial markets, including the existence of closed-end investment fund discounts, price reactions to the release of earnings information, returns of initial public offerings, and the predictability of returns based on prior information.

Closed-End Investment Fund Discounts

A closed-end investment fund issues a fixed number of shares at inception and does not sell any additional shares after the initial offering. Therefore, the fund capitalization is fixed unless a secondary public offering is made. The shares of closed-end funds trade on stock markets like any other shares in the equity market (i.e., their prices are determined by supply and demand).

Theoretically, these shares should trade at a price approximately equal to their net asset value (NAV) per share, which is simply the total market value of the fund's security holdings less any liabilities divided by the number of shares outstanding. An abundance of research, however, has documented that, on average, closed-end funds trade at a discount from NAV. Most studies have documented average discounts in the 4–10 percent range, although individual funds have traded at discounts exceeding 50 percent and others have traded at large premiums.[35]

The closed-end fund discount presents a puzzle because conceptually, an investor could purchase all the shares in the fund, liquidate the fund, and end up making a profit. Some researchers have suggested that these discounts are attributed to management fees or expectations of the managers' performance, but these explanations are not supported by the evidence.[36] An alternative explanation for the discount is that tax liabilities are associated with unrealized capital gains and losses that exist prior to when the investor bought the shares, and hence, the investor does not have complete control over the timing of the realization of gains and losses.[37] Although the evidence supports this hypothesis to a certain extent, the tax effect is not large enough to explain the entire discount. Finally, it has often been argued that the discounts exist because of liquidity problems and errors in calculating NAV. The illiquidity explanation is plausible if shares are recorded at the same price as more liquid, publicly traded stocks; some evidence supports this assertion. But as with tax reasons, liquidity issues explain only a portion of the discount effect.

Can these discounts be exploited to earn abnormal returns if transaction costs are taken into account? No. First, the transaction costs involved in exploiting the discount—buying all the shares and liquidating the fund—would eliminate any profit.[38] Second, these discounts tend to revert to zero over time. Hence, a strategy to trade on the basis of these discounts would not likely be profitable.[39]

Earnings Surprise

Although most event studies have supported semi-strong market efficiency, some researchers have provided evidence that questions semi-strong market efficiency. One of these studies relates to the extensively examined adjustment of stock prices

---

35 See Dimson and Minio-Kozerski (1999) for a review of this literature.
36 See Lee, Sheifer, and Thaler (1990).
37 The return to owners of closed-end fund shares has three parts: 1) the price appreciation or depreciation of the shares themselves, 2) the dividends earned and distributed to owners by the fund, and 3) the capital gains and losses earned by the fund that are distributed by the fund. The explanation of the anomalous pricing has to do with the timing of the distribution of capital gains.
38 See, for example, the study by Pontiff (1996), which shows how the cost of arbitraging these discounts eliminates the profit.
39 See Pontiff (1995).

to earnings announcements.[40] The unexpected part of the earnings announcement, or **earnings surprise**, is the portion of earnings that is unanticipated by investors and, according to the efficient market hypothesis, merits a price adjustment. Positive (negative) surprises should cause appropriate and rapid price increases (decreases). Several studies have been conducted using data from numerous markets around the world. Most of the results indicate that earnings surprises are reflected quickly in stock prices, but the adjustment process is not always efficient. In particular, although a substantial adjustment occurs prior to and at the announcement date, an adjustment also occurs after the announcement.[41]

As a result of these slow price adjustments, companies that display the largest positive earnings surprises subsequently display superior stock return performance, whereas poor subsequent performance is displayed by companies with low or negative earnings surprises.[42] This finding implies that investors could earn abnormal returns using publicly available information by buying stocks of companies that had positive earnings surprises and selling those with negative surprises.

Although there is support for abnormal returns associated with earnings surprises, and some support for such returns beyond the announcement period, there is also evidence indicating that these observed abnormal returns are an artifact of studies that do not sufficiently control for transaction costs and risk.[43]

Initial Public Offerings (IPOs)

When a company offers shares of its stock to the public for the first time, it does so through an initial public offering (or IPO). This offering involves working with an investment bank that helps price and market the newly issued shares. After the offering is complete, the new shares trade on a stock market for the first time. Given the risk that investment bankers face in trying to sell a new issue for which the true price is unknown, it is perhaps not surprising to find that, on average, the initial selling price is set too low and that the price increases dramatically on the first trading day. The percentage difference between the issue price and the closing price at the end of the first day of trading is often referred to as the degree of underpricing.

The evidence suggests that, on average, investors who are able to buy the shares of an IPO at their offering price may be able to earn abnormal profits. For example, during the internet bubble of 1995–2000, many IPOs ended their first day of trading up by more than 100 percent. Such performance, however, is not always the case. Sometimes the issues are priced too high, which means that share prices drop on their first day of trading. In addition, the evidence also suggests that investors buying after the initial offering are not able to earn abnormal profits because prices adjust quickly to the "true" values, which supports semi-strong market efficiency. In fact, the subsequent long-term performance of IPOs is generally found to be below average. Taken together, the IPO underpricing and the subsequent poor performance suggests that the markets are overly optimistic initially (i.e., investors overreact).

---

40 See Jones, Rendleman, and Latané (1984).
41 Not surprisingly, it is often argued that this slow reaction contributes to a momentum pattern.
42 A similar pattern has been documented in the corporate bond market, where bond prices react too slowly to new company earnings announcements as well as to changes in company debt ratings.
43 See Brown (1997) for a summary of evidence supporting the existence of this anomaly. See Zarowin (1989) for evidence regarding the role of size in explaining abnormal returns to surprises; Alexander, Goff, and Peterson (1989) for evidence regarding transaction costs and unexpected earnings strategies; and Kim and Kim (2003) for evidence indicating that the anomalous returns can be explained by risk factors.

Other Anomalies, Implications of Market Pricing Anomalies

Some researchers have examined closely why IPOs may appear to have anomalous returns. Because of the small size of the IPO companies and the method of equally weighting the samples, what appears to be an anomaly may simply be an artifact of the methodology.[44]

Predictability of Returns Based on Prior Information

A number of researchers have documented that equity returns are related to prior information on such factors as interest rates, inflation rates, stock volatility, and dividend yields.[45] But finding that equity returns are affected by changes in economic fundamentals is not evidence of market inefficiency and would not result in abnormal trading returns.[46]

Furthermore, the relationship between stock returns and the prior information is not consistent over time. For example, in one study, the relationship between stock prices and dividend yields changed from positive to negative in different periods.[47] Hence, a trading strategy based on dividend yields would not yield consistent abnormal returns.

Implications for Investment Strategies

Although it is interesting to consider the anomalies just described, attempting to benefit from them in practice is not easy. In fact, most researchers conclude that observed anomalies are not violations of market efficiency but, rather, are the result of statistical methodologies used to detect the anomalies. As a result, if the methodologies are corrected, most of these anomalies disappear.[48] Another point to consider is that in an efficient market, overreactions may occur, but then so do under-reactions.[49] Therefore, on average, the markets are efficient. In other words, investors face challenges when they attempt to translate statistical anomalies into economic profits. Consider the following quote regarding anomalies from the *Economist* ("Frontiers of Finance Survey," 9 October 1993):

> Many can be explained away. When transactions costs are taken into account, the fact that stock prices tend to over-react to news, falling back the day after good news and bouncing up the day after bad news, proves unexploitable: price reversals are always within the bid-ask spread. Others such as the small-firm effect, work for a few years and then fail for a few years. Others prove to be merely proxies for the reward for risk taking. Many have disappeared since (and because) attention has been drawn to them.

It is difficult to envision entrusting your retirement savings to a manager whose strategy is based on buying securities on Mondays, which tends to have negative returns on average, and selling them on Fridays. For one thing, the negative Monday returns are merely an average, so on any given week, they could be positive. In addition, such a strategy would generate large trading costs. Even more importantly, investors would likely be uncomfortable investing their funds in a strategy that has no compelling underlying economic rationale.

---

44 See Brav, Geczy, and Gompers (1995).
45 See, for example, Fama and Schwert (1977) and Fama and French (1988).
46 See Fama and French (2008).
47 Schwert (2003, Chapter 15).
48 Fama (1998).
49 This point is made by Fama (1998).

8 BEHAVIORAL FINANCE

☐ describe behavioral finance and its potential relevance to understanding market anomalies

Behavioral finance examines investor behavior to understand how people make decisions, individually and collectively. Behavioral finance does not assume that people consider all available information in decision-making and act rationally by maximizing utility within budget constraints and updating expectations consistent with Bayes' formula. The resulting behaviors may affect what is observed in the financial markets.

In a broader sense, behavioral finance attempts to explain why individuals make the decisions that they do, whether these decisions are rational or irrational. The focus of much of the work in this area is on the behavioral biases that affect investment decisions. The behavior of individuals, in particular their behavioral biases, has been offered as a possible explanation for a number of pricing anomalies.

Most asset-pricing models assume that markets are rational and that the intrinsic value of a security reflects this rationality. But market efficiency and asset-pricing models do not require that each individual is rational—rather, only that the market is rational. If individuals deviate from rationality, other individuals are assumed to observe this deviation and respond accordingly. These responses move the market toward efficiency. If this does not occur in practice, it may be possible to explain some market anomalies referencing observed behaviors and behavioral biases.

Loss Aversion

In most financial models, the assumption is that investors are risk averse. **Risk aversion** refers to the tendency of people to dislike risk and to require higher expected returns to compensate for exposure to additional risk. Behavioral finance allows for the possibility that the dissatisfaction resulting from a loss exceeds the satisfaction resulting from a gain of the same magnitude. **Loss aversion** refers to the tendency of people to dislike losses more than they like comparable gains. This results in a strong preference for avoiding losses as opposed to achieving gains.[50] Some argue that behavioral theories of loss aversion can explain observed overreaction in markets. If loss aversion is more important than risk aversion, researchers should observe that investors overreact.[51] Although loss aversion can explain the overreaction anomaly, evidence also suggests that under reaction is just as prevalent as overreaction, which counters these arguments.

Herding

Herding behavior has been advanced as a possible explanation of under reaction and overreaction in financial markets. **Herding** occurs when investors trade on the same side of the market in the same securities, or when investors ignore their own private information and/or analysis and act as other investors do. Herding is clustered trading that may or may not be based on information.[52] Herding may result in under- or over-reaction to information depending upon the direction of the herd.

---

50 See DeBondt and Thaler (1985) and Tversky and Kahneman (1981).
51 See Fama (1998).
52 The term used when there is herding without information is "spurious herding."

Overconfidence

A behavioral bias offered to explain pricing anomalies is overconfidence. If investors are overconfident, they overestimate their ability to process and interpret information about a security. Overconfident investors may not process information appropriately, and if there is a sufficient number of these investors, stocks will be mispriced.[53] But most researchers argue that this mispricing is temporary, with prices correcting eventually. If it takes a sufficiently long time for prices to become correctly priced and the mispricing is predictable, it may be possible for investors to earn abnormal profits.

Evidence has suggested that overconfidence results in mispricing for US, UK, German, French, and Japanese markets.[54] This overconfidence, however, is predominantly in higher-growth companies, whose prices react slowly to new information.[55]

Information Cascades

An application of behavioral theories to markets and pricing focuses on the role of personal learning in markets. Personal learning is what investors learn by observing outcomes of trades and what they learn from "conversations"—ideas shared among investors about specific assets and the markets.[56] Social interaction and the resultant contagion is important in pricing and may explain such phenomena as price changes without accompanying news and mistakes in valuation.

Biases that investors possess can lead to herding behavior or information cascades. Herding and information cascades are related but not identical concepts. An **information cascade** is the transmission of information from those participants who act first and whose decisions influence the decisions of others. Those who are acting on the choices of others may be ignoring their own preferences in favor of imitating the choices of others. In particular, information cascades may occur with respect to the release of accounting information because accounting information may be difficult to interpret and may be noisy. For example, the release of earnings is difficult to interpret because it is necessary to understand how the number was arrived at and noisy because it is uncertain what the current earnings imply about future earnings.

Information cascades may result in serial correlation of stock returns, which is consistent with overreaction anomalies. Do information cascades result in correct pricing? Some argue that if a cascade is leading toward an incorrect value, this cascade is "fragile" and will be corrected because investors will ultimately give more weight to public information or the trading of a recognized informed trader.[57] Information cascades, although documented in markets, do not necessarily mean that investors can exploit knowledge of them as profitable trading opportunities.

Are information cascades rational? If the informed traders act first and uninformed traders imitate the informed traders, this behavior is consistent with rationality. The imitation trading by the uninformed traders may help the market incorporate relevant information and improve market efficiency.[58] However, the imitation trading may lead

---

53 Another aspect to overconfidence is that investors who are overconfident in their ability to select investments and manage a portfolio tend to use less diversification, investing in what is most familiar. Therefore, investor behavior may affect investment results—returns and risk—without implications for the efficiency of markets.
54 Scott, Stumpp, and Xu (2003) and Boujelbene Abbes, Boujelbene, and Bouri (2009).
55 Scott, Stumpp, and Xu (2003).
56 Hirshleifer and Teoh (2009).
57 Avery and Zemsky (1999).
58 Another alternative is that the uninformed traders are the majority of the market participants and the imitators are imitating not because they agree with the actions of the majority but because they are looking to act on the actions of the uninformed traders.

to an overreaction to information. The empirical evidence indicates that information cascades are greater for a stock when the information quality regarding the company is poor.[59] Information cascades may enhance the information available to investors.

Other Behavioral Biases

Other behavioral biases that have been put forth to explain observed investor behavior include the following:

- **representativeness**—investors assess new information and probabilities of outcomes based on similarity to the current state or to a familiar classification;
- **mental accounting**—investors keep track of the gains and losses for different investments in separate mental accounts and treat those accounts differently;
- **conservatism**—investors tend to be slow to react to new information and continue to maintain their prior views or forecasts; and
- **narrow framing**—investors focus on issues in isolation and respond to the issues based on how the issues are posed.[60]

The basic idea behind behavioral finance is that investors are humans and, therefore, imperfect. These observed less than rational behaviors may help explain observed pricing anomalies. The beliefs investors have about a given asset's value may not be homogeneous. But an issue, which is controversial, is whether these insights can help someone identify and exploit any mispricing. In other words, can investors use knowledge of behavioral biases to predict how asset prices will be affected and act based on the predictions to earn abnormal profits?

Behavioral Finance and Investors

Behavior biases can affect all market participants, from the novice investor to the most experienced investment manager. An understanding of behavioral finance can help market participants recognize their own and others' behavioral biases. As a result of this recognition, they may be able to respond and make improved decisions, individually and collectively.

Behavioral Finance and Efficient Markets

The use of behavioral finance to explain observed pricing is an important part of the understanding of how markets function and how prices are determined. Whether there is a behavioral explanation for market anomalies remains a debate. Pricing anomalies are continually being uncovered, and then statistical and behavioral explanations are offered to explain these anomalies.

On the one hand, if investors must be rational for efficient markets to exist, then all the imperfections of human investors suggest that markets cannot be efficient. On the other hand, if all that is required for markets to be efficient is that investors cannot consistently beat the market on a risk-adjusted basis, then the evidence does support market efficiency.

---

59 Avery and Zemsky (1999) and Bikhchandani, Hirshleifer, and Welch (1992).
60 For a review of these behavioral issues, see Hirshleifer (2001).

SUMMARY

This reading has provided an overview of the theory and evidence regarding market efficiency and has discussed the different forms of market efficiency as well as the implications for fundamental analysis, technical analysis, and portfolio management. The general conclusion drawn from the efficient market hypothesis is that it is not possible to beat the market on a consistent basis by generating returns in excess of those expected for the level of risk of the investment.

Additional key points include the following:

- The efficiency of a market is affected by the number of market participants and depth of analyst coverage, information availability, and limits to trading.

- There are three forms of efficient markets, each based on what is considered to be the information used in determining asset prices. In the weak form, asset prices fully reflect all market data, which refers to all past price and trading volume information. In the semi-strong form, asset prices reflect all publicly known and available information. In the strong form, asset prices fully reflect all information, which includes both public and private information.

- Intrinsic value refers to the true value of an asset, whereas market value refers to the price at which an asset can be bought or sold. When markets are efficient, the two should be the same or very close. But when markets are not efficient, the two can diverge significantly.

- Most empirical evidence supports the idea that securities markets in developed countries are semi-strong-form efficient; however, empirical evidence does not support the strong form of the efficient market hypothesis.

- A number of anomalies have been documented that contradict the notion of market efficiency, including the size anomaly, the January anomaly, and the winners–losers anomalies. In most cases, however, contradictory evidence both supports and refutes the anomaly.

- Behavioral finance uses human psychology, such as behavioral biases, in an attempt to explain investment decisions. Whereas behavioral finance is helpful in understanding observed decisions, a market can still be considered efficient even if market participants exhibit seemingly irrational behaviors, such as herding.

REFERENCES

Alexander, John C., Delbert Goff, Pamela P. Peterson. 1989. "Profitability of a Trading Strategy Based on Unexpected Earnings." Financial Analysts Journal, vol. 45, no. 4:65–71. 10.2469/faj.v45.n4.65

Bessembinder, Hendrik, Kalok Chan. 1998. "Market Efficiency and the Returns to Technical Analysis." Financial Management, vol. 27, no. 2:5–17. 10.2307/3666289

Bikhchandani, Sushil, David Hirshleifer, Ivo Welch. 1992. "A Theory of Fads, Fashion, Custom, and Cultural Change as Informational Cascades." Journal of Political Economy, vol. 100, no. 5:992–1026. 10.1086/261849

Brav, Alon, Christopher Geczy, Paul A. Gompers. 1995. "The Long-Run Underperformance of Seasoned Equity Offerings Revisited." Working paper, Harvard University.

Brealey, Richard. 1983. "Can Professional Investors Beat the Market?" An Introduction to Risk and Return from Common Stocks, 2nd edition. Cambridge, MA: MIT Press.

Bris, Arturo, William N. Goetzmann, Ning Zhu. 2009. "Efficiency and the Bear: Short Sales and Markets around the World." Journal of Finance, vol. 62, no. 3:1029–1079. 10.1111/j.1540-6261.2007.01230.x

Brown, Laurence D. 1997. "Earning Surprise Research: Synthesis and Perspectives." Financial Analysts Journal, vol. 53, no. 2:13–19. 10.2469/faj.v53.n2.2067

Capaul, Carlo, Ian Rowley, William Sharpe. 1993. "International Value and Growth Stock Returns." Financial Analysts Journal, vol. 49:27–36. 10.2469/faj.v49.n1.27

Chen, Kong-Jun, Xiao-Ming Li. 2006. "Is Technical Analysis Useful for Stock Traders in China? Evidence from the Szse Component A-Share Index." Pacific Economic Review, vol. 11, no. 4:477–488. 10.1111/j.1468-0106.2006.00329.x

Chordia, Tarun, Richard Roll, Avanidhar Subrahmanyam. 2005. "Evidence on the Speed of Convergence to Market Efficiency." Journal of Financial Economics, vol. 76, no. 2:271–292. 10.1016/j.jfineco.2004.06.004

DeBondt, Werner, Richard Thaler. 1985. "Does the Stock Market Overreact?" Journal of Finance, vol. 40, no. 3:793–808. 10.2307/2327804

Deng, Xiaohu, Sandra Mortal, Vishal Gupta. 2017. "The Real Effects of Short Selling Constraints: Cross-Country Evidence." Working paper.

Dimson, Elroy, Carolina Minio-Kozerski. 1999. "Closed-End Funds: A Survey." Financial Markets, Institutions & Instruments, vol. 8, no. 2:1–41. 10.1111/1468-0416.00027

Fama, Eugene F. 1970. "Efficient Capital Markets: A Review of Theory and Empirical Work." Journal of Finance, vol. 25, no. 2:383–417. 10.2307/2325486

Fama, Eugene F. 1976. *Foundations* of Finance. New York: Basic Books.

Fama, Eugene F. 1998. "Market Efficiency, Long-Term Returns, and Behavioral Finance." Journal of Financial Economics, vol. 50, no. 3:283–306. 10.1016/S0304-405X(98)00026-9

Fama, Eugene F., Kenneth R. French. 1988. "Dividend Yields and Expected Stock Returns." Journal of Financial Economics, vol. 22, no. 1:3–25. 10.1016/0304-405X(88)90020-7

Fama, Eugene F., Kenneth R. French. 1995. "Size and Book-to-Market Factors in Earnings and Returns." Journal of Finance, vol. 50, no. 1:131–155. 10.2307/2329241

Fama, Eugene F., Kenneth R. French. 1998. "Value versus Growth: The International Evidence." Journal of Finance, vol. 53:1975–1999. 10.1111/0022-1082.00080

Fama, Eugene F., Kenneth R. French. 2008. "Dissecting Anomalies." Journal of Finance, vol. 63, no. 4:1653–1678. 10.1111/j.1540-6261.2008.01371.x

Grossman, Sanford J., Joseph E. Stiglitz. 1980. "On the Impossibility of Informationally Efficient Markets." American Economic Review, vol. 70, no. 3:393–408.

Hirshleifer, David. 2001. "Investor Psychology and Asset Pricing." Journal of Finance, vol. 56, no. 4:1533–1597. 10.1111/0022-1082.00379

Hirshleifer, David, Siew Hong Teoh. 2009. "Thought and Behavior Contagion in Capital Markets." In Handbook of Financial Markets: Dynamics and Evolution. Edited by Klaus Reiner Schenk-Hoppe and Thorstein Hens. Amsterdam: North Holland.

Jacobs, Bruce I., Kenneth N. Levy. 1988. "Calendar Anomalies: Abnormal Returns at Calendar Turning Points." Financial Analysts Journal, vol. 44, no. 6:28–39. 10.2469/faj.v44.n6.28

References

Jaffe, Jeffrey. 1974. "Special Information and Insider Trading." Journal of Business, vol. 47, no. 3:410–428. 10.1086/295655

Jegadeesh, Narayan, Sheridan Titman. 2001. "Profitability of Momentum Strategies: An Evaluation of Alternative Explanations." Journal of Finance, vol. 56:699–720. 10.1111/0022-1082.00342

Johnson, Timothy C. 2002. "Rational Momentum Effects." Journal of Finance, vol. 57, no. 2:585–608. 10.1111/1540-6261.00435

Kim, Donchoi, Myungsun Kim. 2003. "A Multifactor Explanation of Post-Earnings Announcement Drift." Journal of Financial and Quantitative Analysis, vol. 38, no. 2:383–398. 10.2307/4126756

Kim, Dongcheol. 2006. "On the Information Uncertainty Risk and the January Effect." Journal of Business, vol. 79, no. 4:2127–2162. 10.1086/503659

Lee, Charles M.C., Andrei Sheifer, Richard H. Thaler. 1990. "Anomalies: Closed-End Mutual Funds." Journal of Economic Perspectives, vol. 4, no. 4:153–164.

Malkiel, Burton G. 1995. "Returns from Investing in Equity Mutual Funds 1971 to 1991." Journal of Finance, vol. 50:549–572. 10.2307/2329419

Mobarek, Asma, A. Sabur Mollah, Rafiqul Bhuyan. 2008. "Market Efficiency in Emerging Stock Market." Journal of Emerging Market Finance, vol. 7, no. 1:17–41. 10.1177/097265270700700102

Pontiff, Jeffrey. 1995. "Closed-End Fund Premia and Returns: Implications for Financial Market Equilibrium." Journal of Financial Economics, vol. 37:341–370. 10.1016/0304-405X(94)00800-G

Pontiff, Jeffrey. 1996. "Costly Arbitrage: Evidence from Closed-End Funds." Quarterly Journal of Economics, vol. 111, no. 4:1135–1151. 10.2307/2946710

Roll, Richard. 1983. "On Computing Mean Returns and the Small Firm Premium." Journal of Financial Economics, vol. 12:371–386. 10.1016/0304-405X(83)90055-7

Rozeff, Michael S., Mir A. Zaman. 1988. "Market Efficiency and Insider Trading: New Evidence." Journal of Business, vol. 61:25–44. 10.1086/296418

Schwert, G. William. 2003. "Anomalies and Market Efficiency." Handbook of the Economics of Finance. Edited by George M. Constantinides, M. Harris, and Rene Stulz. Amsterdam: Elsevier Science, B. V.

Scott, James, Margaret Stumpp, Peter Xu. 2003. "Overconfidence Bias in International Stock Prices." Journal of Portfolio Management, vol. 29, no. 2:80–89. 10.3905/jpm.2003.319875

Tversky, Amos, Daniel Kahneman. 1981. "The Framing of Decisions and the Psychology of Choice." Science, vol. 211, no. 30:453–458. 10.1126/science.7455683

Yau, Jot, Thomas Schneeweis, Thomas Robinson, Lisa Weiss. 2007. "Alternative Investments Portfolio Management." Managing Investment Portfolios: A Dynamic Process. Hoboken, NJ: John Wiley & Sons.

Zarowin, P. 1989. "Does the Stock Market Overreact to Corporate Earnings Information?" Journal of Finance, vol. 44:1385–1399. 10.2307/2328649

PRACTICE PROBLEMS

1. If markets are efficient, the difference between the intrinsic value and market value of a company's security is:
   A. negative.
   B. zero.
   C. positive.

2. The intrinsic value of an undervalued asset is:
   A. less than the asset's market value.
   B. greater than the asset's market value.
   C. the value at which the asset can currently be bought or sold.

3. The market value of an undervalued asset is:
   A. greater than the asset's intrinsic value.
   B. the value at which the asset can currently be bought or sold.
   C. equal to the present value of all the asset's expected cash flows.

4. In an efficient market, the change in a company's share price is *most likely* the result of:
   A. insiders' private information.
   B. the previous day's change in stock price.
   C. new information coming into the market.

5. Regulation that restricts some investors from participating in a market will *most likely*:
   A. impede market efficiency.
   B. not affect market efficiency.
   C. contribute to market efficiency.

6. With respect to efficient market theory, when a market allows short selling, the efficiency of the market is *most likely* to:
   A. increase.
   B. decrease.
   C. remain the same.

7. Which of the following regulations will *most likely* contribute to market efficiency? Regulatory restrictions on:
   A. short selling.

Practice Problems

   B. foreign traders.

   C. insiders trading with nonpublic information.

8. Which of the following market regulations will *most likely* impede market efficiency?

   A. Restricting traders' ability to short sell.

   B. Allowing unrestricted foreign investor trading.

   C. Penalizing investors who trade with nonpublic information.

9. An increase in the time between when an order to trade a security is placed and when the order is executed *most likely* indicates that market efficiency has:

   A. decreased.

   B. remained the same.

   C. increased.

10. With respect to the efficient market hypothesis, if security prices reflect *only* past prices and trading volume information, then the market is:

    A. weak-form efficient.

    B. strong-form efficient.

    C. semi-strong-form efficient.

11. Which one of the following statements *best* describes the semi-strong form of market efficiency?

    A. Empirical tests examine the historical patterns in security prices.

    B. Security prices reflect all publicly known and available information.

    C. Semi-strong-form efficient markets are not necessarily weak-form efficient.

12. If prices reflect all public and private information, the market is *best* described as:

    A. weak-form efficient.

    B. strong-form efficient.

    C. semi-strong-form efficient.

13. If markets are semi-strong efficient, standard fundamental analysis will yield abnormal trading profits that are:

    A. negative.

    B. equal to zero.

    C. positive.

14. If markets are semi-strong-form efficient, then passive portfolio management strategies are *most likely* to:

    A. earn abnormal returns.

B. outperform active trading strategies.

C. underperform active trading strategies.

15. If a market is semi-strong-form efficient, the risk-adjusted returns of a passively managed portfolio relative to an actively managed portfolio are *most likely*:

    A. lower.

    B. higher.

    C. the same.

16. Technical analysts assume that markets are:

    A. weak-form efficient.

    B. weak-form inefficient.

    C. semi-strong-form efficient.

17. Fundamental analysts assume that markets are:

    A. weak-form inefficient.

    B. semi-strong-form efficient.

    C. semi-strong-form inefficient.

18. If a market is weak-form efficient but semi-strong-form inefficient, then which of the following types of portfolio management is *most likely* to produce abnormal returns?

    A. Passive portfolio management.

    B. Active portfolio management based on technical analysis.

    C. Active portfolio management based on fundamental analysis.

19. Which of the following is *least likely* to explain the January effect anomaly?

    A. Tax-loss selling.

    B. Release of new information in January.

    C. Window dressing of portfolio holdings.

20. If a researcher conducting empirical tests of a trading strategy using time series of returns finds statistically significant abnormal returns, then the researcher has *most likely* found:

    A. a market anomaly.

    B. evidence of market inefficiency.

    C. a strategy to produce future abnormal returns.

21. Researchers have found that value stocks have consistently outperformed growth stocks. An investor wishing to exploit the value effect should purchase the stock

of companies with above-average:

  A. dividend yields.

  B. market-to-book ratios.

  C. price-to-earnings ratios.

22. Which of the following market anomalies is inconsistent with weak-form market efficiency?

  A. Earnings surprise.

  B. Momentum pattern.

  C. Closed-end fund discount.

23. With respect to efficient markets, a company whose share price changes gradually after the public release of its annual report *most likely* indicates that the market where the company trades is:

  A. semi-strong-form efficient.

  B. subject to behavioral biases.

  C. receiving additional information about the company.

24. With respect to rational and irrational investment decisions, the efficient market hypothesis requires:

  A. only that the market is rational.

  B. that all investors make rational decisions.

  C. that some investors make irrational decisions.

25. Observed overreactions in markets can be explained by an investor's degree of:

  A. risk aversion.

  B. loss aversion.

  C. confidence in the market.

26. Like traditional finance models, the behavioral theory of loss aversion assumes that investors dislike risk; however, the dislike of risk in behavioral theory is assumed to be:

  A. leptokurtic.

  B. symmetrical.

  C. asymmetrical.

SOLUTIONS

1. B is correct. A security's intrinsic value and market value should be equal when markets are efficient.

2. B is correct. The intrinsic value of an undervalued asset is greater than the market value of the asset, where the market value is the transaction price at which an asset can be currently bought or sold.

3. B is correct. The market value is the transaction price at which an asset can be currently bought or sold.

4. C is correct. Today's price change is independent of the one from yesterday, and in an efficient market, investors will react to new, independent information as it is made public.

5. A is correct. Reducing the number of market participants can accentuate market imperfections and impede market efficiency (e.g., restrictions on foreign investor trading).

6. A is correct. According to theory, reducing the restrictions on trading will allow for more arbitrage trading, thereby promoting more efficient pricing. Although regulators argue that short selling exaggerates downward price movements, empirical research indicates that short selling is helpful in price discovery.

7. C is correct. Regulation to restrict unfair use of nonpublic information encourages greater participation in the market, which increases market efficiency. Regulators (e.g., US SEC) discourage illegal insider trading by issuing penalties to violators of their insider trading rules.

8. A is correct. Restricting short selling will reduce arbitrage trading, which promotes market efficiency. Permitting foreign investor trading increases market participation, which makes markets more efficient. Penalizing insider trading encourages greater market participation, which increases market efficiency.

9. A is correct. Operating inefficiencies reduce market efficiency.

10. A is correct. The weak-form efficient market hypothesis is defined as a market where security prices fully reflect all market data, which refers to all past price and trading volume information.

11. B is correct. In semi-strong-form efficient markets, security prices reflect all publicly available information.

12. B is correct. The strong-form efficient market hypothesis assumes all information, public or private, has already been reflected in the prices.

13. B is correct. If all public information should already be reflected in the market price, then the abnormal trading profit will be equal to zero when fundamental analysis is used.

14. B is correct. Costs associated with active trading strategies would be difficult to recover; thus, such active trading strategies would have difficulty outperforming passive strategies on a consistent after-cost basis.

15. B is correct. In a semi-strong-form efficient market, passive portfolio strategies

Solutions

should outperform active portfolio strategies on a risk-adjusted basis.

16. B is correct. Technical analysts use past prices and volume to predict future prices, which is inconsistent with the weakest form of market efficiency (i.e., weak-form market efficiency). Weak-form market efficiency states that investors cannot earn abnormal returns by trading on the basis of past trends in price and volume.

17. C is correct. Fundamental analysts use publicly available information to estimate a security's intrinsic value to determine if the security is mispriced, which is inconsistent with the semi-strong form of market efficiency. Semi-strong-form market efficiency states that investors cannot earn abnormal returns by trading based on publicly available information.

18. C is correct. If markets are not semi-strong-form efficient, then fundamental analysts are able to use publicly available information to estimate a security's intrinsic value and identify misvalued securities. Technical analysis is not able to earn abnormal returns if markets are weak-form efficient. Passive portfolio managers outperform fundamental analysis if markets are semi-strong-form efficient.

19. B is correct. The excess returns in January are not attributed to any new information or news; however, research has found that part of the seasonal pattern can be explained by tax-loss selling and portfolio window dressing.

20. A is correct. Finding significant abnormal returns does not necessarily indicate that markets are inefficient or that abnormal returns can be realized by applying the strategy to future time periods. Abnormal returns are considered market anomalies because they may be the result of the model used to estimate the expected returns or may be the result of underestimating transaction costs or other expenses associated with implementing the strategy, rather than because of market inefficiency.

21. A is correct. Higher than average dividend yield is a characteristic of a value stock, along with low price-to-earnings and low market-to-book ratios. Growth stocks are characterized by low dividend yields and high price-to-earnings and high market-to-book ratios.

22. B is correct. Trading based on historical momentum indicates that price patterns exist and can be exploited by using historical price information. A momentum trading strategy that produces abnormal returns contradicts the weak form of the efficient market hypothesis, which states that investors cannot earn abnormal returns on the basis of past trends in prices.

23. C is correct. If markets are efficient, the information from the annual report is reflected in the stock prices; therefore, the gradual changes must be from the release of additional information.

24. A is correct. The efficient market hypothesis and asset-pricing models only require that the market is rational. Behavioral finance is used to explain *some* of the market anomalies as irrational decisions.

25. B is correct. Behavioral theories of loss aversion can explain observed overreaction in markets, such that investors dislike losses more than comparable gains (i.e., risk is not symmetrical).

26. C is correct. Behavioral theories of loss aversion allow for the possibility that the dislike for risk is not symmetrical, which allows for loss aversion to explain observed overreaction in markets such that investors dislike losses more than they

like comparable gains.

LEARNING MODULE 4

Overview of Equity Securities

by Ryan C. Fuhrmann, CFA, and Asjeet S. Lamba, PhD, CFA.

Ryan C. Fuhrmann, CFA, is at Fuhrmann Capital LLC (USA). Asjeet S. Lamba, PhD, CFA, is at the University of Melbourne (Australia).

LEARNING OUTCOMES	
Mastery	The candidate should be able to:
☐	describe characteristics of types of equity securities
☐	describe differences in voting rights and other ownership characteristics among different equity classes
☐	compare and contrast public and private equity securities
☐	describe methods for investing in non-domestic equity securities
☐	compare the risk and return characteristics of different types of equity securities
☐	explain the role of equity securities in the financing of a company's assets
☐	contrast the market value and book value of equity securities
☐	compare a company's cost of equity, its (accounting) return on equity, and investors' required rates of return

1. IMPORTANCE OF EQUITY SECURITIES

Equity securities represent ownership claims on a company's net assets. As an asset class, equity plays a fundamental role in investment analysis and portfolio management because it represents a significant portion of many individual and institutional investment portfolios.

The study of equity securities is important for many reasons. First, the decision on how much of a client's portfolio to allocate to equities affects the risk and return characteristics of the entire portfolio. Second, different types of equity securities have different ownership claims on a company's net assets, which affect their risk and return characteristics in different ways. Finally, variations in the features of equity securities are reflected in their market prices, so it is important to understand the valuation implications of these features.

This reading provides an overview of equity securities and their different features and establishes the background required to analyze and value equity securities in a global context. It addresses the following questions:

- What distinguishes common shares from preference shares, and what purposes do these securities serve in financing a company's operations?
- What are convertible preference shares, and why are they often used to raise equity for unseasoned or highly risky companies?
- What are private equity securities, and how do they differ from public equity securities?
- What are depository receipts and their various types, and what is the rationale for investing in them?
- What are the risk factors involved in investing in equity securities?
- How do equity securities create company value?
- What is the relationship between a company's cost of equity, its return on equity, and investors' required rate of return?

The remainder of this reading is organized as follows. Section 2 provides an overview of global equity markets and their historical performance. Section 3 examines the different types and characteristics of equity securities, and Section 4 outlines the differences between public and private equity securities. Section 5 provides an overview of the various types of equity securities listed and traded in global markets. Section 6 discusses the risk and return characteristics of equity securities. Section 7 examines the role of equity securities in creating company value and the relationship between a company's cost of equity, its return on equity, and investors' required rate of return. The final section summarizes the reading.

Equity Securities in Global Financial Markets

This section highlights the relative importance and performance of equity securities as an asset class. We examine the total market capitalization and trading volume of global equity markets and the prevalence of equity ownership across various geographic regions. We also examine historical returns on equities and compare them to the returns on government bonds and bills.

Exhibit 1 summarizes the contributions of selected countries and geographic regions to global gross domestic product (GDP) and global equity market capitalization. Analysts may examine the relationship between equity market capitalization and GDP as a rough indicator of whether the global equity market (or a specific country's or region's equity market) is under, over, or fairly valued, particularly compared to its long-run average.

Exhibit 1 illustrates the significant value that investors attach to publicly traded equities relative to the sum of goods and services produced globally every year. It shows the continued significance, and the potential over-representation, of US equity markets relative to their contribution to global GDP. That is, while US equity markets contribute around 51 percent to the total capitalization of global equity markets, their contribution to the global GDP is only around 25 percent. Following the stock market turmoil in 2008, however, the market capitalization to GDP ratio of the United States fell to 59 percent, which is significantly lower than its long-run average of 79 percent.

As equity markets outside the United States develop and become increasingly global, their total capitalization levels are expected to grow closer to their respective world GDP contributions. Therefore, it is important to understand and analyze equity securities from a global perspective.

Importance of Equity Securities

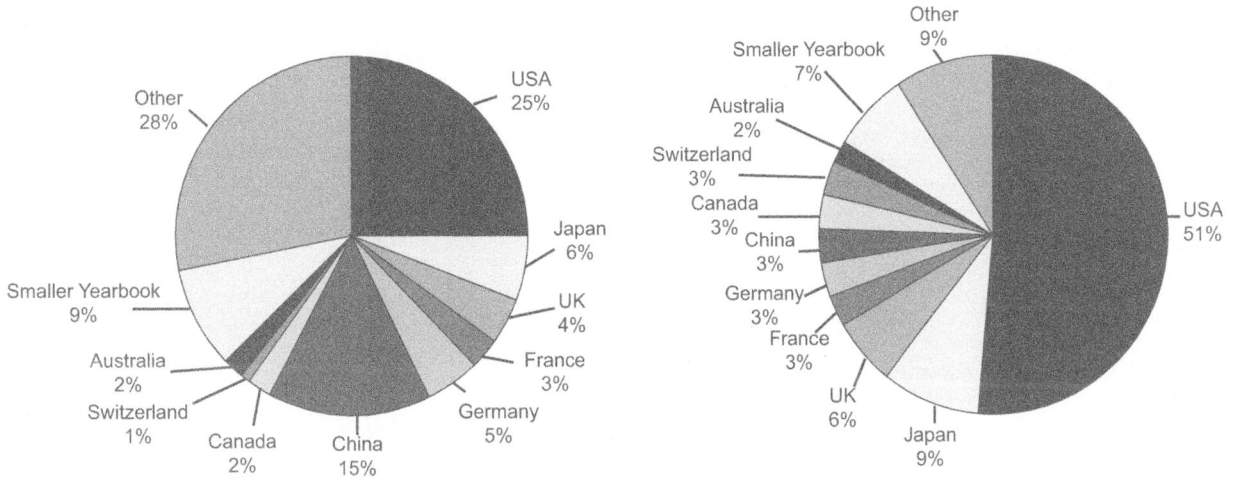

Exhibit 1: Country and Regional Contributions to Global GDP and Equity Market Capitalization (2017)

Source: The WorldBank Databank *2017*, and Dimson, Marsh, and Staunton (2018).

Exhibit 2 lists the top 10 equity markets at the end of 2017 based on total market capitalization (in billions of US dollars), trading volume, and the number of listed companies.[1] Note that the rankings differ based on the criteria used. For example, the top three markets based on total market capitalization are the NYSE Euronext (US), NASDAQ OMX, and the Japan Exchange Group; however, the top three markets based on total US dollar trading volume are the Nasdaq OMX, NYSE Euronext (US), and the Shenzhen Stock Exchange, respectively.[2]

Exhibit 2: Equity Markets Ranked by Total Market Capitalization at the End of 2017 (Billions of US Dollars)

Rank	Name of Market	Total US Dollar Market Capitalization	Total US Dollar Trading Volume	Number of Listed Companies
1	NYSE Euronext (US)	$22,081.4	$16,140.1	2,286
2	NASDAQ OMX	$10,039.4	$33,407.1	2,949
3	Japan Exchange Group[a]	$6,220.0	$6,612.1	3,604
4	Shanghai Stock Exchange	$5,084.4	$7,589.3	1,396
5	Euronext[b]	$4,393.0	$1,981.6	1,255
6	Hong Kong Exchanges	$4,350.5	$1,958.8	2,118
7	Shenzhen Stock Exchanges	$3,617.9	$9,219.7	2,089

---

1 The market capitalization of an individual stock is computed as the share price multiplied by the number of shares outstanding. The total market capitalization of an equity market is the sum of the market capitalizations of each individual stock listed on that market. Similarly, the total trading volume of an equity market is computed by value weighting the total trading volume of each individual stock listed on that market. Total dollar trading volume is computed as the average share price multiplied by the number of shares traded.
2 NASDAQ is the acronym for the National Association of Securities Dealers Automated Quotations.

Rank	Name of Market	Total US Dollar Market Capitalization	Total US Dollar Trading Volume	Number of Listed Companies
8	National Stock Exchange of India	$2,351.5	$1,013.3	1,897
9	BSE Limited[c]	$2,331.6	$183.0	5,616
10	Deutsche Börse	$2,262.2	$1,497.9	499

Notes:

[a] Japan Exchange Group is the merged entity containing the Tokyo Stock Exchange and Osaka Securities Exchange.

[b] From 2001, includes Netherlands, France, England, Belgium, and Portugal.

[c] Bombay Stock Exchange.

Source: Adapted from the *World Federation of Exchanges 2017 Report* (see http://www.world-exchanges.org). Note that market capitalization by company is calculated by multiplying its stock price by the number of shares outstanding. The market's overall capitalization is the aggregate of the market capitalizations of all companies traded on that market. The number of listed companies includes both domestic and foreign companies whose shares trade on these markets.

Exhibit 3 compares the *real* (or inflation-adjusted) compounded returns on government bonds, government bills, and equity securities in 21 countries plus the world index ("Wld"), the world ex-US ("WxU"), and Europe ("Eur") during the 118 years 1900–2017.[3] In real terms, government bonds and bills have essentially kept pace with the inflation rate, earning annualized real returns of less than 2 percent in most countries.[4] By comparison, real returns in equity markets have generally been around 3.5 percent per year in most markets—with a world average return of around 5.2 percent and a world average return excluding the United States just under 5 percent. During this period, South Africa and Australia were the best performing markets followed by the United States, New Zealand, and Sweden.

---

3 The real return for a security is approximated by taking the nominal return and subtracting the observed inflation rate in that country.

4 The exceptions are Austria, Belgium, Finland, France, Germany, Portugal, and Italy—where the average real returns on government bonds and/or bills have been negative. In general, that performance reflects the very high inflation rates in these countries during the World War years.

Importance of Equity Securities

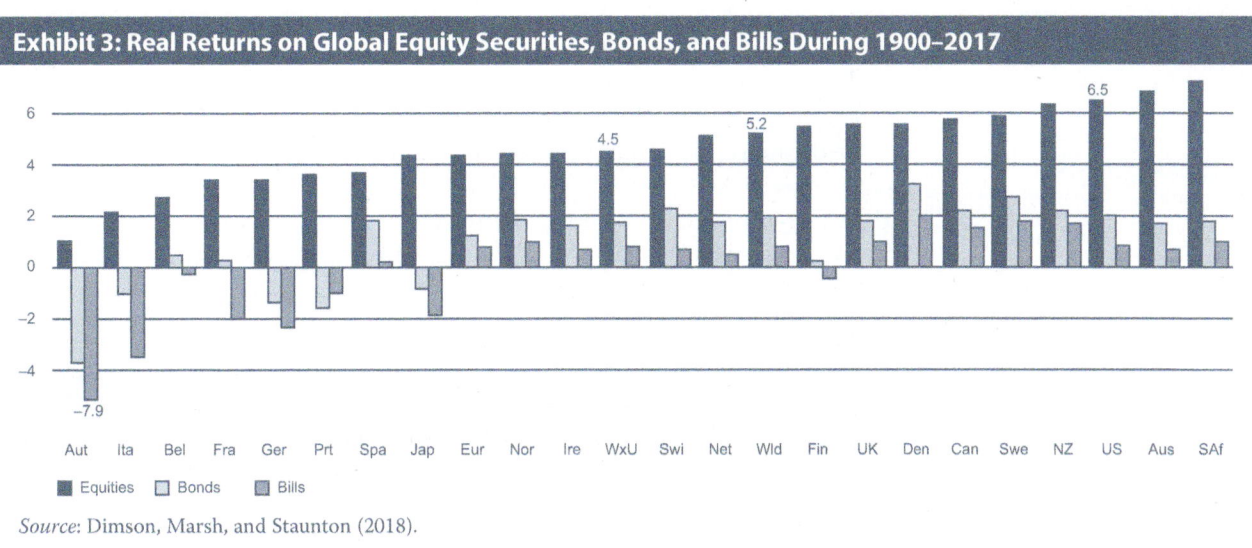

Exhibit 3: Real Returns on Global Equity Securities, Bonds, and Bills During 1900–2017

Source: Dimson, Marsh, and Staunton (2018).

Exhibit 4 shows the annualized real returns on major asset classes for the world index over 1900–2017.

Exhibit 4: Annualized Real Returns on Asset Classes for the World Index, 1900–2017

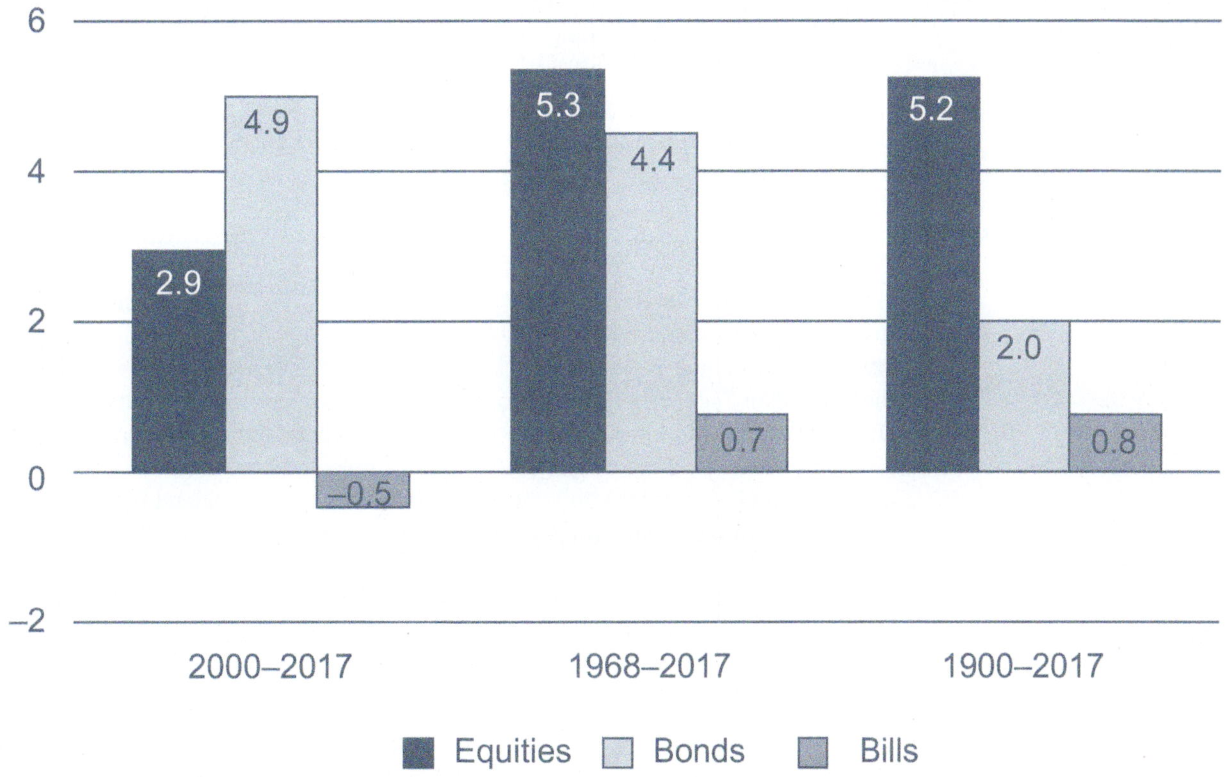

Period	Equities	Bonds	Bills
2000–2017	2.9	4.9	−0.5
1968–2017	5.3	4.4	0.7
1900–2017	5.2	2.0	0.8

Source: Dimson, Marsh, and Staunton (2018).

The volatility in asset market returns is further highlighted in Exhibit 5, which shows the annualized risk premia for equity relative to bonds (EP Bonds), and equity relative to treasury bills (EP Bills). Maturity premium for government bond returns relative to treasury bill returns (Mat Prem) is also shown.

These observations and historical data are consistent with the concept that the return on securities is directly related to risk level. That is, equity securities have higher risk levels when compared with government bonds and bills, they earn higher rates of return to compensate investors for these higher risk levels, and they also tend to be more volatile over time.

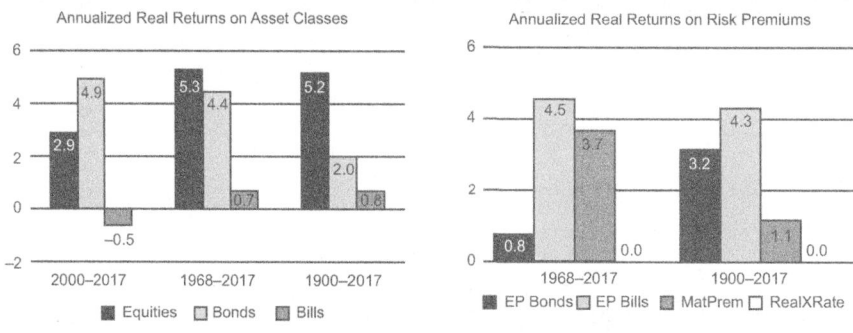

Exhibit 5: Annualized Real Returns on Asset Classes and Risk Premiums for the World Index since 1900–2017

Notes: Equities are total returns, including reinvested dividend income. Bonds are total return, including reinvested coupons, on long-term government bonds. Bills denotes the total return, including any income, from Treasury bills. All returns are adjusted for inflation and are expressed as geometric mean returns. EP bonds denotes the equity risk premium relative to long-term government bonds. EP Bills denotes the equity premium relative to Treasury bills. MatPrem denotes the maturity premium for government bond returns relative to bill returns. RealXRate denotes the real (inflation-adjusted) change in the exchange rate against the US dollar.

Source: Dimson, Marsh, and Staunton (2018).

Given the high risk levels associated with equity securities, it is reasonable to expect that investors' tolerance for risk will tend to differ across equity markets. This is illustrated in Exhibit 6, which shows the results of a series of studies conducted by the Australian Securities Exchange on international differences in equity ownership. During the 2004–2014 period, equity ownership as a percentage of the population was lowest in South Korea (averaging 9.0 percent), followed by Germany (14.5 percent) and Sweden (17.7 percent). In contrast, Australia and New Zealand had the highest equity ownership as a percentage of the population (averaging more than 20 percent). In addition, there has been a relative decline in share ownership in several countries over recent years, which is not surprising given the recent overall uncertainty in global economies and the volatility in equity markets that this uncertainty has created.

Exhibit 6: International Comparisons of Stock Ownership: 2004–2014[5]

	2004	2006	2008	2010	2012	2014
Australia – Direct/Indirect	55%	46%	41%	43%	38%	36%
South Korea – Shares	8	7	10	10	10	N/A
Germany – Shares/Funds	16	16	14	13	15	13
Sweden – Shares	22	20	18	17	15	14
United Kingdom – Shares/Funds	22	20	18	N/A	17	N/A
New Zealand – Direct	23	26	N/A	22	23	26

Source: Adapted from the *2014 Australian Share Ownership Study* conducted by the Australian Securities Exchange (see http://www.asx.com.au). For Australia and the United States, the data pertain to direct and indirect ownership in equity markets; for other countries, the data pertain to direct ownership in shares and share funds. Data not available in specific years are shown as "N/A."

An important implication from the above discussion is that equity securities represent a key asset class for global investors because of their unique return and risk characteristics. We next examine the various types of equity securities traded on global markets and their salient characteristics.

CHARACTERISTICS OF EQUITY SECURITIES

2

- [ ] describe characteristics of types of equity securities
- [ ] describe differences in voting rights and other ownership characteristics among different equity classes

Companies finance their operations by issuing either debt or equity securities. A key difference between these securities is that debt is a liability of the issuing company, whereas equity is not. This means that when a company issues debt, it is contractually obligated to repay the amount it borrows (i.e., the principal or face value of the debt) at a specified future date. The cost of using these funds is called interest, which the company is contractually obligated to pay until the debt matures or is retired.

When the company issues equity securities, it is not contractually obligated to repay the amount it receives from shareholders, nor is it contractually obligated to make periodic payments to shareholders for the use of their funds. Instead, shareholders have a claim on the company's assets after all liabilities have been paid. Because of this residual claim, equity shareholders are considered to be owners of the company. Investors who purchase equity securities are seeking total return (i.e., capital or price appreciation and dividend income), whereas investors who purchase debt securities (and hold until maturity) are seeking interest income. As a result, equity investors expect the company's management to act in their best interest by making operating decisions that will maximize the market price of their shares (i.e., shareholder wealth).

---

5 The percentages reported in the exhibit are based on samples of the adult population in each country who own equity securities either directly or indirectly through investment or retirement funds. For example, 36 percent of the adult population of Australia in 2014 (approximately 6.5 million people) owned equity securities either directly or indirectly. As noted in the study, it is not appropriate to make absolute comparisons across countries given the differences in methodology, sampling, timing, and definitions that have been used in different countries. However, trends across different countries can be identified.

In addition to common shares (also known as ordinary shares or common stock), companies may also issue preference shares (also known as preferred stock), the other type of equity security. The following sections discuss the different types and characteristics of common and preference securities.

Common Shares

Common shares represent an ownership interest in a company and are the predominant type of equity security. As a result, investors share in the operating performance of the company, participate in the governance process through voting rights, and have a claim on the company's net assets in the case of liquidation. Companies may choose to pay out some, or all, of their net income in the form of cash dividends to common shareholders, but they are not contractually obligated to do so.[6]

Voting rights provide shareholders with the opportunity to participate in major corporate governance decisions, including the election of its board of directors, the decision to merge with or take over another company, and the selection of outside auditors. Shareholder voting generally takes place during a company's annual meeting. As a result of geographic limitations and the large number of shareholders, it is often not feasible for shareholders to attend the annual meeting in person. For this reason, shareholders may **vote by proxy**, which allows a designated party—such as another shareholder, a shareholder representative, or management—to vote on the shareholders' behalf.

Regular shareholder voting, where each share represents one vote, is referred to as **statutory voting**. Although it is the common method of voting, it is not always the most appropriate one to use to elect a board of directors. To better serve shareholders who own a small number of shares, **cumulative voting** is often used. Cumulative voting allows shareholders to direct their total voting rights to specific candidates, as opposed to having to allocate their voting rights evenly among all candidates. Total voting rights are based on the number of shares owned multiplied by the number of board directors being elected. For example, under cumulative voting, if four board directors are to be elected, a shareholder who owns 100 shares is entitled to 400 votes and can either cast all 400 votes in favor of a single candidate or spread them across the candidates in any proportion. In contrast, under statutory voting, a shareholder would be able to cast only a maximum of 100 votes for each candidate.

The key benefit to cumulative voting is that it allows shareholders with a small number of shares to apply all of their votes to one candidate, thus providing the opportunity for a higher level of representation on the board than would be allowed under statutory voting.

Exhibit 7 describes the rights of Viacom Corporation's shareholders. In this case, a dual-share arrangement allows the founding chairman and his family to control more than 70 percent of the voting rights through the ownership of Class A shares. This arrangement gives them the ability to exert control over the board of director election process, corporate decision making, and other important aspects of managing the company. A cumulative voting arrangement for any minority shareholders of Class A shares would improve their board representation.

---

[6] It is also possible for companies to pay more than the current period's net income as dividends. Such payout policies are, however, generally not sustainable in the long run.

Characteristics of Equity Securities

> **Exhibit 7: Share Class Arrangements at Viacom Corporation[7]**
>
> Viacom has two classes of common stock: Class A, which is the voting stock, and Class B, which is the non-voting stock. There is no difference between the two classes except for voting rights; they generally trade within a close price range of each other. There are, however, far more shares of Class B outstanding, so most of the trading occurs in that class.
>
> - **Voting Rights**—Holders of Class A common stock are entitled to one vote per share. Holders of Class B common stock do not have any voting rights, except as required by Delaware law. Generally, all matters to be voted on by Viacom stockholders must be approved by a majority of the aggregate voting power of the shares of Class A common stock present in person or represented by proxy, except as required by Delaware law.
> - **Dividends**—Stockholders of Class A common stock and Class B common stock will share ratably in any cash dividend declared by the Board of Directors, subject to any preferential rights of any outstanding preferred stock. Viacom does not currently pay a cash dividend, and any decision to pay a cash dividend in the future will be at the discretion of the Board of Directors and will depend on many factors.
> - **Conversion**—So long as there are 5,000 shares of Class A common stock outstanding, each share of Class A common stock will be convertible at the option of the holder of such share into one share of Class B common stock.
> - **Liquidation Rights**—In the event of liquidation, dissolution, or winding-up of Viacom, all stockholders of common stock, regardless of class, will be entitled to share ratably in any assets available for distributions to stockholders of shares of Viacom common stock subject to the preferential rights of any outstanding preferred stock.
> - **Split, Subdivision, or Combination**—In the event of a split, subdivision, or combination of the outstanding shares of Class A common stock or Class B common stock, the outstanding shares of the other class of common stock will be divided proportionally.
> - **Preemptive Rights**—Shares of Class A common stock and Class B common stock do not entitle a stockholder to any preemptive rights enabling a stockholder to subscribe for or receive shares of stock of any class or any other securities convertible into shares of stock of any class of Viacom.

As seen in Exhibit 7, companies can issue different classes of common shares (Class A and Class B shares), with each class offering different ownership rights.[8] For example, as shown in Exhibit 8, the Ford Motor Company has Class A shares ("Common Stock"), which are owned by the investing public. It also has Class B shares, which are owned only by the Ford family. The exhibit contains an excerpt from Ford's *2017 Annual Report* (p. 144). Class A shareholders have 60 percent voting rights, whereas Class B shareholders have 40 percent. In the case of liquidation, however, Class B shareholders will not only receive the first US$0.50 per share that is available for dis-

---

7 This information has been adapted from Viacom's investor relations website and its 10-K filing with the US Securities and Exchange Commission; see www.viacom.com.

8 In some countries, including the United States, companies can issue different classes of shares, with Class A shares being the most common. The role and function of different classes of shares is described in more detail in Exhibit 8.

tribution (as will Class A shareholders), but they will also receive the next US$1.00 per share that is available for distribution before Class A shareholders receive anything else. Thus, Class B shareholders have an opportunity to receive a larger proportion of distributions upon liquidation than do Class A shareholders.[9]

> **Exhibit 8: Share Class Arrangements at Ford Motor Company[10]**
>
> ### NOTE 21. CAPITAL STOCK AND AMOUNTS PER SHARE
>
> All general voting power is vested in the holders of Common Stock and Class B Stock. Holders of our Common Stock have 60% of the general voting power and holders of our Class B Stock are entitled to such number of votes per share as will give them the remaining 40%. Shares of Common Stock and Class B Stock share equally in dividends when and as paid, with stock dividends payable in shares of stock of the class held.
>
> If liquidated, each share of Common Stock is entitled to the first $0.50 available for distribution to holders of Common Stock and Class B Stock, each share of Class B Stock is entitled to the next $1.00 so available, each share of Common Stock is entitled to the next $0.50 so available, and each share of Common and Class B Stock is entitled to an equal amount thereafter.

Preference Shares

Preference shares (or preferred stock) rank above common shares with respect to the payment of dividends and the distribution of the company's net assets upon liquidation.[11] However, preference shareholders generally do not share in the operating performance of the company and do not have any voting rights, unless explicitly allowed for at issuance. Preference shares have characteristics of both debt securities and common shares. Similar to the interest payments on debt securities, the dividends on preference shares are fixed and are generally higher than the dividends on common shares. However, unlike interest payments, preference dividends are not contractual obligations of the company. Similar to common shares, preference shares can be perpetual (i.e., no fixed maturity date), can pay dividends indefinitely, and can be callable or putable.

Exhibit 9 provides an example of callable preference shares issued by the GDL Fund to raise capital to redeem the remaining outstanding Series B Preferred shares. In this case, the purchaser of the shares will receive an ongoing dividend from the GDL Fund. If the GDL Fund chooses to buy back the shares, it must do so at the $50 a share liquidation preference price. The purchasers of the shares also have the right to put back the shares to GDL at the $50 a share price.

---

9 For example, if US$2.00 per share is available for distribution, the Common Stock (Class A) shareholders will receive US$0.50 per share, while the Class B shareholders will receive US$1.50 per share. However, if there is US$3.50 per share available for distribution, the Common Stock shareholders will receive a total of US$1.50 per share and the Class B shareholders will receive a total of US$2.00 per share.
10 Extracted from Ford Motor Company's *2017 Annual Report* (http://s22.q4cdn.com/857684434/files/doc_financials/2017/annual/Final-Annual-Report-2017.pdf).
11 Preference shares have a lower priority than debt in the case of liquidation. That is, debt holders have a higher claim on a firm's assets in the event of liquidation and will receive what is owed to them first, followed by preference shareholders and then common shareholders.

Characteristics of Equity Securities

> **Exhibit 9: Callable Stock offering by the GDL Fund[12]**
>
> RYE, NY—March 26, 2018—The GDL Fund (NYSE:GDL) (the "Fund") is pleased to announce the completion of a rights offering (the "Offering") in which the Fund issued 2,624,025 Series C Cumulative Puttable and Callable Preferred Shares (the "Series C Preferred"), totaling $131,201,250. Pursuant to the Offering, the Fund issued one non-transferable right (a "Right") for each outstanding Series B Cumulative Puttable and Callable Preferred Share (the "Series B Preferred") of the Fund to Series B Preferred shareholders of record as of February 14, 2018. Holders of Rights were entitled to purchase the Series C Preferred with any combination of cash or surrender of the Series B Preferred at liquidation preference. Therefore, one Right plus $50.00, or one Right plus one share of Series B Preferred with a liquidation value of $50.00 per share, was required to purchase each share of the Series C Preferred. The Offering expired at 5:00 PM Eastern Time on March 20, 2018.

Dividends on preference shares can be cumulative, non-cumulative, participating, non-participating, or some combination thereof (i.e., cumulative participating, cumulative non-participating, non-cumulative participating, non-cumulative non-participating).

Dividends on **cumulative preference shares** accrue so that if the company decides not to pay a dividend in one or more periods, the unpaid dividends accrue and must be paid in full before dividends on common shares can be paid. In contrast, **non-cumulative preference shares** have no such provision. This means that any dividends that are not paid in the current or subsequent periods are forfeited permanently and are not accrued over time to be paid at a later date. However, the company is still not permitted to pay any dividends to common shareholders in the current period unless preferred dividends have been paid first.

Participating preference shares entitle the shareholders to receive the standard preferred dividend plus the opportunity to receive an additional dividend if the company's profits exceed a pre-specified level. In addition, participating preference shares can also contain provisions that entitle shareholders to an additional distribution of the company's assets upon liquidation, above the par (or face) value of the preference shares. **Non-participating preference shares** do not allow shareholders to share in the profits of the company. Instead, shareholders are entitled to receive only a fixed dividend payment and the par value of the shares in the event of liquidation. The use of participating preference shares is much more common for smaller, riskier companies where the possibility of future liquidation is more of a concern to investors.

Preference shares can also be convertible. **Convertible preference shares** entitle shareholders to convert their shares into a specified number of common shares. This conversion ratio is determined at issuance. Convertible preference shares have the following advantages:

- They allow investors to earn a higher dividend than if they invested in the company's common shares.
- They allow investors the opportunity to share in the profits of the company.
- They allow investors to benefit from a rise in the price of the common shares through the conversion option.
- Their price is less volatile than the underlying common shares because the dividend payments are known and more stable.

---

12 https://www.businesswire.com/news/home/20180326005609/en/GDL-Fund-Successfully-Completes-Offering-Issues-131

As a result, the use of convertible preference shares is a popular financing option in venture capital and private equity transactions in which the issuing companies are considered to be of higher risk and when it may be years before the issuing company "goes public" (i.e., issues common shares to the public).

Exhibit 10 provides examples of the types and characteristics of preference shares as issued by Tsakos Energy Navigation Ltd (TNP.PRE).

> **Exhibit 10: Examples of Preference Shares Issued by TEN Ltd[13]**
>
> Athens, Greece, June 21, 2018—TEN Ltd. ("TEN") (NYSE: TNP), a leading diversified crude, product and LNG tanker operator, today announced the pricing of its public offering of its Series F Fixed-to-Floating Rate Cumulative Redeemable Perpetual Preferred Shares, par value $1.00 per share, liquidation preference $25.00 per share ("Series F Preferred Shares"). TEN will issue 5,400,000 Series F Preferred Shares at a price to the public of $25.00 per share. Dividends will be payable on the Series F Preferred Shares to July 30, 2028 at a fixed rate equal to 9.50% per annum and from July 30, 2028, if not redeemed, at a floating rate. In connection with the offering, TEN has granted the underwriters a 30-day option to purchase 810,000 additional Series F Preferred Shares, which, if exercised in full, would result in total gross proceeds of $155,250,000. TEN intends to use the net proceeds from the offering for general corporate purposes, which may include making vessel acquisitions and/or strategic investments and preferred share redemptions. Following the offering, TEN intends to file an application to list the Series F Preferred Shares on the New York Stock Exchange. The offering is expected to close on or about June 28, 2018.

3

PRIVATE VERSUS PUBLIC EQUITY SECURITIES

compare and contrast public and private equity securities

Our discussion so far has focused on equity securities that are issued and traded in public markets and on exchanges. Equity securities can also be issued and traded in private equity markets. **Private equity securities** are issued primarily to institutional investors via non-public offerings, such as private placements. Because they are not listed on public exchanges, there is no active secondary market for these securities. As a result, private equity securities do not have "market determined" quoted prices, are highly illiquid, and require negotiations between investors in order to be traded. In addition, financial statements and other important information needed to determine the fair value of private equity securities may be difficult to obtain because the issuing companies are typically not required by regulatory authorities to publish this information.

There are three primary types of private equity investments: venture capital, leveraged buyouts, and private investment in public equity (or PIPE). **Venture capital** investments provide "seed" or start-up capital, early-stage financing, or mezzanine financing to companies that are in the early stages of development and require additional capital for expansion. These funds are then used to finance the company's product development and growth. Venture capitalists range from family and friends to wealthy

---

13 https://www.tenn.gr/wp-content/uploads/2018/06/tenn062118.pdf

individuals and private equity funds. Because the equity securities issued to venture capitalists are not publicly traded, they generally require a commitment of funds for a relatively long period of time; the opportunity to "exit" the investment is typically within 3 to 10 years from the initial start-up. The exit return earned by these private equity investors is based on the price that the securities can be sold for if and when the start-up company first goes public, either via an **initial public offering** (IPO) on the stock market or by being sold to other investors.

A **leveraged buyout** (LBO) occurs when a group of investors (such as the company's management or a private equity partnership) uses a large amount of debt to purchase all of the outstanding common shares of a publicly traded company. In cases where the group of investors acquiring the company is primarily comprised of the company's existing management, the transaction is referred to as a **management buyout** (MBO). After the shares are purchased, they cease to trade on an exchange and the investor group takes full control of the company. In other words, the company is taken "private" or has been privatized. Companies that are candidates for these types of transactions generally have large amounts of undervalued assets (which can be sold to reduce debt) and generate high levels of cash flows (which are used to make interest and principal payments on the debt). The ultimate objective of a buyout (LBO or MBO) is to restructure the acquired company and later take it "public" again by issuing new shares to the public in the primary market.

The third type of private investment is a **private investment in public equity**, or PIPE.[14] This type of investment is generally sought by a public company that is in need of additional capital quickly and is willing to sell a sizeable ownership position to a private investor or investor group. For example, a company may require a large investment of new equity funds in a short period of time because it has significant expansion opportunities, is facing high levels of indebtedness, or is experiencing a rapid deterioration in its operations. Depending on how urgent the need is and the size of the capital requirement, the private investor may be able to purchase shares in the company at a significant discount to the publicly-quoted market price. Exhibit 11 contains a recent PIPE transaction for the health care company TapImmune, which also included the proposed merger with Maker Therapeutics.

Exhibit 11: Example of a PIPE Transaction[15]

JACKSONVILLE, Florida, June 8, 2018—TapImmune Inc. (NASDAQ: TPIV), a clinical-stage immuno-oncology company, today announced that it has entered into security purchase agreements with certain institutional and accredited investors in connection with a private placement of its equity securities. The private placement will be led by New Enterprise Associates (NEA) with participation from Aisling Capital and Perceptive Advisors, among other new and existing investors. The private placement is expected to be completed concurrently with the closing of the proposed merger between TapImmune Inc. and Marker Therapeutics, Inc., which was previously announced on May 15, 2018.

Upon closing the private placement, TapImmune will issue 17,500,000 shares of its common stock at a price of $4.00 per share. The aggregate offering size, before deducting the placement agent fees and other offering expenses, is expected to be $70 million. Additionally, TapImmune will issue warrants to purchase 13,125,000 shares of TapImmune common stock at an exercise price of $5.00 per share that will be exercisable for a period of five years from the date of issuance. The closing of the transaction, which is subject to the closing of the

---

14 The term PIPE is widely used in the United States and is also used internationally, including in emerging markets.
15 https://tapimmune.com/2018/06/tapimmune-announces-pricing-of-70-million-private-placement/

> merger with Marker, the approval by TapImmune's stockholders as required by NASDAQ Stock Market Rules, and other customary closing conditions, is anticipated to occur by the end of the third quarter of 2018.

While the global private equity market is relatively small in comparison to the global public equity market, it has experienced considerable growth over the past three decades. According to a study of the private equity market sponsored by the *World Economic Forum* and spanning the period 1970–2007, approximately US$3.6 trillion in debt and equity were acquired in leveraged buyouts. Of this amount, approximately 75 percent or US$2.7 trillion worth of transactions occurred during 2001–2007.[16] This pace continued with a further US$2.9 trillion in transactions occurring during 2008-2017.[17] While the US and the UK markets were the focus of most private equity investments during the 1980s and 1990s, private equity investments outside of these markets have grown substantially in recent years. In addition, the number of companies operating under private equity ownership has also grown. For example, during the mid-1990s, fewer than 2,000 companies were under LBO ownership compared to more than 20,000 companies that were under LBO ownership globally at the beginning of 2017. The holding period for private equity investments has also increased during this time period from 3 to 5 years (1980s and 1990s) to approximately 10 years.[18]

The move to longer holding periods has given private equity investors the opportunity to more effectively and patiently address any underlying operational issues facing the company and to better manage it for long-term value creation. Because of the longer holding periods, more private equity firms are issuing convertible preference shares because they provide investors with greater total return potential through their dividend payments and the ability to convert their shares into common shares during an IPO.

In operating a publicly traded company, management often feels pressured to focus on short-term results[19] (e.g., meeting quarterly sales and earnings targets from analysts biased toward near-term price performance) instead of operating the company to obtain long-term sustainable revenue and earnings growth. By "going private," management can adopt a more long-term focus and can eliminate certain costs that are necessary to operate a publicly traded company—such as the cost of meeting regulatory and stock exchange filing requirements, the cost of maintaining investor relations departments to communicate with shareholders and the media, and the cost of holding quarterly analyst conference calls.

As described above, public equity markets are much larger than private equity networks and allow companies more opportunities to raise capital that is subsequently actively traded in secondary markets. By operating under public scrutiny, companies are incentivized to be more open in terms of corporate governance and executive compensation to ensure that they are acting for the benefit of shareholders. In fact, some studies have shown that private equity firms score lower in terms of corporate governance effectiveness, which may be attributed to the fact that shareholders, analysts, and other stakeholders are able to influence management when corporate governance and other policies are public.

---

16 Strömberg (2008).
17 https://www.statista.com/statistics/270195/global-private-equity-deal-value/
18 See, for example, Bailey, Wirth, and Zapol (2005).
19 See, for example, Graham, Harvey, and Rajgopal (2005).

NON-DOMESTIC EQUITY SECURITIES

☐ describe methods for investing in non-domestic equity securities

Technological innovations and the growth of electronic information exchanges (electronic trading networks, the internet, etc.) have accelerated the integration and growth of global financial markets. As detailed previously, global capital markets have expanded at a much more rapid rate than global GDP in recent years; both primary and secondary international markets have benefited from the enhanced ability to rapidly and openly exchange information. Increased integration of equity markets has made it easier and less expensive for companies to raise capital and to expand their shareholder base beyond their local market. Integration has also made it easier for investors to invest in companies that are located outside of their domestic markets. This has enabled investors to further diversify and improve the risk and return characteristics of their portfolios by adding a class of assets with lower correlations to local country assets.

One barrier to investing globally is that many countries still impose "foreign restrictions" on individuals and companies from other countries that want to invest in their domestic companies. There are three primary reasons for these restrictions. The first is to limit the amount of control that foreign investors can exert on domestic companies. For example, some countries prevent foreign investors from acquiring a majority interest in domestic companies. The second is to give domestic investors the opportunity to own shares in the foreign companies that are conducting business in their country. For example, the Swedish home furnishings retailer IKEA abandoned efforts to invest in parts of the Asia/Pacific region because local governments did not want IKEA to maintain complete ownership of its stores. The third reason is to reduce the volatility of capital flows into and out of domestic equity markets. For example, one of the main consequences of the Asian Financial Crisis in 1997–98 was the large outflow of capital from such emerging market countries as Thailand, Indonesia, and South Korea. These outflows led to dramatic declines in the equity markets of these countries and significant currency devaluations and resulted in many governments placing restrictions on capital flows. Today, many of these same markets have built up currency reserves to better withstand capital outflows inherent in economic contractions and periods of financial market turmoil.

Studies have shown that reducing restrictions on foreign ownership has led to improved equity market performance over the long term.[20] Although restrictions vary widely, more countries are allowing increasing levels of foreign ownership. For example, Australia has sought tax reforms as a means to encourage international demand for its managed funds in order to increase its role as an international financial center.

Over the past two decades, three trends have emerged: a) an increasing number of companies have issued shares in markets outside of their home country; b) the number of companies whose shares are traded in markets outside of their home has increased; and c) an increasing number of companies are dual listed, which means that their shares are simultaneously issued and traded in two or more markets. Companies located in emerging markets have particularly benefited from these trends because they no longer have to be concerned with capital constraints or lack of liquidity in their domestic markets. These companies have found it easier to raise capital in the markets of developed countries because these markets generally have higher levels of liquidity and more stringent financial reporting requirements and accounting standards.

---

20 See, for example, Henry and Chari (2004).

Being listed on an international exchange has a number of benefits. It can increase investor awareness about the company's products and services, enhance the liquidity of the company's shares, and increase corporate transparency because of the additional market exposure and the need to meet a greater number of filing requirements.

Technological advancements have made it easier for investors to trade shares in foreign markets. The German insurance company Allianz SE recently delisted its shares from the NYSE and certain European markets because international investors increasingly traded its shares on the Frankfurt Stock Exchange. Exhibit 12 illustrates the extent to which the institutional shareholder base at BASF, a large German chemical corporation, has become increasingly global in nature.

Exhibit 12: Example of Increased Globalization of Share Ownership[21]

BASF is one of the largest publicly owned companies with over 500,000 shareholders and a high free float. An analysis of the shareholder structure carried out in March 2018 showed that, at 21% of share capital, the United States and Canada made up the largest regional group of institutional investors. Institutional investors from Germany made up 12%. Shareholders from United Kingdom and Ireland held 12% of BASF shares, while a further 17% are held by institutional investors from the rest of Europe. Around 28% of the company's share capital is held by private investors, most of whom are resident in Germany.

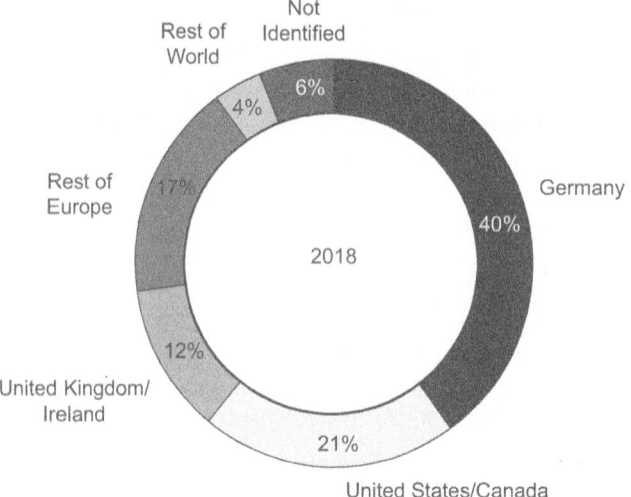

Direct Investing

Investors can use a variety of methods to invest in the equity of companies outside of their local market. The most obvious is to buy and sell securities directly in foreign markets. However, this means that all transactions—including the purchase and sale of shares, dividend payments, and capital gains—are in the company's, not the investor's, domestic currency. In addition, investors must be familiar with the trading, clearing, and settlement regulations and procedures of that market. Investing directly often results in less transparency and more volatility because audited financial information may not be provided on a regular basis and the market may be less liquid. Alternatively, investors can use such securities as depository receipts and global registered shares,

---

21 Adapted from BASF's investor relations website (www.basf.com). **Free float** refers to the extent that shares are readily and freely tradable in the secondary market.

Non-Domestic Equity Securities

which represent the equity of international companies and are traded on local exchanges and in the local currencies. With these securities, investors have to worry less about currency conversions (price quotations and dividend payments are in the investor's local currency), unfamiliar market practices, and differences in accounting standards. The sections that follow discuss various securities that investors can invest in outside of their home market.

Depository Receipts

A **depository receipt**[22] (DR) is a security that trades like an ordinary share on a local exchange and represents an economic interest in a foreign company. It allows the publicly listed shares of a foreign company to be traded on an exchange outside its domestic market. A depository receipt is created when the equity shares of a foreign company are deposited in a bank (i.e., the depository) in the country on whose exchange the shares will trade. The depository then issues receipts that represent the shares that were deposited. The number of receipts issued and the price of each DR is based on a ratio, which specifies the number of depository receipts to the underlying shares. Consequently, a DR may represent one share of the underlying stock, many shares of the underlying stock, or a fractional share of the underlying stock. The price of each DR will be affected by factors that affect the price of the underlying shares, such as company fundamentals, market conditions, analysts' recommendations, and exchange rate movements. In addition, any short-term valuation discrepancies between shares traded on multiple exchanges represent a quick arbitrage profit opportunity for astute traders to exploit. The responsibilities of the **depository bank** that issues the receipts include acting as custodian and as a registrar. This entails handling dividend payments, other taxable events, stock splits, and serving as the transfer agent for the foreign company whose securities the DR represents. The Bank of New York Mellon is the largest depository bank; however, Deutsche Bank, JPMorgan, and Citibank also offer depository services.[23]

A DR can be **sponsored** or **unsponsored**. A sponsored DR is when the foreign company whose shares are held by the depository has a direct involvement in the issuance of the receipts. Investors in sponsored DRs have the same rights as the direct owners of the common shares (e.g., the right to vote and the right to receive dividends). In contrast, with an unsponsored DR, the underlying foreign company has no involvement with the issuance of the receipts. Instead, the depository purchases the foreign company's shares in its domestic market and then issues the receipts through brokerage firms in the depository's local market. In this case, the depository bank, not the investors in the DR, retains the voting rights. Sponsored DRs are generally subject to greater reporting requirements than unsponsored DRs. In the United States, for example, sponsored DRs must be registered (meet the reporting requirements) with the US Securities and Exchange Commission (SEC). Exhibit 13 contains an example of a sponsored DR issued by Alibaba in September 2014.

Exhibit 13: Sponsored Depository Receipts[24]

NEW YORK—(BUSINESS WIRE)—Citi today announced that Alibaba Group Holding Limited ("Alibaba Group") has appointed Citi's Issuer Services business, acting through Citibank, N.A., as the depositary bank for its American Depositary

---

22 Note that the spellings *depositary* and *depository* are used interchangeably in financial markets. In this reading, we use the spelling *depository* throughout.
23 Boubakri, Cosset, and Samet (2010).
24 https://www.businesswire.com/news/home/20140924005984/en/Citi-Appointed-Depositary-Bank-Alibaba-Group-Holding

Receipt ("ADR") program. Alibaba Group's ADRs, which began trading on September 19, 2014, represent the largest Depositary Receipt program in initial public offering market history.

Alibaba Group's ADR program was established through a $25.03 billion initial public offering of 368,122,000 American Depositary Shares ("ADSs"), representing ordinary shares of Alibaba Group, which was priced at $68 per ADS on September 18, 2014. The IPO ranks as the largest in history. The ADRs are listed on the New York Stock Exchange (the "NYSE") under the trading symbol BABA. Each ADS represents one ordinary share of the Company. In its role as depositary bank, Citibank will hold the underlying ordinary shares through its local custodian and issue ADSs representing such shares. Alibaba Group's ADSs trade on the NYSE in ADR form.

There are two types of depository receipts: Global depository receipts (GDRs) and American depository receipts (ADRs), which are described below.

Global Depository Receipts

A **global depository receipt** (GDR) is issued outside of the company's home country and outside of the United States. The depository bank that issues GDRs is generally located (or has branches) in the countries on whose exchanges the shares are traded. A key advantage of GDRs is that they are not subject to the foreign ownership and capital flow restrictions that may be imposed by the issuing company's home country because they are sold outside of that country. The issuing company selects the exchange where the GDR is to be traded based on such factors as investors' familiarity with the company or the existence of a large international investor base. The London and Luxembourg exchanges were the first ones to trade GDRs. Some other stock exchanges trading GDRs are the Dubai International Financial Exchange and the Singapore Stock Exchange. Currently, the London and Luxembourg exchanges are where most GDRs are traded because they can be issued in a more timely manner and at a lower cost. Regardless of the exchange they are traded on, the majority of GDRs are denominated in US dollars, although the number of GDRs denominated in pound sterling and euros is increasing. Note that although GDRs cannot be listed on US exchanges, they can be privately placed with institutional investors based in the United States.

American Depository Receipts

An **American depository receipt** (ADR) is a US dollar-denominated security that trades like a common share on US exchanges. First created in 1927, ADRs are the oldest type of depository receipts and are currently the most commonly traded depository receipts. They enable foreign companies to raise capital from US investors. Note that an ADR is one form of a GDR; however, not all GDRs are ADRs because GDRs cannot be publicly traded in the United States. The term **American depository share** (ADS) is often used in tandem with the term ADR. A depository share is a security that is actually traded in the issuing company's domestic market. That is, while American depository receipts are the certificates that are traded on US markets, American depository shares are the underlying shares on which these receipts are based.

There are four primary types of ADRs, with each type having different levels of corporate governance and filing requirements. Level I Sponsored ADRs trade in the over-the-counter (OTC) market and do not require full registration with the Securities and Exchange Commission (SEC). Level II and Level III Sponsored ADRs can trade on the New York Stock Exchange (NYSE), NASDAQ, and American Stock Exchange (AMEX). Level II and III ADRs allow companies to raise capital and make acquisitions using these securities. However, the issuing companies must fulfill all SEC requirements.

Non-Domestic Equity Securities

The fourth type of ADR, an SEC Rule 144A or a Regulation S depository receipt, does not require SEC registration. Instead, foreign companies are able to raise capital by privately placing these depository receipts with qualified institutional investors or to offshore non-US investors. Exhibit 14 summarizes the main features of ADRs.

Exhibit 14: Summary of the Main Features of American Depository Receipts

	Level I (Unlisted)	Level II (Listed)	Level III (Listed)	Rule 144A (Unlisted)
Objectives	Develop and broaden US investor base with existing shares	Develop and broaden US investor base with existing shares	Develop and broaden US investor base with existing/new shares	Access qualified institutional buyers (QIBs)
Raising capital on US markets?	No	No	Yes, through public offerings	Yes, through private placements to QIBs
SEC registration	Form F-6	Form F-6	Forms F-1 and F-6	None
Trading	Over the counter (OTC)	NYSE, NASDAQ, or AMEX	NYSE, NASDAQ, or AMEX	Private offerings, resales, and trading through automated linkages such as PORTAL
Listing fees	Low	High	High	Low
Size and earnings requirements	None	Yes	Yes	None

Source: Adapted from Boubakri, Cosset, and Samet (2010): Table 1.

More than 2,000 DRs, from over 80 countries, currently trade on US exchanges. Based on current statistics, the total market value of DRs issued and traded is estimated at approximately US$2 trillion, or 15 percent of the total dollar value of equities traded in US markets.[25]

Global Registered Share

A **global registered share** (GRS) is a common share that is traded on different stock exchanges around the world in different currencies. Currency conversions are not needed to purchase or sell them, because identical shares are quoted and traded in different currencies. Thus, the same share purchased on the Swiss exchange in Swiss francs can be sold on the Tokyo exchange for Japanese yen. As a result, GRSs offer more flexibility than depository receipts because the shares represent an actual ownership interest in the company that can be traded anywhere and currency conversions are not needed to purchase or sell them. GRSs were created and issued by Daimler Chrysler in 1998 and by UBS AG in 2011.

Basket of Listed Depository Receipts

Another type of global security is a **basket of listed depository receipts** (BLDR), which is an exchange-traded fund (ETF) that represents a portfolio of depository receipts. An ETF is a security that tracks an index but trades like an individual share on an exchange. An equity-ETF is a security that contains a portfolio of equities that tracks an index. It trades throughout the day and can be bought, sold, or sold short, just like an individual share. Like ordinary shares, ETFs can also be purchased on margin and used in hedging or arbitrage strategies. The BLDR is a specific class of

---

[25] *JPMorgan Depositary Receipt Guide* (2005):4.

ETF security that consists of an underlying portfolio of DRs and is designed to track the price performance of an underlying DR index. For example, the Invesco BLDRS Asia 50 ADR Index Fund is a capitalization-weighted ETF designed to track the performance of 50 Asian market-based ADRs.

5. RISK AND RETURN CHARACTERISTICS

> compare the risk and return characteristics of different types of equity securities

Different types of equity securities have different ownership claims on a company's net assets. The type of equity security and its features affect its risk and return characteristics. The following sections discuss the different return and risk characteristics of equity securities.

Return Characteristics of Equity Securities

There are two main sources of equity securities' total return: price change (or capital gain) and dividend income. The price change represents the difference between the purchase price (P_{t-1}) and the sale price (P_t) of a share at the end of time $t - 1$ and t, respectively. Cash or stock dividends (D_t) represent distributions that the company makes to its shareholders during period t. Therefore, an equity security's total return is calculated as:

$$\text{Total return, } R_t = (P_t - P_{t-1} + D_t)/P_{t-1} \tag{1}$$

For non-dividend-paying stocks, the total return consists of price appreciation only. Companies that are in the early stages of their life cycle generally do not pay dividends because earnings and cash flows are reinvested to finance the company's growth. In contrast, companies that are in the mature phase of their life cycle may not have as many profitable growth opportunities; therefore, excess cash flows are often returned to investors via the payment of regular dividends or through share repurchases.

For investors who purchase depository receipts or foreign shares directly, there is a third source of return: **foreign exchange gains (or losses)**. Foreign exchange gains arise because of the change in the exchange rate between the investor's currency and the currency that the foreign shares are denominated in. For example, US investors who purchase the ADRs of a Japanese company will earn an additional return if the yen appreciates relative to the US dollar. Conversely, these investors will earn a lower total return if the yen depreciates relative to the US dollar. For example, if the total return for a Japanese company was 10 percent in Japan and the yen depreciated by 10 percent against the US dollar, the total return of the ADR would be (approximately) 0 percent. If the yen had instead appreciated by 10 percent against the US dollar, the total return of the ADR would be (approximately) 20 percent.

Investors that only consider price appreciation overlook an important source of return: the compounding that results from reinvested dividends. Reinvested dividends are cash dividends that the investor receives and uses to purchase additional shares. As Exhibit 15 shows, in the long run total returns on equity securities are dramatically influenced by the compounding effect of reinvested dividends. Between 1900 and 2016, US$1 invested in US equities in 1900 would have grown in *real* terms to US$1,402 with dividends reinvested, but to just US$11.9 when taking only the price appreciation or capital gain into account. This corresponds to a real compounded return of 6.4 percent per year with dividends reinvested, versus only 2.1 percent per year without dividends reinvested. The comparable ending real wealth for bonds and bills are US$9.8 and US$2.60, respectively. These ending real wealth figures correspond to annualized real compounded returns of 2.0 percent on bonds and 0.8 percent on bills.

Exhibit 15: Impact of Reinvested Dividends on Cumulative Real Returns in the US and UK Equity Market: 1900–2016

Source: Dimson, Marsh, and Staunton (2017). This chart is updated annually and can be found at http://publications.credit-suisse.com/index.cfm/publikationen-shop/research-institute/.

Risk of Equity Securities

The risk of any security is based on the uncertainty of its future cash flows. The greater the uncertainty of its future cash flows, the greater the risk and the more variable or volatile the security's price. As discussed above, an equity security's total return is determined by its price change and dividends. Therefore, the risk of an equity security can be defined as the uncertainty of its expected (or future) total return. Risk is most often measured by calculating the standard deviation of the equity's expected total return.

A variety of different methods can be used to estimate an equity's expected total return and risk. One method uses the equity's average historical return and the standard deviation of this return as proxies for its expected future return and risk. Another method involves estimating a range of future returns over a specified period of time, assigning probabilities to those returns, and then calculating an expected return and a standard deviation of return based on this information.

The type of equity security, as well as its characteristics, affects the uncertainty of its future cash flows and therefore its risk. In general, preference shares are less risky than common shares for three main reasons:

1. Dividends on preference shares are known and fixed, and they account for a large portion of the preference shares' total return. Therefore, there is less uncertainty about future cash flows.

2. Preference shareholders receive dividends and other distributions before common shareholders.

3. The amount preference shareholders will receive if the company is liquidated is known and fixed as the par (or face) value of their shares. However, there is no guarantee that investors will receive that amount if the company experiences financial difficulty.

With common shares, however, a larger portion of shareholders' total return (or all of their total return for non-dividend shares) is based on future price appreciation and future dividends are unknown. If the company is liquidated, common shareholders will receive whatever amount (if any) is remaining after the company's creditors and preference shareholders have been paid. In summary, because the uncertainty surrounding the total return of preference shares is less than common shares, preference shares have lower risk and lower expected return than common shares.

It is important to note that some preference shares and common shares can be riskier than others because of their associated characteristics. For example, from an investor's point of view, putable common or preference shares are less risky than their callable or non-callable counterparts because they give the investor the option to sell the shares to the issuer at a pre-determined price. This pre-determined price establishes a minimum price that investors will receive and reduces the uncertainty associated with the security's future cash flow. As a result, putable shares generally pay a lower dividend than non-putable shares.

Because the major source of total return for preference shares is dividend income, the primary risk affecting all preference shares is the uncertainty of future dividend payments. Regardless of the preference shares' features (callable, putable, cumulative, etc.), the greater the uncertainty surrounding the issuer's ability to pay dividends, the greater risk. Because the ability of a company to pay dividends is based on its future cash flows and net income, investors try to estimate these amounts by examining past trends or forecasting future amounts. The more earnings and the greater amount of cash flow that the company has had, or is expected to have, the lower the uncertainty and risk associated with its ability to pay future dividends.

Callable common or preference shares are riskier than their non-callable counterparts because the issuer has the option to redeem the shares at a pre-determined price. Because the call price limits investors' potential future total return, callable shares generally pay a higher dividend to compensate investors for the risk that the shares could be called in the future. Similarly, putable preference shares have lower risk than non-putable preference shares. Cumulative preference shares have lower risk than non-cumulative preference shares because the cumulative feature gives investors the right to receive any unpaid dividends before any dividends can be paid to common shareholders.

6. EQUITY AND COMPANY VALUE

- ☐ explain the role of equity securities in the financing of a company's assets
- ☐ contrast the market value and book value of equity securities
- ☐ compare a company's cost of equity, its (accounting) return on equity, and investors' required rates of return

Companies issue equity securities on primary markets to raise capital and increase liquidity. This additional liquidity also provides the corporation an additional "currency" (its equity), which it can use to make acquisitions and provide stock option-based incentives to employees. The primary goal of raising capital is to finance the company's revenue-generating activities in order to increase its net income and maximize the wealth of its shareholders. In most cases, the capital that is raised is used to finance the purchase of long-lived assets, capital expansion projects, research and development, the entry into new product or geographic regions, and the acquisition of other companies. Alternatively, a company may be forced to raise capital to ensure that it continues to operate as a going concern. In these cases, capital is raised to fulfill regulatory requirements, improve capital adequacy ratios, or to ensure that debt covenants are met.

The ultimate goal of management is to increase the book value (shareholders' equity on a company's balance sheet) of the company and maximize the market value of its equity. Although management actions can directly affect the book value of the company (by increasing net income or by selling or purchasing its own shares), they can only indirectly affect the market value of its equity. The book value of a company's equity—the difference between its total assets and total liabilities—increases when the company retains its net income. The more net income that is earned and retained, the greater the company's book value of equity. Because management's decisions directly influence a company's net income, they also directly influence its book value of equity.

The market value of the company's equity, however, reflects the collective and differing expectations of investors concerning the amount, timing, and uncertainty of the company's future cash flows. Rarely will book value and market value be equal. Although management may be accomplishing its objective of increasing the company's book value, this increase may not be reflected in the market value of the company's equity because it does not affect investors' expectations about the company's future cash flows. A key measure that investors use to evaluate the effectiveness of management in increasing the company's book value is the accounting return on equity.

Accounting Return on Equity

Return on equity (ROE) is the primary measure that equity investors use to determine whether the management of a company is effectively and efficiently using the capital they have provided to generate profits. It measures the total amount of net income available to common shareholders generated by the total equity capital invested in the company. It is computed as net income available to ordinary shareholders (i.e., after preferred dividends have been deducted) divided by the average total book value of equity (BVE). That is:

$$\text{ROE}_t = \frac{\text{NI}_t}{\text{Average BVE}_t} = \frac{\text{NI}_t}{(\text{BVE}_t + \text{BVE}_{t-1})/2} \qquad (2)$$

where NI_t is the net income in year t and the average book value of equity is computed as the book values at the beginning and end of year t divided by 2. Return on equity assumes that the net income produced in the current year is generated by the equity existing at the beginning of the year and any new equity that was invested during the year. Note that some formulas only use shareholders' equity at the beginning of year t (that is, the end of year $t-1$) in the denominator. This assumes that only the equity existing at the beginning of the year was used to generate the company's net income during the year. That is:

$$\text{ROE}_t = \frac{\text{NI}_t}{\text{BVE}_{t-1}} \qquad (3)$$

Both formulas are appropriate to use as long as they are applied consistently. For example, using beginning of the year book value is appropriate when book values are relatively stable over time or when computing ROE for a company annually over a period of time. Average book value is more appropriate if a company experiences more volatile year-end book values or if the industry convention is to use average book values in calculating ROE.

One caveat to be aware of when computing and analyzing ROE is that net income and the book value of equity are directly affected by management's choice of accounting methods, such as those relating to depreciation (straight line versus accelerated methods) or inventories (first in, first out versus weighted average cost). Different accounting methods can make it difficult to compare the return on equity of companies even if they operate in the same industry. It may also be difficult to compare the ROE of the same company over time if its accounting methods have changed during that time.

Exhibit 16 contains information on the net income and total book value of shareholders' equity for three **blue chip** (widely held large market capitalization companies that are considered financially sound and are leaders in their respective industry or local stock market) pharmaceutical companies: Pfizer, Novartis AG, and GlaxoSmithKline. The data are for their financial years ending December 2015 through December 2017.[26]

Exhibit 16: Net Income and Book Value of Equity for Pfizer, Novartis AG, and GlaxoSmithKline (in Thousands of US Dollars)

	Financial Year Ending		
	31 Dec 2015	31 Dec 2016	31 Dec 2017
Pfizer			
Net income	$6,960,000	$7,215,000	$21,308,000
Total stockholders' equity	$64,998,000	$59,840,000	$71,287,000
Novartis AG			
Net income	$17,783,000	$6,712,000	$7,703,000
Total stockholders' equity	$77,122,000	$74,891,000	$74,227,000
GlaxoSmithKline			
Net income	$12,420,000	$1,126,000	$2,070,700
Total stockholders' equity	$11,309,250	$6,127,800	$4,715,800

Using the average book value of equity, the return on equity for Pfizer for the years ending December 2016 and 2017 can be calculated as:

Return on equity for the year ending December 2016

$$\text{ROE}_{2016} = \frac{\text{NI}_{2016}}{(\text{BVE}_{2015} + \text{BVE}_{2016})/2} = \frac{7,215,000}{(64,998,000 + 59,840,000)/2} = 11.6\%$$

Return on equity for the year ending December 2017

$$\text{ROE}_{2017} = \frac{\text{NI}_{2017}}{(\text{BVE}_{2016} + \text{BVE}_{2017})/2} = \frac{21,308,000}{(59,840,000 + 71,287,000)/2} = 32.5\%$$

Exhibit 17 summarizes the return on equity for Novartis and GlaxoSmithKline in addition to Pfizer for 2016 and 2017.

---

26 Pfizer uses US GAAP to prepare its financial statements; Novartis and GlaxoSmithKline use International Financial Reporting Standards. Therefore, it would be inappropriate to compare the ROE of Pfizer to that of Novartis or GlaxoSmithKline.

Equity and Company Value

Exhibit 17: Return on Equity for Pfizer, Novartis AG, and GlaxoSmithKline

	31 Dec 2016 (%)	31 Dec 2017 (%)
Pfizer	11.6	32.5
Novartis AG	8.8	10.3
GlaxoSmithKline	12.9	38.2

In the case of Pfizer, the ROE of 32.5 percent in 2017 indicates that the company was able to generate a return (profit) of US$0.325 on every US$1.00 of capital invested by shareholders. GlaxoSmithKline almost tripled its return on equity over this period, from 12.9 percent to 38.2 percent. Novartis's ROE remained relatively unchanged.

ROE can increase if net income increases at a faster rate than shareholders' equity or if net income decreases at a slower rate than shareholders' equity. In the case of GlaxoSmithKline, ROE almost tripled between 2016 and 2017 due to its net income almost doubling during the period and due to its average shareholder's fund decreasing by almost 45 percent during the period. Stated differently, in 2017 compared to 2016, GlaxoSmithKline was significantly more effective in using its equity capital to generate profits. In the case of Pfizer, its ROE increased dramatically from 11.6 percent to 32.5 percent in 2017 versus 2016 even though its average shareholder equity increased by around 5 percent due to a nearly tripling of net income during the period.

An important question to ask is whether an increasing ROE is always good. The short answer is, "it depends." One reason ROE can increase is if net income decreases at a slower rate than shareholders' equity, which is not a positive sign. In addition, ROE can increase if the company issues debt and then uses the proceeds to repurchase some of its outstanding shares. This action will increase the company's leverage and make its equity riskier. Therefore, it is important to examine the source of changes in the company's net income *and* shareholders' equity over time. The DuPont formula, which is discussed in a separate reading, can be used to analyze the sources of changes in a company's ROE.

The book value of a company's equity reflects the historical operating and financing decisions of its management. The market value of the company's equity reflects these decisions as well as investors' collective assessment and expectations about the company's future cash flows generated by its positive net present value investment opportunities. If investors believe that the company has a large number of these future cash flow-generating investment opportunities, the market value of the company's equity will exceed its book value. Exhibit 18 shows the market price per share, the total number of shares outstanding, and the total book value of shareholders' equity for Pfizer, Novartis AG, and GlaxoSmithKline at the end of December 2017. This exhibit also shows the total market value of equity (or market capitalization) computed as the number of shares outstanding multiplied by the market price per share.

Exhibit 18: Market Information for Pfizer, Novartis AG, and GlaxoSmithKline (in Thousands of US Dollars except market price)

	Pfizer	Novartis AG	GlaxoSmithKline
Market price	$35.74	$90.99	$18.39
Total shares outstanding	5,952,900	2,317,500	4,892,200
Total shareholders' equity	$71,287,000	$74,227,000	$4,715,800
Total market value of equity	$212,756,646	$210,869,325	$89,967,558

Note that in Exhibit 18, the total market value of equity for Pfizer is computed as:

Market value of equity = Market price per share × Shares outstanding

Market value of equity = US$35.74 × 5,952,900 = US$212,756,646.

The book value of equity per share for Pfizer can be computed as:

Book value of equity per share = Total shareholders' equity/Shares outstanding

Book value of equity per share = US$71,287,000/5,952,900 = US$11.98.

A useful ratio to compute is a company's price-to-book ratio, which is also referred to as the market-to-book ratio. This ratio provides an indication of investors' expectations about a company's future investment and cash flow-generating opportunities. The larger the price-to-book ratio (i.e., the greater the divergence between market value per share and book value per share), the more favorably investors will view the company's future investment opportunities. For Pfizer the price-to-book ratio is:

Price-to-book ratio = Market price per share/Book value of equity per share

Price-to-book ratio = US$35.74/US$11.98 = 2.98

Exhibit 19 contains the market price per share, book value of equity per share, and price-to-book ratios for Novartis and GlaxoSmithKline in addition to Pfizer.

Exhibit 19: Pfizer, Novartis AG, and GlaxoSmithKline

	Pfizer	Novartis AG	GlaxoSmithKline
Market price per share	$35.74	$90.99	$18.39
Book value of equity per share	$11.98	$32.03	$0.96
Price-to-book ratio	2.98	2.84	19.16

The market price per share of all three companies exceeds their respective book values, so their price-to-book ratios are all greater than 1.00. However, there are significant differences in the sizes of their price-to-book ratios. GlaxoSmithKline has the largest price-to-book ratio, while the price-to-book ratios of Pfizer and Novartis are similar to each other. This suggests that investors believe that GlaxoSmithKline has substantially higher future growth opportunities than either Pfizer or Novartis.

It is not appropriate to compare the price-to-book ratios of companies in different industries because their price-to-book ratios also reflect investors' outlook for the industry. Companies in high growth industries, such as technology, will generally have higher price-to-book ratios than companies in slower growth (i.e., mature) industries, such as heavy equipment. Therefore, it is more appropriate to compare the price-to-book ratios of companies in the same industry. A company with relatively high growth opportunities compared to its industry peers would likely have a higher price-to-book ratio than the average price-to-book ratio of the industry.

Book value and return on equity are useful in helping analysts determine value but can be limited as a primary means to estimate a company's true or intrinsic value, which is the present value of its future projected cash flows. In Exhibit 20, Warren Buffett, one of the most successful investors in the world and CEO of Berkshire Hathaway, provides an explanation of the differences between the book value of a company and its intrinsic value in a letter to shareholders. As discussed above, market value reflects the collective and differing expectations of investors concerning the amount, timing, and uncertainty of a company's future cash flows. A company's intrinsic value can only be estimated because it is impossible to predict the amount and timing of its future cash flows. However, astute investors—such as Buffett—have been able to profit from discrepancies between their estimates of a company's intrinsic value and the market value of its equity.

> ### Exhibit 20: Book Value versus Intrinsic Value[27]
>
> We regularly report our per-share book value, an easily calculable number, though one of limited use. Just as regularly, we tell you that what counts is intrinsic value, a number that is impossible to pinpoint but essential to estimate.
>
> For example, in 1964, we could state with certitude that Berkshire's per-share book value was $19.46. However, that figure considerably overstated the stock's intrinsic value since all of the company's resources were tied up in a sub-profitable textile business. Our textile assets had neither going-concern nor liquidation values equal to their carrying values. In 1964, then, anyone inquiring into the soundness of Berkshire's balance sheet might well have deserved the answer once offered up by a Hollywood mogul of dubious reputation: "Don't worry, the liabilities are solid."
>
> Today, Berkshire's situation has reversed: Many of the businesses we control are worth far more than their carrying value. (Those we don't control, such as Coca-Cola or Gillette, are carried at current market values.) We continue to give you book value figures, however, because they serve as a rough, understated, tracking measure for Berkshire's intrinsic value.
>
> We define intrinsic value as the discounted value of the cash that can be taken out of a business during its remaining life. Anyone calculating intrinsic value necessarily comes up with a highly subjective figure that will change both as estimates of future cash flows are revised and as interest rates move. Despite its fuzziness, however, intrinsic value is all-important and is the only logical way to evaluate the relative attractiveness of investments and businesses.
>
> To see how historical input (book value) and future output (intrinsic value) can diverge, let's look at another form of investment, a college education. Think of the education's cost as its "book value." If it is to be accurate, the cost should include the earnings that were foregone by the student because he chose college rather than a job.
>
> For this exercise, we will ignore the important non-economic benefits of an education and focus strictly on its economic value. First, we must estimate the earnings that the graduate will receive over his lifetime and subtract from that figure an estimate of what he would have earned had he lacked his education. That gives us an excess earnings figure, which must then be discounted, at an appropriate interest rate, back to graduation day. The dollar result equals the intrinsic economic value of the education.

The Cost of Equity and Investors' Required Rates of Return

When companies issue debt (or borrow from a bank) or equity securities, there is a cost associated with the capital that is raised. In order to maximize profitability and shareholder wealth, companies attempt to raise capital efficiently so as to minimize these costs.

When a company issues debt, the cost it incurs for the use of these funds is called the cost of debt. The cost of debt is relatively easy to estimate because it reflects the periodic interest (or coupon) rate that the company is contractually obligated to pay

---

27 Extracts from Berkshire Hathaway's *2008 Annual Report* (www.berkshirehathaway.com).

to its bondholders (lenders). When a company raises capital by issuing equity, the cost it incurs is called the cost of equity. Unlike debt, however, the company is not contractually obligated to make any payments to its shareholders for the use of their funds. As a result, the cost of equity is more difficult to estimate.

Investors require a return on the funds they provide to the company. This return is called the investor's minimum required rate of return. When investors purchase the company's debt securities, their minimum required rate of return is the periodic rate of interest they charge the company for the use of their funds. Because all of the bondholders receive the same periodic rate of interest, their required rate of return is the same. Therefore, the company's cost of debt and the investors' minimum required rate of return on the debt are the same.

When investors purchase the company's equity securities, their minimum required rate of return is based on the future cash flows they expect to receive. Because these future cash flows are both uncertain and unknown, the investors' minimum required rate of return must be estimated. In addition, the minimum required return may differ across investors based on their expectations about the company's future cash flows. As a result, the company's cost of equity may be different from the investors' minimum required rate of return on equity.[28] Because companies try to raise capital at the lowest possible cost, the company's cost of equity is often used as a proxy for the investors' *minimum* required rate of return.

In other words, the cost of equity can be thought of as the minimum expected rate of return that a company must offer its investors to purchase its shares in the primary market and to maintain its share price in the secondary market. If this expected rate of return is not maintained in the secondary market, then the share price will adjust so that it meets the minimum required rate of return demanded by investors. For example, if investors require a higher rate of return on equity than the company's cost of equity, they would sell their shares and invest their funds elsewhere resulting in a decline in the company's share price. As the share price declined, the cost of equity would increase to reach the higher rate of return that investors require.

Two models commonly used to estimate a company's cost of equity (or investors' minimum required rate of return) are the dividend discount model (DDM) and the capital asset pricing model (CAPM). These models are discussed in detail in other curriculum readings.

The cost of debt (after tax) and the cost of equity (i.e., the minimum required rates of return on debt and equity) are integral components of the capital budgeting process because they are used to estimate a company's weighted average cost of capital (WACC). Capital budgeting is the decision-making process that companies use to evaluate potential long-term investments. The WACC represents the minimum required rate of return that the company must earn on its long-term investments to satisfy all providers of capital. The company then chooses among those long-term investments with expected returns that are greater than its WACC.

SUMMARY

Equity securities play a fundamental role in investment analysis and portfolio management. The importance of this asset class continues to grow on a global scale because of the need for equity capital in developed and emerging markets, technological innovation, and the growing sophistication of electronic information exchange. Given

---

[28] Another important factor that can cause a firm's cost of equity to differ from investors' required rate of return on equity is the flotation cost associated with equity

Equity and Company Value

their absolute return potential and ability to impact the risk and return characteristics of portfolios, equity securities are of importance to both individual and institutional investors.

This reading introduces equity securities and provides an overview of global equity markets. A detailed analysis of their historical performance shows that equity securities have offered average real annual returns superior to government bills and bonds, which have provided average real annual returns that have only kept pace with inflation. The different types and characteristics of common and preference equity securities are examined, and the primary differences between public and private equity securities are outlined. An overview of the various types of equity securities listed and traded in global markets is provided, including a discussion of their risk and return characteristics. Finally, the role of equity securities in creating company value is examined as well as the relationship between a company's cost of equity, its accounting return on equity, investors' required rate of return, and the company's intrinsic value.

We conclude with a summary of the key components of this reading:

- Common shares represent an ownership interest in a company and give investors a claim on its operating performance, the opportunity to participate in the corporate decision-making process, and a claim on the company's net assets in the case of liquidation.

- Callable common shares give the issuer the right to buy back the shares from shareholders at a price determined when the shares are originally issued.

- Putable common shares give shareholders the right to sell the shares back to the issuer at a price specified when the shares are originally issued.

- Preference shares are a form of equity in which payments made to preference shareholders take precedence over any payments made to common stockholders.

- Cumulative preference shares are preference shares on which dividend payments are accrued so that any payments omitted by the company must be paid before another dividend can be paid to common shareholders. Non-cumulative preference shares have no such provisions, implying that the dividend payments are at the company's discretion and are thus similar to payments made to common shareholders.

- Participating preference shares allow investors to receive the standard preferred dividend plus the opportunity to receive a share of corporate profits above a pre-specified amount. Non-participating preference shares allow investors to simply receive the initial investment plus any accrued dividends in the event of liquidation.

- Callable and putable preference shares provide issuers and investors with the same rights and obligations as their common share counterparts.

- Private equity securities are issued primarily to institutional investors in private placements and do not trade in secondary equity markets. There are three types of private equity investments: venture capital, leveraged buyouts, and private investments in public equity (PIPE).

- The objective of private equity investing is to increase the ability of the company's management to focus on its operating activities for long-term value creation. The strategy is to take the "private" company "public" after certain profit and other benchmarks have been met.

- Depository receipts are securities that trade like ordinary shares on a local exchange but which represent an economic interest in a foreign company. They allow the publicly listed shares of foreign companies to be traded on an exchange outside their domestic market.
- American depository receipts are US dollar-denominated securities trading much like standard US securities on US markets. Global depository receipts are similar to ADRs but contain certain restrictions in terms of their ability to be resold among investors.
- Underlying characteristics of equity securities can greatly affect their risk and return.
- A company's accounting return on equity is the total return that it earns on shareholders' book equity.
- A company's cost of equity is the minimum rate of return that stockholders require the company to pay them for investing in its equity.

REFERENCES

Bailey, Elizabeth, Meg Wirth, David Zapol. 2005. "Venture Capital and Global Health." Financing Global Health Ventures, Discussion Paper (September 2005): http://www.commonscapital.com/downloads/Venture_Capital_and_Global_Health.pdf

Boubakri, Narjess, Jean-Claude Cosset, Anis Samet. 2010. "The Choice of ADRs." Journal of Banking and Finance, vol. 34, no. 9:2077–2095.

Dimson, Elroy, Paul Marsh, Mike Staunton. 2018. Credit Suisse Global Investment Returns Sourcebook 2017. Credit Suisse Research Institute.

Graham, John R., Campbell R. Harvey, Shiva Rajgopal. 2005. "The Economic Implications of Corporate Financial Reporting." Journal of Accounting and Economics, vol. 40, no. 1–3:3–73.

Henry, Peter Blair, Anusha Chari. 2004. "Risk Sharing and Asset Prices: Evidence from a Natural Experiment." Journal of Finance, vol. 59, no. 3:1295–1324.

Strömberg, Per. 2008. "The New Demography of Private Equity." The Global Economic Impact of Private Equity Report 2008, World Economic Forum.

PRACTICE PROBLEMS

1. Which of the following is *not* a characteristic of common equity?
   A. It represents an ownership interest in the company.
   B. Shareholders participate in the decision-making process.
   C. The company is obligated to make periodic dividend payments.

2. The type of equity voting right that grants one vote for each share of equity owned is referred to as:
   A. proxy voting.
   B. statutory voting.
   C. cumulative voting.

3. All of the following are characteristics of preference shares *except*:
   A. They are either callable or putable.
   B. They generally do not have voting rights.
   C. They do not share in the operating performance of the company.

4. Participating preference shares entitle shareholders to:
   A. participate in the decision-making process of the company.
   B. convert their shares into a specified number of common shares.
   C. receive an additional dividend if the company's profits exceed a pre-determined level.

5. Which of the following statements about private equity securities is *incorrect*?
   A. They cannot be sold on secondary markets.
   B. They have market-determined quoted prices.
   C. They are primarily issued to institutional investors.

6. Venture capital investments:
   A. can be publicly traded.
   B. do not require a long-term commitment of funds.
   C. provide mezzanine financing to early-stage companies.

7. Which of the following statements *most accurately* describes one difference between private and public equity firms?
   A. Private equity firms are focused more on short-term results than public firms.

Practice Problems

   B. Private equity firms' regulatory and investor relations operations are less costly than those of public firms.

   C. Private equity firms are incentivized to be more open with investors about governance and compensation than public firms.

8. Emerging markets have benefited from recent trends in international markets. Which of the following has *not* been a benefit of these trends?

   A. Emerging market companies do not have to worry about a lack of liquidity in their home equity markets.

   B. Emerging market companies have found it easier to raise capital in the markets of developed countries.

   C. Emerging market companies have benefited from the stability of foreign exchange markets.

9. When investing in unsponsored depository receipts, the voting rights to the shares in the trust belong to:

   A. the depository bank.

   B. the investors in the depository receipts.

   C. the issuer of the shares held in the trust.

10. With respect to Level III sponsored ADRs, which of the following is *least likely* to be accurate? They:

    A. have low listing fees.

    B. are traded on the NYSE, NASDAQ, and AMEX.

    C. are used to raise equity capital in US markets.

11. A basket of listed depository receipts, or an exchange-traded fund, would *most likely* be used for:

    A. gaining exposure to a single equity.

    B. hedging exposure to a single equity.

    C. gaining exposure to multiple equities.

12. Calculate the total return on a share of equity using the following data:
    Purchase price: $50
    Sale price: $42
    Dividend paid during holding period: $2

    A. −12.0%

    B. −14.3%

    C. −16.0%

13. If a US-based investor purchases a euro-denominated ETF and the euro subsequently depreciates in value relative to the dollar, the investor will have a total

return that is:

A. lower than the ETF's total return.

B. higher than the ETF's total return.

C. the same as the ETF's total return.

14. Which of the following is *incorrect* about the risk of an equity security? The risk of an equity security is:

A. based on the uncertainty of its cash flows.

B. based on the uncertainty of its future price.

C. measured using the standard deviation of its dividends.

15. From an investor's point of view, which of the following equity securities is the *least* risky?

A. Putable preference shares.

B. Callable preference shares.

C. Non-callable preference shares.

16. Which of the following is *least likely* to be a reason for a company to issue equity securities on the primary market?

A. To raise capital.

B. To increase liquidity.

C. To increase return on equity.

17. Which of the following is *not* a primary goal of raising equity capital?

A. To finance the purchase of long-lived assets.

B. To finance the company's revenue-generating activities.

C. To ensure that the company continues as a going concern.

18. Which of the following statements is *most accurate* in describing a company's book value?

A. Book value increases when a company retains its net income.

B. Book value is usually equal to the company's market value.

C. The ultimate goal of management is to maximize book value.

19. Calculate the book value of a company using the following information:

Number of shares outstanding	100,000
Price per share	€52
Total assets	€12,000,000
Total liabilities	€7,500,000
Net Income	€2,000,000

Practice Problems

    A. €4,500,000.

    B. €5,200,000.

    C. €6,500,000.

20. Which of the following statements is *least accurate* in describing a company's market value?

    A. Management's decisions do not influence the company's market value.

    B. Increases in book value may not be reflected in the company's market value.

    C. Market value reflects the collective and differing expectations of investors.

21. Calculate the return on equity (ROE) of a stable company using the following data:

Total sales	£2,500,000
Net income	£2,000,000
Beginning of year total assets	£50,000,000
Beginning of year total liabilities	£35,000,000
Number of shares outstanding at the end of the year	1,000,000
Price per share at the end of the year	£20

    A. 10.0%.

    B. 13.3%.

    C. 16.7%.

22. Holding all other factors constant, which of the following situations will *most likely* lead to an increase in a company's return on equity?

    A. The market price of the company's shares increases.

    B. Net income increases at a slower rate than shareholders' equity.

    C. The company issues debt to repurchase outstanding shares of equity.

23. Which of the following measures is the *most difficult* to estimate?

    A. The cost of debt.

    B. The cost of equity.

    C. Investors' required rate of return on debt.

24. A company's cost of equity is often used as a proxy for investors':

    A. average required rate of return.

    B. minimum required rate of return.

    C. maximum required rate of return.

SOLUTIONS

1. C is correct. The company is not obligated to make dividend payments. It is at the discretion of the company whether or not it chooses to pay dividends.

2. B is correct. Statutory voting is the type of equity voting right that grants one vote per share owned.

3. A is correct. Preference shares do not have to be either callable or putable.

4. C is correct. Participating preference shares entitle shareholders to receive an additional dividend if the company's profits exceed a pre-determined level.

5. B is correct. Private equity securities do not have market-determined quoted prices.

6. C is correct. Venture capital investments can be used to provide mezzanine financing to companies in their early stage of development.

7. B is correct. Regulatory and investor relations costs are lower for private equity firms than for public firms. There are no stock exchange, regulatory, or shareholder involvements with private equity, whereas for public firms these costs can be high.

8. C is correct. The trends in emerging markets have not led to the stability of foreign exchange markets.

9. A is correct. In an unsponsored DR, the depository bank owns the voting rights to the shares. The bank purchases the shares, places them into a trust, and then sells shares in the trust—not the underlying shares—in other markets.

10. A is correct. The listing fees on Level III sponsored ADRs are high.

11. C is correct. An ETF is used to gain exposure to a basket of securities (equity, fixed income, commodity futures, etc.).

12. A is correct. The formula states $R_t = (P_t - P_{t-1} + D_t)/P_{t-1}$. Therefore, total return = $(42 - 50 + 2)/50 = -12.0\%$.

13. A is correct. The depreciated value of the euro will create an additional loss in the form of currency return that is lower than the ETF's return.

14. C is correct. Some equity securities do not pay dividends, and therefore the standard deviation of dividends cannot be used to measure the risk of all equity securities.

15. A is correct. Putable shares, whether common or preference, give the investor the option to sell the shares back to the issuer at a pre-determined price. This pre-determined price creates a floor for the share's price that reduces the uncertainty of future cash flows for the investor (i.e., lowers risk relative to the other two types of shares listed).

16. C is correct. Issuing shares in the primary (and secondary) market *reduces* a company's return on equity because it increases the total amount of equity capital invested in the company (i.e., the denominator in the ROE formula).

17. C is correct. Capital is raised to ensure the company's existence only when it is

required. It is not a typical goal of raising capital.

18. A is correct. A company's book value increases when a company retains its net income.

19. A is correct. The book value of the company is equal to total assets minus total liabilities, which is €12,000,000 − €7,500,000 = €4,500,000.

20. A is correct. A company's market value is affected by management's decisions. Management's decisions can directly affect the company's *book* value, which can then affect its market value.

21. B is correct. A company's ROE is calculated as (NI_t/BVE_{t-1}). The BVE_{t-1} is equal to the beginning total assets minus the beginning total liabilities, which equals £50,000,000 − £35,000,000 = £15,000,000. Therefore, ROE = £2,000,000/£15,000,000 = 13.3%.

22. C is correct. A company's ROE will increase if it issues debt to repurchase outstanding shares of equity.

23. B is correct. The cost of equity is not easily determined. It is dependent on investors' required rate of return on equity, which reflects the different risk levels of investors and their expectations about the company's future cash flows.

24. B is correct. Companies try to raise funds at the lowest possible cost. Therefore, cost of equity is used as a proxy for the minimum required rate of return.

LEARNING MODULE 5

Company Analysis: Past and Present

LEARNING OUTCOMES

Mastery	The candidate should be able to:
☐	describe the elements that should be covered in a thorough company research report
☐	determine a company's business model
☐	evaluate a company's revenue and revenue drivers, including pricing power
☐	evaluate a company's operating profitability and working capital using key measures
☐	evaluate a company's capital investments and capital structure

INTRODUCTION

An insightful and well-written company research report helps investors understand a company and make better investment decisions about the company's securities. This module is the first of three that will provide a framework to prepare a company research report by applying methods covered in previous modules to assess a company's business model, financial performance, and financial position.

> **LEARNING MODULE OVERVIEW**
>
> - Company research reports analyze a company's past and present financials, its industry and competitors, and forecast its future financial statements. Reports end with a valuation, an investment recommendation, and investment risks.
> - The first step of company analysis requires an understanding of the issuer's business model, for which analysts rely on both issuer and third-party information sources.
> - An understanding of the issuer's business model and analysis of historical financial statements will allow the analyst to identify key drivers of revenues, profitability, cash flows, and financial position.

- Revenue analysis can be done using a bottom-up or top-down approach. A bottom-up approach breaks down revenues into drivers such as sales volumes and prices, by product line or segment. A top-down approach expresses revenue as a function of drivers such as market share, market size, and GDP growth.
- While a company can change its prices at will, its ability to do so successfully (i.e., not causing a loss of volume) and relative to costs is driven by the company's pricing power. Pricing power is primarily a function of industry structure and competitive strategy.
- Cost analysis assesses a company's profitability and working capital management. Analysts calculate and interpret several cost and profitability measures, including gross, operating, and net margins.
- While a fixed versus variable cost analysis is useful, the analysis is often limited by issuer disclosures and accounting standards that emphasize cost reporting by function or nature.
- The degree of operating leverage measures the sensitivity of operating profit to changes in sales. Operating leverage is primarily driven by the fixed and variable cost composition of the issuer's operating expenses.
- The degree of financial leverage measures the sensitivity of net income to changes in operating income. Financial leverage is primarily driven by the issuer's capital structure.

LEARNING MODULE SELF-ASSESSMENT

These initial questions are intended to help you gauge your current level of understanding of this learning module.

1. Identify two elements that are common to *all* company research reports and two elements that are common to *initial* research reports.

    Solution:

    Common to all research reports:

    - Analyst's investment recommendation and target buy or sell prices
    - Risks such as evaluation of material downside and upside risks

    Common to initial research reports:

    - Discussion of issuer's business model and strategy, and explanatory charts and figures that disaggregate revenues and profits by product or geography
    - Detailed financial analysis and models
    - Industry overview and competitive positioning such as industry size, growth rate, market share trends, and industry profitability. Evaluation of the company's competitive position and strategy in each product line or segment is also common.

Introduction

2. Identify three information sources that analysts commonly use to determine and analyze a company's business model.

   Solution:

   - Regulatory filings if the issuer is public, especially the annual and quarterly reports
   - Investor events and presentations by the issuer
   - Visiting the company's properties and/or websites

3. Last year, a distributor of dental care products earned EUR800 million in revenues. Management estimated that its market share was 10%. Based on management's estimate, the market size for distribution of dental care products in this geography last year was *closest* to (in millions of EUR):

   A. 80
   B. 7,200
   C. 8,000

   Solution:

   C is correct.

   $$\text{Market share} = \frac{\text{Revenue}}{\text{Market Size}}$$

   Which can be rearranged to:

   $$\text{Market size} = \frac{\text{Revenue}}{\text{Market Share}}$$

   $$\text{Market size} = \frac{\text{EUR 800 million}}{10\%}$$

   $$\text{Market size} = \text{EUR 8,000 million (8 billion)}$$

4. A beverage manufacturer recently introduced a new line of healthy tea-based drinks. The average selling price was USD20 a case last year and the company sold 2 million cases. This year, an analyst forecasts sales of 3 million cases and an increase in the average selling price—from a reduction in discounts and promotions—of 5%. The analyst's forecast for net sales growth this year over the prior year is *closest* to:

   A. 50%
   B. 55%
   C. 58%

   Solution:

   C is correct.

   Net sales = average selling price × cases sold

   Net sales last year = USD20 × 2 million = USD40 million

   Net sales forecast this year = (USD20 × 1.05) × 3 million = USD63 million

   Forecasted net sales growth rate = 63/40 − 1 = 0.575 or 58%

5. Impression Ltd. is a fictional company that designs, manufactures, and sells skin care and beauty products. Identify whether each expense line below

from Impression Ltd.'s last annual income statement is *most likely* a fixed or variable cost.

I. Amortization of acquired intangible assets	Fixed	Variable
II. Interest expense	Fixed	Variable
III. Costs of goods sold	Fixed	Variable
IV. General and administrative expenses	Fixed	Variable
V. Sales commissions	Fixed	Variable

Solution:

I. Fixed. Amortization expense generally does not change with levels of sales volume, as definite-lived intangible assets are amortized on a straight-line basis over the assets' useful lives.

II. Fixed. Interest expense is a function of the quantity of debt and its interest rate, not sales volume.

III. Variable. Costs of goods sold are incurred when sales are made.

IV. Fixed. General and administrative expenses are usually not related to sales volume each year.

V. Variable. Sales commissions, a form of performance-based compensation for salespeople, are a function of sales and are therefore variable.

6. Based on the data below, the degree of operating leverage for Company XYZ for the year ended 31 December 20X1 is *closest* to:

Company XYZ: Statement of Income for the Year Ended (in millions of EUR)

	31 December 20X1	31 December 20X0
Revenue	9,707	9,256
Costs of goods sold	4,850	4,637
Selling, general, and administrative expenses	993	1,090
Research and development expenses	1,700	1,554
Other operating expenses	491	448
Interest expense	309	325
Other (income) expense	24	(71)
Income before income taxes	1,340	1,273
Provision for income taxes	295	255
Net income	1,045	1,018

A. 0.51

B. 1.08

C. 1.96

C is correct.

20X1 Operating Income = 9,707 − 4,850 − 993 − 1,700 − 491 = 1,673

20X0 Operating Income = 9,256 − 4,637 − 1,090 − 1,554 − 448 = 1,527

$DOL = \% \Delta$ Operating Income$/\% \Delta$ Sales

$DOL = (1{,}673/1{,}527 - 1)/(9{,}707/9{,}256 - 1)$

$DOL = 1.96$

A is incorrect, as it inverts the equation; it is the ratio of the change in sales to the change in operating income.

B is incorrect; it is the ratio of the percentage change in pre-tax income, rather than operating income, to the percentage change in sales.

7. If a company reported trailing 12 months' operating cash flow of USD150 million, current assets excluding cash of USD40 million, and current liabilities of USD60 million, the company *most likely*:

   A. was inefficient in managing its financing.
   B. used trade credit to manage working capital.
   C. over-extended itself and is at risk of bankruptcy.

   Solution:

   B is correct. Negative net working capital typically indicates that the company uses suppliers' trade credit to lengthen days payable, while also efficiently managing inventory days and days sales outstanding.

   A is incorrect. Negative working capital is a source rather than a use of financing and gives an issuer more financial flexibility, as capital is not tied up in working capital.

   C is incorrect. There is not enough information here to determine bankruptcy risk, but positive operating cash flows and negative net working capital are not bankruptcy risk indicators.

8. A company's management may choose *not* to use financial leverage because the company has:

   A. an investment-grade credit rating.
   B. a high degree of operating leverage.
   C. a lower net debt to EBITDA ratio than its peers.

   Solution:

   B is correct. The degree of financial leverage and the degree of operating leverage together equal the degree of total leverage in the business. If the company already has a high degree of operating leverage, using financial leverage may increase total leverage and risk to too high a level.

   A is incorrect. An investment-grade credit rating generally indicates that the company could borrow economically, which would be a reason to use financial leverage.

   C is incorrect. A lower net debt to EBITDA ratio than its peers is an indicator of borrowing capacity, which would be a reason to use financial leverage.

COMPANY RESEARCH REPORTS

2

☐ describe the elements that should be covered in a thorough company research report

Analysts value and make investment recommendations on issuers' equity securities using scenarios of future earnings, cash flows, and financial position. These future scenarios are structured in the form of financial statements and are known as financial statement models. While a financial statement model is quantitative, it is not a mathematics problem to solve with a correct answer, but rather a quantitative expression of an analyst's forward-looking views. These views should be based on supporting evidence and justified by analysis.

The process of forming and justifying a view of an issuer's future financial results and position involves company and industry analysis and is the subject of this module and the next two. Exhibit 1 introduces a framework for company and industry analysis. This module focuses on the foundational block Company Analysis: Past and Present.

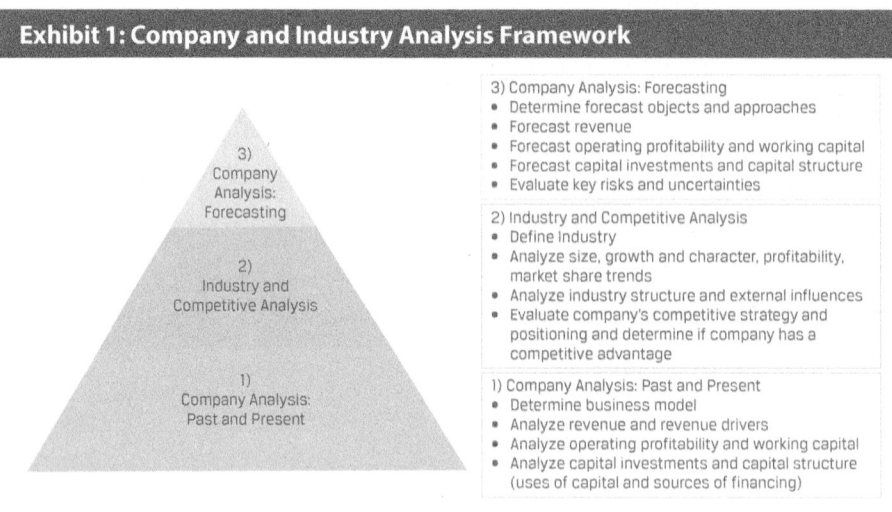

Analysts present their company and industry analysis, as well as their valuation and investment recommendation, in a **company research report**. The structure, content, and tone of the report depend on the analyst's setting. Reports on a public issuer's equity securities for distribution to external clients (a "sell-side report"), for example, often consist of an extensive initial report (an "initiating coverage" report, or "initiation") when the analyst begins covering the security, followed by shorter reports on specific topics or that make updates to a recommendation after the analyst receives new information or conducts additional analyses, particularly after the issuer reports financial results. Analysts' reports solely for internal distribution to an audience already familiar with the issuer might be far shorter and delivered verbally or in a handful of presentation slides.

An example of the structure of an *initial* company research report for external distribution is shown in Exhibit 2. The primary audience is those who are not already knowledgeable about the issuer or security.

Exhibit 2: Initial Company Research Report Elements

Front Matter	- Issuer name and security identifiers (e.g., symbol, CUSIP) - Analysts' recommendation (buy, hold, sell) and target buy or sell prices - Disclosures, disclaimers, and other legally required information
Recommendation	- Analysts' recommendation - Summary of key reasons supporting the recommendation
Company Description	- Discussion of issuer's business model and strategy - Explanatory charts and figures—for example, disaggregation of revenues and profits by product, geography, etc.
Industry Overview & Competitive Positioning	- Industry size, growth rate and key drivers, market share trends, profitability—historical and outlook - Competitive analysis such as Porter's Five Forces - Analysis of external industry influences such as political, economic, social, technological, legal, and environmental ("PESTLE" analysis) - Evaluation of company's position and strategy in the industry
Financial Analysis and Model	- Evaluation of key drivers of revenue, costs, profitability, cash flows, and the issuer's uses and sources of capital - Forecasts of key drivers and supporting discussion - Historical and forecasted financial statements
Valuation	- Estimates of company and security values with target price - Typically includes relative and present value approaches - Discussion of key inputs and scenario and sensitivity analyses
Environmental, Social, and Governance (ESG) Considerations	- Evaluation of ESG indicators and risks - Ownership structure and management composition - Executive compensation
Risks	- Evaluation of material downside and upside risks and discussion of how they are considered in the financial analysis and valuation

THE CFA INSTITUTE RESEARCH CHALLENGE

For examples of initial company research reports, we encourage you to visit the Past Research Challenge Champions section of cfainstitute.org, which has winning reports and presentations from the research competition that CFA Institute and CFA Societies around the world host each year. Teams of university students are assigned a public company to research by a local CFA Society and compete on the quality of their research and modeling, valuation, and communication skills.

Subsequent company research reports are often shorter than initial reports. Their primary audience is those who are already familiar with the issuer or security and require an update based on new information and analyses or a change in the analyst's recommendation. Such a report for a company that recently reported quarterly financial results may be structured in the form shown in Exhibit 3. The structure of a subsequent report depends on the analyst's setting and the nature of the report.

Exhibit 3: Subsequent Company Research Report Elements

Front Matter	- Analysts' names - Issuer name - Security and exchange identifiers (e.g., symbol, CUSIP) - Analysts' recommendation: buy, hold, sell - Current security price and analysts' target price - Disclosures, disclaimers, and other legally required information
Recommendation	- Analysts' recommendation - Summary of changes to the recommendation and support explanations
Analysis of New Information	- Comparison of quarterly actual results with expected results - Analysts' interpretation of new information and changes to forecasts - Historical and updated forecasted financial statements
Valuation	- Estimates of company and security values - Discussion of changes from valuation in prior report
Risks	- Update of risk factors from prior report with discussion of changes

QUESTION SET

1. Which of the following statements about initiation reports is true?

   A. The structure, content, and tone of the report are independent of the analyst's setting.

   B. The report makes updates to the recommendation after the issuer reports financial results.

   C. The primary audience is those who are not already knowledgeable about the issuer or security.

   Solution:

   C is correct. The primary audience is those who are not already knowledgeable about the issuer or security.

   A is incorrect, because the structure, content, and tone of the report are dependent on the analyst's setting. Examples include whether the report is meant for internal or external distribution and whether it is an in-depth initiation report or a subsequent report updating the reader after a change in recommendation or the release of the issuer's quarterly results.

   B is incorrect, because the initial report is to help those who are not already knowledgeable to understand the issuer or security. A subsequent research report is used to update the audience after the release of financial results.

2. If you read a research report that includes both a Porter's Five Forces analysis and a PESTLE analysis, then *most likely*:

   A. the authoring analyst is initiating coverage.

   B. the report is updating a recommendation after an earnings release.

> C. the report is written by a firm's analyst who has covered the company for many years.
>
> **Solution:**
>
> A is correct. A Porter's Five Forces analysis and a PESTLE analysis are common elements in initiations and are less common in subsequent research reports, as they tend to evolve more slowly than other report elements such as financial analyses and models.
>
> B and C are incorrect; these elements are common in subsequent rather than initial research reports.

> 3. The evaluation of a company's competitive strategy takes place before the:
>
>   A. analysis of revenue and revenue drivers.
>
>   B. analysis of operating profitability and working capital.
>
>   C. forecasting of revenue, operating profitability, and working capital.
>
>   **Solution:**
>
>   C is correct. Forecasting takes place only after company analysis and industry and competitive analysis are complete. The evaluation of a company's competitive strategy is part of the industry and competitive analysis.
>
>   A is incorrect, because the analysis of revenue and revenue drivers is part of the first stage of analysis, where the analyst studies the company's past and present financial statements. As we shall see in Lesson 3, analysts start by analyzing the revenue line items first.
>
>   B is incorrect, because the analysis of operating profitability and working capital typically takes place before the industry and competitive analysis. The evaluation of the company's competitive strategy is usually part of the industry and company analysis, which takes place after completion of the analysis of operating profitability and working capital.

DETERMINING THE BUSINESS MODEL

☐ determine a company's business model

Determining the business model is the first step in our industry and company analysis framework because it summarizes important drivers of an issuer's financial results and position, focuses the analyst on what requires further investigation, and should begin setting the analyst's expectations for the issuer. A discussion of the business model is usually in the first part of a company research report (see the "Company Description" section in Exhibit 2).

Recall that a business model describes a company's operations and includes the following elements, which analysts investigate by answering several key questions discussed in prior learning modules.

Business Model Element	Key Questions for Analysts
The product(s) or service(s) the company sells	What is the firm selling?
Customers and key customer groups	To whom does the company sell?

Business Model Element	Key Questions for Analysts
Sales channels, including customer acquisition and product/service delivery mechanisms	How does the company reach potential and current customers and how does it deliver products?
How the product(s) or service(s) are priced and paid for	How much does the company charge and how are prices and payment terms structured?
Resource, supplier, and partner relationships need to operate effectively	What does the company buy and rely on?

There are many corollary questions for each of the key questions, such as determining whether customers are few and concentrated, whether suppliers and resources are specialized or hard to replace, and so on. The answers to these questions are company specific, but the key questions to ask are common across industries and companies. Also, recall that many companies have a conventional business model, such as retailer or natural resource producer, which simplifies business model identification in practice. Analysts will often focus their analysis on the differences in a company's business model, if any, from a conventional model or those of its competitors.

Information sources that analysts use to answer these questions include the following, grouped by origin: the issuer, public third party, proprietary third party, and proprietary primary research.

- Issuer sources (available freely if the company is public)

  - Regulatory filings, especially the annual and quarterly reports
  - Quarterly or semi-annual earnings conference calls
  - Presentations and events for investors
  - Press releases
  - Issuer management, investor relations, or other personnel
  - Company website or properties that the analyst may be able to visit as either a customer or an investor. It is often useful to experience an issuer's and its competitors' products firsthand, though it is not always possible (e.g., pharmaceuticals).

- Public third-party sources

  - Free industry white papers or analyst reports from a consultancy
  - Economic or industry indicators from governments and other organizations
  - General news outlets
  - Industry-specific news outlets
  - Social media
  - Miscellaneous sources available via search engines

- Proprietary third-party sources

  - Analyst reports and communications, including from "sell-side" or "Wall Street" analysts and credit rating agencies
  - Reports and data from platforms such as Bloomberg and FactSet
  - Reports and data from consultancies, often industry specific, such as Rystad in energy, IQVIA and Evaluate in biopharma, Gartner and IDC in information technology

- Proprietary primary research

Determining the Business Model

- Surveys, conversations, product comparisons, and other studies commissioned by the analyst or conducted directly

Analysts in an institutional investment setting (e.g., an asset management firm) are often able to conduct this initial research quickly, as they enjoy broad access to a variety of proprietary third-party sources, may have industry knowledge and experience themselves, can access prior analyses of the company or industry, and often have access to the issuer investor relations personnel and management.

We will demonstrate the determination of an issuer's business model with a fictional example adapted from a real company. We will use this case study throughout this module and the next two to demonstrate the use of the company and industry analysis framework. Another case study of a different company in the same industry is in the self-assessment section at the end of each lesson, so you can practice using the framework on your own.

CASE STUDIES

Warehouse Club Inc.

Elaine Nguyen is an analyst at Fyleton Investments. To find investment candidates for one of Fyleton's funds, Nguyen ran a screen for companies in developed markets that exceeded a certain level of sales growth and return on invested capital over the last five years while also performing well in the last recession. One company that passed the screen is Warehouse Club Inc. ("Warehouse"). Neither Nguyen nor her colleagues have ever worked on Warehouse before. A portfolio manager suggested that Nguyen research the company and its industry for several days and then discuss initial findings with colleagues before writing a formal research report.

Warehouse is a public company, so Nguyen compiles several issuer information sources, including the company's latest annual report and a transcript of management's presentation at a recent investor event. The following paragraphs and figures are excerpts from these sources.

> Warehouse Club Inc. ("we," "our," "us," "the company") is a leading discount retailer, consistently offering customers more than 20% savings on a broad range of food and other merchandise compared to supermarket, department store, convenience store, and e-commerce competitors. Warehouse operated 149, 145, and 141 stores as of 31 December 2X19, 2X18, and 2X17, respectively.
>
> We sell a core assortment of packaged food and beverages, fresh foods, and non-food merchandise such as apparel, appliances, electronics and entertainment, housewares, and sporting goods. In addition to our core assortment, our stores feature a changing assortment of seasonal or discounted items based on the latest consumer trends and availability from suppliers, which vary by store. We also offer ancillary products and services such as petrol stations co-located with our stores, in-store takeaway prepared foods, pharmacy and optician centers, and hearing aids. In addition to carrying the leading branded goods, we also sell packaged food and household goods under our exclusive private-label brand that we source from contract manufacturers, which account for over 15% of our net sales and carry higher than average profitability.
>
> We operate a member-based model that requires customers to show their membership card to enter and shop in our stores. The annual membership fee is $60 per household. We estimate that members' annual savings versus shopping at competitors for the same basket of goods amounts to over five times their annual membership fee. Our membership fee revenues

were $601, $576, and $553 million in fiscal years 2X19, 2X18, and 2X17, respectively. Besides providing us with a source of recurring revenue, membership engenders shopper loyalty and drives our industry-low levels of inventory theft of less than 20 basis points as a percentage of net sales, which we believe is at least one-fifth that of competitors. Total memberships were 10.2, 9.8, and 9.4 million as of 31 December 2X19, 2X18, and 2X17, respectively.

Our strategy is based on price and cost leadership. We stock a limited selection of high-quality branded and private-label products in a wide range of categories that produce high sales volumes and rapid inventory turnover. We limit items to fast-selling models, sizes, and colors and carry an average of approximately 4,000 unique products per store, less than a quarter of the assortment of our supermarket and supercenter competitors. Most items are sold only in bulk sizes. Wherever possible, we utilize direct-from-manufacturer distribution and move merchandise immediately to the sales floor, presenting on pallets in a no-frills warehouse atmosphere. Our high-volume purchases of a limited number of products, direct from manufacturer distribution, and reduced handling of merchandise enable us to hold a low-cost position in the retail industry in terms of merchandise and labor costs. Our low costs and membership fee revenues enable us to operate profitably while charging significantly lower prices than other retailers. Low prices for quality products drive greater membership and net sales over time, leveraging our selling, general, and administrative expenses, reducing them as a percentage of net sales.

Our stores operate on a seven-day, 70-hour week with predictable shifts for employees. Because the hours of operation are shorter than other retailers, and due to other efficiencies inherent in a warehouse-type operation, labor costs are lower relative to the volume of sales. We look to maintain a large base of full-time employees with above-average wages and benefits to establish long tenures, as we believe this maximizes productivity and customer service at our stores. Our employee retention rate for employees who have been with us for at least a year is 90%, which we believe is substantially higher than the retail industry average.

Our retail operations, which represent substantially all our consolidated net sales, are our only reportable segment. We do not have significant sales outside our domestic geography: the United States. No single customer or supplier represents a material amount of revenues or merchandise costs, respectively.

Determining the Business Model

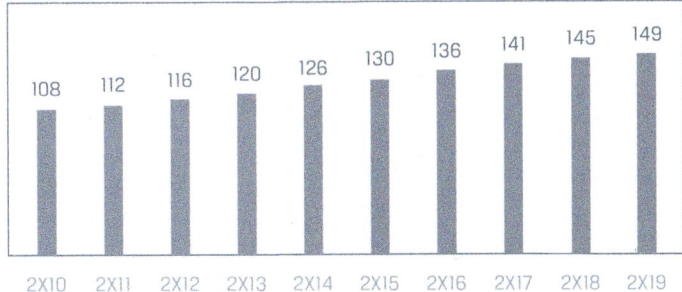

Warehouse Club Inc.
Number of Stores at Year-End, 2X10–2X19

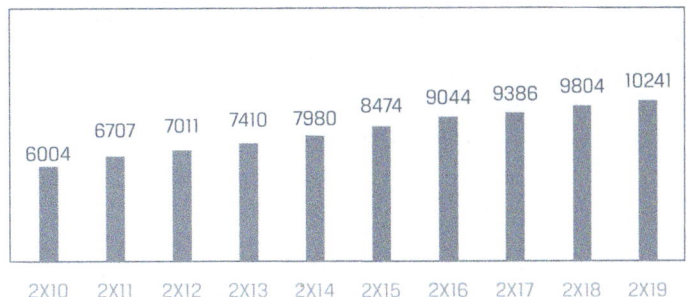

Warehouse Club Inc.
Number of Members (thousands) at Year-End, 2X10–2X19

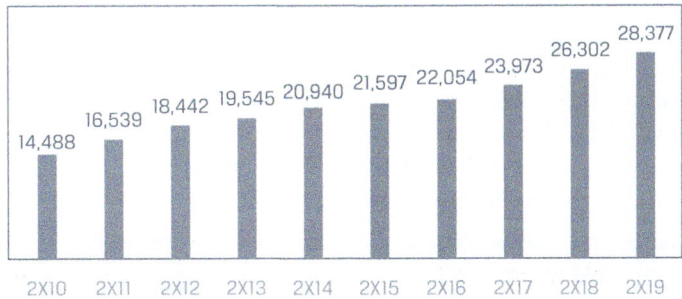

Warehouse Club Inc.
Annual Net Sales (USD millions), 2X10–2X19

Warehouse Club Inc. Income Statements for the Years Ended ... (amounts in USD millions except per share amounts)

	31 December 2X17	31 December 2X18	31 December 2X19
Net sales	23,973	26,302	28,377
Membership fees	553	576	601
Total revenues	24,526	26,878	28,978
Merchandise costs	(21,258)	(23,399)	(25,248)
Selling, general, and administrative expenses	(2,201)	(2,363)	(2,566)
Depreciation and amortization	(260)	(273)	(283)
New-store opening expenses	(16)	(13)	(16)

	31 December 2X17	31 December 2X18	31 December 2X19
Operating income	791	830	865
Interest expense	(25)	(30)	(29)
Interest income	10	14	24
Income before taxes	776	814	860
Income tax expense	(178)	(187)	(198)
Net income	598	627	662
Shares outstanding	83	83	84
Earnings per share	7.20	7.55	7.88

During its presentation at a recent investor event, Warehouse management made the following statements that were not in the annual report:

- Three years ago, the company launched "Buy Online, Pick-Up in Store," which enables members to shop on Warehouse's website or mobile app and pick up their order, assembled by Warehouse employees, at a store. The company does not plan to offer e-commerce or delivery itself or through third-party services.

- Membership is $60 per year, paid upfront, and refundable on a prorated basis for days remaining in the year. Management has increased the price of membership every five years by $5 and expects to continue to do so. The last price increase was three years ago.

- Management intends to open four new stores per year for the next five years.

- The company operates stores in urban and suburban areas in a single country. Over 90% of current members live within 10 kilometers of a store, and while membership has grown around existing stores over time, management believes the primary driver of membership growth is opening stores in new areas.

- Management does not plan to open stores in another country for the foreseeable future. An immaterial amount of merchandise is imported.

EXAMPLE 1

Determining Warehouse Club Inc.'s Business Model

Nguyen answers the following questions to determine Warehouse Club Inc.'s business model and to identify areas to conduct further research.

- What is the firm selling?

Warehouse sells a range of consumer goods, mostly consumables and perishables, approximately 4,000 unique items. For customers to shop at the stores, they must hold a membership, which Warehouse sells for $60 per year, per household. Nguyen graphs the following net sales by category data with descriptions supplied by Warehouse, and notes that the composition of net sales by category has not changed materially in the last 10 years.

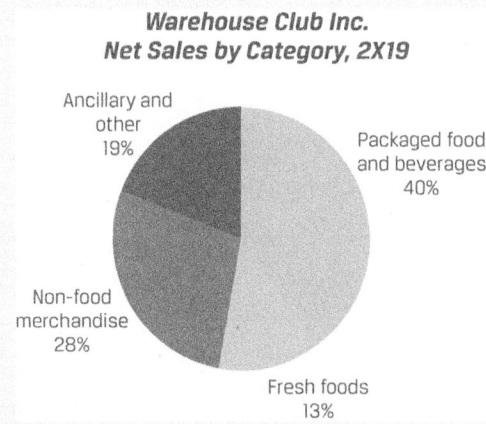

"Non-food merchandise" includes a broad range of items such as appliances, electronics, health and personal care products, hardware, outdoor and sporting goods, jewelry, furniture, and housewares.

"Ancillary and other" are service businesses that operate in or next to Warehouse's stores and include takeaway prepared foods, prescription pharmacies, petrol stations, optician centers, and hearing aids.

- To whom?

Warehouse's members are primarily consumer households that live within 10 kilometers of a store, are value-conscious, are willing to forgo a more extensive selection for lower unit prices on bulk-sized goods, and are able to afford the annual membership fee.

- How?

Warehouse sells products and services both in and around its stores. Members can either shop at the store or shop online and pick up at the store (Nguyen notes that management did not disclose the size of this in terms of net sales). Management said that it does minimal advertising (besides promotional mail) in an area before it opens a store and also sends out membership renewal reminders; the company primarily relies on word of mouth and its stores' physical presence to drive interest and foot traffic.

Memberships can be purchased online, by phone, or at any Warehouse store. Management said that over three-quarters of members purchase and renew their memberships online.

- For how much?

Warehouse has two revenue streams: goods and services (for which it earns net sales) and membership (for which it earns membership fees).

Management sets the prices of its merchandise by item. Gross margin and markup on aggregate net sales for the last three fiscal years were as follows:

	31 December 2X17	31 December 2X18	31 December 2X19
Net sales	23,973	26,302	28,377
Merchandise costs	(21,258)	(23,399)	(25,248)
Gross margin	2,715	2,903	3,129
Gross margin % of net sales	11.33%	11.04%	11.03%
Markup	12.77%	12.41%	12.39%

Therefore, the average good or service is sold at a price that is a little over 12% of the cost for Warehouse to purchase and ready the item for sale. While management claims that the company is a cost and price leader, Nguyen will have to corroborate that.

Membership is $60 per year, per household. Membership is required to shop at Warehouse stores, thus effectively raising the price of all its goods and services.

- What does the company buy and rely on to operate effectively?
  - Merchandise from a broad range of manufacturers and private-label goods from contract manufacturers
  - Human capital in stores and in management
  - Fixed assets including land in attractive locations, buildings, fixtures, refrigerators and freezers, and a range of information technology systems such as point-of-sale payment systems
  - Credit and debit card payment networks and financial institutions to receive and make electronic payments

While these are all broadly available and the company has not had supply or service interruptions in the past, a key partner appears to be merchandise manufacturers, particularly those that manufacture Warehouse's private-label products. Since Warehouse is strict on cost and quality and carries a limited selection, the company does rely heavily on these contract manufacturers.

In summary, Warehouse's business model is aimed at creating a virtuous cycle whereby low prices drive memberships, which drive further sales, which drive negotiating leverage with suppliers to enable low prices at low costs.

DISCUSSION BOARD QUESTION

Based on the information provided, what would you change about or add to Elaine Nguyen's analysis of Warehouse Club Inc.'s business model? Why?

We encourage you to post your response, as well as read and reply to others' responses, on the Learning Ecosystem discussion board.

QUESTION SET

Iliso Marketplace Ltd. ("we," "our," "us," "the Company," "Iliso") is redefining e-commerce by delivering superior customer experiences at competitive prices through our Iliso Marketplace mobile app and website. While e-commerce customers have historically been forced to compromise on shipping times, product quality, and hassles with returns, we've built a vertically integrated system that delivers a vast selection of products with one-day delivery on most orders. We continue to make significant investments in both technology and our fulfillment infrastructure to improve the customer experience and expand into new product categories and geographies.

Customer Experience

> We're committed to delighting our customers every day. Hallmarks of our customer experience include:
>
> - Next-Day or Faster Delivery. Customers are eligible for one-day delivery 365 days a year. In 2X19, over 93% of orders were delivered within 24 hours of receiving the order.
> - Free Shipping. Customers are eligible for free shipping on orders greater than $25, which we believe is the industry-leading minimum order threshold, and no membership fee is required.
> - Vast Selection of Items, Including Fresh Groceries. Customers can order from a selection of items across almost every category of goods—from fresh produce to consumer electronics to home décor and furniture. To continue offering the highest-quality items, we modify our selection continuously based on customer reviews. We enforce strict standards for third-party merchants to protect customers from counterfeit goods.
> - Frictionless Returns. Our customers simply tap a button on our app and leave the item outside their door for pickup. Refunds are initiated the moment the item is picked up at the door.
>
> The number of active customer accounts as of the fourth quarter for the years ended 31 December 2X17, 2X18, and 2X19, were 29, 31, and 36 million, respectively. Active customer account refers to a unique email address and at least one purchase in the indicated period; we do not charge membership fees or require minimum purchases to maintain an account.
>
> **Our Fulfillment Network**
>
> To achieve our differentiated customer experience, we focus on urban markets and have built a vertically integrated system in which we control every step, from a customer's purchase on our app to the photo confirmation of the delivery at the customer's front door. We receive most of our products directly from manufacturers at our fulfillment centers and minimize the use of third-party carriers and contractors by directly employing over 65,000 people in fulfillment and delivery. We believe direct employment and control of fulfillment assets such as delivery trucks enable speed, efficiency, and waste reduction, which is especially important for product categories such as fresh foods.
>
> We've made the strategic decision to focus on urban markets in the United States for the foreseeable future to achieve an economical route density for customer deliveries and returns and one-day shipping.
>
> **Merchant Services**
>
> In 2X13, we launched Merchant Services, allowing third-party merchants to sell products on Iliso Marketplace and utilize our fulfillment network. When multiple merchants (including us) sell the same product, our algorithm shows the customer the lowest price, including shipping cost, though the customer can manually choose a different seller. Third-party merchants must meet our rigorous quality standards but otherwise have discretion in product assortment and description, pricing, and shipping terms.
>
> We receive sales commissions on third-party merchants' sales, as well as service revenues if the merchant utilizes our fulfillment network for warehousing and delivery. We record revenue on a "net" basis for third-party merchant-related transactions because we act as an agent; the Company is not the seller of record, nor does it take control of the goods inventory. The number of active third-party merchants as of the fourth quarter for the years ended 31 December 2X17, 2X18, and 2X19 was 25,500, 31,500, and 40,500, respectively. Active third-party merchant refers to a unique email address and at least one sale in the indicated period; we do not charge merchant membership fees, nor do we require minimum sales levels.

Our annual gross merchandise value (GMV)—which includes the value of all products sold on our marketplace by us and third-party merchants, net of sales taxes and returns allowances but including any applicable shipping fees—was $5,721, $6,950, and $8,605 million for the years ended 31 December 2X17, 2X18, and 2X19, respectively. GMV by product category for the year ended 31 December 2X19 was as follows:

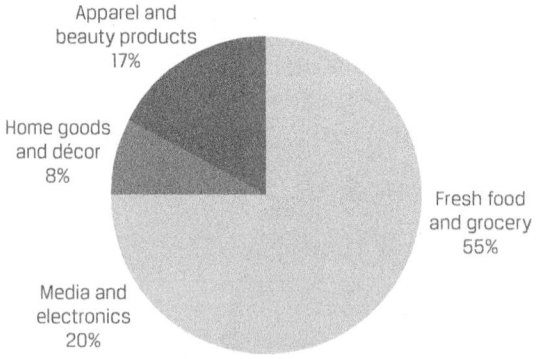

**Iliso Marketplace Ltd.
GMV by Product Category, 2X19**

- Apparel and beauty products 17%
- Home goods and décor 8%
- Media and electronics 20%
- Fresh food and grocery 55%

Iliso recently went public, so financial information is available only for the five years ended 31 December 2X19. Amounts are in millions of USD (except per share amounts).

Iliso Marketplace Ltd. GMV, Customer, and Merchant Counts for the Years Ended 31 December

	2X15	2X16	2X17	2X18	2X19
Iliso retail sales	2,589	3,424	5,100	6,052	7,336
Third-party merchant sales	279	432	621	898	1,269
Total GMV	2,868	3,856	5,721	6,950	8,605
Active customer accounts (millions)	16	23	29	31	36
Third-party merchants (#)	14,850	18,000	25,500	31,500	40,500

Iliso Marketplace Ltd. Income Statements for the Years Ended 31 December

	2X15	2X16	2X17	2X18	2X19
Net retail sales	2,589	3,424	5,100	6,052	7,336
Third-party merchant fees	42	65	94	134	190
Total revenues	2,631	3,489	5,194	6,186	7,526
Costs of revenues	(1,894)	(2,506)	(3,729)	(4,446)	(5,414)
Operating, general, and administrative expenses	(685)	(895)	(1,300)	(1,544)	(1,831)
Advertising and marketing	(53)	(70)	(104)	(124)	(151)

Determining the Business Model

	2X15	2X16	2X17	2X18	2X19
Operating income	(1)	18	61	72	130
Interest income	6	7	9	9	10
Interest expense	(5)	(13)	(15)	(12)	(8)
Pre-tax income	0	12	55	69	132
Provision for income taxes	0	(3)	(13)	(16)	(32)
Net income	0	9	42	52	100
Basic EPS	0.00	0.03	0.15	0.18	0.34
Diluted EPS	0.00	0.03	0.14	0.18	0.34
Basic share count	274	280	284	288	291
Diluted share count	274	280	291	288	297

The notes to Iliso's financial statements provide the following descriptions of accounts.

Net retail sales

Retail sales are earned from the Company's online product sales to consumers. Retail revenue is recognized when control of the goods is transferred to the customer, which occurs upon delivery to the customer.

Third-party merchant fees

Third-party merchant fees revenue includes commissions and service fees earned from merchants that sell their products through the Company's online business. The revenue is recognized when the order is completed and transmitted to the third-party merchant.

Costs of revenues

Costs of revenues primarily comprise the purchase price of products sold to customers where the Company records revenue gross, and include logistics center costs. Inbound shipping and handling costs to receive products from suppliers are included in inventory and recognized in costs of revenues as products are sold. Additionally, costs of revenues include outbound shipping and logistics-related expenses, delivery service costs from our Merchant Services business (where the Company is the delivery service provider), and depreciation expense.

Operating, general, and administrative expenses

Operating, general, and administrative expenses include costs incurred in operating and staffing the Company's fulfillment centers (including costs attributable to receiving, inspecting, picking, packaging, and preparing customer orders), customer service costs, payment processing fees, costs related to the design, execution, and maintenance of the Company's technology infrastructure and online offerings, and general corporate function costs.

Advertising and marketing expenses

Advertising and marketing expenses are expensed as incurred and include brand and performance advertising such as television and digital advertising, sponsored search, email marketing campaigns, and other similar initiatives.

1. What forms the customer base (the "who") for Iliso's merchant services segment?

    A. Third-party merchants

    B. E-commerce customers

C. Fresh food and grocery consumers

Solution:

A is correct. In merchant services, Iliso acts as an agent for third-party merchants. Iliso is paid commissions and service fees by merchants that sell their products through the company's online business. Third-party merchants are therefore the customer base for this business segment.

B is incorrect, because e-commerce customers are customers of Iliso's retail sales segment. Iliso is paid by e-commerce customers for goods purchased through its online platform. The purchases of third-party merchant products by these e-commerce customers belong to the third-party merchant and are not recognized in Iliso's retail sales.

C is incorrect, because fresh food and grocery consumers are a product line segmentation of both its retail sales and its third-party merchant GMV. In addition, fresh food and grocery forms only 55% of the overall GMV and does not encompass all of Iliso's GMV sales.

2. Iliso's business model(s) is(are) likely to benefit from _____ effects.

   A. network
   B. value chain
   C. supply chain

   Solution:

   A is correct. Iliso's business model—in particular, merchant services—is an example of a two-sided network effect. Network effect refers to a network in which the value increases as more participants join the network. By providing an excellent service to merchants and to consumers, Iliso is able to attract both buyers and sellers to its online marketplace. The growth of users on Iliso's platform attracts more merchants, which in turn attracts more users.

   B is incorrect, because value chain refers to the systems and processes within a firm that create value for its customers—which answers the "how" aspect of a business model.

   C is incorrect, because the supply chain is the network inside and outside the company involved in producing the product/service and delivering it to the end user.

3. Which of the following business features is *least likely* to increase consumer retention ("stickiness") on Iliso's platform?

   A. A focus on urban markets
   B. Next-day or faster delivery
   C. No membership fee is required.

   Solution:

   A is correct. A focus on urban markets does not change customer stickiness. The customer experience for those in urban markets would not necessarily change if the company began shipping to rural markets as well.

   B is incorrect. The company states that next-day or faster delivery is a hallmark of its customer experience and may provide a competitive advantage.

   C is incorrect, because the lack of a membership fee is likely to decrease the cost of a customer's staying on the platform, thus increasing retention for some customers.

4. The gross margin of Iliso's merchant services segment is *most likely* _____ the gross margin of Iliso's retail sales segment.

   A. higher than
   B. the same as
   C. lower than

   Solution:

   A is correct. The cost of revenues for Iliso's retail sales includes the purchase price of products sold to customers, including shipping and handling costs, whereas the cost of revenues for merchant services includes only the outbound shipping and logistics expenses. The purchase price of products is a far higher proportion of total GMV sold to customers compared with shipping and logistics costs. Accordingly, the exclusion of the purchase price of products in both the numerator and the denominator will raise the reported gross margin of the merchant services segment.

   B is incorrect, because the gross margin for merchant services cannot be the same as that of retail sales. The retail sales segment includes the purchase price of products sold and associated inbound logistics costs, which means the numerator and the denominator are significantly higher than in the merchant services segment.

   C is incorrect, because the gross margin for merchant services cannot be lower than that of retail sales. Assuming a positive gross margin for both segments, the gross margin for merchant services must be higher since the denominator is smaller (being only the service commissions and service fees charged to merchants).

REVENUE ANALYSIS

4

☐ evaluate a company's revenue and revenue drivers, including pricing power

Revenue Drivers

After determining the business model, we turn to the analysis of historical financial results and position for the company. This analysis will be used as a basis for forecasting a financial statement model that supports security valuation. For most companies—perhaps with the exception of banks, for which the balance sheet comes first—analysts start by analyzing revenues. As with other financial statement lines, the analysis involves identifying **drivers**, which are causative factors that explain the level of and changes in an output variable (here, revenues), and understanding the evolution of the drivers over time.

Analysts can take a bottom-up or top-down approach to determining revenue drivers. A bottom-up approach decomposes revenues into drivers such as sales volume and price, or revenues by product line, segment, or geography, which may be further broken down into other drivers. A top-down approach expresses revenues as a function of drivers such as market share, the addressable market or market size, and GDP growth. The two approaches are often used together.

> **CASE STUDIES**
>
> ### Bottom-Up Approach to Revenue Analysis: Warehouse Club Inc.
>
>
>
> Warehouse's revenues are composed of net sales and membership fees.
>
> Based on her business model work, Nguyen knows that net sales are sales of merchandise and services in Warehouse stores (the company does not operate an e-commerce business). A logical driver of net sales each year, therefore, is the number of stores open that year. Nguyen decomposes Warehouse's net sales into two drivers: the *average* number of stores open and net sales per average store. Nguyen also calculates the change in these drivers: the absolute change in stores each year (new-store openings; so far, Warehouse has never closed a store) and the annual percentage change in net sales per store.

	2X10	2X11	2X12	2X13	2X14	2X15	2X16	2X17	2X18	2X19
Stores, year-end	108	112	116	120	126	130	136	141	145	149
New-store openings	5	4	4	4	6	4	6	5	4	4
Average stores (#)	106	110	114	118	123	128	133	139	143	147
Net sales per average store	138	150	162	166	170	169	166	173	184	193
Growth rate		9%	8%	2%	3%	−1%	−2%	4%	6%	5%
Net sales	14,488	16,539	18,442	19,545	20,940	21,597	22,054	23,973	26,302	28,377

> Net sales in 2X19 were 96% higher than in 2X10, driven by similar growth contributions from the two drivers: the average number of stores increased by 39% and sales per average store increased by 40%.
>
> An encouraging sign for forecasting this company's results is that each driver appears relatively stable, indicating that they might be somewhat predictable. Sometimes, however, key revenue drivers are volatile, such as interest rates and oil prices for banks and oil producers, respectively. Volatility does not mean that the analyst has selected an incorrect driver; drivers are based on the business model.
>
> Nguyen then decomposes Warehouse's membership fee revenues into the annual price of membership and the average number of members.

Members

	2X10	2X11	2X12	2X13	2X14	2X15	2X16	2X17	2X18	2X19
Members, end of year	6,004	6,707	7,011	7,410	7,980	8,474	9,044	9,386	9,804	10,241
Members, annual average	5,900	6,360	6,855	7,218	7,691	8,218	8,764	9,217	9,600	10,017
Avg. per member fee	50.00	50.00	55.00	55.00	55.00	55.00	55.00	60.00	60.00	60.00
Membership fee revenues	295	318	377	397	423	452	482	553	576	601

> Membership growth has been a larger driver of membership fee revenue growth than price increases, as the number of members has grown by 70% from 2X10 to 2X19 while prices have increased by 20% over the same period.

> Management indicated that over 90% of members live within 10 kilometers of a store and, from 2X10 to 2X19, the company opened 46 new stores. Nguyen adds to her membership analysis by calculating the average number of members per store; if this number has been falling over time, it could mean that existing stores are losing members and sales to new stores the company opens, an example of **cannibalization**.

	2X10	2X11	2X12	2X13	2X14	2X15	2X16	2X17	2X18	2X19
Avg. members per store	57,282	57,818	60,128	61,171	62,528	64,205	65,892	66,546	67,133	68,141
Growth rate		0.9%	4.0%	1.7%	2.2%	2.7%	2.6%	1.0%	0.9%	1.5%

> Not only has the average number of members per store not declined, but it has also grown by 19%, indicating no cannibalization and that new-store openings are not the only driver of membership growth. This is a positive sign, though Nguyen notes that additional analysis is needed to estimate a ceiling on the number of members a store can reasonably support, and to determine whether stores that opened many years ago have already hit this ceiling.

Pricing Power

Prices are a driver of revenue for every firm, and it may appear that pricing is a unilateral decision by management (e.g., Warehouse management chooses its markups on merchandise net sales and has chosen to increase its annual membership fee by $5 every five years). In fact, prices are constrained by a company's **pricing power**. Pricing power refers to a company's ability to set prices and other economic terms with customers without affecting its sales volumes. While Warehouse's management could choose to increase the price of membership from $60 to $600, such a decision would likely result in the loss of all its members. The membership price is constrained by the savings Warehouse can offer members on purchases, which itself is the subject of competition from other retailers that also use low prices to attract customers and of negotiations with suppliers that desire higher prices. Pricing power is primarily a function of both market structure (covered earlier in Economics) and a company's competitive positioning in its market.

In the most competitive markets, where firms are selling nearly identical products, firms are price *takers*—that is, price is dictated by the forces of supply and demand—and all firms generally sell at the same price. If a firm prices above the prevailing market price, it will sell a fraction or none of its output, as customers will buy elsewhere. It is also generally not rational for a firm to price below the market price, as doing so would not only reduce its profits but also cause competitors to do the same, leading to a price war. Returns on capital in highly competitive markets move in cycles based on supply and demand, but over the long run approximate firms' cost of capital as competition forces prices down to marginal cost. A **low-cost producer** (with costs below—in some cases, *well* below—those of a marginal producer) can, however, earn long-run returns above its cost of capital in a highly competitive industry, but it requires the low-cost position to be sustained against competition over time. A prominent example is state-owned oil producers that benefit from monopoly ownership of low-cost oil reserves in certain countries.

Other attributes of highly competitive markets include little to no product differentiation, low barriers to firm entry, available substitutes, a lack of customer loyalty, and low switching costs for customers. Many markets fit this description, including retail, oil and gas and other natural resources, bank loans and deposits, insurance, fresh food, off-patent pharmaceuticals, transportation, and some types of technology hardware. Highly competitive markets often do not start as highly competitive but, rather, become more competitive as new firms enter, the pace of innovation slows, and imitation becomes widespread, a process known as **commoditization**.

Firms operating in less competitive markets, such as monopolistic competition, oligopoly, or monopoly structures, tend to have some degree of pricing power. They can raise prices or change other economic terms (contract length, late fees, etc.) without materially affecting sales volumes. Attributes of these markets include product differentiation, barriers to entry, lack of economical substitutes, switching costs for customers, and a high degree of customer loyalty or retention. Markets and companies that fit this description include branded consumer goods, utilities, patented pharmaceuticals, software, restaurants, payment networks, medical devices, and some types of real estate. Firms with pricing power often apply value- or cost-based pricing as well as price discrimination strategies (outlined in the previous module). While product differentiation is most visible, differentiation can also include convenience, wrap-around services, and a secondary resale market.

Analysts evaluate pricing power not just by examining a firm's prices over time or relative to competitors, but also by comparing a firm's prices with its costs—in other words, its profit margins. While a company may be increasing prices by 3% per year, if its costs are rising by 5%, it is showing both an inability to pass along price increases to customers and declining profitability for investors. A company without pricing power may be unable to increase prices even as costs rise, because it is constrained by the availability of substitutes and customers can easily switch. For example, a movie theater might be unable to increase prices in line with costs, because streaming video subscriptions are cheaper and the company would likely lose customers if it raised prices significantly. Therefore, an important sign of pricing power is rising profitability over time, which demonstrates both an ability to retain economics for investors and that competitors, new entrants, or substitutes are not driving down prices faster than costs.

> **EXAMPLE 2**
>
> Nestlé SA is a global packaged food and beverage company headquartered in Switzerland. The company sells products with proprietary brand trademarks (such as Nespresso, Purina, Perrier, Maggi, and Stouffer's) that it acquires and develops with marketing and R&D investments, which totaled CHF19 billion in 2021, or 20% of the company's revenues. The distinctiveness of its products through branding can confer pricing power. From 2011 to 2021, the company demonstrated its pricing power through a record of increasing prices while increasing volumes and its operating profitability.
>
> **Nestle SA Pricing Power**
>
>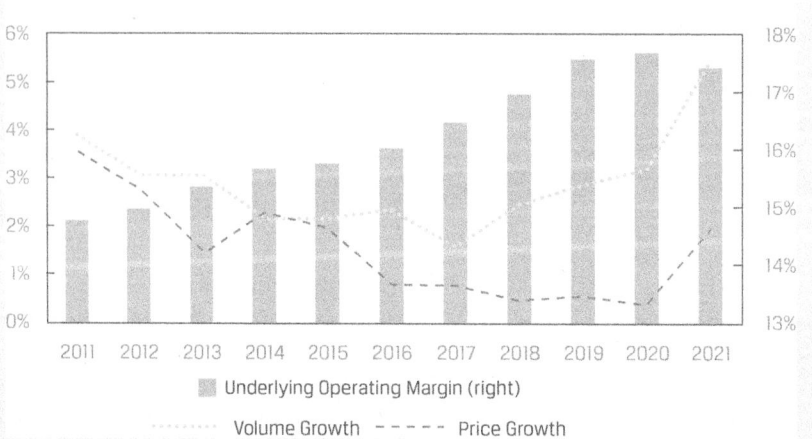

Top-Down Revenue Analysis

Analysts can also take a top-down approach to analyzing revenue by expressing it as a function of drivers such as market size and a company's share of that market. This approach will be discussed in more detail in the next module (on industry and competitive analysis), but we will demonstrate this approach for Warehouse Club Inc.

CASE STUDIES

Top-Down Approach to Revenue Analysis: Warehouse Club Inc.

A government agency reports total national retail and food services sales each month for the country that Warehouse operates in (the United States). The data capture consumer spending at hundreds of thousands of retailers and restaurants. Sales are categorized by the type of retailer or restaurant, which reflects the primary type of product or service it sells. An excerpt of a monthly release is shown below.

National Retail Sales, January 2X19 (billions of USD)	
Total retail and food services sales	456,012
Total retail sales	399,359
Automobile and parts dealers	88,152
Petrol stations	36,539
Pharmacies and drug stores	24,273
Grocery stores	57,392
Total food services sales	56,653
Full-service restaurants	24,730
Limited-service restaurants	25,273
Pubs, bars, and other	6,650

Warehouse sells a broad range of retail goods in most cities, so US national retail spending is generally representative of Warehouse's **market size**—the existing demand for goods or services offered by a company. By expressing Warehouse's revenues as a percentage of the market, or its **market share**, over time, we can assess whether the company has been gaining or losing relevance with its customers relative to competitors and substitutes.

A challenge for analysts is determining market size. The data might be difficult to gather (not the case here), and judgment is required for determining what to include and exclude: only sales of products identical to the company's, sales of similar products, all sales of competitors, and so on. The common practice is to include all sales of *similar* products and to consider *substitutes* separately (discussed in the next module on industry analysis). A substitute serves the same function as a product but differs in form (e.g., movie theater and streaming video, grocery stores and restaurants, print and digital advertising). This practice is subject to a wide range of opinions, however, and some analysts include sales of substitutes in market size estimates. The share of market that a firm does not have (i.e., 100% − x% market share) represents sales potential.

Elaine Nguyen decides to use total US retail sales as the market size for Warehouse, with one exclusion: automobiles and parts. Warehouse does not sell automobiles or automobile parts, nor does it sell substitute means of transportation or repair. Nguyen considers food service substitutes (restaurants and pubs) for Warehouse.

Warehouse Club Inc. Market Share (%, left) of Retail Sales excl. Autos and Parts (USD millions, right)

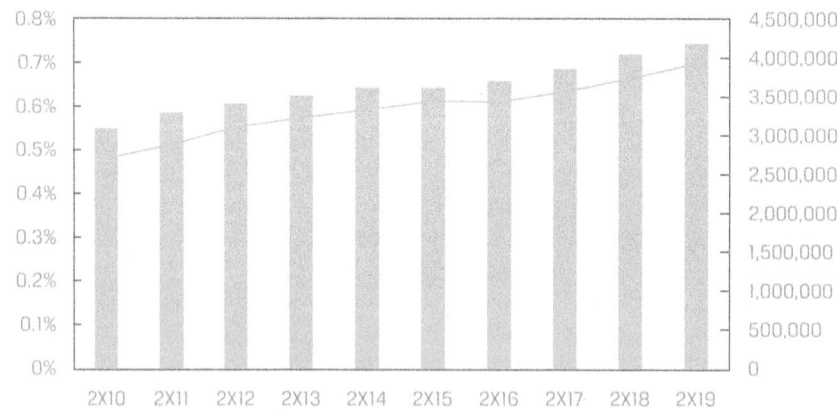

Nguyen makes three observations:

- The market is large and growth has been positive, albeit at a slow (3.4%) rate. This finding aligns with Nguyen's expectations, because this is a developed market that represents a broad range of consumer spending (a large portion of which is for necessities) and the country has been in an economic expansion.

- Warehouse Club Inc. has a small (70 basis points in 2X19) but growing share of the market (up from 48 basis points in 2X10), indicating that its value proposition relative to other retailers has been resonating with consumers.

- Warehouse's market share increased in most years, with the exception of 2X16, when its share was flat from the prior year. Nguyen will have to investigate further.

DISCUSSION BOARD QUESTION

Which of Nguyen's analyses was more helpful to you in understanding Warehouse's historical revenue growth: the bottom-up or the top-down approach? Why?

We encourage you to post your response, as well as read and reply to others' responses, on the Learning Ecosystem discussion board.

QUESTION SET

Questions 1–4 refer to the earlier vignette on Iliso Marketplace Ltd.

Revenue Analysis

1. In 2X19, the percentage of GMV that Iliso collected from third-party merchants (the company's "take rate") was *closest* to:

   A. 2.2%.

   B. 14.7%.

   C. 15.0%.

   Solution:

   C is correct. For e-commerce businesses, the take rate refers to the retention percentage of the value of transactions facilitated by the platform. In 2X19, Iliso third-party merchant fees were $190 million against third-party gross merchandise value (GMV) of $1,269 million on its platform. The take rate is therefore:

   $190/1{,}269 = 0.1497 \approx 15.0\%$

   A is incorrect, because it results from dividing third-party merchant fees by total GMV. B is incorrect, because 14.7% is the percentage of Iliso's GMV attributable to third-party merchant sales.

2. Which of the following measures would be used to best assess Iliso's pricing power?

   A. Take rate

   B. GMV year-on-year growth rate

   C. GMV per active customer account

   Solution:

   A is correct. The percentage of transaction value retained by the platform reflects the price Iliso charges third-party merchants to use its platform. Both the stability and the level of its take rate reflect the state of competition that Iliso faces from other e-commerce platforms.

   B is incorrect, because the GMV year-on-year growth rate can be affected by numerous factors, including customer volumes, product mix, and basket size. It does not carry information for analysts to estimate pricing power.

   C is incorrect, because GMV per active customer account can be affected by product mix and the average basket size, which is driven by its $25 minimum for free shipping. This measure does not carry information for analysts to estimate the pricing power of the platform.

3. Referring to the data table earlier in this lesson titled "National Retail Sales, January 2X19" and assuming 2X19 US monthly retail and food sales of $456 billion and assuming Iliso's addressable geography is the United States, Iliso's market share of retail and food sales was *closest* to:

   A. 0.134%.

   B. 0.138%.

   C. 0.157%.

   Solution:

   C is correct. In 2X19, annual US retail and food sales were: 456 × 12 = $5,472 billion. Since GMV reflects the value of retail sales on Iliso's platform, the appropriate estimate of Iliso's market share is therefore:

2X19 GMV/2X19 US retail and food sales = 8,605/5,472,000 = 0.157%

A is incorrect, because this measure uses only Iliso's retail sales and ignores third-party GMV, even though the vignette states that merchants may sell the same products.

B is incorrect, because this measure uses Iliso's net revenues as a percentage of the market. This measure is inappropriate, since Iliso's net revenues do not reflect the gross value of third-party merchant sales on its platform.

4. Which of the following is an appropriate bottom-up driver of Iliso's revenues?

   A. Iliso's market share of US retail and food sales
   B. GMV per average active customer account
   C. Iliso's revenue as a function of GDP growth

   Solution:

   B is correct. In a bottom-up approach, analysts decompose the revenues into logical revenue drivers such as product line or segment. A driver of Iliso's net sales must be the average number of active customer accounts during the period and the net retail sales per account. We use GMV, since this measure accurately reflects the total amount of retail sales (both Iliso's first-party and third-party sales).

   A and C are incorrect, because they are top-down, not bottom-up, drivers.

5. OPERATING PROFITABILITY AND WORKING CAPITAL ANALYSIS

☐ evaluate a company's operating profitability and working capital using key measures

Operating Costs and Their Classification

Generally, operating costs are incurred in generating—or are otherwise related to—*current period* revenue: all costs related to the acquisition, production, sale, improvement, and delivery of goods and services; the management of business activities; and compliance with laws and regulations. Investing costs are related to the acquisition and production of long-term assets, including tangible assets like property and equipment and intangible assets such as software, trademarks, and patents. Financing costs include payments to debt and equity investors as a return on their investment.

> **MINDING THE GAAP: CLASSIFICATION OF COSTS**
>
> IFRS and US GAAP do not classify operating, investing, or financing costs in an intuitive manner, and there are differences in classification on the income statement and statement of cash flows. Several prominent examples include:

Cost	Intuition	IFRS and US GAAP Classification: Income Statement	IFRS and US GAAP Classification: Statement of Cash Flows
Research and development	Investing	Operating	Operating
Depreciation and amortization*	Investing	Operating	Non-cash add-back to Operating *Capital expenditures* in Investing
Interest expense	Financing	Other (not operating)	US GAAP: Operating IFRS: Operating or Financing
Income taxes	Separate	Other (not operating)	Operating

Recall that IFRS and US GAAP require the costs of acquiring and constructing long-term tangible and intangible assets to be capitalized and then, for those with a finite useful life, systematically expensed over time on the income statement as non-cash depreciation and amortization expense. The most common allocation method is straight line, where the cost is expensed evenly over the useful life of the asset.

Unless specified otherwise, we use the IFRS classifications of costs on the income statement in our discussion.

For most companies, operating costs account for the majority of costs and are primarily determined by the company's business model and size. As shown in Exhibit 4, a company's operating costs can be categorized and analyzed in three ways: by their behavior with output, their nature, or their function.

Exhibit 4: Categorization of Operating Costs

Behavior with Output *Whether the cost varies or not with output in the short run*	Nature *What the cost is*	Function *The purpose of the cost*
• Variable costs vary with output • Fixed costs do not vary with output	• Compensation of employees • Raw materials • Merchandise • Office supplies	• Cost of goods sold • Sales and Marketing • Genral and administrative • Research and development

Behavior with Output: Fixed and Variable Costs

A useful classification of operating costs for analysts is fixed versus variable, which was introduced in an earlier module. The distinction is useful because the proportion of fixed to variable costs in operating costs affects the stability and predictability of operating profit. Using a fixed/variable operating cost classification, operating profit is defined in Equation 1.

$$\text{Operating profit} = [Q \times (P - VC)] - FC \qquad (1)$$

Q = units of outputs sold in a period.

P = price per unit of output.

VC = variable operating costs expressed per unit of output. Examples include merchandise costs for a retailer like Warehouse Club Inc. and materials and direct labor costs for a manufacturer.

FC = fixed operating costs, which do not change within a given range of output in the short run. Examples include compensation for salaried employees, depreciation and amortization, software and IT expenses, insurance, and certain utilities costs. FC is stated on a total dollar, not per unit, basis.

For a firm to be profitable, it's clear from Equation 1 that $(P - VC)$, or the **contribution margin**, must be positive and that Q must be high enough such that FC is exceeded. Recall that the amount of fixed costs in the operating cost structure of an issuer is referred to as operating leverage and that it presents both benefits and risks. If operating costs are largely fixed and the contribution margin is positive, operating profit can increase rapidly with increases in Q. However, the reverse is true if Q declines, since fixed costs do not change, so operating profit will fall. As shown in Equation 2, operating leverage can be measured and compared across firms by using the **degree of operating leverage** (DOL):

$$DOL = \%\,\Delta\,\text{Operating Profit}/\%\,\Delta\,\text{Sales} \qquad (2)$$

A firm can increase its degree of operating leverage by increasing the fixed costs and decreasing the variable costs in its cost base.

EXAMPLE 3

Variable and Fixed Cost Analysis

While analyzing operating costs using the variable and fixed framework is insightful, its use by independent investment analysts is limited because disclosure of fixed and variable costs is not required by IFRS or US GAAP, nor is the disclosure of output volume. Additionally, many companies have several lines of business that have different volume, price, and cost structures, the details of which are lost in the presentation of highly aggregated financial statements that investors receive. However, in some industries, it is common for issuers to disclose these figures, or it is relatively easy for an analyst to make assumptions. A prominent example is oil and gas producers, for which we provide an example here.

Ribbon Energy Ltd. ("Ribbon") is a fictional oil and natural gas company focused on the exploration and development of oil and natural gas reserves. Selected operating and financial data for the last 12 months are as follows:

	Last 12 Months
Sales volume (thousands of barrels of oil equivalent)	154,812
Average price, per barrel of oil equivalent	$49.66
Total revenues (millions)	$7,688
Production costs, per barrel of oil equivalent:	
Lease operating expense	11.21
Production and ad valorem taxes	3.40

Operating Profitability and Working Capital Analysis

	Last 12 Months
Gathering and transportation expense	2.63
Production costs	$17.24
Other operating expenses (millions of USD):	
Depreciation, depletion, and accretion (DD&A)	1,275
General and administrative expenses (G&A)	150

Production costs are variable costs stated on a per barrel of oil equivalent basis, while other operating expenses (DD&A and G&A) are fixed and stated on an aggregate dollar basis.

Ribbon's management provides the following guidance for the next 12 months. Management does not provide guidance for prices (and therefore revenue), since it sells in a commodity market with volatile prices that are difficult to predict. Ribbon does not hedge. At the time guidance was provided, the average oil price per barrel was $62.50.

	Next 12 Months
Sales volume (thousands of barrels of oil equivalent)	156,360–167,197
Production costs, per barrel of oil equivalent	$17.34
Other operating expenses (millions of USD):	
Depreciation, depletion, and accretion (DD&A)	1,415
General and administrative expenses (G&A)	150

1. Ribbon's contribution margin per barrel for the last 12 months is *closest* to:

   A. $23.2.

   B. $32.4.

   C. $45.3.

   Solution:

   B is correct. Recall that the contribution margin per barrel is $P - VC$. The average price per barrel, P, in the past 12 months was $49.66, and the variable cost per barrel, VC, was $17.24. Therefore, the contribution margin was $49.66 − $17.24 = $32.42.

   A is incorrect, because this amount is the company's EBIT, or operating profit, per barrel.

   C is incorrect, because it results from using the current rather than the last 12 months' average oil price per barrel to calculate the contribution margin.

2. At the high end of management's guidance, Ribbon's operating profit for the next 12 months is *closest* to:

   A. $5,496 million.

   B. $5,986 million.

   C. $6,002 million.

   Solution:

   B is correct.

   Operating profit = $[Q \times (P - VC)] - FC$

Operating profit = [167.197 million × ($62.50 − $17.34)] − ($1,415 + $150)

Operating profit = $5,986 million

A is incorrect, because this amount is the operating profit using the low end of guided sales volume of 156.360 million barrels.
C is incorrect, because it relies on last year's production costs of $17.24 per barrel.

3. Some analysts covering Ribbon believe that volume will be lower than what management expects. Assuming a 5% reduction over last year's volume, Ribbon's operating profit for the next 12 months is *closest* to:

   A. $5,077 million.
   B. $5,091 million.
   C. $5,776 million.

   Solution:
   A is correct.
   The last 12 months' volume was 154.812 million. A 5% reduction is 154.812 × 0.95 = 147,071 million barrels.

   Operating profit = [Q × (P − VC)] − FC

   Operating profit = [147,071 million × ($62.50 − $17.34)] − ($1,415 + $150)

   Operating profit = $5,076.7 million

   B is incorrect, because it uses last year's production costs.
   C is incorrect, because it assumes a 5% increase rather than decrease in volume from the prior year.

4. Ribbon's degree of operating leverage for the next 12 months at the low end of management's guidance is _____ at the high end of management's guidance.

   A. lower than
   B. the same as
   C. higher than

   Solution:
   C is correct.
   Last 12 months' sales: $7,688
   Last 12 months' operating profit: $1,244
   Low end of guidance
   Next 12 months' sales: 156.360 × $62.50 = $9,773
   Next 12 months' operating profit: $9,773 − (156.360 × 17.34) − 1,565 = 5,496
   Degree of operating leverage: (5,496/1,244 − 1)/(9,773/7,688 − 1) = 1.95
   High end of guidance
   Next 12 months' sales: 167.197 × $62.50 = $10,450
   Next 12 months' operating profit: $10,450 − (167.197 × 17.34) − 1,565 = 5,986
   Degree of operating leverage: (5,986/1,244 − 1)/(10,450/7,688 − 1) = 1.85

Natural and Functional Operating Cost Classifications and Measures of Operating Profitability

Rather than fixed and variable, IFRS and US GAAP require issuers to disclose operating costs using either a natural or a functional cost classification based on "historical and industry factors and the nature of the entity." Most issuers, including Warehouse Club Inc., choose a functional classification. This approach leads to all issuers' income statements appearing similar in structure, with lines related to functional areas such as "cost of sales," "selling, general, and administrative expenses," and "research and development," even though their business models (and fixed versus variable cost composition) can differ significantly. The functional classification of operating costs is used to calculate and distinguish key profitability measures used in analysis and forecasting, as shown in Exhibit 5.

Exhibit 5: Measures of Operating Profitability

Gross Profit:	EBITDA:	Operating Profit:
Revenue	Revenue	Revenue
Cost of Sales	Cost of Sales	Cost of Sales
Gross Profit	Operating Expenses i.e. SG&A, R&D, etc.	Operating Expenses i.e. SG&A, R&D, etc.
	EBITDA	Depreciation and Amortization
		Operating Profit (EBIT)

Gross Margin:	EBITDA Margin:	Operating/EBIT Margin:
Gross Profit	EBITDA	Operating Profit (EBIT)
Revenue	Revenue	Revenue

Gross profit, EBITDA, and EBIT are measures of operating profitability that capture different functional costs in their definitions. Generally, a significant amount of cost of sales is variable, so gross margin is an approximate measure of contribution margin. Other operating expenses such as sales and marketing, general and administrative, and research and development costs tend to be largely fixed, though they may have a variable component such as sales commissions. Depreciation and amortization expenses are fixed unless the issuer uses units of output as the depreciation method. An issuer's notes to its financial statements contain useful information about the composition and nature of operating costs.

For most companies, the major driver of operating costs over the long run is output, even for fixed costs, because output growth often requires growth in assets, human capital, and purchased goods and services. Warehouse Club Inc., for example, might be able to grow membership fee revenues to an extent without incurring costs, but growing net sales requires more stores and employees. This has been true even for so-called asset-light companies in the internet and software industries, which have shown large increases in operating costs along with large increases in revenue over time. Since output or revenue is a major cost driver, analysts often express operating costs as a percentage of revenue. Additional considerations include industry profitability, **economies of scale**, and **economies of scope**.

Industry profitability will be discussed in detail in the next module, but recall from the earlier discussion on pricing power that prices relative to costs (i.e., profitability) are largely dictated by market structure and a company's competitive positioning. Since industry participants are competing in the same product and factor markets, competitive forces within them determine industry profitability in the long run; analysts should not analyze profitability only on a company-by-company basis.

Economies of scale refer to a decline in costs per unit as output grows and generally result from having fixed costs in the cost structure that are spread over more units of output. A company with entirely variable costs can also exhibit some economies of scale over time if it increases its bargaining power over suppliers as it grows, driving down variable costs per unit. Economies of scale are usually evident from the business model and can be found empirically by comparing a company's size in revenues with its operating costs as percentages of sales or margins.

Economies of scope refer to a decline in costs per unit as the number of product or business lines increases and generally result from shared costs between the product lines. Economies of scope are usually evident from the business model and can be found empirically by comparing the profitability of an integrated company with that of a standalone company. Examples of economies of scope can be found in financial services, where there are customer, client service, compliance, technology, and back-office similarities (and thus cost efficiencies) across commercial banking, consumer banking, brokerage, asset management, payment processing, and investment banking. Economies of scope have resulted in large global firms competing in many lines of business.

Recall that Warehouse Club Inc.'s management claimed that it has economies of scale, saying that "low prices for quality products drive greater membership and net sales over time, leveraging our selling, general, and administrative expenses, reducing them as a percentage of net sales." While this makes intuitive sense as there is probably a fixed amount of SG&A costs each year to operate a store, Elaine Nguyen must corroborate it empirically.

CASE STUDIES

Warehouse Club Inc. Operating Profitability Analysis

Warehouse Club Inc.'s operating costs are composed of merchandise costs (costs of sales), SG&A expenses, depreciation and amortization, and costs associated with opening new stores.

Based on her business model work, Elaine Nguyen believes the following about drivers for each of these operating costs.

Operating Cost	Driver(s)
Merchandise costs (costs of sales)	Sales
SG&A expenses	Sales Number of employees and per-employee compensation
Depreciation and amortization	Long-term assets Useful lives
Store opening expenses	Store openings

Based on these drivers, Nguyen calculates Warehouse's gross margin (1 − cost of sales as % of net sales), SG&A expenses as a percentage of net sales, gross fixed assets to depreciation and amortization (implied useful life), store opening expenses per new-store opening, and, finally, profit margins. Profit margins include membership fee revenues.

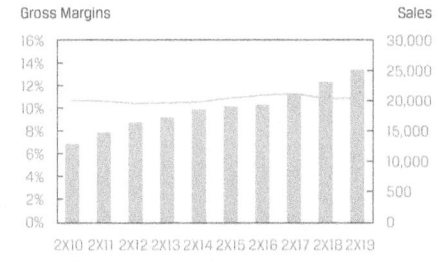
Warehouse Club Inc. Gross Margin (line, left) and Cost of Sales (bars, right, USD millions)

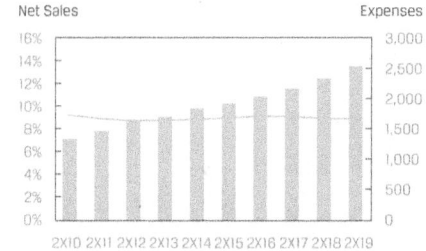
Warehouse Club Inc. SG&A % of Net Sales (line, left) & SG&A Expenses (bars, right, USD millions)

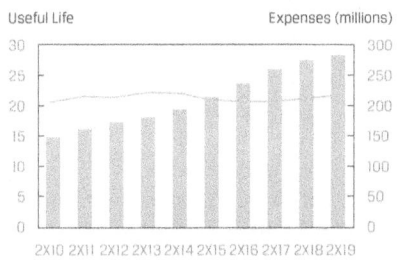
Warehouse Club Inc. Implied Useful Life (line, left) & D&A Expense (bars, right, USD millions)

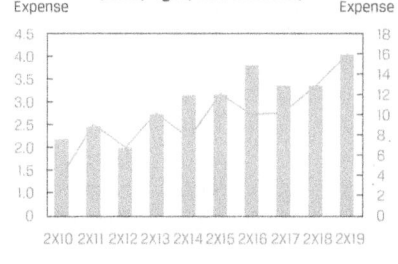
Warehouse Club Inc. Store Opening Expense per Opening (line, left) & Store Opening Expense (bars, right, USD millions)

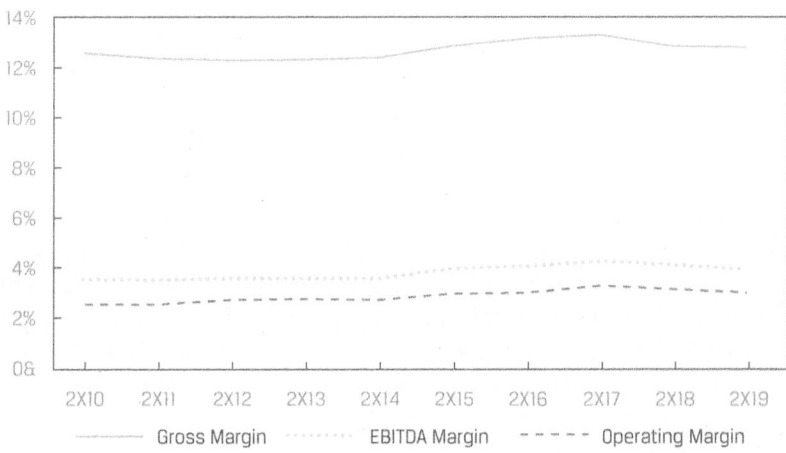
Warehouse Club Inc. Operating Profitability

Nguyen makes the following observations:

- Operating costs have increased significantly on an absolute basis from 2X10 to 2X19, but on a relative-to-sales basis have remained stable over the same period, indicating that the driver of the increase has been net sales growth.

- One exception is store opening expenses per store opening, which have quadrupled from 2X10 to 2X19, though in aggregate remain a small cost (less than 1/100 of SG&A expenses). Note that these are operating costs related to store openings, such as employee training before opening, not the investing cost of land and fixed assets.

- SG&A expenses do not appear to be fixed relative to net sales, as they have remained roughly the same percentage of net sales over time.

- Margins have remained mostly stable, though they did increase from 2X15 to 2X17 before coming back down in 2X18 and 2X19. Margins are low for Warehouse, with EBITDA and operating margins of 4% and 3%, respectively, in 2X19.
- The amount of operating profit is similar to the amount of membership fee revenues each year. Nguyen creates the following chart:

Warehouse Club Inc. Membership Fee Revenue as % of Operating Profit

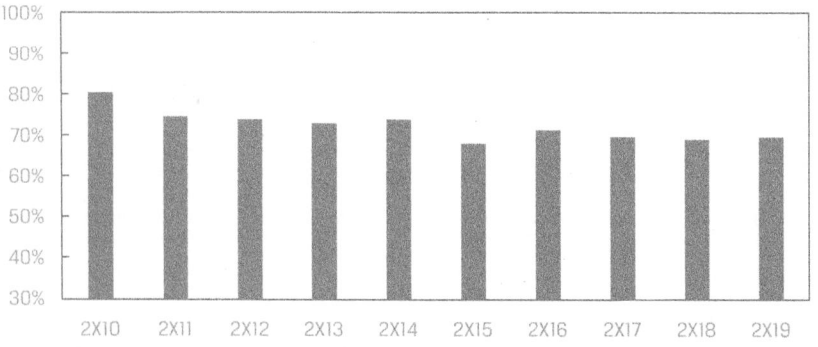

This chart implies that net sales from its stores—after deducting costs of sales, SG&A expenses, D&A, and store opening expenses—account for the remaining 30% of operating profit. This percentage is likely an understatement, since some amount of SG&A expenses is associated with membership fee revenues (marketing, customer service, payment processing, management), but it does align with Warehouse management's assertion in its annual report that prices provide members with a significant return on membership: the company earns a thin margin on net sales, and it is membership fees that allow the company to run profitably.

Working Capital

Recall from earlier modules on working capital that the primary measures of a company's working capital management are activity ratios that determine its cash conversion cycle and the ratio of net working capital to sales. A short cash conversion cycle means that the company requires less external financing to fund operations, while net working capital requirements determine a minimum level of investment, in addition to capital investments, that cannot be distributed to investors. Negative net working capital means that suppliers are a source of financing.

CASE STUDIES

Warehouse Club Inc. Working Capital Management

Elaine Nguyen calculates the working capital measures for Warehouse.

Operating Profitability and Working Capital Analysis

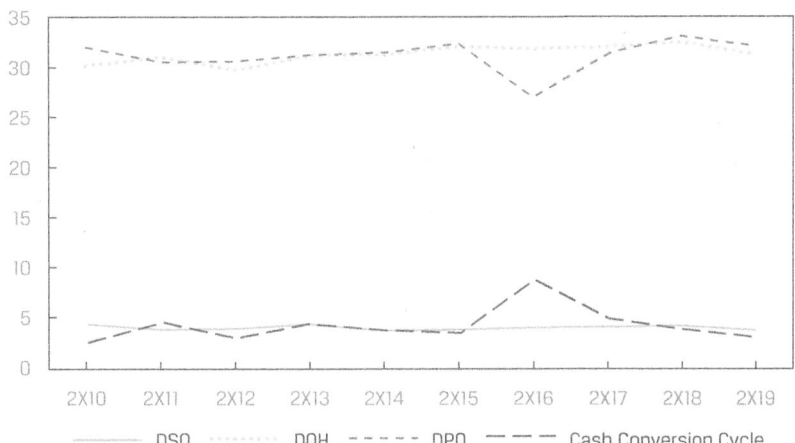

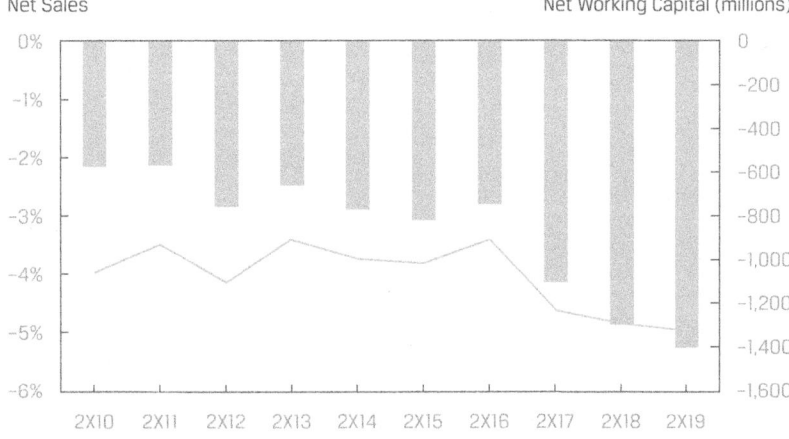

Nguyen makes the following observations:

- The cash conversion cycle is short, less than a week, primarily as a result of a DSO of 4, because Warehouse's customers pay in cash or with credit or debit cards that settle in less than five business days, and days of inventory on hand is nearly equal to days payable outstanding, indicating that inventory is financed by suppliers.
- Net working capital is negative, now down to −5.0% of net sales, indicating that it is a source of financing for the company.
- Generally, all the activity ratios have been stable since 2X10, except for a one-year increase in 2X16 from a decline in days payable outstanding. Nguyen looked into this increase in the notes to the financial statements in a historical annual report. The company indicated that it changed accounting information systems in early 2X17 and made accelerated payments to suppliers at the end of 2X16, in advance of the system change in case there were problems.

QUESTION SET

Questions 1–4 relate to the working capital data below for Iliso Marketplace, as well as to Iliso's financial statements in the lesson "Determining the Business Model".

Working Capital	2X15	2X16	2X17	2X18	2X19
Accounts receivable, net	29	50	50	52	58
DSO	*4*	*5*	*4*	*3*	*3*
Inventories, net	190	250	325	384	439
DOH	*37*	*36*	*32*	*32*	*30*
Prepayments and other	23	32	35	56	59
% of total revenue	*1%*	*1%*	*1%*	*1%*	*1%*
Accounts payable	138	190	272	321	410
DPO	*27*	*28*	*27*	*26*	*28*
Taxes payable	2	8	10	12	29
% of total revenue	*0%*	*0%*	*0%*	*0%*	*0%*
Accrued expenses and other current	111	193	232	295	354
% of total revenue	*4%*	*6%*	*4%*	*5%*	*5%*
Net working capital	(8)	(59)	(104)	(136)	(237)
NWC to sales	*0%*	*-2%*	*-2%*	*-2%*	*-3%*
Cash conversion cycle	14	14	9	8	5

1. Compared with 2X18, Iliso's operating margin change in 2X19 is *closest* to:

    A. 0.07%.

    B. 0.57%.

    C. 80.56%.

    Solution:

    B is correct. Operating (EBIT) margin is Operating profit/Revenue:

    2X18: 72/6,186 = 1.163%

    2X19: 130/7,526 = 1.727%

    Subtracting 2X18 EBIT margin from 2X19 EBIT margin gives:

    1.727% − 1.163% = 0.564%

    A is incorrect, because it is the change in gross profit margin.
    C is incorrect, because it is the year-over-year change in operating profit.

2. What is the *most likely* explanation for Iliso's improvement in inventory days on hand from 2X15 to 2X19?

    A. More customers paying in cash

    B. Strong growth in net retail sales

C. Rising proportion of GMV from third-party merchant sales

Solution:

C is correct. With third-party merchant sales, Iliso acts as an agent for the third-party merchant and does not take control of inventory. Accordingly, as the proportion of third-party merchant sales rises in GMV and Iliso's revenues, the portion of revenues associated with inventories falls.

A is incorrect, because there is no indication that Iliso accepts cash on delivery (as is common in China and other geographies). It appears that, like other e-commerce platforms, Iliso accepts only online payments.

B is incorrect, because growth in retail sales is likely to grow accounts receivable as well; days sales outstanding should be unaffected.

3. Which of the following expenses are *most likely* to vary with output?

   A. depreciation

   B. costs of sales

   C. interest expense

   Solution:

   B is correct. Costs of sales are inventory costs that are recognized when a sale is made.

   A is incorrect, because depreciation varies with fixed assets. This expense is a fixed cost in the short run. Recall that fixed operating costs do not change within a given range of output in the short run.

   C is incorrect, because interest expense is a fixed cost component that arises from the company's capital structure, not its revenues.

4. Iliso doesn't disclose gross profit on third-party merchant sales. However, an analyst observes that a competing marketplace platform makes 85% gross profit margin on third-party merchant sales. Assuming that Iliso's gross profit margin is similar, what proportion of Iliso's gross profit *most likely* came from third-party merchant sales in 2X19?

   A. 7.6%

   B. 15.0%

   C. 28.1%

   Solution:

   A is correct.

   Gross profit of third-party merchant sales = 85% × 190 = $162

   Gross profit of Iliso = Total revenues − Costs of revenues = $7,526 − $5,414 = $2,112

   Proportion of gross profit arising from merchant sales = $162/$2,112 = 7.6%

   B is incorrect; it is the cost of revenues on third-party merchant sales.

   C is incorrect; it is Iliso's gross profit margin in 2X19.

6. CAPITAL INVESTMENTS AND CAPITAL STRUCTURE

 evaluate a company's capital investments and capital structure

Sources and Uses of Capital

Firms invest capital from debt and equity investors to earn returns above their investors' required rates of return. An important consideration in company analysis is to evaluate whether required rates of return have been met or exceeded (i.e., whether economic value is created for investors) over the longer run and to assess risks and opportunities associated with the capital structure, such as the use of financial leverage. Before evaluation, a first step is to determine a company's sources and uses of capital on a historical basis, as shown generically in Exhibit 6.

Exhibit 6: Sources and Uses of Capital

Sources of Capital	Uses of Capital
Cash flows from operations, including net working capital (if negative)	Cash and investments on hand
Debt issuance	Net working capital (if positive)
Equity issuance	Capital expenditures and additions to intangibles
Asset disposals	Acquisitions
	Debt paydown
	Dividends and share repurchases

CASE STUDIES

Warehouse Club Inc.'s Sources and Uses of Capital

Elaine Nguyen calculates the following information on Warehouse over 2X10–2X19. Cash flows from operations include the effect of additional net working capital financing (i.e., Warehouse's net working capital became more negative over time).

Capital Investments and Capital Structure

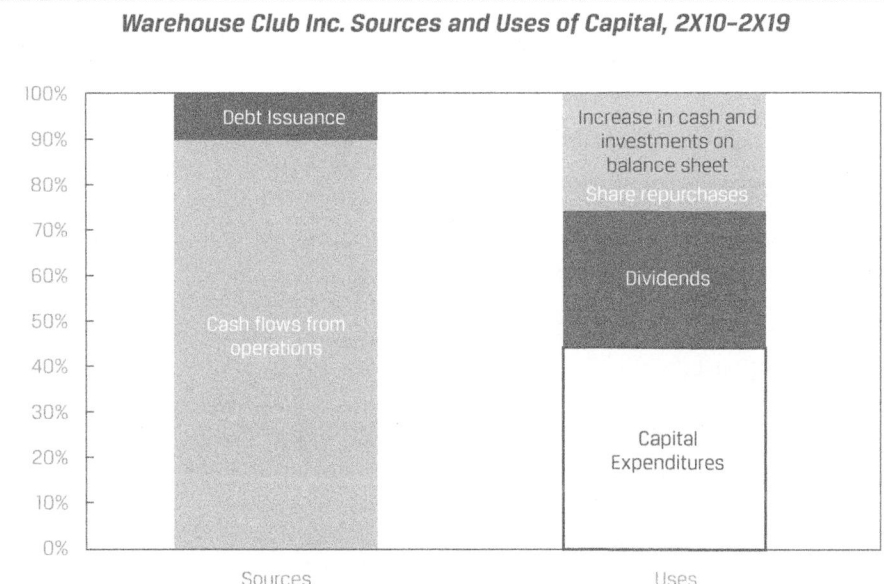

Nguyen makes the following observations:

- Capital expenditures and returns to shareholders (dividends and share repurchases) are almost equal, which is surprising considering that new-store openings performed well; Nguyen expected the company to devote a greater amount to capital expenditures for new stores.
- The company has made no acquisitions.
- Even after returns to shareholders, the company seems to prefer equity financing to debt financing. This preference is logical considering the company's thin operating margin, though the fact that it primarily sells a wide range of necessities reduces its sales risks (i.e., from changes in the business cycle and in technology or fashion) and membership fees are a source of predictable income.
- The fact that debt issuance is smaller than the increase in cash and investments on the balance sheet indicates that the company's net debt has decreased over time, implying a decline in financial leverage.

Evaluating Capital Investments and Capital Structure

Returns on invested capital over the longer run, compared with investors' required rates of return, can be used to evaluate whether management has used investors' capital wisely. Recall that independent investment analysts do not have access to the same information that management uses to assess individual projects with IRRs and NPVs, so analysts have to use more aggregated measures to discern whether there have been worsening or improving trends in value creation.

Risks related to the capital structure can be measured using leverage and coverage ratios, credit ratings by third-party rating agencies, and the sensitivity of net income to changes in operating income known as the **degree of financial leverage**, as shown in Equation 3. The degree of financial leverage is increased by higher interest expenses that are fixed with respect to operating income. The degree of financial leverage is analogous to the degree of operating leverage but is determined by financing costs rather than fixed operating costs.

$$DFL = \%\,\Delta\text{ Net income}/\%\,\Delta\text{ Operating income} \qquad (3)$$

CASE STUDIES

Evaluating Warehouse Club Inc.'s Capital Investments and Capital Structure

Elaine Nguyen calculates the following information on Warehouse over 2X10–2X19. Additionally, the company's interest coverage ratio (EBIT to interest expense) has been over 20 times and recently reached 30 times in 2X19, and the company's credit is rated investment grade by major credit rating agencies.

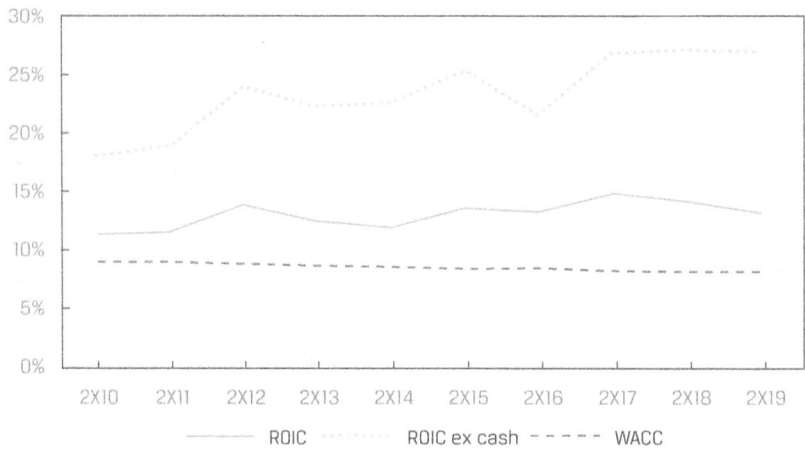

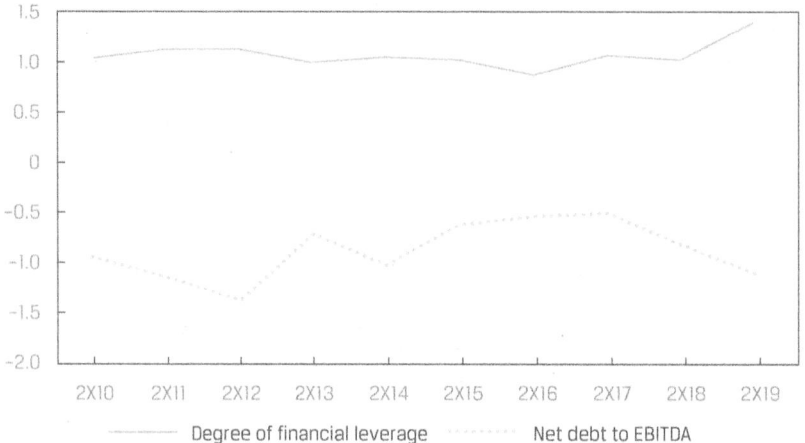

Nguyen makes the following observations:

- The company has created value for investors, with a spread of ROIC over WACC of 200–700 basis points since 2X10. WACC has declined slightly over time as interest rates have fallen; this calculation assumes a constant required rate of return on equity of 9%.

- The company's returns on capital are far higher than its low operating and net margins would suggest, owing to its high asset turnover and negative net working capital as a low-cost means of financing from suppliers, requiring less capital from investors.

Capital Investments and Capital Structure

- The company has a conservative capital structure, with negative net debt and a degree of financial leverage close to 1.0 because interest expense is largely covered by interest income on cash holdings (i.e., net and operating income move together).
- The capital structure conservatism is evidenced in the counterfactual ROIC, which excludes cash and investments on the balance sheet. While an exaggeration (the company would need *some* cash on hand), ROIC could be almost 15 percentage points higher if the company reduced net cash by investing in value-creating projects or by returning capital.

Unlevered returns, as measured by ROIC or return on assets, are augmented by financial leverage to produce levered returns, or return on equity, which was introduced in an earlier module. We can use return on equity and its decomposition as a comprehensive measure of profitability for an issuer. The ROE decomposition for Warehouse Club Inc. illustrates the drivers of the company's levered returns, which are well in excess of its net margin.

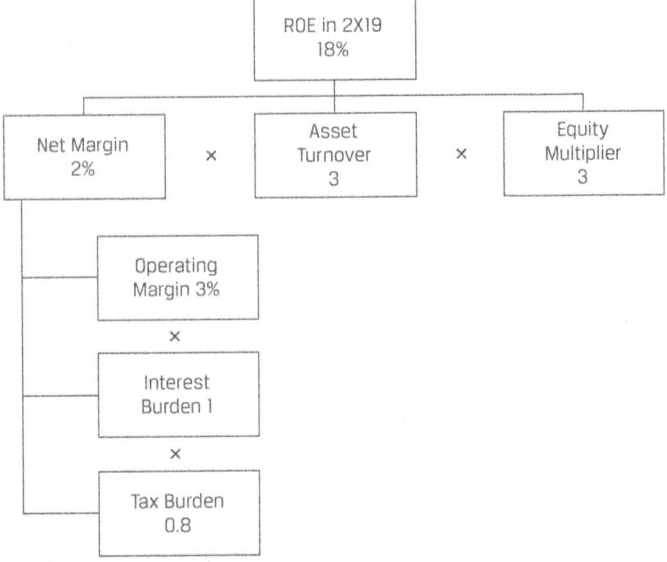

QUESTION SET

Questions 1–4 relate to Iliso's financial statements in the lesson "Determining the Business Model".

1. In 2X19, the market value of Iliso's equity was $1,178 million, and the book value of debt, which was approximately equal to the market value, was $144 million. Assuming a cost of debt of 5.5%, cost of equity of 12%, tax rate of 24%, and price-to-book ratio of 1.0, Iliso's WACC is *closest* to:

    A. 11.15%.
    B. 11.30%.
    C. 12.00%.

    Solution:

    A is correct. Recall that:

WACC = [weighting of debt × gross cost of debt × (1 − tax rate)] + (weighting of equity × cost of equity).

Total capital is $1,178 + $144 = $1,322 million. Weighting of debt is therefore $144/$1,322 = 10.89%, and Weighting of equity is 1 − Weight of debt = 89.11%.

Therefore, WACC = [10.89% × 5.5% × (1 − 24%)] + (89.11% × 12%) = 11.15%.
B is incorrect, because it incorrectly calculates WACC using a pre-tax rather than after-tax cost of debt.
C is incorrect; it is the cost of equity.

2. Why might Iliso's WACC be significantly higher than Warehouse Club's WACC, as calculated earlier in the module?

   A. Warehouse Club's business model is less risky than e-commerce.
   B. Warehouse Club's capital structure, with degree of financial leverage close to 1.0, is less conservative than Iliso's.
   C. Iliso is an established retailer with an investment-grade rating.

   Solution:

   A is correct. The cost of equity is the compensation that equity investors demand for the business and financial risks of investing in an issuer's equity securities. Iliso's cost of equity is 12%, whereas Warehouse Club's is 9%, reflecting Warehouse Club's longer operating history, more proven business model, and competitive positioning.
   B is incorrect, because Warehouse Club's capital structure, with degree of financial leverage of 1.0, would imply almost 100% weighting of equity, whereas Iliso has an 11% debt weighting and therefore Warehouse's capital structure is *more* conservative.
   C is incorrect, because an investment-grade rating would reduce Iliso's cost of debt and WACC.

3. Iliso's degree of financial leverage in 2X19 is *closest* to:

   A. 0.77.
   B. 1.13.
   C. 1.84.

   Solution:

   B is correct, calculated as Change in net income/Change in operating income = (100/52 − 1) divided by (130/72 − 1) = 1.146.
   A is incorrect, because it is incorrectly calculated as 2X19 Net income/Operating income = 100/130 = 0.77.
   C is incorrect, because it is Iliso's equity multiplier: Total assets/Equity = 2,168/(592 + 586) = 1.84.

4. Explain why Iliso's ROE differs from Warehouse Club's ROE.

   Solution:

   Iliso's ROE is lower than Warehouse Club's ROE.

   ROE = Net margin × Asset turnover × Equity multiplier

ROE = 1.3% × 3.5 × 1.84

= 8.37%, which is less than half of Warehouse Club's 18% ROE.

This primarily results from Iliso's lower net margin (1% versus 2%) and an equity multiplier that is 40% lower (1.84 versus 3), which is somewhat offset by Iliso's higher asset turnover (3.5 versus 3).

PRACTICE PROBLEMS

The following information relates to questions 1-7

Joshua Hu, a research analyst, is initiating coverage on several companies in the ocean freight shipping industry. OldShips is a mature company with high fixed costs and a high capital expenditure to sales ratio because it owns and operates its own fleet of ships. CleanYards is a technologically advanced, sustainable shipyard with a focus on specialized repairs and ship construction. Hu has compiled the following data for the two companies:

	OldShips	CleanYards
Degree of Financial Leverage (DFL)	2.0	2.0
Degree of Operating Leverage (DOL)	1.0	2.0
Asset turnover ratio	0.84×	0.42×
DSO	27	98
DOH	12	46
DPO	55	40

NewShips, a third company, is a web-based shipping technology platform that connects ship operators such as OldShips with customers in a wide variety of industries who need ocean freight shipping. NewShips' customers place orders online and pay for freight to be placed on a container to any destination in the world. NewShips' partners, like OldShips, provide vessels on both long- and short-term charters.

In 2X19, NewShips' platform brokered orders for 900,000 twenty-foot equivalent unit (TEU) containers in aggregate, with an average gross freight rate of USD3,848 per TEU. On average, NewShips' commission, which it receives as a broker from the customer, was 6% of the freight rate.

1. Which of the following is *most likely* to be an element of Hu's subsequent reports?

    A. Industry size, growth rate, and key drivers

    B. Summary of changes to the recommendation

    C. Ownership structure and management composition

2. Shipping is a highly cyclical industry. Which of the following companies *most likely* has the most ability to ramp up capacity to meet increased demand for shipping services?

    A. OldShips

    B. NewShips

    C. CleanYards

Practice Problems

3. In 2X19, NewShips' revenue was *closest* to:

   A. $173 million.

   B. $1.46 billion.

   C. $3.63 billion.

4. Assuming both companies have similar equity multipliers, OldShips is *most likely* to have a:

   A. much lower ROE than CleanYards.

   B. similar ROE to CleanYards'.

   C. much higher ROE than CleanYards.

5. When conducting company analysis, which of the following is *least* relevant to determining a company's business model?

   A. Company annual report describing the firm's product lines

   B. Comments by management about competing products and substitutes

   C. Industry white papers regarding the company's product pricing strategy

6. OldShips' cash conversion cycle (CCC) is:

   A. lower than CleanYards'.

   B. similar to CleanYards'.

   C. higher than CleanYards'.

7. The first step in reviewing a company's capital investments is to:

   A. evaluate management's investments.

   B. identify operating cash flow drivers.

   C. determine the major sources and uses of cash.

SOLUTIONS

1. B is correct. A subsequent company research report focuses on updating investors on new information or changes in an analyst's price target and recommendation.

   A and C are incorrect, because in-depth information regarding industry size, growth rate, and key drivers or ownership structure and management composition is more suited to an initiation report.

2. B is correct. Only NewShips has a capital-light business model. Both OldShips and CleanYards require substantial capital investment in order to increase supply capacity. New ship construction (for OldShips) and acquiring new yards (for CleanYards) take time and cannot be met immediately.

3. A is correct. NewShips acts as a broker and earns 5% of the freight rate in commissions. In 2X19, NewShips brokered 900,000 TEUs at an average freight rate of 3,848 per TEU, earning a 5% commission: 900,000 × 3,848 × 0.05 = $173 million.

4. B is correct; ROE = DTL × Asset turnover × Equity multiplier.

   OldShips has half the degree of CleanYards' total leverage. However, its asset turnover is double CleanYards' (0.84× versus 0.42×). Since the equity multiplier is the same, their ROEs must be similar.

   Degree of total leverage (DTL) = DFL × DOL = (% Δ Net income/% Δ Operating income) × (% Δ Operating income/% Δ Q).

   Thus, OldShips' DTL = 2 × 1 = 2, whereas CleanYards' DTL = 2 × 2 = 4.

   A and C are incorrect, because both companies must have similar ROEs.

5. B is correct. Competing products and substitutes are analyzed in Porter's Five Forces. This analysis is usually performed to better understand a company's industry and its competitive positioning. Management comments are unlikely to guide the analyst to better understand the company's business model.

   A and C are incorrect, because both are relevant sources for an analyst in determining the company's business model.

6. A is correct.

   CCC = DOH + DSO − DPO, so:

   OldShips' CCC = 12 + 27 − 55 = −16 days

   CleanYards' CCC = 46 + 98 − 40 = 104 days

   OldShips, in fact, has a negative cash conversion cycle. OldShips takes advantage of the favorable credit terms granted by its suppliers.

   B and C are incorrect, because OldShips' CCC is lower than CleanYards'.

7. C is correct. Before a review of a company's capital investments, the first step is to determine the company's sources and uses of capital on a historical basis.

   A and B are incorrect, because both take place after the analyst has identified the company's sources and uses of cash and determined what to focus on.

LEARNING MODULE 6

Industry and Competitive Analysis

LEARNING OUTCOMES

Mastery	The candidate should be able to:
☐	describe the purposes of, and steps involved in, industry and competitive analysis
☐	describe industry classification methods and compare methods by which companies can be grouped
☐	determine an industry's size, growth characteristics, profitability, and market share trends
☐	analyze an industry's structure and external influences using Porter's Five Forces and PESTLE frameworks
☐	evaluate the competitive strategy and position of a company

INTRODUCTION 1

It is essential for analysts to understand the industry context for a company's financial performance and its evaluation. For example, is a company's revenue growth driven by a macroeconomic or industry-wide factor (such as an economic expansion) or a company-specific factor (such as increasing market share)? The answer has important implications for forecasting and valuation.

In this learning module, we discuss how an industry is defined and address the challenges associated with grouping companies that operate in multiple industries. Next, we introduce methods to survey an industry in terms of size, profitability, and market share trends. Further analysis includes frameworks to interpret a competitive environment using Porter's Five Forces and external trends using PESTLE analysis. Finally, we combine these approaches to understand a company's competitive strategy and its position relative to its industry peers.

> **LEARNING MODULE OVERVIEW**
>
> - Analysts use industry and competitive analysis to understand an industry's structural factors, relative competitive strengths and weaknesses, and their contribution to a company's economic profits.

- An analyst's first step in an industry and competitive analysis is to define the boundaries of the industry in question and its constituents. Industries are commonly defined as companies that sell similar products or services. However, this definition can be challenging to apply in practice, as companies can sell diverse products or services across many industries and product similarity is subjective.
- To define an industry, analysts can use third-party classification systems such as GICS but need to be aware of the methodologies and limitations of these systems.
- After defining the industry, the analyst surveys the industry by estimating its total annual sales, historical growth rate, and profitability metrics and then determining market shares and trends of key players.
- Industry metrics can be compared against broader economic trends during recessions or expansions to determine the industry's level of maturity, sensitivity to business cycles, and competitive rivalry.
- Analysts use Porter's Five Forces to understand an industry's structure, as defined by the level of competitive rivalry, through an assessment of the threat of new entrants, the threat of substitutes, customer bargaining power, and the bargaining power of suppliers.
- To supplement this research, analysts use PESTLE analysis to understand the external influences on and potential changes to an industry's growth rate and market share dynamics.
- To evaluate a company's competitive strategy, an analyst should determine whether the strategy creates a defense against industry forces and is aligned with the external forces acting on the industry, and whether the company has the resources and capabilities necessary to execute it.

LEARNING MODULE SELF-ASSESSMENT

These initial questions are intended to help you gauge your current level of understanding of this learning module.

1. When assigning a company to an industry, which of the following is a limitation of using third-party industry classification schemes?

    A. Currency differences
    B. Single-product companies
    C. Strictly hierarchical taxonomies

    Solution:

    C is correct. Commercial classification schemes such as GICS, IBC, and TRBC are examples of strictly hierarchical taxonomies that classify a company to a single group, regardless of whether the company sells multiple types of products or services.

2. A factor that determines sensitivity to the business cycle is *most likely*:

    A. customer migration to substitute products.
    B. interest rate exposure of the business model.

Introduction

C. growth rates in line with broader economic activity.

Solution:

B is correct. Factors that determine sensitivity to the business cycle include the degree to which sales are discretionary or necessary for consumers, pricing power, the interest rate exposure of the business model, and whether the product is a durable or capital good versus a recurring purchase such as consumables and subscription services.

A and C are incorrect, as they reflect features of a mature industry but are not necessarily more cyclical.

3. A common measure of industry concentration is:

    A. Porter's Five Forces.
    B. the PESTLE framework.
    C. the Herfindahl-Hirschman Index.

Solution:

C is correct. The Herfindahl-Hirschman Index (HHI) is a common measure of industry concentration that is calculated as the sum of the squares of competitor market shares. Porter's Five Forces model evaluates an industry's level of competitive rivalry and profitability. The PESTLE framework is more concerned with an industry's growth rate and market share dynamics.

4. Identify the following statement as true or false. Justify your answer.

    Some of the forces included in Porter's Five Forces framework are the threat of new entrants, sensitivity to the business cycle, and the bargaining power of customers.

Solution:

False. Porter's Five Forces model uses the threat of substitutes, the threat of new entrants, the bargaining power of customers, and the bargaining power of suppliers to determine the rivalry among existing competitors. Sensitivity to the business cycle is *not* one of the forces.

5. The price competition historically demonstrated by automakers and aircraft manufacturers is *best* described as an example of:

    A. the threat of substitutes.
    B. the bargaining power of suppliers.
    C. the rivalry among existing competitors.

Solution:

C is correct. Despite relatively low risks from the other Five Forces, automakers and aircraft manufacturers compete fiercely on price, offering promotions and generous financing and warranty terms in an attempt to capture every sale.

6. Standardization of a product will _____ (increase/decrease/have no effect on) the bargaining power of customers.

Solution:

Standardization of a product will *increase* the bargaining power of customers. For example, oil refiners pay for crude oil based on its grade, not on its specific oil producer; crude oil within a grade is interchangeable.

7. Impression Ltd. is a fictional company that designs, manufactures, and sells skin care and beauty products. A PESTLE analysis for Impression Ltd. would *most likely* identify which of the following?

   A. A customer of Impression Ltd., a large e-commerce retailer, is acquiring a private-label manufacturer of skin care products.
   B. Increased discussion by legislatures around instituting an excise tax on disposable plastic packaging as part of a package of carbon taxes
   C. An online, direct sales competitor has launched a suite of photo filters that integrate with leading social media apps based on its beauty products.

   Solution:

   B is correct. PESTLE analysis is concerned with identifying and evaluating *external* forces on an industry, which include political forces such as a packaging tax. A and C are incorrect, as they are competitor moves within the beauty industry.

8. As a venture capital investor, you are on the board of Ridge Inc., a fictional company that is entering the auto industry, which is characterized by high capital intensity, minimal switching costs for customers because regulations require standardization of many features, and price consciousness of customers except among a relatively small percentage of affluent consumers.

   Based on these observations, recommend and justify a competitive strategy to the rest of Ridge Inc.'s board.

   Solution:

   A cost leadership strategy is one competitive strategy that might be successful for Ridge Inc. Since most customers are price conscious and face minimal switching costs between automakers or models, a low selling price can be an effective way to gain market share. Combined with high capital intensity, such a strategy might enable Ridge to operate at an economic profit if it produces and sells enough volume and maintains fixed-cost discipline to keep unit costs low. Other competitive strategies that might be successful for Ridge include a differentiation strategy aimed at luxury or performance customers.

2. USES OF INDUSTRY ANALYSIS

☐ describe the purposes of, and steps involved in, industry and competitive analysis

The next step in our company and industry analysis framework (Exhibit 1), introduced in the last module, is industry and competitive analysis, which involves the study of the drivers of an industry's size, profitability, and market shares and the evaluation of a company's competitive positioning in its industry.

Exhibit 1: Company and Industry Analysis Framework

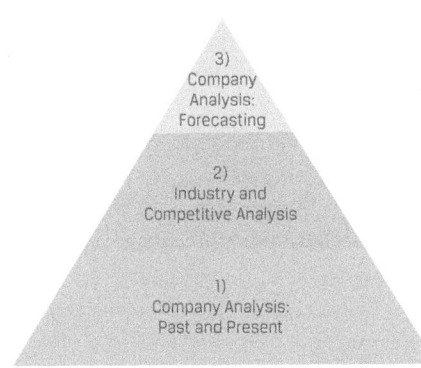

3) Company Analysis: Forecasting
- Determine forecast objects and approaches
- Forecast revenue
- Forecast operating profitability and working capital
- Forecast capital investments and capital structure
- Evaluate key risks and uncertainties

2) Industry and Competitive Analysis
- Define Industry
- Analyze size, growth and character, profitability, market share trends
- Analyze industry structure and external influences
- Evaluate company's competitive strategy and positioning and determine if company has a competitive advantage

1) Company Analysis: Past and Present
- Determine business model
- Analyze revenue and revenue drivers
- Analyze operating profitability and working capital
- Analyze capital investments and capital structure (uses of capital and sources of financing)

Why Analyze an Industry?

Many industry participants have similar business models. They often compete in the same or similar product markets as sellers and in factor markets as buyers, so they tend to be exposed to the same demand and supply opportunities and risk factors. As will be discussed later with Porter's Five Forces model, these industry structural factors result in profitability differences by industry in the long run, with company-specific factors like business model variation, competitive strategy, size, and execution creating variance around the industry median.

McGahan and Porter (1997) estimated the relative importance of industry versus company-specific effects on both the emergence of economic profits (ROIC in excess of WACC) and their sustainability over time, finding that industry was the most important factor in the sustainability of economic profits. Importantly, they found that company-specific effects were much larger for low performers than for high performers in an industry, suggesting that industry and competitive forces can act as a ceiling on a company's returns but not as a floor.

A useful way to think about this dynamic is that competition "pulls" company profitability to an industry base rate over time. Industry and competitive analysis is used to estimate that base rate and its determinants, to form a forward-looking perspective on potential structural changes, and, finally, to analyze firms' relative strengths and weaknesses to determine their position against the base rate. It is important to emphasize, though, that these measures and outcomes are dynamic and that some companies have outperformed or underperformed their industry in economic profitability for many years.

Improve Forecasts

Competitive forces from industry incumbents, substitutes, suppliers, and customers discipline companies' prices and costs, market share, and thus profitability. By taking an industry perspective and better understanding these drivers—as well as building a database of past competitive actions and strategies by firms in an industry and their track records of success—analysts can sharpen their forecasts and alertness to what is most important. Guan, Wong, and Zhang (2014) found that sell-side investment analysts who covered both companies and their suppliers made more accurate earnings forecasts than those who did not cover the suppliers. Without a broader perspective, an analyst may underrate competitive forces and overrate the degree to which a company controls its destiny.

Identify Investment Opportunities

Industry analysis may uncover an attractive investment candidate that an analyst was previously unaware of or had not fully appreciated until assessing its strengths and weaknesses relative to industry peers and competitors. In addition, some investors may conclude that it is the industry, not any specific company, that they want exposure to, and in fact would like to diversify away the company-specific risks. These investors might take a basket approach by investing in several companies with position sizes scaled by size, liquidity, or relative attractiveness.

Industry and Competitive Analysis Steps

We approach industry and competitive analysis through the process shown in Exhibit 2, which begins with defining an industry and ends with evaluating a company's competitive positioning in the context of that industry.

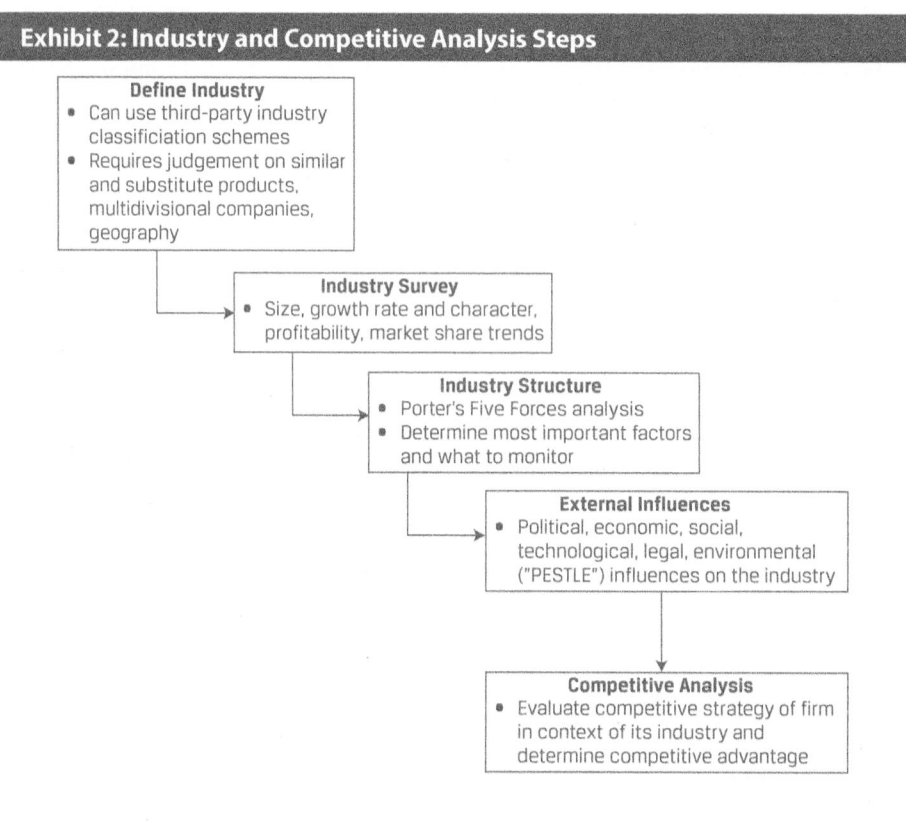

QUESTION SET

1. Over the long run:

    A. business cycles result in profitability differences by industry.

> B. company-specific factors such as competitive strategy result in profitability differences by industry.
>
> C. structural factors result in profitability differences by industry.
>
> **Solution:**
>
> C is correct. Structural factors, such as Porter's Five Forces, drive profitability and profitability differences by industry in the long run. Company-specific factors result in company profitability levels around the industry median, while changes in the business cycle drive *short-run* profitability for both industries and companies.

> 2. Which of the following is an industry, *not* a company-specific, attribute?
>
>   A. Competitive strategy
>
>   B. Business model variation
>
>   C. Sensitivity to the business cycle
>
>   **Solution:**
>
>   C is correct. Sensitivity to the business cycle is an example of a factor that influences an entire industry.
>
>   A and B are examples of company-specific attributes, which also include company size and strategy execution.

> 3. Explain why industry has a significant effect on company growth and profitability.
>
>   **Solution:**
>
>   Companies in the same industry compete in similar product markets as sellers and in factor markets as buyers, so they tend to be exposed to the same demand and supply opportunities and risk factors. For example, while a restaurant company that sells chicken has a different product than a restaurant that sells pastries, both are competing for a similar customer need (prepared food), employ similarly skilled workers, and have capital equipment and real estate.

INDUSTRY CLASSIFICATION

☐ describe industry classification methods and compare methods by which companies can be grouped

An industry is commonly defined as companies that sell similar products or services, from the perspective of a customer. Challenges in defining an industry include whether to include substitutes, classifying companies that operate in multiple industries, geographical considerations, and making updates since business models are always evolving. To help analysts contend with these difficulties, third-party organizations maintain industry classification schemes that are widely used in investment management.

Third-Party Industry Classification Schemes

Early third-party industry classification schemes such as SIC, NACE, and ISIC were devised by government agencies, tended to be country-specific, and grouped companies by their production characteristics into industries such as agriculture, manufacturing, distribution, retail, and services. The schemes were not updated frequently and became less useful as new technologies and business models emerged and both issuers and investors became increasingly global. These legacy schemes used by investment analysts were largely replaced with commercial schemes such as the Global Industry Classification Standard (GICS) by MSCI and S&P Dow Jones Indices, Industry Classification Benchmark (ICB) by FTSE Russell, and The Refinitiv Business Classification (TRBC) by Refinitiv. These schemes are global, reviewed and updated at least annually, with new companies added more frequently, and group companies by the similarity of the products or services they sell—a "demand" approach rather than the "supply" approach of the legacy schemes. GICS and ICB cover public companies, while TRBC also covers private companies, non-profits, and government entities. Data aggregators (such as Bloomberg, FactSet, and CapIQ) and stock exchange operators (such as the London Stock Exchange) either use these industry classification schemes or have their own that are substantially similar.

GICS, ICB, and TRBC are strictly hierarchical taxonomies, analogous to the species, genus, family, etc., taxonomy used in biology. In each scheme, a company is classified to a *single* group in the lowest tier, with the groups themselves making up the higher tiers. In other words, continuing with the biology metaphor, a company is classified to a single species, which automatically assigns it to a genus, family, and so on. GICS, ICB, and TRBC have slightly different groupings, tiers, and names. Exhibit 3 shows the names and hierarchy of each scheme's tiers, the number of groups in each tier, and the composition of the highest tier.

Industry Classification

Exhibit 3: GICS, ICB, and TRBC Structures

GICS by S&P DJI and MSCI

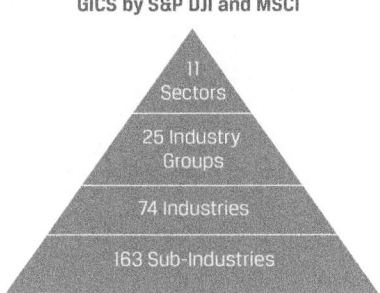

- 11 Sectors
- 25 Industry Groups
- 74 Industries
- 163 Sub-Industries

GICS Sectors
1. Energy
2. Financials
3. Materials
4. Information Technology
5. Industrials
6. Communication Services
7. Consumer Discretionary
8. Utilities
9. Consumer Staples
10. Real Estate
11. Health care

ICB by FTSE Russell

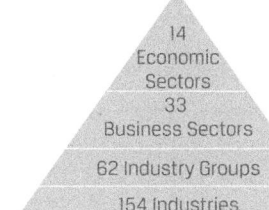

- 11 Industries
- 20 Supersectors
- 45 Sectors
- 173 Subsectors

ICB Industries
1. Energy
2. Financials
3. Basic Materials
4. Information Technology
5. Industrials
6. Telecommunications
7. Consumer Discretionary
8. Utilities
9. Consumer Staples
10. Real Estate
11. Health care

TRBC by Refinitiv

- 14 Economic Sectors
- 33 Business Sectors
- 62 Industry Groups
- 154 Industries
- 898 Activities

TRBC Economic Sectors
1. Energy
2. Financials
3. Basic Materials
4. Technology
5. Industrials
6. Communication Services
7. Consumer Cyclicals
8. Utilities
9. Consumer Non-Cyclicals
10. Real Estate
11. Healthcare
12. Institutions, Associations, and Organizations
13. Government Activity
14. Academic and Educational Services

GICS, ICB, and TRBC also have slightly different rules for companies operating in multiple industries, all of which use some discretion. While each scheme differs slightly, the general process is shown in Exhibit 4. The goal is to assign a company to a single grouping that describes the majority of its business.

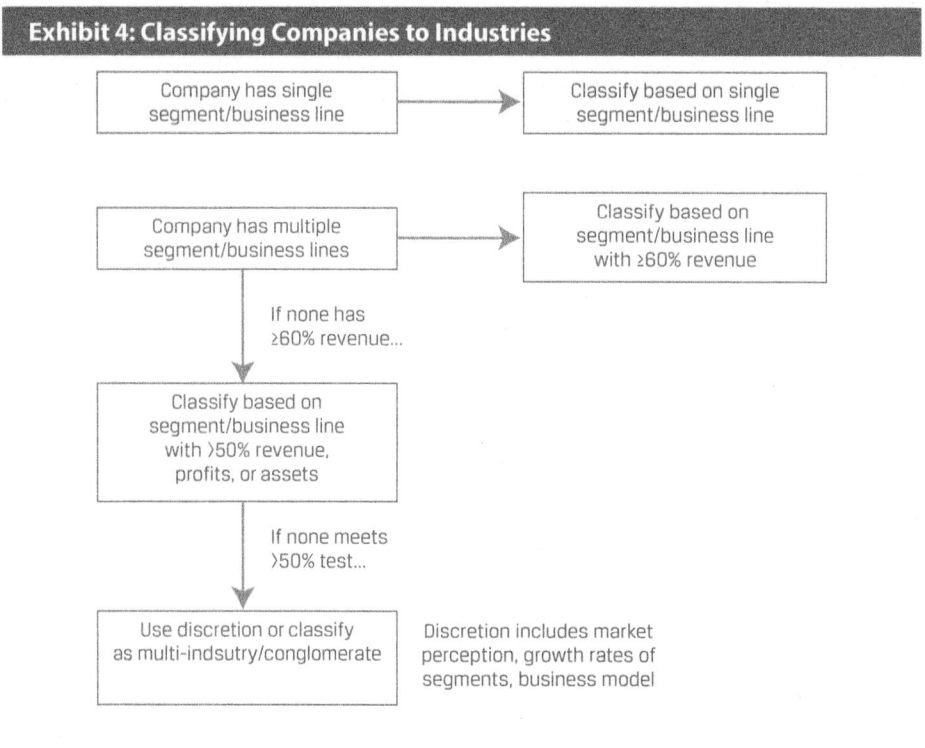

Limitations of Third-Party Industry Classification Schemes

While these classification schemes are a useful starting place for research (and they have other uses like index construction and investment performance attribution, described elsewhere in the curriculum), they have four important limitations that analysts must contend with in doing industry research:

1. Groupings of companies with business model variations or that sell substitute products
2. The classification of multi-product companies
3. Geographical considerations
4. Changes in groupings over time that affect prior-period comparability of industry statistics

Analysts may find that industry groupings in the third-party schemes are either too narrow or too broad, as the scheme providers use discretion in constructing groups based on product similarity and business model. Therefore, analysts must either use classification tiers at a higher or lower level or modify the groupings based on their own discretion and purposes of analysis. On the one hand, many companies classified as "application software" sell products with completely different functionality and do not compete with one another—for example, Shopify, the Canadian company that sells front-end and payment processing software to small and mid-sized e-commerce companies, is grouped with Check Point Software, an Israeli security software company. On the other hand, as will be shown with Warehouse Club Inc., retailers are classified into numerous sub-industries and even across sectors, although many of their product offerings overlap and are thus competing for the same consumer dollar.

Because GICS, ICB, and TRBC are strict taxonomies, multi-product companies are assigned to a single grouping. This treatment can be a problem for an analyst identifying competitors if a competitor is a division of a company classified in a

Industry Classification

different industry or even sector. The most prominent examples are in technology. A large software market is cloud infrastructure and platform services (sometimes called "public cloud"), which are computing, storage, and other IT-related capabilities sold on a metered basis to clients over the internet. Large players include Amazon Web Services, Microsoft Azure, Google Cloud Platform, and Alibaba Cloud, which are all divisions of larger parent companies with other segments that differ materially by business model. While Amazon and Alibaba are classified in the same industry, Alphabet (parent of Google Cloud Platform) and Microsoft are each classified in different sectors. Amazon's classification as a consumer discretionary retailer has long inspired consternation, as most of its operating profits come from its Amazon Web Services segment, not e-commerce.

With their global nature, GICS, ICB, and TRBC are useful for some sectors and industries that are in fact global (primarily those that manufacture physical goods and digital products), but they can be less useful for more service-oriented companies that compete nationally or even locally because of customer behavior or regulations that restrict competition. For example, only a small minority of people travel a significant distance from their home to receive healthcare services, and insurers (whether private or government) typically restrict the choice of provider geographically. Governments also regulate the practice of medicine through the licensing of facilities, physicians, and other practitioners. Therefore, the healthcare services industry is best examined on a national or regional basis; the economics of hospitals in the UAE have little relevance to those in France. However, this approach should not be taken for granted, as industries can globalize or localize based on business model changes. While media (pay TV) companies were once regional, the shift to internet-based streaming video has resulted in a global industry with new, larger players.

Finally, industry classification scheme providers change groupings and classifications, which can affect industry statistics. One of the largest changes, for example, was the creation of the Real Estate sector, composed primarily of Real Estate Investment Trusts carved out of the Financials sector. Additionally, public offerings and de-listings from acquisitions and bankruptcies change the composition of the groupings over time (introducing survivorship bias in historical returns statistics). Analysts should be aware of these issues, make sure that historical statistics are restated to conform to the latest groupings, and construct survivorship bias–free datasets if possible.

CASE STUDIES

Defining Warehouse Club Inc.'s Industry

Warehouse Club Inc. has a single line of business and would be assigned to the "Consumer Staples Merchandise Retail" sub-industry in GICS.

Sector	Industry Group	Industry	Sub-Industry	Other Sub-Industry Constituents
Consumer Staples	Consumer Staples Distribution & Retail	Consumer Staples Distribution & Retail	Consumer Staples Merchandise Retail	Costco, Walmart, BJ's, Carrefour, Sun Art Retail Group, Coles Group, PriceSmart

> While this classification is logical, the sub-industry includes companies outside Warehouse's domestic geography that are less relevant to its customers and does not include many companies in its domestic geography that sell similar products to the same types of customers. For example, grocers and drugstores are included in a different sub-industry (Food Retail and Drug Retail, respectively), and e-commerce retailers that it competes with are in a different sector entirely (Consumer Discretionary).
>
> The challenge in placing Warehouse in an industry is that it sells several categories of consumer goods, both staples and discretionary goods like apparel, as do many other companies. Retailers also have varying business models—including membership-based warehouses, e-commerce, and co-locations with other services like pharmacies—and have varying location, assortment, and pricing strategies.
>
> Elaine Nguyen chooses to define Warehouse's industry more broadly than its GICS sub-industry by taking a customer perspective: retailers of all kinds operating in Warehouse's domestic geography, except for automobile and auto parts retailers as Warehouse does not sell those products or even substitutes for them (and it is a large category of domestic retail sales). Nguyen also does not include restaurants and food services, instead considering them substitutes.

Alternative Methods of Grouping Companies

An industry or product approach to grouping companies is not the only grouping method and may be less useful in contexts outside industry analysis. Other approaches that are used in contexts such as index construction and investment performance evaluation include the following:

- Geography, in which companies are classified by country and then countries are aggregated into categories such as developed, emerging, and frontier markets. Classification by country is typically by the country where the issuer is incorporated, the country of the primary listing of its equity securities, the location of its headquarters, or market perception. Note that classification by the geographic composition of revenue is generally *not* the approach taken, though this aspect may be the foremost concern for an analyst. For example, Toyota is universally classified as a Japanese company. However, its largest market by revenues is North America, which is also the location of most of its assets. The classification of developed, emerging, and frontier markets is more controversial, and third parties like index providers use greater discretion. It is not a quantitative determination but considers variables such as the size and liquidity of equity securities markets in the country, income per capita, and legal restrictions on foreign investment.

- Sensitivity to the business cycle, with groupings such as "defensive" and "cyclical." Defensive companies are those whose sales growth, profitability, and valuations are less affected by changes in broad macroeconomic activity (e.g., GDP growth), while the opposite is true of cyclicals. Generally, this classification is done by grouping entire sectors from the industry classification schemes discussed earlier. Sectors such as consumer staples, healthcare, and utilities are considered defensive, while financials, basic materials, consumer discretionary, and industrials are considered cyclical. This grouping method can be combined with other methods—such as a geographic approach (e.g., Japanese cyclicals), because countries may vary with respect to their current position in the business cycle, or credit ratings (e.g., Japanese cyclicals with high-yield credit)—to further isolate exposure to certain risk factors.

Industry Classification

- Statistical similarities, or the use of clustering analysis to group companies based on similarities of financial ratios and market data or co-movements of their securities' investment returns. This approach includes grouping by size according to market capitalization or by other characteristics such as the following:
  - Valuation ratios
  - Growth rates of sales or earnings
  - Profitability ratios
  - Statistics based on price performance such as volatility and momentum
- ESG characteristics, such as the ratio of carbon emissions to revenues, measures of board and executive personnel diversity, and exposure to certain businesses such as tobacco and gambling. These metrics can be aggregated into composite ESG ratings or scores that enable cross-issuer comparability.

These groupings are usually relative (e.g., companies with dividend yields at or above the 75th percentile as of the measurement date) and tend to show far more turnover in their constituents than groupings based on industries and countries, because these statistics are less stable by company and companies' rankings change.

QUESTION SET

1. Contrast the Global Industry Classification Standard (GICS) commercial scheme with the Standard Industrial Classification (SIC) third-party classification system in terms of geographic coverage, update frequency, and the addition of new companies.

   Solution:

   The GICS commercial scheme is determined on a global basis, updated at least annually, and adds new companies frequently, while the SIC is US-only, infrequently updated, and does not regularly add new companies.

2. The GICS, ICB, and TRBC commercial industry classification schemes suffer from which common problem when used by analysts?

   A. They quickly become out of date.

   B. They cover a limited number of countries.

   C. They often classify multi-industry companies inaccurately.

   Solution:

   C is correct. Commercial industry classification schemes are strictly hierarchical and assign each company to a single industry. Multi-industry companies are classified using evaluations of segment revenues, profits, or assets or the discretion of the scheme creator. This approach often results in classifications that are different from analyst expectations or in "multi-industry" classifications that are challenging to use in practice.

3. Identify whether each of the following sectors is generally considered "cyclical" or "defensive."

I. Consumer Staples	Cyclical	Defensive
II. Consumer Discretionary	Cyclical	Defensive
III. Energy	Cyclical	Defensive

IV. Healthcare	Cyclical	Defensive
V. Utilities	Cyclical	Defensive
VI. Financials	Cyclical	Defensive
VII. Industrials	Cyclical	Defensive
VIII. Technology	Cyclical	Defensive
IX. Materials	Cyclical	Defensive
X. Real Estate	Cyclical	Defensive

Solution:

I. Defensive
II. Cyclical
III. Cyclical
IV. Defensive
V. Defensive
VI. Cyclical
VII. Cyclical
VIII. Defensive
IX. Cyclical
X. Defensive

4. INDUSTRY SURVEY

☐ determine an industry's size, growth characteristics, profitability, and market share trends

After defining an industry, the next step in industry and competitive analysis is to survey the industry by estimating its size, calculating its historical growth rate, evaluating the character of that growth rate, measuring its profitability, and identifying major industry players and market share trends over time. This industry survey provides a basis for the industry evaluation in the next step and makes an analyst aware of the main issues and opportunities.

Industry Size and Historical Growth Rate

Industry size is typically measured by total annual sales from the product or customer perspective, which is not necessarily all sales of each industry constituent. For example, Amazon's retail segment sales would be included in sizing the retail industry, while sales for its Amazon Web Services segment would not. The growth rate is calculated either as year-over-year rates each year or as a compounded annual growth rate over a multi-year period. If possible, industry growth should be broken out by contributions from volume and price/mix drivers.

Except for some industries that are dominated by large, publicly traded companies (e.g., autos, smartphones, airlines, pharmaceuticals), industry size will often include a potentially large amount in sales from private companies, sometimes small businesses, for which data are unavailable or impractical to tabulate. It's common practice to estimate industry size for these industries using economic indicators published by government agencies, data from third-party consultancies that use surveys, or industry data from issuers' investor presentations based on proprietary sources. These all need to be corroborated for reasonableness by the analyst. For Warehouse Club Inc., for example, we use retail sales published by a government agency for industry size, because the retail industry includes hundreds of thousands of small retailers.

Characterizing Industry Growth

The pattern of historical growth of an industry can be used to characterize it based on the magnitude of its growth rate and sensitivity to the business cycle. One approach to characterizing an industry's growth rate is a style box, as shown in Exhibit 5. Essential to this approach is comparing the industry's historical growth rate with a broader measure of economic growth during recessions and expansions.

Exhibit 5: Industry Growth Style Box

	Mature	Growth
Defensive	–Utilities –Beverages –Pharmaceuticals	–Biotechnology –Software –Gaming
Cyclical	–Crude oil –Natural gas –Freight transportation	–Semiconductors –Fintech –Digital advertising

Source: Authors' analysis.

Growth industries include those that have not yet reached full saturation or penetration of their total addressable market, and thus have idiosyncratic growth drivers separate from broader economic growth. Growth industries are often based on or benefit from an emerging technology. Key questions for analysts related to growth industries include whether historically high growth rates will persist and what the peak penetration rate is—which are more challenging to answer the "newer" the industry is. Conversely, mature industries have fully penetrated their addressable market and have growth rates either in line with broader economic activity (approximately zero) or declining as customer demand migrates to a substitute. Key issues for investors in a mature industry include monitoring for disruptive threats, changes in competitive intensity, and the speed of decline.

Sensitivity to the business cycle is driven by the business models of companies in an industry and correlates with industry maturity. Factors that determine sensitivity include the degree to which sales are discretionary or necessary for consumers, prices, the interest rate exposure of the business model, and whether the product is a durable or capital good versus a recurring purchase such as consumables and subscription services. Although most investors expect greater variability in returns from firms in cyclical industries, differing investor views as to the length and magnitude of such cycles lead to wide variations in the valuations of issuers over time.

Although commonly used by market participants, these distinctions can sometimes be of limited usefulness. For example, a severe economic downturn is likely to have a negative impact on all firms, so differences will be a matter of degree but not categorical. Second, companies in different stages of the life cycle within an industry can differ materially in terms of growth, defensiveness, and cyclicality; for example, growth firms based on an emerging technology may exist within a cyclical industry that is far less affected by an economic downturn.

Industry Profitability Measures

The best measure of industry profitability is a time series of the distribution of returns on invested capital (e.g., 25th, 50th, 75th percentiles), which captures after-tax operating profits for each dollar of invested capital and is agnostic about capital structure. However, unless the industry is dominated by public companies, obtaining these data is seldom feasible.

Two common methods to overcome this challenge in practice are to measure the profitability of the publicly traded players and assume that the profitability of private competitors is similar—either using various sources to estimate the profitability of non-public companies (e.g., for state-owned energy companies, there are estimates of their production costs per barrel, production, and capital expenditures, and prices are generally uniform throughout the industry) or obtaining data from a government agency or third-party consultancy. For Warehouse Club Inc., the same government agency that publishes retail sales data each month also does an annual survey of retailers' gross margins and operating expenses, which can be used to calculate industry operating margins.

Clearly, a profitable industry is preferable to an unprofitable one, but often more important than a point estimate of profitability is the time series: is industry profitability rising or falling? If there is a discernible trend, it will be an important point of investigation for the analyst.

Market Share Trends and Major Players

Finally, market shares are measured by expressing industry participants' annual revenues as percentages of the industry size each year. Given the aforementioned measurement problems with estimating industry size, market shares should be interpreted as a range rather than a definitive point estimate. Again, more important than each company's market share is the trend over time, which can reveal whether customers have judged the company's products superior to competitors'. An important consideration is acquisitions, particularly large ones; a company buying a competitor is a market share gain, but more important is whether the company is increasing or decreasing its share on an organic (non-acquired) basis.

An additional consideration in this analysis is the degree of industry concentration. Lower concentration—that is, many small competitors in the market—is usually associated with a high degree of competitive intensity unless the industry is very service-oriented, is local in nature, or has high product differentiation. Rising concentration (consolidation) is associated with falling competitive intensity and higher profitability. A common measure of industry concentration is the **Herfindahl-Hirschman Index (HHI)**, calculated as the sum of the squares of competitor market shares:

$$HHI = \sum_{i=1}^{\infty} s_i^2 ,$$

where s is the market share of market participant i stated as a whole number (i.e., 50% share = 50, not 0.50).

A market consisting of four firms with shares of 30, 30, 20, and 20 has an HHI of $30^2 + 30^2 + 20^2 + 20^2 = 2{,}600$. The maximum HHI is for a monopoly, with a value of $100^2 = 10{,}000$. Antitrust regulators in some countries consider markets with an HHI between 1,500 and 2,500 moderately concentrated and consider markets with an HHI over 2,500 highly concentrated. A rule of thumb is that acquisitions in highly concentrated markets that increase the HHI by more than 200 points are often subject to regulatory challenges.

CASE STUDIES

Industry Survey for Warehouse Club Inc. and Iliso Marketplace Ltd.

Industry Size and Growth Rate

Elaine Nguyen sizes the US retail (excluding autos) industry using three measures: total annual revenues, annual revenues on a per capita basis, and the number of retailers. For all these measures, Nguyen uses data from the US Census Bureau, since the industry consists mostly of small businesses with no public filings and the data are high quality; the Bureau has been collecting such data since 1952.

At the end of 2X19, there were 556,531 firms in the industry, but over 92% of them employed fewer than 20 people. Just 470 large firms with over 5,000 employees accounted for 62% of total industry employment. Of these large firms, 144 were publicly traded.

US Retailers (ex autos) as of 2X19	
< 20 employees	516,766
Between 20 and 5,000 employees	39,295
> 5,000 employees	470

US Retailers (ex autos) as of 2X19	
Total	556,531
Note: public companies	144

Character of Industry Growth

The retail industry has existed for hundreds of years in the USA, though there have been many changes in both form (e.g., department stores, discounters, e-commerce) and the products sold. Comparing industry sales growth with GDP growth since the early 1990s shows that the two are tightly related. However, the industry does not show extreme cyclicality, unlike the auto industry.

Elaine Nguyen classifies the industry as mature and moderately cyclical.

Annual Growth Rates: US Retail Sales ex Autos, Autos, and GDP

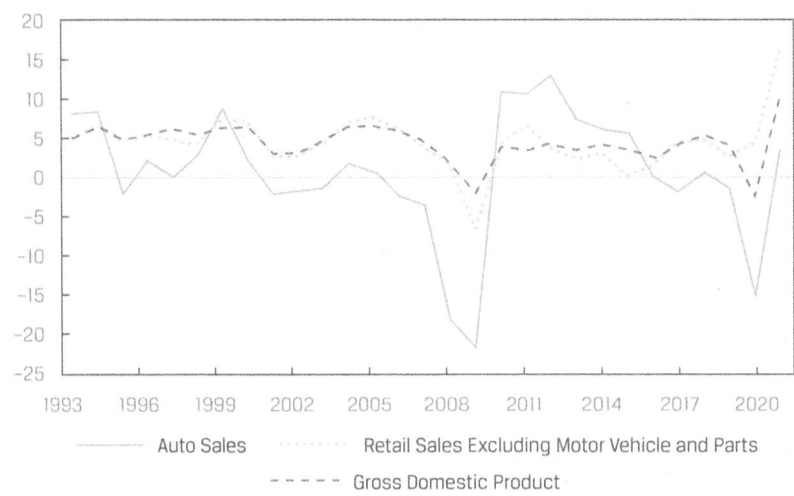

Industry Profitability

Nguyen analyzes industry profitability in two ways: (1) the gross and operating margins of all retailers (except autos) in the USA using Census Bureau data and (2) the profitability of the 10 largest publicly traded retailers in the USA by 2X19 sales. Because of segment disclosure changes, M&A, and other corporate transactions, Nguyen examines the last 5 rather than 10 years of data.

Gross and Operating Margins of US Retailers ex Autos

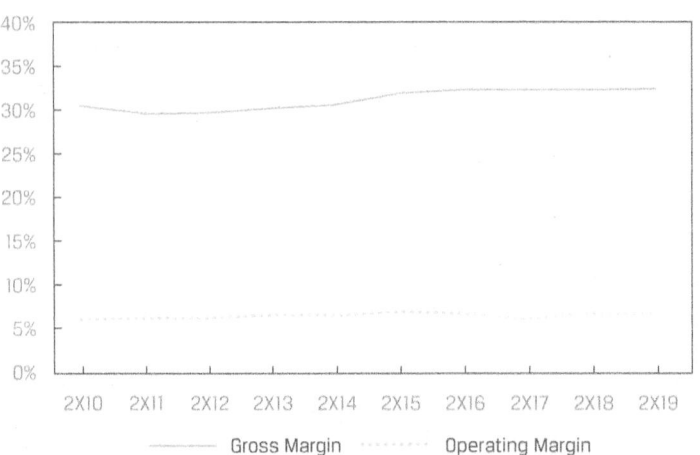

Industry Survey

Operating Margins	2X15	2X16	2X17	2X18	2X19
Walmart (US segment)	6.4%	5.8%	5.3%	5.2%	5.1%
Walmart (Sam's Club segment)	3.2%	2.9%	1.5%	2.6%	2.8%
Amazon.com (North America segment)	2.2%	3.0%	2.7%	5.1%	4.1%
Costco Wholesale (US segment)	2.7%	2.7%	2.8%	2.7%	2.7%
The Home Depot, Inc.	13.3%	14.2%	14.5%	14.4%	14.4%
Kroger Co.	3.3%	3.0%	2.1%	2.1%	1.8%
Target Corp.	6.9%	7.1%	5.8%	5.5%	6.0%
Lowe's Companies, Inc.	8.4%	9.0%	9.6%	7.9%	8.8%
Albertsons Companies, Inc.	0.7%	1.1%	0.3%	1.0%	1.5%
Ahold Delhaize (US segment)	4.0%	3.9%	4.1%	4.5%	4.3%
The TJX Companies, Inc. (US segments)	13.0%	12.8%	11.8%	11.8%	11.6%

Market Share Trends

The most significant market share trend in US retail is the shift toward e-commerce, which has been ongoing since the late 1990s. This shift has accrued largely to Amazon.com, the pioneer in US e-commerce, with its share of e-commerce at roughly 40% (Amazon has a large third-party merchant business but does not disclose GMV, so its exact share is unknown).

US E-Commerce % of Retail Sales ex Autos and Petrol

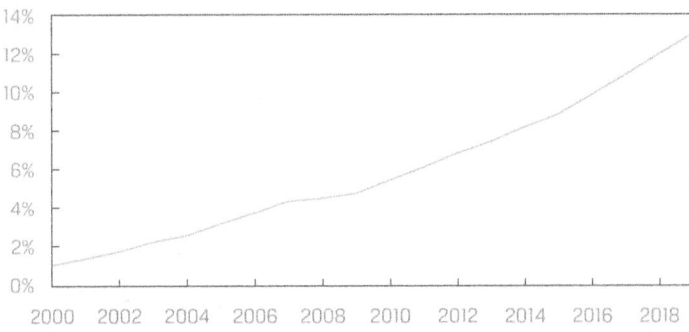

The industry is fragmented, with the top 10 largest firms holding less than 30% market share, the 10th largest holding less than 1%, with a large amount of share held by over 500,000 small retail businesses. However, the top 10 largest firms have gained share (~2%, from 26.3% in 2X15 to 28.6% in 2X19).

US Net Sales	2X15	2X16	2X17	2X18	2X19
Walmart US and Sam's Club	355,206	365,198	377,693	389,505	399,796
Amazon.com*	63,708	79,785	106,110	141,366	170,773
Costco Wholesale (US segment)	84,351	86,579	93,889	102,286	111,751
The Home Depot, Inc.	80,550	86,615	92,413	99,386	101,333
Kroger Co.	109,830	115,337	123,280	121,852	122,286
Target Corp.	73,717	69,414	71,786	74,433	77,130
Lowe's Companies, Inc.	59,074	61,311	63,263	65,872	67,147
Albertsons Companies, Inc.	58,734	59,678	56,925	60,535	62,455
Ahold Delhaize (US segment)	42,482	42,946	43,194	44,174	44,841
The TJX Companies, Inc. (US segments)	23,899	25,651	27,365	29,845	32,021

US Net Sales	2X15	2X16	2X17	2X18	2X19
Total top 10	951,551	992,514	1,055,918	1,129,254	1,189,533
Share of US retail sales ex autos	26.3%	26.9%	27.4%	27.9%	28.6%

*Amazon.com's "North America" segment only.

QUESTION SET

1. Identify the following statement as true or false. Justify your answer.

   Industry size is typically measured by the total annual sales of all industry constituents.

   Solution:

   False. Industry size is typically measured by the total annual sales from the product or customer perspective, which is not necessarily the sum of total sales of each industry constituent as some constituents may have segments in other industries.

2. A section of the fast-food market consists of 10 firms operating 1,840 restaurant locations across North America and currently has a Herfindahl-Hirschman Index (HHI) of 1,516. The market leader announces plans to acquire its closest competitor and commits to not closing any locations at either company. As a result, the HHI will *most likely*:

   A. decrease.
   B. not change.
   C. increase.

   Solution:

   C is correct. The Herfindahl-Hirschman Index (HHI) is calculated as the sum of the squares of competitor market shares. In this example, the market share of the leading company would increase and the number of competitors would decrease, which would increase the HHI. The number of store locations does not affect the HHI.

3. Identify the following statement as true or false. Justify your answer.

   Companies in different stages of the life cycle within the same industry can differ materially in terms of cyclicality.

   Solution:

   True. An industry is defined as companies with similar products or services from the perspective of a customer. A new entrant in an industry may have low but increasing market share, which can serve as a growth driver in addition to an economic expansion. The new entrant may therefore be less affected than a mature company by a recession.

   Please refer to the Industry Survey for Warehouse Club Inc. and Iliso Marketplace Ltd. earlier in the lesson to answer the following questions.

4. Amazon.com's change in US retail market share from 2X15 to 2X19 is *best* described as an example of:

   A. a disruptive threat.

   B. achieving peak penetration rate.

   C. saturation of its addressable market.

   Solution:

   A is correct. As the pioneer in US e-commerce, Amazon achieved roughly 40% market share by using Amazon.com as an online shopping platform. Therefore, Amazon.com is an example of a disruptive threat to the established retail industry. Based on US net sales from 2X15 to 2X19, it is uncertain whether Amazon achieved its peak penetration rate or saturated its addressable market, as it continued to increase its market share component of the top 10 retailers' share from 7% to 14%.

5. Current economic forecasts call for an increase of 3% in US GDP, an inflation rate of 1.5%, and decreasing consumer sentiment. Therefore, over the next fiscal year, Nguyen would *most likely* expect Warehouse Club Inc.'s total sales to:

   A. decrease.

   B. increase 2%–5%.

   C. increase 5%–8%.

   Solution:

   B is correct. Nguyen classifies the industry as mature and moderately cyclical, and Warehouse Club Inc. operates a single line of business with no new products or services defined. As a result, Warehouse Club Inc.'s total sales would move in line with broader US GDP growth as a stable company in a mature industry.

INDUSTRY STRUCTURE AND EXTERNAL INFLUENCES

☐ analyze an industry's structure and external influences using Porter's Five Forces and PESTLE frameworks

Recall from earlier lessons in economics that Porter's Five Forces is a framework for assessing industry structure that determines an industry's long-run profitability measure by its returns on invested capital.

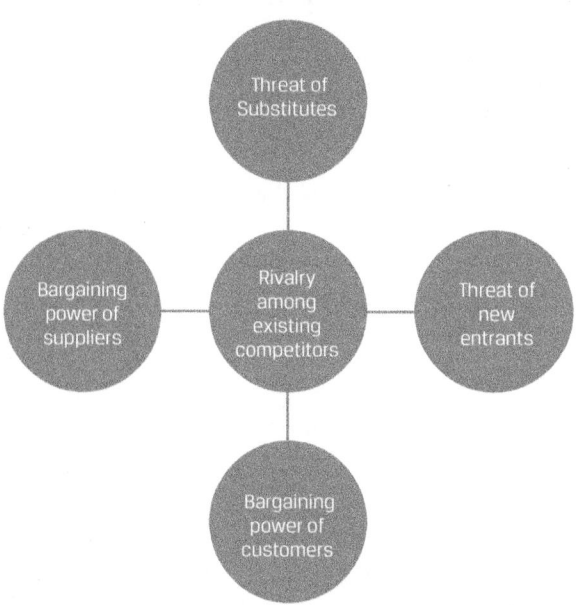

If some or all of the five industry forces are intense, almost no company earns attractive returns on capital, while benign forces lead to highly profitable industries. From the industry survey work in the previous lesson, we may have already measured the industry's profitability on a historical basis. The analysis of structural forces is aimed at not simply measuring profitability but rather characterizing its drivers in a qualitative fashion and improving alertness to key issues to monitor that can affect industry profitability. For new industries for which data are unavailable or which are still in an early, unprofitable stage, the analysis of industry structure can help point to potential profitability levels.

Assessing the Five Forces: A Checklist Approach

The assessment of the five forces is similar to the determination of a company's business model, from the prior module, in that it is a qualitative research investigation that is difficult to generalize. We provide illustrative questions to answer as an analyst and offer examples of real industry observations for each question.

Assessing the Threat of New Entrants

- Have there been significant numbers of new industry entrants in recent history?
    - In the USA, more than 50,000 new restaurants are opened per year. Conversely, from 2010 to 2021, fewer than three new commercial bank charters were issued per year in the USA.
- Are there network effects with the industry's product or service, such that its value to users is greater as the number of users increases and a new entrant would have a low-value product that has to achieve scale?
    - Payment networks such as Visa, Mastercard, JCB, and China UnionPay enable payments between hundreds of millions of cardholders and millions of merchants by connecting thousands of financial institutions on their network.
- Do incumbents benefit from economies of scale from significant fixed costs in the cost structure, such that a new entrant would require time and unprofitable economics to reach competitiveness?

- Cloud computing services require enormous fixed assets in terms of servers and networking equipment. These services have virtually no variable cost, however, and large incumbents have decreased unit prices substantially over time while gaining scale.

- Do incumbents benefit from economies of scope across multiple business lines—from increased convenience in terms of customers and market share and/or from joint costs that can be leveraged across the businesses?

  - Warehouse Club Inc. operates pharmacies and gas stations, which leverages real estate costs and drives increased foot traffic. Many commercial banks operate consumer banks, asset and investment management, broker-dealers, and investment bank businesses, as there are common customers and joint operating costs.

- Are customers loyal to brands?

  - A common threat to branded consumer merchandise sold to retailers is merchandise manufactured by contract manufacturers at the direction of the retailer and sold under retailer-owned "private label" or "generic" brands. In some categories, such as dairy milk and packaged baked goods, private label has over 50% volume share, which has risen over time. Consumers do not appear to be driven by brands in these categories. However, energy drinks, alcoholic beverages, and tobacco products have a very low private label market share over time, with consumers making repeat purchases of the same brand. Note that an important consideration for the value of brands is the legal environment that protects trademarks, trade dress, copyright, and other intangible assets in a jurisdiction. Without these legal protections, brands and their likeness can be imitated by competitors.

- Are there significant switching costs for customers in terms of time, training, or replacement?

  - So-called infrastructure software such as SAP for businesses requires lengthy implementation processes led by third-party consulting firms, and connections to other mission-critical software systems need to be established. Switching from SAP to another provider is a costly and lengthy endeavor. Conversely, customers can and do switch between food delivery apps, as minimal useful information is needed (or stored) to switch apps (payment information).

- Do incumbents have exclusive or preferential access to hard-to-obtain inputs or end-customer interfaces?

  - In the beverages business, incumbents have shelf space arrangements with retailers, often own distribution assets, and in some countries have the same arrangements with restaurants and pubs. This advantage is a potent deterrent for the beverage companies' customers to start carrying new entrants' products.

- Are there government policies that restrict or slow industry entry?

  - These policies can take many forms, such as regulations that only larger companies can afford to comply with, subsidies for domestic companies, patents, and licenses.

Note that experience and expertise among incumbents are not sustainable barriers to industry entry. Entrants can imitate, poach employees, purchase inputs and services from the incumbents' suppliers, and engage with industry consultants to obtain industry expertise.

Assessing the Threat of Substitutes

- Is there another product or service that fulfills the same or similar customer need? Is it lower priced?
    - Video conference calls and collaboration software are a low-price substitute for business travel and office real estate.
- Can customers go without the industry's product?
    - Aesthetic and elective medical procedures can be canceled or deferred without loss of function for a patient.
- Is the substitute product improving in performance relative to the industry's product?
    - While digital advertising was rudimentary in the early 2000s, with pop-ups and display ads, and was not a material threat to television advertising, digital advertising improved to include highly targeted videos and advertising disguised as content from third-party influencers and has taken market share from television advertising.
- Is it difficult for customers to switch to a substitute?
    - In most countries, prescriptions for a branded pharmaceutical are automatically substituted with a generic at a pharmacy if there is one approved.

Assessing the Bargaining Power of Customers

- Are there few, concentrated customers for the industry?
    - For many electronic component companies, mobile device makers such as Apple, Samsung, and Xiaomi account for a significant percentage of their revenues.
- Are the industry's products standardized or undifferentiated?
    - Crude oil is graded (e.g., Brent, West Texas Intermediate) by its density and sulfur content, which determine its cost and the effort to refine it into products such as petroleum. Oil refiners pay for crude oil based on its grade, not by specific oil producer; crude oil within a grade is interchangeable.
- Are the industry's products critical for customers?
    - Pesticides and seeds, especially those made with biotechnology, are sold at high prices but are vital to sustaining high agricultural yields and the high prices are outweighed by the cost of crops lost to disease and insects.
- Are the industry's products a large part of customers' budget?
    - Customers may be more motivated to seek alternatives and negotiate for products that account for a large part of their budget and for which quality is not a paramount concern. For livestock farmers, the cost of feed

Industry Structure and External Influences

   accounts for over 60% of annual operating costs, while pharmaceuticals and vaccines for livestock account for a small percentage but come with a high cost of failure, which has given animal-pharmaceutical companies a strong bargaining position.

- Can customers backward-integrate—that is, "build" rather than "buy" what the industry is selling?

  - Streaming video services first licensed content from existing studios and media companies, but over time they vertically integrated by producing their own video content.

Assessing the Bargaining Power of Suppliers

- Are there few, concentrated suppliers for the industry?

  - Apple's "A" and "M" series processors for its iPhones and MacBooks are manufactured exclusively by TSMC. While Apple has more supplier choice for its other components, it is beholden to a single company for this crucial component.

- Are there significant costs for switching suppliers?

  - Asset managers need performance data and analytics on equity, fixed income, and other indexes for investment processes and client reporting of benchmarks. Indexes are owned by a small number of companies and charge licensing fees for data permissions and commercial use. An, Benetton, Song, and Index Providers (2021) found that managers of indexed exchange-traded funds paid index licensing fees equal to 35% of their management fee revenue. While asset managers can switch because each provider offers similar catalogues of indexes, doing so would require changing investment processes, client reporting, and conversations with clients—and can look bad to prospects.

- Are suppliers differentiated or specialized?

  - Healthcare providers, airlines, investment banks, technology companies, and professional services firms all require skilled, credentialed, or licensed labor, for which there is limited supply.

- Are there substitutes for the products from suppliers?

  - Retailers can substitute branded merchandise for private label merchandise from contract manufacturers.

Assessing Rivalry among Existing Competitors

- Is there a history of price competition among competitors?

  - Despite a low risk from every other industry force, automakers and aircraft manufacturers compete fiercely on price, offering promotions and generous financing and warranty terms to try to capture every sale.

- Are there numerous, roughly equal-sized competitors?

  - There are approximately a dozen automakers with an annual global market share over 1%. However, the largest company (Toyota) has had less than 15% market share for many years.

- Are products differentiated?

- Pharmaceuticals without a patent (generics) are legally required to be chemically equivalent to their originator drug in order to be approved by regulators in an abbreviated process that doesn't involve a clinical trial. Pharmacies are indifferent as to whether an approved generic is sold by one company or another and manufacturers' costs are largely fixed, so the companies compete fiercely on price for volume. Price competition increases with the number of approved generics per originator drug; Dave, Hartzema, and Kesselheim (2017) found that a drug with one generic competitor had prices that were, on average, six times higher than the prices of one for which there were nine generic manufacturers.

- Are there high barriers to exiting?
  - If exiting an industry is difficult or costly, such as shutting down natural resource–producing assets, companies with low profitability may remain in the industry for much longer than in other industries, which can result in lingering competition.

- Is industry growth slow?
  - If penetration of the addressable market is low, companies may not feel a need to compete for customers using price and other economic terms. This was the case for mobile wireless plans until the mid-2010s, when penetration plateaued and companies began engaging in aggressive promotional activity in competition for one another's customers.

After completing the evaluation of industry structure, an analyst must judge which are the most and least important factors. It is often clear that one or two forces are strongest, but there isn't a quantitative test or threshold by which to judge definitively. Posing scenarios to experienced industry insiders is often useful, such as asking, "What do you think would happen if company X increased its prices by 10% tomorrow?" If their answer is that a large percentage of customers are willing and able to switch to a competitor or substitute—perhaps it has happened before—it's likely that customer bargaining power and the threat of substitutes warrant further investigation.

> **CASE STUDIES**
>
> ### Porter's Five Forces Analysis for US Retail (ex autos)
>
>
>
> #### Threat of New Entrants: Very High
>
> Opening a retailer, especially an e-commerce retailer that utilizes third-party merchant services, is relatively easy and common. In the USA, retailers are the most common type of business formed—by a wide margin, with over 40,000 new firms filing formation papers each month (the next most common is transportation and warehousing, with around half the number of retailer formations). Customers can easily switch retailers, as most do not have an ongoing relationship such as a subscription fee or contract, and there are minimal regulatory barriers such as licenses and patents.
>
> #### Threat of Substitutes: Low
>
> Broadly speaking, the substitute for retail is consumer services (e.g., restaurants, travel, healthcare), which also includes digital services (such as streaming video subscriptions and gaming). Most categories of goods, however, are not

easily replaceable with services (e.g., apparel and home décor), or they enjoy a cost advantage because of lower labor intensity (e.g., fresh food). There have been periods when services grew faster than goods, but as shown in an earlier exhibit, retail sales have grown essentially in line with US nominal output/income. Retail is arguably one of the oldest industries, and while it has evolved over time, it has yet to be replaced.

Bargaining Power of Customers: Moderate

Retail customers are highly fragmented, with each consumer representing a distinct decision-maker, as there are generally no group purchasing organizations. However, many products are sold by many retailers, and the internet has enabled easy comparison shopping at retailers. Customers are price sensitive with respect to identical products sold by different retailers.

Bargaining Power of Suppliers: Low to Moderate

Key suppliers for retailers include manufacturers of goods, employees, and lessors of retail or fulfillment space. In most cases, numerous options are available. However, branded goods are sold exclusively by a sole manufacturer that may impose high prices and other economic terms, like shelf space and visibility, and may want to sell only to certain retailers (e.g., makers of luxury goods may not sell to discount retailers in order to maintain exclusivity).

Rivalry among Existing Competitors: High

Given the sheer number of similarly sized firms selling similar or identical products, retailers compete fiercely, often with price promotions and discounts as price is one of the few ways they can lure customers away from competitors.

External Influences on Industry Growth

Analyzing the structure of an industry primarily involves looking *inside* the industry and at close adjacencies such as customers, suppliers, and substitutes. It is important for analysts to look *outside* the industry for factors that influence the industry's economic outcomes. One framework for this purpose is a **PESTLE analysis** of the *p*olitical, *e*conomic, *s*ocial, *t*echnological, *l*egal, and *e*nvironmental influences on an industry. While Porter's Five Forces is concerned with the determinants of industry profitability, a PESTLE analysis is more concerned with an industry's growth rate and market share dynamics. For example, athletic apparel companies such as lululemon athletica inc. have long benefited from increasing consumer interest in fitness and wellness, a social influence on the apparel industry. This trend is not apparent from Porter's Five Forces but is obviously important for growth in athletic apparel. When the trend eventually plateaus or declines, it's likely to result in declining sales growth or sales for lululemon, so analysts carefully monitor the trend using a variety of metrics. PESTLE analysis is a framework for identifying "themes" or "narratives" that investors may take a perspective on and desire exposure to.

While analysts must look broadly for influences, several factors make this search easier in practice. First, external influences often do not change very quickly (though their magnitude and direction can), so this analysis does not need to be done every quarter. Second, analysts develop industry expertise, and those in an institutional setting can access industry specialists who offer their perspectives and surveillance of industry trends as a paid service. Finally, it is usually the case that some influences are far more important than others for a given industry.

Political Influences

Political influences on an industry include changing fiscal and monetary policies, governments' direct selling and purchasing activities, regulatory changes, and geopolitical conditions and actions. We highlight three sectors and their constituent industries for which political influences are often significant: energy, healthcare, and defense.

The energy sector is subject to three important political influences: the political appeal of low and stable energy prices in the short run, climate agreements and legislation calling for emissions reductions, and the actions of OPEC (Organization of the Petroleum Exporting Countries). Most governments desire low energy prices in the short run to maintain their appeal to consumers and businesses that have inelastic demand with respect to price. However, in the long run, higher energy prices (perhaps because of a carbon tax) might be preferable in order to curb demand and meet emissions targets, for which the consumption of fossil fuels is the main driver. Investors and producers may worry about the longer-term outlook, since governments are intending to shrink fossil fuels as a percentage of the energy mix, but reductions in fossil fuel production are at odds with low energy prices in the short run. Finally, energy companies owned by member states of OPEC produced 35% of crude oil globally in 2021 (*BP Statistical Review of World Energy*) and set production quotas as a bloc. Actions taken by OPEC significantly affect global and regional energy prices. OPEC members may choose to keep prices low enough to slow the transition to renewables, exploiting governments' need for low energy prices in the short run.

Governments are the largest buyers of healthcare products and services and, in most cases, are the exclusive buyers of defense goods and services globally. For political appeal and to shore up fiscal deficits, governments have at times pursued reforms such as expansions of healthcare coverage and subsidies, price controls or reductions, and restrictions on certain healthcare services or products.

Defense spending is determined by countries' geopolitical objectives, perceived threat environment, and alliance commitments. From the late 1990s to 2010, global military spending rose markedly, increasing as a share of global GDP, which benefited defense companies. Future defense spending depends on geopolitical events and other competing budget priorities. Finally, governments also extensively regulate healthcare and defense, the stringency of which changes over time. From 2000-2007, several high-profile pharmaceutical scandals led to a period of heightened regulatory scrutiny and a declining number of drug approvals. This scrutiny was relaxed by the mid-2010s. Countries are selective about which countries they permit domestic defense companies to do business with, and the contracting process is highly complex, involving third-party costs and performance audits.

Economic Influences

Economic influences on an industry include changes in GDP or personal income, inflation, interest rates, and exchange rates. These influences can be related to the business cycle (cyclical) or structural, such as how longer-run population and productivity growth rates have differed across countries, which affects the sales and costs of companies operating in different countries. Economic influences are most important for cyclical sectors such as financials, basic materials, and consumer discretionary, and exchange rate changes are most important for industries and companies operating in multiple currencies—especially if there are large currency compositional mismatches in revenues and costs and if the company does business in an illiquid currency with more volatile exchange rates.

The auto industry is among the most affected by economic influences, because it sells high-priced durable goods, the purchase of which can be delayed (consumer keeps current car longer) or substituted (used car) based on consumer confidence. Structural economic influences are important for many multinational companies that have sought to increase exposure to faster-growing emerging markets over time. As of 2022, over 40% of Nestlé SA's sales were in emerging markets, which have long shown faster volume growth than its developed-market sales.

Social Influences

Social influences include cultural and consumer trends, demographic changes such as the relative growth rates among different population cohorts, and changes in lifestyles. These influences are not entirely external to an industry, as companies influence culture through political advocacy, advertising, and a variety of other efforts such as product placements in media. There is growing reputational risk and/or pressure on companies via social media and the press to source sustainable inputs, as well as increased scrutiny of supply chains for violations of human rights.

Social influences are often more significant for industries that sell to consumers rather than to other businesses. In concert with technological and economic influences, the global beauty industry (comprising skin care, color cosmetics, hair care, fragrances, and select personal care product categories) has grown briskly since 2010, particularly premium products. High-quality cameras on mobile devices and social media have increased the salience of people's physical appearance and created efficient marketing channels for beauty companies that utilize third-party influencers and video tutorials.

Technological Influences

Technological changes can create new or improved products or render existing products obsolete, radically changing industries and companies. Based on the pioneering work of Clayton Christensen, we distinguish between two kinds of technological changes: sustaining and disruptive innovations.

Sustaining innovations are improvements in product or service performance and the addition of marginal features, but without a fundamental change in functionality or operation. These innovations are often led by industry incumbents making improvements to better serve existing or adjacent customers' needs. Successive improvements to cable television—including digital transmission, improved video quality, premium programming, DVRs, and additional channels—represent sustaining innovations. Disruptive innovation is a change that creates a new market or enters an existing one but with a very different value proposition that may not immediately appeal to existing customers who are happy with the current product. Cable television was disrupted by streaming video delivered over the internet. At first a rudimentary offering that appealed to people who did not have cable subscriptions, it eventually grew to overtake cable in the number of subscribers.

Disruptive innovation is most likely to come from new entrants, because they do not have an existing profitable business to protect. The difficulty faced by incumbents with disruptive innovation is termed the "innovator's dilemma": they can either invest in the disruptive innovation themselves, speeding the decline of their existing business (and potentially harming employees) but not losing market share, or ignore the innovation and lose market share while continuing to generate strong profits in the near to medium term.

Legal Influences

Legal influences on an industry include changes in laws and regulations from courts and policymakers that alter an industry's business practices or economic outcomes. These influences, which are in addition to the fiscal and monetary policy changes discussed earlier under political influences, are often more subtle changes to the "rules of the road" governing industry affairs. Companies look to shape these influences through policy advocacy and in legal proceedings of their own.

Examples of industries strongly affected by legal influences include tobacco and cannabis. Jurisdictions have wide-ranging laws and regulations on the manufacturing, distribution, marketing, sale, and use of tobacco products to discourage consumption and the associated adverse health consequences, including secondhand smoke. Laws cover advertising prohibitions, graphic images on packaging, minimum purchase age, bans on smoking in public places, and limitations on nicotine content and flavorings. These laws are in addition to the generally high taxes levied on tobacco, which encourage non-taxable counterfeit activity that governments must police. Adoption of or changes in these laws in various jurisdictions significantly affect tobacco industry sales. In response to these influences, as well as broader social influences that have resulted in declining cigarette sale volumes, the tobacco industry is primarily focused on developing so-called reduced risk products that may pose fewer health risks and therefore create a more favorable legal environment.

The cannabis industry is in an evolving legal environment, where certain jurisdictions have legalized its production, sale, and use (Canada), while some have varying laws at the sub-sovereign level (the USA) and most others still completely prohibit cannabis (most of Asia).

Environmental Influences

Finally, environmental influences are often closely associated with legal influences and include risks and opportunities related to the transition to a lower-carbon economy, laws and practices concerning waste and land use, and environmental protections.

Transition risks and opportunities are important influences for sectors such as energy, airlines, utilities, and autos, as they are involved in the production or consumption of fossil fuels, which are responsible for carbon emissions. Due to changes in regulations, taxes, consumer preferences, or voluntary actions, companies in these sectors must evolve their business operations or face share losses to competing solutions with lower-carbon emissions.

QUESTION SET

1. In 2009, Amazon.com started Amazon Publishing, extending its business into publishing books in addition to book retailing. From the perspective of a competing publisher, this is an example of:

    A. decreasing the threat of substitutes.

    B. decreasing the bargaining power of suppliers.

    C. increasing the bargaining power of customers.

    Solution:

    C is correct. Amazon Publishing is an example of backward-integration, as it could now produce and sell its own published content as well as other publishers' content. The creation of Amazon Publishing increased the bargaining power of Amazon as a customer and increased the level of competitive rivalry in the publishing industry. Amazon Publishing would also increase the threat of substitutes and the bargaining power of suppliers, as authors and end users could work directly with Amazon.

2. Proposed government regulations for the restaurant industry would introduce new compliance requirements for all new and existing facilities to reduce the environmental impact of take-out and delivery options. These regulations would apply only to restaurants with a physical address and

would not apply to mobile restaurants (i.e., food trucks). For an existing restaurant with several physical locations, these regulations would:

A. reduce competitive rivalry by increasing the barriers to entry.

B. increase competitive rivalry by increasing the threat of substitutes.

C. both reduce and increase competitive rivalry.

Solution:

C is correct. The proposed regulatory changes would have a mixed impact on the level of competitive rivalry in the restaurant industry. These environmental regulations would increase the entry barriers by increasing the costs of setting up a new restaurant, while also increasing the threat of substitutes by making it easier to open mobile restaurants, which do not have to comply with these regulations.

Please refer to the Industry Survey for Warehouse Club Inc. and Iliso Marketplace Ltd. in the previous lesson to answer the following questions.

3. To compete with online retailers, Warehouse Club Inc. is considering installing a sophisticated image recognition system in its stores to track and analyze consumer behavior in order to identify clothing items that were tried on but not purchased. For Warehouse, this change would be a _____ (*sustaining* or *disruptive*) innovation.

Solution:

For Warehouse, this change would be a *sustaining* innovation. Sustaining improvements focus on adding marginal features without a fundamental change in functionality or operation. For example, the proposed system would provide incremental customer and product knowledge but would not represent a fundamental change in Warehouse's go-to-market strategy. Disruptive innovation is a change that creates a new market or enters an existing one with a different value proposition.

4. Identify the following statement as true or false. Justify your answer.

The CEO of Iliso Marketplace Ltd. expects revenue growth to be in line with US GDP growth for the next two fiscal years. As a result, the CEO approves an extension to an existing aggressive sales promotion and discount strategy that has been in place for the past 18 months. This extension will increase the competitive rivalry in the industry.

Solution:

False. The sales promotion and discount strategy is already in place within this mature industry, thus demonstrating a history of price competition among the competitors.

5. A PESTLE analysis for Iliso Marketplace Ltd. would *most likely* identify which of the following items?

A. A competitor is acquiring a fleet of delivery vehicles instead of using third-party parcel carriers.

B. The increasing political discussion around instituting a tax on parcel deliveries of less than 2 kilograms

> **C.** A competitor is launching an augmented reality application to allow tech-savvy consumers to view home décor and furniture products in real time.
>
> **Solution:**
>
> B is correct. The political discussion around potential applications of a tax is an example of a political trend changing over time. This theme could potentially affect Iliso Marketplace Ltd. A (fleet of delivery vehicles) and C (augmented reality) are examples of competitive actions that could affect the level of competitive rivalry in the industry.

6. COMPETITIVE POSITIONING

☐ evaluate the competitive strategy and position of a company

All companies have a competitive strategy, whether intentional or not. An intentional strategy results from company-wide planning, performance measurement, and feedback loops to sharpen the strategy. An unintentional strategy results from various teams within a firm pursuing their own incentives, doing whatever they did in prior years, or following industry or professional norms. An unintentional strategy is rarely the best and often exacerbates communication and coordination problems present at every company, although the approach might perform well in areas such as discovery-oriented research. Munos (2009) found evidence of diseconomies of scale in pharmaceutical R&D, with most new drugs discovered by small companies operating in a relatively "unmanaged" way.

Ultimately, an effective competitive strategy is evidenced by a company's track record of value added for its stakeholders, such as economic profits. Its effectiveness can be judged only in hindsight. To evaluate a competitive strategy on a forward-looking basis, an analyst should assess the strategy along three dimensions:

- Does the strategy create a defense against the five industry forces?
- Does the strategy benefit from, or is at least not at odds with, the expected external industry influences identified in the PESTLE analysis?
- Does the company have the resources and capabilities to execute the strategy?

Clearly, the analysis and the answers to these questions are company and industry specific (CFA Institute has published a helpful industry-by-industry reference titled *Sector Analysis: A Framework for Investors* with examples). We can, however, identify three well-known competitive strategies that have worked in a variety of industries, as shown in Exhibit 6: cost leadership, differentiation, and focus. These three generic strategies are based on Michael Porter's research on competition. While companies do tend to have specific variations, generic strategies explain a large percentage of strategies in practice—similar to how many companies' business models are well described using conventional models. A poor situation is for a company to be "stuck in the middle"—not a cost leader, not differentiated, not focused.

Competitive Positioning

Exhibit 6: Generic Competitive Strategies

	Cost Leadership	Differentiation	Focus
Means of executing strategy	<ul><li>Economies of scale from fixed costs</li><li>Favorable access to raw materials</li><li>Culture of strict cost control</li><li>Aggressive pricing to gain high volume</li><li>Low-cost distribution</li><li>Economies of scope</li></ul>	<ul><li>Investments in advertising, brand, customer service, proprietary distribution channels</li><li>Protection using trademarks, copyright, patents</li><li>Superior quality, unique features</li><li>Culture of strong customer experience</li><li>Premium pricing</li><li>Integration of services, software, and hardware</li></ul>	<ul><li>Proximity to customers and strong understanding of their needs</li><li>May incorporate elements of strategy from both cost leadership and differentiation, but focused on particular group</li></ul>
Which of the Five Forces it defends against (why it works)	<ul><li>Threat of new entrants: Capital requirements and scale advantages deter entrants</li><li>Bargaining power of customers: Customers can only bring prices down to the costs of the marginal producer, leaving margin for the cost leaders</li><li>Industry rivalry: Rivals may not be able to compete on price with cost leaders</li></ul>	<ul><li>Threat of new entrants and of substitutions: Customer loyalty to unique product can deter switching, protect market share</li><li>Bargaining power of customers: Customers may be unable to unwilling to comparison shop or switch</li><li>Bargaining power of suppliers: The company may have the ability to pass along price increases to customers and/or margin to absorb cost increases</li></ul>	<ul><li>Threat of new entrants and of substitutes: Customer loyalty to unique product can deter switching, protect market share</li><li>Bargaining power of customers: Customers may be unable or unwilling to comparison shop or switch</li></ul>
Industry appropriateness	<ul><li>Capital intensive</li><li>Price-conscious customers</li><li>Customers do not value or notice product differences</li><li>Minimal innovation in industry</li></ul>	<ul><li>Price is not foremost concern for customers</li><li>Customers value distinctiveness</li><li>Innovation in industry, with products varying in features and forms</li></ul>	<ul><li>Difficult (or uneconomical) to serve customer group, product, or geography for other players</li></ul>
Risks to the strategy	<ul><li>Cost inflation, loss of discipline</li><li>Technological change that results in loss of cost leadership or market share</li><li>Desire for premiumization among customers</li></ul>	<ul><li>Imitation by competitors</li><li>Buyers become sophisticated, no longer demand level of service</li><li>Pricing premium becomes too high for customers to bear</li><li>May preclude high market share, as customers value exclusivity</li></ul>	<ul><li>Larger competitors outcompete on price</li><li>The differences in demand between the between the narrow group and industry as a whole narrow</li><li>Buyers become sophisticated, no longer demand level of service</li></ul>

QUESTION SET

1. Manitou Resorts is a 25-room boutique hotel located in a rural mountain area approximately three hours from a major urban center. It provides accommodations, high-end dining options, and an on-site health and wellness spa. Manitou's primary customers are young professional couples

in the middle-to-upper-income brackets. The CEO is contemplating several options for expansion, as the resort is frequently at full capacity. Which of the following initiatives would be consistent with Manitou's current competitive strategy?

A. The development of 10 stand-alone lakefront cottages to accommodate families of up to six people, providing access to family-related activities such as pools, water sports, and evening entertainment

B. The addition of conference room facilities to accommodate corporate events that could be priced at a 10%–15% discount to a 150-room franchise hotel approximately 30 minutes from Manitou

C. Developing a management and reservation system to identify recommendations to referral partners such as golf courses, taxi/shuttle services, or other guest experiences to increase fee revenue

Solution:

C is correct. Manitou Resorts' current competitive strategy is a focus strategy targeting a specific customer segment: young professionals in middle-to-upper-income brackets located in a nearby city and focused on wellness and relaxation. The other options represent an expansion into new customer segments (family vacations and corporate events), which could be inconsistent with its current customer base. A represents a cost leadership competitive strategy, while B represents a differentiation strategy.

2. Warehouse Club Inc. is considering launching a "private label" brand of non-perishable food products. Based on its current competitive strategy, which of the following is the *most appropriate* rationale to support?

A. Customers do not notice product differences.

B. Customers value new product features and forms.

C. Products can be segmented into regular and premium brands.

Solution:

A is correct. Warehouse Club Inc.'s current competitive strategy is cost leadership. In a cost leadership strategy, industry appropriateness is determined by capital intensity, price-conscious customers, customers not valuing or noticing product differences, and minimal innovation in the industry. B represents an example of a differentiation strategy. C represents an example of a focus strategy.

3. To defend against the bargaining power of suppliers, customers may be unable or unwilling to comparison shop or switch in which of the following competitive strategies (select all that apply):

___ Cost leadership

___ Differentiation

___ Focus

Solution:

Both differentiation and focus. That "customers may be unable or unwilling to comparison shop or switch" is a common feature of both differentiation and focus strategies. In a cost leadership strategy, "customers can only bring prices down to the costs of the marginal producer, leaving margin for the cost leaders."

4. A risk to a differentiation competitive strategy is:
   A. limited market share due to exclusivity.
   B. larger competitors outcompete on price.
   C. technological change that results in loss of market share.

   Solution:

   A is correct. Since a differentiation strategy pursues a unique product or service offering, it creates a risk that the strategy may preclude high market share, as customers value exclusivity. B is a risk to a focus strategy where larger competitors outcompete on price. C is a risk to a cost leadership strategy where the technological change results in cost leadership or market share loss.

5. A large online retailer in the USA has begun to offer a "price-matching" guarantee on its website to match any competitor's online price for an identical product, including Iliso Marketplace. Recommend and justify whether Iliso should launch a similar guarantee to protect its market share.

   Solution:

   No, Iliso should not launch a similar guarantee. A price-matching guarantee is a strategy pursued by companies with a cost leadership approach by using aggressive pricing to gain volume. Iliso Marketplace Ltd. operates with a differentiation strategy that permits premium pricing if aligned with a strong customer experience. If Iliso maintained its customer experience offering and began to reduce its revenue to match cost leaders, the company would likely decrease its overall profitability.

REFERENCES

Guan, Yuyan, M.H. Franco Wong, Yue Zhang. Analyst Following Along the Supply Chain (March 17, 2014). INSEAD Working Paper No. 2014/21/ACC, Available at SSRN: https://ssrn.com/abstract=2410151 or 10.2139/ssrn.2410151

McGahan, A. M., M. E. Porter. July 1997. ""How Much Does Industry Matter, Really?" Special Issue on Organizational and Competitive Influences on Strategy and Performance." Strategic Management Journal18 (no. S1): 15–30. 10.1002/(SICI)1097-0266(199707)18:1+<15::AID-SMJ916>3.0.CO;2-1

An, Yu, Matteo Benetton, Yang Song. Whales Behind the Scenes of ETFs (July 30, 2021). Available at SSRN: https://ssrn.com/abstract=3855836 or 10.2139/ssrn.3855836

Dave, C. V., A. Hartzema, A. S. Kesselheim. 28 Dec, 2017. "Prices of Generic Drugs Associated with Numbers of Manufacturers." New England Journal of Medicine377 (26): 2597–98. 10.1056/NEJMc1711899

Munos, B. Dec 2009. "Lessons from 60 years of pharmaceutical innovation." Nature Reviews. Drug Discovery8 (12): 959–68. 10.1038/nrd2961

PRACTICE PROBLEMS

1. An alternative method of grouping companies by geography is *least likely* to be completed using:

   A. location of head office.

   B. geographic composition of revenue.

   C. primary listing of its equity securities.

2. A market consists of three firms with market shares of 50%, 30%, and 20%. The Herfindahl-Hirschman Index (HHI) is *closest* to:

   A. 0.38.

   B. 2,500.

   C. 3,800.

3. Lower industry concentration is usually associated with a high degree of competitive intensity unless the industry is *most likely*:

   A. global.

   B. service-oriented.

   C. one with low product differentiation.

4. Increased environmental regulations on automotive manufacturers will *most likely* have which of the following effects on the threat of new entrants?

   A. An increase

   B. A decrease

   C. No change

5. The CEO of a large law firm is concerned about a new mobile application that uses algorithms to auto-complete legal forms and questions in discovery and provides recommendations for small-claims matters at a much lower cost than a traditional law firm charges. As a result, the CEO is contemplating whether the firm should develop and launch its own branded application, which would affect its short-term profitability but maintain its existing customer base, or give up market share to focus on more complex claims with higher profitability. This scenario is an example of:

   A. defensiveness.

   B. innovator's dilemma.

   C. sustaining innovation.

6. PESTLE analysis is a framework for identifying:

   A. industry themes.

   B. the level of industry concentration.

C. determinants of industry profitability.

7. The means of executing cost leadership competitive strategies *do not include* which of the following?
    A. proximity to customers
    B. favorable access to raw materials
    C. economies of scale from fixed costs

8. Which of the following is *most likely* a risk of executing a differentiation competitive strategy?
    A. pricing premiums become too high
    B. larger competitors outcompete on price
    C. a desire for premium-ization among customers

SOLUTIONS

1. B is correct. Classification by country is typically by the country where the issuer is incorporated, the country of the primary listing of its equity securities, the location of its headquarters, or market perception. Note that classification by the geographic composition of revenue is generally *not* the approach taken, though this aspect may be the foremost concern for an analyst.

2. C is correct. The Herfindahl-Hirschman Index (HHI) is calculated as the sum of the squares of competitor market shares. In this example, the HHI is calculated as ($50^2 + 30^2 + 20^2 = 3,800$). A incorrectly calculates the HHI using the percentage market shares ($0.5^2 + 0.3^2 + 0.2^2 = 0.38$). B incorrectly calculates the HHI using only the market leader concentration ($50^2 = 2,500$).

3. B is correct. Lower industry concentration, defined as many small competitors in the market, is usually associated with a high degree of competitive intensity unless the industry is service-oriented, is local in nature, or has high product differentiation.

4. B is correct. Increased environmental regulations on automotive manufacturers represent an additional cost for compliance when building a new manufacturing facility and increase the barriers to entry into the industry.

5. B is correct. The described mobile application represents a fundamental change in the business model of a law firm. The application is a disruptive, not sustaining, innovation, as it brings new entrants into the market but with a very different value proposition. The CEO's decision represents the "innovator's dilemma": the firm can either invest in the disruptive innovation, speeding the decline of its existing business but not losing market share, or ignore the innovation and lose market share while continuing to generate strong profits in the near term.

6. A is correct. PESTLE analysis is a framework for identifying "themes" or "narratives" that investors may take a perspective on and desire exposure to. B refers to the Herfindahl-Hirschman Index. C refers to Porter's Five Forces.

7. A is correct. Proximity to customers is a means of executing a focus strategy. The means of executing a cost leadership strategy include economies of scale from fixed costs, favorable access to raw materials, a culture of strict cost control, aggressive pricing to gain high volume, low-cost distribution, and economies of scope.

8. A is correct. The risks of a differentiation strategy include imitation by competitors, buyers becoming sophisticated and no longer demanding level of service, and pricing premiums becoming too high for customers to beat; such a strategy may also preclude high market share, as customers value exclusivity. B relates to a focus strategy, while C relates to a cost leadership strategy.

LEARNING MODULE 7

Company Analysis: Forecasting

LEARNING OUTCOMES

Mastery	The candidate should be able to:
☐	explain principles and approaches to forecasting a company's financial results and position
☐	explain approaches to forecasting a company's revenues
☐	explain approaches to forecasting a company's operating expenses and working capital
☐	explain approaches to forecasting a company's capital investments and capital structure
☐	describe the use of scenario analysis in forecasting

INTRODUCTION

Forecasts of companies' financial statements are used by analysts in valuation and to make investment recommendations. Developing the forecasts or projections is an important aspect of an analyst's job and is the focus of this module. In the first lesson, what to forecast, approaches to forecasting, and selecting a forecast horizon are discussed. The next three lessons focus on particular forecasts: revenues, operating expenses and working capital, and capital investments and capital structure. The final lesson discusses the use of scenario analysis in considering multiple outcomes.

> **LEARNING MODULE OVERVIEW**
>
> - Four common types of forecast objects are drivers of financial statement lines, individual financial statement lines, summary measures, and ad hoc objects. An analyst's choice of forecast object depends on available information, efficiency, accuracy, explanatory value, and verifiability.
> - Forecast approaches generally are based on historical results, historical base rates and convergence, management guidance, or analyst discretion. An analyst's choice of forecast approach depends on the company's industry structure, sensitivity to the business cycle, and business model, as well as the reliability and availability of information.

- The choice of the forecast time horizon is determined by the investment strategy for which the security is being considered, the cyclicality of the industry, company-specific factors, and the analyst's employer's preferences.
- Revenue forecasts may be based on top-down or bottom-up forecast objects, using any of the four forecast approaches. Using different forecast objects and approaches to project revenue can be useful in uncovering implicit assumptions or errors in any single approach.
- Top-down revenue drivers include growth relative to GDP growth, and market growth and market share. Bottom-up revenue drivers include volumes and average selling prices; revenue by product line, geographic area, or reporting segment; capacity-based measures; and return-based measures.
- Analysts often use aggregated forecast objects or summary measures to forecast operating expenses because of a lack of disaggregated information. However, forecasts for operating expenses should be coherent with revenue forecasts. The choice of forecast object can vary depending on the forecast horizon.
- Working capital forecasts typically use efficiency ratios combined with revenue and operating expense forecasts to project accounts receivable, inventory, accounts payable, and other current assets and liabilities.
- Forecasts for capital expenditures may differentiate between maintenance and growth capital expenditures. Maintenance capital expenditure forecasts are often based on depreciation and amortization expenses. Growth capital expenditure forecasts are tied to a company's strategy, expansion plans, and revenue growth.
- Forecasts about a company's capital structure consider historical leverage ratios and capital structure, the company's financial strategy, and capital expenditure forecasts.
- Based on a company's risk factors, an analyst may develop several forecast scenarios rather than develop a single forecast. The analyst will judge the likelihood of each scenario occurring.

LEARNING MODULE SELF-ASSESSMENT

These initial questions are intended to help you gauge your current level of understanding of this learning module.

1. A benefit of using summary measures as forecast objects is *most likely*:

    A. efficiency.

    B. transparency.

    C. explanatory value.

    Solution:

    A is correct. The benefit of using summary measures as a forecast object is efficiency, as fewer variables need to be forecast, but a disadvantage is less transparency. Forecasting financial statement lines or their drivers has the benefit of improved explanatory value.

Introduction

2. Which of the following approaches is *most* appropriate for forecasting annual revenues for a company in a cyclical industry?

    A. Historical results
    B. Management guidance
    C. Analyst's discretionary forecast

    Solution:

    C is correct. An analyst's discretionary forecast is most appropriate, because it allows the analyst to consider both the current phase and the expected future phase of the business cycle. Historical results are a less appropriate forecast approach for companies in cyclical industries, because a future period is likely to be at a different point in the business cycle than the current or past period, and so results will differ. The use of guidance for companies that are highly sensitive to the business cycle is less appropriate, as management does *not* have an informational advantage over investors in forecasting macroeconomic variables like GDP or the prices of commodities.

3. An example of a top-down driver for revenue is a company's:

    A. market share.
    B. sales growth rate.
    C. products' average selling price.

    Solution:

    A is correct. Top-down drivers of revenue include the company's market share and the industry's market growth. The company's sales growth rate and products' average selling price are bottom-up drivers of revenue.

4. In developing a revenue forecast, non-recurring revenue *most likely*:

    A. has the same drivers as recurring revenue.
    B. will be disclosed by a company's management.
    C. is considered separately from recurring revenue.

    Solution:

    C is correct. Non-recurring items and effects should be considered separately. The non-recurring objects, such as changes in exchange rates or provisions for legal costs, generally do not have the same drivers as the recurring objects. While management may disclose some non-recurring items and effects, there are also non-recurring items and effects that management does not disclose, which require analyst judgment.

5. An analyst should consider the effects of changing commodity prices when forecasting:

    A. revenue only.
    B. cost of sales only.
    C. both revenue and cost of sales.

    Solution:

    C is correct. Both a company's cost of sales through input prices and its revenue may be affected by commodity prices. The effect on revenue depends on the company's competitive positioning and the price elasticity of demand for the company's products.

6. Working capital forecasts for a mature company with a unique business model are *most likely* made by:

   A. increasing the current assets and liabilities by the sales growth rate.
   B. using the company's efficiency ratios combined with sales and operating forecasts.
   C. using a historical base rate and convergence approach to develop forecasts of revenue, operating expenses, and efficiency ratios.

   Solution:

   B is correct. For a company with a unique business model, using a historical results approach is appropriate. Working capital forecasts are typically made by using efficiency ratios, which are combined with sales and operating cost forecasts to project accounts receivable, inventories, accounts payable, and other current assets and liabilities. The historical base rate and convergence approach is appropriate if the company is converging toward the norm for the industry. Adjusting current assets and liabilities by the sales growth rate is not appropriate, because changes in sales will affect each item differently.

7. Depreciation and amortization expenses are often used as the basis for:

   A. growth capital expenditures only.
   B. maintenance capital expenditures only.
   C. both growth and maintenance capital expenditures.

   Solution:

   B is correct. Maintenance capital expenditure forecasts are often based on depreciation and amortization expenses. Growth capital expenditure forecasts are more discretionary and are tied to management's expansion plans and revenue growth.

8. Which of the following generic risk factors is *most likely* to affect an established company in the consumer staples sector?

   A. Inflation or deflation
   B. Technological developments
   C. Changes in the business cycle

   Solution:

   A is correct. While all of these choices are generic risk factors, inflation or deflation is the one most likely to affect an established company in the consumer staples sector. The consumer staples sector is not likely to experience significant technological developments and is generally not sensitive to changes in the business cycle.

2. FORECAST OBJECTS, PRINCIPLES, AND APPROACHES

☐ explain principles and approaches to forecasting a company's financial results and position

Forecast Objects, Principles, and Approaches

Approaches to forecasting vary by analyst and setting. Analysts who publish company research for external distribution tend to maintain quarterly forecasts and invest a great deal of effort to achieve forecast accuracy of revenue and earnings per share estimates. An investor with a controlling position in a private company has access to far more information, which may be used to build highly detailed models with a multi-year or even multi-decade perspective. Additionally, there are forecasting norms that vary by business model of the target company, such that models for banks appear markedly different from those for oil and gas producers.

In this module, we take the perspective of a longer-term-oriented analyst forecasting relatively straightforward public issuers—Warehouse Club Inc. and Iliso Marketplace Ltd., introduced in the prior two modules—but the principles discussed are broadly applicable. The more technical details of financial statement modeling using spreadsheets are covered in lessons in Financial Statement Analysis.

What to Forecast?

Analysts may focus on different **forecast objects** related to issuers' financial statements. Below are four common forecast objects.

1. *Drivers of financial statement lines*, which were illustrated in the earlier module on company analysis. Recall that for Warehouse Club Inc., net sales each year was analyzed using two bottom-up drivers: the average number of stores open and the average net sales per store, both of which were also analyzed using year-over-year percentage changes over the last 10 years. Forecasts of net sales (at the top of Warehouse's income statement) can be made by forecasting these drivers individually and multiplying them. Gross margin and SG&A expenses as percentages of net sales were identified as key drivers of operating expenses, which can be forecast and then multiplied by the net sales forecast to obtain the forecast cost of sales and SG&A expenses. Forecasting drivers rather than financial statement lines outright has the benefit of improved explanatory value and may improve accuracy; a financial statement line item can have multiple drivers moving in different directions, which might be difficult to forecast on an aggregated basis.

2. *Individual financial statement lines*. Rather than drivers, analysts can also directly forecast individual financial statement lines. This approach is often used for lines without clear drivers, for less-material items, and for items that the analyst does not have a perspective on. In some cases, the analyst may look for an estimate by management or simply assume the quantity will remain the same in future periods as in the past. Examples include lines such as amortization expense on the income statement (a forecast for which is often provided by management in the annual report), "other non-current assets" on the balance sheet (when small), and various lines on statements of cash flows for which minimal disclosures are provided.

3. *Summary measures* such as free cash flow, earnings per share, and total assets. The benefit of using these as forecast objects is efficiency. The disadvantage is less transparency, making it difficult to audit the forecast. This approach is most appropriate if the summary measure is stable and predictable, or if issuer disclosures are severely limited.

4. *Ad hoc objects*, which may not yet be reported on historical financial statements. In some cases, an analyst may need to forecast a loss or gain and its timing to make an investment decision with respect to the company's equity or debt securities before the issuer recognizes an accrual on its

financial statements. Examples of such cases include an issuer's announcing a material legal proceeding, government regulatory action, a tax dispute, or a natural disaster.

Focus on Objects That Are Regularly Disclosed

We recommend using forecast objects that either are disclosed regularly or can be directly calculated using what is disclosed regularly (e.g., for Warehouse Club: net sales, number of stores, net sales per store, national retail sales published monthly by a government agency). Information that is *not* disclosed regularly (such as the size of a market from a third-party consultancy's report) is suitable for *informing* forecasts but can be problematic for direct use because forecasts cannot be confirmed in a timely manner. While it may be intuitive to forecast sales and gross margin by individual product line for a company, if gross margin is disclosed only on a consolidated basis, it will be difficult for the analyst to verify product-line gross margin estimates. If the company's reported gross margin results differ from gross margin estimates, is the forecast off on product A, B, or C? Similarly, if a quantity is disclosed only on an annual basis, a forecast of it can be confirmed only once a year.

We also caution against overly complex models, because they require more forecasts and take more time to update, often without any improvement in accuracy. For example, the Swiss pharmaceutical company Novartis AG discloses revenues on a quarterly basis for over 35 individual drugs by US and Rest of World regions. Most of the drugs are approved for more than one type of illness. The company also has over 50 drugs in late-stage clinical development that may drive future revenue. While an analyst could forecast Novartis AG's revenues by forecasting sales for each of its individual drugs by illness and geography, it would take months to create such a model and weeks to update it every quarter, and the forecasts by illness are not verifiable over time based on the company's disclosures. Instead, the analyst should use judgment to focus on the most important drivers and use aggregations and shortcuts where the value-added of discrete forecasting is low. For example, it would not be a good use of an analyst's time to forecast sales for drugs with small addressable markets or those that have reached maturity and will exhibit slow growth until they lose patent protection.

Forecast Approaches

For any object, there are four general forecast approaches, as shown in Exhibit 1. In practice, they are often combined.

Forecast Objects, Principles, and Approaches

Exhibit 1: Forecast Approaches for Financial Statement Objects

Historical Results: Assume Past is Precedent

This approach uses past observed or calculated values (such as a historical median) as a forecast. This is the easiest approach and is, perhaps, the default. Because the past occurred at least once before, it seems plausible to expect that it will again. However, past results were produced in past conditions, which may differ from current and future conditions.

> **USING HISTORICAL RESULTS AS FORECASTS**
>
> An analyst is forecasting the market size for energy drinks, a type of non-alcoholic ready-to-drink beverage. The analyst uses two drivers: a forecast of the market for non-alcoholic ready-to-drink beverages and energy drinks' share of that market. Sales of non-alcoholic ready-to-drink beverages have grown, on average, by 3% per year for the last 10 years. Since the analyst does not expect any material changes in conditions, she forecasts that the market will continue to grow by 3% per year.
>
> The analyst believes that energy drinks bear some similarities to sports drinks, another type of non-alcoholic ready-to-drink beverage, which has achieved a market share of 20%. The analyst thus forecasts that energy drinks will also reach a market of 20% by 2035. These two forecasts are multiplied to arrive at a forecast market size for energy drinks.

This approach may be appropriate for companies operating in industries where the analyst does not expect the industry structure (e.g., Porter's Five Forces, PESTLE influences) to change, as well as for companies that have a low sensitivity to changes in the business cycle. This approach is also commonly used for forecast objects that are not material or that the analyst does not hold an opinion on.

Historical results are a less appropriate forecast approach for companies in cyclical industries, because a future period is likely to be at a different point in the business cycle than the current or past period, and so results will differ. An "over the cycle" average or median may be appropriate for a multi-year forecast for a cyclical company, but less appropriate for a specific year as such an average or median disguises the year-to-year volatility. This forecast approach is also less appropriate for companies that are changing their competitive strategy or restructuring in some way, such as making a large acquisition or divestiture that renders historical results non-comparable.

Historical Base Rates and Convergence

This approach uses an industry or peer group average or median, computed over a long period of time, as a "base rate" for forecasting that an object will converge to over some time frame. The base rate could also be a macroeconomic variable such as GDP growth. This approach is not a rote historical exercise, as analyst discretion is required in selecting the object, the sample to calculate the base rate, and a time frame for convergence to the base rate.

> **HISTORICAL BASE RATES AND CONVERGENCE**
>
> Tesla is a relatively new entrant in the automotive industry, with an innovative suite of electric vehicles. An analyst may forecast Tesla's income statement by forecasting that its sales growth, gross and operating margins, capital intensity, and capital structure will converge to historical automotive industry averages (using a peer group of publicly traded global automakers) over the next 10 years.
>
> This forecast may be contested by other analysts who believe that the shift from internal combustion to electric vehicles, Tesla's innovative battery technology, and its direct-to-consumer sales approach make historical auto industry averages irrelevant for Tesla.

Historical base rates and convergence may be appropriate for forecasting companies in well-established industries with many publicly traded peers, such as banks, airlines, restaurants, automakers, and retailers, especially when the analyst's industry analysis does not call for material changes in industry structure or external industry influences. This approach is also logical for smaller companies that are "maturing into" a financial profile similar to that of larger peers with scale. For example, a biotechnology company that recently launched its first drug likely spends more than half its revenues on R&D, a ratio that is likely to decline toward the industry norm as the company scales.

This approach is less appropriate for companies in changing or new industries for which calculating a base rate is difficult or less relevant, for companies in highly cyclical industries for which a longer-term base rate and smooth convergence to it would obscure year-to-year volatility, and for companies that are industry leaders by a wide margin and account for a substantial proportion of any industry base rate. For example, "digital advertising industry" averages for sales growth and operating margins would be dominated by Alphabet and Meta, such that using them to forecast Alphabet's and Meta's financial results would simply be using their own historical results as the forecast, which may ignore any benefit from economies of scale (as the companies were smaller in the past).

Management guidance

Management of public companies may publicly provide targets for earnings, revenues, and other measures (e.g., capital expenditures) for the next quarter, year, or longer term, known as **management guidance** (or simply as guidance). Guidance can be detailed or rather directional and is often updated throughout the year. Initial guidance for next fiscal year might be provided during the fourth-quarter earnings call and updated for completed quarters, and new information provided at the first-, second-, and third-quarter earnings calls. Beyer et al. (2010) found that guidance accounts for a majority of the quarterly financial reporting information used by investors. Its importance stems from its forward-looking rather than backward-looking nature, and because management has an abundance of industry and company information that investors do not.

Guidance is often provided as a range (e.g., "sales growth of 2%–4%") and embeds many sub-forecasts and assumptions by management, including macroeconomic growth, cost inflation, market share changes, pricing actions, and changes in exchange rates. If management's estimates for these change, so will guidance, and it is not uncommon for companies to suspend guidance altogether in periods of high uncertainty, such as during the COVID-19 pandemic or in recessions. A key focus of investors is understanding management's assumptions embedded in guidance and scrutinizing their plausibility.

While the midpoint of a guidance range might be intuitively interpreted as management's "true" expectations, Ciconte et al. (2013) found that the upper bound often better represents management's expectations, which are "padded" by associating it with a pessimistic lower bound to create a hurdle that is more easily cleared, for which management can be rewarded.

SHORT- AND LONG-TERM MANAGEMENT GUIDANCE

Novo Nordisk A/S is a large biopharmaceutical company with shares and American Depositary Receipts (ADRs) listed on the NASDAQ Copenhagen and NYSE, respectively. Its management provides annual guidance that it updates each quarter, as well as less detailed but longer-term "strategic aspirations" during its annual Capital Markets Day presentations. Guidance includes management's point and range estimates for the following (for each fiscal year):

- Sales growth
- Operating profit growth
- Net interest income/expense
- Effective tax rate
- Capital expenditures
- Depreciation and amortization
- Free cash flow

Using guidance for forecasts is appropriate when it is provided and when management has demonstrated a track record of reliable estimates (analysts should analyze past guidance versus actuals). We caution against the use of guidance for companies that are highly sensitive to the business cycle, as management does *not* have an informational advantage over investors at forecasting macroeconomic variables like GDP or the prices of commodities. Hutton et al. (2012) found that investors have an informational advantage at the macroeconomic level, while management has an advantage at the firm level and tends to make more accurate forecasts for objects under greater management control, such as operating expenses and capital expenditures.

Analyst's discretionary forecast

We group all other forecast approaches as analysts' discretionary forecasts, which include those based on surveys, quantitative models, probability distributions, analogies to historical precedents that differ from comparable companies or industry averages, and other unobservable inputs. This approach is most common for companies in cyclical industries, companies that have no or few comparables, those that do not provide management guidance, and/or those undergoing a fundamental change like a shift in the competitive or regulatory environment. For example, while shifts in energy production have happened before (e.g., coal to natural gas), climate change and the potential shift to renewable energy and adoption of technologies like electric vehicles are unprecedented, with no historical observations to use as forecasts. Instead, an energy sector analyst must make discretionary forecasts based on many sources, such as government emission reduction commitments, proposed legislation, capital expenditure constraints, and so on.

> **DISCRETIONARY FORECASTS**
>
> An analyst is building a financial statement model for a medical technology company developing a new device to treat a type of stroke for which no other effective treatments exist. The analyst uses information from the device's clinical trials and epidemiology data from various medical journals to estimate the total addressable market of patients that are treatable with the device. The analyst also conducts a survey of specialist physicians to gauge their interest in using the device and to estimate the number of patients they would use it for (depending on the results of the clinical trials), and uses recent launches of other medical devices for neuro- and cardiovascular diseases to estimate market share for this device for the next 10 years. The analyst develops several market share scenarios based on the results of the clinical trials (i.e., the safer and more effective the device, the higher sales growth will be). While the analyst uses comparable, historical results as inputs, significant judgment is also required because this situation is unique.

Selecting a Forecast Horizon

The choice of the forecast time horizon is determined by the investment strategy for which the security is being considered, the cyclicality of the industry, company-specific factors, and the analyst's employer's preferences. Most professionally managed investment strategies describe the investment time frame and average holding period in the investment objectives of the strategy. For example, long-term-oriented fund managers may focus their forecasting primarily on a time period of three to five years, while shorter-term-oriented managers may focus more on the next one or two quarters.

The cyclicality of the industry could also influence the analyst's choice of time frame, because the forecast period should be long enough to allow the business to reach an expected mid-cycle level of sales and profitability. Similar to cyclicality, various company-specific factors, including recent acquisition or restructuring activity, can influence the selection of the forecast period to allow enough time for the realization of the expected benefits from such activity to be reflected in the financial statements. In other cases, there might be no individual analyst choice in the sense that the analyst's employer has specified fixed parameters.

> **QUESTION SET**
>
> 1. A company discloses financial results by geographic area, and the economic exposure of each geographic area is similar. Explain why an analyst should or should not develop forecasts by geographic area and aggregate the results.
>
>   **Solution:**
>
>   An analyst should *not* develop forecasts by geographic area, because each area has similar economic exposure. Developing forecasts for each geographic area would require more time to develop and update, without a significant improvement in accuracy over an aggregate forecast.

2. Which approach is *most* appropriate for an analyst to use to forecast revenue for an industry leader in a mature, non-cyclical industry?

   A. Historical results
   B. Analyst's discretionary forecast
   C. Historical base rates and convergence

   Solution:

   A is correct. Historical results is appropriate for companies operating in mature industries where the analyst does not expect the industry structure to change and for companies with low sensitivity to the business cycle. Analyst's discretionary forecast is most common for companies that have no or few comparables, do not provide management guidance, and/or are undergoing a fundamental change. Historical base rates and convergence is not appropriate, because the company is an industry leader and would account for a substantial proportion of any industry base rate.

3. Which of the following statements about management guidance is *most* accurate?

   A. The availability of guidance increases during periods of high uncertainty.
   B. The midpoint of guidance best represents management's "true" expectations.
   C. Understanding the assumptions behind the guidance is critical to assessing the guidance.

   Solution:

   C is correct. A key focus of an analyst is to understand management's assumptions embedded in guidance and to scrutinize their plausibility. It is not uncommon for companies to suspend guidance altogether in periods of high uncertainty. While the midpoint of a guidance range might be intuitively interpreted as management's "true" expectations, management may provide a range specifically intended to create a hurdle that is more easily cleared, for which management can be rewarded.

4. Which of the following is an example of an ad hoc forecast object?

   A. Amortization expense
   B. Average sales per store
   C. Pending legal proceedings

   Solution:

   C is correct. Ad hoc objects are those that may not yet be reflected in historical financial statements. Amortization expense is an individual financial statement line. Average sales per store is a bottom-up driver of a financial statement line (revenue).

FORECASTING REVENUES

3

☐ explain approaches to forecasting a company's revenues

After the forecast time horizon is determined, a revenue forecast requires the selection of the forecast objects and approach.

Forecast Objects for Revenues

Forecast objects for revenues are typically either top-down or bottom-up drivers, as discussed in the earlier module on company analysis. Common top-down forecast objects include "growth relative to GDP growth" and "market growth and market share."

Growth relative to GDP growth. The analyst first forecasts the growth rate of nominal GDP. The analyst then considers how the growth rate of the specific company being examined will compare with nominal GDP growth. The analyst can use a forecast for real GDP growth to project volumes and a forecast for inflation to project prices. Analysts often think in terms of percentage point premiums or discounts derived from a company's position in its life cycle (e.g., growth, mature, or decline) or business cycle sensitivity. Thus, an analyst's conclusion might be that a healthcare company's revenue will grow at a rate of 200 bps above the nominal GDP growth rate. The forecast could also be in relative terms. Thus, if GDP is forecast to grow at 4% and the company's revenue is forecast to grow at a 50% faster rate, the forecast percentage change in revenue would be 4% × (1 + 0.50) = 6.0%, or 200 bps higher than the GDP growth rate forecast in absolute terms.

Market growth and market share. The analyst first forecasts a growth rate for a company's product market, and then considers the company's current market share and how that share is likely to change over time. For example, if a company is expected to maintain an 8% market share of a given product market and the product market is forecast to grow from CNY144 billion to CNY154 billion in annual revenue, the forecast growth in company revenue goes from a level of 8% × CNY144 billion = CNY11.5 billion to a level of 8% × CNY154 billion = CNY12.3 billion (considering this product market alone). If the product market revenue has a predictable relationship with GDP, regression analysis might be used to estimate the relationship.

In contrast, an analyst could select bottom-up drivers as the forecast objects, which are then aggregated to arrive at a forecast of total revenue for the company. Examples of bottom-up drivers for revenue forecasts include the following:

- *Volumes and average selling prices.* Forecasts for volumes and prices of the company's products are prepared individually and multiplied to arrive at a revenue forecast. This approach is commonly used for companies that disclose these quantities, such as media and internet companies (users and revenues per user), airlines, asset managers (i.e., AUM and management fee rates), and commodity producers. Many companies disclose price and volume contributions to overall revenue growth, which can be used as the forecast object as well.

- *Product-line or segment revenues.* Forecasts for individual products, product or business lines, geographic areas, or reporting segments are made and then aggregated into a total revenue forecast. This approach is commonly used if a company makes such disclosures and if the objects have different economic exposures.

- *Capacity-based measures.* Forecasts, for example, in retailing, based on the number of stores and sales per store, or same-store sales growth (for stores that have been open for at least 12 months) and sales related to new-store openings.

- *Return- or yield-based measures.* Forecasts based on account balances and revenue yields on them. For example, net interest income for a bank can be calculated as loans multiplied by the average interest rate minus the product of deposits and liabilities and their average interest rate.

Using elements of both top-down and bottom-up objects can be useful for uncovering implicit assumptions or errors that could arise from using a single approach (e.g., forecasting revenues using bottom-up drivers but checking against what this approach would imply for the company's market size and share).

Separating Recurring and Non-Recurring Revenue or Revenue Growth

An important principle is that non-recurring items and effects should be excluded from a forecast object and considered separately. The non-recurring objects generally do not have the same drivers as the recurring object and may inflate or deflate its size. There are two types of non-recurring items and effects: those that are disclosed by a company's management and those that are not, which require analyst judgment to identify.

For revenue, the first type includes the effect of changes in exchange rates, extra selling days and weeks in the period, acquisitions/divestitures, and other "one-time" revenues or gains. These are separated from a revenue forecast object so that "underlying" revenue or growth can be forecast apart from the non-recurring items (for which a discrete forecast may not be made at all). This is generally a straightforward task unless the credibility of an issuer's financial reporting is in doubt, in which case the analyst may judge certain "non-recurring" items as, in fact, recurring. Some analysts may also use proprietary exchange rate forecasts in revenue projections.

The second type of non-recurring items is those *not* quantified by management and that require analyst judgment to estimate. For example, the COVID-19 pandemic had numerous economic effects, including a rapid increase in e-commerce sales as a percentage of retail sales in most geographies. Many believed that this effect was a "new normal," that the increase in e-commerce sales would recur and subsequent periods would show growth from the newly achieved level. By the second half of 2021, this belief was called into question, because e-commerce sales as a percentage of retail sales began to decline, returning to a trend established prior to the pandemic. Many e-commerce companies saw revenue decelerate or decline in 2022, confirming that some amount of e-commerce's COVID-19-related growth was, in fact, non-recurring. As a second example, graphic processing units (GPUs) are types of semiconductors used in a variety of applications, including gaming PCs. GPU manufacturers saw a large increase in sales in the late 2010s, which many believed was partly attributable to the use of GPUs in cryptocurrency mining, but the companies either could not or would not quantify the precise amount. Although that amount is unknown, an analyst may judge such sales as non-recurring (e.g., due to government restrictions on cryptocurrency mining) and forecast these GPU sales separately from those attributable to gaming.

Forecast Approaches for Revenues

Any of the four forecast approaches introduced in Exhibit 1 in the prior lesson (historical results, historical base rates and convergence, management guidance, discretionary forecasts) can be used for forecasting revenue objects, with the selection based on the analyst's judgment, the information environment, and the issuer's business model. We illustrate how Elaine Nguyen might use the four approaches to forecast revenues for Warehouse Club Inc. in Exhibit 2.

Exhibit 2: Forecast Approaches for Warehouse Club Inc.'s Revenues

Forecast Object	Forecast Approach	Example of Object and Approach for Warehouse Club Inc.
Top-down drivers (e.g., market size, market share)	Historical results	US retail sales excluding autos has grown on average by 3.4% each year for the last 10 years and the company's share of that (70 basis points in 2X19) has increased by 2 basis points per year. Nguyen can forecast revenues by assuming 3.4% market growth and 2 basis points of market share gain each year going forward.
	Historical base rates and convergence	Rather than assuming continued share gains, Nguyen may forecast that Warehouse's sales growth rate will converge to the market growth rate over the next five years, and forecast revenues by assuming a smooth decline in annual market share gains to 0 basis points by 2X25.
	Management guidance	If Warehouse provides annual or longer-term expectations for market size, market share, or sales, Nguyen can use these in her revenue forecast.
	Analyst's discretionary forecast	Warehouse has operated stores in some regional geographies for a long time. Nguyen may commission a study or survey to determine Warehouse's market share in its most established markets (which could be multiples of its all-in market share) and develop market size and share estimates by established/growing/new regions for Warehouse and aggregate them into a sales forecast.

Forecast Object	Forecast Approach	Example of Object and Approach for Warehouse Club Inc.
Bottom-up drivers (e.g., stores, sales per store, membership, membership annual price)	Historical results	Warehouse has opened 4–6 new stores, grown net sales per store by 3.8%, and added ~450,000 members per year for the last 10 years. Nguyen could assume these same quantities going forward as the revenue forecast.
	Historical base rates and convergence	There are several mature retailers in the USA that ceased opening new stores several years ago. Nguyen may slow the rate of new-store openings gradually to zero in the USA.
	Management guidance	Management has provided guidance on new-store openings per year and the annual price of membership, which are bottom-up drivers for the revenue forecast.
	Analyst's discretionary forecast	Nguyen may develop a discretionary forecast for stores and members by determining stores per capita and the ratio of members to stores in Warehouse's more mature regional geographies and then applying these quantities, or fractions of them, to different regions where Warehouse is opening stores today. This approach would require a geographic analysis of stores and commissioning surveys to determine regional membership counts or the use of third-party or government data, if available.

Analysts must incorporate their view (implicitly or explicitly) on key risk factors in their revenue forecasts. Four risk factors to consider for all companies are competition, changes in the business cycle, inflation and deflation, and technological developments. For Warehouse Club Inc., two key risk factors are competition and technological developments, embodied in e-commerce, which has been taking share in US retail for many years. Views on these risk factors are also embedded in forecasts of profitability,

Forecasting Revenues

working capital, capital investments, and capital structure. Given the potential wide range of outcomes, analysts often construct several forecasts for an issuer's financial statements called *scenarios*, each based on different views of key risk factors. We discuss scenario analysis in the last lesson of this module, after forecasting other key financial statement drivers.

QUESTION SET

An analyst gathers the following information for Iliso Marketplace Ltd. (Iliso), the e-commerce retailer introduced in earlier modules. Recall that sales by third-party merchants are recognized on a net basis, because Iliso does not take control of the inventory. Iliso receives 15% of the gross merchandise value (GMV) of third-party sales as commission.

	2X19 (USD millions)
National retail sales excluding autos	4,165,000
Iliso's retail sales	7,336
Iliso's third-party merchant sales	1,269
Total GMV	8,605
Iliso's retail sales	7,336
Third-party merchant fees	190
Total Revenues	7,526

Gross merchandise value has increased by an average of 3.6% per year from 2X15 to 2X19 and by 2.7% from 2X18 to 2X19. Iliso's GMV as a percentage of national retail sales has increased steadily, from 0.08% in 2X15 to 0.21% in 2X19.

	2X19	Average Growth per Year, 2X15 to 2X19	Growth from 2X18 to 2X19
Average sales/customer account (USD)	204	5.9%	4.6%
# accounts (millions)	36	22.5%	16.1%
Iliso's retail sales (USD millions)	7,336	29.7%	21.4%
Average sales/third-party merchant (USD)	31,300	13.6%	9.8%
# third-party merchants	40,500	28.5%	28.6%
Third-party merchant sales (USD millions)	1,269	46.0%	41.2%

1. Explain how an analyst would use top-down drivers to forecast Iliso's 2X20 GMV.

    Solution:

    An analyst would first forecast national retail sales excluding autos and then forecast Iliso's GMV as a percentage of that market, which represents Iliso's market share. National retail sales excluding autos have been increasing each year, and the analyst is likely to use a growth rate between 2.7% and 3.6%, depending on economic conditions. Iliso's market share in 2X19 was 0.21%, and given past increases, an increase of 2 to 3 bps seems reasonable.

2. Explain why an analyst using top-down drivers needs to allocate Iliso's forecast GMV sales between its own retail sales and sales by third-party merchants. Describe two alternative approaches to doing so.

Solution:

It is important that an analyst allocate the forecast total GMV between Iliso and third-party merchants, because Iliso's revenue and cost structure differs for each. Iliso recognizes revenue on a gross basis for its own retail sales and on a net basis for sales made by third-party merchants. Iliso's take rate is 15% on third-party merchant sales, but its gross margin percentage is far greater.

Currently, Iliso's retail sales account for 85% of its GMV, while third-party merchant sales account for the remaining 15%. An analyst could allocate the forecast increase in GMV sales based on those percentages. Alternatively, an analyst could allocate an increasing proportion to third-party merchant sales, because they have been growing at a faster rate than Iliso's retail sales.

3. Given the following assumptions, the analyst's forecast of Iliso's 2X20 total revenues is *closest* to:

   - National retail sales excluding autos grows by 3.4%.
   - Iliso's market share (i.e., its GMV as a percentage of national retail sales excluding autos) increases by 2 bps.
   - GMV is split 75%/25% between retail sales and third-party merchant sales.
   - The take rate on third-party merchant sales remains the same as in 2X19.

   A. 7,800.
   B. 8,441.
   C. 9,906.

   Solution:

   A is correct.

   Forecast of national retail sales excluding autos = 1.034 × 4,165,000 = 4,306,610

   Forecast of Iliso's 2X20 GMV = 4,307,000 × (0.21% + 2 bps) = 9,906

   Forecast of Iliso's 2X20 retail sales = 9,905 × 75% = 7,430

   Forecast of 2X20 third-party merchant sales = 9,905 × 25% = 2,477

   Forecast of 2X20 third-party merchant fees = 2,476 × 15% = 371

   Forecast of Iliso's 2X20 total revenues = 7,429 + 371 = 7,801

4. An analyst who uses bottom-up drivers forecasts the number of customer accounts to increase by 15%, the average sales per customer to increase by 5%, the number of third-party merchants to increase by 28%, and the aver-

age sales per third-party merchant to increase by 40%. The analyst's forecast for Iliso's 2X20 GMV (in USD millions) is *closest* to:

A. 8,860.

B. 9,210.

C. 11,140.

Solution:

C is correct.

Forecast of Iliso's 2X20 retail sales = 204(1.05) × 36(1.15) = 8,868 or = 7,336(1.05)(1.15)

= 8,858

Forecast of 2X20 third-party merchant sales = [40,500(1.28) × 31,300(1.40)]/1,000,000 = 2,272 or = 1,269(1.28)(1.40)

= 2,274

Forecast of Iliso's 2X20 GMV = 8,868 + 2,272 = 11,140

FORECASTING OPERATING EXPENSES AND WORKING CAPITAL

☐ explain approaches to forecasting a company's operating expenses and working capital

Issuers' disclosures about operating costs are typically less detailed than revenue disclosures. Rather than modeling costs separately for different geographic regions, business segments, or product lines, analysts are often forced to use more aggregated forecast objects such as consolidated financial statement lines (e.g., cost of sales, SG&A) or summary measures like EBITDA margins on a consolidated or segment basis. The forecasts for revenues and costs should still be coherent. If sales of a relatively low-margin product, segment, or geography are forecast to grow faster than other revenues, some level of overall profit margin deterioration should be forecast, even if the analyst is uncertain about the precise margins earned on each object. For example, food and grocery typically has low gross profit margins, so an analyst of a grocery chain that also sells higher-margin items, such as alcoholic products or pharmaceutical products, would want to forecast any change in product mix sold.

Cost of Sales and Gross Margins

Cost of sales (cost of goods sold, or COGS) is typically the single largest cost for companies that make and/or sell products. Because it has a direct link with sales, forecasting this item as a percentage of sales (or as a gross margin) is usually a good approach. If a company is losing market share to new substitute products with lower prices, gross margins are likely to decline. But if the company is gaining market share because it has introduced differentiated products—especially if it has done so in combination with achieving cost advantages—gross margins are likely to rise.

Cost of sales is typically a large cost, so even a single basis point in a gross margin forecast can have a material impact on forecasts of operating profit and free cash flow. Analysts should consider whether a more detailed analysis of these costs (e.g., by segment, input, or product line, or by volume and price components) is possible to better justify the forecast. For example, some companies face fluctuating input costs that can be passed on to customers only with a time lag. Particularly for companies with low gross margins, sudden shocks in input costs can affect operating profit significantly. A good example is the sensitivity of airlines' profits to unhedged changes in jet fuel costs. In these cases, a breakdown of both costs and sales into volume and price components is essential for developing short-term forecasts, even if analysts use the overall relationship between sales and input costs for developing longer-term forecasts, as shown in Exhibit 3.

Exhibit 3: The Effect of Prices and Costs on Gross Profit and Margin

Assume that a company's COGS as a percentage of sales equals 25% and that the quantity sold is the same in Period 2 as in Period 1. If input costs double in Period 2 and the company can pass the entire increase on to its customers through a 25% price increase, COGS as a percentage of sales will increase (to 40%) because an equal absolute amount has been added to the numerator and to the denominator.

	Period 1	Period 2
Sales	100.0	125.0
COGS	25.0	50.0
Gross profit	75.0	75.0
COGS as % of sales	25%	40%
Gross margin %	75%	60%

Thus, although the absolute amount of gross profit will remain constant, the gross margin will decrease (from 75% to 60%).

Analysts should incorporate a company's hedging strategy into a forecast. For example, commodity-driven companies' gross margins almost automatically decline if input prices of needed commodities increase significantly, because the variable costs increase at a faster rate than output prices. Through hedging strategies, a company can mitigate the impact on profitability. For example, brewers often hedge the cost of barley, a key raw material needed for brewing beer, one year in advance. Although companies usually do not disclose specific hedging positions, their hedging strategy is often disclosed in the notes to the financial statements. Further, the negative impact of increasing sales prices on sales volume (if product demand is price elastic) can be mitigated by a policy of gradual sales price increases. For example, if the brewer expects higher barley prices because of a poor harvest, the brewer can slowly increase prices to avoid a strong price jump next year.

While competitors' gross margins can provide a useful cross-check for forecasting gross margin, the margins may not be comparable given differences in business models. For example, some retailers own and operate their own stores, whereas other companies operate as wholesalers with franchised retail operations. In the franchise model, most of the operating costs are incurred by the franchisee; the wholesaler sells products with only a small markup to these franchisees. Compared with a retailer with its own stores, a wholesaler will have a much lower gross margin but also much lower operating costs.

SG&A Expenses

SG&A expenses are the other main type of operating costs. In contrast to cost of sales, SG&A expenses often have a less direct relationship with revenues. As an illustration of the profit impact of COGS and SG&A, consider the case of a Thai cement and building materials company, Siam Cement Group, from 2017 to 2018. A summary of the company's key income statement items is shown in Exhibit 4.

Exhibit 4: Siam Cement Group 2017–18 Financials

	2017 (THB billions)	2018 (THB billions)	YoY%	Percentage of Sales 2017	Percentage of Sales 2018
Net sales	450.92	478.44	6.1	100.0	100.0
COGS	349.31	383.46	9.8	77.5	80.1
Gross profit	101.61	94.98	−6.5	22.5	19.9
SG&A	52.58	55.09	4.8	11.7	11.5
Selected SG&A items:					
Salary and personnel expenses	24.24	23.98	−1.1	5.4	5.0
Freight costs	11.63	11.55	−0.7	2.6	2.4
Research and development	4.18	4.67	11.7	0.9	1.0
Promotion and advertising	2.62	2.58	−1.5	0.6	0.5
Operating income	49.03	39.89	−18.6	10.8	8.4

Note: "YoY%" means year-over-year percentage change.
Source: Based on information in Siam Cement Group's annual reports.

As shown in Exhibit 4, Siam Cement was affected in 2018 by higher input costs that could not be fully passed on to customers. Consequently, despite sales growth of 6.1%, gross profit fell by 6.5% and gross margin declined. The company was able to limit its other operating costs; SG&A expenses grew 4.8%, declining slightly as a percentage of revenue. Operating income fell 18.6%. This experience contrasts with the company's experience in 2016 (not shown), when lower input costs resulted in a widening of the gross margin by 240 basis points versus the prior year.

Although SG&A expenses overall are generally less closely linked to revenue than is cost of sales, certain SG&A expenses could be more variable than others. Specifically, selling and distribution expenses often have a large variable component and can be modeled as a percentage of sales, while general corporate costs are more fixed and might be better modeled using a fixed growth rate based on expected wage inflation.

Segment disclosures often include operating and EBITDA margin profitability by segment, but generally do not include cost items such as cost of sales, SG&A, etc., by segment. If an analyst is constructing a model based on segment forecasts, the analyst might instead use summary measures on a segment basis, as shown in Example 1.

EXAMPLE 1

Analysis of a Consumer Goods Company with Multiple Segments

A consumer goods company reported an overall underlying operating margin of 19.1% in 2X19. As shown in Exhibit 5, the operating margin is lowest in its fastest-growing segment, Home Care. The other two segments enjoy higher margins but are growing more slowly.

Exhibit 5: Segment Revenue and Profits (EUR millions, unless noted)

Segment	2X19	2X18	'19/'18 YoY	Avg. Growth Rate, 2X17–2X19
Beauty & Personal Care	21,868	20,624	6%	3%
Foods & Refreshments	19,287	20,227	–5%	–5%
Home Care	10,825	10,131	7%	3%
Total revenues	51,980	50,982	2%	0%
Underlying operating profit				
Beauty & Personal Care	4,960	4,543	9%	
Foods & Refreshments	3,382	3,576	–5%	
Home Care	1,605	1,344	19%	
Total	9,947	9,463	5%	
Underlying operating profit margin				
Beauty & Personal Care	22.7%	22.0%		
Foods & Refreshments	17.5%	17.7%		
Home Care	14.8%	13.3%		
Total	19.1%	18.6%		

Note: Underlying operating profit is a non-IFRS operating profit measure, equal to IFRS operating profit adjusted for items such as restructuring costs.

Source: Example adapted from Unilever.

1. Determine the estimated sales, operating profit, and operating profit margin by using the following two approaches: (A) Assume total sales growth of 2.0% and overall underlying operating margin of 19.1% for the next five years, and (B) assume each individual segment's sales growth and underlying operating margin continue at the same rate reported in 2019. Which approach will result in a higher estimated underlying operating profit after five years?

   Solution:

   Exhibit 6 shows that operating profit after five years will be EUR10,962 million under Approach A and EUR11,549 million under Approach B.

Forecasting Operating Expenses and Working Capital

Exhibit 6: Sales and Operating Profit, 2X19–2X24E (EUR millions, unless noted)

Approach A	2X19A	2X20E	2X21E	2X22E	2X23E	2X24E
Total revenues	51,980	53,020	54,080	55,162	56,265	57,390
Growth rate		2%	2%	2%	2%	2%
Underlying operating profit	9,947	10,127	10,329	10,536	10,747	10,962
Growth rate		2%	2%	2%	2%	2%
Underlying operating profit margin	19.1%	19.1%	19.1%	19.1%	19.1%	19.1%

Approach B						
Sales	2X19A	2X20E	2X21E	2X22E	2X23E	2X24E
Beauty & Personal Care	21,868	23,187	24,586	26,069	27,641	29,308
Growth rate		6%	6%	6%	6%	6%
Foods & Refreshments	19,287	18,391	17,536	16,721	15,944	15,203
Growth rate		−5%	−5%	−5%	−5%	−5%
Home Care	10,825	11,567	12,359	13,205	14,110	15,077
Growth rate		7%	7%	7%	7%	7%
Total revenues	51,980	53,144	54,481	55,995	57,695	59,588

Margins	2X19A	2X20E	2X21E	2X22E	2X23E	2X24E
Beauty & Personal Care	22.7%	22.7%	22.7%	22.7%	22.7%	22.7%
Foods & Refreshments	17.5%	17.5%	17.5%	17.5%	17.5%	17.5%
Home Care	14.8%	14.8%	14.8%	14.8%	14.8%	14.8%

Underlying operating profit	2X19A	2X20E	2X21E	2X22E	2X23E	2X24E
Beauty & Personal Care	4,960	5,259	5,576	5,913	6,269	6,648
Foods & Refreshments	3,382	3,225	3,075	2,932	2,796	2,666
Home Care	1,605	1,715	1,832	1,958	2,092	2,235
Total	9,947	10,199	10,484	10,803	11,157	11,549

2. Compare and explain the results under the two alternative approaches (A and B) in Question 1.

   Solution:

   Approach A assumes a constant 2% total sales growth rate and a stable 19.1% underlying operating margin. Thus, the operating profit growth rate is in line with the revenue growth rate and constant at 2%, which therefore assumes no difference in growth rates and profitability of the segments. Approach B assumes growth rates of 6%, −5%, and 7% of sales for the Beauty & Personal Care, Foods & Refreshments, and Home Care segments. This approach results in a faster overall compounded growth rate than under Approach A (3% versus 2%) and an annual increase, on average, in the total underlying operating profit margin of 6 bps due to the mix effect of different segment margins. In 2024E, Approach A yields an underlying operating profit margin of 19.1%.

3. Assume the company can grow segment revenues over the next five years at the following rates: Beauty & Personal Care, 3.0%; Foods & Refreshments, 2.0%; Home Care, 4.0%. But underlying operating profit margins in Beauty & Personal Care will fall 20 bps annually for the next five years (because of high competition, limited growth, and costs resulting from the adoption of sustainable packaging), and operating profit margins in the Foods & Refreshments and Home Care segments will increase by 15 and 50 bps, respectively, each year for the next five years (helped by increasing demand for the company's products and better utilization of its factories). Calculate the overall underlying operating profit margin in each of the next five years.

Solution:

As shown in Exhibit 7, the overall underlying operating profit margin improves from 19.1% in 2X19 to 19.5% in 2X24, because the margin decline in Beauty & Personal Care is more than offset by the margin increase in Foods & Refreshments and the faster-growing Home Care segment.

Exhibit 7: Sales and Operating Profit, 2X19–2X24E (EUR millions, unless noted)

Sales	2X19A	2X20E	2X21E	2X22E	2X23E	2X24E
Beauty & Personal Care	21,868	22,524	23,200	23,896	24,613	25,351
Growth rate		3%	3%	3%	3%	3%
Foods & Refreshments	19,287	19,673	20,066	20,468	20,877	21,294
Growth rate		2%	2%	2%	2%	2%
Home Care	10,825	11,258	11,708	12,177	12,664	13,170
Growth rate		4%	4%	4%	4%	4%
Total revenues	51,980	53,455	54,974	56,540	58,153	59,816

Margins	2X19A	2X20E	2X21E	2X22E	2X23E	2X24E
Beauty & Personal Care	22.7%	22.5%	22.3%	22.1%	21.9%	21.7%
Foods & Refreshments	17.5%	17.7%	17.8%	18.0%	18.1%	18.3%
Home Care	14.8%	15.3%	15.8%	16.3%	16.8%	17.3%

Underlying operating profit	2X19A	2X20E	2X21E	2X22E	2X23E	2X24E
Beauty & Personal Care	4,960	5,064	5,169	5,277	5,386	5,496
Foods & Refreshments	3,382	3,479	3,579	3,681	3,786	3,894
Home Care	1,605	1,725	1,853	1,988	2,131	2,282
Total	9,947	10,268	10,601	10,946	11,303	11,672
Margin	19.1%	19.2%	19.3%	19.4%	19.4%	19.5%

Working Capital Forecasts

Working capital forecasts are typically made by using efficiency ratios, discussed in earlier modules, as the forecast object, which are combined with sales and costs forecasts to project accounts receivable, inventories, accounts payable, and other current assets and liabilities, as demonstrated in Example 2.

Forecasting Operating Expenses and Working Capital

EXAMPLE 2

Working Capital Forecasts with Efficiency Ratios

Exhibit 8 shows revenue, COGS, and year-end working capital account balances for YY Ltd., a fictional company, for years 1–3. Based on the data in the exhibit, answer Questions 1–3.

Exhibit 8: YY Ltd. Financial Data (CNY millions)

Year	1	2	3
Revenue	174,915	205,839	245,866
COGS	152,723	177,285	209,114
Accounts receivable	5,598	6,949	10,161
Inventory	29,481	32,585	41,671
Accounts payable	46,287	59,528	72,199

1. Calculate days sales outstanding (DSO), inventory days on hand (DOH), and days payable outstanding (DPO) for years 1, 2, and 3, using year-end balances and assuming a 365-day fiscal year.

   Solution:

   Recall that days sales outstanding is equal to accounts receivable/(revenues/365), inventory days on hand is equal to inventories/(COGS/365), and days payable outstanding is equal to accounts payable/(COGS/365). Using the data in Exhibit 8, the three ratios for years 1–3 are as follows:

Year	1	2	3
Days sales outstanding	12	12	15
Inventory days on hand	70	67	73
Days payable outstanding	111	123	126

2. Your colleague Liang forecasts revenue growth of 18%, 16%, and 13% and gross margins of 17%, 17%, and 16% in years 4, 5, and 6, respectively, for YY Ltd. Using Liang's forecasts, calculate expected revenue and COGS in years 4, 5, and 6.

   Solution:

   Using Liang's forecasts for annual revenue growth and gross margins and the data in Exhibit 8, expected revenue and COGS for years 4–6 are as follows:

Year (CNY millions)	1	2	3	4	5	6
Revenue	174,915	205,839	245,866	290,122	336,541	380,292
Growth rate		18%	19%	18%	16%	13%
COGS	152,723	177,285	209,114	240,801	279,329	319,445
Gross margin	13%	14%	15%	17%	17%	16%

3. Liang forecasts that days sales outstanding, inventory days on hand, and days payable outstanding in years 4, 5, and 6 will remain the same as the year 3 amounts. Using Liang's forecasts as well as forecast revenue and COGS, calculate expected accounts receivable, inventories, and accounts payable year-end balances for years 4, 5, and 6.

Solution:

Each of the efficiency ratios can be rearranged to yield working capital balances, because we have values for two of the three variables in them: the efficiency ratios are assumed to remain constant from year 3 levels, and revenue and COGS have already been forecast.

Days sales outstanding is equal to accounts receivable/(revenues/365); thus, accounts receivable is equal to days sales outstanding × (revenues/365). Similarly, inventories is equal to inventory days on hand × (COGS/365), and accounts payable is equal to days payable outstanding × (COGS/365).

Using the data in Exhibit 8 and the revenue and COGS forecasts, year-end working capital account balances are as follows:

Year (CNY millions)	1	2	3	4	5	6
Revenue	174,915	205,839	245,866	290,122	336,541	380,292
COGS	152,723	177,285	209,114	240,801	279,329	319,445
Accounts receivable	5,598	6,949	10,161	11,990	13,908	15,716
Inventories	29,481	32,585	41,671	47,985	55,663	63,657
Accounts payable	46,287	59,528	72,199	83,139	96,442	110,292
Days sales outstanding	12	12	15	15	15	15
Inventory days on hand	70	67	73	73	73	73
Days payable outstanding	111	123	126	126	126	126

While a historical results approach is common for working capital efficiency ratios, analysts can also use the other forecast approaches. Exhibit 9 discusses forecast objects and approaches that Elaine Nguyen can use for Warehouse Club Inc.'s operating costs and working capital.

Exhibit 9: Forecast Approaches for Warehouse Club Inc.'s Operating Costs and Working Capital

Forecast Object	Forecast Approach	Example of Object and Approach for Warehouse Club Inc.
Gross margin (on net sales)	Historical results	From 2X10 to 2X19, Warehouse's gross margin increased by an average of 2 bps per year. Such an increase may reflect increasing bargaining power over suppliers with scale, and Nguyen can use the same 2 bps per year increase in gross margin as a forecast.
	Historical base rates and convergence	Both the industry average gross margin and that of larger, more mature retailers such as Walmart are much greater than Warehouse's gross margin. But Warehouse's business model is to use a low gross margin on net sales to drive high-margin membership revenues. Therefore, Nguyen probably will not use this approach.
	Management guidance	If Warehouse management provides guidance on margins, Nguyen can use this approach as the forecast, after evaluating management's forecasting credibility.
	Analyst's discretionary forecast	Nguyen may formulate a discretionary forecast for gross margin by exploring the relationship between it, inflation/deflation in Warehouse's product categories, and management's desire for member savings vs. competitors to equal 5× the annual price of membership.

Forecast Object	Forecast Approach	Example of Object and Approach for Warehouse Club Inc.
Selling, general, and administrative expenses (SG&A) as a percentage of sales	Historical results	SG&A, which captures the cost of operating stores and some merchandise distribution, is primarily composed of employee payroll. Relative to sales, it has remained mostly stable at or around 9%. Nguyen may forecast it to remain the same.
	Historical base rates and convergence	Warehouse's SG&A as a percentage of sales is already lower than that of larger retailer competitors (and substantially lower than the retail industry average), owing to its business model differences that emphasize store productivity and cost leadership. Nguyen will therefore probably not use this approach to forecast SG&A.
	Management guidance	If Warehouse management provides guidance on SG&A, Nguyen can use this approach as the forecast, after evaluating management's forecasting credibility.
	Analyst's discretionary forecast	Since SG&A is primarily composed of employee payroll, Nguyen may forecast it based on projected employee productivity (e.g., employees to stores) and projected wage rates, which may be based on macroeconomic variables like projected economy-wide wage growth.

Forecast Object	Forecast Approach	Example of Object and Approach for Warehouse Club Inc.
Working capital ratios (e.g., DSO, DOH, DPO)	Historical results	As of 2X19, Warehouse's DSO, DOH, and DPO were 3, 30, and 28, respectively. DSO and DPO have been stable for the last 10 years, while DOH has decreased by 7 days since 2X10. Nguyen might forecast a stable DSO and DPO and a modestly declining DOH over the next several years.
	Historical base rates and convergence	Warehouse's working capital ratios and cash conversion cycle are materially better than the industry average and some larger peers and have been for many years, owing to its business model differences. Nguyen will therefore probably not use this forecast approach, unless Warehouse changes its business model (e.g., it launches an e-commerce business).
	Management guidance	If Warehouse management provides guidance on working capital (e.g., a projection for the net working capital to sales ratio), Nguyen can use this approach as the forecast, after evaluating management's forecasting credibility.
	Analyst's discretionary forecast	Nguyen may develop a discretionary forecast for working capital by, for example, estimating net working capital to sales ratios by product category (e.g., fresh foods, packaged foods, non-food merchandise) and applying them to a net sales forecast also broken down by category.

QUESTION SET

Iliso Marketplace Ltd., the e-commerce retailer introduced in prior modules, reports its GMV by product category: in 2X19, the mix was 55% food and grocery, 20% media and electronics, 8% home goods and décor, and 17% apparel and beauty products. However, Iliso presents only aggregated financial results (no segment disclosures).

Iliso's cost of revenue is primarily composed of the inventory costs of products sold to customers where Iliso records revenue gross. Inventory costs include shipping and handling costs. Additionally, cost of revenue includes outbound shipping and logistics-related expenses, as well as delivery service costs from the third-party merchant business, where Iliso is the delivery service provider. Cost of revenue also includes depreciation expense related to inventory handling and shipping assets.

Iliso's operating, general, and administrative expenses include costs incurred in operating and staffing its fulfillment centers, customer service costs, payment processing fees, costs related to the design, execution, and maintenance of Iliso's technology infrastructure, and general corporate function costs.

Iliso has minimal accounts receivable, because customers pay with credit cards that settle in less than a week. Iliso does have significant inventory, accounts payable, and accrued expenses on its balance sheet.

1. How might an analyst use Iliso's disclosure of GMV by product category?

   Solution:

   An analyst could estimate cost of sales/sales and gross profit margin by category by looking at other retailers that primarily sell products in the specific category. Information on those companies could be used to check whether Iliso's gross profit margin is consistent with that implied by the product category mix. Also, if the mix is expected to change, an analyst can adjust the aggregate cost of sales/sales and gross profit margins accordingly. The information should probably not be used directly to develop detailed forecasts by category, because those forecasts would not be verifiable and would not be an efficient use of the analyst's time.

2. It is *most* appropriate to forecast Iliso's cost of revenue as a percentage of its:

   A. retail sales.
   B. total revenues.
   C. total GMV sales.

   Solution:

   A is correct. Cost of revenue should be based on Iliso's retail sales. Cost of revenue is unaffected by third-party merchandise sales unless the merchant uses Iliso's fulfillment network for warehousing and delivery. The company does not provide information on such use by third parties, and it would be a small cost compared with cost of revenue for Iliso's retail sales. Iliso's cost of revenue is primarily composed of the inventory costs of products sold to customers where Iliso records revenue gross.

3. Discuss the use of a historical base rates and convergence approach, calculated using other retailers' financial results, for forecasting Iliso's operating expenses.

   Solution:

   Iliso's e-commerce business model and the breadth of the retail sales industry may make industry averages inappropriate to use for Iliso. However, if there are larger, more mature e-commerce retailers to calculate statistics for, this approach may be appropriate.

4. If food and grocery increases as a proportion of Iliso's retail sales, which of the following would *most likely* increase?

   A. Inventory turnover
   B. Gross profit margin
   C. Current assets/sales

   Solution:

   A is correct. Inventory turnover would increase because of the perishable nature of food and grocery. Inventory as a percentage of sales would decrease, resulting in a decrease in current assets to sales.

FORECASTING CAPITAL INVESTMENTS AND CAPITAL STRUCTURE

5

- explain approaches to forecasting a company's capital investments and capital structure

Projections for long-term assets are based on cash flow statement and income statement projections, because net PP&E and intangible assets on the balance sheet primarily increase due to capital expenditures and decrease due to depreciation and amortization expenses. Capital expenditures can be broken down into maintenance capital expenditures necessary to sustain the current business and growth capital expenditures needed to expand the business. Maintenance capital expenditure forecasts are often based on historical depreciation and amortization expenses, usually with a small adjustment upward to account for inflation in capital goods. For businesses with low fixed asset turnover, maintenance capital expenditure requirements can be quite high. Growth capital expenditure forecasts are more discretionary and are tied to management's expansion plans and revenue growth. Depreciation and amortization forecasts are based on net PP&E and intangibles on the balance sheet (which increase due to capital expenditures) and their useful lives as assumed by management's accounting policies, which can be approximated by the ratio of gross fixed assets to depreciation and amortization expenses. Information may also be found in the notes to the financial statements.

Analysts must also make projections about a company's future capital structure. Leverage ratios—such as debt to capital, debt to equity, and debt to EBITDA—are often used as the forecast object to project future debt and equity levels. Analysts should consider historical company practice, management's financial strategy, and the capital requirements implied by the capital expenditure assumptions when projecting the future capital structure. Management may provide guidance on target capital structure, debt covenant ratios (e.g., net debt to EBITDA), and capital expenditures, sometimes broken down into maintenance, growth, and acquisitions. Example 3 demonstrates the use of these forecast objects for YY Ltd., the same company in Example 2.

EXAMPLE 3

Balance Sheet Modeling

Exhibit 10 shows financial data for YY Ltd. related to its PP&E and intangible assets. Based on the data in Exhibit 10 and the data and analysis in Example 2, answer Questions 1 and 2.

Exhibit 10: YY Ltd. Long-Term Asset Data (CNY millions)

Year	1	2	3
PP&E, net	5,068	6,992	6,306
Goodwill	282	248	253
Intangible assets, net	1,779	1,424	4,013
Total fixed assets	7,129	8,664	10,572
Capital expenditures – PP&E	3,785	3,405	3,026
Capital expenditures – intangibles	333	142	3,310
Depreciation expense	220	324	518
Amortization expense	529	486	666

Note: PP&E and intangibles asset account balances were also affected each year by changes in exchange rates and by disposals, which are not shown in the exhibit. Assume that such effects are zero in years 4–6.

1. Calculate the following:

   A. Capital expenditures (for both PP&E and intangibles) as a percentage of revenue (for years 1–3)

B. Depreciation expense as a percentage of beginning-of-year PP&E, net (for years 2 and 3)

C. Amortization expense as a percentage of beginning-of-year intangible assets, net (for years 2 and 3).

Solution:

Using the data, the following percentages were calculated.

Year	1	2	3
Revenue	174,915	205,839	245,866
Capital expenditures – PP&E (% of revenue)	2.2%	1.7%	1.2%
Capital expenditures – intangibles (% of revenue)	0.2%	0.1%	1.3%
Depreciation (% of beginning PP&E)		6%	7%
Amortization (% of beginning intangibles)		27%	47%

2. Given the following assumptions and forecast revenue from Example 2, calculate expected total fixed assets for years 4–6.

   - Capital expenditures for PP&E as a percentage of revenue to remain at the year 3 level
   - Capital expenditures for intangibles as a percentage of revenue to remain at the year 1 level
   - Goodwill to remain at the year 3 level
   - Depreciation and amortization expenses as a percentage of beginning-of-year PP&E, net, and intangible assets, net, to remain at year 3 levels

Solution:

Using the data provided, expected total fixed assets for years 4–6 was calculated as CNY12,351 million; CNY15,179 million; and CNY18,662 million, respectively. PP&E, net, for each year was calculated as the prior period balance plus capital expenditures minus depreciation expense. Intangible assets, net, for each year was calculated in a similar fashion. Goodwill was held constant at CNY253 million.

Year	1	2	3	4	5	6
Revenue	174,915	205,839	245,866	290,122	336,541	380,292
PP&E, net	5,068	6,992	6,306	9,410	12,854	16,583
Goodwill	282	248	253	253	253	253
Other intangible assets, net	1,779	1,424	4,013	2,688	2,072	1,827
Total fixed assets	7,129	8,664	10,572	12,351	15,179	18,662
Capital expenditures – PP&E	3,785	3,405	3,026	3,571	4,142	4,680

Year	1	2	3	4	5	6
Capital expenditures – PP&E (% of revenue)	2.2%	1.7%	1.2%	1.2%	1.2%	1.2%
Capital expenditures – intangibles	333	142	3,310	552	641	724
Capital expenditures – intangibles (% of revenue)	0.2%	0.1%	1.3%	0.2%	0.2%	0.2%
Depreciation expense	220	324	518	467	697	952
Depreciation (% of beginning PP&E)		6%	7%	7%	7%	7%
Amortization expense	529	486	666	1,877	1,257	969
Amortization (% of beginning intangibles)		27%	47%	47%	47%	47%

3. Based on Exhibit 11, which shows financial data for YY Ltd. related to its capital structure and profitability, answer Question 3.

Exhibit 11: YY Ltd. Debt and Profitability Data (CNY millions)

Year	1	2	3
Gross debt	10,931	17,624	17,597
Revenue	174,915	205,839	245,866
EBITDA	9,304	12,343	14,190
EBITDA margin	5.3%	6.0%	5.8%

YY Ltd. management has a year 6 gross debt to EBITDA ratio target of 2.0.

A. Assuming an EBITDA margin of 6.0%, revenue forecasts from Example 2, and gross debt to EBITDA ratios of 1.25, 1.50, and 2.0 for years 4, 5, and 6, respectively, calculate expected gross debt for years 4–6.

B. Given the results of part A, how much incremental borrowing does the forecast imply from year 3 to year 6?

Solution:

Gross debt of CNY21,579 million; CNY30,289 million; and CNY45,635 million are estimated for years 4–6, respectively, for YY Ltd. This forecast is made by first multiplying forecast revenue by the forecast EBITDA margin to calculate forecast EBITDA. Then, the expected gross debt to EBITDA ratio is multiplied by the forecast EBITDA to calculate forecast gross debt.

Year	1	2	3	4	5	6
Gross debt	10,931	17,624	17,597	21,759	30,289	45,635
Revenue	174,915	205,839	245,866	290,122	336,541	380,292

Year	1	2	3	4	5	6
EBITDA	9,304	12,343	14,190	17,407	20,192	22,818
EBITDA margin	5.3%	6.0%	5.8%	6.0%	6.0%	6.0%
Gross debt to EBITDA	1.17	1.43	1.24	1.25	1.50	2.00

Exhibit 12 discusses forecast objects and approaches that Elaine Nguyen can use for Warehouse Club Inc.'s capital expenditures and gross debt to EBITDA.

Exhibit 12: Forecast Approaches for Warehouse Club Inc.'s Capital Expenditures and Structure

Forecast Object	Forecast Approach	Example of Object and Approach for Warehouse Club Inc.
Capital expenditures as a percentage of net sales	Historical results	Warehouse has spent 2% of net sales on capital expenditures for the last 10 years, which Nguyen can use as the forecast going forward.
	Historical base rates and convergence	More mature retailers (e.g., Walmart in the USA) have all but stopped opening new stores, which has reduced their capital requirements to maintenance and new initiatives like e-commerce. If Warehouse does not intend to go to new geographies or launch an e-commerce business, Nguyen might forecast capital expenditures trending down to maintenance level, along with a decline in new-store openings per year, as Warehouse matures.
	Management guidance	Warehouse management provides guidance on new-store openings, which Nguyen can use to forecast capital expenditures (along with a maintenance capital expenditure forecast and a forecast for growth capital expenditures per new store).
	Analyst's discretionary forecast	Nguyen might instead use a discretionary forecast for capital expenditures by projecting a maintenance CAPEX amount (not disclosed by management) and growth CAPEX associated with new-store openings.

Forecast Object	Forecast Approach	Example of Object and Approach for Warehouse Club Inc.
Gross debt to EBITDA	Historical results	For the last five years, Warehouse's ratio of debt to trailing twelve months EBITDA has been 1.10, which Nguyen can project going forward. The product of this ratio and projected EBITDA (from earlier forecasts of sales and operating expenses) is Warehouse's gross debt.
	Historical base rates and convergence	Warehouse's more mature competitors and peers use a greater amount of debt in their capital structure, and return more capital to shareholders with buybacks and dividends. Nguyen might forecast the same for Warehouse over time, with an increasing ratio of debt to EBITDA and percentage of free cash flow returned to shareholders.
	Management guidance	Warehouse's management may provide a target capital structure through a target debt to EBITDA ratio or credit rating, which Nguyen can use as the forecast.
	Analyst's discretionary forecast	Nguyen might instead make a discretionary forecast linked to her free cash flow forecast, projecting a debt to EBITDA ratio and return of capital to shareholders. Depending on Fyleton Investments' strategy, Nguyen might engage with Warehouse's management to advocate for such a capital structure.

QUESTION SET

An analyst gathers the following information related to Iliso's capital expenditures and capital structure (USD millions):

Forecasting Capital Investments and Capital Structure

	2X15	2X16	2X17	2X18	2X19
Iliso's retail sales	2,589	3,424	5,100	6,052	7,336
Operating income	−1	18	61	72	130
Depreciation expense	25	43	65	91	123
PP&E (net)	198	294	435	590	768
Short-term debt	56	255	198	66	0
Long-term debt	43	157	168	144	144
Equity	548	732	858	1,006	1,178
Capital expenditures	79	140	208	247	301

1. Which of the following would the analyst *most likely* use in estimating Iliso's maintenance capital expenditures?

    A. Operating income

    B. Depreciation expense

    C. Earnings before interest, taxes, depreciation, and amortization (EBITDA)

    Solution:

    B is correct. Depreciation expense can serve as the basis for maintenance capital expenditures, as it is management's estimate of the cost of fixed assets expensed on the income statement in a manner that tracks its use.

2. Which of the following approaches is *most* appropriate for forecasting Iliso's capital expenditures?

    A. Historical results

    B. Analyst's discretionary forecast

    C. Historical base rates and convergence

    Solution:

    A is correct. Capital expenditures have been 4.1% of retail sales for the past four years (2X16–2X19). The historical results approach—using the bottom-up driver retail sales—is most appropriate. An analyst's discretionary forecast is not required, because Iliso is not in a cyclical industry or undergoing a fundamental change. Iliso's unique model and the breadth of the industry make the approach using historical base rates and convergence to the industry inappropriate.

3. The analyst forecasts 2X20 total revenues of 8,411 million, operating income of 2% of total revenues, capital expenditures of 4% of total revenues, depreciation expense of 20% of opening PP&E (net), and debt/EBITDA of 0.50. The analyst's forecast for debt (in millions) is *closest* to:

    A. 84.

    B. 161.

> **C.** 195.
>
> **Solution:**
>
> B is correct.
>
> 2X20 operating income = 0.02(8,411) = 168
>
> 2X20 depreciation expense = 0.20(768) = 154
>
> EBITDA = 168 + 154 = 322
>
> Debt = 0.50(322) = 161
>
> 4. The analyst notes that Iliso's common stock and paid-in capital accounts increased, in total, by 75 million from 2X18 to 2X19, but only 42 million was reported as stock issuance on the statement of cash flows. Retained earnings increased by the amount of net income. Which of the following *most likely* explains the difference of 33 million?
>
>   **A.** A stock split
>
>   **B.** A stock dividend
>
>   **C.** Stock-based compensation
>
>   **Solution:**
>
>   C is correct. Stock-based compensation is a non-cash expense in the income statement and is reported as an addition to net income in the indirect method of reporting cash flow from operations. The issuance also increases common stock and paid-in capital. A stock split typically simply increases the number of shares outstanding and decreases any stated par value per share. A stock dividend increases common stock and paid-in capital and reduces retained earnings by the same amount.

6. SCENARIO ANALYSIS

☐ describe the use of scenario analysis in forecasting

Recall from earlier lessons that industry and business risks may result in future outcomes that differ from expectations. The final step in forecasting involves incorporating the possibility of different outcomes based on key risk factors as well as judging their likelihood of occurrence. Generic risk factors that affect all companies—but to varying degrees—include changes in the business cycle, competition, inflation and deflation, and technological developments. Rather than develop single point estimate forecasts, analysts make several forecast scenarios that vary based on different outcomes with respect to key risk factors. Investors compare these scenarios with other analysts' (e.g., sell-side analysts) forecasts for a company, as well as forecasts implied by current valuations, to make investment decisions.

We demonstrate the use of scenario analysis for technological developments that threaten to cannibalize demand for an existing product in the following historical case study. Technological developments can affect demand for a product, the quantity supplied of a product, or both. When changes in technology lead to lower manufacturing

Scenario Analysis

costs, the supply curve will shift to the right as suppliers produce more of the product at the same price. Conversely, if changes in technology result in the development of attractive substitute products, the demand curve will shift to the left.

EXAMPLE 4

Quantifying the Tablet Market's Potential to Cannibalize Demand for Personal Computers

The worldwide tablet market experienced a major technological development with the introduction of the Apple iPad tablet in April 2010, which was expected to have (and indeed did have) important implications for the manufacturers of desktop and laptop computers. A tablet promised to offer the capabilities of a portable personal computer (PC) with a touchscreen interface instead of a keyboard. Another distinguishing feature of the then-new tablets was that—unlike the majority of PCs, which run on the Microsoft Windows platform—they would run on a non-Microsoft operating system: Apple's iOS or Google's Android. Given the tablet's ability to perform many of the most common tasks of a PC—including emailing, browsing the web, sharing photos, playing music, watching movies, playing games, keeping a calendar, and managing contacts—an analyst at that time might reasonably have wondered to what extent sales of tablets might cannibalize demand for PCs and what the potential impact might be on Microsoft's sales and earnings. Exhibit 13 presents one approach to answering these questions. It is set at the start of 2012, just over a year after the launch of the iPad. It is presented from the position of an analyst assessing the impact of the tablet on the PC market and Microsoft.

Exhibit 13: Unit and Revenue Projections (in thousands, unless noted)

Pre-Cannibalization PC Projections	FY2011	FY2012E	FY2013E	FY2014E	3-Year CAGR
Consumer PC shipments	170,022	174,430	184,120	193,811	4.5%
Non-consumer PC shipments	180,881	185,570	195,880	206,189	4.5%
Total global PC shipments	350,903	360,000	380,000	400,000	4.5%
% of which is consumer	48%	48%	48%	48%	
% of which is non-consumer	52%	52%	52%	52%	
Consumer tablet shipments	36,785	82,800	111,250	148,750	59.3%
Non-consumer tablet shipments	1,686	7,200	13,750	26,250	149.7%
Total global tablet shipments	38,471	90,000	125,000	175,000	65.7%
% of which is consumer	96%	92%	89%	85%	
% of which is non-consumer	4%	8%	11%	15%	

Pre-Cannibalization PC Projections	FY2011	FY2012E	FY2013E	FY2014E	3-Year CAGR
Cannibalization factor, consumer	30%	30%	30%	30%	
Cannibalization factor, non-consumer	10%	10%	10%	10%	
# of consumer PCs cannibalized by tablets	11,036	24,840	33,375	44,625	
# of non-consumer PCs cannibalized by tablets	169	720	1,375	2,625	
Total PCs cannibalized by tablets	11,205	25,560	34,750	47,250	
% of total PCs cannibalized by tablets	3.2%	7.1%	9.1%	11.8%	
Post-Cannibalization PC Projections					
Consumer PC shipments	158,987	149,590	150,745	149,186	−2.1%
Non-consumer PC shipments	180,712	184,850	194,505	203,564	4.0%
Total global PC shipments	339,699	334,440	345,250	352,750	1.3%
Microsoft implied average selling price (USD)					
Consumer	85	85	85	85	
Non-consumer	155	155	155	155	
Revenue impact for Microsoft (USD millions)					
Consumer	938	2,111	2,837	3,793	
Non-consumer	26	112	213	407	
Total revenue impact	964	2,223	3,050	4,200	

Note: CAGR is compound annual growth rate. Non-consumer includes enterprise, education, and government purchasers.

Sources: Based on data from Gartner, JPMorgan, Microsoft, and authors' analysis.

Worldwide market shipments of PCs in FY2011 totaled 350.9 million units, while worldwide shipments of tablets totaled 38.5 million units (source: Gartner Personal Computer Quarterly Statistics Worldwide Database). Shipments to consumers represented 96% of total tablet shipments during fiscal year 2011. We next estimate the magnitude of the potential substitution effect, or cannibalization factor, that tablets will have on the PC market. Because the cannibalization factor depends on many different variables—including user preferences, end-use application, and whether the purchaser already owns a PC—we use a range of potential estimates. Moreover, we also divide the worldwide PC market into consumer and non-consumer (enterprise, education, and government purchasers), because the degree of substitution is likely to differ between the two. For purposes of illustration, we assume a cannibalization factor of 30% for the consumer market and 10% for the non-consumer market in our base case scenario.

In addition, the base case scenario assumes that non-consumer adoption of tablets increases to 15% of the market from 4% in 2011. Moreover, although the composition of the global PC market is roughly evenly divided between consumers and non-consumers (48% and 52% in fiscal year 2011, respectively), the non-consumer segment is significantly more profitable for Microsoft, because approximately 80% of the company's Office products are sold to enterprise, education, and government institutions. The average selling price (ASP) estimates are derived by dividing Microsoft's estimated average revenue by customer type for the prior three years by Microsoft's estimated PC shipments for each type of customer. By multiplying the projected number of PCs cannibalized by tablets by the estimated ASP, we can derive an estimate of the revenue impact for Microsoft. For example, in FY2012, it is projected that 24.8 million consumer PCs will be cannibalized by sales of tablets. With a consumer ASP of USD85, this cannibalization implies a revenue loss for Microsoft of USD2.1 billion (24.8 million units × USD85 per unit = USD2.1 billion).

Once the revenue impact has been projected, the next step is to estimate the impact of lower PC unit volumes on operating costs and margins. We begin by analyzing the cost structure of Microsoft and, more specifically, the breakdown between fixed and variable costs. Most software companies have a cost structure with a relatively high proportion of fixed costs and a low proportion of variable costs, because costs related to product development and marketing (mostly fixed) are sunk and unrecoverable, whereas the cost of producing an additional copy of the software (mostly variable) is relatively low. Because very few, if any, companies provide an explicit breakdown of fixed versus variable costs, an estimate almost always needs to be made. One method is to use the formula

$$\%\Delta \text{ (Cost of revenue + Operating expenses)}/\%\Delta \text{ revenue},$$

where %Δ is "percentage change in," used as a proxy for variable cost percentage. Another approach is to assign an estimate of the percentage of fixed and variable costs to the various components of operating expenses. The two approaches are illustrated in Exhibit 14 and Exhibit 15.

Exhibit 14: Estimation of Variable Costs for Microsoft, Method 1 (USD millions)

Selected Operating Segments	FY2009	FY2010	FY2011	FY2011/FY2009 Percentage Change
Revenue:				
Windows and Windows Live	15,563	18,792	18,778	
Microsoft business division	19,211	19,345	21,986	
Total segment revenue	34,774	38,137	40,764	17%
Operating expenses:				
Windows and Windows Live	6,191	6,539	6,810	

Selected Operating Segments	FY2009	FY2010	FY2011	FY2011/FY2009 Percentage Change
Microsoft business division	8,058	7,703	8,159	
Total operating expenses	14,249	14,242	14,969	5%

%Variable cost estimate ≈ %Δ (Cost of revenue + Operating expenses)/%Δ revenue ≈ 5%/17% ≈ **29%**

%Fixed cost ≈ 1 − %Variable cost ≈ 1 − 29% ≈ **71%**

Exhibit 15: Estimation of Variable Costs for Microsoft, Method 2 (USD millions)

Operating Expenses	FY2009	FY2010	FY2011	FY2009–FY2011 Average	% of Total Op. Expenses	Estimated % of Fixed Costs	Fixed Cost Contribution
Cost of revenue (excl. depreciation)	10,455	10,595	13,577	11,542	29%	20%	6%
Depreciation expense	1,700	1,800	2,000	1,833	5%	100%	5%
Total cost of revenue	12,155	12,395	15,577	13,376	34%		10%
R&D	9,010	8,714	9,043	8,922	22%	100%	22%
Sales and marketing	12,879	13,214	13,940	13,344	34%	80%	27%
General and admin.	4,030	4,063	4,222	4,105	10%	100%	10%
Total operating expenses	38,074	38,386	42,782	39,747	100%		60%
Estimated percentage of Microsoft's total cost structure that is fixed:							70%

Note: Fiscal year ends in June.

Sources: Microsoft 2011 Form 10-K and authors' analysis.

As can be seen, Microsoft's cost structure appears to consist of approximately 70% fixed costs and 30% variable costs. Note, however, that a growing company like Microsoft will typically re-invest in PP&E to support future growth, so even those expenses that appear to be "fixed" will increase over time. To adjust for this expected growth in fixed costs, this example includes an assumption that the change in fixed costs will be half the rate of the change in sales. Variable costs are projected to change at the same rate as sales. As shown in Exhibit 16, after incorporating these assumptions into the projections, an assumed 7.0% compound annual growth rate (CAGR) in revenue through FY2014 would translate into a 10.6% CAGR in operating income $[(36{,}757/27{,}161)^{1/3} - 1 = 0.106$, or 10.6%]. In addition, these assumptions would result in an operating margin expansion of 410 bps over the same period (42.9% − 38.8% = 4.1 pps, or 410 bps), because of the significant amount of operating leverage that exists as a result of

Scenario Analysis

a relatively large fixed cost base. With the further assumptions of no change in other income, a constant effective tax rate, and no change in shares outstanding, the pre-cannibalization model, shown in Exhibit 16, results in projected revenue of USD85.7 billion, operating income of USD36.8 billion, an operating margin of 42.9%, and EPS that increases at a CAGR of 10.3% to USD3.62 in FY2014.

Exhibit 16: Microsoft Pre-Cannibalization EPS Projections (USD millions, except EPS)

	FY2011	FY2012E	FY2013E	FY2014E	3-Year CAGR
Revenue	69,943	74,839	80,078	85,683	7.0%
YoY%		7.0%	7.0%	7.0%	
Operating Expenses					
Fixed (70%)	29,947	30,996	32,080	33,203	3.5%
Variable (30%)	12,835	13,733	14,694	15,723	7.0%
Total operating expenses	42,782	44,729	46,774	48,926	4.6%
Operating income	27,161	30,110	33,303	36,757	10.6%
Operating margin	38.83%	40.23%	41.59%	42.90%	
Other income (expense)	910	910	910	910	
Pre-tax income	28,071	31,020	34,213	37,667	
Provision for income taxes	4,921	5,438	5,998	6,603	
Effective tax rate	17.53%	17.53%	17.53%	17.53%	
Net income	23,150	25,582	28,215	31,064	
Weighted average shares outstanding, diluted	8,593	8,593	8,593	8,593	
Estimated EPS pre-cannibalization	2.69	2.98	3.28	3.62	10.3%

In the post-cannibalization scenario, as shown in Exhibit 17, revenue is reduced each year to reflect the expected impact of cannibalization, which results in a decrease in the CAGR of revenue over the period to 5.2%, down from 7.0% in the pre-cannibalization scenario. Given the reduction in revenue growth and holding the cost structure constant at 70/30 fixed versus variable costs, operating income growth slows to a CAGR of 8.0%, down from 10.6% in the pre-cannibalization scenario. Operating margin at the end of the period is reduced by approximately 100 bps, from 42.9% to 41.9%, because the company is unable to leverage its fixed cost base to the same degree as a result of slower revenue growth. Overall, in the post-cannibalization scenario, Microsoft is expected to generate revenue of USD81.5 billion, operating income of USD34.2 billion, an operating margin of 41.9%, and EPS that increases at a CAGR of 7.7%

to USD3.37 in FY2014. Thus, the cannibalization of PCs as a result of projected growth in the tablet market is expected to reduce the company's annual revenues in FY2014 by USD4.2 billion, operating income by USD2.6 billion, operating margins by 96 bps, and EPS by USD0.25.

Exhibit 17: Microsoft Post-Cannibalization EPS Projections, Base Case Scenario (USD millions, except EPS and unless noted)

	FY2011	FY2012E	FY2013E	FY2014E	3-Year CAGR
Revenue	69,943	72,616	77,028	81,483	5.2%
YoY%		3.8%	6.1%	5.8%	
Operating Expenses					
Fixed (70%)	29,947	30,520	31,447	32,356	2.6%
Variable (30%)	12,835	13,325	14,135	14,952	5.2%
Total operating expenses	42,782	43,845	45,581	47,308	3.4%
Operating income	27,161	28,771	31,446	34,175	8.0%
Operating margin	38.83%	39.62%	40.82%	41.94%	
Other income (expense)	910	910	910	910	
Pre-tax income	28,071	29,681	32,356	35,085	
Provision for income taxes	4,921	5,203	5,672	6,151	
Effective tax rate	17.53%	17.53%	17.53%	17.53%	
Net income	23,150	24,478	26,684	28,934	
Weighted average shares outstanding, diluted	8,593	8,593	8,593	8,593	
Estimated EPS post-cannibalization	2.69	2.85	3.11	3.37	7.7%
Compared with pre-cannibalization:					
Estimated impact on operating margin		−61 bps	−77 bps	−96 bps	
Estimated impact on EPS (USD)		−0.13	−0.17	−0.25	−2.6%

KNOWLEDGE CHECK

Answer the following questions using the data from the exhibits on Microsoft:

1. Estimate post-cannibalization global PC shipments in FY2012 assuming a cannibalization factor of 40% for consumers and 15% for non-consumers.

   Solution:

   The number of PCs cannibalized by tablets is equal to the product of the expected number of global tablet shipments, the percentage representation of each category, and the cannibalization factor for the category. Tablet

Scenario Analysis

shipments in FY2012 are projected to be 90 million units; (90 million tablets × 92% consumer representation × 40% consumer cannibalization factor = 33.12 million consumer PCs cannibalized by tablets) + (90 million tablets × 8% non-consumer representation × 15% cannibalization = 1.08 million non-consumer PCs cannibalized by tablets) = 34.2 million total PCs cannibalized by tablets. Post-cannibalization shipments are equal to pre-cannibalization shipments minus expected cannibalization, or 360 million − 34.2 million = 325.8 million.

2. Using the results derived in Question 1, estimate the post-cannibalization revenue in FY2012 for Microsoft.

   Solution:

   The estimated impact on revenue is equal to the product of the number of PCs cannibalized and the ASP. Using the results obtained in Question 1 and the ASP data, the expected revenue impact can be calculated as (33.12 million consumer PCs cannibalized by tablets × USD85 ASP = USD2.815 billion) + (1.08 million non-consumer PCs cannibalized by tablets × USD155 ASP = USD167.4 million) = USD2.983 billion total impact on revenue for Microsoft. Post-cannibalization revenue is equal to pre-cannibalization revenue minus the estimated impact of cannibalization on revenue, or USD74.839 billion − USD2.983 billion = USD71.856 billion.

3. Using the estimate for post-cannibalization revenue derived in Question 2 and the cost structure provided, estimate post-cannibalization operating income and operating margin in FY2012 for Microsoft. Assume that fixed costs change at half the rate of the change in sales.

   Solution:

Exhibit 18: Solution to Question 3 (USD millions)

	FY2011	FY2012E	Notes
Revenue	69,943	71,856	Derived from Question 2
YoY%		2.74%	Rate of change in sales used to estimate operating expenses
Operating Expenses			
Fixed (70%)	29,947	30,357	Fixed costs change at half the rate of the change in sales, or 29,947 × (1 + 2.74%/2)
Variable (30%)	12,835	13,186	Variable costs change at the same rate as the change in sales, or 12,835 × (1 + 2.74%)
Total operating expenses	42,782	43,543	Although not shown, operating expenses include COGS

	FY2011	FY2012E	Notes
Operating income	27,161	28,313	Revenue minus total operating expenses, or 71,856 − 43,543 = 28,313
Operating margin	38.8%	39.4%	Operating income divided by revenue, or 28,313/71,856 = 39.4%

Post-cannibalization operating income and operating margin in FY2012 for Microsoft are USD28,314 million and 39.4%, respectively.

4. Using the estimate for operating income derived in Question 3 and the data in the exhibits, calculate the expected post-cannibalization EPS in FY2012 for Microsoft. Assume that other income (expense), the effective tax rate, and the diluted weighted average shares outstanding provided for FY2011 remain constant in FY2012.

Solution:

Exhibit 19: Solution to Question 4 (USD millions, except EPS and unless noted)

	FY2011	FY2012E	Notes
Revenue	69,943	71,856	
YoY%		2.74%	
Operating Expenses			
Fixed (70%)	29,947	30,357	
Variable (30%)	12,835	13,186	
Total operating expenses	42,782	43,543	
Operating income	27,161	28,314	
Operating margin	38.8%	39.4%	
Other income (expense)	910	910	
Pre-tax income	28,071	29,224	Operating income + Other income (expense), or 28,314 + 910 = 29,224
Provision for income taxes	4,921	5,123	Pre-tax income × Effective tax rate, or 29,224 × 17.53% = 5,123
Effective tax rate	17.53%	17.53%	
Net income	23,150	24,101	Pre-tax income − Provision for income taxes, or 29,224 − 5,123 = 24,101

Scenario Analysis

	FY2011	FY2012E	Notes
Weighted average shares outstanding, diluted	8,593	8,593	
Estimated EPS post-cannibalization (USD)	2.69	2.80	Net income/Wtd. avg. shs. out., or 24,101/8,593 = USD2.80

Whenever one is estimating something that depends on many different variables that are difficult to measure, we recommend altering some of the assumptions to generate a range of estimates based on various scenarios. Thus, having developed a forecast under a base case cannibalization scenario, we can analyze the sensitivity of the results by altering the cannibalization assumptions. The base case scenario corresponds to the assumptions reflected in the boxed center of the table in Exhibit 20. Exhibit 21 summarizes the results of both bull and bear case scenarios, showing the estimated FY2014 EPS under alternative estimated cannibalization factors.

Exhibit 20: Estimated FY2014 EPS Sensitivity to Changes in Cannibalization Rates (USD)

		Non-Consumer Cannibalization				
		0%	5%	10%	15%	20%
Consumer Cannibalization	15%	−0.11	−0.12	−0.14	−0.15	−0.16
	20%	−0.15	−0.16	−0.17	−0.19	−0.20
	25%	−0.19	−0.20	−0.21	−0.22	−0.23
	30%	−0.22	−0.24	−0.25	−0.26	−0.27
	35%	−0.26	−0.27	−0.28	−0.30	−0.31
	40%	−0.30	−0.31	−0.32	−0.33	−0.35
	45%	−0.34	−0.35	−0.36	−0.37	−0.38

Exhibit 21: Post-Cannibalization EPS Projections for Bull and Bear Case Scenarios (USD millions, except EPS and unless noted)

Bull Case Scenario (Cannibalization Factor: 15% Consumer/5% Non-Consumer)

	FY2011	FY2012E	FY2013E	FY2014E	3-Year CAGR
Revenue	69,943	73,728	78,553	83,583	6.1%
YoY%		5.4%	6.5%	6.4%	
Operating Expenses					
Fixed (70%)	29,947	30,758	31,764	32,781	3.1%
Variable (30%)	12,835	13,529	14,414	15,338	6.1%
Total operating expenses	42,782	44,287	46,178	48,119	4.0%

Bull Case Scenario (Cannibalization Factor: 15% Consumer/5% Non-Consumer)					
	FY2011	FY2012E	FY2013E	FY2014E	3-Year CAGR
Operating income	27,161	29,441	32,374	35,464	9.3%
Operating margin	38.83%	39.93%	41.21%	42.43%	
Other income (expense)	910	910	910	910	
Pre-tax income	28,071	30,351	33,284	36,374	
Provision for income taxes	4,921	5,321	5,835	6,377	
Effective tax rate	17.53%	17.53%	17.53%	17.53%	
Net income	23,150	25,030	27,449	29,998	
Weighted average shares outstanding, diluted	8,593	8,593	8,593	8,593	
Estimated EPS post-cannibalization (USD)	**2.69**	**2.91**	**3.19**	**3.49**	**9.0%**
Compared with pre-cannibalization:					
Estimated impact on operating margin		−30 bps	−38 bps	−47 bps	
Estimated impact on EPS (USD)		−0.07	−0.09	−0.13	−1.3%

Bear Case Scenario (cannibalization factor: 40% consumer, 20% non-consumer)					
	FY2011	FY2012E	FY2013E	FY2014E	3-Year CAGR
Revenue	69,943	71,801	75,869	79,812	4.5%
YoY%		2.7%	5.7%	5.2%	
Operating Expenses					
Fixed (70%)	29,947	30,345	31,205	32,016	2.3%
Variable (30%)	12,835	13,175	13,922	14,646	4.5%
Total operating expenses	42,782	43,520	45,127	46,662	2.9%
Operating income	27,161	28,280	30,742	33,151	6.9%
Operating margin	38.83%	39.39%	40.52%	41.54%	
Other income (expense)	910	910	910	910	
Pre-tax income	28,071	29,190	31,652	34,061	
Provision for income taxes	4,921	5,117	5,549	5,971	
Effective tax rate	17.53%	17.53%	17.53%	17.53%	
Net income	23,150	24,073	26,103	28,090	

Scenario Analysis

Bear Case Scenario (cannibalization factor: 40% consumer, 20% non-consumer)

	FY2011	FY2012E	FY2013E	FY2014E	3-Year CAGR
Weighted average shares outstanding, diluted	8,593	8,593	8,593	8,593	
Estimated EPS post-cannibalization (USD)	2.69	2.80	3.04	3.27	6.7%
Compared with pre-cannibalization:					
Estimated impact on operating margin		−84 bps	−107 bps	−136 bps	
Estimated impact on EPS (USD)		−0.18	−0.24	−0.35	−3.6%

QUESTION SET

1. For which of the following companies is it *most* crucial for an analyst to conduct scenario analysis to estimate a decline in earnings from a recession?

   A. A bank
   B. A chain of large grocery stores
   C. A provider of residential electricity

   Solution:

   A is correct, because both lending volume and interest rates typically fall in recessions, which results in declining earnings for banks. Demand for both food-at-home and residential electricity is generally not as sensitive to changes in the business cycle.

2. An analyst is preparing scenarios for a company's gross margin. Selected financial data from the prior period include the following:

   Average selling price per product EUR6.50

   Quantity sold (000s) 2,300

   Total revenues (EUR 000s) 14,950

   Cost of sales (EUR 000s) 7,475

   Gross profit (EUR 000s) 7,475

   Gross profit margin 50%

   If input prices increase by 20%, the analyst expects the company to increase selling prices by 10%, resulting in a 5% decrease in volume sold. The forecast decrease in gross profit margin is *closest* to:

   A. 4.5%
   B. 7.4%.

C. 15.0%

Solution:

A is correct.

Average selling price = EUR6.50(1.10) = EUR7.15

Quantity sold in 000s = 2,300(0.95) = 2,185

Average input cost = (7,475/2,300)(1.20) = EUR3.90

Total revenues in 000s = 2,185(EUR7.15) = 15,622.75

Gross profit in 000s = 2,185(EUR7.15 − EUR3.90) = 7,101.25

Gross profit margin
= 7,101.25/15,622.75 ≈ 45.5%, which is 4.5% less than 50%

3. The invention of a new technology that leads to lower product manufacturing costs in a highly competitive industry is *most likely* to result in:

   A. lower gross profit margins.

   B. higher gross profit margins.

   C. no impact on gross profit margins.

   Solution:

   C is correct. In a highly competitive industry, savings in manufacturing costs are likely to be passed on to customers through competition in the form of lower prices.

REFERENCES

Beyer, Anne, Daniel A. Cohen, Thomas Z. Lys, Beverly R. Walther. 2010. "The financial reporting environment: Review of the recent literature." December.Journal of Accounting and Economics, Elsevier50 (2-3): 296–343. 10.1016/j.jacceco.2010.10.003

Ciconte, Will, Marcus Kirk, Jenny Wu Tucker. 2013. Does the Midpoint of Range Earnings Forecasts Represent Managers' Expectations? (February 1, 2013). Review of Accounting Studies, 19(2): 628-660., Available at SSRN: https://ssrn.com/abstract=2061440 or

Hutton, A. P., L. F. Lee, S. Z. Shu. 2012. "Do Managers Always Know Better? The Relative Accuracy of Management and Analyst Forecasts." Journal of Accounting Research50:1217–44. 10.1111/j.1475-679X.2012.00461.x

PRACTICE PROBLEMS

1. Forecast objects should be:
   A. based on independent third-party reports.
   B. based on individual discrete items, not aggregations.
   C. disclosed regularly or based on items that are disclosed regularly.

2. Management guidance is *most* appropriately used by analysts in forecasting:
   A. capital expenditures of a company.
   B. pricing of commodities sold by a company.
   C. revenue of a company sensitive to the business cycle.

3. Which of the following is an example of a top-down driver of revenues for a passenger airline?
   A. Market share of routes
   B. Number of planes in fleet
   C. Average ticket price per mile flown

4. An analyst forecasts a company's sales using a historical results approach and top-down drivers (expected industry sales and expected market share). The analyst observes that the forecast is within the range of management guidance on sales but is toward the upper end and not closer to the midpoint. Which of the following is the *most likely* explanation for this observation?
   A. The analyst has been overly optimistic in estimating the company's expected market share.
   B. Management's true expectations are toward the upper end, but management has created a range using a pessimistic lower bound that is more easily cleared.
   C. The midpoint represents management's true expectations, and management has a lower and better estimate of market growth based on macroeconomic variables.

5. A clothing company, which initially produced designer clothing, has increasingly entered into the mass market. Which of the following approaches to forecasting revenues is *least* appropriate?
   A. Historical results
   B. Analyst's discretionary forecast
   C. Historical base rates and convergence

6. An analyst is forecasting operating costs for a company with relatively high fixed costs, sensitivity to economic conditions, and commodity inputs with volatile pricing. The company does not follow a hedging strategy for commodity purchases but tries to buy when prices are low. Which of the following is *most* appropri-

Practice Problems

ate to use in forecasting operating costs? The analyst uses:

A. analyst discretion to forecast all operating costs.

B. management guidance to forecast all operating costs.

C. management guidance to forecast fixed operating costs and analyst discretion to forecast variable operating costs.

7. An analyst notes that a company's capital expenditures do not follow a discernible pattern; the company seems to have periods of very low capital expenditures and periods of high capital expenditures. Management does not provide any guidance on capital expenditures. The analyst should develop a forecast of capital expenditures based on:

A. the company's usage of PP&E capacity.

B. the industry's average capital expenditures.

C. the company's average capital expenditures.

8. An analyst predicts that if a company's technological developments are a success, the company's operating costs will be reduced by 15%. As a result of the reduction in costs, the company will reduce the average selling price of its products by 5% and the volume of sales will increase by 8%. The company's current gross profit margin is 40%. If technological developments occur, the company's gross profit margin will be *closest* to:

A. 44.8%.

B. 46.3%.

C. 47.5%.

SOLUTIONS

1. C is correct. Forecast objects should either be disclosed regularly or be directly calculable using what is disclosed regularly. Information that is *not* disclosed regularly (such as a third-party consultancy's report) is suitable to *inform* forecasts but can be problematic for direct use, because forecasts cannot be confirmed in a timely manner. While it may be intuitive to forecast individual discrete items, such as sales and gross margin by individual product line, if gross margin is disclosed only on a consolidated basis, it will be difficult for analysts to verify their product-line gross margin estimates.

2. A is correct. Management has an advantage at the firm level and tends to make more accurate forecasts for objects that are subject to management actions, such as capital expenditures. Management does *not* have an informational advantage over investors in forecasting macroeconomic variables, such as GDP, the business cycle, or the prices of commodities. Hutton et al. (2012) found that investors have an informational advantage over management at the macroeconomic level.

3. A is correct. Market share of routes is a top-down driver of revenues and can be used to estimate an airline's market share. The number of planes in fleet and the average ticket price per mile flown are bottom-up drivers of revenues.

4. B is correct. Management has a tendency to pad its guidance to make it easier to achieve the forecast results for which management will be rewarded. Management does not have an informational advantage at the macroeconomic level.

5. A is correct. Historical results is least appropriate, because the company has changed its competitive strategy. Analyst's discretionary forecast may be appropriate, because the company is undergoing a fundamental change. The company is growing and may be transitioning to be more like the industry, in which case historical base rates and convergence may be an appropriate approach.

6. C is correct. Management has an advantage in forecasting for objects that are subject to its actions (such as capital expenditures and inventories, which affect fixed costs). The analyst is likely to have an informational advantage when it comes to forecasting economic conditions and commodity prices, which affect revenues and variable costs.

7. A is correct. Based on the company's spending pattern, it most likely makes capital expenditures based on capacity needs as it grows. If it is approaching full usage of existing capacity, it will expand.

8. B is correct.

    Sales = 100(0.95)(1.08) = 102.6

    Cost of sales = 60(0.85)(1.08) = 55.1

    Gross profit = 102.2 − 55.1 = 47.5

    Gross profit margin = 47.5/102.6 = 46.3%

LEARNING MODULE 8

Equity Valuation: Concepts and Basic Tools

by John J. Nagorniak, CFA, and Stephen E. Wilcox, PhD, CFA.

John J. Nagorniak, CFA (USA). Stephen E. Wilcox, PhD, CFA, is at Minnesota State University, Mankato (USA).

LEARNING OUTCOMES	
Mastery	The candidate should be able to:
☐	evaluate whether a security, given its current market price and a value estimate, is overvalued, fairly valued, or undervalued by the market
☐	describe major categories of equity valuation models
☐	describe regular cash dividends, extra dividends, stock dividends, stock splits, reverse stock splits, and share repurchases
☐	describe dividend payment chronology
☐	explain the rationale for using present value models to value equity and describe the dividend discount and free-cash-flow-to-equity models
☐	explain advantages and disadvantages of each category of valuation model
☐	calculate the intrinsic value of a non-callable, non-convertible preferred stock
☐	calculate and interpret the intrinsic value of an equity security based on the Gordon (constant) growth dividend discount model or a two-stage dividend discount model, as appropriate
☐	identify characteristics of companies for which the constant growth or a multistage dividend discount model is appropriate
☐	explain the rationale for using price multiples to value equity, how the price to earnings multiple relates to fundamentals, and the use of multiples based on comparables
☐	calculate and interpret the following multiples: price to earnings, price to an estimate of operating cash flow, price to sales, and price to book value
☐	describe enterprise value multiples and their use in estimating equity value
☐	describe asset-based valuation models and their use in estimating equity value

1. INTRODUCTION

Analysts gather and process information to make investment decisions, including buy and sell recommendations. What information is gathered and how it is processed depend on the analyst and the purpose of the analysis. Technical analysis uses such information as stock price and trading volume as the basis for investment decisions. Fundamental analysis uses information about the economy, industry, and company as the basis for investment decisions. Examples of fundamentals are unemployment rates, gross domestic product (GDP) growth, industry growth, and quality of and growth in company earnings. Whereas technical analysts use information to predict price movements and base investment decisions on the direction of predicted change in prices, fundamental analysts use information to estimate the value of a security and to compare the estimated value to the market price and then base investment decisions on that comparison.

This reading introduces equity valuation models used to estimate the **intrinsic value** (synonym: **fundamental value**) of a security; intrinsic value is based on an analysis of investment fundamentals and characteristics. The fundamentals to be considered depend on the analyst's approach to valuation. In a top-down approach, an analyst examines the economic environment, identifies sectors that are expected to prosper in that environment, and analyzes securities of companies from previously identified attractive sectors. In a bottom-up approach, an analyst typically follows an industry or industries and forecasts fundamentals for the companies in those industries in order to determine valuation. Whatever the approach, an analyst who estimates the intrinsic value of an equity security is implicitly questioning the accuracy of the market price as an estimate of value. Valuation is particularly important in active equity portfolio management, which aims to improve on the return–risk trade-off of a portfolio's benchmark by identifying mispriced securities.

This reading is organized as follows. Section 2 discusses the implications of differences between estimated value and market price. Section 3 introduces three major categories of valuation model. Section 4 presents an overview of present value models with a focus on the dividend discount model. Section 5 describes and examines the use of multiples in valuation. Section 6 explains asset-based valuation and demonstrates how these models can be used to estimate value. Section 7 states conclusions and summarizes the reading.

2. ESTIMATED VALUE AND MARKET PRICE

☐ evaluate whether a security, given its current market price and a value estimate, is overvalued, fairly valued, or undervalued by the market

By comparing estimates of value and market price, an analyst can arrive at one of three conclusions: The security is *undervalued*, *overvalued*, or *fairly valued* in the marketplace. For example, if the market price of an asset is $10 and the analyst estimates intrinsic value at $10, a logical conclusion is that the security is fairly valued. If the security is selling for $20, the security would be considered overvalued. If the security is selling for $5, the security would be considered undervalued. Basically, by estimating value, the analyst is assuming that the market price is not necessarily the best estimate of intrinsic value. If the estimated value exceeds the market price, the analyst infers the security is *undervalued*. If the estimated value equals the market price, the analyst infers the security is *fairly valued*. If the estimated value is less than the market price, the analyst infers the security is *overvalued*.

In practice, the conclusion is not so straightforward. Analysts must cope with uncertainties related to model appropriateness and the correct value of inputs. An analyst's final conclusion depends not only on the comparison of the estimated value and the market price but also on the analyst's confidence in the estimated value (i.e., in the model selected and the inputs used in it). One can envision a spectrum running from relatively high confidence in the valuation model *and* the inputs to relatively low confidence in the valuation model *and/or* the inputs. When confidence is relatively low, the analyst might demand a substantial divergence between his or her own value estimate and the market price before acting on an apparent mispricing. For instance, if the estimate of intrinsic value is $10 and the market price is $10.05, the analyst might reasonably conclude that the security is fairly valued and that the 1/2 of 1 percent market price difference from the estimated value is within the analyst's confidence interval.

Confidence in the convergence of the market price to the intrinsic value over the investment time horizon relevant to the objectives of the portfolio must also be taken into account before an analyst acts on an apparent mispricing or makes a buy, sell, or hold recommendation: The ability to benefit from identifying a mispriced security depends on the market price converging to the estimated intrinsic value.

In seeking to identify mispricing and attractive investments, analysts are treating market prices with skepticism, but they are also treating market prices with respect. For example, an analyst who finds that many securities examined appear to be overvalued will typically recheck models and inputs before acting on a conclusion of overvaluation. Analysts also often recognize and factor into recommendations that different market segments—such as securities closely followed by analysts versus securities relatively neglected by analysts—may differ in how common or persistent mispricing is. Mispricing may be more likely in securities neglected by analysts.

EXAMPLE 1

Valuation and Analyst Response

1. An analyst finds that all the securities analyzed have estimated values higher than their market prices. The securities all appear to be:

   A. overvalued.

   B. undervalued.

   C. fairly valued.

Solution to 1:

B is correct. The estimated intrinsic value for each security is greater than the market price. The securities all appear to be undervalued in the market. Note, however, that the analyst may wish to reexamine the model and inputs to check that the conclusion is valid.

2. An analyst finds that nearly all companies in a market segment have common shares which are trading at market prices above the analyst's estimate of the shares' values. This market segment is widely followed by analysts. Which of the following statements describes the analyst's *most appropriate* first action?

   A. Issue a sell recommendation for each share issue.

> B. Issue a buy recommendation for each share issue.
>
> C. Reexamine the models and inputs used for the valuations.
>
> **Solution to 2:**
>
> C is correct. It seems improbable that all the share issues analyzed are overvalued, as indicated by market prices in excess of estimated value—particularly because the market segment is widely followed by analysts. Thus, the analyst will not issue a sell recommendation for each issue. The analyst will *most appropriately* reexamine the models and inputs prior to issuing any recommendations. A buy recommendation is not an appropriate response to an overvalued security.
>
> 3. An analyst, using a number of models and a range of inputs, estimates a security's value to be between ¥250 and ¥270. The security is trading at ¥265. The security appears to be:
>
>   A. overvalued.
>
>   B. undervalued.
>
>   C. fairly valued.
>
> **Solution to 3:**
>
> C is correct. The security's market price of ¥265 is within the range estimated by the analyst. The security appears to be fairly valued.

Analysts often use a variety of models and inputs to achieve greater confidence in their estimates of intrinsic value. The use of more than one model and a range of inputs also helps the analyst understand the sensitivity of value estimates to different models and inputs.

3. CATEGORIES OF EQUITY VALUATION MODELS

| | describe major categories of equity valuation models

Three major categories of equity valuation models are as follows:

- **Present value models** (synonym: **discounted cash flow models**). These models estimate the intrinsic value of a security as the present value of the future benefits expected to be received from the security. In present value models, benefits are often defined in terms of cash expected to be distributed to shareholders (**dividend discount models**) or in terms of cash flows available to be distributed to shareholders after meeting capital expenditure and working capital needs (**free-cash-flow-to-equity models**). Many models fall within this category, ranging from the relatively simple to the very complex. In Section 4, we discuss in detail two of the simpler models, the Gordon (constant) growth model and the two-stage dividend discount models.

- **Multiplier models** (synonym: **market multiple models**). These models are based chiefly on share price multiples or enterprise value multiples. The former model estimates intrinsic value of a common share from a price multiple for some fundamental variable, such as revenues, earnings, cash flows, or book value. Examples of the multiples include price to earnings (P/E, share price divided by earnings per share) and price to sales (P/S, share price divided by sales per share). The fundamental variable may be stated on a forward basis (e.g., forecasted EPS for the next year) or a trailing basis (e.g., EPS for the past year), as long as the usage is consistent across companies being examined. Price multiples are also used to compare relative values. The use of the ratio of share price to EPS—that is, the P/E multiple—to judge relative value is an example of this approach to equity valuation.

Enterprise value (EV) multiples have the form (Enterprise value)/(Value of a fundamental variable). Two possible choices for the denominator are earnings before interest, taxes, depreciation, and amortization (EBITDA) and total revenue. Enterprise value, the numerator, is a measure of a company's total market value from which cash and short-term investments have been subtracted (because an acquirer could use those assets to pay for acquiring the company). An estimate of common share value can be calculated indirectly from the EV multiple; the value of liabilities and preferred shares can be subtracted from the EV to arrive at the value of common equity.

- **Asset-based valuation models**. These models estimate intrinsic value of a common share from the estimated value of the assets of a corporation minus the estimated value of its liabilities and preferred shares. The estimated market value of the assets is often determined by making adjustments to the **book value** (synonym: **carrying value**) of assets and liabilities. The theory underlying the asset-based approach is that the value of a business is equal to the sum of the value of the business's assets.

As already mentioned, many analysts use more than one type of model to estimate value. Analysts recognize that each model is a simplification of the real world and that there are uncertainties related to model appropriateness and the inputs to the models. The choice of model(s) will depend on the availability of information to input into the model(s) and the analyst's confidence in the information and in the appropriateness of the model(s).

EXAMPLE 2

Categories of Equity Valuation Models

1. An analyst is estimating the intrinsic value of a new company. The analyst has one year of financial statements for the company and has calculated the average values of a variety of price multiples for the industry in which the company operates. The analyst plans to use at least one model from each of the three categories of valuation models. The analyst is *least likely* to rely on the estimate(s) from the:

   A. multiplier model(s).
   B. present value model(s).
   C. asset-based valuation model(s).

   ### Solution to 1:

   B is correct. Because the company has only one year of data available, the analyst is *least likely* to be confident in the inputs for a present value model. The values on the balance sheet, even before adjustment, are likely to be close to market values because the assets are all relatively new. The multiplier models are based on average multiples from the industry.

2. Based on a company's EPS of €1.35, an analyst estimates the intrinsic value of a security to be €16.60. Which type of model is the analyst *most likely* to be using to estimate intrinsic value?

   A. Multiplier model.
   B. Present value model.
   C. Asset-based valuation model.

Solution to 2:

A is correct. The analyst is using a multiplier model based on the P/E multiple. The P/E multiple used was 16.60/1.35 = 12.3.

As you begin the study of specific equity valuation models in the next section, you must bear in mind that any model of value is, by necessity, a simplification of the real world. Never forget this simple fact! You may encounter models much more complicated than the ones discussed here, but even those models will be simplifications of reality.

4 BACKGROUND FOR THE DIVIDEND DISCOUNT MODEL

☐ describe regular cash dividends, extra dividends, stock dividends, stock splits, reverse stock splits, and share repurchases

☐ describe dividend payment chronology

Present value models follow a fundamental tenet of economics which states that individuals defer consumption—that is, they invest—for the future benefits expected. Individuals and companies make an investment because they expect thereby to earn a rate of return over the investment period. Logically, the value of an investment should be equal to the present value of the expected future benefits. For common shares, an analyst can equate benefits to the cash flows to be generated by the investment. The simplest present value model of equity valuation is the dividend discount model (DDM), which specifies cash flows from a common stock investment to be dividends.

The next section describes aspects of dividends that users of dividend discount models should understand.

Dividends: Background for the Dividend Discount Model

Generally, there are two sources of return from investing in equities: (1) cash dividends received by an investor over his or her holding period and (2) the change in the market price of equities over that holding period.

A **dividend** is a distribution paid to shareholders based on the number of shares owned, and a cash dividend is a cash distribution made to a company's shareholders. Cash dividends are typically paid out regularly at known intervals; such dividends are known as regular cash dividends. By contrast, an **extra dividend** or **special dividend** is a dividend paid by a company that does not pay dividends on a regular schedule or a dividend that supplements regular cash dividends with an extra payment. Companies in cyclical industries and companies undergoing corporate and/or financial restructuring are among those observed to use extra dividends.[1]

The payment of dividends is not a legal obligation: dividends must be declared (i.e., authorized) by a company's board of directors; in some jurisdictions, they must also be approved by shareholders. Regular cash dividends are customarily declared and paid out quarterly in the United States and Canada; semiannually in Europe and Japan; and annually in some other countries, including China.

Dividend discount models address discounting expected cash dividends. A **stock dividend** (also known as a **bonus issue of shares**) is a type of dividend in which a company distributes additional shares of its common stock (typically, 2%–10% of the shares then outstanding) to shareholders instead of cash. A stock dividend divides the "pie" (the market value of shareholders' equity) into smaller pieces without affecting the value of the pie or any shareholder's proportional ownership in the company. Thus, stock dividends are not relevant for valuation. Stock splits and reverse stock splits are similar to stock dividends in that they have no economic effect on the company or shareholders. A **stock split** involves an increase in the number of shares outstanding with a consequent decrease in share price. An example of a stock split is a two-for-one stock split in which each shareholder is issued an additional share for each share currently owned. A **reverse stock split** involves a reduction in the number of shares outstanding with a corresponding increase in share price. In a one-for-two reverse stock split, each shareholder would receive one new share for every two old shares held, thereby reducing the number of shares outstanding by half.

In contrast to stock dividends and stock splits, share repurchases are an alternative to cash dividend payments. A **share repurchase** (or **buyback**) is a transaction in which a company uses cash to buy back its own shares. Shares that have been repurchased are not considered for dividends, voting, or computing earnings per share. A share repurchase is viewed as equivalent to the payment of cash dividends of equal value in terms of the effect on shareholders' wealth, all other things being equal. Company managements have expressed several key reasons for engaging in share repurchases—namely, (1) signaling a belief that their shares are undervalued (or, more generally, to support share prices), (2) flexibility in the amount and timing of distributing cash to shareholders, (3) tax efficiency in markets where tax rates on dividends exceed tax rates on capital gains, and (4) the ability to absorb increases in outstanding shares because of the exercise of employee stock options.

The payout of regular cash dividends to common shareholders follows a fairly standard chronology that is set in motion once the company's board of directors votes to pay the dividend. First is the **declaration date**, the day that the company issues a statement declaring a specific dividend. Next comes the **ex-dividend date** (or ex-date), the first date that a share trades without (i.e., "ex") the dividend. This is followed closely (one or two business days later) by the **holder-of-record date** (also called the owner-of-record date, shareholder-of-record date, record date, date of record, or date of book closure), the date that a shareholder listed on the company's books will be deemed to have ownership of the shares for purposes of receiving the upcoming dividend; the amount of time between the ex-date and the holder-of-record date is linked to the trade settlement cycle in force. The final milestone is the **payment date** (or **payable date**), which is the day that the company actually mails out (or electronically transfers) a dividend payment to shareholders.

---

[1] Another type of dividend is a liquidating dividend, which is a return of capital rather than a distribution from earnings or retained earnings. Liquidating dividends are used when a company goes out of business and distributes its net assets, sells a portion of its business for cash and distributes the sale's proceeds, or pays a dividend that exceeds its accumulated retained earnings.

> **EXAMPLE 3**
>
> ### Total S.A. Dividend Payment Time Line
>
> On 26 May 2017, Total S.A., one of the world's largest integrated energy companies, declared an annual dividend of €2.48 per share, payable on a quarterly basis. The first quarterly dividend of €2.48/4 = €0.62 was payable on 12 October 2017. The holder-of-record date was 26 September, and the ex-dividend date was 25 September. A timeline for the upcoming Total S.A. quarterly dividend is shown in Exhibit 1.
>
> **Exhibit 1: Timeline for Total S.A. Quarterly Dividend**
>
>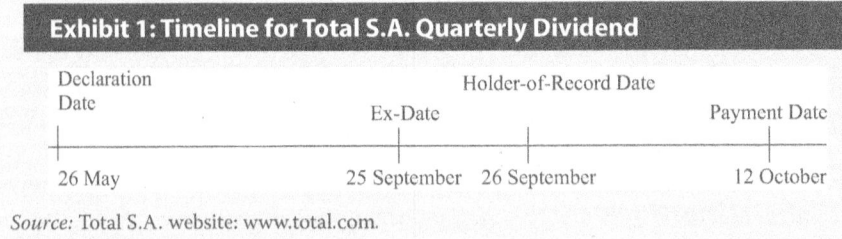
>
> *Source:* Total S.A. website: www.total.com.

Because buyers of a company's shares on the ex-dividend date are no longer eligible to receive the upcoming dividend, all else being equal, on that day the company's share price immediately decreases by the amount of the foregone dividend. Exhibit 2 illustrates the decrease in share price that occurs for a hypothetical company that has declared a $1.00 per share dividend as trading begins on its ex-dividend date.

Exhibit 2: Stock Price Change for Hypothetical Company on Ex-Dividend Date

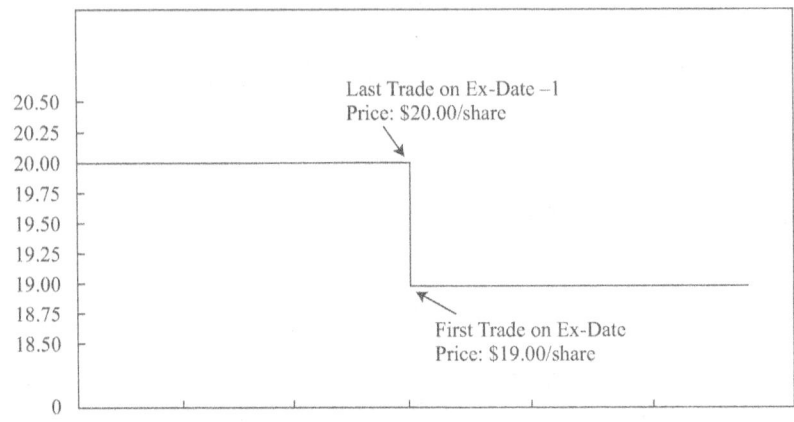

Note: Assumes dividend declared is $1 per share and convention for stock trade settlement is $T + 3$.

DIVIDEND DISCOUNT MODEL (DDM) AND FREE-CASH-FLOW-TO-EQUITY MODEL (FCFE)

5

- ☐ explain the rationale for using present value models to value equity and describe the dividend discount and free-cash-flow-to-equity models
- ☐ explain advantages and disadvantages of each category of valuation model

If the issuing company is assumed to be a going concern, the intrinsic value of a share is the present value of expected future dividends. If a constant required rate of return is also assumed, then the DDM expression for the intrinsic value of a share is Equation 1:

$$V_0 = \sum_{t=1}^{\infty} \frac{D_t}{(1+r)^t} \qquad (1)$$

where

V_0 = value of a share of stock today, at $t = 0$

D_t = expected dividend in year t, assumed to be paid at the end of the year

r = required rate of return on the stock

At the shareholder level, cash received from a common stock investment includes any dividends received and the proceeds when shares are sold. If an investor intends to buy and hold a share for one year, the value of the share today is the present value of two cash flows—namely, the expected dividend *plus* the expected selling price in one year:

$$V_0 = \frac{D_1 + P_1}{(1+r)^1} = \frac{D_1}{(1+r)^1} + \frac{P_1}{(1+r)^1} \qquad (2)$$

where P_1 = the expected price per share at $t = 1$.

To estimate the expected selling price, P_1, the analyst could estimate the price another investor with a one-year holding period would pay for the share in one year. If V_0 is based on D_1 and P_1, it follows that P_1 could be estimated from D_2 and P_2:

$$P_1 = \frac{D_2 + P_2}{(1+r)}$$

Substituting the right side of this equation for P_1 in Equation 2 results in V_0 estimated as

$$V_0 = \frac{D_1}{(1+r)} + \frac{D_2 + P_2}{(1+r)^2} = \frac{D_1}{(1+r)} + \frac{D_2}{(1+r)^2} + \frac{P_2}{(1+r)^2}$$

Repeating this process, we find the value for n holding periods is the present value of the expected dividends for the n periods plus the present value of the expected price in n periods:

$$V_0 = \frac{D_1}{(1+r)^1} + \cdots + \frac{D_n}{(1+r)^n} + \frac{P_n}{(1+r)^n}$$

Using summation notation to represent the present value of the n expected dividends, we arrive at the general expression for an n-period holding period or investment horizon:

$$V_0 = \sum_{t=1}^{n} \frac{D_t}{(1+r)^t} + \frac{P_n}{(1+r)^n} \qquad (3)$$

The expected value of a share at the end of the investment horizon—in effect, the expected selling price—is often referred to as the **terminal stock value** (or **terminal value**).

> **EXAMPLE 4**
>
> ## Estimating Share Value for a Three-Year Investment Horizon
>
> 1. For the next three years, the annual dividends of a stock are expected to be €2.00, €2.10, and €2.20. The stock price is expected to be €20.00 at the end of three years. If the required rate of return on the shares is 10 percent, what is the estimated value of a share?
>
> ### Solution:
>
> The present values of the expected future cash flows can be written as follows:
>
> $$V_0 = \frac{2.00}{(1.10)^1} + \frac{2.10}{(1.10)^2} + \frac{2.20}{(1.10)^3} + \frac{20.00}{(1.10)^3}$$
>
> Calculating and summing these present values gives an estimated share value of V_0 = 1.818 + 1.736 + 1.653 + 15.026 = €20.23.
> The three dividends have a total present value of €5.207, and the terminal stock value has a present value of €15.026, for a total estimated value of €20.23.

Extending the holding period into the indefinite future, we can say that a stock's estimated value is the present value of all expected future dividends as shown in Equation 1.

Consideration of an indefinite future is valid because businesses established as corporations are generally set up to operate indefinitely. This general form of the DDM applies even in the case in which the investor has a finite investment horizon. For that investor, stock value today depends *directly* on the dividends the investor expects to receive before the stock is sold and depends *indirectly* on the expected dividends for periods subsequent to that sale, because those expected future dividends determine the expected selling price. Thus, the general expression given by Equation 1 holds irrespective of the investor's holding period.

In practice, many analysts prefer to use a free-cash-flow-to-equity (FCFE) valuation model. These analysts assume that dividend-paying *capacity* should be reflected in the cash flow estimates rather than *expected dividends*. FCFE is a measure of dividend-paying capacity. Analysts may also use FCFE valuation models for a non-dividend-paying stock. To use a DDM, the analyst needs to predict the timing and amount of the first dividend and all the dividends or dividend growth thereafter. Making these predictions for non-dividend-paying stock accurately is typically difficult, so in such cases, analysts often resort to FCFE models.

The calculation of FCFE starts with the calculation of cash flow from operations (CFO). CFO is simply defined as net income plus non-cash expenses minus investment in working capital. FCFE is a measure of cash flow generated in a period that is available for distribution to common shareholders. What does "available for distribution" mean? The entire CFO is *not* available for distribution; the portion of the CFO needed for fixed capital investment (FCInv) during the period to maintain the value of the company as a going concern is *not* viewed as available for distribution to

Dividend Discount Model (DDM) and Free-Cash-Flow-to-Equity Model (FCFE)

common shareholders. Net amounts borrowed (borrowings minus repayments) are considered to be available for distribution to common shareholders. Thus, FCFE can be expressed as

$$\text{FCFE} = \text{CFO} - \text{FCInv} + \text{Net borrowing} \qquad (4)$$

The information needed to calculate historical FCFE is available from a company's statement of cash flows and financial disclosures. Frequently, under the assumption that management is acting in the interest of maintaining the value of the company as a going concern, reported capital expenditure is taken to represent FCInv. Analysts must make projections of financials to forecast future FCFE. Valuation obtained by using FCFE involves discounting expected future FCFE by the required rate of return on equity; the expression parallels Equation 1:

$$V_0 = \sum_{t=1}^{\infty} \frac{\text{FCFE}_t}{(1+r)^t}$$

EXAMPLE 5

Present Value Models

1. An investor expects a share to pay dividends of $3.00 and $3.15 at the end of Years 1 and 2, respectively. At the end of the second year, the investor expects the shares to trade at $40.00. The required rate of return on the shares is 8 percent. If the investor's forecasts are accurate and the market price of the shares is currently $30, the *most likely* conclusion is that the shares are:

    A. overvalued.
    B. undervalued.
    C. fairly valued.

    Solution to 1:

    B is correct.

    $$V_0 = \frac{3.00}{(1.08)^1} + \frac{3.15}{(1.08)^2} + \frac{40.00}{(1.08)^2} = 39.77$$

    The value estimate of $39.77 exceeds the market price of $30, so the conclusion is that the shares are undervalued.

2. Two investors with different holding periods but the same expectations and required rate of return for a company are estimating the intrinsic value of a common share of the company. The investor with the shorter holding period will *most likely* estimate a:

    A. lower intrinsic value.
    B. higher intrinsic value.
    C. similar intrinsic value.

    Solution to 2:

    C is correct. The intrinsic value of a security is independent of the investor's holding period.

3. An equity valuation model that focuses on expected dividends rather than the capacity to pay dividends is the:

    A. dividend discount model.

B. free cash flow to equity model.

C. cash flow return on investment model.

Solution to 3:

A is correct. Dividend discount models focus on expected dividends.

How is the required rate of return for use in present value models estimated? To estimate the required rate of return on a share, analysts frequently use the capital asset pricing model (CAPM):

$$\text{Required rate of return on share } i = \text{Current expected risk-free rate of return} + \text{Beta}_i \left[\text{Market (equity) risk premium}\right] \quad (5)$$

Equation 5 states that the required rate of return on a share is the sum of the current expected risk-free rate plus a risk premium that equals the product of the stock's beta (a measure of non-diversifiable risk) and the market risk premium (the expected return of the market in excess of the risk-free return, where in practice, the "market" is often represented by a broad stock market index). However, even if analysts agree that the CAPM is an appropriate model, their inputs into the CAPM may differ. Thus, there is no uniquely correct answer to the question: What is the required rate of return?

Other common methods for estimating the required rate of return for the stock of a company include adding a risk premium that is based on economic judgments, rather than the CAPM, to an appropriate risk-free rate (usually a government bond) and adding a risk premium to the yield on the company's bonds. Good business and economic judgment is paramount in estimating the required rate of return. In many investment firms, required rates of return are determined by firm policy.

6 PREFERRED STOCK VALUATION

- [ ] calculate the intrinsic value of a non-callable, non-convertible preferred stock
- [ ] explain advantages and disadvantages of each category of valuation model

General dividend discount models are relatively easy to apply to preferred shares. In its simplest form, **preferred stock** is a form of equity (generally, non-voting) that has priority over common stock in the receipt of dividends and on the issuer's assets in the event of a company's liquidation. It may have a stated maturity date at which time payment of the stock's par (face) value is made or it may be perpetual with no maturity date; additionally, it may be callable or convertible.

For a non-callable, non-convertible perpetual preferred share paying a level dividend D and assuming a constant required rate of return over time, Equation 1 reduces to the formula for the present value of a perpetuity. Its value is:

$$V_0 = \frac{D_0}{r} \quad (6)$$

For example, a $100 par value non-callable perpetual preferred stock offers an annual dividend of $5.50. If its required rate of return is 6 percent, the value estimate would be $5.50/0.06 = $91.67.

Preferred Stock Valuation

For a non-callable, non-convertible preferred stock with maturity at time n, the estimated intrinsic value can be estimated by using Equation 3 but using the preferred stock's par value, F, instead of P_n:

$$V_0 = \sum_{t=1}^{n} \frac{D_t}{(1+r)^t} + \frac{F}{(1+r)^n} \qquad (7)$$

When Equation 7 is used, the most precise approach is to use values for n, r, and D that reflect the payment schedule of the dividends. This method is similar to the practice of fixed-income analysts in valuing a bond. For example, a non-convertible preferred stock with a par value of £20.00, maturity in six years, a nominal required rate of return of 8.20 percent, and semiannual dividends of £2.00 would be valued by using an n of 12, an r of 4.10 percent, a D of £2.00, and an F of £20.00. The result would be an estimated value of £31.01. Assuming payments are annual rather than semiannual (i.e., assuming that $n = 6$, $r = 8.20$ percent, and $D = £4.00$) would result in an estimated value of £30.84.

Preferred stock issues are frequently callable (redeemable) by the issuer at some point prior to maturity, often at par value or at prices in excess of par value that decline to par value as the maturity date approaches. Such call options tend to reduce the value of a preferred issue to an investor because the option to redeem will be exercised by the issuer when it is in the issuer's favor and ignored when it is not. For example, if an issuer can redeem shares at par value that would otherwise trade (on the basis of dividends, maturity, and required rate of return) above par value, the issuer has motivation to redeem the shares.

Preferred stock issues can also include a retraction option that enables the holder of the preferred stock to sell the shares back to the issuer prior to maturity on prespecified terms. Essentially, the holder of the shares has a put option. Such put options tend to increase the value of a preferred issue to an investor because the option to retract will be exercised by the investor when it is in the investor's favor and ignored when it is not. Although the precise valuation of issues with such embedded options is beyond the scope of this reading, Example 6 includes a case in which Equation 7 can be used to approximate the value of a callable, retractable preferred share.

EXAMPLE 6

Preferred Share Valuation: Two Cases

Case 1: Non-callable, Non-convertible, Perpetual Preferred Shares

The following facts concerning the Union Electric Company 4.75 percent perpetual preferred shares are as follows:

- Issuer: Union Electric Co. (owned by Ameren)
- Par value: US$100
- Dividend: US$4.75 per year
- Maturity: perpetual
- Embedded options: none
- Credit rating: Moody's Investors Service/Standard & Poor's Ba1/BB
- Required rate of return on Ba1/BB rated preferred shares as of valuation date: 7.5 percent.

1. Estimate the intrinsic value of this preferred share.

   Solution

   Basing the discount rate on the required rate of return on Ba1/BB rated preferred shares of 7.5 percent gives an intrinsic value estimate of US$4.75/0.075 = US$63.33.

2. Explain whether the intrinsic value of this issue would be higher or lower if the issue were callable (with all other facts remaining unchanged).

   Solution

   The intrinsic value would be lower if the issue were callable. The option to redeem or call the issue is valuable to the issuer because the call will be exercised when doing so is in the issuer's interest. The intrinsic value of the shares to the investor will typically be lower if the issue is callable. In this case, because the intrinsic value without the call is much less than the par value, the issuer would be unlikely to redeem the issue if it were callable; thus, callability would reduce intrinsic value, but only slightly.

Case 2: Retractable Term Preferred Shares

Retractable term preferred shares are a type of preferred share that has been previously issued by Canadian companies, and have now began to be offered by companies in other jurisdictions, including Japan. This type of issue specifies a "retraction date" when the preferred shareholders have the option to sell back their shares to the issuer at par value (i.e., the shares are "retractable" or "putable" at that date).[2] At predetermined dates prior to the retraction date, the issuer has the option to redeem the preferred issue at predetermined prices (which are always at or above par value).

An example of a retractable term preferred share currently outstanding is TMC (Toyota Motor Corporation), First Series Model AA class shares, with a 0.5 percent dividend rate, increasing by 0.5 percent every year until 2020 and thereafter, becoming fixed at 2.5 percent. TMC is leading global automobile manufacturer, with headquarters in Japan and global operations. The issue is in Japanese Yen. The shares have a ¥10,598 par value and pay a semiannual dividend of ¥26.5 [= (0.5 percent × ¥10,598)/2] on 31 March 2016. The semiannual dividend is expected to increase to ¥132.5 [= (2.5 percent × ¥10,598)/2] on 31 March 2020 and beyond. As of 31 December 2017 the company carried ratings from Moody's and Standard & Poor's of Aa3 and AA–, respectively. Thus, the shares are viewed by Moody's and Standard & Poor's as having "adequate" credit quality, qualified by "Aa3 and AA–," which means relatively high quality within that group. Beginning from 2 April 2021, the shares are redeemable at the option of TMC at ¥10,598 (par value). The retraction date is the last day of March, June, September, and December of each year, starting from 1 September 2020, with the shares retractable at par value. The Series AA shares have voting rights and may exercise their voting rights and other rights held by holders of common shares of TMC in the same manner. The Series AA shares were issued at a 20% premium to the common shares price in 2015, and since then the share price has decreased to ¥7,243 as at 31 December 2017, and with a current required rate of 3.05 per year (1.525 percent semiannual). Because the issue's market price is so far below the prices at which TMC could redeem or call the issue, redemption is considered to be unlikely by TMC, whereas the retraction option for the Series

---

[2] "Retraction" refers to this option, which is a put option. The terminology is not completely settled: The type of share being called "retractable term preferred" is also known as "hard retractable preferred," with "hard" referring to payment in cash rather than common shares at the retraction date.

AA holders appears to have a significant value since they will potentially be able to put back the shares to TMC at approximately 45 percent over the current market value (¥10,598 compared to ¥7,243).

3. Assume that the issue will be retracted in December 2020; the holders of the shares will put the shares to the company in December 2020. Based on the information given, estimate the intrinsic value of a share. Assume it is December 2017.

Solution

An intrinsic value estimate of a share of this preferred issue is ¥10,279. Expected semiannual dividends:

Year ended March 31, 2018: ¥79.5 [= (1.5 percent × ¥10,598)/2]

Year ended March 31, 2019: ¥106 [= (2.0 percent × ¥10,598)/2]

Year ended March 31, 2020: ¥132.5 [= (2.5 percent × ¥10,598)/2]

$$V_0 = \left[\frac{¥79.5}{1.01525} + \frac{¥79.5}{1.01525^2} + \frac{¥106}{1.01525^3} + \frac{¥106}{1.01525^4} + \frac{¥132.5}{1.01525^5} + \frac{¥132.5}{1.01525^6} + \frac{¥10,598}{1.01525^6}\right]$$
$$\approx ¥10,279$$

The difference between the current market price of ¥7,243 and the intrinsic value of ¥10,279 is the implied value of retractable option given to the holders of the Series AA shares.

THE GORDON GROWTH MODEL 7

- ☐ calculate and interpret the intrinsic value of an equity security based on the Gordon (constant) growth dividend discount model or a two-stage dividend discount model, as appropriate
- ☐ identify characteristics of companies for which the constant growth or a multistage dividend discount model is appropriate
- ☐ explain advantages and disadvantages of each category of valuation model

A rather obvious problem when one is trying to implement Equation 1 for common equity is that it requires the analyst to estimate an infinite series of expected dividends. To simplify this process, analysts frequently make assumptions about how dividends will grow or change over time. The Gordon (constant) growth model (Gordon, 1962) is a simple and well-recognized DDM. The model assumes dividends grow indefinitely at a constant rate.

Because of its assumption of a constant growth rate, the Gordon growth model is particularly appropriate for valuing the equity of dividend-paying companies that are relatively insensitive to the business cycle and in a mature growth phase. Examples might include an electric utility serving a slowly growing area or a producer of a staple food product (e.g., bread). A history of increasing the dividend at a stable growth rate is another practical criterion if the analyst believes that pattern will hold in the future.

With a constant growth assumption, Equation 1 can be written as Equation 8, where g is the constant growth rate:

$$V_0 = \sum_{t=1}^{\infty} \frac{D_0(1+g)^t}{(1+r)^t} = D_0\left[\frac{(1+g)}{(1+r)} + \frac{(1+g)^2}{(1+r)^2} + \ldots + \frac{(1+g)^\infty}{(1+r)^\infty}\right] \quad (8)$$

If required return r is assumed to be strictly greater than growth rate g, then the square-bracketed term in Equation 8 is an infinite geometric series and sums to $[(1 + g)/(r - g)]$. Substituting into Equation 8 produces the Gordon growth model as presented in Equation 9:

$$V_0 = \frac{D_0(1+g)}{r-g} = \frac{D_1}{r-g} \quad (9)$$

For an illustration of the expression, suppose the current (most recent) annual dividend on a share is €5.00 and dividends are expected to grow at 4 percent per year. The required rate of return on equity is 8 percent. The Gordon growth model estimate of intrinsic value is, therefore, €5.00(1.04)/(0.08 − 0.04) = €5.20/0.04 = €130 per share. Note that the numerator is D_1 not D_0. (Using the wrong numerator is a common error.)

The Gordon growth model estimates intrinsic value as the present value of a growing perpetuity. If the growth rate, g, is assumed to be zero, Equation 8 reduces to the expression for the present value of a perpetuity, given earlier as Equation 6.

In estimating a long-term growth rate, analysts use a variety of methods, including assessing the growth in dividends or earnings over time, using the industry median growth rate, and using the relationship shown in Equation 10 to estimate the sustainable growth rate:

$$g = b \times \text{ROE} \quad (10)$$

where

g = dividend growth rate

b = earnings retention rate = (1 − Dividend payout ratio)

ROE = return on equity

Example 7 illustrates the application of the Gordon growth model to the shares of a large industrial manufacturing company. The analyst believes it will continue to grow at a rate that it achieved in the previous three years and remain stable in the future. The example asks how much the dividend growth assumption adds to the intrinsic value estimate. The question is relevant to valuation because if the amount is high on a percentage basis, a large part of the value of the share depends on the realization of the growth estimate. One can answer the question by subtracting from the intrinsic value estimate determined by Equation 9 the value determined by Equation 6, which assumes no dividend growth.[3]

EXAMPLE 7

Applying the Gordon Growth Model

Siemens AG operates in the capital goods and technology space. It is involved in the engineering, manufacturing, automation, power, and transportation sectors. It operates globally and is one of the largest companies in the sectors in which it operates. It is a substantial employer in both its original, domestic German market, as well as dozens of countries around the world. Selected financial information for Siemens appears in Exhibit 3.

---

[3] A related concept, the present value of growth opportunities (PVGO), is discussed in more advanced readings.

The Gordon Growth Model

Exhibit 3: Selected Financial Information for Siemens AG

Year	2017	2016	2015	2014	2013
EPS	€7.45	€6.74	€8.85	€6.37	€5.08
DPS	€3.7	€3.6	€3.5	€3.3	€3.0
Payout ratio	50%	53%	40%	52%	59%
ROE	15.6%	15.9%	22.3%	18.2%	14.6%
Share price (XETRA - Frankfurt)	€119.2	€104.2	€79.94	€94.37	€89.06

Note: DPS stands for "dividends per share."

Source: Morningstar, www.siemens.com.

The analyst estimates the growth rate to be approximately 5.4 percent based on the dividend growth rate over the period 2013 to 2017 [$3(1 + g)^4 = 3.7$, so $g = 5.4\%$]. To verify that the estimated growth rate of 5.4 percent is feasible in the future, the analyst also uses the average of Siemens's retention rate and ROE for the previous five years ($g \approx 0.49 \times 17.3\% \approx 8.5\%$) to estimate the sustainable growth rate.

Using a number of approaches, including adding a risk premium to a long-term German government bond and using the CAPM, the analyst estimates a required return of 7.5 percent. The most recent dividend of €3.70 is used for D_0.

1. Use the Gordon growth model to estimate Siemens's intrinsic value.

Solution to 1:

$$V_0 = \frac{€3.70(1 + 0.054)}{0.075 - 0.054} = €185.70$$

2. How much does the dividend growth assumption add to the intrinsic value estimate?

Solution to 2:

$$€185.70 - \frac{€3.70}{0.075} = €136.37$$

3. Based on the estimated intrinsic value, is a share of Siemens undervalued, overvalued, or fairly valued?

Solution to 3:

A share of Siemens appears to be undervalued. The analyst, before making a recommendation, might consider how realistic the estimated inputs are and check the sensitivity of the estimated value to changes in the inputs.

4. What is the intrinsic value if the growth rate estimate is lowered to 4.4 percent?

Solution to 4:

$$V_0 = \frac{€3.70(1 + 0.044)}{0.075 - 0.044} = €124.61$$

5. What is the intrinsic value if the growth rate estimate is lowered to 4.4 percent and the required rate of return estimate is increased to 8.5 percent?

Solution to 5:

$$V_0 = \frac{€3.70(1 + 0.044)}{0.085 - 0.044} = €94.21$$

The Gordon growth model estimate of intrinsic value is extremely sensitive to the choice of required rate of return r and growth rate g. It is possible that the growth rate assumption and the required return assumption used initially were too high. Worldwide economic growth is typically in the low single digits, which may mean that a large company such as Siemens may struggle to grow dividends at 5.4 percent into perpetuity. Exhibit 4 presents a further sensitivity analysis of Siemens's intrinsic value to the required return and growth estimates.

Exhibit 4: Sensitivity Analysis of the Intrinsic-Value Estimate for Siemens AG

	g = 2.5%	g = 3.5%	g = 4.5%	g = 5.5%	g = 6.5%
r = 6%	€108.4	€153.2	€257.8	€780.7	—
r = 7%	€84.3	€109.4	€154.7	€260.2	€788.1
r = 8%	€69.0	€85.1	€110.5	€156.1	€262.7
r = 9%	€58.3	€69.6	€85.9	€111.5	€157.6
r = 10%	€50.6	€58.9	€70.3	€86.7	€112.6

Note that no value is shown when the growth rate exceeds the required rate of return. The Gordon growth model assumes that the growth rate cannot be greater than the required rate of return.

The assumptions of the Gordon model are as follows:

- Dividends are the correct metric to use for valuation purposes.
- The dividend growth rate is forever: It is perpetual and never changes.
- The required rate of return is also constant over time.
- The dividend growth rate is strictly less than the required rate of return.

An analyst might be dissatisfied with these assumptions for many reasons. The equities being examined might not currently pay a dividend. The Gordon assumptions might be too simplistic to reflect the characteristics of the companies being evaluated. Some alternatives to using the Gordon model are as follows:

- Use a more robust DDM that allows for varying patterns of growth.
- Use a cash flow measure other than dividends for valuation purposes.
- Use some other approach (such as a multiplier method) to valuation.

Applying a DDM is difficult if the company being analyzed is not currently paying a dividend. A company may not be paying a dividend if 1) the investment opportunities the company has are all so attractive that the retention and reinvestment of funds is preferable, from a return perspective, to the distribution of a dividend to shareholders or 2) the company is in such shaky financial condition that it cannot afford to pay a dividend. An analyst might still use a DDM to value such companies by assuming that dividends will begin at some future point in time. The analyst might further assume that constant growth occurs after that date and use the Gordon growth model for

The Gordon Growth Model

valuation. Extrapolating from no current dividend, however, generally yields highly uncertain forecasts. Analysts typically choose to use one or more of the alternatives instead of or as a supplement to the Gordon growth model.

EXAMPLE 8

Gordon Growth Model in the Case of No Current Dividend

1. A company does not currently pay a dividend but is expected to begin to do so in five years (at $t = 5$). The first dividend is expected to be $4.00 and to be received five years from today. That dividend is expected to grow at 6 percent into perpetuity. The required return is 10 percent. What is the estimated current intrinsic value?

Solution:

The analyst can value the share in two pieces:

1. The analyst uses the Gordon growth model to estimate the value at $t = 5$; in the model, the year-ahead dividend is $4(1.06)$. Then the analyst finds the present value of this value as of $t = 0$.
2. The analyst finds the present value of the $4 dividend not "counted" in the estimate in Piece 1 (which values dividends from $t = 6$ onward). Note that the statement of the problem implies that D_0, D_1, D_2, D_3, and D_4 are zero.

Piece 1: The value of this piece is $65.818:

$$V_n = \frac{D_n(1+g)}{r-g} = \frac{D_{n+1}}{r-g}$$

$$V_5 = \frac{\$4(1+0.06)}{0.10-0.06} = \frac{\$4.24}{0.04} = \$106$$

$$V_0 = \frac{\$106}{(1+0.10)^5} = \$65.818$$

Piece 2: The value of this piece is $2.484:

$$V_0 = \frac{\$4}{(1+0.10)^5} = \$2.484$$

The sum of the two pieces is $65.818 + $2.484 = $68.30.
Alternatively, the analyst could value the share at $t = 4$, the point at which dividends are expected to be paid in the following year and from which point they are expected to grow at a constant rate.

$$V_4 = \frac{\$4.00}{0.10-0.06} = \frac{\$4.00}{0.04} = \$100$$

$$V_0 = \frac{\$100}{(1+0.10)^4} = \$68.30$$

The next section addresses the application of the DDM with more flexible assumptions as to the dividend growth rate.

8
MULTISTAGE DIVIDEND DISCOUNT MODELS

- calculate and interpret the intrinsic value of an equity security based on the Gordon (constant) growth dividend discount model or a two-stage dividend discount model, as appropriate
- identify characteristics of companies for which the constant growth or a multistage dividend discount model is appropriate
- explain advantages and disadvantages of each category of valuation model

Multistage growth models are often used to model rapidly growing companies. The *two-stage DDM* assumes that at some point the company will begin to pay dividends that grow at a constant rate, but prior to that time the company will pay dividends that are growing at a higher rate than can be sustained in the long run. That is, the company is assumed to experience an initial, finite period of high growth, perhaps prior to the entry of competitors, followed by an infinite period of sustainable growth. The two-stage DDM thus makes use of two growth rates: a high growth rate for an initial, finite period followed by a lower, sustainable growth rate into perpetuity. The Gordon growth model is used to estimate a terminal value at time n that reflects the present value at time n of the dividends received during the sustainable growth period.

Equation 11 will be used here as the starting point for a two-stage valuation model. The two-stage valuation model is similar to Example 8 except that instead of assuming zero dividends for the initial period, the analyst assumes that dividends will exhibit a high rate of growth during the initial period. Equation 11 values the dividends over the short-term period of high growth and the terminal value at the end of the period of high growth. The short-term growth rate, g_S, lasts for n years. The intrinsic value per share in year n, V_n, represents the year n value of the dividends received during the sustainable growth period or the terminal value at time n. V_n can be estimated by using the Gordon growth model as shown in Equation 12, where g_L is the long-term or sustainable growth rate. The dividend in year $n + 1$, D_{n+1}, can be determined by using Equation 13:

$$V_0 = \sum_{t=1}^{n} \frac{D_0(1+g_S)^t}{(1+r)^t} + \frac{V_n}{(1+r)^n} \tag{11}$$

$$V_n = \frac{D_{n+1}}{r - g_L} \tag{12}$$

$$D_{n+1} = D_0(1+g_S)^n(1+g_L) \tag{13}$$

EXAMPLE 9

Applying the Two-Stage Dividend Discount Model

1. The current dividend, D_0, is $5.00. Growth is expected to be 10 percent a year for three years and then 5 percent thereafter. The required rate of return is 15 percent. Estimate the intrinsic value.

Solution:

$D_1 = \$5.00(1 + 0.10) = \$5.50$

Multistage Dividend Discount Models

$D_2 = \$5.00(1 + 0.10)^2 = \$6.05$

$D_3 = \$5.00(1 + 0.10)^3 = \$6.655$

$D_4 = \$5.00(1 + 0.10)^3(1 + 0.05) = \$6.98775$

$V_3 = \frac{\$6.98775}{0.15 - 0.05} = \$69.8775$

$V_0 = \frac{\$5.50}{(1 + 0.15)} + \frac{\$6.05}{(1 + 0.15)^2} + \frac{\$6.655}{(1 + 0.15)^3} + \frac{\$69.8775}{(1 + 0.15)^3} \approx \$59.68$

The DDM can be extended to as many stages as deemed appropriate. For most publicly traded companies (that is, companies beyond the start-up stage), practitioners assume growth will ultimately fall into three stages: 1) growth, 2) transition, and 3) maturity. This assumption supports the use of a *three-stage DDM*, which makes use of three growth rates: a high growth rate for an initial finite period, followed by a lower growth rate for a finite second period, followed by a lower, sustainable growth rate into perpetuity.

One can make the case that a three-stage DDM would be most appropriate for a fairly young company, one that is just entering the growth phase. The two-stage DDM would be appropriate to estimate the value of an older company that has already moved through its growth phase and is currently in the transition phase (a period with a higher growth rate than the sustainable growth rate) prior to moving to the maturity phase (the period with a lower, sustainable growth rate).

However, the choice of a two-stage DDM need not rely solely on the age of a company. Long-established companies sometimes manage to restart above-average growth through, for example, innovation, expansion to new markets, or acquisitions. Or a company's long-run growth rate may be interrupted by a period of subnormal performance. If growth is expected to moderate (in the first case) or improve (in the second case) toward some long-term growth rate, a two-stage DDM may be appropriate. Thus, we chose a two-stage DDM to value International Business Machines Corporation in Example 10.

EXAMPLE 10

Two-Stage Dividend Discount Model: International Business Machines Corporation

International Business Machines Corporation (IBM) is a US based leading technology company. IBM was founded in 1911, initially as a company that manufactured machinery for sale and lease, ranging from commercial scales and industrial time recorders, meat and cheese slicers, to punched cards. IBM introduced the personal computer in 1981; however, by the 1990s, it began to suffer losses in its core computer manufacturing business and by the 2000s, it had begun to diversify into business consulting, which was finalized in 2005 when it sold its personal computer business to Chinese company Lenovo. IBM now operates through five segments: Cognitive Solutions, Global Business Services (GBS), Technology Services & Cloud Platforms, Systems, and Global Financing. The Cognitive Solutions segment delivers a spectrum of capabilities from descriptive, predictive, and prescriptive analytics to cognitive systems. Cognitive Solutions includes Watson, a cognitive computing platform that has the ability to interact in natural language, process big data, and learn from interactions with people and computers. The GBS segment provides clients with consulting, application management services, and global process services. The Technology Services & Cloud Platforms segment provides information technology infrastructure services. The Systems segment provides clients with infrastructure technologies. The Global Financing segment includes client financing, commercial financing, and remanufacturing and remarketing.

The 30 July 2018 *Value Line* report on IBM appears in Exhibit 5. IBM has increased its dividends every year over the past 15 years. Information from *Value Line* shows that the dividend growth is around 17.0 percent for the past 10 years, 13.5 percent for the past 5 years, and estimated to be 4.5 percent for 2015 to 2023. After a period of growth through acquisition and merger, the pattern suggests that IBM may be transitioning to a mature growth phase.

The two-stage DDM is arguably a good choice for valuing IBM because the company appears to be transitioning from a high-growth phase (note the 13.5 percent dividend growth for the past 5 years) to a lower-growth phase (note the forecast of 4.5 percent dividend growth to 2015–2023).

The CAPM can be used to estimate the required return, r, for IBM. The *Value Line* report (in the top left corner) estimates beta to be 0.95. Using the yield of about 2.0 percent on 10-year US Treasury notes as a proxy for the risk-free rate and assuming an equity risk premium of 5.0 percent, we find the estimate for r would be 6.75 percent [2.0% + 0.95(5.0%)].

To estimate the intrinsic value at the end of 2018, we use the 2018 dividend of US$6.21 from the *Value Line* report. The dividend is assumed to grow at a rate of 5.0 percent for one year and then 2.33 percent thereafter. The growth rate assumption for the first stage is consistent with the *Value Line* forecast for the 2018 and 2019 dividends. Our assumption of a 2.33 percent perpetual growth rate produces an 8-year growth rate assumption near 4.5%,[4] which is consistent with the *Value Line* forecast of 4.5 percent growth from 2015–2022. Thus:

$$D_{2019} = US\$6.21(1 + 0.05) = US\$6.5205$$

$$D_{2020} = US\$6.21(1 + 0.05)(1 + 0.0233) = US\$6.6724$$

$$D_{2021} = US\$6.21(1 + 0.05)(1 + 0.0233)^2 = US\$6.8279$$

$$V_{2020} = \frac{US\$6.8279}{0.0675 - 0.0233} = US\$154.4774$$

$$V_{2018} = \frac{US\$6.5205}{(1 + 0.0675)} + \frac{US\$6.6724}{(1 + 0.0675)^2} + \frac{US\$154.4774}{(1 + 0.0675)^2} \approx US\$147.523$$

Given a recent price of US$148.56, as noted at the top left corner of the *Value Line* report, the intrinsic-value estimate of US$147.523 suggests that IBM is approximately fairly valued.

---

[4] The exact geometric average annual growth rate for 2015–2023 can be determined as $[(1 + 0.10)(1 + 0.0727)(1 + 0.0525)(1 + 0.499)(1 + 0.022)(1 + 0.022)(1 + 0.022)(1 + 0.022)]^{1/8} - 1 = 4.5\%$.

Exhibit 5: *Value Line* Report on IBM

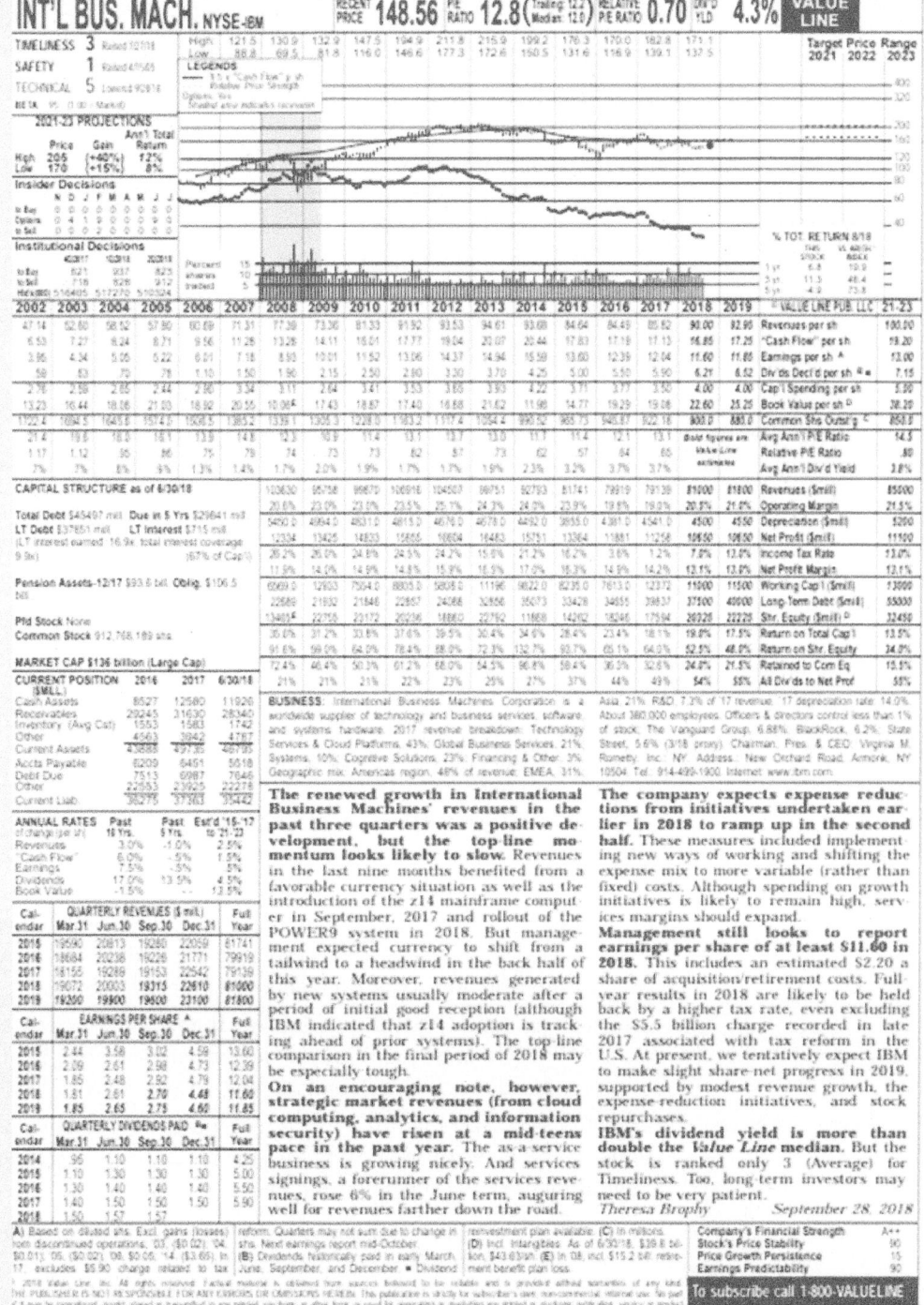

Source: © 2018 Value Line, Inc. All Rights Reserved Worldwide. "Value Line" is a registered trademark of Value Line, Inc. Value Line Geometric and Arithmetic Indices calculated by Thomson Reuters. Information supplied by Thomson Reuters.

9 MULTIPLER MODELS AND RELATIONSHIP AMONG PRICE MULTIPLES, PRESENT VALUE MODELS, AND FUNDAMENTALS

☐ explain the rationale for using price multiples to value equity, how the price to earnings multiple relates to fundamentals, and the use of multiples based on comparables

☐ calculate and interpret the following multiples: price to earnings, price to an estimate of operating cash flow, price to sales, and price to book value

☐ explain advantages and disadvantages of each category of valuation model

The term **price multiple** refers to a ratio that compares the share price with some sort of monetary flow or value to allow evaluation of the relative worth of a company's stock. Some practitioners use price ratios as a screening mechanism. If the ratio falls below a specified value, the shares are identified as candidates for purchase, and if the ratio exceeds a specified value, the shares are identified as candidates for sale. Many practitioners use ratios when examining a group or sector of stocks and consider the shares for which the ratio is relatively low to be attractively valued securities.

Price multiples that are used by security analysts include the following:

- Price-to-earnings ratio (P/E). This measure is the ratio of the stock price to earnings per share. P/E is arguably the price multiple most frequently cited by the media and used by analysts and investors (Block 1999). The seminal works of McWilliams (1966), Miller and Widmann (1966), Nicholson (1968), Dreman (1977), and Basu (1977) presented evidence of a return advantage to low-P/E stocks.

- Price-to-book ratio (P/B). The ratio of the stock price to book value per share. Considerable evidence suggests that P/B multiples are inversely related to future rates of return (Fama and French 1995).

- Price-to-sales ratio (P/S). This measure is the ratio of stock price to sales per share. O'Shaughnessy (2005) provided evidence that a low P/S multiple is the most useful multiple for predicting future returns.

- Price-to-cash-flow ratio (P/CF). This measure is the ratio of stock price to some per-share measure of cash flow. The measures of cash flow include free cash flow (FCF) and operating cash flow (OCF).

A common criticism of all of these multiples is that they do not consider the future. This criticism is true if the multiple is calculated from trailing or current values of the divisor. Practitioners seek to counter this criticism by a variety of techniques, including forecasting fundamental values (the divisors) one or more years into the future. The resulting forward (leading or prospective) price multiples may differ markedly from the trailing price multiples. In the absence of an explicit forecast of fundamental values, the analyst is making an implicit forecast of the future when implementing such models. The choice of price multiple—trailing or forward—should be used consistently for companies being compared.

Besides the traditional price multiples used in valuation, just presented, analysts need to know how to calculate and interpret other ratios. Such ratios include those used to analyze business performance and financial condition based on data reported in financial statements. In addition, many industries have specialized measures of business performance that analysts covering those industries should be familiar with. In analyzing cable television companies, for example, the ratio of total market value of the company to the total number of subscribers is commonly used. Another common measure is revenue per subscriber. In the oil industry, a commonly cited ratio is proved reserves per common share. Industry-specific or sector-specific ratios such as these can be used to understand the key business variables in an industry or sector as well as to highlight attractively valued securities.

Relationships among Price Multiples, Present Value Models, and Fundamentals

Price multiples are frequently used independently of present value models. One price multiple valuation approach, the method of comparables, does not involve cash flow forecasts or discounting to present value. A price multiple is often related to fundamentals through a discounted cash flow model, however, such as the Gordon growth model. Understanding such connections can deepen the analyst's appreciation of the factors that affect the value of a multiple and often can help explain reasons for differences in multiples that do not involve mispricing. The expressions that are developed can be interpreted as the *justified value* of a multiple—that is, the value justified by (based on) fundamentals or a set of cash flow predictions. These expressions are an alternative way of presenting intrinsic-value estimates.

As an example, using the Gordon growth model identified previously in Equation 9 and assuming that price equals intrinsic value ($P_0 = V_0$), we can restate Equation 9 as follows:

$$P_0 = \frac{D_1}{r-g} \tag{14}$$

To arrive at the model for the justified forward P/E given in Equation 15, we divide both sides of Equation 14 by a forecast for next year's earnings, E_1. In Equation 15, the dividend payout ratio, p, is the ratio of dividends to earnings:

$$\frac{P_0}{E_1} = \frac{D_1/E_1}{r-g} = \frac{p}{r-g} \tag{15}$$

Equation 15 indicates that the P/E is inversely related to the required rate of return and positively related to the growth rate; that is, as the required rate of return increases, the P/E declines, and as the growth rate increases, the P/E increases. The P/E and the payout ratio appear to be positively related. This relationship may not be true, however, because a higher payout ratio may imply a slower growth rate as a result of the company retaining a lower proportion of earnings for reinvestment. This phenomenon is referred to as the dividend displacement of earnings.

EXAMPLE 11

Value Estimate Based on Fundamentals

1. Petroleo Brasileiro SA, commonly known as Petrobras, was once labeled "the most expensive oil company" by Bloomberg.com. Data for Petrobras and the oil industry, including the trailing twelve-month (TTM) P/E and payout ratios, appear below.

	Petrobras	Industry
P/E ratio (TTM)	39.61	13.0
Return on assets (TTM) (%)	3.0	3.2

	Petrobras	Industry
EPS 3-year growth rate (%)	NM	66.00
EPS (MRQ) vs. Qtr. 1 yr. ago (% change)	138.96	−12.0

Note: NM stands for non-quantifiable. Petrobras EPS has decreased from a loss of BRL 1.14 per share to a profit of BRL 0.16 per share in the most recent period. MRQ stands for "most recent quarter."

Source: Reuters.

Explain how the information shown supports a higher P/E for Petrobras than for the industry.

Solution:

The data support a higher P/E for Petrobras because its (MRQ) EPS growth rate exceed those of the industry. Equation 15 implies a positive relationship between the payout ratio and the P/E multiple. Petrobras has had a negative EPS for the period 2014 to 2017, and has paid no dividend during that period. A higher payout ratio supports a higher P/E. Furthermore, to the extent that higher EPS growth implies a high growth rate in dividends, the high EPS growth rate supports a high P/E. The higher P/E ratio is due to an improvement in the underlying financial performance of the company and the expected higher growth potential of the stock compared to the median firms in the industry.

EXAMPLE 12

Determining Justified Forward P/E

Heinrich Gladisch, CFA, is estimating the justified forward P/E for Nestlé, one of the world's leading nutrition and health companies. Gladisch notes that sales for 2017 were SFr89.78 billion (US$90.3 billion) and that net income was SFr7.18 billion (US$7.25 billion). He organizes the data for EPS, dividends per share, and the dividend payout ratio for the years 2013–2017 in the following table:

	2013	2014	2015	2016	2017
Earnings per share	SFr3.24	SFr4.54	SFr2.90	SFr2.76	SFr2.32
Year over year % change		44.6%	−36.1%	−4.8%	−15.9%
Dividend per share	SFr2.15	SFr2.2	SFr2.25	SFr2.3	SFr2.35
Year over year % change		2.3%	2.3%	2.2%	2.2%
Dividend payout ratio	68.5%	48.5%	77.6%	83.3%	99.2%

Gladisch calculates that ROE averaged 15.5 percent in the period 2013–2017 but was below that level at 11.7 percent in 2017. In that year, however, Nestlé's reported net income included a large nonrecurring component. The company reported 2017 "underlying earnings," which it defined as net income "from continuing operations before impairments, restructuring costs, results on disposals and significant one-off items," to be SFr2.93, giving an adjusted 14.8% ROE. Predicting increasing improvement in Nestlé's profit margins from growth in its product markets, Gladisch estimates a long-run ROE of 21.5 percent.

Multipler Models and Relationship Among Price Multiples, Present Value Models, and Fundamentals

Gladisch decides that the dividend payout ratios of the 2013–2016 period—averaging 67.7 percent—are more representative of Nestlé's future payout ratio than is the high 2017 dividend payout ratio (when based on reported earnings). The dividend payout ratio in 2017 was higher because management apparently based the 2017 dividend on the components of net income that were expected to continue into the future. But basing a dividend on net income including non-recurring items creates the potential need to increase dividends in the future. Rounding up the 2013–2017 average, Gladisch settles on an estimate of 68 percent for the dividend payout ratio for use in calculating a justified forward P/E using Equation 15.

Gladisch's firm estimates that the required rate of return for Nestlé's shares is 9 percent per year. Gladisch also finds the following data at the opposite ends of the spectrum of external research analyst forecasts:

	2018E	2019E
Most optimistic analyst forecast:		
EPS	SFr3.99	SFr4.33
Year over year % change	71.9%	8.5%
P/E (based on a target price of SFr105)	26.3	24.2
Least optimistic analyst forecast:		
EPS	SFr3.52	SFr3.59
Year over year % change	51.7%	2.0%
P/E (based on a target price of SFr68)	19.3	18.9

1. Based only on information and estimates developed by Gladisch and his firm, estimate Nestlé's justified forward P/E.

Solution to 1:

The estimate of the justified forward P/E is 32.38. The dividend growth rate can be estimated by using Equation 10 as (1 − Dividend payout ratio) × ROE = (1 − 0.68) × 0.215 = 0.069, or 6.9 percent. Therefore,

$$\frac{P_0}{E_1} = \frac{\text{Payout}}{r - g} = \frac{0.68}{0.09 - 0.069} = 32.38$$

2. Compare and contrast the justified forward P/E estimate from Question 1 to the estimates from each end of the spectrum of external research analysts forecasts.

Solution to 2:

The estimated justified forward P/E of 32.38 is higher than the justified 2018 P/E estimates of 26.3 and 19.3 of the two analysts. Using a required rate of return of 9.5 percent rather than 9 percent results in a justified forward P/E estimate of 26.2 = 0.68/(0.095 − 0.069). Using an ROE of 16.5 percent (the average ROE of the 2013–2016 period) rather than 21.5 percent results in a justified forward P/E estimate of 18.4 = 0.68/[0.09 − (0.32)(0.165)] = 0.68/(0.09 − 0.053). The justified forward P/E is very sensitive to changes in the inputs.

Justified forward P/E estimates can be sensitive to small changes in assumptions. Therefore, analysts can benefit from carrying out a sensitivity analysis, as shown in Exhibit 6, which is based on Example 12. Exhibit 6 shows how the justified forward

P/E varies with changes in the estimates for the dividend payout ratio (columns) and return on equity. The dividend growth rate (rows) changes because of changes in the retention rate (1 − Payout rate) and ROE. Recall g = ROE times retention rate.

Exhibit 6: Estimates for Nestlé's Justified Forward P/E (Required Rate of Return = 9 Percent)

Constant Dividend Growth Rate (%)	Dividend Payout Ratio				
	55%	60%	65%	70%	75%
4.0	11.0	12.0	13.0	14.0	15.0
4.5	12.2	13.3	14.4	15.6	16.7
5.0	13.8	15.0	16.3	17.5	18.8
5.5	15.7	17.1	18.6	20.0	21.4
6.0	18.3	20.0	21.7	23.3	25.0
6.5	22.0	24.0	26.0	28.0	30.0
7.0	27.5	30.0	32.5	35.0	37.5
7.5	36.7	40.0	43.3	46.7	50.0

10. METHOD OF COMPARABLES AND VALUATION BASED ON PRICE MULTIPLES

- [ ] explain the rationale for using price multiples to value equity, how the price to earnings multiple relates to fundamentals, and the use of multiples based on comparables
- [ ] calculate and interpret the following multiples: price to earnings, price to an estimate of operating cash flow, price to sales, and price to book value
- [ ] explain advantages and disadvantages of each category of valuation model

The method of comparables is the most widely used approach for analysts reporting valuation judgments on the basis of price multiples. This method essentially compares relative values estimated using multiples or the relative values of multiples. The economic rationale underlying the method of comparables is the **law of one price**: Identical assets should sell for the same price. The methodology involves using a price multiple to evaluate whether an asset is fairly valued, undervalued, or overvalued in relation to a benchmark value of the multiple. Choices for the benchmark multiple include the multiple of a closely matched individual stock or the average or median value of the multiple for the stock's industry. Some analysts perform trend or time-series analyses and use past or average values of a price multiple as a benchmark.

Identifying individual companies or even an industry as the "comparable" may present a challenge. Many large corporations operate in several lines of business, so the scale and scope of their operations can vary significantly. When identifying comparables (sometimes referred to as "comps"), the analyst should be careful to identify companies that are most similar according to a number of dimensions. These dimensions include (but are not limited to) overall size, product lines, and growth rate. The type of analysis shown in Section 5.1 relating multiples to fundamentals is a productive way to identify the fundamental variables that should be taken into account in identifying comparables.

EXAMPLE 13

Method of Comparables (1)

1. As noted previously, P/E is a price multiple frequently used by analysts. Using P/E in the method of comparables can be problematic, however, as a result of business cycle effects on EPS. An alternative valuation tool that is useful during periods of economic slowdown or extraordinary growth is the P/S multiple. Although sales will decline during a recession and increase during a period of economic growth, the change in sales will be less than the change in earnings in percentage terms because earnings are heavily influenced by fixed operating and financing costs (operating and financial leverage).

    The following data provide the P/S for most of the major automobile manufacturers as at December 2017:

Company	P/S
Peugeot	0.28
Ford Motor	0.33
General Motors	0.36
Nissan Motor	0.38
Honda Motor	0.46
Tata Motors	0.49
Daimler	0.55
BMW	0.57
Toyota Motor	0.80

    Sources: Morningstar and company websites.

    Based on the data presented, which stock appears to be undervalued when compared with the others?

Solution:

The P/S analysis suggests that Peugeot shares offer the best value. An analyst must be alert for a range of potential explanations of apparently low or high multiples when performing comparables analysis, rather than just assuming a relative mispricing.

EXAMPLE 14

Method of Comparables (2)

1. Incorporated in the Netherlands, Airbus is active in the aerospace and defense industry. It is a dominant aerospace company in Europe. Its largest business, Airbus Commercial Aircraft, is a manufacturing company with bases in several European countries and accounts for the majority of Airbus SE profits. Airbus and its primary competitor, Boeing, control most of the global commercial airplane industry.

   Comparisons are frequently made between Airbus and Boeing. As noted in Exhibit 7, the companies are broadly similar in size as measured by total revenues. Converting total forecast revenues from euros to US dollars using the average exchange rate for 2017 of US$1.13/€ results in a value of $75.5 billion for Airbus's total revenues. Thus, total revenues for Boeing are expected to be about a fifth higher than those for Airbus.

   The companies do differ, however, in several important areas. Airbus derives a greater share of its revenue from commercial aircraft production than does Boeing, and the order backlog for Airbus is much higher than that for Boeing. Converting the Airbus order backlog from euros to US dollars using the quarter-end rate for September 2017 of $1.1813/€ results in a value of $1.12 billion for Airbus's order backlog. Thus, the order backlog for Airbus is more than twice as high as the backlog for Boeing.[5]

   Exhibit 7: Data for EADS and Boeing

	Airbus	Boeing
Total revenues (billions, 2017)	€66.8	$92.2
Annual revenue growth (2015–2017 average)	1.8%	−2.1%
Percent of revenues from commercial aircraft	75%	69%
Order backlog (billions)	€945	$474
Share price, 12/Dec/17	€86.96	$283.73
EPS (basic)	€3.33	$10.18
DPS	€1.48	$5.7
Dividend payout ratio	44%	56%
P/E ratio	26.1	27.9

   Note: 2017 forecast data and YTD average exchange rate as of 12 December 2017. Order backlog as of 30 September 2017.

   Sources: Company websites: www.airbus.com and www.boeing.com, *Financial Times*.

   What data shown in Exhibit 7 support a higher P/E for Boeing than for Airbus?

---

5 Exchange rate data are available from FRED (Federal Reserve Economic Data) at http://research.stlouisfed.org/fred2/. Each company uses slightly different methodology for calculating order backlog.

Method of Comparables and Valuation Based on Price Multiples

Solution:

Recall from Equation 14 and the discussion that followed it that P/E is directly related to the payout ratio and the dividend growth rate. The P/E is inversely related to the required rate of return. The only data presented in Exhibit 7 that support a higher P/E for Boeing is the company's higher dividend payout ratio (expected at 56 percent versus 44 percent for Airbus).

The following implicitly supports a higher P/E for Airbus: Airbus has higher revenue growth (as reported for 2016 and expected for 2017) and a higher backlog of orders, suggesting that it may have a higher future growth rate.

EXAMPLE 15

Method of Comparables (3)

1. Canon Inc. is a leading worldwide manufacturer of business machines, cameras, and optical products. Canon was founded in 1937 as a camera manufacturer and is incorporated in Tokyo. The corporate philosophy of Canon is *kyosei* or "living and working together for the common good." The following data can be used to determine a P/E for Canon over the time period 2013–2017. Analyze the P/E of Canon over time and discuss the valuation of Canon.

Year	Price (a)	EPS (b)	P/E (a) ÷ (b)
2013	¥3,330	¥200.8	16.6
2014	¥3,840.5	¥229.0	16.8
2015	¥3,675	¥201.7	18.2
2016	¥3,295	¥138	23.9
2017	¥4,200	¥222.88	18.8

Sources: EPS, year-end prices, and P/E data are from Capital IQ and the *Financial Times*.

Solution:

Trend analysis of Canon's P/E reveals a peak of 23.9 at the end of 2016. The 2013 P/E of 16.6 is the lowest of the five years reported. This finding suggests that Canon's share price may be fairly price as of year-end 2017. A bearish case for Canon's stock can be made if an analyst believes that P/E will return to its historical low (16.6 over this five-year period) or be lower. Such a bearish prediction requires that a decrease in P/E not be offset by an increase in EPS. A bullish case can be made if the analyst believes the stock deserves re-rating and an even higher than trend P/E.

Illustration of a Valuation Based on Price Multiples

Telefónica S.A., a world leader in the telecommunication sector, provides communication, information, and entertainment products and services in Europe, Africa, and Latin America. It has operated in its home country of Spain since 1924, but as of 2017, more than 75 percent of its business was outside its home market.

Deutsche Telekom AG provides network access, communication services, and value-added services via fixed and mobile networks. It generates more than half of its revenues outside its home country, Germany.

Exhibit 8 provides comparable data for these two communication giants for 2015–2017.

Exhibit 8: Data for Telefónica and Deutsche Telekom

	Telefónica			Deutsche Telekom		
	2017	2016	2015	2017	2016	2015
(1) Total assets (€ billions)	115.0	123.6	120.3	141.3	148.5	143.9
Asset growth	−6.9%	2.7%	—	−4.9%	3.2%	—
(2) Net revenues (€ billions)	52.0	52.0	54.9	77.3	75.2	71.3
Revenue growth	0%	−5.2%	—	2.8%	5.5%	—
(3) Net cash flow from operating activities (€ billions)	13.8	13.3	13.6	17.2	15.5	15.0
Cash flow growth	3.4%	−2.0%	—	11.0%	3.3%	—
(4) Book value of common shareholders' equity (€ billions)	16.9	18.2	15.8	42.5	38.8	38.2
Debt ratio: $1 - [(4) \div (1)]$	85.3%	85.3%	86.9%	70.0%	73.9%	73.5%
(5) Net profit (€ billions)	2.9	2.1	0.4	3.5	2.7	3.3
Earnings growth	38.1%	425.0%	—	29.6%	−18.2%	—
(6) Weighted average number of shares outstanding (millions)	5,122.9	4,896.6	4,833.6	4,740.2	4,654.9	4,584.8
(7) Price per share (€)	7.93	9.52	9.13	13.42	16.21	15.44
Price-to-revenue ratio (P/R): $(7) \div [(2) \div (6)]$	0.8	0.9	0.8	0.8	1.0	1.0
P/CF: $(7) \div [(3) \div (6)]$	2.9	3.5	3.2	3.7	4.9	4.7
P/B: $(7) \div [(4) \div (6)]$	2.4	2.6	2.8	1.5	1.9	1.9
P/E: $(7) \div [(5) \div (6)]$	14.0	22.2	110.3	18.2	27.9	21.5

Sources: Company websites: www.telefonica.es and www.deutschetelekom.com.

Time-series analysis of all price multiples in Exhibit 8 suggests that both companies are currently attractively valued. For example, the 2017 price-to-revenue ratio (P/R) of 0.78 for Telefónica is below the 2015–2017 average for this ratio of approximately 0.83. The 2017 P/CF of 3.7 for Deutsche Telekom is below the 2015–2017 average for this ratio of approximately 4.4.

A comparative analysis produces somewhat mixed results. The 2017 values for Deutsche Telekom for the P/R, P/CF, P/E multiples are higher than those for Telefónica. This result suggests that Telefónica is attractively valued when compared with Deutsche Telekom. The 2017 P/B for Telefónica, however, is higher than for Deutsche Telekom.

An analyst investigating these contradictory results would look for information not reported in Exhibit 8. For example, the earnings before interest, taxes, depreciation, and amortization (EBITDA) for Telefónica was €16.4 billion in 2017. The EBITDA value for Deutsche Telekom was €20.7 billion in 2017. The 2017 price-to-EBITDA ratio for Telefónica is [(7.93 × 5,123)/16,400] or [7.92/(16,400/5,123] = 2.5, whereas the 2017 price-to-EBITDA ratio for Deutsche Telekom is 3.1. Thus, the higher P/E for Deutsche Telekom can-not be explained by higher depreciation charges, higher interest costs, and/or a greater tax burden, but appears to be due to a better quality of earnings.

In summary, the major advantage of using price multiples is that they allow for relative comparisons, both cross-sectional (versus the market or another comparable) and in time series. The approach can be especially beneficial for analysts who are assigned to a particular industry or sector and need to identify the expected best performing stocks within that sector. Price multiples are popular with investors because the multiples can be calculated easily and many multiples are readily available from financial websites and newspapers.

Caution is necessary. A stock may be relatively undervalued when compared with its benchmarks but overvalued when compared with an estimate of intrinsic value as determined by one of the discounted cash flow methodologies. Furthermore, differences in reporting rules among different markets and in chosen accounting methods can result in revenues, earnings, book values, and cash flows that are not easily comparable. These differences can, in turn, result in multiples that are not easily comparable. Finally, the multiples for cyclical companies may be highly influenced by current economic conditions.

ENTERPRISE VALUE   11

- ☐ describe enterprise value multiples and their use in estimating equity value
- ☐ explain advantages and disadvantages of each category of valuation model

An alternative to estimating the value of equity is to estimate the value of the enterprise. Enterprise value is most frequently determined as market capitalization plus market value of preferred stock plus market value of debt minus cash and investments (cash equivalents and short-term investments). Enterprise value is often viewed as the cost of a takeover: In the event of a buyout, the acquiring company assumes the acquired company's debt but also receives its cash. Enterprise value is most useful when comparing companies with significant differences in capital structure.

Enterprise value (EV) multiples are widely used in Europe, with EV/EBITDA arguably the most common. EBITDA is a proxy for operating cash flow because it excludes depreciation and amortization. EBITDA may include other non-cash expenses, however, and non-cash revenues. EBITDA can be viewed as a source of funds to pay interest, dividends, and taxes. Because EBITDA is calculated prior to payment to any of the company's financial stakeholders, using it to estimate enterprise value is logically appropriate.

Using enterprise value instead of market capitalization to determine a multiple can be useful to analysts. Even where the P/E is problematic because of negative earnings, the EV/EBITDA multiple can generally be computed because EBITDA is usually positive. An alternative to using EBITDA in EV multiples is to use operating income.

In practice, analysts may have difficulty accurately assessing enterprise value if they do not have access to market quotations for the company's debt. When current market quotations are not available, bond values may be estimated from current quotations for bonds with similar maturity, sector, and credit characteristics. Substituting the book value of debt for the market value of debt provides only a rough estimate of the debt's market value. This is because market interest rates change and investors' perception of the issuer's credit risk may have changed since the debt was issued.

EXAMPLE 16

Estimating the Market Value of Debt and Enterprise Value

1. Cameco Corporation is one of the world's largest uranium producers; it accounts for 16 percent of world production from its mines in Canada and the United States. Cameco estimates it has about 458 million kilograms of proven and probable reserves and holds premier land positions in the world's most promising areas for new uranium discoveries in Canada and Australia. Cameco is also a leading provider of processing services required to produce fuel for nuclear power plants. It generates 1,000 megawatts of electricity through a partnership in North America's largest nuclear generating station located in Ontario, Canada.

   For simplicity of exposition in this example, we will present share counts in thousands and all dollar amounts in thousands of Canadian dollars. In 2017, Cameco had 395,793 shares outstanding. Its 2017 year-end share price was $14.11. Therefore, Cameco's 2017 year-end market capitalization was $5,584,640.

   In its 2017 Annual Report (available at www.cameco.com), Cameco reported total debt and other liabilities of $2,919,100. The company presented the following schedule for long-term debt payments:

Year	Payment
2018	$69,000
2019 and 2020	610,000
2021 and 2022	482,000
Thereafter	744,000
Total	$1,905,000

   Cameco's longest maturity debt matures in 2042. We will assume that the amounts paid in 2019 and 2020, and in 2021 and 2022, will be paid equally during the two years. The "thereafter" period includes two debenture tranches, the first one maturing in 2024 for a total value of $620,000 and the second tranche maturing in 2042 for the remaining $124,000. A yield curve for zero-coupon Canadian government securities was available from the Bank of Canada. The yield-curve data and assumed risk premiums in Exhibit 9 were used to estimate the market value of Cameco's long-term debt:

Enterprise Value

Exhibit 9: Estimated Market Value

Year	Yield on Zero-Coupon Government Security (%)	Assumed Risk Premium (%)	Discount Rate (%)	Book Value	Market Value
2018	0.89	0.50	1.39	$69,000	$68,054
2019	1.11	1.00	2.11	$305,000	$292,525
2020	1.39	1.50	2.89	$305,000	$280,014
2021	1.65	2.00	3.65	$241,000	$208,804
2022	1.88	2.50	4.38	$241,000	$194,505
2023	2.10	3.00	5.10	$0	$0
2024	2.30	3.50	5.80	$620,000	$417,823
2025	2.50	4.00	6.50	$0	$0
...	...	...	...	$...	$...
2042	2.92	5.00	7.92	$124,000	$18,445
				$1,905,000	$1,480,170

Note from Exhibit 9 that the book value of long-term debt is $1,905,000 and its estimated market value is $1,480,170. The book value of total debt and liabilities of $2,919,100 minus the book value of long-term debt of $1,905,000 is $1,014,100. If we assume that the market value of that remaining debt is equal to its book value of $1,014,100 an estimate of the market value of total debt and liabilities is that amount plus the estimated market value of long-term debt of $1,480,170 or $2,494,270.

At the end of 2017, Cameco had cash and equivalents of $591,600. Enterprise value can be estimated as the $5,584,640 market value of stock plus the $2,494,270 market value of debt minus the $591,600 cash and equivalents, or $7,487,310. Cameco's 2017 EBITDA was $606,000; an estimate of EV/EBITDA is, therefore, $7,487,310 divided by $606,000, or 12.4.

EXAMPLE 17

EV/Operating Income

1. Exhibit 10 presents data for twelve major mining companies. Based only on the information in Exhibit 10, which two mining companies seem to be the *most* undervalued?

Exhibit 10: Data for Twelve Major Mining Companies

Company	EV (US$ millions)	Operating Income (OI) (US$ millions)	EV/OI
BHP Billiton	119,712.3	11,753	10.19
Rio Tinto	93,856.1	6,471	14.5
Vale	82,051.2	6,366	12.89

Company	EV (US$ millions)	Operating Income (OI) (US$ millions)	EV/OI
Glencore	80,772.0	−549	−147.13
Southern Copper	37,817.0	1,564	24.18
Freeport-McMoRan	33,452.0	−2,766	−12.09
Anglo American	32,870.3	2,562	12.83
Norilsk Nickel	22,483.0	3,377	6.66
Coal India	21,652.1	1,382	15.67
Barrick Gold	21,549.8	2,424	8.89
Newmont Mining	20,683.0	−65	−318.20
Goldcorp	12,986.7	369	35.19

Source: www.miningfeeds.com, Morningstar.

Solution:

Norilsk Nickel and Barrick Gold have the lowest EV/OI and thus appear to be the *most* undervalued or favorably priced on the basis of the EV/OI. Note the negative ratio for Glencore, Freeport-McMoRan, and Newmont Mining. Negative ratios are difficult to interpret, so other means are used to evaluate companies with negative ratios.

12 ASSET-BASED VALUATION

☐ describe asset-based valuation models and their use in estimating equity value

☐ explain advantages and disadvantages of each category of valuation model

An asset-based valuation of a company uses estimates of the market or fair value of the company's assets and liabilities. Thus, asset-based valuations work well for companies that do not have a high proportion of intangible or "off the books" assets and that do have a high proportion of current assets and current liabilities. The analyst may be able to value these companies' assets and liabilities in a reasonable fashion by starting with balance sheet items. For most companies, however, balance sheet values are different from market (fair) values, and the market (fair) values can be difficult to determine.

Asset-based valuation models are frequently used together with multiplier models to value private companies. As public companies increase reporting or disclosure of fair values, asset-based valuation may be increasingly used to supplement present value and multiplier models of valuation. Important facts that the practitioner should realize are as follows:

- Companies with assets that do not have easily determinable market (fair) values—such as those with significant property, plant, and equipment—are very difficult to analyze using asset valuation methods.

- Asset and liability fair values can be very different from the values at which they are carried on the balance sheet of a company.

Asset-Based Valuation

- Some assets that are "intangible" are shown on the books of the company. Other intangible assets, such as the value from synergies or the value of a good business reputation, may not be shown on the books. Because asset-based valuation may not consider some intangibles, it can give a "floor" value for a situation involving a significant amount of intangibles. When a company has significant intangibles, the analyst should prefer a forward-looking cash flow valuation.
- Asset values may be more difficult to estimate in a hyper-inflationary environment.

We begin by discussing asset-based valuation for hypothetical nonpublic companies and then move on to a public company example. Analysts should consider the difficulties and rewards of using asset-based valuation for companies that are suited to this measure. Owners of small privately held businesses are familiar with valuations arrived at by valuing the assets of the company and then subtracting any relevant liabilities.

EXAMPLE 18

An Asset-Based Valuation of a Family-Owned Laundry

1. A family owns a laundry and the real estate on which the laundry stands. The real estate is collateral for an outstanding loan of $100,000. How can asset-based valuation be used to value this business?

Solution:

The analyst should get at least two market appraisals for the real estate (building and land) and estimate the cost to extinguish the $100,000 loan. This information would provide estimated values for everything except the laundry as a going concern. That is, the analyst has market values for the building and land and the loan but needs to value the laundry business. The analyst can value the assets of the laundry: the equipment and inventory. The equipment can be valued at depreciated value, inflation-adjusted depreciated value, or replacement cost. Replacement cost in this case means the amount that would have to be spent to buy equivalent used machines. This amount is the market value of the used machines. The analyst will recognize that any intangible value of the laundry (prime location, clever marketing, etc.) is being excluded, which will result in an inaccurate asset-based valuation.

Example 18 shows some of the subtleties present in applying asset-based valuation to determine company value. It also shows how asset-based valuation does not deal with intangibles. Example 19 emphasizes this point.

EXAMPLE 19

An Asset-Based Valuation of a Restaurant

1. The business being valued is a restaurant that serves breakfast and lunch. The owner/proprietor wants to sell the business and retire. The restaurant space is rented, not owned. This particular restaurant is hugely popular

> because of the proprietor's cooking skills and secret recipes. How can the analyst value this business?
>
> ### Solution:
>
> Because of the intangibles, setting a value on this business is challenging. A multiple of income or revenue might be considered. But even those approaches overlook the fact that the proprietor may not be selling his secret recipes and, furthermore, does not intend to continue cooking. Some (or all) of the intangible assets may vanish when the business is sold. Asset-based valuation for this restaurant would begin with estimating the value of the restaurant equipment and inventory and subtracting the value of any liabilities. This approach will provide only a good baseline, however, for a minimum valuation.

For public companies, the assets will typically be so extensive that a piece-by-piece analysis will be impossible, and the transition from book value to market value is a nontrivial task. The asset-based valuation approach is most applicable when the market value of the corporate assets is readily determinable and the intangible assets, which are typically difficult to value, are a relatively small proportion of corporate assets. Asset-based valuation has also been applied to financial companies, natural resource companies, and formerly going-concerns that are being liquidated. Even for other types of companies, however, asset-based valuation of tangible assets may provide a baseline for a minimal valuation.

EXAMPLE 20

An Asset-Based Valuation of an Airline

1. Consider the value of an airline company that has few routes, high labor and other operating costs, has stopped paying dividends, and is losing millions of dollars each year. Using most valuation approaches, the company will have a negative value. Why might an asset-based valuation approach be appropriate for use by one of the company's competitors that is considering acquisition of this airline?

Solution:

The airline's routes, landing rights, leases of airport facilities, and ground equipment and airplanes may have substantial value to a competitor. An asset-based approach to valuing this company would value the company's assets separately and aside from the money-losing business in which they are presently being utilized.

Analysts recognizing the uncertainties related to model appropriateness and the inputs to the models frequently use more than one model or type of model in valuation to increase their confidence in their estimates of intrinsic value. The choice of models will depend on the availability of information to put into the models. Example 21 illustrates the use of three valuation methods.

Asset-Based Valuation

EXAMPLE 21

A Simple Example of the Use of Three Major Equity Valuation Models

Company data for dividend per share (DPS), earnings per share (EPS), share price, and price-to-earnings ratio (P/E) for the most recent five years are presented in Exhibit 11. In addition, estimates (indicated by an "E" after the amount) of DPS and EPS for the next five years are shown. The valuation date is at the end of Year 5. The company has 1,000 shares outstanding.

Exhibit 11: Company DPS, EPS, Share Price, and P/E Data

Year	DPS	EPS	Share Price	TTM P/E
10	$3.10E	$5.20E	—	—
9	$2.91E	$4.85E	—	—
8	$2.79E	$4.65E	—	—
7	$2.65E	$4.37E	—	—
6	$2.55E	$4.30E	—	—
5	$2.43	$4.00	$50.80	12.7
4	$2.32	$3.90	$51.48	13.2
3	$2.19	$3.65	$59.86	16.4
2	$2.14	$3.60	$54.72	15.2
1	$2.00	$3.30	$46.20	14.0

The company's balance sheet at the end of Year 5 is given in Exhibit 12.

Exhibit 12: Balance Sheet as of End of Year 5

Cash	$ 5,000
Accounts receivable	15,000
Inventories	30,000
Net fixed assets	50,000
Total assets	$100,000
Accounts payable	$ 3,000
Notes payable	17,000
Term loans	25,000
Common shareholders' equity	55,000
Total liabilities and equity	$100,000

1. Using a Gordon growth model, estimate intrinsic value. Use a discount rate of 10 percent and an estimate of growth based on growth in dividends over the next five years.

Solution to 1:

$$D_5(1+g)^5 = D_{10} \quad 2.43(1+g)^5 = 3.10$$

$$g \approx 5.0\%$$

Estimate of value = V_5 = 2.55/(0.10 − 0.05) = $51.00

2. Using a multiplier approach, estimate intrinsic value. Assume that a reasonable estimate of P/E is the average trailing twelve-month (TTM) P/E ratio over Years 1 through 4.

Solution to 2:

Average P/E = (14.0 + 15.2 + 16.4 + 13.2)/4 = 14.7

Estimate of value = $4.00 × 14.7 = $58.80

3. Using an asset-based valuation approach, estimate value per share from adjusted book values. Assume that the market values of accounts receivable and inventories are as reported, the market value of net fixed assets is 110 percent of reported book value, and the reported book values of liabilities reflect their market values.

Solution to 3:

Market value of assets = 5,000 + 15,000 + 30,000 + 1.1(50,000) = $105,000

Market value of liabilities = $3,000 + 17,000 + 25,000 = $45,000

Adjusted book value = $105,000 − 45,000 = $60,000

Estimated value (adjusted book value per share) = $60,000 ÷ 1,000 shares = $60.00

Given the current share price of $50.80, the multiplier and the asset-based valuation approaches indicate that the stock is undervalued. Given the intrinsic value estimated using the Gordon growth model, the analyst is likely to conclude that the stock is fairly priced. The analyst might examine the assumptions in the multiplier and the asset-based valuation approaches to determine why their estimated values differ from the estimated value provided by the Gordon growth model and the market price.

SUMMARY

The equity valuation models used to estimate intrinsic value—present value models, multiplier models, and asset-based valuation—are widely used and serve an important purpose. The valuation models presented here are a foundation on which to base analysis and research but must be applied wisely. Valuation is not simply a numerical analysis. The choice of model and the derivation of inputs require skill and judgment.

When valuing a company or group of companies, the analyst wants to choose a valuation model that is appropriate for the information available to be used as inputs. The available data will, in most instances, restrict the choice of model and influence the way it is used. Complex models exist that may improve on the simple valuation models described in this reading; but before using those models and assuming that complexity increases accuracy, the analyst would do well to consider the "law of parsimony:" A

Asset-Based Valuation

model should be kept as simple as possible in light of the available inputs. Valuation is a fallible discipline, and any method will result in an inaccurate forecast at some time. The goal is to minimize the inaccuracy of the forecast.

Among the points made in this reading are the following:

- An analyst estimating intrinsic value is implicitly questioning the market's estimate of value.

- If the estimated value exceeds the market price, the analyst infers the security is *undervalued*. If the estimated value equals the market price, the analyst infers the security is *fairly valued*. If the estimated value is less than the market price, the analyst infers the security is *overvalued*. Because of the uncertainties involved in valuation, an analyst may require that value estimates differ markedly from market price before concluding that a misvaluation exists.

- Analysts often use more than one valuation model because of concerns about the applicability of any particular model and the variability in estimates that result from changes in inputs.

- Three major categories of equity valuation models are present value, multiplier, and asset-based valuation models.

- Present value models estimate value as the present value of expected future benefits.

- Multiplier models estimate intrinsic value based on a multiple of some fundamental variable.

- Asset-based valuation models estimate value based on the estimated value of assets and liabilities.

- The choice of model will depend upon the availability of information to input into the model and the analyst's confidence in both the information and the appropriateness of the model.

- Companies distribute cash to shareholders using dividend payments and share repurchases.

- Regular cash dividends are a key input to dividend valuation models.

- Key dates in dividend chronology are the declaration date, ex-dividend date, holder-of-record date, and payment date.

- In the dividend discount model, value is estimated as the present value of expected future dividends.

- In the free cash flow to equity model, value is estimated as the present value of expected future free cash flow to equity.

- The Gordon growth model, a simple DDM, estimates value as $D_1/(r - g)$.

- The two stage dividend discount model estimates value as the sum of the present values of dividends over a short-term period of high growth and the present value of the terminal value at the end of the period of high growth. The terminal value is estimated using the Gordon growth model.

- The choice of dividend model is based upon the patterns assumed with respect to future dividends.

- Multiplier models typically use multiples of the form: P/ measure of fundamental variable or EV/ measure of fundamental variable.

- Multiples can be based upon fundamentals or comparables.

- Asset-based valuations models estimate value of equity as the value of the assets less the value of liabilities.

REFERENCES

Basu, S. 1977. "Investment Performance of Common Stocks in Relation to Their Price-Earnings Ratios: A Test of the Efficient Market Hypothesis." Journal of Finance, vol. 32, no. 3:663–682. 10.2307/2326304

Block, S. 1999. "A Study of Financial Analysts: Practice and Theory." Financial Analysts Journal, vol. 55, no. 4:86–95. 10.2469/faj.v55.n4.2288

Dreman, D. 1977. Psychology of the Stock Market. New York: AMACOM.

Fama, E., K. French. 1995. "Size and Book-to-Market Factors in Earnings and Returns." Journal of Finance, vol. 50, no. 1:131–155. 10.2307/2329241

McWilliams, J. 1966. "Prices, Earnings and P-E Ratios." Financial Analysts Journal, vol. 22, no. 3:137. 10.2469/faj.v22.n3.137

Miller, P., E. Widmann. 1966. "Price Performance Outlook for High & Low P/E Stocks." 1966 Stock & Bond Issue, Commercial & Financial Chronicle: 26–28.

Nicholson, S. 1968. "Price Ratios in Relation to Investment Results." Financial Analysts Journal, vol. 24, no. 1:105–109. 10.2469/faj.v24.n1.105

O'Shaughnessy, J. 2005. What Works on Wall Street. New York: McGraw-Hill.

PRACTICE PROBLEMS

1. An analyst estimates the intrinsic value of a stock to be in the range of €17.85 to €21.45. The current market price of the stock is €24.35. This stock is *most likely*:

   A. overvalued.

   B. undervalued.

   C. fairly valued.

2. An analyst determines the intrinsic value of an equity security to be equal to $55. If the current price is $47, the equity is *most likely*:

   A. undervalued.

   B. fairly valued.

   C. overvalued.

3. In asset-based valuation models, the intrinsic value of a common share of stock is based on the:

   A. estimated market value of the company's assets.

   B. estimated market value of the company's assets plus liabilities.

   C. estimated market value of the company's assets minus liabilities.

4. Which of the following is *most likely* used in a present value model?

   A. Enterprise value.

   B. Price to free cash flow.

   C. Free cash flow to equity.

5. Book value is *least likely* to be considered when using:

   A. a multiplier model.

   B. an asset-based valuation model.

   C. a present value model.

6. An analyst is attempting to calculate the intrinsic value of a company and has gathered the following company data: EBITDA, total market value, and market value of cash and short-term investments, liabilities, and preferred shares. The analyst is *least likely* to use:

   A. a multiplier model.

   B. a discounted cash flow model.

   C. an asset-based valuation model.

7. An analyst who bases the calculation of intrinsic value on dividend-paying capac-

ity rather than expected dividends will *most likely* use the:

A. dividend discount model.

B. free cash flow to equity model.

C. cash flow from operations model.

8. An investor expects to purchase shares of common stock today and sell them after two years. The investor has estimated dividends for the next two years, D_1 and D_2, and the selling price of the stock two years from now, P_2. According to the dividend discount model, the intrinsic value of the stock today is the present value of:

A. next year's dividend, D_1.

B. future expected dividends, D_1 and D_2.

C. future expected dividends and price—D_1, D_2 and P_2.

9. In the free cash flow to equity (FCFE) model, the intrinsic value of a share of stock is calculated as:

A. the present value of future expected FCFE.

B. the present value of future expected FCFE plus net borrowing.

C. the present value of future expected FCFE minus fixed capital investment.

10. With respect to present value models, which of the following statements is *most accurate*?

A. Present value models can be used only if a stock pays a dividend.

B. Present value models can be used only if a stock pays a dividend or is expected to pay a dividend.

C. Present value models can be used for stocks that currently pay a dividend, are expected to pay a dividend, or are not expected to pay a dividend.

11. A Canadian life insurance company has an issue of 4.80 percent, $25 par value, perpetual, non-convertible, non-callable preferred shares outstanding. The required rate of return on similar issues is 4.49 percent. The intrinsic value of a preferred share is *closest to*:

A. $25.00.

B. $26.75.

C. $28.50.

12. Two analysts estimating the value of a non-convertible, non-callable, perpetual preferred stock with a constant dividend arrive at different estimated values. The *most likely* reason for the difference is that the analysts used different:

A. time horizons.

B. required rates of return.

C. estimated dividend growth rates.

Practice Problems

13. The Beasley Corporation has just paid a dividend of $1.75 per share. If the required rate of return is 12.3 percent per year and dividends are expected to grow indefinitely at a constant rate of 9.2 percent per year, the intrinsic value of Beasley Corporation stock is *closest* to:

   A. $15.54.

   B. $56.45.

   C. $61.65.

14. An investor is considering the purchase of a common stock with a $2.00 annual dividend. The dividend is expected to grow at a rate of 4 percent annually. If the investor's required rate of return is 7 percent, the intrinsic value of the stock is *closest* to:

   A. $50.00.

   B. $66.67.

   C. $69.33.

15. The Gordon growth model can be used to value dividend-paying companies that are:

   A. expected to grow very fast.

   B. in a mature phase of growth.

   C. very sensitive to the business cycle.

16. Which of the following is *most likely* considered a weakness of present value models?

   A. Present value models cannot be used for companies that do not pay dividends.

   B. Small changes in model assumptions and inputs can result in large changes in the computed intrinsic value of the security.

   C. The value of the security depends on the investor's holding period; thus, comparing valuations of different companies for different investors is difficult.

17. An analyst gathers or estimates the following information about a stock:

Current price per share	€22.56
Current annual dividend per share	€1.60
Annual dividend growth rate for Years 1–4	9.00%
Annual dividend growth rate for Years 5+	4.00%
Required rate of return	12%

   Based on a dividend discount model, the stock is *most likely*:

   A. undervalued.

   B. fairly valued.

   C. overvalued.

18. An analyst is attempting to value shares of the Dominion Company. The company has just paid a dividend of $0.58 per share. Dividends are expected to grow by 20 percent next year and 15 percent the year after that. From the third year onward, dividends are expected to grow at 5.6 percent per year indefinitely. If the required rate of return is 8.3 percent, the intrinsic value of the stock is *closest* to:

    A. $26.00.

    B. $27.00.

    C. $28.00.

19. Hideki Corporation has just paid a dividend of ¥450 per share. Annual dividends are expected to grow at the rate of 4 percent per year over the next four years. At the end of four years, shares of Hideki Corporation are expected to sell for ¥9000. If the required rate of return is 12 percent, the intrinsic value of a share of Hideki Corporation is *closest* to:

    A. ¥5,850.

    B. ¥7,220.

    C. ¥7,670.

20. The best model to use when valuing a young dividend-paying company that is just entering the growth phase is *most likely* the:

    A. Gordon growth model.

    B. two-stage dividend discount model.

    C. three-stage dividend discount model.

21. An equity analyst has been asked to estimate the intrinsic value of the common stock of Omega Corporation, a leading manufacturer of automobile seats. Omega is in a mature industry, and both its earnings and dividends are expected to grow at a rate of 3 percent annually. Which of the following is *most likely* to be the best model for determining the intrinsic value of an Omega share?

    A. Gordon growth model.

    B. Free cash flow to equity model.

    C. Multistage dividend discount model.

22. A price earnings ratio that is derived from the Gordon growth model is inversely related to the:

    A. growth rate.

    B. dividend payout ratio.

    C. required rate of return.

23. The primary difference between P/E multiples based on comparables and P/E multiples based on fundamentals is that fundamentals-based P/Es take into account:

    A. future expectations.

    B. the law of one price.

Practice Problems

C. historical information.

24. An analyst makes the following statement: "Use of P/E and other multiples for analysis is not effective because the multiples are based on historical data and because not all companies have positive accounting earnings." The analyst's statement is *most likely*:

    A. inaccurate with respect to both historical data and earnings.

    B. accurate with respect to historical data and inaccurate with respect to earnings.

    C. inaccurate with respect to historical data and accurate with respect to earnings.

25. An analyst has gathered the following information for the Oudin Corporation:

    Expected earnings per share = €5.70
    Expected dividends per share = €2.70
    Dividends are expected to grow at 2.75 percent per year indefinitely
    The required rate of return is 8.35 percent

    Based on the information provided, the price/earnings multiple for Oudin is *closest* to:

    A. 5.7.

    B. 8.5.

    C. 9.4.

26. An analyst has prepared a table of the average trailing twelve-month price-to-earning (P/E), price-to-cash flow (P/CF), and price-to-sales (P/S) for the Tanaka Corporation for the years 2014 to 2017.

Year	P/E	P/CF	P/S
2014	4.9	5.4	1.2
2015	6.1	8.6	1.5
2016	8.3	7.3	1.9
2017	9.2	7.9	2.3

    As of the date of the valuation in 2018, the trailing twelve-month P/E, P/CF, and P/S are, respectively, 9.2, 8.0, and 2.5. Based on the information provided, the analyst may reasonably conclude that Tanaka shares are *most likely*:

    A. overvalued.

    B. undervalued.

    C. fairly valued.

27. An analyst gathers the following information about two companies:

	Alpha Corp.	Delta Co.
Current price per share	$57.32	$18.93

Last year's EPS	$3.82	$1.35
Current year's estimated EPS	$4.75	$1.40

Which of the following statements is *most accurate*?

A. Delta has the higher trailing P/E multiple and lower current estimated P/E multiple.

B. Alpha has the higher trailing P/E multiple and lower current estimated P/E multiple.

C. Alpha has the higher trailing P/E multiple and higher current estimated P/E multiple.

28. An analyst gathers the following information about similar companies in the banking sector:

	First Bank	Prime Bank	Pioneer Trust
P/B	1.10	0.60	0.60
P/E	8.40	11.10	8.30

Which of the companies is *most likely* to be undervalued?

A. First Bank.

B. Prime Bank.

C. Pioneer Trust.

29. The market value of equity for a company can be calculated as enterprise value:

A. minus market value of debt, preferred stock, and short-term investments.

B. plus market value of debt and preferred stock minus short-term investments.

C. minus market value of debt and preferred stock plus short-term investments.

30. Which of the following statements regarding the calculation of the enterprise value multiple is *most likely* correct?

A. Operating income may be used instead of EBITDA.

B. EBITDA may not be used if company earnings are negative.

C. Book value of debt may be used instead of market value of debt.

31. An analyst has determined that the appropriate EV/EBITDA for Rainbow Company is 10.2. The analyst has also collected the following forecasted information for Rainbow Company:

EBITDA = $22,000,000

Market value of debt = $56,000,000

Cash = $1,500,000

The value of equity for Rainbow Company is *closest* to:

Practice Problems

    A. $169 million.

    B. $224 million.

    C. $281 million.

32. Enterprise value is most often determined as market capitalization of common equity and preferred stock minus the value of cash equivalents plus the:

    A. book value of debt.

    B. market value of debt.

    C. market value of long-term debt.

33. A disadvantage of the EV method for valuing equity is that the following information may be difficult to obtain:

    A. Operating income.

    B. Market value of debt.

    C. Market value of equity.

34. Asset-based valuation models are best suited to companies where the capital structure does not have a high proportion of:

    A. debt.

    B. intangible assets.

    C. current assets and liabilities.

35. Which of the following is *most likely* a reason for using asset-based valuation?

    A. The analyst is valuing a privately held company.

    B. The company has a relatively high level of intangible assets.

    C. The market values of assets and liabilities are different from the balance sheet values.

36. Which type of equity valuation model is *most likely* to be preferable when one is comparing similar companies?

    A. A multiplier model.

    B. A present value model.

    C. An asset-based valuation model.

SOLUTIONS

1. A is correct. The current market price of the stock exceeds the upper bound of the analyst's estimate of the intrinsic value of the stock.

2. A is correct. The market price is less than the estimated intrinsic, or fundamental, value.

3. C is correct. Asset-based valuation models calculate the intrinsic value of equity by subtracting liabilities from the market value of assets.

4. C is correct. FCFE can be used in a form of present value, or discounted cash flow, model. Both EV and price to free cash flow are forms of multiplier models.

5. C is correct. Multiplier valuation models (in the form of P/B) and asset-based valuation models (in the form of adjustments to book value) use book value, whereas present value models typically discount future expected cash flows.

6. B is correct. To use a discounted cash flow model, the analyst will require FCFE or dividend data. In addition, the analyst will need data to calculate an appropriate discount rate.

7. B is correct. The FCFE model assumes that dividend-paying capacity is reflected in FCFE.

8. C is correct. According to the dividend discount model, the intrinsic value of a stock today is the present value of all future dividends. In this case, the intrinsic value is the present value of D_1, D_2, and P_2. Note that P_2 is the present value at Period 2 of all future dividends from Period 3 to infinity.

9. A is correct. In the FCFE model, the intrinsic value of stock is calculated by discounting expected future FCFE to present value. No further adjustments are required.

10. C is correct. Dividend discount models can be used for a stock that pays a current dividend or a stock that is expected to pay a dividend. FCFE can be used for both of those stocks and for stocks that do not, or are not expected to, pay dividends in the near future. Both of these models are forms of present value models.

11. B is correct. The expected annual dividend is 4.80% × $25 = $1.20. The value of a preferred share is $1.20/0.0449 = $26.73.

12. B is correct. The required rate of return, r, can vary widely depending on the inputs and is not unique. A preferred stock with a constant dividend would not have a growth rate to estimate, and the investor's time horizon would have no effect on the calculation of intrinsic value.

13. C is correct. $P_0 = D_1/(r - g) = 1.75(1.092)/(0.123 - 0.092) = \$61.65$.

14. C is correct. According to the Gordon growth model, $V_0 = D_1/(r - g)$. In this case, $D_1 = \$2.00 \times 1.04 = \$2.08$, so $V_0 = \$2.08/(0.07 - 0.04) = \$69.3333 = \$69.33$.

15. B is correct. The Gordon growth model (also known as the constant growth model) can be used to value dividend-paying companies in a mature phase of growth. A stable dividend growth rate is often a plausible assumption for such companies.

Solutions

16. B is correct. Very small changes in inputs, such as required rate of return or dividend growth rate, can result in large changes to the valuation model output. Some present value models, such as FCFE models, can be used to value companies without dividends. Also, the intrinsic value of a security is independent of the investor's holding period.

17. A is correct. The current price of €22.56 is less than the intrinsic value (V_0) of €24.64; therefore, the stock appears to be currently undervalued. According to the two-stage dividend discount model:

$$V_0 = \sum_{t=1}^{n} \frac{D_0(1+g_S)^t}{(1+r)^t} + \frac{V_n}{(1+r)^n} \text{ and } V_n = \frac{D_{n+1}}{r-g_L}$$

$D_{n+1} = D_0(1+g_S)^n(1+g_L)$

$D_1 = €1.60 \times 1.09 = €1.744$

$D_2 = €1.60 \times (1.09)^2 = €1.901$

$D_3 = €1.60 \times (1.09)^3 = €2.072$

$D_4 = €1.60 \times (1.09)^4 = €2.259$

$D_5 = [€1.60 \times (1.09)^4](1.04) = €2.349$

$V_4 = €2.349/(0.12 - 0.04) = €29.363$

$$V_0 = \frac{1.744}{(1.12)^1} + \frac{1.901}{(1.12)^2} + \frac{2.072}{(1.12)^3} + \frac{2.259}{(1.12)^4} + \frac{29.363}{(1.12)^4}$$

$= 1.557 + 1.515 + 1.475 + 1.436 + 18.661$

$= €24.64$ (which is greater than the current price of €22.56)

18. C is correct.

$$V_0 = \frac{D_1}{(1+r)} + \frac{D_2}{(1+r)^2} + \frac{P_2}{(1+r)^2}$$

$$= \frac{0.70}{(1.083)} + \frac{0.80}{(1.083)^2} + \frac{31.29}{(1.083)^2}$$

$= \$28.01$

Note that $D_1 = 0.58(1.20) = 0.70$, $D_2 = 0.58(1.20)(1.15) = 0.80$, and $P_2 = D_3/(k-g) = 0.80(1.056)/(0.083 - 0.056) = 31.29$

19. B is correct.

$$V_0 = \frac{D_1}{(1+r)} + \frac{D_2}{(1+r)^2} + \frac{D_3}{(1+r)^3} + \frac{D_4}{(1+r)^4} + \frac{P_4}{(1+r)^4}$$

$$= \frac{468}{(1.12)} + \frac{486.72}{(1.12)^2} + \frac{506.19}{(1.12)^3} + \frac{526.44}{(1.12)^4} + \frac{9000}{(1.12)^4}$$

$= ¥7,220$

20. C is correct. The Gordon growth model is best suited to valuing mature companies. The two-stage model is best for companies that are transitioning from a growth stage to a mature stage. The three-stage model is appropriate for young companies just entering the growth phase.

21. A is correct. The company is a mature company with a steadily growing dividend rate. The two-stage (or multistage) model is unnecessary because the dividend growth rate is expected to remain stable. Although an FCFE model could be used, that model is more often chosen for companies that currently pay no dividends.

22. C is correct. The justified forward P/E is calculated as follows:

$$\frac{P_0}{E_1} = \frac{\frac{D_1}{E_1}}{r-g}$$

P/E is inversely related to the required rate of return, r, and directly related to the growth rate, g, and the dividend payout ratio, D/E.

23. A is correct. Multiples based on comparables are grounded in the law of one price and take into account historical multiple values. In contrast, P/E multiples based on fundamentals can be based on the Gordon growth model, which takes into account future expected dividends.

24. A is correct. The statement is inaccurate in both respects. Although multiples can be calculated from historical data, forecasted values can be used as well. For companies without accounting earnings, several other multiples can be used. These multiples are often specific to a company's industry or sector and include price-to-sales and price-to-cash flow.

25. B is correct.

$$\frac{P_0}{E_1} = \frac{\frac{D_1}{E_1}}{r-g} = \frac{\frac{2.7}{5.7}}{0.0835 - 0.0275} = 8.5$$

26. A is correct. Tanaka shares are most likely overvalued. As the table below shows, all the 2018 multiples are currently above their 2014–2017 averages.

Year	P/E	P/CF	P/R
2014	4.9	5.4	1.2
2015	6.1	8.6	1.5
2016	8.3	7.3	1.9
2017	9.2	7.9	2.3
Average	7.1	7.3	1.7

27. B is correct. P/E = Current price/EPS, and Estimated P/E = Current price/Estimated EPS.

    Alpha P/E = $57.32/$3.82 = 15.01

    Alpha estimated P/E = $57.32/4.75 = 12.07

    Delta P/E = $18.93/$1.35 = 14.02

    Delta estimated P/E = $18.93/$1.40 = 13.52

28. C is correct. Relative to the others, Pioneer Trust has the lowest P/E multiple and the P/B multiple is tied for the lowest with Prime Bank. Given the law of one price, similar companies should trade at similar P/B and P/E levels. Thus, based on the information presented, Pioneer is most likely to be undervalued.

29. C is correct. Enterprise value is calculated as the market value of equity plus the market value of debt and preferred stock minus short-term investments. Therefore, the market value of equity is enterprise value minus the market value of debt and preferred stock plus short-term investments.

30. A is correct. Operating income may be used in place of EBITDA when calculating the enterprise value multiple. EBITDA may be used when company earnings

are negative because EBITDA is usually positive. The book value of debt cannot be used in place of market value of debt.

31. A is correct.

    EV = 10.2 × 22,000,000 = $224,400,000

    Equity value = EV − Debt + Cash
    = 224,400,000 − 56,000,000 + 1,500,000
    = $169,900,000

32. B is correct. The market value of debt must be calculated and taken out of the enterprise value. Enterprise value, sometimes known as the cost of a takeover, is the cost of the purchase of the company, which would include the assumption of the company's debts at market value.

33. B is correct. According to the reading, analysts may have not have access to market quotations for company debt.

34. B is correct. Intangible assets are hard to value. Therefore, asset-based valuation models work best for companies that do not have a high proportion of intangible assets.

35. A is correct. Asset-based valuations are most often used when an analyst is valuing private enterprises. Both B and C are considerations in asset-based valuations but are more likely to be reasons to avoid that valuation model rather than reasons to use it.

36. A is correct. Although all models can be used to compare various companies, multiplier models have the advantage of reducing varying fundamental data points into a format that allows direct comparisons. As long as the analyst applies the data in a consistent manner for all the companies, this approach provides useful comparative data.

Glossary

Abandonment option The option to terminate an investment at some future time if the financial results are disappointing.

Abnormal return The return on an asset in excess of the asset's required rate of return; the risk-adjusted return.

Absolute dispersion The amount of variability present without comparison to any reference point or benchmark.

Accelerated book build An offering of securities by an investment bank acting as principal that is accomplished in only one or two days.

Accounting profit Income as reported on the income statement, in accordance with prevailing accounting standards, before the provisions for income tax expense. Also called *income before taxes* or *pretax income*.

Accredited investors Investors that meet certain minimum regulatory net worth or other requirements in order to invest in certain types of alternative assets.

Accrued interest The amount of interest in currency or par value terms of a fixed-income instrument that accumulates from the last coupon payment until the trade settlement date. The amount is paid by the buyer to the seller.

Action lag Delay from policy decisions to implementation.

Active investment An approach to investing in which the investor seeks to outperform a given benchmark.

Active return The return on a portfolio minus the return on the portfolio's benchmark.

Activist Short for "activist shareholder." Managers secure sufficient equity holdings to allow them to seek a position in a company's board and influence corporate policies or direction.

Activity ratios Ratios that measure how well a company is managing key current assets and working capital over time.

Ad hoc committee A small group of lenders or bondholders who negotiate with an issuer on debt restructuring and refinancing before the issuer submits a final proposal to the wider group of all lenders and bondholders.

Add-on pricing A pricing approach based on high-margin optional features, customizations, and additional content.

Add-on rate A yield or pricing convention for money market instrument quotations. It is the interest earned on an instrument, derived from the difference between the price and face value, expressed as a percentage of the price and multiplied by the periodicity of the annual rate.

Agency costs Direct and indirect costs borne by the principal in a principal-agent relationship owing primarily to information asymmetries. Agency costs include the costs of monitoring and assessing the agent as well as missed opportunities.

Agency RMBS Securities created by the pooling of residential mortgage-backed securities in the United States by either the Federal National Mortgage Association (Fannie Mae) or the Federal Home Loan Mortgage Corporation (Freddie Mac). These RMBS carry the full faith and credit of the government, essentially a guarantee with respect to timely payment of interest and repayment of principal.

All-or-nothing (AON) orders An order that includes the instruction to trade only if the trade fills the entire quantity (size) specified.

Allocationally efficient A characteristic of a market, a financial system, or an economy that promotes the allocation of resources to their highest value uses.

Altcoin A cryptocurrency other than Bitcoin.

Alternative data Data that are generated from non-traditional sources, such as social media and sensor networks.

Alternative hypothesis The hypothesis that is accepted if the null hypothesis is rejected.

Alternative investment markets Market for investments other than traditional securities investments (i.e., traditional common and preferred shares and traditional fixed income instruments). The term usually encompasses direct and indirect investment in real estate (including timberland and farmland) and commodities (including precious metals); hedge funds, private equity, and other investments requiring specialized due diligence.

Alternative trading systems Trading venues that function like exchanges but that do not exercise regulatory authority over their subscribers except with respect to the conduct of the subscribers' trading in their trading systems. Also called *electronic communications networks* or *multilateral trading facilities*.

American depository receipt A US dollar-denominated security that trades like a common share on US exchanges.

American depository share The underlying shares on which American depository receipts are based. They trade in the issuing company's domestic market.

American options Options that may be exercised at any time from contract inception until maturity.

American-style Type of option contract that can be exercised at any time up to the option's expiration date.

Amortization The process of allocating the cost of intangible long-term assets having a finite useful life to accounting periods; the allocation of the amount of a bond premium or discount to the periods remaining until bond maturity.

Amortizing debt A loan or bond with a payment schedule that calls for periodic payments of interest and repayments of principal.

Analysis of variance (ANOVA) A table that presents the sums of squares, degrees of freedom, mean squares, and F-statistic for a regression model.

Analytical duration Estimates of duration using mathematical formulas. Estimates of the impact of yield changes on bond prices using analytical duration implicitly assume that benchmark yields and spreads are independent variables and are uncorrelated.

Anchoring and adjustment bias An information-processing bias in which the use of a psychological heuristic influences the way people estimate probabilities.

Annual general meeting (AGM) A yearly meeting of the corporate board of directors and shareholders, typically held in person and digitally, during which votes on directors, compensation plans, shareholder resolutions, and any other matters properly brought forward at the meeting are held. Issuer management may also make presentations and hold events.

Anomalies Apparent deviations from market efficiency.

Antidilutive With reference to a transaction or a security, one that would increase earnings per share (EPS) or result in EPS higher than the company's basic EPS—antidilutive securities are not included in the calculation of diluted EPS.

Arbitrage 1) The simultaneous purchase of an undervalued asset or portfolio and sale of an overvalued but equivalent asset or portfolio, in order to obtain a riskless profit on the price differential. Taking advantage of a market inefficiency in a risk-free manner. 2) The condition in a financial market in which equivalent assets or combinations of assets sell for two different prices, creating an opportunity to profit at no risk with no commitment of money. In a well-functioning financial market, few arbitrage opportunities are possible. 3) A risk-free operation that earns an expected positive net profit but requires no net investment of money.

Arbitrageurs Traders who engage in arbitrage. See *arbitrage*.

Arithmetic mean The sum of the observations divided by the number of observations.

Artificial intelligence (AI) Computer systems that are capable of performing tasks that previously required human intelligence. AI methods are sometimes better suited to identify complex, non-linear relationships than are traditional quantitative and statistical methods.

Ask The price at which a dealer or trader is willing to sell an asset, typically qualified by a maximum quantity (ask size). See *offer*.

Ask size The maximum quantity of an asset that pertains to a specific ask price from a trader. For example, if the ask for a share issue is $30 for a size of 1,000 shares, the trader is offering to sell at $30 up to 1,000 shares.

Asset allocation The process of determining how investment funds should be distributed among asset classes.

Asset class A group of assets that have similar characteristics, attributes, and risk–return relationships.

Asset utilization ratios Ratios that measure how efficiently a company performs day-to-day tasks, such as the collection of receivables and management of inventory.

Asset-backed commercial paper Secured form of commercial paper issuance. Loans or receivables are sold to a special purpose entity that issues the ABCP and makes interest and principal payments to investors from asset cash flows.

Asset-backed securities (ABS) A type of bond issued by a legal entity called a special purpose entity created solely to own assets such as loans, receivables, and mortgages and to distribute cash flows to ABS investors. Generally, ABS backed by mortgages are known as mortgage-backed securities (MBS) while ABS refer to non-mortgage ABS.

Asset-backed token A token that represents the ownership of a physical asset that does not exist on the blockchain and whose value is based on the underlying asset.

Asset-based valuation models Valuation based on estimates of the market value of a company's assets.

Asymmetric information Also known as *information asymmetry*; the differential of information between corporate insiders and outsiders regarding the company's performance and prospects. Managers typically have more information about the company's performance and prospects than owners and creditors.

At-the-money Describes a unique situation in which the price of the underlying is equal to an option's exercise price. Like an out-of-the-money option, the intrinsic value is zero.

Auction/reverse auction models Pricing models that establish prices through bidding (by sellers in the case of reverse auctions).

Autarky Countries seeking political self-sufficiency with little or no external trade or finance. State-owned enterprises control strategic domestic industries.

Automatic stabilizer A countercyclical factor that automatically comes into play as an economy slows and unemployment rises.

Availability bias An information-processing bias in which people take a heuristic approach to estimating the probability of an outcome based on how easily the outcome comes to mind.

Available-for-sale Under US GAAP, debt securities not classified as either held-to-maturity or held-for-trading securities. The investor is willing to sell but not actively planning to sell. In general, available-for-sale debt securities are reported at fair value on the balance sheet, with unrealized gains included as a component of other comprehensive income.

Average revenue (AR) Total revenue divided by quantity sold.

Backfill Bias A problem whereby certain surviving hedge funds may be added to databases and various hedge fund indexes only after they are initially successful and start to report their returns. Also see *survivorship bias*.

Backup line of credit A type of credit enhancement provided by a bank to an issuer of commercial paper to ensure that the issuer will have access to sufficient liquidity to repay maturing commercial paper if issuing new paper is not a viable option.

Backwardation A downward-sloping, or inverted, forward curve in a futures market.

Balance sheet ratios Financial ratios involving balance sheet items only.

Balanced With respect to a government budget, one in which spending and revenues (taxes) are equal.

Balloon payment A large payment required at maturity to retire a bond's outstanding principal amount.

Base rates The reference rate on which a bank bases lending rates to all other customers.

Base-rate neglect A type of representativeness bias in which the base rate or probability of the categorization is not adequately considered.

Basic EPS Net earnings available to common shareholders (i.e., net income minus preferred dividends) divided by the weighted average number of common shares outstanding.

Basis risk The possibility that the expected value of a derivative differs unexpectedly from that of the underlying.

Basket of listed depository receipts (BLDR) An exchange-traded fund (ETF) that represents a portfolio of depository receipts.

Bayes' formula The rule for updating the probability of an event of interest—given a set of prior probabilities for the event, information, and information given the event—if you receive new information.

Bearer bonds Bonds for which ownership is not recorded; only the clearing system knows who the bond owner is.

Behavioral finance A field of finance that examines the psychological variables that affect and often distort the investment decision making of investors, analysts, and portfolio managers.

Behind the market Said of prices specified in orders that are worse than the best current price; e.g., for a limit buy order, a limit price below the best bid.

Benchmark A bond used to compare against another bond to discern attributes, often a government bond with the same or similar time-to-maturity as the bond under analysis.

Benchmark spread The difference in yield-to-maturity between a bond and that of a benchmark bond.

Best bid The highest bid in the market.

Best effort offering An offering of a security using an investment bank in which the investment bank, as agent for the issuer, promises to use its best efforts to sell the offering but does not guarantee that a specific amount will be sold.

Best offer The lowest offer (ask price) in the market.

Best-in-class An ESG implementation approach that seeks to identify the most favorable companies in an industry based on ESG considerations.

Beta A measure of systematic risk that is based on the covariance of an asset's or portfolio's return with the return of the overall market; a measure of the sensitivity of a given investment or portfolio to movements in the overall market.

Bid The price at which a dealer or trader is willing to buy an asset, typically qualified by a maximum quantity.

Bid size The maximum quantity of an asset that pertains to a specific bid price from a trader.

Big data The vast amount of information being generated by both traditional sources—for example, stock exchanges, companies, governments—and non-traditional sources—for example, electronic devices, social media, sensor networks, and company exhaust.

Bilateralism The conduct of political, economic, financial, or cultural cooperation between two countries. Countries engaging in bilateralism may have relations with many different countries but in one-at-a-time agreements without multiple partners. Typically, countries exist on a spectrum between bilateralism and multilateralism.

Bimodal A distribution that has two most frequently occurring values.

Bitcoin A cryptocurrency using blockchain technology that was created in 2009.

Bivariate correlation Also known as Pearson correlation. A parametric measure of the relationship between two variables.

Black swan risk An event that is rare and difficult to predict but has an important impact.

Block brokers A broker (agent) that provides brokerage services for large-size trades.

Blockchain A type of digital ledger in which information is recorded sequentially and then linked together and secured using cryptographic methods.

Blue chip Widely held large market capitalization companies that are considered financially sound and are leaders in their respective industry or local stock market.

Board of directors A body or individual selected by a limited company's member(s) or shareholder(s), in a manner determined by the company's charter, that manages the company. Typically, for larger companies, boards of directors appoint and oversee executive management.

Bond equivalent yield A money market interest rate quoted on a 365-day add-on rate basis.

Bond indenture A legal document between a bond issuer and investors that governs each party's rights and responsibilities.

Bond market vigilantes Bond market participants who might reduce their demand for long-term bonds, thus pushing up their yields.

Bondholders Investors in an entity's securitized debt claims, such as commercial paper, notes, and bonds. Common types of bondholders include investment funds and institutional investors.

Bonds Contractual agreements between an issuer and bondholders.

Bonus issue of shares A type of dividend in which a company distributes additional shares of its common stock to shareholders instead of cash.

Book building Investment bankers' process of compiling a "book" or list of indications of interest to buy part of an offering.

Book value The net amount shown for an asset or liability on the balance sheet; book value may also refer to the company's excess of total assets over total liabilities. Also called *carrying value*.

Boom An expansionary phase characterized by economic growth "testing the limits" of the economy.

Bootstrap A resampling method that repeatedly draws samples with replacement of the selected elements from the original observed sample. Bootstrap is usually conducted by using computer simulation and is often used to find standard error or construct confidence intervals of population parameters.

Bottom-up analysis An investment selection approach that focuses on company-specific circumstances rather than emphasizing economic cycles or industry analysis.

Box and whisker plot A graphic for visualizing the dispersion of data across quartiles. It consists of a box with "whiskers" connected to the box.

Breakeven point Represents the price of the underlying in a derivative contract in which the profit to both counterparties would be zero.

Bridge financing Interim financing that provides funds until permanent financing can be arranged.

Broker An agent who executes orders to buy or sell securities on behalf of a client in exchange for a commission.

Brokered market A market in which brokers arrange trades among their clients.

Broker–dealer A financial intermediary (often a company) that may function as a principal (dealer) or as an agent (broker) depending on the type of trade.

Brownfield investments The third stage of development of an infrastructure asset. Brownfield investments involve expanding existing facilities and may involve privatization of public assets or a sale leaseback of completed greenfield projects. They are characterized by a shorter investment period with immediate cash flows and an operating history.

Budget surplus/deficit The difference between government revenue and expenditure for a stated fixed period of time.

Bullet bond A bond whose principal repayment is made entirely at maturity.

Bundling A pricing approach that refers to combining multiple products or services so that customers are incentivized or required to buy them together.

Business cycles Are recurrent expansions and contractions in economic activity affecting broad segments of the economy.

Business model A concise description of how a business works and makes revenues and profits, including its customers, products or services, channels for reaching customers, and pricing.

Businesses Organization entities formed and managed for the purpose of providing a return or economic benefits to its investors and owners.

Buy-side firm An investment management company or other investor that uses the services of brokers or dealers (i.e., the client of the sell side firms).

Buyback A transaction in which a company buys back its own shares. Unlike stock dividends and stock splits, share repurchases use corporate cash.

Cabotage The right to transport passengers or goods within a country by a foreign firm. Many countries—including those with multilateral trade agreements—impose restrictions on cabotage across transportation subsectors, meaning that shippers, airlines, and truck drivers are not allowed to transport goods and services within another country's borders.

Call market A market in which trades occur only at a particular time and place (i.e., when the market is called).

Call money rate The interest rate that buyers pay for their margin loan.

Call option The right to buy an underlying.

Call period The time during which the issuer of a callable bond can exercise the call option.

Call price The price at which the issuer of a callable bond has the right to purchase the bond from investors.

Call protection period The time during which the issuer of a callable bond is not allowed to exercise the call option.

Call risk The uncertain maturity and limited price appreciation associated with callable bonds.

Callable bond A bond containing an embedded call option that gives the issuer the right to buy the bond back from the investor at specified prices on predetermined dates.

Cannibalization A transfer of sales or market share from one product to another product owned by the same company. It tends to occur when the two products are actual or perceived substitutes.

Capacity The ability of the borrower to make its debt payments on time.

Capital Other company resources available that reduce reliance on debt.

Capital allocation The process that companies use for decision making on capital investments—those projects with a life of one year or longer.

Capital allocation line (CAL) A graph line that describes the combinations of expected return and standard deviation of return available to an investor from combining the optimal portfolio of risky assets with the risk-free asset.

Capital asset pricing model (CAPM) An equation describing the expected return on any asset (or portfolio) as a linear function of its beta relative to the market portfolio.

Capital expenditure Expenditure on physical capital (fixed assets).

Capital investments An expenditure for an asset or resource with a useful life of more than one year.

Capital market expectations (CME) Expectations concerning the risk and return prospects of asset classes.

Capital market line (CML) The line with an intercept point equal to the risk-free rate that is tangent to the efficient frontier of risky assets; represents the efficient frontier when a risk-free asset is available for investment.

Capital market securities Fixed-income securities with original maturities greater than one year.

Capital markets Financial markets that trade securities of longer duration, such as bonds and equities.

Capital restrictions Controls placed on foreigners' ability to own domestic assets and/or domestic residents' ability to own foreign assets.

Capital structure The mix of debt and equity that a company uses to finance its business; a company's specific mix of long-term financing.

Capital-indexed bond A type of index-linked bond for which changes in the index are captured with adjustments to the principal. A common example is Treasury Inflation Protected Securities (TIPS) issued by the United States government.

Capital-intensive businesses Companies or business activities that are characterized by a relatively low fixed asset turnover, a high percentage of capital expenditures to sales, or a high net-working-capital-to-sales ratio.

Capital-light businesses Also known as *asset light businesses*, companies or business activities characterized by relatively high fixed asset turnover, a low percentage of capital expenditures to sales, or a low net-working-capital-to-sales ratio.

Carried interest A performance fee (also referred to as an incentive fee, or carry) that is applied based on excess returns above a hurdle rate.

Carrying Investing and holding an asset for a period of time.

Carrying amount The amount at which an asset or liability is valued according to accounting principles.

Carrying value Of a fixed-income instrument is the purchase price plus (minus) the amortized amount of the discount (premium) if the bond is purchased at a price below (above) par value.

Cartel Participants in collusive agreements that are made openly and formally.

Cash conversion cycle The amount of time between an issuer paying its suppliers in cash and receiving cash from its customers.

Cash flow additivity principle The principle that dollar amounts indexed at the same point in time are additive.

Cash flow from operations A cash profit measure over a period for an issuer's primary business activities. It includes cash from customers as well as interest and dividends received from financial investments, less cash paid to employees and suppliers as well as taxes paid to governments and interest paid to lenders.

Cash flow hedge Refers to a specific **hedge accounting** classification in which a derivative is designated as absorbing the variable cash flow of a floating-rate asset or liability, such as foreign exchange, interest rates, or commodities.

Cash markets Markets in which specific assets are exchanged at current prices. Cash markets are often referred to as **spot markets**.

Cash prices The current prices prevailing in **cash markets**.

Cash ratio A measure of liquidity that is the ratio of cash and marketable securities to current liabilities.

Catch-up clause A clause in an agreement that favors the GP. For a GP who earns a 20% performance fee, a catch-up clause allows the GP to receive 100% of the distributions above the hurdle rate *until* she receives 20% of the profits generated, and then every excess dollar is split 80/20 between the LPs and GP.

CDS credit spread Reflects the credit spread of a credit default swap (CDS) derivative contract. As with cash bonds, CDS credit spreads depend on the probability of default (POD) and the loss given default (LGD).

Central bank digital currencies (CBDCs) A tokenized version of the currency issued by the central bank, such as a digital bank note or coin, and a digital liability of the central bank.

Central bank funds market The market in which deposit-taking banks that have an excess reserve with their national central bank can lend money to banks that need funds for maturities ranging from overnight to one year. Called the federal or fed funds market in the United States.

Central bank funds rate The interest rate at which central bank funds are bought (borrowed) and sold (lent) for maturities ranging from overnight to one year. Called federal or fed funds rate in the United States.

Central clearing mandate A requirement instituted by global regulatory authorities following the 2008 global financial crisis that most **over-the-counter (OTC)** derivatives be **cleared** by a **central counterparty (CCP)**.

Central counterparty (CCP) An economic entity that assumes the **counterparty credit risk** between derivative **counterparties**, one of which is typically a financial intermediary. CCPs provide **clearing** and **settlement** for most **derivative contracts**.

Central limit theorem The theorem that states the sum (and the mean) of a set of independent, identically distributed random variables with finite variances is normally distributed, whatever distribution the random variables follow.

Certificate of deposit (CD) An instrument that represents a specified amount of funds on deposit with a bank for a specified maturity and interest rate. CDs are issued in various denominations and can be negotiable or non-negotiable.

Channels Venues where a company markets and/or delivers its products and services.

Character The quality of a debt issuer's management.

Checking accounts Bank deposits with no stated maturity available for transactional purposes that pay little or no interest. Also known as a *demand deposit*.

Circuit breaker A pause in intraday trading for a brief period if a price limit is reached.

Classical cycle Refers to fluctuations in the level of economic activity when measured by GDP in volume terms.

Clawback A requirement that the general partner return any funds distributed as incentive fees until the limited partners have received their initial investment and a percentage of the total profit.

Clearing An exchange's process of verifying the execution of a transaction, exchange of payments, and recording of participants.

Clearing instructions Instructions that indicate how to arrange the final settlement ("clearing") of a trade.

Clearinghouse An entity associated with a futures market that acts as middleman between the contracting parties and guarantees to each party the performance of the other.

Closed-end fund A mutual fund in which no new investment money is accepted. New investors invest by buying existing shares, and investors in the fund liquidate by selling their shares to other investors.

Cluster sampling A procedure that divides a population into subpopulation groups (clusters) representative of the population and then randomly draws certain clusters to form a sample.

Co-investing In co-investing, the investor invests in assets *indirectly* through the fund but also possesses rights (known as co-investment rights) to invest *directly* in the same assets. Through co-investing, an investor is able to make an investment *alongside* a fund when the fund identifies deals.

Code of ethics An established guide that communicates an organization's values and overall expectations regarding member behavior. A code of ethics serves as a general guide for how community members should act.

Coefficient of determination (R^2) The percentage of the variation of the dependent variable that is explained by the independent variable. It is a measure of goodness of fit of a regression model.

Coefficient of variation The ratio of a set of observations' standard deviation to the observations' mean value.

Cognitive cost The effort involved in processing new information and updating beliefs.

Cognitive dissonance The mental discomfort that occurs when new information conflicts with previously held beliefs or cognitions.

Cognitive errors Behavioral biases resulting from faulty reasoning; cognitive errors stem from basic statistical, information-processing, or memory errors.

Coincident economic indicators Turning points that are usually close to those of the overall economy; they are believed to have value for identifying the economy's present state.

Collateral Assets or financial guarantees underlying a debt obligation that are above and beyond the issuer's promise to pay.

Collateral manager Buys and sells debt obligations for and from the CDO's collateral pool to generate sufficient cash flows to meet the obligations to the CDO bondholders.

Collateralized bond obligations (CBOs) CDOs backed by high-yield corporate and emerging market bonds.

Collateralized debt obligations (CDOs) Securities backed by a diversified pool of one or more debt obligations. CDOs can be backed by a broad range of debt.

Collateralized loan obligations (CLOs) CDOs backed by leveraged bank loans.

Collateralized mortgage obligations Securitize mortgage pass-through securities or multiple pools of loans. CMOs are structured to redistribute the cash flows to different bond classes or tranches and create securities that have different exposures to prepayment risk.

Commercial paper (CP) Short-term, negotiable, unsecured promissory note that represents a debt obligation of the issuer.

Committed (regular) lines of credit Bank commitments to extend credit; the commitment is considered a short-term liability and is usually in effect for 364 days (one day short of a full year).

Committed capital The amount that the limited partners have agreed to provide to the private equity fund.

Commodities A product or service from a firm that is indistinguishable from products or services of competing firms, usually conforming to a common standard or grade imposed by convention or regulation.

Commoditization A process by which competing products become less differentiated over time and become interchangeable "commodities" in the eyes of customers. This process is typically associated with declining profitability for the selling firms.

Commodity producers A firm that makes and/or sells commodities.

Commodity swap A type of swap involving the exchange of payments over multiple dates as determined by specified reference prices or indexes relating to commodities.

Common market Level of economic integration that incorporates all aspects of the customs union and extends it by allowing free movement of factors of production among members.

Common shares A type of security that represents an ownership interest in a company. Also called *common stock*.

Common stock A type of security that represents an ownership interest in a company. Also called *common shares*.

Common-size analysis The restatement of financial statement items using a common denominator or reference item that allows one to identify trends and major differences; an example is an income statement in which all items are expressed as a percent of revenue.

Companies Organization entities formed and managed for the purpose of providing a return or economic benefits to its investors and owners.

Company research report A document that presents an analyst's investment recommendation on an issuer and its securities, supported by financial modeling, industry overviews and competitive analyses, valuation scenarios, ESG considerations, and investment risks.

Complete markets Informally, markets in which the variety of distinct securities traded is so broad that any desired payoff in a future state-of-the-world is achievable.

Concession agreement A contractual arrangement under which an entity (also known as a grantor) establishes terms and conditions with a developer or operator (referred to as a concessionaire) to plan, build, operate, finance, and maintain an infrastructure asset for a specific period.

Conditional expected value The expected value of a stated event given that another event has occurred.

Conditional pass-through covered bonds Convert to pass-through securities after the original maturity date if all bond payments have not yet been made.

Conditional variances The variance of one variable, given the outcome of another.

Conditions The general economic, competitive, and business environment faced by all borrowers that may affect their ability to service or refinance debt.

Confidence level The complement of the level of significance.

Confirmation bias A belief perseverance bias in which people tend to look for and notice what confirms their beliefs, to ignore or undervalue what contradicts their beliefs, and to misinterpret information as support for their beliefs.

Consensus protocol A set of rules governing how blocks can join the blockchain that is designed to resist attempts at malicious manipulation up to a certain level of security; it can be either a proof of work or a proof of stake.

Conservatism bias A belief perseverance bias in which people maintain their prior views or forecasts by inadequately incorporating new information.

Constant yield-price trajectory A graphical depiction of the relationship between time to maturity and a bond price, assuming no default, that shows that a bond price approaches par as time passes.

Constituent securities With respect to an index, the individual securities within an index.

Contango Refers to spot price below forward price in a futures market.

Contingency provision Clause in a legal document that allows for some action if a specific event or circumstance occurs.

Contingency table A table of the frequency distribution of observations classified on the basis of two discrete variables.

Contingent claim A type of derivative in which one of the *counterparties* determines whether and when the trade will settle. An *option* is a common type of contingent claim.

Contingent convertible bonds Bonds that automatically convert to equity if a specific event or circumstance occurs, such as the issuer's equity capital falling below the minimum requirement set by regulators.

Continuous trading market A market in which trades can be arranged and executed any time the market is open.

Continuously compounded return The natural logarithm of 1 plus the holding period return, or equivalently, the natural logarithm of the ending price over the beginning price.

Contract manufacturers Companies that make products for other companies that meet specific terms and specifications.

Contract size Amount(s) used for calculation to price and value the derivative. The contract size is often referred to as "notional amount or notional principal."

Contraction The period of a business cycle after the peak and before the trough; often called a *recession* or, if exceptionally severe, called a *depression*.

Contraction risk The risk of earlier repayment of a mortgage-backed security than expected.

Contractionary Tending to cause the real economy to contract.

Contractionary fiscal policy A fiscal policy that has the objective to make the real economy contract.

Contribution margin A profitability measure using variable costs: unit price less unit variable cost. It can also be expressed as a percentage of price or sales.

Controlling shareholder An individual or entity that owns a majority of the voting rights in a corporation.

Convenience sampling A procedure of selecting an element from a population on the basis of whether or not it is accessible to a researcher or how easy it is for a researcher to access the element.

Convenience yield A non-cash benefit of holding a physical commodity versus a derivative.

Conversion price For a convertible bond, the price per share at which the bond can be converted into shares.

Conversion ratio Number of common shares received in exchange for each preferred share after a predetermined period.

Conversion value For a convertible bond, the value of the bond if it is converted at the market price of the shares. Also called *parity value*.

Convertible bond A bond that gives the bondholder the right to exchange the bond for a specified number of common shares in the issuing company.

Convertible debt A debt instrument that gives the holder the right to exchange the instrument for a specified number of common shares in the issuing company.

Convertible preference shares A type of equity security that entitles shareholders to convert their shares into a specified number of common shares.

Convexity An interest rate risk measure used in conjunction with duration; captures the degree of nonlinearity (curvature) in the relation between price change and yield change.

Convexity adjustment A measure that is used to complement modified duration to capture the second-order effect of yield changes on a bond's price. It is equal to the annual convexity statistic times one-half times the given change in the yield-to-maturity squared.

Convexity bias Refers to the difference in price changes for a given change in yield between interest rate futures and interest rate forward contracts. That is, interest rate

Glossary

forwards exhibit a non-linear or convex relationship between price and yield, while the price–yield relationship is linear for interest rate futures.

Cooperation The process by which countries work together toward some shared goal or purpose. These goals may, and often do, vary widely—from strategic or military concerns, to economic influence, to cultural preferences.

Cooperative country A country that engages and reciprocates in rules standardization; harmonization of tariffs; international agreements on trade, immigration, or regulation; and allowing the free flow of information, including technology transfer.

Core real estate strategies Strategies with exposure to well-leased, high-quality commercial and residential real estate in the best markets, generally offered by open-end funds. Investors expect core real estate to deliver stable returns, primarily from income from the property.

Core-plus real estate strategies Value-add investments that require modest redevelopment or upgrades to lease any vacant space together with possible alternative use of the underlying properties. Compared to core real estate strategies, these may be appealing for investors seeking higher returns and willing to accept additional risks from development, redevelopment, repositioning, and leasing.

Corporate issuers Limited companies or corporations that seek financing in financial markets by, for example, issuing debt or equity securities.

Corporations Another term for limited companies, though often used to refer to public limited companies. See *limited company*, *private limited company*, and *public limited company*.

Correlation A measure of the linear relationship between two random variables.

Correlation coefficient A number between −1 and +1 that measures the consistency or tendency for two investments to act in a similar way. It is used to determine the effect on portfolio risk when two assets are combined.

Cost averaging The periodic investment of a fixed amount of money.

Cost of capital The cost of financing for a company; the rate of return that suppliers of capital require as compensation for their contribution of capital (also called *opportunity cost of funds*).

Cost of carry The net of the costs and benefits related to owning an underlying asset for a specific period.

Cost of debt The required return on debt financing for a company, such as when it issues a bond, takes out a bank loan, or leases an asset through a finance lease.

Cost of equity The return required by equity investors to compensate for both the time value of money and the risk. Also referred to as the required rate of return on common stock or the required return on equity.

Counterparty Legal entities entering a **derivative contract**.

Counterparty credit risk The likelihood that a **counterparty** is unable to meet its financial obligations under the contract.

Counterparty risk The risk that the other party to a contract will fail to honor the terms of the contract.

Country The geopolitical environment as well as the legal and political system faced by all issuers in a jurisdiction that may affect debt payment.

Coupon Periodic interest payments paid by a bond issuer to investors, typically expressed as a percentage of par on an annual basis.

Cournot assumption Assumption in which each firm determines its profit-maximizing production level assuming that the other firms' output will not change.

Covariance A measure of the co-movement (linear association) between two random variables.

Covenants The terms and conditions of lending agreements that the issuer must comply with; they specify the actions that an issuer is obligated to perform (affirmative covenant) or prohibited from performing (negative covenant).

Credit default swap (CDS) A type of credit derivative in which one party, the credit protection buyer who is seeking credit protection against a third party, makes a series of regularly scheduled payments to the other party, the credit protection seller. The seller makes no payments until a credit event occurs.

Credit enhancements Provisions or methods that allow a borrower improve their creditworthiness in a structured transaction.

Credit event An event that defines a payout in a credit derivative. Events are usually defined as bankruptcy, failure to pay an obligation, or an involuntary debt restructuring.

Credit facilities Loan agreements with pre-specified terms and limits but with fluctuating balances based on borrower-specific needs at different points in time, analogous to a credit card.

Credit migration risk The risk that a bond issuer's creditworthiness deteriorates, or migrates lower, leading investors to believe the risk of default is higher. Also called **downgrade risk**.

Credit rating Letter-grade, qualitative measures of an issuer's ability to meet its debt obligations based on both the probability of default and the expected loss under a default scenario.

Credit rating agencies Institutions that issue and maintain credit ratings. The three largest are Standard & Poor's, Moody's, and Fitch Ratings.

Credit risk The expected economic loss under a potential borrower default over the life of the contract

Credit spread A premium over and above the current government bond yield.

Credit spread risk The risk of greater expected loss due to changes in credit conditions as a result of macroeconomic, market, and/or issuer-related factors.

Credit tranching Internal credit enhancement where cash flows into a senior/subordinate structure.

Credit-linked notes Bonds whose coupon changes when the bonds' credit rating changes.

Critical values Values of the test statistic at which the decision changes from fail to reject the null hypothesis to reject the null hypothesis.

Cross-default clause Covenant or contract clause that specifies borrowers are considered in default if they default on another debt obligation.

Cross-sectional analysis Also called relative analysis. Analysis that involves comparisons across individuals in a group over a given time period or at a given point in time.

Crossing networks Trading systems that match buyers and sellers who are willing to trade at prices obtained from other markets.

Crowdsourcing A business model that enables users to contribute directly to a product, service, or online content.

Cryptocurrency An electronic medium of exchange that lacks physical form.

Cryptocurrency wallet A storage unit for public and/or private keys for cryptocurrency transactions. These wallets may be a physical device, program, or service.

Cryptography An algorithmic process to encrypt data, making the data unusable if received by unauthorized parties.

Cumulative preference shares Preference shares for which any dividends that are not paid accrue and must be paid in full before dividends on common shares can be paid.

Cumulative voting A voting process whereby shareholders can accumulate and vote all their shares for a single candidate in an election, as opposed to having to allocate their voting rights evenly among all candidates.

Currencies Monies issued by national monetary authorities.

Currency Money issued by national monetary authorities.

Currency swap A swap in which each party makes interest payments to the other in different currencies.

Current government spending With respect to government expenditures, spending on goods and services that are provided on a regular, recurring basis including health, education, and defense.

Current ratio A measure of liquidity that is the ratio of current assets to current liabilities.

Current yield The sum of the coupon payments received over the year divided by the flat price. Also called the income, interest yield, or running yield.

Customs union Extends the free trade area (FTA) by not only allowing free movement of goods and services among members, but also creating a common trade policy against nonmembers.

CVaR Conditional VaR, a tail loss measure. The weighted average of all loss outcomes in the statistical distribution that exceed the VaR loss.

Daily settlement A specific process of *mark-to-market* by a central clearing party in which the profits and losses of all counterparties to derivatives contracts are determined using settlement prices for each contract.

Dark pools Alternative trading systems that do not display the orders that their clients send to them.

Data mining The practice of determining a model by extensive searching through a dataset for statistically significant patterns.

Data science An interdisciplinary field that harnesses advances in computer science, statistics, and other disciplines for the purpose of extracting information from big data (or data in general).

Data snooping The practice of determining a model by extensive searching through a dataset for statistically significant patterns.

Day order An order that is good for the day on which it is submitted. If it has not been filled by the close of business, the order expires unfilled.

Days of inventory on hand (DOH) The average number of days it would take to sell the amount of inventory on hand. It is calculated as either the ending or average balance of inventories divided by (cost of goods sold/days in the period).

Days payable outstanding (DPO) The average number of days it takes a company to pay its suppliers. It is calculated as either the ending or average balance of accounts payable divided by (cost of goods sold/days in the period).

Days sales outstanding (DSO) The average number of days it takes for a company to receive payment from customers who purchase goods or services on credit. It is calculated as either the ending or average balance of accounts receivable divided by (revenues/days in the period).

Dealers Financial intermediaries, such as commercial banks or investment banks, who transact as **counterparties** with derivative end users.

Debt A claim against an entity to receive cash, stock, or other assets at a future date. From the perspective of the debtor or borrower, an obligation to pay cash, stock, or other assets at a future date. Generally, debt claims are unconditional and are senior to equity claims.

Debt service coverage ratio A ratio in which the net operating income of a real estate investment for a specific period is divided by the amount of debt service to be paid during the same time period.

Debt tax shield The tax benefit from interest paid on debt being tax deductible from income, equal to the marginal tax rate multiplied by the value of the debt.

Debt-to-assets ratio A solvency ratio calculated as total debt divided by total assets.

Debt-to-capital ratio A solvency ratio calculated as total debt divided by total debt plus total shareholders' equity.

Debt-to-equity ratio A solvency ratio calculated as total debt divided by total shareholders' equity.

Debt-to-income ratio (DTI) Residential lending metric that compares an individual's monthly debt payments to their monthly pre-tax, gross income.

Debut issuer An issuer approaching the bond market for the first time.

Deciles Quantiles that divide a distribution into 10 equal parts.

Declaration date The day that the corporation issues a statement declaring a specific dividend.

Decreasing returns to scale When a production process leads to increases in output that are proportionately smaller than the increase in inputs.

Deductible temporary differences Temporary differences that result in a reduction of or deduction from taxable income in a future period when the balance sheet item is recovered or settled.

Deep learning An area of artificial intelligence in which a system uses neural networks to perform multistage, non-linear data processing to identify patterns. Also called *deep learning nets*.

Deep learning nets See *Deep learning*.

Deep-in-the-money option An option that is highly likely to be exercised.

Deep-out-of-the-money option An option that is highly unlikely to be exercised.

Default When a borrower on a mortgage loan fails to meet the obligations of the loan.

Default risk premium An extra return that compensates investors for the possibility that the borrower will fail to make a promised payment at the contracted time and in the contracted amount.

Defeasance Mechanism that allows prepayment on mortgage, but the borrower must purchase a portfolio of government securities that fully replicates the cash flows of the remaining scheduled principal and interest payments, including the balloon loan balance, on the loan.

Defensive interval ratio A liquidity ratio that estimates the number of days that an entity could meet cash needs from liquid assets; calculated as (cash + short-term marketable investments + receivables) divided by daily cash expenditures.

Deferred coupon bonds Bonds that pay no coupons for their first few years but then pay a higher coupon than they otherwise normally would for the remainder of their life. Also called *split coupon bonds*.

Deferred tax assets A balance sheet asset that arises when an excess amount is paid for income taxes relative to accounting profit. The taxable income is higher than accounting profit and income tax payable exceeds tax expense. The company expects to recover the difference during the course of future operations when tax expense exceeds income tax payable.

Deferred tax liabilities A balance sheet liability that arises when a deficit amount is paid for income taxes relative to accounting profit. The taxable income is less than the accounting profit and income tax payable is less than tax expense. The company expects to eliminate the liability over the course of future operations when income tax payable exceeds tax expense.

Defined benefit pension plans (DB plans) Plans in which the company promises to pay a certain annual amount (defined benefit) to the employee after retirement. The company bears the investment risk of the plan assets.

Defined contribution pension plans Individual accounts to which an employee and typically the employer makes contributions during their working years and expect to draw on the accumulated funds at retirement. The employee bears the investment and inflation risk of the plan assets.

Deflation Negative inflation.

Degree of financial leverage The ratio of percentage change in net income to percentage change in operating income over a period. It is a measure of how sensitive net income is to changes in operating income, driven by the firm's use of debt in its capital structure.

Degree of operating leverage (DOL) The ratio of percentage change in operating income to percentage change in sales over a period. It is a measure of how sensitive operating income is to changes in sales, driven by the fixed and variable cost composition of operating expenses.

Delta The relationship between the option price and the underlying price, which reflects the sensitivity of the price of the option to changes in the price of the underlying. Delta is a good approximation of how an option price will change for a small change in the stock.

Demand shock A typically unexpected disturbance to demand, such as an unexpected interruption in trade or transportation.

Dependent variable The variable that is explained by a regression model.

Depository bank A bank that raises funds from depositors and other investors and lends it to borrowers.

Depository institutions Commercial banks, savings and loan banks, credit unions, and similar institutions that raise funds from depositors and other investors and lend it to borrowers.

Depository receipt A security that trades like an ordinary share on a local exchange and represents an economic interest in a foreign company.

Depreciation The process of systematically allocating the cost of long-lived (tangible) assets to the periods during which the assets are expected to provide economic benefits.

Derivative A financial instrument that derives its value from the performance of an underlying asset.

Derivative contract A legal agreement between counterparties with a specific **maturity**, or length of time, until the closing of the transaction, or **settlement**.

Derivative pricing rule A pricing rule used by crossing networks in which a price is taken (derived) from the price that is current in the asset's primary market.

Derivatives A financial instrument whose value depends on the value of some underlying asset or factor (e.g., a stock price, an interest rate, or exchange rate).

Differentiated products A product or service from a firm that is distinguishable or distinct from those of competing firms. It is customers who determine and value whether a product is differentiated.

Diffuse prior The assumption of equal prior probabilities.

Diffusion index Reflects the proportion of the index's components that are moving in a pattern consistent with the overall index.

Digital assets The umbrella term covering assets that can be created, stored, and transmitted electronically and have associated ownership or use rights. Digital assets include a variety of assets, such as cryptocurrencies, tokens (security and utility), and digital collectables.

Diluted EPS The EPS that would result if all dilutive securities were converted into common shares.

Dilution An increase in the number of shares outstanding from share issuance that decreases the percentage of shares owned by existing shareholders.

Direct investing Occurs when an investor makes a direct investment in an asset without the use of an intermediary.

Direct lending Providing capital directly from private debt investors.

Direct listing Where the equity of a security is floated on the public markets directly, without underwriters, reducing the complexity and cost of the transaction.

Direct sales Marketing and/or delivering products and services to customers without an intermediary or third party between the customer and seller.

Direct taxes Taxes levied directly on income, wealth, and corporate profits.

Discount factor The price equivalent of a zero rate. Also may be stated as the present value of a currency unit on a future date.

Discount rate A yield or pricing convention for money market instrument quotations. It is the interest earned on an instrument, derived from the difference between the price and face value, expressed as a percentage of the face value and multiplied by the periodicity of the annual rate.

Discounted cash flow models Valuation models that estimate the intrinsic value of a security as the present value of the future benefits expected to be received from the security.

Discriminatory pricing rule A pricing rule used in continuous markets in which the limit price of the order or quote that first arrived determines the trade price.

Diseconomies of scale Increase in cost per unit resulting from increased production.

Dispersion The variability of a population or sample of observations around the central tendency.

Display size The size of an order displayed to public view.

Disposition effect As a result of loss aversion, an emotional bias whereby investors are reluctant to dispose of losers. This results in an inefficient and gradual adjustment to deterioration in fundamental value.

Distressed debt Debt of mature companies in financial difficulty, in bankruptcy, or likely to default on debt.

Distressed/restructuring These strategies focus on securities of companies either in or perceived to be near bankruptcy. In one approach, hedge funds simply purchase fixed-income securities trading at a significant discount to par but that are still senior enough to be backed by sufficient corporate assets.

Distributed ledger A type of database that can be shared among entities in a network.

Distributed ledger technology (DLT) Technology based on a distributed ledger.

Diversification ratio The ratio of the standard deviation of an equally weighted portfolio to the standard deviation of a randomly selected security.

Dividend A distribution paid to shareholders based on the number of shares owned.

Dividend discount model (DDM) A present value model of stock value that views the intrinsic value of a stock as present value of the stock's expected future dividends.

Dividend payout ratio The ratio of cash dividends paid to earnings for a period.

Dividends Distributions of profits and/or net assets from a corporation to its shareholders. While often in cash, dividends can be also be paid in stock or assets, such as property.

Divisor A number (denominator) used to determine the value of a price return index. It is initially chosen at the inception of an index and subsequently adjusted by the index provider, as necessary, to avoid changes in the index value that are unrelated to changes in the prices of its constituent securities.

Domestic bonds A type of bond for which the issuer's domicile and jurisdiction of issuance are the same.

Domestic content provisions Stipulate that some percentage of the value added or components used in production should be of domestic origin.

Double taxation The taxation of business income at both the entity and personal or owner levels. In most jurisdictions, this taxation scheme applies to public limited companies.

Downside risk The potential for loss.

Drag on liquidity An action or event that reduces available funds or delays cash inflows.

Drivers Causative factors that explain the level of and changes in an output variable.

DSC ratio A property's annual net operating income (NOI) divided by the debt service.

Dual-class structure A capital structure that includes at least two classes of equity shares with unequal voting rights.

Dupont analysis An approach to decomposing return on investment, e.g., return on equity, as the product of other financial ratios.

Duration The percentage change in bond price given an unanticipated small change in interest rates.

Duration gap The difference between a bond's Macaulay duration and its investor's investment horizon.

Dynamic pricing A pricing approach that charges different prices at different times. Specific examples include off-peak pricing, "surge" pricing, and "congestion" pricing.

Early repayment option May entitle the borrower to prepay all or part of the outstanding mortgage principal prior to maturity. This creates a risk from the lender's or investor's viewpoint because the cash flow amounts and timing cannot be known with certainty.

Earnings surprise The portion of a company's earnings that is unanticipated by investors and, according to the efficient market hypothesis, merits a price adjustment.

Economic indicators Economic statistics provided by government and established private organizations that contain information on an economy's recent past activity or its current or future position in the business cycle.

Economic infrastructure investments A category of infrastructure investments that support economic activity through transportation assets, information and communication technology assets, and utility and energy assets.

Economic stabilization Reduction of the magnitude of economic fluctuations.

Economic union Incorporates all aspects of a common market and in addition requires common economic institutions and coordination of economic policies among members.

Economies of scale A decline in costs per unit as output grows, generally resulting from having fixed costs in the cost structure that are spread over more units of output.

Economies of scope A decline in costs per unit as the number of product or business lines increases, generally resulting from having shared costs between the product lines.

Effective annual rate An interest rate with a periodicity of one.

Effective convexity An interest rate risk statistic that measures the non-linear/second-order effect of changes in the benchmark yield curve on a bond's price.

Effective duration The sensitivity of the bond's price to an instantaneous parallel shift in a benchmark yield curve—for example, the government par curve.

Efficient market A market in which asset prices reflect new information quickly and rationally. See also, *informationally efficient market*.

Either/or fee A custom fee arrangement whereby major investors are offered a structure where managers agree to charge *either* a lower management fee *or* a higher incentive fee, whichever is greater.

Electronic communications networks (ECNs) See *alternative trading systems* and *multilateral trading facilities*.

Embedded derivative A derivative within an underlying, such as a callable, putable, or convertible bond.

Embedded options Contingency provisions found in a bond's indenture representing rights that enable their holders to take advantage of interest rate movements. They can be exercised by the issuer, by the bondholder, or automatically depending on the course of interest rates.

Emotional biases Behavioral biases resulting from reasoning influenced by feelings; emotional biases stem from impulse or intuition.

Empirical duration Estimates of duration calculated over time and in different interest rate environments. Unlike analytical duration, empirical duration estimates do not assume that benchmark yields and spreads are independent variables and are uncorrelated.

Employee stock ownership plan (ESOP) A type of employee benefit plan in which a company sets up a trust fund to receive contributions of newly issued shares or cash to buy existing shares. Contributions are tax deductible up to certain limits. Shares in the trust fund are allocated to individual employees based on relative pay or a formula.

Endowment bias An emotional bias in which people value an asset more when they hold rights to it than when they do not.

Enterprise risk management An overall assessment of a company's risk position. A centralized approach to risk management sometimes called firmwide risk management.

Enterprise value (EV) Total company value (the market value of debt, common equity, and preferred equity) minus the value of cash and investments.

Equal weighting An index weighting method in which an equal weight is assigned to each constituent security at inception.

Equity Ownership interest in an entity. A residual claim on the assets of an entity after more senior claims, such as debt, have been satisfied. Also known as *net assets*.

Equity swap A swap transaction in which at least one cash flow is tied to the return on an equity portfolio position, often an equity index.

Error term Represents the difference between the observed value of the independent variable and that expected from the true underlying population relation between the dependent and independent variable.

Estimated parameters In a simple linear regression, the estimated parameters are the intercept and slope of the fitted line.

Ether A programmable cryptocurrency created on the Ethereum blockchain in 2015 that allows for the execution of smart contracts.

Ethical principles Beliefs regarding what is good, acceptable, or obligatory behavior and what is bad, unacceptable, or forbidden behavior.

Ethics The study of moral principles or of making good choices. Ethics encompasses a set of moral principles and rules of conduct that provide guidance for our behavior.

Eurobonds A type of bond issued internationally, outside the jurisdiction of the country in whose currency the bond is denominated.

European options Options that may be exercised only at contract maturity.

European-style Said of an option contract that can only be exercised on the option's expiration date.

Event risk Risk that evolves around set dates, such as elections, new legislation, or other date-driven milestones, such as holidays or political anniversaries, known in advance. Example: Brexit referendum.

Ex-dividend date The first date that a share trades without (i.e., "ex") the right to receive the declared dividend for the period.

Excess kurtosis Degree of kurtosis (fatness of tails) relative to the kurtosis of the normal distribution.

Excess spread Surplus difference of yield remaining after payments to bondholders are made after expenses are made and losses are covered.

Exchange A rules-based, open access market venue where financial instruments are traded, with price and volume transparency accessible by issuers, investors, and their intermediaries.

Exchange-traded derivative (ETD) Futures, options, and other financial contracts available on exchanges.

Exchanges Places where traders can meet to arrange their trades.

Execution instructions Instructions that indicate how to fill an order.

Exercise The decision to transact the underlying by an option holder.

Exercise date The day that an option is exercised by its holder. For a call option, the day the strike price is paid and underlying is purchased. For a put option, when the strike price is received and the underlying is sold.

Exercise price The pre-agreed execution price specified in an option contract. Sometimes, this price is referred to as the strike price.

Exogenous risk A sudden or unanticipated risk that impacts either a country's cooperative stance, the ability of non-state actors to globalize, or both. Examples include sudden uprisings, invasions, or the aftermath of natural disasters.

Expansion The period of a business cycle after its lowest point and before its highest point.

Expansionary Tending to cause the real economy to grow.

Expansionary fiscal policy Fiscal policy aimed at achieving real economic growth.

Expected exposure (EE) The size of the investor's claim at the time of default.

Expected loss (EL) Default probability times loss severity given default.

Expected return on the portfolio Denoted as $(E(R_p))$. The weighted average of the expected returns (R_1 to R_n) on the component securities using their respective weights (w_1 to w_n).

Expected value of a random variable The probability-weighted average of the possible outcomes of a random variable.

Expert system A type of computer programming, often based on "if–then" rules, that attempts to simulate the knowledge base and analytical abilities of human experts in specific problem-solving contexts.

Export subsidy Paid by the government to the firm when it exports a unit of a good that is being subsidized.

Exposure at default (EAD) The size of the investor's claim at the time of default.

Extension risk The risk of later repayment of a mortgage-backed security than expected.

External credit enhancements Provisions or methods from a third party that allow a borrower improve their creditworthiness in a structured transaction.

External debt Sovereign debt owed to foreign creditors.

Extra dividend A dividend paid by a company that does not pay dividends on a regular schedule, or a dividend that supplements regular cash dividends with an extra payment.

Extraordinary general meetings (EGMs) Meetings besides an AGM of the corporate board and shareholders, typically held to deliberate and vote on urgent matters. Corporate charters and bylaws specify who can call an EGM and under what conditions.

Extreme value theory A branch of statistics that focuses primarily on extreme outcomes.

Face value The amount of principal on a bond, also known as par value.

Factoring arrangement When a company sells its accounts receivable to a lender (known as a factor) that assumes responsibility for the credit-granting and collection process.

Fair value A market-based measure of an investment based on observable or derived assumptions to determine a price that market participants would use to exchange an asset or liability in an orderly transaction at a specific time.

Fair value hedge Refers to a specific **hedge accounting** designation that applies when a derivative is deemed to offset the fluctuation in fair value of an asset or liability.

Fallen angels Formerly investment-grade issuers whose credit quality has deteriorated since the time of issuance.

Fat-Tailed Describes a distribution that has fatter tails than a normal distribution (also called leptokurtic).

Fed funds rate The US interbank lending rate on overnight borrowings of reserves.

Federal funds rate The US interbank lending rate on overnight borrowings of reserves. Also known as *Fed Funds rate*.

Fiat money Money that is not convertible into any other commodity.

Fiduciary call A combination of a purchased call option and investment in a risk-free bond with face value of the option's exercise price.

Fill or kill See *immediate or cancel order*.

Finance lease A type of lease which is more akin to the purchase or sale of the underlying asset.

Financial leverage The use of debt in the capital structure. Measured using ratios such as operating income to operating income less interest expense, total assets to total equity, or debt to equity.

Financial leverage ratio A measure of financial leverage calculated as average total assets divided by average total equity.

Financial risk The risk arising from a company's capital structure and, specifically, from the level of debt and debt-like obligations.

Fintech Technological innovation in the financial services industry, specifically with the design and delivery of financial services and products. It may also refer more broadly to companies involved in developing the new technologies and their applications, as well as the business sector that includes such companies.

Firm commitment A pre-determined amount (price and quantity) is agreed to be exchanged at settlement. Examples of firm commitments include forward contracts, futures contracts, and swaps.

First lien Security interest in a property that gives the lender the right to seize the collateral if the borrower does not pay as agreed.

First lien debt Debt secured by a pledge of certain assets that could include buildings, but it may also include property and equipment, licenses, patents, brands, etc.

First mortgage debt Debt secured by a pledge of a specific property.

Fiscal multiplier The ratio of a change in national income to a change in government spending.

Fiscal policy The use of taxes and government spending to affect the level of aggregate expenditures.

Fixed charge coverage A solvency ratio measuring the number of times interest and lease payments are covered by operating income, calculated as (EBIT + lease payments) divided by (interest payments + lease payments).

Fixed charge coverage ratio A measure of how well a company's earnings covers its fixed expenses, which may include debt payments, interest expense, and lease costs.

Fixed-income instruments Debt instruments such as loans or bonds.

Fixed-income securities Fixed-income instruments designed to be more easily tradeable than a loan, such as a bond.

Fixed-price call A contingency provision that grants an issuer the right to buy back a bond at a predetermined price in the future.

Fixed-rate payer The counterparty paying fixed cash flows in a swap contract. May also be referred to as the floating-rate receiver.

Flat price The full price of a bond minus accrued interest. Flat prices are usually quoted by bond dealers.

Float-adjusted market-capitalization weighting An index weighting method in which the weight assigned to each constituent security is determined by adjusting its market capitalization for its market float.

Floating-rate notes Notes on which interest payments are not fixed but instead vary from period to period depending on the current level of a reference interest rate. Also known as *floaters*.

Floating-rate payer The counterparty paying the variable cash flows in a swap contract. May also be referred to as the fixed-rate receiver.

Forecast object A variable on or related to an issuer's financial statements that an analyst makes a projection for. Examples include drivers of financial statements, financial statement lines, and summary measures like EBITDA.

Foreclosure Allows a lender to take possession of the property and ultimately sell the property to recover funds toward satisfying the outstanding debt obligation.

Foreign bonds A type of bond for which the issuer's domicile and jurisdiction of issuance are different.

Foreign currency reserves Holding by the central bank of non-domestic currency deposits and non-domestic bonds.

Foreign direct investments (FDI) Long-term investments in the productive capacity of a foreign country.

Foreign exchange gains (or losses) Gains (or losses) that occur when the exchange rate changes between the investor's currency and the currency that foreign securities are denominated in.

Forward contract A **derivative contract** for the future exchange of an **underlying** at a fixed price set at contract signing.

Forward price Represents the price agreed upon in a forward contract to be exchanged at the contract's maturity date, T. This price is shown in equations as $F_0(T)$.

Forward price-to-earnings ratio A P/E calculated on the basis of a forecast of EPS; a stock's current price divided by next year's expected earnings.

Forward rate agreement (FRA) An OTC derivatives contract in which counterparties agree to apply a specific interest rate to a future time period.

Founders class shares A way to entice early participation in startup funds whereby managers offer incentives that entitle investors to a lower fee structure and/or other favorable terms.

Framing bias An information-processing bias in which a person answers a question differently based on the way in which it is asked (framed).

Franchising A situation where an owner of an asset and associated intellectual property divests the asset and licenses intellectual property to a third-party operator (franchisee) in exchange for royalties. Franchisees operate under the constraints of a franchise agreement.

Free cash flow The actual cash that would be available to the company's investors after making all investments necessary to maintain the company as an ongoing enterprise (also referred to as free cash flow to the firm); the internally generated funds that can be distributed to the company's investors (e.g., shareholders and bondholders) without impairing the value of the company.

Free cash flow hypothesis The hypothesis that higher debt levels discipline managers by forcing them to make fixed debt service payments and by reducing the company's free cash flow.

Free float The portion of a listed company's equity securities that are not held by insiders, strategic investors, sponsors, founders, and so on, that are more freely available for trading.

Free trade areas One of the most prevalent forms of regional integration, in which all barriers to the flow of goods and services among members have been eliminated.

Free-cash-flow-to-equity models Valuation models based on discounting expected future free cash flow to equity.

Freemium business model A pricing approach that allows customers a certain level of usage or functionality at no charge. Those who wish to use more must pay.

Frequency table A representation of the frequency of occurrence of two discrete variables.

Full price The price of a bond including any accrued interest owed to the seller. It is the flat price plus accrued interest.

Fully amortizing loan A loan or bond with a payment schedule that calls for the complete repayment of principal over the instrument's time to maturity.

Fund investing In fund investing, the investor invests in assets indirectly by contributing capital to a fund as part of a group of investors. Fund investing is available for all major alternative investment types.

Fund of funds Funds that hold a portfolio of hedge funds; also called *funds of hedge funds*.

Fundamental analysis The examination of publicly available information and the formulation of forecasts to estimate the intrinsic value of assets.

Fundamental growth These strategies use fundamental analysis to identify companies expected to exhibit high growth and capital appreciation.

Fundamental long/short In this strategy, the hedge fund takes a long position in companies that are trading at inexpensive levels compared to their potential intrinsic value and shorts those that trade in the other direction, with the intention of reversing this trade to obtain alpha.

Fundamental value These strategies use fundamental analysis to identify undervalued and unloved companies for which there is a possibility that a corporate turnaround, with future revenue and cash flow growth, will result in higher valuations.

Fundamental weighting An index weighting method in which the weight assigned to each constituent security is based on its underlying company's size. It attempts to address the disadvantages of market-capitalization weighting by using measures that are independent of the constituent security's price.

Fungible Freely exchangeable, interchangeable, or substitutable with other things of the same type. Money and commodities are the most common examples.

Futures contract A variation of a forward contract that has essentially the same basic definition but with some additional features, such as a clearinghouse guarantee against credit losses, a daily settlement of gains and losses, and an organized electronic or floor trading facility.

Futures contract basis point value (BPV) The change in price of a futures contract given a 1 basis point (0.01%) change in yield.

Futures contracts Forward contracts with standardized sizes, dates, and underlyings that trade on futures exchanges.

Futures margin account An account held by an exchange clearinghouse for each derivatives counterparty. The funds in such an account are used to ensure that counterparties do not default on their contract obligation.

Futures price The pre-agreed price at which a futures contract buyer (seller) agrees to pay (receive) for the underlying at the maturity date of the futures contract.

FX swap The combination of a spot and a forward FX transaction.

G-spread Yield spread in basis points between a bond's yield-to-maturity and that of an actual or interpolated government bond. It represents the return for bearing risks relative to the government bond.

Game theory The set of tools decision makers use to incorporate responses by rival decision makers into their strategies.

Gamma A numerical measure of how sensitive an option's delta (the sensitivity of the derivative's price) is to a change in the value of the underlying.

Gate A provision that when implemented limits or restricts redemptions for a period of time.

General collateral repo Rather than involving a specific security, a repo that instead references a specific group of securities as eligible collateral (such as government bonds of a specific maturity).

General collateral repo rate The interest rate on a general collateral repo.

General obligation (GO) bonds Unsecured bonds issued by a non-sovereign government which are backed by the taxing authority of the issuer.

General obligation bonds Also known as GO bonds. Bonds issued by non-sovereign governments for general purposes and repaid from tax cash flows.

General partners (GPs) Owners of a general partnership or limited partnership with unlimited liability and other attributes as specified in the partnership agreement.

General partnership A business organizational form owned entirely by general partners.

Geophysical resource endowment Includes such factors as livable geography and climate as well as access to food and water, which are necessary for sustainable growth. Geophysical resource endowment is highly unequal among countries.

Geopolitics The study of how geography affects politics and international relations. These relations matter for investments because they contribute to important drivers of investment performance, including economic growth, business performance, market volatility, and transaction costs.

Gilts Bonds issued by the UK government.

Global depository receipt (GDR) A depository receipt that is issued outside of the company's home country and outside of the United States.

Global minimum-variance portfolio The portfolio on the minimum-variance frontier with the smallest variance of return.

Global registered share (GRS) A common share that is traded on different stock exchanges around the world in different currencies.

Globalization The process of interaction and integration among people, companies, and governments worldwide. It is marked by the spread of products, information, jobs, and culture across borders.

Gold standard With respect to a currency, if a currency is on the gold standard a given amount can be converted into a prespecified amount of gold.

Good-on-close An execution instruction specifying that an order can only be filled at the close of trading. Also called *market-on-close*.

Good-on-open An execution instruction specifying that an order can only be filled at the opening of trading.

Good-till-cancelled order An order specifying that it is valid until the entity placing the order has cancelled it (or, commonly, until some specified amount of time such as 60 days has elapsed, whichever comes sooner).

Goodwill An intangible asset that represents the excess of the purchase price of an acquired company over the value of the net identifiable assets acquired.

Governance tokens In permissionless networks, governance tokens serve as votes to determine how the particular network is run.

Government debt management Government policies that relate to the issuance of debt securities, typically handled by a treasurer or finance ministry.

Government equivalent yield Measures quoted using actual/actual day counts.

Grant date The day that terms of compensation are communicated by an issuer and accepted by an employee recipient.

Green bonds Bonds used in green finance whereby the proceeds are earmarked toward environmental-related products.

Greenfield investments The first stage of development of an infrastructure asset. Greenfield investments involve developing new assets and new infrastructure with the intention either to lease or sell the assets to the government after construction or to hold and operate the assets. Greenfield investors typically invest alongside strategic investors or developers that specialize in developing the underlying assets.

Gross profit margin The ratio of gross profit to revenues.

Groupthink The practice of thinking or making decisions as a group in a way that discourages creativity or individual responsibility. For scenario analysis to be useful in portfolio management, teams must work hard to build creative processes, identify scenarios, track these scenarios, and assess the need for action on a regular cadence.

Growth cycle Refers to fluctuations in economic activity around the long-term potential trend growth level, focusing on how much actual economic activity is below or above trend growth in economic activity.

Growth option The option to make additional investments in a project at some future time if the financial results are strong. Also called an *expansion option*.

Growth rate cycle Refers to fluctuations in the growth rate of economic activity.

Haircut The difference between the market value of the security used as collateral and the value of the loan. Also called *repo margin*.

Halo effect An emotional bias that extends a favorable evaluation of some characteristics to other characteristics.

Hard commodities Traded natural resources, such as crude oil and metals, with markets often involving the physical delivery of the underlying upon settlement.

Hard hurdle rate Hurdle ratewhere the manager earns fees on annual returns in excess of the hurdle rate.

Hard-bullet covered bonds Type of security where if payments do not occur according to the original schedule of a covered bond, a bond default is triggered and bond payments are accelerated.

Harmonic mean A type of weighted mean computed as the reciprocal of the arithmetic average of the reciprocals.

Hedge The **derivative contract** used in **hedging** an exposure.

Hedge accounting Accounting standard(s) that allow an issuer to offset a hedging instrument (usually a derivative) against a hedged transaction or balance sheet item to reduce financial statement volatility.

Hedge funds Private investment vehicles that may invest in public equities or publicly traded fixed-income assets, private capital, and/or real assets, but they are distinguished by their investment *approach* rather than by the investments themselves.

Hedge ratio The proportion of an underlying that will offset the risk associated with a derivative position.

Hedging The use of a derivative contract to offset or neutralize existing or anticipated exposure to an **underlying**.

Hegemony Countries that are regional or even global leaders and use their political or economic influence of others to control resources.

Held-to-maturity Debt (fixed-income) securities that a company intends to hold to maturity; these are presented at their original cost, updated for any amortisation of discounts or premiums.

Herding Clustered trading that may or may not be based on information.

Herfindahl-Hirschman Index (HHI) A measure of market concentration, calculated as the sum of the squares of competitor market shares. Antitrust regulators in some countries consider markets with an HHI between 1,500 and 2,500 moderately concentrated and consider markets with an HHI over 2,500 highly concentrated.

Heteroskedasticity Non-constant variance across all observations.

Hidden order An order that is exposed not to the public but only to the brokers or exchanges that receive it.

Hidden revenue business model Business models that provide services to users at no charge and generate revenues elsewhere.

High yield Bond issuers and issues rated BB+ (Ba1 on Moody's scale) or lower. Also known as speculative grade and junk.

High-water mark The highest value, net of fees, that a fund has reached in history. It reflects the highest cumulative return used to calculate an incentive fee.

Hindsight bias A bias with selective perception and retention aspects in which people may see past events as having been predictable and reasonable to expect.

Holder-of-record date The date that a shareholder listed on the corporation's books will be deemed to have ownership of the shares for purposes of receiving an upcoming dividend.

Holding period return The single-period internal rate of return for a real estate property that includes property income and the change in property value over the period.

Home bias A preference for securities listed on the exchanges of one's home country.

Homogeneity of expectations The assumption that all investors have the same economic expectations and thus have the same expectations of prices, cash flows, and other investment characteristics.

Homoskedasticity Constant variance across all observations.

Horizon yield An investor's total rate of return on a fixed income instrument over their holding period, including reinvested coupon payments. It is an internal rate of return expressed as an annualized rate.

Hostile takeover When a potential acquirer seeks to acquire a company (the target) against the wishes of the target's board of directors. Typically, a tender offer is used to carry out the hostile takeover, against which a board might use a poison pill in its defense.

Household A person or a group of people living in the same residence, taken as a basic unit in economic analysis.

Human capital The present value of an individual's future expected labor income.

Hurdle rate The rate of return that a project's IRR must exceed for the project to be accepted by the company.

Hypothesis A proposed explanation or theory that can be tested.

Hypothesis testing The process of testing of hypotheses about one or more populations using statistical inference.

I-spread Also known as interpolated spread, it is the yield spread for a bond over the standard swap rate in that currency of the same tenor.

Iceberg order An order in which the display size is less than the order's full size.

If-converted method A method for accounting for the effect of convertible securities on earnings per share (EPS) that specifies what EPS would have been if the convertible securities had been converted at the beginning of the period, taking account of the effects of conversion on net income and the weighted average number of shares outstanding.

Illusion of control bias A bias in which people tend to believe that they can control or influence outcomes when, in fact, they cannot.

Immediate or cancel order An order that is valid only upon receipt by the broker or exchange. If such an order cannot be filled in part or in whole upon receipt, it cancels immediately. Also called *fill or kill*.

Impact lag The lag associated with the result of actions affecting the economy with delay.

Implied forward rate An interest rate or yield over a future period implied by the current term structure of interest rates.

Import license Specifies the quantity of a good that can be imported into a country.

In-the-money Describes an option with a positive intrinsic value.

Income tax paid The actual amount paid for income taxes in the period; not a provision, but the actual cash outflow.

Income tax payable The income tax owed by the company on the basis of taxable income.

Increasing returns to scale When a production process leads to increases in output that are proportionately larger than the increase in inputs.

Incurrence test A financial ratio or other measurement taken prior to an action such as debt issuance, usually on a pro forma basis taking the action into account. Satisfaction of the test (e.g., leverage ratio below a certain value) is linked to covenants between the issuer and investors.

Indenture A written contract between a lender and borrower that specifies the terms of the loan, such as interest rate, interest payment schedule, or maturity.

Independent With reference to events, the property that the occurrence of one event does not affect the probability of another event occurring. With reference to two random variables X and Y, they are independent if and only if $P(X,Y) = P(X)P(Y)$.

Independent directors Members of a corporation's board of directors who do not have an employment or familial relationship with the company, nor do they have a relationship that would impair their independence such as an economic interest in a vendor or competitor of the company.

Independent variable An explanatory variable in a regression model.

Independently and identically distributed With respect to random variables, the property of random variables that are independent of each other but follow the identical probability distribution.

Index-linked bonds A bond whose coupon payments or principal repayment is linked to a specified index.

Indexing An investment strategy in which an investor constructs a portfolio to mirror the performance of a specified index.

Indicator variable A variable that takes on only one of two values, 0 or 1, based on a condition. In simple linear regression, the slope is the difference in the dependent variable for the two conditions. Also referred to as a *dummy variable*.

Indifference curve A curve representing all the combinations of two goods or attributes such that the consumer is entirely indifferent among them.

Indirect taxes Taxes such as taxes on spending, as opposed to direct taxes.

Inflation premium An extra return that compensates investors for expected inflation.

Inflation reports A type of economic publication put out by many central banks.

Inflation-linked bonds Debt instruments that link the principal and interest to inflation.

Information cascade The transmission of information from those participants who act first and whose decisions influence the decisions of others.

Information-motivated traders Traders that trade to profit from information that they believe allows them to predict future prices.

Informationally efficient market A market in which asset prices reflect new information quickly and rationally.

Infrastructure A type of real asset that is intended for public use and provides essential services. These assets are typically long-lived fixed assets, such as bridges and toll roads.

Initial coin offering (ICO) An unregulated process whereby companies raise capital by selling crypto-tokens to investors in exchange for fiat money or another agreed-upon cryptocurrency.

Initial margin The ratio of the price of collateral to the value of cash exchanged in a repo; a value over 1.0 or 100% indicates overcollateralization.

Initial margin requirement The margin requirement on the first day of a transaction as well as on any day in which additional margin funds must be deposited.

Initial public offering (IPO) The first issuance of common shares to the public by a formerly private corporation.

Inside directors Members of a corporation's board of directors who are not independent. Typically, inside directors are employees or founders (and their family) of the company.

Insolvency Refers to the condition in which firm value is below the face value of debt used to finance the firm's assets.

Institution An established organization or practice in a society or culture. An institution can be a formal structure, such as a university, organization, or process backed by law; or it can be informal, such as a custom or behavioral pattern important to society. Institutions can, but need not be, formed by national governments. Examples of institutions include non-governmental organizations, charities, religious customs, family units, the media, political parties, and educational practice.

Intangible assets Assets without a physical form, such as patents and trademarks.

Interbank market The market of loans and deposits between banks for maturities ranging from overnight to one year.

Intercept The estimated value of the dependent variable when the independent variable is zero.

Interest coverage A solvency ratio calculated as EBIT divided by interest payments.

Interest coverage ratio A measure of an issuer's ability to service its debt, typically the ratio of operating income or EBIT to interest expense.

Interest rate A rate of return that reflects the relationship between differently dated cash flows; a discount rate.

Interest rate swap A swap in which the underlying is an interest rate. Can be viewed as a currency swap in which both currencies are the same and can be created as a combination of currency swaps.

Interest-indexed bond A type of index-linked bond for which changes in the index are captured with adjustments to interest payments.

Internal credit enhancements Provisions or methods a borrower initiates to improve their creditworthiness in a structured transaction, such as overcollateralization or excess spread.

Internal rate of return The discount rate that makes net present value equal 0; the discount rate that makes the present value of an investment's costs (outflows) equal to the present value of the investment's benefits (inflows).

Internal rate of return (IRR) The discount rate that makes net present value equal 0; the discount rate that makes the present value of an investment's costs (outflows) equal to the present value of the investment's benefits (inflows).

Internet of things The vast array of physical devices, home appliances, smart buildings, vehicles, and other items that are embedded with electronics, sensors, software, and network connections that enable the objects in the system to interact and share information.

Interquartile range The difference between the third and first quartiles of a dataset.

Intrinsic value The amount gained (per unit) by an option buyer if an option is exercised at any given point in time. May be referred to as the exercise value of the option.

Investment banks Financial intermediaries that provide advice to their mostly corporate clients and help them arrange transactions such as initial and seasoned securities offerings.

Investment grade Bond issuers and issues rated BBB- (Baa3 on Moody's scale).

Investment policy statement A written planning document that describes a client's investment objectives and risk tolerance over a relevant time horizon, along with the constraints that apply to the client's portfolio.

Issue rating A rating which seeks to capture the probability of default or expected loss of the issuer's senior unsecured bonds.

Issuer rating A rating which seeks to capture the credit risk of a specific financial obligation of an issuer which takes such factors as seniority into account.

J-curve effect Represents the initial negative return in the capital commitment phase followed by an acceleration of returns through the capital deployment phase.

Jackknife A resampling method that repeatedly draws samples by taking the original observed data sample and leaving out one observation at a time (without replacement) from the set.

January effect Calendar anomaly that stock market returns in January are significantly higher compared to the rest of the months of the year, with most of the abnormal returns reported during the first five trading days in January. Also called *turn-of-the-year effect*.

Joint probability function A function giving the probability of joint occurrences of values of stated random variables.

Judgmental sampling A procedure of selectively handpicking elements from the population based on a researcher's knowledge and professional judgment.

Junior debt Debt obligation with lower priority of payment than senior debt obligations.

Key rate duration Also known as partial duration, is a measure of a bond's sensitivity to a change in the benchmark yield at a specific maturity.

Keynesians Economists who believe that fiscal policy can have powerful effects on aggregate demand, output, and employment when there is substantial spare capacity in an economy.

Kurtosis The statistical measure that indicates the combined weight of the tails of a distribution relative to the rest of the distribution.

Lagging economic indicators Turning points that take place later than those of the overall economy; they are believed to have value in identifying the economy's past condition.

Law of one price A principle that states that if two investments have the same or equivalent future cash flows regardless of what will happen in the future, then these two investments should have the same current price.

Lead underwriter The lead investment bank in a syndicate of investment banks and broker–dealers involved in a securities underwriting.

Leading economic indicators Turning points that usually precede those of the overall economy; they are believed to have value for predicting the economy's future state, usually near-term.

Legal tender Something that must be accepted when offered in exchange for goods and services.

Lender of last resort An entity willing to lend money when no other entity is ready to do so.

Leptokurtic Describes a distribution that has fatter tails than a normal distribution (also called fat-tailed).

Lessee Tenant or property user that enters a lease with a property owner or lessor.

Lessor Property owner or manager that leases a property to a tenant or property user.

Level of significance The probability of a Type I error in testing a hypothesis.

Leverage A measure for identifying a potentially influential high-leverage point.

Leveraged buyout A transaction whereby the target company management team converts the target to a privately held company by using heavy borrowing to finance the purchase of the target company's outstanding shares.

Leveraged buyout (LBO) An acquirer (typically an investment fund specializing in LBOs) uses a significant amount of debt to finance the acquisition of a target and then pursues restructuring actions, with the goal of exiting the target with a sale or public listing.

Leveraged buyouts Buyout equity transactions that utilize a high proportion of debt financing to make a company acquisition.

Leveraged loan Where private debt investor firms borrow money to make a direct loan to a borrower.

Leveraged loans Loans made to a borrower or issuer with relatively lower credit quality and/or higher leverage.

Liability-driven investing An investment industry term that generally encompasses asset allocation that is focused on funding an investor's liabilities in institutional contexts.

Licensing arrangements Rights to produce a product or have access to intangible assets using someone else's brand name in return for a royalty (often a percentage of revenues).

Lien A legal right or claim to property by a creditor.

Likelihood The probability of an observation, given a particular set of conditions.

Limit order Instructions to a broker or exchange to obtain the best price immediately available when filling an order, but in no event accept a price higher than a specified (limit) price when buying or accept a price lower than a specified (limit) price when selling.

Limit order book The book or list of limit orders to buy and sell that pertains to a security.

Limited company A business organizational form owned by shareholders or members with limited liability who elect a board of directors to appoint management. Generally, limited companies have indefinite life and easier transfer of ownership interests than limited partnerships.

Limited liability partnership (LLP) A business organizational form available in some jurisdictions owned entirely by limited partners with limited liability.

Limited partners (LPs) Owners of a limited partnership with limited liability and other attributes as specified in the partnership agreement.

Limited partnership A business organizational form owned by a general partner and limited partners.

Limited partnership agreement (LPA) A legal document that outlines the rules of the partnership and establishes the framework that ultimately guides the fund's operations throughout its life.

Lin-log model A functional form for transforming regression model data in which the dependent variable is linear but the independent variable is logarithmic.

Linear derivatives Firm commitment derivative contracts in which the contract's payoff/profit function is linear with respect to the price of the underlying.

Liquid market Said of a market in which traders can buy or sell with low total transaction costs when they want to trade.

Liquidity The extent to which a company is able to meet its short-term obligations using cash flows and those assets that can be readily transformed into cash.

Liquidity premium An extra return that compensates investors for the risk of loss relative to an investment's fair value if the investment needs to be converted to cash quickly.

Liquidity ratios Financial ratios measuring the company's ability to meet its short-term obligations to creditors as they come due.

Liquidity risk A divergence in the cash flow timing of a derivative versus that of an underlying transaction.

Liquidity trap A condition in which the demand for money becomes infinitely elastic (horizontal demand curve) so that injections of money into the economy will not lower interest rates or affect real activity.

Load fund A mutual fund in which, in addition to the annual fee, a percentage fee is charged to invest in the fund and/or for redemptions from the fund.

Loan-to-value ratio (LTV) Ratio of the amount of the mortgage to the property's value. The lower the LTV, the higher the borrower's equity. From the lender's perspective, the higher the borrower's equity, the less likely the borrower is to default.

Loans Debt instruments agreed to between a borrower and lender, typically a bank.

Lockout or revolving period For an ABS with a non-amortizing collateral pool, such as credit card debt, is the period in which the cash proceeds from principal repayments are reinvested in additional loans with a principal equal to the principal repaid. During this period, there is no prepayment risk and potential default risk is generally limited. When the lockout period is over, principal repayments are used to pay off the outstanding principal on the ABS. Lockout period and revolving period are interchangeable.

Lockup period The minimum holding period before investors are allowed to make withdrawals or redeem shares from a fund. Its purpose is to allow the hedge fund manager the required time to implement and potentially realize a strategy's expected results.

Log-lin model A functional form for transforming regression model data in which the dependent variable is logarithmic but the independent variable is linear.

Log-log model A functional form for transforming regression model data in which both the dependent and independent variables are in logarithmic form.

Long A trading position in a **derivative contract** that gains value as the price of the **underlying** moves higher.

Long position A position in an asset or contract in which one owns the asset or has an exercisable right under the contract.

Long-run average total cost The curve describing average total cost when no costs are considered fixed.

Loss aversion The tendency of people to dislike losses more than they like comparable gains.

Loss given default (LGD) The investor's loss conditional on an issuer event of default.

Loss severity Portion of a bond's value (including unpaid interest) an investor loses in the event of default.

Loss-aversion bias A bias in which people tend to strongly prefer avoiding losses as opposed to achieving gains.

Low-cost producer A firm with lower production costs than its industry competitors.

M^2 An appraisal measure that indicates what a portfolio would have returned, assuming the same total risk as the market index.

M^2 alpha Difference between the risk-adjusted performance of the portfolio and the performance of the benchmark.

Macaulay duration The present-value weighted average time to receipt of cash flows for fixed-income instrument, also the holding period needed to balance coupon reinvestment risk and price risk for a one-time instantaneous "parallel" shift in the yield curve once the bond purchase is settled. It is named after Frederick Macaulay, the Canadian economist who introduced the concept in 1938.

Machine learning (ML) Involves computer-based techniques that seek to extract knowledge from large amounts of data without making any assumptions about the data's underlying probability distribution. The goal of ML algorithms is to automate decision-making processes by generalizing, or "learning," from known examples to determine an underlying structure in the data.

Maintenance capital expenditures Investments in assets to keep them in operation or increase their efficiency without extending their useful lives.

Maintenance margin Minimum balance set below the initial margin that each contract buyer and seller must hold in the futures margin account from trade initiation until final settlement at maturity.

Maintenance margin requirement The margin requirement on any day other than the first day of a transaction.

Management buy-in A type of leveraged buyout where the current management team is replaced with the acquiring team involved in managing the company.

Management buyout A type of leveraged buyout where the current management team participates in the acquisition.

Management guidance Management of public companies may publicly provide targets for earnings, revenues, and other measures (e.g., capital expenditures) for the next quarter, year, or longer term. Guidance can be detailed or rather directional and is often updated throughout the year. Initial guidance for next fiscal year might be provided during the fourth-quarter earnings call and updated for completed quarters, and new information provided at the first-, second-, and third-quarter earnings calls. Also known simply as *guidance*.

Margin call Request to a derivatives contract counterparty to immediately deposit funds to return the futures margin account balance to the initial margin.

Margin financing A financing arrangement whereby the prime broker lends shares, bonds, or derivatives and the hedge fund (or investment manager) deposits cash or other collateral into a margin account at the prime broker based on certain fractions of the investment positions.

Margin loan Money borrowed from a broker to purchase securities.

Marginal propensity to consume The proportion of an additional unit of disposable income that is consumed or spent; the change in consumption for a small change in income.

Marginal propensity to save The proportion of an additional unit of disposable income that is saved (not spent).

Mark to market (MTM) The practice in which a central clearing party assigns profits and losses to counterparties to derivative contracts. In exchange-traded markets, this practice takes place daily and is often referred to as daily settlement.

Market anomaly Change in the price or return of a security that cannot directly be linked to current relevant information known in the market or to the release of new information into the market.

Market bid–ask spread The difference between the best bid and the best offer.

Market discount rate The rate of return required by investors given the risk of the bond investment, also known as the required yield or required rate of return.

Market float The number of shares that are available to the investing public.

Market makers Over-the-counter (OTC) dealers who typically enter into offsetting bilateral transactions with one another to transfer risk to other parties.

Market model A regression equation that specifies a linear relationship between the return on a security (or portfolio) and the return on a broad market index.

Market multiple models Valuation models based on share price multiples or enterprise value multiples.

Market neutral These strategies use quantitative, fundamental, and technical analysis to identify under- and overvalued equity securities. The hedge fund takes long positions in undervalued securities and short positions in overvalued securities, while seeking to maintain a market-neutral net position.

Market order Instructions to a broker or exchange to obtain the best price immediately available when filling an order.

Market reference rate A market-determined interest rate used as the underlying in financial instruments and contracts such as variable-rate debt and interest rate swaps. An example is the Secured Overnight Financing Rate (SOFR), which is an overnight cash borrowing rate collateralized by US Treasuries. Other MRRs include the euro short-term rate (€STR) and the Sterling Overnight Index Average (SONIA).

Market reference rate (MRR) The interest rate underlying used in interest rate swaps. These rates typically match those of loans or other short-term obligations. Survey-based Libor rates used as reference rates in the past have been replaced by rates based on a daily average of observed market transaction rates. For example, the Secured Overnight Financing Rate (SOFR) is an overnight cash borrowing rate collateralized by US Treasuries. Other MRRs include the euro short-term rate (€STR) and the Sterling Overnight Index Average (SONIA).

Market risk Risk related to market movements, e.g., unexpected changes in share prices, interest rates, currency exchange rates, and commodity prices.

Market share A company's or product's revenue expressed as a percentage of its market size.

Market size Total sales for a good or service, which can be calculated on a global or more regional basis.

Market value The price at which an asset or security can currently be bought or sold in an open market.

Market-capitalization weighting An index weighting method in which the weight assigned to each constituent security is determined by dividing its market capitalization by the total market capitalization (sum of the market capitalization) of all securities in the index. Also called *value weighting*.

Market-on-close An execution instruction specifying that an order can only be filled at the close of trading.

Marketable limit order A buy limit order in which the limit price is placed above the best offer, or a sell limit order in which the limit price is placed below the best bid. Such orders generally will partially or completely fill right away.

Markowitz efficient frontier The graph of the set of portfolios offering the maximum expected return for their level of risk (standard deviation of return).

Master limited partnership (MLP) Has similar features to limited partnerships but is usually a more liquid investment that is often publicly traded.

Master repurchase agreement A legal document governing all repo trades between two parties.

Match funding Financing an asset with a source, such as a loan or bond, that is aligned with certain attributes of the asset, such as duration and the respective streams of income and financing costs.

Material (materiality) Refers to information that is decision-useful for a reasonable investor.

Matrix pricing An estimation process for financial instruments based on the prices of comparable instruments.

Maturity The date of a fixed-income instrument's final payment to investors.

Maturity premium An extra return that compensates investors for the increased sensitivity of the market value of debt to a change in market interest rates as maturity is extended.

Maturity structure of interest rates Also known as the term structure of interest rates, refers to the difference in interest rates or benchmark yields by time-to-maturity.

Mean absolute deviation With reference to a sample, the mean of the absolute values of deviations from the sample mean.

Mean square error (MSE) Calculated as the sum of squares error (SSE) divided by the degrees of freedom, which are the number of observations minus the number of independent variables minus one. Since simple linear regression has just one independent variable, the degrees of freedom calculation is the number of observations minus 2.

Mean square regression (MSR) Calculated as the sum of squares regression (SSR) divided by the number of independent variables in the regression model. In simple linear regression, there is only one independent variable, so MSR equals SSR.

Mean–variance analysis An approach to portfolio analysis using expected means, variances, and covariances of asset returns.

Measure of central tendency A quantitative measure that specifies where data are centered.

Measures of location Quantitative measures that describe the location or distribution of data. They include not only measures of central tendency but also other measures, such as percentiles.

Median The value of the middle item of a set of items that has been sorted into ascending or descending order (i.e., the 50th percentile).

Meme coin A type of altcoin that is often inspired by a joke.

Mental accounting bias An information-processing bias in which people treat one sum of money differently from another equal-sized sum based on which mental account the money is assigned to.

Merger arbitrage Generally, these strategies involve going long (buying) the stock of the company being acquired at a discount to its announced takeover price and going short (selling) the stock of the acquiring company when the merger or acquisition is announced.

Mesokurtic Describes a distribution with kurtosis equal to that of the normal distribution, namely, kurtosis equal to three.

Mezzanine debt Refers to private credit subordinated to senior secured debt but senior to equity in the borrower's capital structure.

Mezzanine-stage financing Mezzanine venture capital that prepares a company to go public as it continues to expand capacity and enhance its growth trajectory. It represents the bridge financing needed to fund a private firm until it can execute an IPO or be sold.

Miner A validator of transactions on the blockchain that locks blocks of transactions into the blockchain and receives compensation for this process in the form of a digital asset.

Minimum efficient scale The smallest output that a firm can produce such that its long-run average total cost is minimized.

Minimum-variance portfolio The portfolio with the minimum variance for each given level of expected return.

Minority shareholder An individual or entity that owns less than a majority of the voting rights in a corporation.

Mode The most frequently occurring value in a distribution.

Modern portfolio theory (MPT) The analysis of rational portfolio choices based on the efficient use of risk.

Modified duration The first derivative of a bond's price with respect to its yield, this statistic is a measure of interest rate risk used to estimate the percentage price change for a given change in yield-to-maturity.

Monetarists Economists who believe that the rate of growth of the money supply is the primary determinant of the rate of inflation.

Monetary policy Actions taken by a nation's central bank to affect aggregate output and prices through changes in bank reserves, reserve requirements, or its target interest rate.

Monetary transmission mechanism The process whereby a central bank's interest rate gets transmitted through the economy and ultimately affects the rate of increase of prices.

Monetary union An economic union in which the members adopt a common currency.

Money convexity A measure that is used to complement modified duration to capture the second-order effect of yield changes on a bond's price, expressed in currency terms.

Money duration A measure of the price change of a fixed-income instrument in currency units from a change in yield-to-maturity. The money duration can be stated per 100 of par value or in terms of the actual position size. In the United States, money duration is commonly called "dollar duration."

Money market The market for short-term debt instruments (one-year maturity or less).

Money market securities Fixed-income securities with original maturities of one year or less.

Money-weighted return The internal rate of return on a portfolio, taking account of all cash flows.

Moneyness Expresses the relationship between an option's value and its exercise price across the full range of possible underlying prices.

Monopolistic competition Highly competitive form of imperfect competition; the competitive characteristic is a notably large number of firms, while the monopoly aspect is the result of product differentiation.

Monopoly In pure monopoly markets, there are no substitutes for the given product or service. There is a single seller, which exercises considerable power over pricing and output decisions.

Monte Carlo simulation A technique that uses the inverse transformation method for converting a randomly generated uniformly distributed number into a simulated value of a random variable of a desired distribution. Each key decision variable in a Monte Carlo simulation requires an assumed statistical distribution; this assumption facilitates incorporating non-normality, fat tails, and tail dependence as well as solving high-dimensionality problems.

Moral principles Beliefs regarding what is good, acceptable, or obligatory behavior and what is bad, unacceptable, or forbidden behavior.

Mortgage loan Agreement to finance real estate by the collateral of a specified property that obliges the borrower to make a predetermined series of payments to the lender.

Mortgage pass-through security Security created when mortgage lenders pool mortgages together and sell securities to investors. The cash flow from the mortgage pool—monthly payments of principal, interest, and prepayments—are "passed through" to the security holders.

Mortgage-backed securities Debt obligations that represent claims to the cash flows from pools of mortgage loans, most commonly on residential property.

Mortgage-backed securities (MBS) Bonds created from the securitization of mortgages.

Multi-factor model A model that explains a variable in terms of the values of a set of factors.

Multi-market indexes Comprised of indexes from different countries, designed to represent multiple security markets.

Multilateral trading facilities See *alternative trading systems*.

Multilateralism The conduct of countries who participate in mutually beneficial trade relationships and extensive rules harmonization. Private firms are fully integrated into global supply chains with multiple trade partners. Examples of multilateral countries include Germany and Singapore.

Multiple of invested capital (MOIC) A simplified calculation that measures the total value of all distributions and residual asset values relative to an initial total investment; also known as a *money multiple*.

Multiple-price auction A debt securities auction in which bidders receive distinct prices based on their bids.

Multiplier models Valuation models based on share price multiples or enterprise value multiples.

Mutual fund A comingled investment pool in which investors in the fund each have a pro-rata claim on the income and value of the fund.

Nash equilibrium When two or more participants in a non-coop-erative game have no incentive to deviate from their respective equilibrium strategies given their opponent's strategies.

Nationalism The promotion of a country's own economic interests to the exclusion or detriment of the interests of other nations. Nationalism is marked by limited economic and financial cooperation. These actors may focus on national production and sales, limited cross-border investment and capital flows, and restricted currency exchange.

Natural language processing (NLP) A field of research within the field of text analytics and at the intersection of computer science, AI, and linguistics that focuses on developing computer programs to analyze and interpret human language.

Natural resources These include commodities (hard and soft), agricultural land (farmland), and timberland.

Negative externalities A cost to a third party because of the production or consumption of a good or service.

Negative pledge clause Limitations on investments, the disposal of assets, or issuance of debt senior to existing obligations. Negative covenants seek to ensure that an issuer maintains the ability to make interest and principal payments.

Net cash An issuer's total debt less cash and marketable securities. When the balance is negative it is referred to as net cash.

Net debt An issuer's total debt less cash and marketable securities. When the balance is positive it is referred to as net debt.

Net investment hedge Refers to a specific **hedge accounting** designation that applies when either a foreign currency bond or a derivative, such as an FX swap or forward, is used to offset the exchange rate risk of the equity of a foreign operation.

Net present value (NPV) The present value of an investment's cash inflows (benefits) minus the present value of its cash outflows (costs).

Net profit margin An indicator of profitability, calculated as net income divided by revenue; indicates how much of each dollar of revenues is left after all costs and expenses. Also called *profit margin* or *return on sales*.

Net tax rate The tax rate net of transfer payments.

Net working capital Working capital excluding short-term items unrelated to business operations, such as cash, marketable securities, and short-term debt.

Network effects A business model that enables users to contribute directly to a product, service, or online content.

Neural networks A type of computer program design based on how the human brain learns and processes information.

Neutral rate of interest The rate of interest that neither spurs on nor slows down the underlying economy.

No-load fund A mutual fund in which there is no fee for investing in the fund or for redeeming fund shares, although there is an annual fee based on a percentage of the fund's net asset value.

Node Each value on a binomial tree from which successive moves or outcomes branch.

Non-agency RMBS MBS backed by residential mortgages that are issued by private entities and not guaranteed by a federal agency or a GSE.

Non-amortizing loans Type of debt where there are no scheduled principal repayments.

Non-cooperative country A country with inconsistent and even arbitrary rules; restricted movement of goods, services, people, and capital across borders; retaliation; and limited technology exchange.

Non-cumulative preference shares Preference shares for which dividends that are not paid in the current or subsequent periods are forfeited permanently (instead of being accrued and paid at a later date).

Non-financial risks Risks that arise from sources other than changes in the external financial markets, such as changes in accounting rules, legal environment, or tax rates.

Non-fungible token (NFT) A unique cryptographic token on the blockchain that cannot be replicated and is used to represent ownership of physical assets, such as artwork, real estate, or other assets.

Non-linear derivatives Derivatives, such as options or other contingent claims, with payoff/profit profiles that are non-linear (asymmetric) with respect to the price of the underlying.

Non-participating preference shares Preference shares that do not entitle shareholders to share in the profits of the company. Instead, shareholders are only entitled to receive a fixed dividend payment and the par value of the shares in the event of liquidation.

Non-probability sampling A sampling plan dependent on factors other than probability considerations, such as a sampler's judgment or the convenience to access data.

Non-recourse loan Loan in which the lender does not have a claim against the borrower and thus can look only to the property to recover the outstanding mortgage balance.

Non-state actors Those that participate in global political, economic, or financial affairs but do not directly control national security or country resources. Examples of non-state actors are non-governmental organizations (NGOs), multinational companies, charities, and even influential individuals, such as business leaders or cultural icons.

Nonparametric test A test that is not concerned with a parameter or that makes minimal assumptions about the population from which a sample comes.

Nonsystematic risk Unique risk that is local or limited to a particular asset or industry that need not affect assets outside of that asset class.

Normal distribution A continuous, symmetric probability distribution that is completely described by its mean and its variance.

Normalized earnings The expected level of mid-cycle earnings for a company in the absence of any unusual or temporary factors that affect profitability (either positively or negatively).

Notching Ratings adjustment methodology where specific issues from the same borrower may be assigned different credit ratings.

Notice period The length of time (typically 30–90 days) in advance that investors may be required to notify a fund of their intent to redeem some or all of their investment. This allows a fund manager to liquidate a position in an orderly fashion without magnifying losses.

Novation process A process that substitutes the initial **swap execution facility (SEF)** contract with identical trades facing the **central counterparty (CCP)**. The CCP serves as **counterparty** for both financial intermediaries, eliminating bilateral **counterparty credit risk** and providing **clearing** and **settlement** services.

Null hypothesis The hypothesis that is tested.

Off-the-run Seasoned government bonds that are often less liquid.

Off-the-run securities Sovereign debt securities outstanding other than on-the-sun securities. Off-the-run securities are less liquid than on-the-run securities.

Offer The price at which a dealer or trader is willing to sell an asset, typically qualified by a maximum quantity (ask size).

Official interest rate An interest rate that a central bank sets and announces publicly; normally the rate at which it is willing to lend money to the commercial banks. Also called *official policy rate* or *policy rate*.

Official policy rate An interest rate that a central bank sets and announces publicly; normally the rate at which it is willing to lend money to the commercial banks.

Oligopoly Market structure with a relatively small number of firms supplying the market.

Omnichannel Refers to a company selling its products or services in multiple channels, such as in store and online.

On-the-run Most recently issued, and liquid, government bonds.

On-the-run securities The most recently issued and liquid sovereign debt securities.

Open interest The number of outstanding contracts.

Open market operations The purchase or sale of bonds by the national central bank to implement monetary policy. The bonds traded are usually sovereign bonds issued by the national government.

Open-end fund A mutual fund that accepts new investment money and issues additional shares at a value equal to the net asset value of the fund at the time of investment.

Operating cycle The length of time between a company's acquisition of goods or raw materials and the collection of cash from sales to customers.

Operating efficiency ratios Ratios that measure how efficiently a company performs day-to-day tasks, such as the collection of receivables and management of inventory.

Operating leases A type of lease which is more akin to the rental of the underlying asset.

Operating leverage The sensitivity of a firm's operating profit to a change in revenues, determined by the composition of fixed and variable operating costs.

Operating profit margin A profitability ratio calculated as operating income (i.e., income before interest and taxes) divided by revenue. Also called *operating margin*.

Operational deposits Bank deposits generated by clearing, custody, and cash management activities.

Operational independence A bank's ability to execute monetary policy and set interest rates in the way it thought would best meet the inflation target.

Operational risk The risk that arises from inadequate or failed people, systems, and internal policies, procedures, and processes, as well as from external events that are beyond the control of the organization but that affect its operations.

Operationally efficient Said of a market, a financial system, or an economy that has relatively low transaction costs.

Opportunistic real estate strategies Include major redevelopment, repurposing of assets, taking on large vacancies, or speculating on significant improvement in market conditions. These may be appealing for investors seeking higher returns and willing to accept additional risks from development, redevelopment, repositioning, and leasing.

Opportunity cost The value that investors forgo by choosing a particular course of action; the value of something in its best alternative use.

Optimal capital structure The capital structure at which the value of the company is maximized.

Option A primary example of a **contingent claim**. A **derivative contract** that provides the buyer the right, but not the obligation, to buy or sell an **underlying**.

Option contract See *option*.

Option premium An amount that is paid upfront from the option buyer to the option seller. Reflects the value of the option buyer's right to exercise in the future.

Option-adjusted price The sum of a bond's flat price and value of an embedded option.

Option-adjusted spread Or OAS for a bond is its Z-spread adjusted for the value of an embedded option.

Option-adjusted yield A yield measure for a bond adjusted for embedded options.

Order A specification of what instrument to trade, how much to trade, and whether to buy or sell.

Order precedence hierarchy With respect to the execution of orders to trade, a set of rules that determines which orders execute before other orders.

Order-driven markets A market (generally an auction market) that uses rules to arrange trades based on the orders that traders submit; in their pure form, such markets do not make use of dealers.

Ordinary shares Equity shares that are subordinate to all other types of equity (e.g., preferred equity). Also called *common stock* or *common shares*.

Organizational form A legal and tax classification of a business, specific to a jurisdiction, that determines the organization's legal identity, owner–manager relationship, owner liability, taxation, and access to financing.

Out-of-the-money Describes an option with zero intrinsic value because the option buyer would not rationally exercise the option. An example of such would be the case in which the price of the underlying is less than the option's exercise price for a call option.

Over-the-counter (OTC) Refers to derivative markets in which **derivative contracts** are created and traded between derivatives end users and **dealers**, or financial intermediaries, such as commercial banks or investment banks.

Overcollateralization Credit enhancement technique where collateral underlying the transaction exceeds the face value of the issued bonds.

Overconfidence bias A bias in which people demonstrate unwarranted faith in their own intuitive reasoning, judgments, and/or cognitive abilities.

Overfitting When a machine learning model learns the input and target dataset too precisely, making the system more likely to discover false relationships or unsubstantiated patterns that will lead to prediction errors.

P-value The smallest level of significance at which the null hypothesis can be rejected.

Par rate A yield-to-maturity that makes the present value of a bond's cash flows equal to par.

Par swap rate The fixed swap rate that equates the present value of all future expected floating cash flows to the present value of fixed cash flows.

Par value The amount of principal on a bond, also known as face value.

Parallel shift When all maturities along a yield curve increase or decrease in yield in the same direction by the same magnitude. A parallel shift in the yield curve is implicitly assumed in analytical duration and convexity.

Parameter A descriptive measure computed from or used to describe a population of data, conventionally represented by Greek letters.

Parametric test Any test (or procedure) concerned with parameters or whose validity depends on assumptions concerning the population generating the sample.

Pari passu clause A covenant or contract clause that ensures a debt obligation is treated the same as the borrower's other senior debt instruments and is not subordinated to similar obligations.

Partially amortizing bond A loan or bond with a payment schedule that calls for the complete repayment of principal over the instrument's time to maturity.

Participating preference shares Preference shares that entitle shareholders to receive the standard preferred dividend plus the opportunity to receive an additional dividend if the company's profits exceed a pre-specified level.

Pass-through businesses Businesses that, by virtue of their organizational form and/or other legal and regulatory attributes, do not pay entity-level taxes on income or loss; income or loss is passed through to owners, who pay personal taxes.

Pass-through rate The coupon rate of a mortgage pass-through security that is received by the investor after administrative charges. It is lower than the weighted average mortgage rate earned on the underlying pool of mortgages because of administrative charges. The pass-through rate that the investor receives is said to be "net interest" or "net coupon."

Passive investment In the fixed-income context, it is investment that seeks to mimic the prevailing characteristics of the overall investments available in terms of credit quality, type of borrower, maturity, and duration rather than express a specific market view.

Payable date The day that the company actually mails out (or electronically transfers) a dividend payment.

Payment date The day that the company actually mails out (or electronically transfers) a dividend payment.

Payment-in-kind A bond feature whereby coupon payments can be fully or partially paid in the form of additional issuance or added to the principal amount.

Payments system The system for the transfer of money.

Pearson correlation A parametric measure of the relationship between two variables.

Pecking order theory The theory that managers consider how their actions might be interpreted by outsiders and thereby order their preferences for various forms of corporate financing. Forms of financing that are least visible to outsiders (e.g., internally generated funds) are most preferable to managers, and those that are most visible (e.g., equity issuance) are least preferable.

Penetration pricing A discount pricing approach used when a firm willingly sacrifices margins in order to build scale and market share.

Percentiles Quantiles that divide a distribution into 100 equal parts that sum to 100.

Perfect competition A market structure in which the individual firm has virtually no impact on market price, because it is assumed to be a very small seller among a very large number of firms selling essentially identical products.

Performance evaluation The measurement and assessment of the outcomes of investment management decisions.

Performance fee Fee paid to the general partner from the limited partner(s) based on realized net profits.

Period costs Costs (e.g., executives' salaries) that cannot be directly matched with the timing of revenues and which are thus expensed immediately.

Periodicity Number of periods in a year, used for compound interest. The periodicity of a fixed-income instrument usually matches the frequency of its coupon payments.

Permanent differences Differences between tax and financial reporting of revenue (expenses) that will not be reversed at some future date. These result in a difference between the company's effective tax rate and statutory tax rate and do not result in a deferred tax item.

Permissioned networks Networks that are fully open only to select participants on a DLT network.

Permissionless networks Networks that are fully open to any user on a DLT network.

Perpetual bonds Bonds with no stated maturity date.

Perpetuity A perpetual annuity, or a set of never-ending level sequential cash flows, with the first cash flow occurring one period from now.

PESTLE analysis A framework for analyzing factors that influence an industry's economic outcomes.

Pet projects A capital investment that is pursued by management but is not economically justifiable by a disinterested party. Motivations for pet projects include self-dealing and vanity.

Physical risks Economic and financial losses from the increase in the severity and frequency of extreme weather due to climate change—for example, the loss of coastal real estate from a storm.

PIPE (private investment in public equity) A private offering to select investors with fewer disclosures and lower transaction costs that allows the issuer to raise capital more quickly and cost effectively.

Platykurtic Describes a distribution that has relatively less weight in the tails than the normal distribution (also called thin-tailed).

Pledge A legal right or claim to property by a creditor. Also called a lien.

Poison pill Officially known as a shareholder rights plan, a poison pill is a hostile-takeover defense adopted by boards of directors according to rules specified in the corporate charter. There are several types of poison pills. Generally, they allow shareholders, *excluding* the shareholder making the hostile bid and their affiliates, to buy newly issued shares at a discounted price. The share issuance would dilute the bidder's ownership percentage, rendering it impossible for the bidder to attain control.

Policy rate An interest rate that a central bank sets and announces publicly; normally the rate at which it is willing to lend money to the commercial banks.

Portfolio companies The individual companies owned by a private equity firm.

Portfolio investment flows Short-term investments in foreign assets, such as stocks or bonds.

Portfolio planning The process of creating a plan for building a portfolio that is expected to satisfy a client's investment objectives.

Position The quantity of an asset that an entity owns or owes.

Posterior probability An updated probability that reflects or comes after new information.

Power of a test The probability of correctly rejecting the null—that is, rejecting the null hypothesis when it is false.

Pre-funding period Allows the trust to acquire during a certain period of time after the close of the transaction.

Preference shares A type of equity interest which ranks above common shares with respect to the payment of dividends and the distribution of the company's net assets upon liquidation. They have characteristics of both debt and equity securities. Also called *preferred stock*.

Preferred stock See *preference shares*.

Premium In the case of bonds, premium refers to the amount by which a bond is priced above its face (par) value. In the case of an option, the amount paid for the option contract.

Prepayment option May entitle the borrower to prepay all or part of the outstanding mortgage principal prior to maturity. This creates a risk from the lender's or investor's viewpoint because the cash flow amounts and timing cannot be known with certainty.

Prepayment risk The risk that the some or all of a mortgage-backed security's principal is repaid at a different speed than expected, either in the form of contraction risk (or earlier repayment than expected) or extension risk (later repayment).

Present value models Valuation models that estimate the intrinsic value of a security as the present value of the future benefits expected to be received from the security. Also called *discounted cash flow models*.

Pretax margin A profitability ratio calculated as earnings before taxes divided by revenue.

Price discrimination A pricing approach that charges different prices to different customers based on their willingness to pay.

Price index Represents the average prices of a basket of goods and services.

Price limits Establish a band relative to the previous day's settlement price within which all trades must occur.

Price multiple A ratio that compares the share price with some sort of monetary flow or value to allow evaluation of the relative worth of a company's stock.

Price priority The principle that the highest priced buy orders and the lowest priced sell orders execute first.

Price return Measures *only* the price appreciation or percentage change in price of the securities in an index or portfolio.

Price return index An index that reflects *only* the price appreciation or percentage change in price of the constituent securities. Also called *price index*.

Price stability In economics, refers to an inflation rate that is low on average and not subject to wide fluctuation.

Price takers Producers that must accept whatever price the market dictates.

Price value of a basis point (PVBP) An estimate of the change in the full price of a bond given a 1 bp change in its yield-to-maturity. The PVBP is also called the "PV01," standing for the "price value of an 01" or "present value of an 01," where "01" means 1 bp. In the United States, it is commonly called the "DV01" for the "dollar value" of 1 bp.

Price weighting An index weighting method in which the weight assigned to each constituent security is determined by dividing its price by the sum of all the prices of the constituent securities.

Price-setting option The option to adjust prices when demand or supply varies from what is forecast.

Price-to-earnings ratio (P/E) The ratio of share price to earnings per share.

Pricing power A company's ability to set prices and other economic terms with customers without affecting its sales volumes.

Primary bond markets Fixed-income markets comprised of issuers issuing bonds to investors to raise capital, often intermediated by a third-party such as an investment bank.

Primary capital markets (primary markets) The market where securities are first sold and the issuers receive the proceeds.

Primary dealer Financial institution that is authorized to deal in new issues of sovereign bonds and that serves primarily as a trading counterparty of the office responsible for issuing sovereign bonds.

Primary market The market where securities are first sold and the issuers receive the proceeds.

Prime broker A broker that provides services that commonly include custody, administration, lending, short borrowing, and trading.

Prime loans Lending made to borrowers of high credit quality with strong employment and credit histories, a low DTI, substantial equity in the underlying property, and a first lien on the mortgaged property serving as the collateral for the loan.

Principal The amount that an issuer agrees to repay the debtholders on the maturity date.

Principal-agent relationship An arrangement in which one party (the agent) has authority to act for or on behalf of another party (the principal). Such an arrangement imposes a duty on the agent to act in the principal's best interest.

Prior probabilities Probabilities reflecting beliefs prior to the arrival of new information.

Priority of claims Priority of payment, with the most senior or highest ranking debt having the first claim on the cash flows and assets of the issuer.
Private capital Funding provided to companies that is not sourced from the public markets.
Private company A company, typically a limited company, that does not list its equity securities on an exchange.
Private debt Capital extended to companies through a loan or other form of debt.
Private debtholders Investors in an entity's non-securitized debt claims, such as a loan or lease. The most common type of private debtholder is a bank.
Private equity Equity investment capital raised from sources other than public markets and traditional institutions.
Private equity fund A hedge fund that seeks to buy, optimize, and ultimately sell portfolio companies to generate profits. See *venture capital fund*.
Private equity securities Securities that are not listed on public exchanges and have no active secondary market. They are issued primarily to institutional investors via non-public offerings, such as private placements.
Private investment in public equity (PIPE) An investment in the equity of a publicly traded firm that is made at a discount to the market value of the firm's shares.
Private limited company A type of limited company in many jurisdictions with pass-through taxation but restrictions on the number of shareholders or members and on the transfer of ownership interest.
Private placement A sale of debt or equity securities to a small group of investors on an unregulated basis. The terms of the offering are negotiated by the issuer and investors.
Probability of default (POD) The likelihood that an issuer fails to make full and timely payments of principal and interest; typically an annualized measure.
Probability sampling A sampling plan that allows every member of the population to have an equal chance of being selected.
Probability tree diagram A diagram with branches emanating from nodes representing either mutually exclusive chance events or mutually exclusive decisions.
Production flexibility option The option to alter production when demand varies from what is forecast.
Profession An occupational group that has specific education, expert knowledge, and a framework of practice and behavior that underpins community trust, respect, and recognition.
Profit margin An indicator of profitability, calculated as net income divided by revenue; indicates how much of each dollar of revenues is left after all costs and expenses.
Profitability ratios Ratios that measure a company's ability to generate profitable sales from its resources (assets).
Prospectus Legal document in securitization that describes the structure of the transaction, including the priority and amount of payments to be made to the servicer, administrators, and the ABS holders, as well as the credit enhancements used in the securitization.
Protective put A strategy of purchasing an underlying asset and purchasing a put on the same asset.
Proxy contest When a shareholder or group of shareholders campaigns for certain matters they have submitted to a shareholder vote, often a slate of directors who oppose the incumbent board and management. The incumbent board and management simultaneously campaign for their side.

Proxy voting A form of casting a ballot in an election in which a voter authorizes a representative to vote on their behalf according to instructions. In corporate elections, proxy ballots are cast by shareholders that direct a representative, typically the corporate secretary, to enter their votes as instructed.
Public (listed) company A company with its equity securities traded on an exchange.
Public limited companies A type of limited company in many jurisdictions with entity-level taxation but no restrictions on the number of shareholders or transferability of ownership interest; the most suitable organizational form for a company that seeks to go public.
Public–private partnership A long-term contractual relationship between the public and private sectors for the purpose of having the private sector deliver a project or service traditionally provided by the public sector. Infrastructure is increasingly being financed privately through public–private partnerships by local, regional, and national governments.
Public–private partnership (PPP) An agreement between the public sector and the private sector to finance, build, and operate public infrastructure, such as hospitals and toll roads.
Pull on liquidity An action or event that accelerates cash outflows.
Purchase agreement Legal document in a securitization transaction that outlines the representations and warranties that the seller makes about the assets sold.
Pure discount bonds Bonds that do not pay interest during their life. They are issued at a discount to par value and redeemed at par. Also called zero-coupon bonds.
Put An option that gives the holder the right to sell an underlying asset to another party at a fixed price over a specific period of time.
Put option The right to sell an underlying.
Putable bonds Bonds that give the bondholder the right to sell the bond back to the issuer at a predetermined price on specified dates.
Put–call forward parity Describes the no-arbitrage condition in which at $t = 0$ the present value of the price of a long forward commitment plus the price of the long put must equal the price of the long call plus the price of the risk-free asset (with face value of the exercise price of both the call and the put).
Put–call parity Describes the no-arbitrage condition in which at $t = 0$ the price of the long underlying asset plus the price of the long put must equal the price of the long call plus the price of the risk-free asset (with face value of the exercise price of both the call and the put).
Quantile A value at or below which a stated fraction of the data lies. Also referred to as a fractile.
Quantitative easing An expansionary monetary policy based on aggressive open market purchase operations.
Quartiles Quantiles that divide a distribution into four equal parts.
Quick ratio A measure of liquidity that is the ratio of cash, marketable securities, and receivables to current liabilities.
Quintiles Quantiles that divide a distribution into five equal parts.
Quota rents Profits that foreign producers can earn by raising the price of their goods higher than they would without a quota.

Quotas Government policies that restrict the quantity of a good that can be imported into a country, generally for a specified period of time.

Quote-driven market A market in which dealers acting as principals facilitate trading.

Quoted margin Specified spread of a floating rate instrument over a market reference rate or benchmark.

Range The difference between the maximum and minimum values in a dataset.

Rapid amortization provisions Provisions in receivable ABS that may require early principal amortization if specific events occur. Such provisions are referred to as early amortization and are included to safeguard the credit quality of the issue, particularly during the revolving period.

Razor, razorblade pricing A pricing approach that combines a low price on a piece of equipment and high-margin pricing on repeat-purchase consumables.

Real assets Generally, these are tangible physical assets, such as real estate, infrastructure, and natural resources, but they also include such intangibles as patents, intellectual property, and goodwill. Real assets generate current or expected future cash flows and/or are considered a store of value.

Real estate Includes borrowed or ownership capital in buildings or land. Developed land includes commercial and industrial real estate, residential real estate, and infrastructure.

Real option A right, but not an obligation, for management to make a decision with respect to a capital investment that alters future cash flows from the original forecasted scenario.

Real risk-free interest rate The single-period interest rate for a completely risk-free security if no inflation were expected.

Rebalancing In the context of asset allocation, a discipline for adjusting the portfolio to align with the strategic asset allocation.

Rebalancing policy The set of rules that guide the process of restoring a portfolio's asset class weights to those specified in the strategic asset allocation.

Recapitalization Recapitalization via private equity describes the steps a firm takes to increase or introduce leverage to its portfolio company and pay itself a dividend out of the new capital structure.

Recognition lag The lag in government response to an economic problem resulting from the delay in confirming a change in the state of the economy.

Recourse loan Loan in which the lender has a claim against the borrower for the shortfall (deficiency) between the amount of the outstanding mortgage balance and the proceeds received from the sale of the property.

Recovery rate (RR) The percentage of an outstanding debt claim recovered when an issuer defaults

Redemption fee A fee charged to discourage redemptions and to offset the transaction costs for remaining investors in the fund.

Refinancing rate A type of central bank policy rate.

Regionalism In between the two extremes of bilateralism and multilateralism. In regionalism, a group of countries cooperate with one another. Both bilateralism and regionalism can be conducted at the exclusion of other groups. For example, regional blocs may agree to provide trade benefits to one another and increase barriers for those outside of that group.

Registered bonds Bonds for which ownership is recorded by either name or serial number.

Regression analysis Allows us to test hypotheses about the relationship between two variables, by quantifying the strength of the relationship between the two variables, and to use one variable to make predictions about the other variable.

Regression coefficients The collective term for the intercept and slope coefficients in the regression model.

Regret The feeling that an opportunity has been missed; typically, an expression of *hindsight bias*.

Regret-aversion bias An emotional bias in which people tend to avoid making decisions that will result in action out of fear that the decision will turn out poorly.

Relative dispersion The amount of dispersion relative to a reference value or benchmark.

Reopening Issuing bonds by increasing the size of an existing bond issue with a price significantly different from par.

Replication A strategy in which a derivative's cash flow stream may be recreated using a combination of long or short positions in an underlying asset and borrowing or lending cash.

Repo rate The interest rate on a repurchase agreement.

Representativeness bias A belief perseverance bias in which people tend to classify new information based on past experiences and classifications.

Repurchase agreement (Repo) A form of collateralized loan involving the sale of a security with a simultaneous agreement by the seller to buy back the same security from the purchaser at an agreed-on price and future date. The party who sells the security at the inception of the repurchase agreement and buys it back at maturity is borrowing money from the other party, and the security sold and subsequently repurchased represents the collateral.

Repurchase date The date when the party who sold the security at the inception of a repurchase agreement buys back the security from the cash lending counterparty.

Repurchase price The price at which the party who sold the security at the inception of the repurchase agreement buys back the security from the cash lending counterparty.

Required margin Yield spread of a floating rate instrument such that the instrument is priced at par value on a rate reset date.

Required rate of return The rate of return required by investors given the risk of the bond investment, also known as the market discount rate or required yield.

Required yield The rate of return required by investors given the risk of the bond investment, also known as the market discount rate of required rate of return.

Required yield spread The difference in yield-to-maturity between a bond and that of a government benchmark bond with the same or similar time-to-maturity.

Resampling A statistical method that repeatedly draws samples from the original observed data sample for the statistical inference of population parameters.

Reserve currency A currency held by global central banks in significant quantities and widely used to conduct international trade and financial transactions.

Reserve requirement The requirement for banks to hold reserves in proportion to the size of deposits.

Residual The amount of deviation of an observed value of the dependent variable from its estimated value based on the fitted regression line.

Restricted domestic currency A currency with limited convertibility into other currencies due to illiquidity.

Return on assets (ROA) A profitability ratio calculated as net income divided by average total assets; indicates a company's net profit generated per dollar invested in total assets.

Return on equity (ROE) A profitability ratio calculated as net income divided by average shareholders' equity.

Return on invested capital (ROIC) A measure of the profitability of a company relative to the amount of capital invested by the equityholders and debtholders.

Return on sales An indicator of profitability, calculated as net income divided by revenue; indicates how much of each dollar of revenues is left after all costs and expenses. Also referred to as *net profit margin*.

Return-generating model A model that can provide an estimate of the expected return of a security given certain parameters and estimates of the values of the independent variables in the model.

Revenue bonds Bonds issued by non-sovereign governments related to a government sponsored project expected to generate future cash flow as a primary source of repayment.

Reverse repurchase agreement A repurchase agreement viewed from the perspective of the cash lending counterparty.

Reverse stock split A reduction in the number of shares outstanding with a corresponding increase in share price, but no change to the company's underlying fundamentals.

Revolving credit agreements The most reliable form of short-term bank borrowing facilities; they are in effect for multiple years (e.g., three to five years) and can have optional medium-term loan features. Also known as *revolvers*.

Rho The change in a given derivative instrument for a given small change in the risk-free interest rate, holding everything else constant. Rho measures the sensitivity of the option to the risk-free interest rate.

Ricardian equivalence An economic theory that implies that it makes no difference whether a government finances a deficit by increasing taxes or issuing debt.

Risk Exposure to uncertainty. The chance of a loss or adverse outcome as a result of an action, inaction, or external event.

Risk averse The assumption that an investor will choose the least risky alternative.

Risk aversion The degree of an investor's inability and unwillingness to take risk.

Risk budgeting The establishment of objectives for individuals, groups, or divisions of an organization that takes into account the allocation of an acceptable level of risk.

Risk exposure The state of being exposed or vulnerable to a risk. The extent to which an organization is sensitive to underlying risks.

Risk governance The top-down process and guidance that directs risk management activities to align with and support the overall enterprise.

Risk management The process of identifying the level of risk an organization wants, measuring the level of risk the organization currently has, taking actions that bring the actual level of risk to the desired level of risk, and monitoring the new actual level of risk so that it continues to be aligned with the desired level of risk.

Risk management framework The infrastructure, process, and analytics needed to support effective risk management in an organization.

Risk premium An extra return expected by investors for bearing some specified risk.

Risk shifting Actions to change the distribution of risk outcomes.

Risk tolerance the level of risk an investor is willing and able to bear.

Risk transfer Actions to pass on a risk to another party, often, but not always, in the form of an insurance policy.

Risk-neutral pricing A no-arbitrage derivative value established separately from investor views on risk that uses underlying asset volatility and the risk-free rate to calculate the present value of future cash flows.

Risk-neutral probability The computed probability used in binomial option pricing by which the discounted weighted sum of expected values of the underlying equal the current option price. Specifically, this probability is computed using the risk-free rate and assumed up gross return and down gross return of the underlying.

Rollover risk The likelihood that a property owner will lose an existing tenant and forgo income until a new one is found.

Safety-first rules Rules for portfolio selection that focus on the risk that portfolio value or portfolio return will fall below some minimum acceptable level over some time horizon.

Sample correlation coefficient A standardized measure of how two variables in a sample move together. It is the ratio of the sample covariance to the product of the two variables' standard deviations.

Sample covariance A measure of how two variables in a sample move together.

Sample excess kurtosis A sample measure of the degree of a distribution's kurtosis in excess of the normal distribution's kurtosis.

Sample mean The sum of the sample observations divided by the sample size.

Sample skewness A sample measure of the degree of asymmetry of a distribution.

Sample standard deviation The positive square root of the sample variance.

Sample variance The sum of squared deviations around the mean divided by the degrees of freedom.

Sample-size neglect A type of representativeness bias in which financial market participants incorrectly assume that small sample sizes are representative of populations (or "real" data).

Sampling distribution The distribution of all distinct possible values that a statistic can assume when computed from samples of the same size randomly drawn from the same population.

Sampling error The difference between the observed value of a statistic and the estimate resulting from using subsets of the population.

Sampling plan The set of rules used to select a sample.

Saving deposits Bank deposits typically held for non-transactional purposes that often have a stated term.

Scatter plot A two-dimensional graphical plot of paired observations of values for the independent and dependent variables in a simple linear regression.

Scenario analysis A variation of the valuation process combining a base case with alternative outcomes, allowing the incorporation of more favorable or adverse scenarios in the valuation process.

Scraping An automated, large-scale, algorithm-driven approach that retrieves otherwise unstructured data available on websites and creates data in a more structured format.

Seasoned offering An offering in which an issuer sells additional units of a previously issued security.

Secondary bond markets Fixed-income markets comprised of investors trading existing bonds amongst themselves.

Secondary market The market where securities are traded among investors.

Secondary precedence rules Rules that determine how to rank orders placed at the same time.

Secondary sale Sale of a private company stake to another private equity firm or group of financial buyers.

Secondary-stage investments The second stage of development of an infrastructure asset. Secondary-stage investments involve existing infrastructure facilities or fully operational assets that do not require further investment or development over the investment horizon. These assets generate immediate cash flow and returns expected over the investment period.

Sector indexes Indexes that represent and track different economic sectors—such as consumer goods, energy, finance, health care, and technology—on either a national, regional, or global basis.

Secured With collateral; secured debt is backed by the cash flows of the issuer and the collateral as a secondary source of repayment.

Secured loans Loans collateralized by an asset of the borrower.

Security Evidence of equity or debt interest or in an entity or a related right, such as a derivative. Often standardized to conform to security exchange requirements.

Security characteristic line A plot of the excess return of a security on the excess return of the market.

Security market index A portfolio of securities representing a given security market, market segment, or asset class.

Security market line The graphical representation of the CAPM formula, showing the relationship between expected return and beta.

Security selection The process of selecting individual securities; typically, security selection has the objective of generating superior risk-adjusted returns relative to a portfolio's benchmark.

Security tokens Digitizes the ownership rights associated with publicly traded securities.

Segmenting A process of identifying and grouping customers by decision-useful attributes.

Self-attribution bias A bias in which people take too much credit for successes (*self-enhancing*) and assign responsibility to others for failures (*self-protecting*).

Self-control bias A bias in which people fail to act in pursuit of their long-term, overarching goals because of a lack of self-discipline.

Self-investment limits With respect to investment limitations applying to pension plans, restrictions on the percentage of assets that can be invested in securities issued by the pension plan sponsor.

Sell-side firm A broker/dealer that sells securities and provides independent investment research and recommendations to their clients (i.e., buy-side firms).

Semi-strong-form efficient market A market in which security prices reflect all publicly known and available information.

Semiannual bond basis yield Also known as a semiannual bond equivalent yield, it is an annualized interest rate with a periodicity of two.

Semiannual bond equivalent yield Also known as a semiannual bond basis yield, it is an annualized interest rate with a periodicity of two.

Senior debt A debt obligation with higher priority of payment than junior debt obligations.

Senior unsecured debt The highest-ranked debt in an issuer's capital structure which is a general obligation of the borrower.

Seniority Priority of payment of various debt obligations.

Sensitivity analysis A form of analysis used to determine the impact of a change in one or more key variables affecting investment returns or valuation.

Separately managed account (SMA) An investment portfolio managed exclusively for the benefit of an individual or institution.

Separately managed accounts Accounts that are managed in accordance with an investor's specific investment preferences and risk tolerance.

Service period The time between the grant and vesting dates for an employee share-based award, usually measured in years.

Settlement The closing date at which the counterparties of a derivative contract exchange payment for the underlying as required by the contract.

Settlement price The price determined by an exchange's clearinghouse in the daily settlement of the mark-to-market process. The price reflects an average of the final futures trades of the day.

Share class Types of equity securities that have different voting rights—for example, an issuer may issue Class A shares that carry one vote per share and Class B shares that carry ten votes per share.

Share repurchase A transaction in which a company buys back its own shares. Unlike stock dividends and stock splits, share repurchases use corporate cash.

Shareholder activism A range of actions by a corporation's shareholders that are intended to result in some change in the corporation, typically a change in the board of directors, management, or business strategy.

Shareholder derivative lawsuit A legal action by a shareholder on behalf of a company, not the shareholder personally, against a third party. Often, the third party is a director or manager who the shareholder believes has harmed the company.

Shareholder engagement Shareholder engagement reflects active ownership by investors in which the investor seeks to influence a corporation's decisions on ESG matters, either through dialogue with corporate officers or votes at a shareholder assembly (in the case of equity).

Shareholder theory of corporate governance Espoused by Milton Friedman in his famous 1970 essay, the shareholder theory holds that the objective of a business is to increase profits and shareholder value.

Shareholders Hold a direct equity position in a firm, and both individual persons and financial institutions can be shareholders. The term comes from the individual or investment firm literally having a share of the company. It is most commonly used when talking about the rights and responsibilities that come with being an "owner" of a company, such as stewardship, voting, and engagement. This differentiates it from a situation where an individual or an investment firm lends money or invests in a bond (in other words, they are not an equityholder of a company). Because bond investors do not have a share and are not owners of a company, they cannot vote. Nonetheless, expectations around engagement are increasing for those who invest in loans and bonds as well, making the difference between the two terms more subtle.

Shares Units of ownership interest in a limited company.

Sharpe ratio The average return in excess of the risk-free rate divided by the standard deviation of return; a measure of the average excess return earned per unit of standard deviation of return. Also known as the *reward-to-variability ratio*.

Shelf registration A type of public offering that allows the issuer to file a single, all-encompassing offering circular that covers a series of bond issues.

Short A trading position in a **derivative contract** that gains value as the price of the **underlying** moves lower.

Short biased These strategies use quantitative, technical, and fundamental analysis to short overvalued equity securities with limited or no long-side exposures.

Short position A position in an asset or contract in which one has sold an asset one does not own, or in which a right under a contract can be exercised against oneself.

Short selling A transaction in which borrowed securities are sold with the intention to repurchase them at a lower price at a later date and return them to the lender.

Short-run average total cost The curve describing average total cost when some costs are considered fixed.

Shortfall risk The risk that portfolio value or portfolio return will fall below some minimum acceptable level over some time horizon.

Shutdown point The point at which average revenue is equal to the firm's average variable cost.

Side letter A side agreement created between the GP and specific LPs. These agreements exist *outside* the LPA. These agreements provide additional terms and conditions related to the investment agreement.

Signpost An indicator, market level, data piece, or event that signals a risk is becoming more or less likely. An analyst can think of signposts like a traffic light.

Simple linear regression (SLR) An approach for estimating the linear relationship between a dependent variable and a single independent variable by minimizing the sum of the squared deviations between the fitted line and the observed values.

Simple random sample A subset of a larger population created in such a way that each element of the population has an equal probability of being selected to the subset.

Simple random sampling The procedure of drawing a sample to satisfy the definition of a simple random sample.

Simple yield The sum of the coupon payments plus the straight-line amortized share of the gain or loss divided by the bond's flat price. Simple yields are used mostly to quote JGBs.

Simulation A technique for exploring how a target variable (e.g. portfolio returns) would perform in a hypothetical environment specified by the user, rather than a historical setting.

Simulation trial A complete pass through the steps of a simulation.

Single-price auction A debt securities auction in which all bidders pay the same price.

Sinking fund Provisions that reduce the credit risk of a bond issue by requiring the issuer to retire a portion of the bond's principal outstanding each year.

Situational influences External factors, such as environmental or cultural elements, that shape our behavior.

Skewed Not symmetrical.

Skewness A quantitative measure of skew (lack of symmetry); a synonym of skew. It is computed as the average cubed deviation from the mean standardized by dividing by the standard deviation cubed.

Slope coefficient The change in the estimated value of the dependent variable for a one-unit change in the value of the independent variable.

Small country A country that is a price taker in the world market for a product and cannot influence the world market price.

Smart beta Involves the use of transparent, rules-based strategies as a basis for investment decisions.

Smart contracts Computer programs that are designed to self-execute on the basis of pre-specified terms and conditions agreed to by parties to a contract.

Social infrastructure investments A category of infrastructure investments that are directed toward human activities and include such assets as educational, health care, social housing, and correctional facilities, with the focus on providing, operating, and maintaining the asset infrastructure.

Soft commodities Standardized agricultural products, such as cattle and corn, with markets often involving the physical delivery of the underlying upon settlement.

Soft hurdle rate Hurdle rate where the fee is calculated on the entire return when the hurdle is exceeded. With a soft hurdle, GPs are able to catch up performance fees once the hurdle threshold is exceeded.

Soft power A means of influencing another country's decisions without force or coercion. Soft power can be built over time through actions, such as cultural programs, advertisement, travel grants, and university exchange.

Soft-bullet covered bonds Delay the bond default and payment acceleration of bond cash flows until a new final maturity date, which is usually up to a year after the original maturity date.

Solvency Refers to the condition in which firm value exceeds the face value of debt used to finance the firm's assets.

Solvency ratios Ratios that measure a company's ability to meet its long-term obligations.

Solvency risk The risk that an organization does not survive or succeed because it runs out of cash, even though it might otherwise be solvent.

Sophisticated investors Individuals or entities that are permitted in a jurisdiction to trade unregistered or, generally, less regulated securities, including shares of privately held companies; also called *accredited investors*.

Sovereign immunity A principle limiting the legal recourse of bondholders holding national government debt from forcing the issuer to declare bankruptcy or liquidate assets to settle debt claims.

Spearman rank correlation coefficient A measure of correlation applied to ranked data.

Special dividend A dividend paid by a company that does not pay dividends on a regular schedule, or a dividend that supplements regular cash dividends with an extra payment.

Special purpose acquisition company A "blank check" company that exists solely for the purpose of acquiring an unspecified private company within a predetermined period or return capital to investors.

Special purpose entity (SPE) Also referred to as a special purpose vehicle or SPV, this legal entity is created for a specific economic purpose. In the case of a project SPV, the entity's sole purpose is to facilitate the construction, operation, and financing of an infrastructure asset over its contractual life.

Special purpose vehicle See *special purpose entity*.

Special situations An area of private capital investment which targets return by investing in stressed, distressed, or event-driven opportunities.

Split ratings Complex risks viewed very differently by rating agencies

Sponsored A type of depository receipt in which the foreign company whose shares are held by the depository has a direct involvement in the issuance of the receipts.

Spot curve Yields-to-maturity on a series of default-risk-free zero-coupon bonds.

Spot markets Markets in which specific assets are exchanged at current prices. Spot markets are often referred to as **cash markets**.

Spot prices The current prices prevailing in **spot markets**.

Spot rates Yields-to-maturity on default-risk-free zero-coupon bonds.

Spread The difference in yield-to-maturity between a bond and that of a another bond.

Spread risk Bond price risk arising from changes in the yield spread on credit-risky bonds; reflects changes in the market's assessment and/or pricing of credit migration (or downgrade) risk and market liquidity risk.

Spurious correlation Refers to: 1) correlation between two variables that reflects chance relationships in a particular dataset; 2) correlation induced by a calculation that mixes each of two variables with a third variable; and 3) correlation between two variables arising not from a direct relation between them but from their relation to a third variable.

Stablecoin A cryptocurrency that aims to maintain a stable value relative to a specified asset or to a pool or basket of assets.

Stackelberg model A prominent model of strategic decision making in which firms are assumed to make their decisions sequentially.

Staggered board A structure of board elections in which only part of the board is elected simultaneously—for example, only one-third of the board may be up for election each year, so the board can be replaced over three years, not in one year if all seats were elected annually. This structure fosters greater continuity of board members but is an obstacle for shareholders seeking to effect change.

Stakeholder theory of corporate governance An expansion of the shareholder theory of corporate governance under which the objective of a business is to maximize value for, and balance the interests of, a broad group of stakeholders, including shareholders, employees, society, and the non-human environment.

Stakeholders Any party with an interest, financial or non-financial, in an entity or its actions.

Standard deviation The positive square root of the variance; a measure of dispersion in the same units as the original data.

Standard error of the estimate A measure of the distance between the observed values of the dependent variable and those predicted from the estimated regression. The smaller this value, the better the fit of the model. Also known as the standard error of the regression and the root mean square error.

Standard error of the forecast Used to provide an interval estimate around the estimated regression line. It is necessary because the regression line does not describe the relationship between the dependent and independent variables perfectly.

Standard error of the slope coefficient Calculated for simple linear regression by dividing the standard error of the estimate by the square root of the variation of the independent variable.

Standardization The process of creating protocols for the production, sale, transport, or use of a product or service. Standardization occurs when relevant parties agree to follow these protocols together. It helps support expanded economic and financial activities, such as trade and capital flows that support higher economic growth and standards of living, across borders.

Standards of conduct Behaviors required by a group; established benchmarks that clarify or enhance a group's code of ethics.

Standing limit orders A limit order at a price below market and which therefore is waiting to trade.

State actors Typically national governments, political organizations, or country leaders that exert authority over a country's national security and resources. The South African President, Sultan of Brunei, Malaysia's Parliament, and the British Prime Minister are all examples of state actors.

Statement of cash flows A financial statement that details the movement of cash over a period. The statement is classified into operating, investing, and financing activities.

Static trade-off theory of capital structure A theory pertaining to a company's optimal capital structure; the optimal level of debt is found at the point where additional debt would cause the costs of financial distress to increase by a greater amount than the benefit of the additional tax shield.

Statistically significant A result indicating that the null hypothesis can be rejected; with reference to an estimated regression coefficient, frequently understood to mean a result indicating that the corresponding population regression coefficient is different from zero.

Status quo bias An emotional bias in which people do nothing (i.e., maintain the status quo) instead of making a change.

Statutory voting A common method of voting where each share represents one vote.

Step-up bonds Bonds for which the coupon, be it fixed or floating, increases by specified margins at specified dates.

Stock dividend A type of dividend in which a company distributes additional shares of its common stock to shareholders instead of cash.

Stock exchange An exchange in which equity securities are traded. See *exchanges*.

Stock split An increase in the number of shares outstanding with a consequent decrease in share price, but no change to the company's underlying fundamentals.

Stockholder overhang The downward pressure on the share price of stock as large blocks of shares are being sold on the open market.

Stop order An order in which a trader has specified a stop price condition. Also called *stop-loss order*.

Stop-loss order See *stop order*.

Stranded assets A resource that is no longer economically valuable owing to changes in demand, regulations, or availability of substitutes—for example, a newly discovered oil well that will not be brought into production.

Strategic asset allocation A long-term strategy that establishes target allocations for various asset classes and aims to optimize the balance between risk and reward by diversifying investments.

Stratified random sampling A procedure that first divides a population into subpopulations (strata) based on classification criteria and then randomly draws samples from each stratum in sizes proportional to that of each stratum in the population.

Street convention For yield measures on fixed-income instruments that assume payments are made on scheduled dates and ignore weekends and holidays.

Stress testing A specific type of scenario analysis that estimates losses in rare and extremely unfavorable combinations of events or scenarios.

Strong-form efficient market A market in which security prices reflect all public and private information.

Structural budget deficit Also known as the cyclically adjusted budget deficit. The deficit that would exist if the economy was at full employment (or full potential output).

Structural subordination Arises in a holding company structure when the debt of operating subsidiaries is serviced by the cash flow and assets of the subsidiaries before funds can be passed to the holding company to service debt at the parent level.

Structured notes A broad category of securities that incorporate the features of debt instruments and one or more embedded derivatives designed to achieve a particular issuer or investor objective.

Subordinated debt A class of unsecured debt that ranks below a firm's senior unsecured obligations.

Subordination A form of internal credit enhancement that relies on creating more than one bond tranche and ordering the claim priorities for ownership or interest in an asset between the tranches. The ordering of the claim priorities is called a senior/subordinated structure, where the tranches of highest seniority are called senior, followed by subordinated or junior tranches. Also called **credit tranching**.

Subprime loans Lending to borrowers with lower credit quality, high DTI, and/or are loans with higher LTV, and include loans that are secured by second liens otherwise subordinated to other loans.

Sum of squares error (SSE) A measure of the total deviation between observed and estimated values of the dependent variable. It is calculated by subtracting each estimated value $\hat{Y}_i$ from its corresponding observed value Y_i, squaring each of these differences, and then summing all of these squared differences.

Sum of squares regression (SSR) A measure of the explained variation in the dependent variable, calculated as the sum of the squared differences between the predicted value of the dependent variable, $\hat{Y}_i$, based on the estimated regression line, and the mean of the dependent variable, $\bar{Y}$.

Sum of squares total (SST) A measure of the total variation in the dependent variable in a simple linear regression. It is calculated by subtracting the mean of the observed values $\bar{Y}$ from each of the observed values Y_i, squaring each of these differences, and then summing all of these squared differences.

Sunk costs A cost that has already been incurred.

Supervised learning A type of machine learning in which the system attempts to learn to model relationships based on labeled training data.

Supervisory board In some jurisdictions, a corporation's board of directors is formally composed of a supervisory board and a management board. The supervisory board appoints and oversees the management board and often includes representatives of employees and other non-shareholder stakeholders.

Supply chain The sequence of processes involved in the creation and delivery of a physical product to the end customer, both within and external to a firm, regardless of whether those steps are performed by a single firm.

Supply shock A typically unexpected disturbance to supply.

Survivorship bias Relates to the inclusion of only current investment funds in a database. As such, the returns of funds that are no longer available in the marketplace (have been liquidated) are excluded from the database. Also see *backfill bias*.

Swap A firm commitment involving a periodic exchange of cash flows.

Swap contract An agreement between two parties to exchange a series of future cash flows.

Swap execution facility (SEF) A swap trading platform accessed by multiple **dealers**.

Swap rate The fixed rate to be paid by the fixed-rate payer specified in a swap contract.

Syndicate A group of lenders, typically made up of banks.

Synthetic protective put The combination of a synthetic long underlying position (i.e., a long forward and risk-free borrowing) and a purchased put on the underlying.

Systematic risk The risk of severe damage to the real economy caused by the impairment of (parts of) the financial system.

Systematic sampling A procedure of selecting every *k*th member until reaching a sample of the desired size. The sample that results from this procedure should be approximately random.

Systemic risk Refers to risks supervisory authorities believe are likely to have broad impact across the financial market infrastructure and affect a wide swath of market participants.

Tactical asset allocation A proactive strategy that adjusts asset class allocations within a portfolio based on short-term market trends, economic conditions, or valuation changes to capitalize on temporary market inefficiencies or opportunities to improve returns or manage risk more effectively.

Target capital structure Management's desired proportions of debt and equity financing, usually stated on a book value basis or indirectly using a financial leverage metric, such as net or gross debt to EBITDA or credit rating.

Target independent A bank's ability to determine the definition of inflation that they target, the rate of inflation that they target, and the horizon over which the target is to be achieved.

Target semideviation A measure of downside risk, calculated as the square root of the average of the squared deviations of observations below the target (also called target downside deviation).

Tariffs Taxes that a government levies on imported goods.

Tax base The amount at which an asset or liability is valued for tax purposes.

Tax expense An aggregate of an entity's income tax payable (or recoverable in the case of a tax benefit) and any changes in deferred tax assets and liabilities. It is essentially the income tax payable or recoverable if these had been determined based on accounting profit rather than taxable income.

Taxable income The portion of an entity's income that is subject to income taxes under the tax laws of its jurisdiction.

Taxable temporary differences Temporary differences that result in a taxable amount in a future period when determining the taxable profit as the balance sheet item is recovered or settled.

Technical analysis A form of security analysis that uses price and volume data, often displayed graphically, in decision making.

Tender offer A solicitation by a current or prospective shareholder to other shareholders to acquire a substantial percentage, including 100%, of shares at a specified price. This action is usually undertaken by a potential acquirer whose bid was rejected by the issuer's board of directors, prompting the potential acquirer to appeal directly to shareholders.

Tenor The remaining time to maturity for a bond or derivative contract. Also called term to maturity.

Term repos Repos with a maturity longer than one day.

Term structure of interest rates Also known as the maturity structure of interest rates, refers to the difference in interest rates or benchmark yields by time-to-maturity.

Terminal stock value The expected value of a share at the end of the investment horizon—in effect, the expected selling price. Also called *terminal value*.

Terminal value The expected value of a share at the end of the investment horizon—in effect, the expected selling price.

Test of the mean of the differences A statistical test for differences based on paired observations drawn from samples that are dependent on each other.

Text analytics Involves the use of computer programs to analyze and derive meaning typically from large, unstructured text- or voice-based datasets, such as company filings, written reports, quarterly earnings calls, social media, email, internet postings, and surveys.

Thematic risks Known risks that evolve and expand over a period of time. Climate change, pattern migration, the rise of populist forces, and the ongoing threat of terrorism fall into this category.

Thin-tailed Describes a distribution that has relatively less weight in the tails than the normal distribution (also called platykurtic).

Tiered pricing A pricing approach that charges different prices to different buyers, commonly based on volume purchased.

Timberland investment management organizations Entities that support institutional investors by managing their investments in timberland by analyzing and acquiring suitable timberland holdings.

Time tranching Structure of a securitization that allows for the redistribution of "prepayment risk" among bond classes by creating bond classes of different expected maturities.

Time value The difference between an option's premium and its intrinsic value.

Time value decay The process by which the time value of an option declines toward zero as the option's expiration date is approached.

Time-weighted rate of return The compound rate of growth of one unit of currency invested in a portfolio during a stated measurement period; a measure of investment performance that is not sensitive to the timing and amount of withdrawals or additions to the portfolio.

Tokenization The process of representing ownership rights to physical assets on a blockchain or distributed ledger.

Top-down analysis An investment selection approach that begins with consideration of macroeconomic conditions and then evaluates markets and industries based upon such conditions.

Total probability rule for expected value A rule explaining the expected value of a random variable in terms of expected values of the random variable conditional on mutually exclusive and exhaustive scenarios.

Total return Measures the price appreciation, or percentage change in price of the securities in an index or portfolio, plus any income received over the period.

Total return index An index that reflects the price appreciation or percentage change in price of the constituent securities plus any income received since inception.

Total working capital The difference between current assets and current liabilities.

Tracking error The standard deviation of the differences between a portfolio's returns and its benchmark's returns; a synonym of active risk. Also called *tracking risk*.

Tracking risk The standard deviation of the differences between a portfolio's returns and its benchmark's returns. Also called *tracking error* and *active risk*.

Trade creation When regional integration results in the replacement of higher cost domestic production by lower cost imports from other members.

Trade diversion When regional integration results in lower-cost imports from non-member countries being replaced with higher-cost imports from members.

Trade sale A portion or division of a private company sold via either direct sale or auction to a strategic buyer interested in increasing the scale and scope of an existing business.

Trade settlement date The date when the buyer and seller transfer consideration and securities.

Traditional investment markets Markets for traditional investments, which include all publicly traded debts and equities and shares in pooled investment vehicles that hold publicly traded debts and/or equities.

Tranches A grouping of securities within an issue with characteristics that vary from other tranches, such as different credit quality and seniority.

Transfer payments Welfare payments made through the social security system that exist to provide a basic minimum level of income for low-income households.

Transition risks Economic and financial losses from the transition to a lower-carbon economy in response to climate change—for example, the abandonment of an oil well that is no longer economical.

Treasury Inflation-Protected Securities (TIPS) US Treasury bonds with a principal that is adjusted for changes in the Consumer Price Index. TIPS are issued in 5-, 10-, and 30-year maturities.

Treynor ratio A measure of risk-adjusted performance that relates a portfolio's returns in excess of the risk-free rate to a portfolio's beta.

Trimmed mean A mean computed after excluding a stated small percentage of the lowest and highest observations.

Triparty repo A repurchase agreement in which the transacting parties agree to use a third-party agent that provides access to a larger collateral pool and multiple counterparties, as well as valuation and safekeeping of assets.

True yield Measures on fixed-income instruments use actual payment dates, accounting for weekends and holidays. The true yield on an instrument is always lower than the street convention yield.

Turn-of-the-year effect Calendar anomaly that stock market returns in January are significantly higher compared to the rest of the months of the year, with most of the abnormal returns reported during the first five trading days in January.

Two-fund separation theorem The theory that all investors regardless of taste, risk preferences, and initial wealth will hold a combination of two portfolios or funds: a risk-free asset and an optimal portfolio of risky assets.

Two-way table A table of the frequency distribution of observations classified on the basis of two discrete variables. Also known as *Contingency table*.

Two-week repo rate The interest rate on a two-week repurchase agreement; may be used as a policy rate by a central bank.

Type I error The error of rejecting a true null hypothesis; a false positive.

Type II error The error of not rejecting a false null hypothesis; false negative.

Uncommitted lines of credit Sources of bank credit that a bank can refuse to honor. Uncommitted credit lines are made up to a certain principal amount for a pre-determined maximum maturity, charging a market reference rate plus an issuer-specific spread on only the principal outstanding for the period of use.

Underfitted When a machine learning model treats true parameters as if they are noise and is unable to recognize relationships in the training data, making the model more likely to fail to fully discover patterns that underlie the data.

Underlying The asset referred to in a **derivative contract**.

Underwritten offering A type of securities issue mechanism in which the investment bank guarantees the sale of the securities at an offering price that is negotiated with the issuer. Also known as *firm commitment offering*.

Unearned revenue A liability account for money that has been collected for goods or services that have not yet been delivered; payment received in advance of providing a good or service. Also called *deferred revenue* or *deferred income*.

Unimodal A distribution with a single value that is most frequently occurring.

Unit economics The expression of revenues and costs on a per-unit basis.

Unitranche debt A hybrid or blended loan structure combining different tranches of secured and unsecured debt into a single loan with a single, blended interest rate.

Unsecured Without collateral; unsecured debt is backed only by cash flows of the issuer.

Unsponsored A type of depository receipt in which the foreign company whose shares are held by the depository has no involvement in the issuance of the receipts.

Unsupervised learning A type of machine learning in which the system tries to learn the structure of unlabeled data.

Utility tokens Tokens that provide services within a network, such as paying for services and network fees.

Validity instructions Instructions which indicate when the order may be filled.

Value added resellers Businesses that distribute a product and also handle more complex aspects of product installation, customization, service, or support.

Value at risk A money measure of the minimum value of losses expected during a specified time period at a given level of probability.

Value chain The systems and processes in a firm that create value for its customers.

Value proposition The product or service attributes valued by a firm's target customer that lead those customers to prefer that firm's offering.

Value-add real estate strategies Strategies that involve larger-scale redevelopment and repositioning of existing assets and that may allow the investor to earn a higher return compared with core-plus real estate strategies.

Value-based pricing Pricing set primarily by reference to the value of the product or service to customers.

VaR See *value at risk*.

Variance The expected value (the probability-weighted average) of squared deviations from a random variable's expected value.

Variance of a random variable The expected value (the probability-weighted average) of squared deviations from a random variable's expected value.

Variation margin The difference between current margin required and the current collateral price in a repurchase agreement.

Vega The change in a given derivative instrument for a given small change in volatility, holding everything else constant. A sensitivity measure for options that reflects the effect of volatility.

Velocity The pace at which geopolitical risk impacts an investor portfolio.

Venture capital Private equity investment in a startup or early-stage company involving high risk and a high rate of failure.

Venture capital fund A hedge fund that seeks to buy, optimize, and ultimately sell portfolio companies to generate profits. See *private equity fund*.

Venture debt Private debt funding that provides venture capital backing to start-up or early-stage companies that may be generating little or negative cash flow.

Vest To become unconditionally entitled to.

Vesting date The day that an employee becomes unconditionally entitled to compensation.

Vintage year The year in which a private capital fund makes its first investment.

Volatility The standard deviation of the continuously compounded returns on the underlying asset.

Vote by proxy A mechanism that allows a designated party—such as another shareholder, a shareholder representative, or management—to vote on the shareholder's behalf.

Voting rights The power of shareholders to cast votes in corporate elections for directors and other matters submitted to a shareholder vote.

Warrant An attached option that gives its holder the right to buy the underlying stock of the issuing company at a fixed exercise price until the expiration date.

Waterfall structures These represent the distribution order for cash flows and risk to different tranches in a financing structure.

Weak-form efficient market hypothesis The belief that security prices fully reflect all past market data, which refers to all historical price and volume trading information.

Weighted average cost of capital (WACC) The expected cost of debt and equity weighted by the proportion of each used in a company's capital structure.

Weighted average coupon rate (WAC) Rate calculated for a mortgage pass-through security by weighting the mortgage rate of each mortgage in the pool by the percentage of the outstanding mortgage balance relative to the outstanding amount of all the mortgages in the pool.

Weighted average maturity (WAM) Calculated for a mortgage pass-through security by weighting the remaining number of months to maturity of each mortgage in the pool by the outstanding mortgage balance relative to the outstanding amount of all the mortgages in the pool.

Winsorized mean A mean computed after assigning a stated percentage of the lowest values equal to one specified low value and a stated percentage of the highest values equal to one specified high value.

Write-off/liquidation Refers to a transaction that has not gone well, and the investment is likely to lose value. The private equity firm revises the value of its investment downward or liquidates the portfolio company.

Yield curve A graphical depiction of yields-to-maturity of bonds from the same issuer across maturities.

Yield spread The difference in yield-to-maturity between a bond and that of a another bond.

Yield-to-call An internal rate of return on a fixed-income instrument's cash flows assuming cash flows are received on scheduled dates and the bond is called at a certain call price and date.

Yield-to-maturity The internal rate of return that an investor earns on a bond assuming no default, the bond is held to maturity, and periodic cash flows are reinvested at the yield-to-maturity. Also called yield-to-redemption or redemption yield.

Yield-to-worst The lowest among a fixed-income instrument's yields-to-call and yield-to-maturity. A commonly cited yield measure for fixed-rate callable bonds.

Z-spread or zero-volatility spread is a constant yield spread for a bond over a government or swap curve.

Zero-coupon bond A bond that does not pay a coupon but is priced at a discount and pays its full face value at maturity.

Zero-coupon bonds Bonds that do not pay interest during their life. They are issued at a discount to par value and redeemed at par. Also called pure discount bond.